LANDLORDS, PEASANTS AND INTELLECTUALS IN MODERN KOREA

Landlords, Peasants and Intellectuals in Modern Korea

Edited by
Pang Kie-chung and Michael D. Shin

East Asia Program
Cornell University
Ithaca NY 14853

The Cornell East Asia Series is published by the Cornell University East Asia Program (distinct from Cornell University Press). We publish affordably priced books on a variety of scholarly topics relating to East Asia as a service to the academic community and the general public. Standing orders, which provide for automatic notification and invoicing of each title in the series upon publication, are accepted.

If after review by internal and external readers a manuscript is accepted for publication, it is published on the basis of camera-ready copy provided by the volume author. Each author is thus responsible for any necessary copy-editing and for manuscript formatting. Address submission inquiries to CEAS Editorial Board, East Asia Program, Cornell University, Ithaca, New York 14853-7601.

The publication of this book was supported by a grant from the Korea Foundation. The Korea Literature Translation Institute assisted with promotion.

Number 128 in the Cornell East Asia Series
Copyright © 2005 by Kie-chung Pang and Michael D. Shin. All rights reserved
ISSN 1050-2955
ISBN-13: 978-1-885445-38-4 hc / ISBN-10: 1-885445-38-5 hc
ISBN-13: 978-1-885445-28-5 pb / ISBN-10: 1-885445-28-8 pb
Library of Congress Control Number: 2005936919
Printed in the United States of America
23 22 21 20 19 18 17 16 15 14 13 12 11 10 09 08 05   9 8 7 6 5 4 3 2 1

Cover design by Sumi Shin.

⊗ The paper in this book meets the requirements for permanence of ISO 9706:1994.

Contents

PART III: INTELLECTUALS

Preface

Pang Kie-chung

Since liberation from Japanese colonial rule, historiography in Korea has made rapid strides within the oppressive political and ideological conditions of national division during the past half century. In particular, historians have devoted much effort to overcoming the work of Japanese historians who created a version of Korean history meant to justify Japan's colonial rule. They have produced a tremendous amount of research as schools of historiography competed with each other that differed in their views of history and their research methodologies. Their work has made possible a new understanding of Korean history, based on objective facts and premised on Korea's autonomy, that reflects the views of the various schools and is narrated in diverse ways.

However, despite these achievements, Korean historians have generally not had much interest in building relations with historians or Korean Studies scholars outside of Korea. There is a strong tendency to being content with remaining within the bounds of Korea. This is true of relations with America, where research on Korean history is relatively active, as in Japan; at most, only scholars of specific standpoints established personal ties in the U.S. It is true that one of the reasons for this situation is that foreign scholars have lacked a deep understanding of Korea's history and current situation or had only a distorted understanding of them. On the other hand, another principal cause is the closed mindset and sense of scholarly superiority of Korean scholars who ignored or looked down on research in other countries, absorbed in the idea that Korea is the center of Korean Studies. This sense of superiority was even stronger among progressive historians, and it is undeniable that their target was Korean Studies in the U.S.

The problem is that Korean scholars are potentially contributing to their own intellectual regression. Because research by Korean scholars has not been systematically introduced to foreign scholars, the difference between the two has become more marked in their views on Korean history, and Korean scholars are unable to absorb deeply the new methodologies and research trends outside of Korea. Even worse, foreign scholars sometimes regard a limited group of Korean scholars as representative of the entire Korean academic world, and there is a repetition of old colonialist views of Korean history. For example, various forms of modernization theory are widespread, asserting that Korea lacked the ability to modernize on its own and was able to do so only through Japanese colonial rule. If the Korean academic world is the center of research on Korean history, it is now necessary to work actively at establishing academic exchanges and at introducing the accumulated research and problematics to scholars and students outside of Korea. By doing so, foreign scholars will be able to understand the current situation of Korean academia, and through serious intellectual debate, scholars will be able to develop a Korean historiography that is open and of universal interest.

This volume is a collection of studies on modern Korean history produced by a group of scholars engaged in progressive scholarship in South Korea. The idea for the book came from Michael D. Shin, who came to Yonsei University's Institute of Korean Studies (Kukhak yŏn'guwŏn) in August 1996 to do his dissertation research. There were two main considerations behind this project. First, there was no work in English introducing the work of progressive historians in Korea. Second, few systematic studies of modern Korean history were available for advanced undergraduate and graduate students in Korean Studies in the U.S. I heartily agreed with Michael Shin's suggestion, and together, we began to make plans for this volume. We formed a joint research group with Professor Kim Yong-sop (Kim Yongsŏp), formerly of Yonsei University, and leading scholars among his students. The main characteristic of their scholarship on modern Korean history is their systematic understanding of the development of modern history based on the historical theory of social formations and the theory of "internal development" and their empirical work in primary source materials. Though I do not know how this research will be received in the U.S., I think that this volume represents a significant effort at intellectual exchange since this is the first time it is introduced to a wider audience.

From the planning stages to its publication, this volume has received a tremendous amount of help from many individuals and institutions. First, both of the editors wish to thank all the writers for their cooperation and patience for the trouble they suffered because of our insistent requests for revisions. Also, we sincerely thank Yonsei University for providing all the funding for the translations. Professor Bruce Cumings not only gave crucial assistance to this project but also wrote an invaluable afterword. I want to thank him for his kind efforts and support, without which it would have been difficult to complete this project.

The main reason that this project has taken so long to complete was the time necessary for translation. Michael Shin supervised the translations and made the final revisions. The translators are all excellent researchers of modern Korean history, and we thank them for their devoted efforts for this project: Professor Charles Armstrong, Professor Kelly Jeong, Howard Kahm, Jeong-Il Lee, Paul S. Nam, and Min Suh Son. Shinyoung Kwon assisted the editors and took care of various administrative tasks during the writing of the chapters and their translation.

We thank the Korea Foundation for their generous support by providing a publication grant for this volume. Two anonymous readers gave comments that were valuable in the process of revision. Professor Lee Injae, Professor Choi Yun-oh, Professor Paek Seung-chul, Dr. Chung Ho-hun, and Oh Jin-seok, all of Yonsei University, were very generous in assisting with the explanation of terminology for additional footnotes and the compilation of biographical information on many of the figures who appear in this volume. Angela Kim, Jiaeh Kim, and Melissa Schwartz of Cornell University proofread the entire manuscript, and Angela Kim and Oh Sunmin prepared the index. Lastly, we also wish to thank Karen Smith and Evangeline Ray of the Cornell East Asia Series for their hard work in bringing this book to publication. Special thanks goes to Evangeline for her meticulous copyediting of several chapters that improved their readability.

Note on Romanization

Korean words and names are romanized by the McCune-Reischauer system. Some well-known names and place names are romanized according to standard usage, such as Seoul and Park Chung Hee. Korean and Japanese names are written in East Asian order with the surname coming first.

We have decided against the use of macrons to indicate long vowels in romanizing Japanese names and words. Such symbols are of little use to those unfamiliar with the language.

The term "Hanmal period" (韓末) generally refers to the period 1876-1910. However, since the meaning of the term can differ slightly from person to person, we have decided to leave it untranslated.

Introduction

Michael D. Shin

One of the central concerns of modern historiography is to explain the transition from feudal to capitalist society. In the case of Korea, this transition involved the violence and turbulence of colonization by Japan, civil war, and national division, but the legacy of colonial rule and the continuing division have posed considerable obstacles to the writing of "Korean" history. To justify Japan's takeover, scholars who supported the empire advocated what is known as "stagnation theory" which held that Korea lacked a history until it came into contact with the modern world. After liberation in 1945, the division of the country led to the establishment of military dictatorships on both sides of the peninsula. The official histories of the two Koreas present contending views of history to claim legitimacy for their respective states as the "true" representative of the Korean people, and both sides employed repressive means to maintain their ideological hegemony. Historians thus faced the multiple tasks of refuting stagnation theory, explaining the historical origins of the division, and providing a version of history that would undermine the legitimacy of the military dictatorship and contribute to reunification.

The objective of this volume is to introduce one of the major "schools" of South Korean historiography to an English-speaking audience. The central figure in this "school" is Professor Kim Yong-sop (Kim Yongsŏp), formerly of Yonsei University. He and his students have been involved in some of the most important intellectual debates of the past few decades. Kim Yong-sop is well known for his extensive work on the socioeconomic history of the Chosŏn period, but his importance as a historian goes beyond his empirical contributions. He has also developed a framework for Korean history that has done much to refute stagnation theory and enabled a deeper understanding of the historical roots of Korea's division. His scholarship represents the achievement of many of the tasks of modern historiography, and it helped lay the foundation for the emergence of a progressive historiography in the 1980s.

Modern historiography began to emerge around the turn of the nineteenth-twentieth century as intellectuals began to shift the writing of history from court-centered annals to narratives centered on the nation (*minjok*). The Unyo Incident of 1875 and the Kanghwa Treaty of 1876 began the process of separating Chosŏn from the Chinese world order. The country suddenly found itself facing an international world that it knew little about and for which existing modes of knowledge appeared to be of limited value. The threat of imperialist takeover made it even more urgent for Chosŏn to study Western forms of knowledge in order to set an effective course of re-form. Part of this effort involved learning a completely new world history, as the Sino-centric worldview was no longer adequate to understanding the historical forces shaping the present. The initial task of modern historiography paralleled that of the modern period itself: to regain control over the country's history.

The introduction of modern historiography involved both the study of Western history and a reexamination of Korea's past. The efforts of intellectuals began to produce results in the 1890s and 1900s when modern schools were established, and modern newspapers began publishing. They translated works on Western history whose narratives focused on the rise and fall of nations, including biographies of famous patriots and heroes of national unification struggles, such as Germany's Bismarck and Italy's Mazzini. The reexamination of Korea's past focused on military heroes such as Admiral Yi Sunsin and Ŭlji Mundŏk of Koguryŏ,[1] and they also began to devote attention to Silhak thought of the eighteenth and early nineteenth centuries. In the first decade of the twentieth century, intellectuals republished a number of texts by leading Silhak scholars. In Silhak thought, they were searching for new traditions that would be more suited to the present as well as for models for combining new and traditional forms of thought. However, the

1. Kang Yŏngju, *Han'guk yŏksa sosŏl ŭi chaeinsik* (A reexamination of the historical novel in Korea) (Seoul: Ch'angjak kwa pip'yŏngsa, 1991), chapter 2.

reexamination of Korean history was only in its early stages. Some of the major works in this period were actually chronicles of recent history, such as Hwang Hyŏn's *Maech'ŏn yarok* and Chŏng Kyo's *Taehan kyenyŏnsa*. Despite their concern for Chosŏn's current situation, these works were still not completely modern in their methodologies and narrative structure.[2]

Modern historiography in Chosŏn did not fully emerge until after the Japanese takeover began in 1910. As is well known, Sin Ch'aeho (1880–1936) was the scholar who brought modern historiography to maturity in the 1920s. He actually did most of his research and writing while working in China with various exile groups, and his major works were published in Chosŏn later, mainly from the mid 1920s to the early 1930s. Though his research focused on the ancient period, it was clear that his main interest was to provide a version of history suited to present concerns. He severely critiqued histories based on the notion of *sadae* (serving the great) that followed the Chinese worldview. His goal was to liberate historiography from the orthodoxy of *sadaejuŭi* and write a version of Chosŏn history that stressed its autonomy. Almost all schools of modern historiography were, at least in some way, indebted to his work.[3]

After the March First Movement in 1919, the colonial government implemented the so-called Cultural Policy (*Bunka Seiji*), which allowed the publication of vernacular newspapers and led to tremendous growth in the colonial intellectual world. The new generation of historians who emerged at this time was the first to have been educated in modern schools, and some of them were able to get faculty positions and become professional historians. However, the development of modern historiography faced two significant challenges. First, the colonial government began to assert more control over the writing of Chosŏn history. Even before the occupation began in 1910, Japan had conducted archaeological research in Chosŏn, and in late 1922, it began a large-scale project to compile a complete history of the country, even persuading some Chosŏn historians to participate such as, most notably,

---

2. Kim Yong-sop (Kim Yongsŏp), "Uri nara kŭndae yŏksahak ŭi sŏngnip" (The establishment of our country's modern historiography), *Han'guk hyŏndaesa*, no. 6 (1970). Reprinted in *Han'guk ŭi yŏksa insik*, vol. 2 (Seoul: Ch'angjak kwa pip'yŏngsa, (1976) 1995).

3. Kim Yong-sop, "Uri nara kŭndae yŏksahak ŭi sŏngnip"; An Pyŏngjik, "Tanje Sin Ch'ae-ho ŭi minjokjuŭi" (The nationalism of Sin Ch'aeho), *Han'guk ŭi yŏksa insik*, vol. 2.

Ch'oe Namsŏn.[4] Second, the ideological splits that emerged in the intellectual world in the 1920s were also reflected in historiography. The surge of interest in Marxism led to the development of a Marxist historiography in the late 1920s. Although debates were lively among Marxists and between Marxists and nationalist historians, they failed to produce much unity, leaving many issues unresolved at liberation. The division of the country brought about both a physical separation and an ideological polarization that made it difficult for historians to continue their work.

During the 1950s and 1960s, many historians attempted to build on the work of colonial period scholars to develop a nationalist historiography that would refute stagnation theory. One culmination of their research was Yi Ki-baek's *Han'guksa sillon* (A New History of Korea), which was published in 1967.[5] According to stagnation theory, the cause of Korea's weakness and poverty in the nineteenth century was that its society had stagnated for centuries. Korea had not undergone a feudal period and remained at the level of ancient village society. Some scholars had even claimed that Korea had been a historical colony of Japan going back to ancient times. The research of postwar historians demonstrated that Korea did have an autonomous history going back to ancient times, passing through all the major historical stages, including feudalism. Historical research concentrated on the pre-modern period though there were some studies on the early modern period. Under military dictatorship, some topics were taboo, especially those related to the occupation period, since many of the elites, including Park Chung Hee, had collaborated with the Japanese. Though it is undeniable that nationalist historians performed a valuable role in refuting stagnation theory, their critique was incomplete since it focused mainly on its empirical claims and not on its theoretical underpinnings.

Until the 1980s, the dominant paradigm in South Korean historiography and the academic world in general was that of modernization theory. As is well known, Talcott Parsons (1902–79) developed modernization theory at Harvard in the mid-twentieth century, and he and his students, such as Neil Smelser, turned it into influential tool for the study of non-Western

4. Yi Tosang, *Ilje ŭi yŏksa ch'imnyak 120nyŏn* (120 years of the Japanese empire's attacks on history) (Seoul: Kyŏng'in munhwasa, 2003), pp. 109-10.
5. For the English translation, see Yi Ki-Baik, *A New History of Korea*, trans. Edward W. Wagner with Edward J. Schultz (Cambridge: Harvard University Press, 1984).

societies. It aimed to articulate an evolutionary model of development that, if properly followed, promised even growth and a peaceful, rather than revolutionary, transition to modernity.[6] Reflecting an Orientalist worldview, it saw non-Western societies as locked in a traditional mindset that was the main obstacle to modernization; unable to free themselves, these societies needed an outside stimulus to put them on the road to development. Edwin Reischauer's (1910-1990) research on Japanese history and society and W. W. Rostow's (1916-2003) theory of the "stages of economic growth" had a tremendous influence in spreading modernization theory among South Korean scholars.[7]

In the context of Korean history, modernization theory represents a continuation of stagnation theory as they share many of the same basic premises. Ironically, certain forms of nationalist historiography have unwittingly given stagnation theory a second life. Many historians influenced by modernization theory see the year 1876 as the beginning of the modern period—the year Korea signed its first Western-style treaty and opened its ports. This chronology privileges the impact of the West, and the underlying assumption is that Korean society lacked the ability to modernize on its own and needed stimulus from the West or Japan to embark on its historical development. These historians have tended to focus on the reform efforts of the most westernized elites, such as the Independence Club (1896-98) which was led by Sŏ Chaep'il (Philip Jaisohn) and Yun Ch'iho. They blamed Korea's annexation by Japan on conservative forces and, implicitly, the ignorance of the masses that obstructed their reforms. These elites came to power in South Korea after liberation in 1945, and thus this scholarship indirectly provided ideological support for state policies from the 1950s-70s.

This historical orthodoxy came under attack in the 1980s with the maturation of a progressive historiography. A new generation of scholars, who went to college during the Yushin years, became further politicized after the Kwangju Democratic Uprising in May 1980, which helped bring Chun Doo Hwan to power. Like many other dictators, Chun unwittingly planted the seeds of his demise. As colleges rapidly increased enrollments in the 1980s,

---

6. Harry Harootunian, *History's Disquiet: Modernity, Cultural Practice, and the Question of Everyday Life* (New York: Columbia University Press, 2000), p. 33.

7. W. W. Rostow, *The Stages of Economic Growth: a non-Communist manifesto* (Cambridge: Cambridge University Press, 1960).

most colleges began to offer core courses in modern Korean history. History departments had to hire more faculty to teach these courses, leading to a tremendous increase in research. The increased enrollments were part of the Chun regime's plan to keep students in classrooms and discourage them from engaging in protest demonstrations. These efforts backfired as a new generation of historians became entrenched in academia and played an important role in creating a critical intellectual community. Many of them turned their attention to the modern period, especially previously ignored or taboo aspects of it, and their research helped to undermine the legitimacy of the military dictatorship. In fact, during that decade, historical practice in South Korea had a relevance that was rarely achieved elsewhere during the twentieth century. As new types of critical historiography emerged, social movements were engaged in reviving certain forms of popular memory.[8] The dialogue between history and memory produced counter-memories that helped mobilize resistance against military dictatorship. After the overthrow of the dictatorship in 1987, progressive historians have continued to contribute to the democratization of popular memory.

It would be no exaggeration to say that the emergence of a progressive historiography in the 1980s would not have been possible without Kim Yong-sop's work on the origins of capitalism. His main interests fall broadly into three areas: the socioeconomic history of the Chosŏn period, socioeconomic thought, and modern historiography. His research on these areas combined to enable him to create an alternate paradigm for Korean history. Over the course of his career, Kim Yong-sop has done a vast number of case studies on agricultural history with a focus on the land system and its relation to the social status system. From the late 1950s, he began to publish research that made innovative use of *yang'an* (land registers) from the mid- to late-Chosŏn period. He has also extended this research both into the modern period and back into the Koryo and earlier periods.

Chapter 1 is a seminal article by Kim Yong-sop that synthesized his decades of case studies on socioeconomic history. Many of his studies focused on an issue that earlier scholars had not treated in depth: the differentiation of

8. For example, see Kim Kwang'ŏk, "Chŏngch'ijŏk tamnon kije rosŏ ŭi minjung munhwa undong: sahoegŭk ŭrosŏ ŭi madanggŭk," *Han'guk munhwa illyuhak* 21 (1989). For an English version of this article, see Kim, Kwang-Ok, "The Role of Madangguk in Contemporary Korea's Popular Culture Movement," *Korea Journal* 37, no. 3 (autumn 1997).

the peasant class during the mid-to-late Chosŏn period. Based on his findings, he argued that the country was in the process of feudal breakdown in the late Chosŏn period. In response, there emerged two conflicting programs of reform: what Kim Yong-sop has called the "landlord course" and the "peasant course." The conflict between the two courses of reform is the key to understanding the fundamental internal dynamic of modern Korean history. The aggressions of the foreign powers in the late nineteenth century obstructed the process of historical resolution between these two courses, and the Japanese occupation only contained the conflict and continued to prevent a resolution. In the end, of course, the landlord course culminated in the formation of the South Korean state, and the peasant course in the North Korean state. The elegance of Kim Yong-sop's paradigm is that it provides a single framework to explain the historical factors behind feudal breakdown in the late Chosŏn period, colonization by Japan, and the division of the country.

Because of his focus on the internal dynamics of Korean history, Kim Yong-sop has often been seen as a proponent of "internal development" theory, though he himself does not use the term in his writings. However, the term is not an entirely appropriate one to characterize his work, nor is a related term, the theory of "capitalist sprouts" (*chabonjuŭi maenga*). The concept of "capitalist sprouts" emerged in the 1930s in Marxist debates in Asia, but in Korea, Paek Nam'un was the only Marxist scholar to use the term. Paek argued that capitalism in Korea began to emerge in the late Chosŏn period, and but Japanese imperialism later distorted its development. His refutation of stagnation theory aimed to undermine Japan's claim to have modernized Korea. After liberation, a debate on "capitalist sprouts" emerged simultaneously and independently on both sides of the peninsula in the 1960s. In the south, Kim Yong-sop's work was one of the foci of the debate. While scholars in the north emphasized the emergence of capitalism, Kim Yong-sop's focus was on the process of feudal breakdown. It is important to note how careful he has been in his use of the term "capitalism." In his analysis of the late Chosŏn period, he mentions economic actors who used capitalist methods to acquire wealth, but he does not talk about full-blown capitalism until after the port opening in 1876. Over time, the use of the term "capitalist sprouts" became confused and even became associated with modernization theory—sometimes used to describe the Korean equivalent to the "Protestant spirit."[9] In short, the term came to be used by proponents of diametrically opposed theories.[10]

The term "internal development" emerged later in historiographical discourse, but it suffered a similar fate. The Japanese historian Kajimura Hideki (1935-1989) first coined the term in the late 1970s.[11] Internal development theory is in agreement with the "sprouts theory" in opposing stagnation theory and emphasizing the internal dynamics of Korean history. Kajimura attempted to achieve terminological clarity by using the term "internal development" to refer to a generally Marxist perspective on Korean history. However, as the use of the term became more widespread, scholars used it more loosely, and its meaning became vague. Like the term "capitalist sprouts," it even came to be associated with its opposite—modernization theory.[12] The vagueness of both terms deprives them of much analytic force. As is evident in the recent "development vs. exploitation" debates on the colonial period,[13] the usefulness of the term "internal development" has become increasingly ideological; it is at times crudely invoked to dismiss certain forms of scholarship, particularly nationalist historiography.

9. For more on this debate, see the sections on the modern period in Han'guk Kyŏngje sahakhoe, ed., *Han'guksa sidae kubunnon* (Debates on the periodization of Korean history) (Seoul: Ŭlyu munhwasa, (1970) 1988).

10. For an analysis of the debate on "capitalist sprouts," see Kajimura Hideki, "Shihon shugi hoga no mondai to hoken makki no nomin toso" (The issue of capitalist sprouts and peasant struggles at the end of the feudal period) in *Chosenshi nyumon* (Tokyo: Taihei shuppansha, 1970), pp. 253-76.

11. For example, see the section on "Naizaiteki hatsuten no tenkai" (The unfolding of internal development) in Kajimura Hideki, *Kajimura Hideki chosakushu, dai 3 kan: Kindai Chosen shakai keisairon* (Tokyo: Akashi shoten, 1993).

12. Yi Seyŏng, "'Naejaejŏk paljŏnnon' ŭl kajanghan tto hana ŭi singminjuŭi yŏksa insik" (Another colonialist view of history disguised as "internal development theory"), *Yŏksa wa hyŏnsil*, no. 7 (1992). See also Kim Ingŏl, "1960, 70nyŏndae 'naejaejŏk paljŏnnon' kwa Han'guk sahak" (Korean historiography and "internal development theory" in the 1960s and 70s) in Kim Yong-sŏp kyosu chŏngnyŏn kinyŏm nonch'ong kanhaeng wiwŏnhoe, ed., *Kim Yongsŏp kyosu chŏngnyŏn kinyŏm Han'guk sahak nonch'ong*, vol. 1: *Han'guksa insik kwa yŏksa iron* (Seoul: Chisik san'ŏpsa, 1997), pp. 113-49.

13. For more on the "development vs. exploitation" debate, see the section on "Singminji wa kŭndae" (Colony and Modernity) in *Ch'angjak kwa pip'yŏng*, no. 98 (winter 1997) and Kim Dongno, "Singminji sidae ŭi kŭndaejŏk sut'al kwa sut'al ŭl t'onghan kŭndaehwa" (Mod-ern exploitation in the colonial period and modernization through exploitation), *Ch'angjak kwa pip'yŏng*, no. 99 (spring 1998).

In the end, the term "internal development theory" simply refers to scholarship opposed to stagnation theory without distinguishing among the variety of theoretical positions that it encompasses. Research to refute these views began in the occupation period, and Paek Nam'un's seminal scholarship is discussed in Pang Kie-chung's contribution to this volume (chapter 7). It is true that one of the main objectives of Kim Yong-sop's research has been to oppose the claims of the "colonial view of history" (*singmin sagwan*) which was based on "stagnation theory." However, he went farther than previous critics of stagnation theory by also critiquing its theoretical foundation, the historical view of modernization theory. What he accomplished was an inversion of stagnation theory—turning it on its head, so to speak. His work suggests that it was Japanese colonialism that retarded the development of Korean history by preventing a resolution of the conflict between the landlord and peasant courses of reform.

While he was engaged in this empirical research, Kim Yong-sop also undertook an examination of the origins of modern historiography, and it was crucial to the development of his scholarship. The scope of his research included historians who were ignored at the time, such as Sin Ch'aeho; in the early 1970s, he played an important role in the restoration of Sin Ch'aeho to his canonical place as one of the founders of modern historiography.[14] He was searching in the recent past for ways to open up new possibilities of writing history. The underlying objective was to revive and build upon a critical historiography to critique his present. His work has contributed to the construction of an alternate genealogy of modern historiography in Korea. During the 1980s and 1990s, historians have filled in the gaps in the genealogy, and the studies of Paek Nam'un, Yi Sunt'ak (chapter 8), and An Chaehong (chapter 9) in this volume are contributions to this effort.

As mentioned above, Kim Yong-sop's scholarship opened up a critical space that contributed to the emergence of a progressive historiography in the 1980s. With its focus on the conflict between landlords and peasants, his historical framework enabled a reinterpretation of modern Korean history as the struggle of the masses to become the agents of their own history. This

---

14. Kim Yong-sop, "Uri nara kŭndae yŏksahak ŭi sŏngnip," pp. 421-49. See also Kim Yong-sop, "Uri nara kŭndae yŏksahak ŭi paldal" which is reprinted in the same volume.

conception of history obviously resonated with the struggles of the democracy movement at the time.[15]

The rewriting of modern history involved a critique of earlier scholarship for its positive evaluation of the role of elites. This critique was also partially indebted to Kim Yong-sop's scholarship. Throughout his career, he has been concerned with the relationship between socioeconomic conditions and intellectual production; in fact, this concern remains a central part of the research agenda of this "school" of historiography. In his work on intellectual history, he demonstrated how thought was rooted in particular socioeconomic conditions and, at the same time, was a response to them. One example is his work on Silhak thought and its relation to the breakdown of the feudal system and the rise of peasant rebellions in the late Chosŏn period. Historians in the 1980s were able to extend his analyses to the modern period. Their aim was to reveal that the so-called modernizing elites, who claimed to be acting for the nation, were actually pursuing narrow class interests. As their research revealed, many of these elites collaborated with the Japanese during the occupation period, placing class above nation.

Progressive historians also began a reexamination of leftist movements and intellectuals during the occupation period, a dangerous topic to address during the years of military dictatorship. State ideology at the time essentially saw leftist ideologies such as Marxism and communism as forms of mass deception. Marxism was an ideology with little relevance to actual conditions of the people whose influence was limited to a group of intellectual elites during the colonial period, and the communist movement was an externally directed movement controlled by the Soviet Union. However, in Kim Yong-sop's framework, the emergence of leftist ideologies in the 1920s can be seen as having indigenous roots since they were a successor to the peasant course of reform. Intellectuals were not mechanically applying Marxism and other leftist ideologies and distorting Korea's reality to fit the theory; rather, they saw it as a way to give the peasants agency by providing a strategy to express and achieve their demands. As Kim Yong-sop discusses in chapter 4, the struggles of the peasants during the colonial period developed beyond an economic movement or a class movement and became a part of

---

15. Yi Seyŏng, "1980, 90nyŏndae minjuhwa munje wa yŏksahak" (Historiography and the issue of democratization in the 1980s and 90s), *Han'guksa insik kwa yŏksa iron: Kim Yongsŏp kyosu chŏngnyŏn kinyŏm Han'guk sahak nonch'ong*, vol. 1.

the national liberation movement. In short, interest in Marxism and the rise of the socialist movement was both an outgrowth of and a concrete response to Korea's political, economic, and social conditions. The critique of the historical orthodoxy on leftist ideologies constituted an attack on the anti-communist "nationalism" of the South Korean state.[16]

Reunification was a central issue in the student movement in the 1980s; it was an issue that struck at the heart of the illegitimacy of the military dictatorship. Progressive historians supported their efforts by examining the historical roots of the division of the country and the liberation period (1945-48) to gain a better understanding of the obstacles to reunification. As mentioned above, another major focus of Kim Yong-sop's work has been to illuminate the historical factors behind Korea's division. His historical framework makes it clear that the division was not simply the result of the cold war conflict between the U.S. and the Soviet Union. Over the course of his career, he has also undertaken a systematic examination of intellectuals' conceptions of the state during the Japanese occupation period in order to illuminate the ideological origins of the country's division, and his students have continued doing research on this problematic. Their analysis is compelling because it helps to explain both the ferocity of the Korean War and the persistence of the division despite the fall of the Soviet Union and the end of the cold war. The implication of this work is that reunification must involve a resolution of deeply rooted historical conflicts in order to create a political and social order that will be stable and lasting.

It is no accident that a progressive historiography was able to develop at Yonsei University. During the Japanese occupation period, the school was known as Yŏnhŭi Chŏnmun Hakgyo or Chosun Christian College, and it was the only nongovernmental institution of higher learning that had a humanities department.[17] Among its faculty, it had three prominent historians: Paek Nam'un (1894-1979), a Marxist; the nationalist Chŏng Inbo (1893-1950); and Paek Nakjun (L. George Paik, 1895-1985), a Christian. The Yŏnhŭi faculty also included the economist Yi Sunt'ak (1897-1950) and the linguists Ch'oe Hyŏnbae (1894-1970) and Kim Yun'gyŏng (1894-

---

16. The work of progressive historians is summarized in the general history of Korea that they collectively wrote. See Han'guk yŏksa yŏn'guhoe, *Han'guk yŏksa* (Seoul: Yŏksa pip'yŏngsa 1992).

17. Kim Yong-sop, "Uri nara kŭndae yŏksahak ŭi paldal," p. 486.

1977). Despite the fact that it was a Christian school, it maintained, for the most part, an intellectually open atmosphere that enabled Korean Studies to flourish.

After liberation, when Yŏnhŭi Chŏnmun Hakgyo became a university, it created a history department in 1946.[18] The next generation of historians at Yonsei included Hong Yi-sup (Hong Isŏp, 1914-74) and Sohn Pow-key (Son Pogi, 1922-), and they made important contributions to the further development of nationalist historiography. Hong Yi-sup studied under Mun Ilp'yŏng (1888-1939) at Paejae Academy and was a student of Chŏng Inbo. Hong wrote one of the first and most influential general histories of Korea from a nationalist point of view—*Chosŏn kwahaksa* (The history of Korean science) which came out in 1944-46.[19] He also contributed to the development of a methodology for studying modern Korean thought.[20] Sohn Pow-key was a graduate of Yŏnhŭi Chŏnmun Hakgyo and, after liberation, studied under Son Chint'ae (1900-?), who was an advocate of "neo-nationalist" historiography (*sin minjokjuŭi sahak*). He later received a Ph.D. from the University of California at Berkeley. Sohn is well known as one of the pioneers in research on Korea's prehistory, and he was the scholar who proved that Old Stone Age culture had existed in the Korean peninsula. In addition, he has done much work on the history of printing in Korea.[21]

Kim Yong-sop himself is actually not a graduate of Yonsei University. He graduated from the Department of History Education of the College of Education at Seoul National University (SNU). His advisor was Sohn Pow-key who recommended that he pursue graduate work at Koryŏ (Korea) University. At Koryŏ, where Kang Man-gil was also studying at the time, Kim Yong-sop was relatively free to pursue his own research and did his master's thesis on Chŏn Pongjun and the Kabo Peasants' War.[22] The results

---

18. On the history of Yonsei University, see *Yŏnse Taehakgyo paeknyŏnsa, 1885-1985* (The one hundred year history of Yonsei University) (Seoul: Yonsei University Press, 1985).

19. Kim Yong-sop, "Urinara kŭndae yŏksahak ŭi paldal" (The development of our country's historiography) in *Han'guk ŭi yŏksa insik*, vol. 2, pp. 486-89. Originally published in *Munhak kwa chisŏng*, no. 4 (summer 1971).

20. Hong Isŏp, "Han'guk kŭndaesa ŭi pangbŏp" and "Han'guk chŏngsinsa sŏsŏl" in *Hong Isŏp chŏnjip* (Seoul: Yŏnse Taehakgyo ch'ulp'anbu, 1994).

21. Sohn Pow-key's books include *Han'guk ŭi kohwalja* (Korea's old moveable type) (Seoul: Pojinjae, 1971) and *Social History of the Early Choson Dynasty* (Seoul: Chisik san'ŏpsa, 2000).

22. Kim Yong-sop, "Tonghaknan sŏnggyŏk ko" (An examination of the nature of the Tonghak Uprising) (master's thesis, Koryŏ University, 1957).

of his research left him unsatisfied by the explanations provided by political history and led him to begin doing research on *yang'an* and socioeconomic history. After completing his thesis in 1957, he became a lecturer at SNU's College of Education and was appointed professor in 1959 when Sohn Pow-key moved to Yonsei. He moved to the College of Arts and Sciences (*Mulli-gwa taehak*) at SNU in 1967 and then accepted a position at Yonsei in 1975 as the successor to Hong Yi-sup, who had passed away the previous year.

Within this "school" of historiography, this volume concentrates on their work on early modern history with a focus on the Japanese occupation period. Of course, a single volume cannot do justice to the amount of research they have produced. The objective is simply to present a combination of their representative work and latest research and to show the diversity of research and differences of opinion within this group of scholars. We have sought to maintain a balance between socioeconomic and intellectual history.

Part I is a brief examination of the period before the Japanese occupation. The increasing severity of peasant rebellions in the nineteenth century was a sign that the foundations of the feudal system in Chosŏn were crumbling. After the Unyo Incident in 1875 and Chosŏn's entrance into the modern world system with the Treaty of Kanghwa in 1876, foreign imperialism exacerbated the process of feudal breakdown while it undermined the ability of the Chosŏn state to address these problems. Both the state and non-state elites tried to learn about Western thought and institutions in an effort to modernize the country and be able to resist the intrusions of the foreign powers. They adopted a range of strategies, including *tongdo sŏgi* (Eastern ways, Western technology) and *munmyŏng kaehwa* (civilization and enlightenment) which called for a more complete westernization.

Chapter 1, which was discussed above, serves as an excellent introduction to the major themes and positions of Kim Yong-sop. It gives an overview of the socioeconomic history of the Chosŏn period and then connects it with developments in the late nineteenth century. The next two chapters utilize Kim Yong-sop's framework to examine modernization efforts in this period and analyze the reasons for their failure. In chapter 2, Chu Chin-Oh provides an alternative interpretation of the thought of the Independence Club from the standpoint of this "school." He examines the influence of Social Darwinism on the leading members of the Independence Club and the political, international, and social and cultural aspects of their reform proposals. Chapter 3 summarizes the results of Choi Won-kyu's recent research on cadastral surveys conducted by the state at the turn of the century. Until the 1990s, research on the late nineteenth century generally focused on peasant movements and the reform efforts of non-state elites, and little work was done on the Chosŏn state.[23] Choi Won-kyu's work is a contribution to the growing body of research on state modernization efforts such as the Kwangmu reforms that began in 1897.

Part II contains a selection of research on the socioeconomic history of the occupation and liberation periods. Chapter 4 is an abridged version of Kim Yong-sop's overview of Japanese agricultural policies and their consequences. He broke down the development of the policies into three stages. The first stage was from 1910-19 and was characterized by the Company Law, which required a permit from the Government-General in order to create a business. The second stage was the 1920s; in 1920, Japan implemented the Program to Increase Rice Production (*Sanmi chŭngsik kyehoek*) in order to turn Chosŏn into its main supplier of rice. The third stage was the 1930s when Japan changed its policies to establish a control economy. In each stage, he demonstrates how the policies' effect on landholding patterns created a situation in which the problems in the agricultural economy became concentrated in the landlord-tenant system. He then goes to analyze the development of the peasant movement during the occupation period, breaking it down into four stages that led to its increasing radicalization.

In chapter 5, Hong Sung-Chan examines developments within the landlord class, based on nearly a decade of case studies on the landlord system in the twentieth century. Focusing on modernizing landlords, he discovered that their business methods could be classified into three types: *nongjang* (agricultural estates), the agricultural trust system, and capitalist agricultural enterprises. In chapter 6, Kim Seong-bo examines the culmination of the "peasant course"—i.e., the North Korean land reform of 1946—using materials he found in archives in the former Soviet Union. His research shows how changes in the international situation and domestic politics combined to radicalize the North's land reform as communist allied with radical peasant forces in the countryside. He suggests that land reform is one of the reasons for the internal unity of the North Korean regime that has continued to the present day.

---

23. "Tae Han cheguk 100 chunyŏn chwadam: Kojong kwa Tae Han cheguk ŭl tullŏssan ch'oegŭn nonjaeng," *Yŏksa pip'yŏng* no. 37 (Summer 1997), p. 249.

Part III examines intellectuals who collectively demonstrate the spectrum of ideological responses during the occupation period and on whom, as yet, there are no studies in the English language. Modern education in Chosŏn experienced significant growth in the 1900s and 1910s, as shown by the leadership of teachers and students in the March First Movement. However, a recognizably modern intellectual world did not emerge until after 1919. The relaxation of publication laws after the March First Movement led to a burst of intellectual activity as daily newspapers and intellectual journals were founded. Along with the rapid rise of an intellectual world, ideological splits also emerged with the introduction of Marxism and other types of anti-capitalist thought. The severity of ideological differences and the inability to overcome them were a reflection of the depth of the internal conflicts of colonial Chosŏn society.

The three intellectuals examined in Part III were part of the generation who emerged in the 1920s. Their generation was the first to get almost a fully modern education, and all three of them attended college in Japan. After their return to Chosŏn, they pursued different intellectual and political paths, and the three chapters examine their thought, views on current affairs, and relation to political movements. Pang Kie-chung's research on the Marxist historian Paek Nam'un has contributed to the rapid growth of research on socialism over the past twenty years by focusing on socialist thought and not just the socialist/communist movement itself. Chapter 7 is a taken from his monograph on Paek Nam'un and his development of a Marxist historiography that could provide a framework to explain all the stages of "Korean" history. While much scholarly attention has been devoted to the ideological splits among intellectuals, this school of historians has also been interested in intellectuals who worked toward a united front during the 1920s and early 30s. In chapter 8, Lee Ji-won analyzes the thought of one of the leaders of the Sin'ganhoe (united-front) movement, An Chaehong. In the last chapter of this volume, Hong Sung-Chan examines the work of the economist Yi Sunt'ak, a social democrat who also worked toward establishing national unity. Their interest in such figures has, in part, grown out of their reflection on the reasons for the failure of such efforts to prevent the eventual division of the country.

In recent years, there has been much talk of a "crisis of the humanities" in academia and in the mass media in South Korea. As sales of humanities books have declined, scholars are concerned about their growing inability to have a social impact, calling for the reform of a university system that no longer seems to suit the needs of the present.[24] The crisis of the humanities is a symptom of a more general crisis that the country has been facing since the 1990s. Though the ideals of the democracy movement have been partially realized, democracy remains an incomplete project. However, the configuration of social forces has changed so much that it is difficult to determine who can be effective agents of social change, despite the emergence of new forms of civic movements. These developments suggest that the problematic of the 1980s has run its course and needs to be reworked to be relevant to the present.

The crisis of the humanities also seems to be a crisis of historical consciousness. The current popularity of historical dramas on TV, even as sales of history-related books are declining, is a sign of a growing disjunction between history and memory. In addition, even at the beginning of the twenty-first century, historical judgments can still "send shock waves through the whole body politic" in East Asia, as Bruce Cumings writes in his afterword to this volume. The task, once again, is to search for new ways of writing history. The achievement of this task also involves reflection and critique of earlier work. During the late 1990s, a generational change occurred among historians as a whole generation of prominent scholars retired. Their retirements have served as an occasion to reflect both on past scholarship and on the future direction of Korean historiography.[25] Recent research shows that a younger generation of historians is trying to develop new ways of

24. See the five volumes of *Inmun chŏngch'aek yŏn'gu ch'ongsŏ 2004* (Research on humanities policy series 2004) published by the Inmun sahoe yŏn'guhoe. For publication statis-tics, see "Wigi e ppajin inmun ch'ulp'an" (Humanities publishing which has fallen into a crisis), *Hangyŏre sinmun*, Dec. 20, 2004.

25. In addition to Kim Yong-sop, Professor Kang Man-gil and Professor Cho Tonggŏl have recently retired. *Han'guksa insik kwa yŏksa iron*, *Han'guk kodae chungse ŭi chibae ch'eje wa nongmin* (Peasants and the ruling structure in ancient and medieval Korean history), *Han'guk kŭnhyŏndae ŭi minjok munje wa singukga kŏnsŏl* (State building and the national issue in modern and contemporary Korean history): *Kim Yongsŏp kyosu chŏngnyŏn kinyŏm Han'guk sahak nonch'ong*, vol. 1, 2, 3; Kang Man-gil (Kang Man'gil), ed., *Chosŏn hugisa yŏn'gu ŭi hyŏnhwang kwa kwaje* (The current state and tasks of research on the late Chosŏn period) (Seoul: Ch'angjak kwa pip'yŏngsa, 2000); Kang Man-gil, ed., *Han'guk chabonjuŭi ŭi yŏksa* (The history of Korean capitalism) (Seoul: Ch'angjak kwa pip'yŏngsa, 2000); Kang Man-gil, et al., eds., *T'ong'il chihyang uri minjok haebang undongsa* (The history of our national liberation movement whose goal is reunification) (Seoul: Yŏksa pip'yŏngsa, 2000). See also Usong Cho Tonggŏl sŏnsaeng chŏngnyŏn kinyŏm nonch'ong kanhaeng wiwŏnhoe, ed., *Usong Cho Tonggŏl sŏnsaeng chŏngnyŏn kinyŏm nonch'ong 1,2* (Seoul: Nanam, 1997).

conceiving power relations, ideology, and the relations between them. To develop a new problematic, it is often necessary to engage in dialogue with people engaged in forms of struggle. But it may also be helpful to open a dialogue with scholars working under different problematics, though with similar political and social concerns. This volume hopes to contribute in a small way to this ongoing dialogue in order to enable readers to participate in current debates on modern Korean history.

PART I

KOREA BEFORE THE JAPANESE OCCUPATION

The Two Courses of Agrarian Reform in Korea's Modernization

Kim Yong-sop
金容燮

In the late nineteenth century, the feudal state of the Yi dynasty was forced to open its ports to the modern capitalist economies and to enter into diplomatic relations with the imperialist powers. The Western powers that had been colonizing small states and undeveloped areas of the world were now focusing their aggressions on East Asia. After forcing China and Japan to open their ports, they began to bring pressure upon Chosŏn. At first, Chosŏn adopted a policy of seclusion toward the West and of driving out the "barbarians," but eventually its ports were opened by Japan, which was westernizing and transforming itself into a capitalist economy in an effort to join the ranks of the imperialist states. In light of these developments, Chosŏn had no choice but to open its ports and extend diplomatic relations to the Western powers as well.

These changes signified Chosŏn's departure from the feudal world order and its incorporation into the modern world capitalist system. Although these changes were inevitable in view of the trends of world history at the time, the transformation that they brought about was no simple matter. The world capitalist system was an imperialist system in which a small number of states established political, economic, and military domination over small, undeveloped countries throughout the world. Many small countries were either incorporated into the territory of the imperialist states through military force or became one of their colonies. With the opening of its ports, Chosŏn now faced the same danger. The country found itself in a crisis whose resolution would determine whether it would be able to survive as a state or fall to the status of a colony.

In such a changing world, the key to the Chosŏn monarchy's survival was to establish a system that could deal with the modern capitalist states and adapt to their world order. It involved the restructuring of the state and thus the implementation of reforms for the modernization of society. After the opening of the ports, various social classes repeatedly attempted to organize social reform movements in order to modernize Chosŏn, but many obstacles stood in the way. The establishment of a new system would affect entrenched class interests. These obstacles were even greater for economic policies that sought to address the agricultural problems of the time. The manner of reform of the feudal economic system would determine whether feudal class relations would be overturned completely or maintained in a changed form. Broadly speaking, within reform movements of the time, there was a conflict between the proposals of the yangban and landlords and those of the peasants. The outcome of this conflict would determine the nature of modernization in Chosŏn society. The main purpose of this chapter is to examine the debates on modernization by focusing on their proposals regarding agriculture.

Problems in the Agricultural Economy and Traditions of Reform Before the Opening of the Ports

Problems in the agricultural economy were a target of reform even before Chosŏn embarked on modernization. In fact, the roots of reform actually date back to the late Chosŏn period, when changes occurred in both the feudal land and tax systems. As agricultural production improved at all levels, agriculture was affected by the growth of a commodity-monetary economy. As a result, conflict among the social classes escalated as traditional rural society was gradually but thoroughly being restructured through its differentiation.

During the Koryŏ and early Chosŏn periods, the land system was managed according to the *chŏnju chŏn'gaek* system, in which the state granted officials the right to collect taxes (*sujogwŏn*) on parcels of land. This system disappeared by the late Chosŏn period, when self-cultivators and the *chijusijak chŏnjak* system (landlord-tenant system) became predominant, both of which were based on the recognition of private property rights. One of the main features of the land system during this period was the lack of class restrictions on private ownership. People of all classes had the right to own land, from the royal family and yangban officials to commoners and the low-born (*ch'ŏnmin*).

It was possible to accumulate large land holdings through the sale and purchase of land. People of wealth did not need to seek out peasants who wanted to sell their land. Many peasants in urgent need of money would take their ownership papers and go in search of a buyer. Rich peasants could accumulate land with little effort.[1] When the agricultural economy was being rebuilt after the Hideyoshi and Mongol invasions, the Chosŏn state implemented the *chŏlsu* system[2] and encouraged the clearing of new farmland.[3] As a result, the royal family and government offices rushed to establish *kung-jangt'o* (palace estate land)[4] and *tunjŏn*[5] and managed these lands through the landlord system.[6] Even yangban landlords engaged in land reclamation and

1. Pak Chiwŏn, *Yŏn'amjip* (The collected works of Yŏn'am Pak Chiwŏn), vol. 16—*hanmin myŏngjŏn ŭi.*

2. Because of the disruptions and destruction caused by the foreign invasions, there was a significant amount of land that was abandoned and whose ownership was unclear. Under the *chŏlsu* system (the characters literally mean "break" and "receive"), the government would grant the right to reclaim a parcel of uncultivated land. Sometimes, it meant the granting of ownership of the land, or it meant the granting of only the right to collect taxes or the right to cultivate it. (editor's note—henceforth, abbreviated as "ed.")

3. Yi Kyŏngsik, "17 segi t'oji chŏlsuje wa chikjŏn pokguron" (The chŏjsu system and the discussion on the restoration of the office land system in the seventeenth century), *Tongbang hakji*, nos. 54-55-56 (combined issue, 1987); Yi Kyŏngsik, "17 segi ŭi t'oji kaegan kwa chijuje ŭi chŏn'gae" (Land reclamation and the development of the landlord system in the seventeenth century), *Han'guksa yŏn'gu*, no. 9 (1973); Song Ch'ansŏp, "17-18 segi sinjŏn kaegan ŭi hwakdae wa kyŏngyŏng hyŏngt'ae" (The expansion and management of land reclamation in the seventeenth and eighteenth centuries), *Han'guk saron*, no. 12 (1985).

4. *Kungjangt'o* (palace estate land) was land that was divided and distributed to members of the royal family. (ed.)

5. Originally, *tunjŏn* or "military colony land" was government owned land that was managed as a type of communal agricultural estate. Peasants were granted the right of cultivation, and the taxes from this land were used to support military units in the area. This type of land first appeared in the Koryo period. Later, this term was used for land distributed and managed in this fashion, even if it was not for military purposes. (ed.)

6. Wada Ichiro, *Chosen no tochi seido oyobi chizei seido chosa hokokusho* (Keijo (Seoul): Chosen Sotokufu, 1920); Chŏng Ch'angnyŏl, "Chosŏn hugi ŭi tunjŏn e taehayŏ," *Yi Haenam paksa hwagap kinyŏm sahak nonch'ong*, (Seoul: Ilchogak, 1970); Pak Kwangsŏng, "Kungbangjŏn ŭi yŏn'gu" (A study of palace estate land), *Inch'ŏn kyodae nonmunjip*, no. 5 (1970), "Sok kungbangjŏn ŭi yŏn'gu" (Part 2: a study of palace estate land), *Inch'ŏn kyodae nonmunjip*, no. 9 (1974), "Yŏngamun tunjŏn ŭi yŏn'gu" (A study of military colony and government office land), *Inch'ŏn kyodae nonmunjip*, no. 10 (1975); An Pyŏngt'ae (An Byonte), "17-18 seiki Chosen kyuboten no kozo to tenkai" (The structure and development of palace estate land in Chosŏn in the seventeenth and eighteenth centuries), *Chosen shakai no kozo to Nihon teikokushugi* (Tokyo: Ryukei shosha, 1977); Pak Chunsŏng, "17-18 segi kungbangjŏn ŭi hwakdae wa soyu hyŏngt'ae

expanded their landholdings.[7] Because of the accumulation of land and the expansion of operations by rich peasants and the large landlord class, an increasing number of peasants gradually lost their land.

The taxation system was based on the principle of local autonomy. All the residents of a county (*kun*) or district (*hyŏn*) were collectively responsible for the payment of taxes (*ch'ong'aekje*).[8] One of main features of the system was that the amount of taxes levied varied, both directly and indirectly, according to an individual's position within the social status system. For example, one of the privileges of the yangban class was exemption from the military service tax (*kunyŏkse*). It was only natural that the tax system functioned to the advantage of elites who were involved in local administration of the countryside.

However, in the late Chosŏn period, the social status system was in turmoil as large numbers of commoners and low-borns rose to yangban status as recorded in household registers (*hojŏk*).[9] Their main objective was to avoid the military service tax and slave service (*nobigong*). These changes in the social status system led to the appearance of peasants of higher social status. Under the *ch'ong'aekje* system, the tax burden of these upwardly mobile peasants was shifted to others who remained in a lower social status. Since their taxes were doubled or even tripled, there were many cases of peasants

ŭi pyŏnhwa" (The expansion of palace estate land and the changes in its forms of ownership in the seventeenth and eighteenth centuries), *Han'guk saron*, no. 11 (1984); Yi Yŏngho, "18-19 segi chidae hyŏngt'ae ŭi pyŏnhwa wa nong'ŏp kyŏng'yŏng ŭi pyŏndong" (Changes in the forms of land rent and changes in agricultural management in the eighteenth and nineteenth centuries), *Han'guk saron*, no. 12 (1984); To Chinsun, "19 segi kungjangt'o esŏ ŭi chungdapju ŭi hangjo" (Tax protests by rich tenant farmers who rent tenant land to small-scale farmers on palace estate land in the nineteenth century), *Han'guk saron*, no. 13 (1895); Yi Yŏnghun, *Chosŏn hugi t'oji soyu ŭi kibon kujo wa nongmin kyŏng'yŏng* (Ph.D. diss., Seoul National University, 1985).

7. Yi Seyŏng, "18-19 segi yangban toho ŭi chiju kyŏng'yŏng" (The landlord management of yangban landowners in the eighteenth and nineteenth centuries), *Han'guk munhwa*, no. 6 (1985).

8. Kim Yong-sop (Kim Yongsŏp), "Chosŏn hugi ŭi puse chedo ijŏngch'aek" (Policies on the revision of the tax system in the late Chosŏn period), *Han'guk kŭndae nong'ŏpsa yŏn'gu*, vol. 1 (Seoul: Ilchogak, 1984).

9. Shikata Hiroshi, "Richo jinko ni kansuru mibun kaikyuteki kansatsu" (An examination of the social class status of the population of the Yi Dynasty), *Chosen shakai keizai kenkyu*, vol. 2 (1976); Chŏng Sŏkjong, "Chosŏn hugi sahoe sinbunje ŭi pyŏnhwa" (Changes in the social status system in the late Chosŏn period), *Chosŏn hugi sahoe pyŏndong yŏn'gu* (Seoul: Ilchogak, 1983); Yi Chun'gu, "Chosŏn hugi yangban sinbun idong e kwanhan yŏn'gu" (A study on changes in yangban social status during the late Chosŏn period), *Yŏksa hakbo*, nos. 96-97, 1982; Kim Sŏkhŭi, "Kyŏngsangdo Tansŏng hojŏk taejang e kwanhan yŏn'gu" (A study of the household registers of Tansŏng, Kyŏngsang province), *Pusan tae inmun nonch'ong*, no. 24 (1983).

falling into ruin in this period. The resulting disruption in the taxation system was called the *samjŏng mullan* (disorder of the three systems).[10]

Agricultural productivity increased as technology improved at all levels of production. In the Chosŏn period, a major development was the dissemination of the technique of rice transplantation which enabled double cropping in wet fields. Compared to the method of direct seeding, rice transplantation required less labor, and the labor saved could now be used for increasing cultivation.[11] One consequence of this development was an accelerated differentiation of rural society.

In this period, farmers were able to produce crops for the market—not just the usual crops such as tobacco, cotton, and vegetables but staple grains as well.[12] Production for the market functioned as the engine for change in rural society. Agricultural production gradually became fully integrated with markets, a process that was accelerated by the partial implementation of a cash payment system for taxes.[13] Agriculture was at the stage of small-scale commodity production, and both landlords and peasants engaged in such production. The ones most suited to engage in commercial agriculture were the rich peasant class and the landlord class, both of whom had plenty of capital. This situation inevitably led to the differentiation of rural society.

10. The *samjŏng* were the three kinds of taxes of the Chosŏn period: the land tax, the military service tax (*kun'yŏkse, kunp'ose*), and the grain loan tax (*hwangok*). (ed.)

11. Song Ch'ansik, "Chosŏn hugi nong'ŏp e issŏsŏ ŭi kwangjak undong" (The movement to expand cultivation in the agriculture of the late Chosŏn period), *Yi Haenam paksa hwagap kinyŏm sahak nonch'ong*; Miyajima Hiroshi, "Richo koki nosho no kenkyu" (A study of agricultural treatises in the late Yi Dynasty), *Jinbun gakuho*, no. 43 (1977); Kim Yong-sop, "Chosŏn hugi ŭi sudojak kisul" (The technique of wet-field rice cultivation in the late Chosŏn period), *Chosŏn hugi nong'ŏpsa yŏn'gu*, vol. II, revised edition (Seoul: Ilchogak, 1990).

12. Miyajima Hiroshi, "Richo koki nosho no kenkyu"; An Pyŏngjik, "Chŏng Yagyong ŭi sang'ŏpjŏk nong'ŏpgwan" (Chŏng Yagyong's views on commercial agriculture), *Taedong munhwa yŏn'gu* 18 (1984); Yi Seyŏng, "18-19 segi kokmul sijang ŭi hyŏngsŏng kwa yut'ong kujo ŭi pyŏndong" (The emergence of grain markets and changes in the circulation structure in the eighteenth and nineteenth centuries), *Han'guk saron*, no. 9 (1983); Yi Yŏnghak, "18 segi yŏnch'o ŭi saengsang kwa yut'ong" (The production and circulation of tobacco in the eighteenth century), *Han'guk saron*, no. 13 (1985); Yi Yungap, "18-19 segi Kyŏngbuk chibang ŭi nong'ŏp pyŏndong" (Changes in agriculture in the north Kyŏngsang province region in the eighteenth and nineteenth centuries), *Han'guksa yŏn'gu*, no. 54 (1985); Kim Yong-sop, "Chosŏn hugi ŭi kyŏngyŏnghyŏng punong kwa sang'ŏpjŏk nong'ŏp" (Managerial rich peasants and commercial agriculture in the late Chosŏn period), *Chosŏn hugi nong'ŏpsa yŏn'gu*, vol. II, revised edition.

13. Pang Kie-chung (Pang Kijung), "17-18 segi chŏnban kŭmnap chose ŭi sŏngnip kwa chŏn'gae" (The establishment and development of the cash payment of taxes in the seventeenth and first half of the eighteenth centuries), *Tongbang hakji*, no. 45 (1984).

It is clear that there were many factors behind the differentiation of rural society. It initially occurred in the commoner and low-born classes but was not restricted to these classes. Social differentiation was also widespread among those with yangban social status.[14] Many impoverished yangban without political connections fell into destitution. In general, land became concentrated in the hands of a small number of landlords and rich peasants, while many others gradually lost their land and became tenant farmers. According to one historical source, for every hundred households, there were five landlord families, twenty-five independent farm households, and seventy tenant farming households in the southwestern Honam region.[15]

Peasants in even worse straits fell to the status of wage laborers or even became wandering migrants. In most cases, poor peasants usually faced the prospect of further decline because landlords who leased farmland tended to choose peasant families with livestock and available labor, rather than poor families with few laboring members.[16] Landlords were mainly composed of members of the royal family, government offices, and the yangban class, but there also were commoners and low-born who became landlords. Similarly, while the majority of tenant farmers and wage-laborers came from commoners and the low-born, a significant number of yangban had also fallen into ruin.

Within this social class structure, there was constant conflict between landlords and tenants and between employers and laborers over wages and the distribution of wealth. Tension also existed between rich and poor peasants over tenant farming land and the landlords' methods of agricultural management.[17] Because of the irrational tax system, peasants and even some of the yangban class were dissatisfied with the government. Ultimately, these conflicts developed into a structural contradiction between the government, local officials, and rich peasants, on the one hand, and small-scale self-cultivators

14. Kim Yong-sop, "Chosŏn hugi yangbanch'ŭng ŭi nongŏp saengsan" (The agricultural production of the yangban class in the late Chosŏn period), *Chosŏn hugi nong'ŏpsa yŏn'gu*, vol. 2, revised edition.

15. Chŏng Yagyong, *Yŏyudang chŏnsŏ* (The complete works of Chŏng Yagyong), volume of verse writings, ŭijŏng ŏmkŭm Honam cheŭb chŏnbu sujojisok ch'aja (A request that the custom of bearing the responsibility of transporting the taxes of the landlords in various ŭp in the Honam region be strictly forbidden), *Chŏnsŏ* vol. 1, p. 198.

16. Chŏng Yagyong, *Kyŏngse yup'yo*, chŏnje 1 (land system 1), "On the well-field system" 2, and chŏnje 4, chŏnsŏ vol. 3, pp. 83, 103.

17. Kim Yong-sop, "18-19 segi ŭi nong'ŏp siljŏng kwa saeroun nong'ŏp kyŏngyŏngnon" (The conditions of agriculture and new theories of agricultural management in the eighteenth and nineteenth centuries), *Han'guk kŭndae nong'ŏpsa yŏn'gu*, vol. 1.

and poor peasants, on the other.[18] In the process, exploited peasants who had a strong political consciousness eventually began to contemplate rebelling against the system.[19] These structural contradictions grew worse at the end of the eighteenth century and in the end brought about large-scale peasant rebellions in the nineteenth century—the peasant war in P'yŏng'an province in 1811 and the peasant rebellion in the three southern provinces in 1862.

Neither the government nor the educated class could afford to ignore these developments in rural society. In order to preserve the existing state and society, it was necessary to suppress the peasant rebellions by any means possible and to search for fundamental solutions that could stabilize the life of the peasantry. There were calls for reform proposals on how to solve the problems in the agricultural economy.

Various solutions were proposed, but in general, they can be divided into two types. The first believed that the turmoil could be resolved by stabilizing the peasant economy through a revision of the irrational system of taxation. The second argued that in order to provide fundamental stability to the peasant economy, it was necessary to reform the land system as well.

First, many scholars and officials put forth proposals to solve problems through a revision of the tax system, and naturally they were the ones supported by the government. In times of crisis, kings would often issue a *kuŏngyo*,[20] requesting both high and low ranking officials to submit certain types of memorials such as a *paekgwan jin'ŏn*,[21] a *min'ŭnso*,[22] a *nongjŏng*-

---

18. Yazawa Yasusuke, "Richo koki ni okeru shakaiteki mujun no tokusitsu" (The special qualities of the social contradictions in the late Yi Dynasty), *Jinbun gakuho*, no. 89 (1972); An Pyŏng'uk, "Chosŏn hugi chach'i wa chŏhang chojik ŭrosŏŭi hyanghoe" (Provincial self-rule and rural associations as resistance organizations in the late Chosŏn period), *Sŏngsim yodae nonmunjip*, no. 18 (1986); An Pyŏng'uk, "19 segi imsul millan e issŏsŏ ŭi hyanghoe wa yoho" (Rural associations and the wealthy in the Imsul (1806) Uprising in the nineteenth century), *Han'guk saron*, no. 14 (1986).

19. Chŏng Yagyong, *Mongmin simsŏ*, vol. 28, *pyŏngjŏn ŭngbyŏn*; Yu Sinhwan, *Pongsŏjip*, vol. 5, *simu pyŏn*.

20. A *kuŏngyo* is a directive from the king to his ministers and the people, seeking their advice on a specific problem. (ed.)

21. Han Ugŭn, "Chŏngjo pyŏng'o sohoe tŭngnok ŭi punsŏkjŏk yŏn'gu" (An analysis of the register of memorials in the year 1786 during King Chŏngjo's reign), *Sŏuldae nonmunjip*, no. 11 (1965). A *paekgwan chin'ŏn* is a statement containing the opinions of all ministers and government officials. (ed.)

22. A *min'ŭnso* is a memorial from commoners revealing their troubles and inner thoughts. (ed.)

so,[23] or a *chinp'ye ch'aekja*.[24] One king also established the Office to Rectify the Samjŏng (Samjŏng ijŏng ch'ŏng)[25] to reform the irrationalities in the administration of the *samjŏng*. Under the existing system, taxes were levied based on the feudal social status system, and intermediary exploitation emerged through the feudal system of local autonomy. Despite small differences of opinion among the proponents of such reform, they all generally agreed on the need for equitable levying and collection of taxes by eliminating intermediary exploitation and also by abolishing status distinctions in the levying of taxes.

During the late Chosŏn period, the government adopted this course of reform and implemented various measures such as the Taedongbŏp,[26] Kyun'yŏkbŏp,[27] Household Cloth Law (*hop'obŏp*),[28] village granary system (*sach'angje*),[29] and the cadastral survey (*yangjŏn*). All of them had the objective of reforming the tax system.[30] What was missing from these policies was a consideration of existing land ownership relations and class conflicts in rural society.

Many obstacles existed to the reform of the tax system. In the existing system, yangban landowners were exempt from certain taxes and could take

23. An Pyŏng'uk, "Chosŏn hugi min'ŭn ŭi ildan kwa min ŭi tonghyang" (A survey of *min'ŭm* and trends of the people in the late Chosŏn period), *Han'guk munhwa*, no. 2 (1981); Kim Yong-sop, "18 segi nongch'on chisik'in ŭi nong'ŏpgwan" (The views on agriculture of rural intellectuals in the eighteenth century), *Chosŏn hugi nong'ŏpsa yŏn'gu*, vol. I, first edition (1970). A *nongjŏngso* is a petition containing opinions on agricultural policy. (ed.)

24. A *chinp'ye ch'aekja* is a book listing and organizing various types of corrupt practices. (ed.)

25. Pak Kwangsŏng, "Chinju millan ŭi yŏn'gu—ijŏngch'ŏng ŭi solch'i wa samjŏng kyoguch'aek ŭl chungsim ŭro" (A study of the Chinju popular rebellion—focusing on the establishment of the Office of Correction and the policies to reform the *samjŏng*), *Inch'ŏn kyodae nonmunjip*, no. 3 (1968); Kim Yong-sop, "Ch'ŏljongjo ŭi ŭngji samjŏngso wa samjŏng ijŏngch'aek" (Petitions on agricultural policy in response to the king's request for advice and the measures to rectify the *samjŏng* policy during King Ch'ŏljong's reign), *Han'guk kŭndae nong'ŏpsa yŏn'gu*, vol. 1.

26. The Taedongbŏp was an attempt to replace the tribute tax with a grain tax on land. Each region of the country had to send to the government a specific amount of locally produced products each year. The Taedongbŏp was designed to eliminate irregularities in the tribute tax system. It was gradually implemented province by province during the early and mid-seventeenth century. (ed.)

27. The *kyun'yŏkbŏp* was a law that attempted to eliminate status distinctions in the military service tax. (ed.)

28. Proposals on the household cloth tax emerged in the seventeenth century. It was designed to replace the military cloth tax (*kunp'oje*) and was intended to expand the tax base by being levied on a great range of people. (ed.)

29. Based on the ideas of Chu Hsi, the *sach'angje* or "Village Granary System" was an attempt to reform the inefficiencies and corrupt practices of the grain loan system. (ed.)

30. See Kim Yong-sop, "Chosŏn hugi ŭi puse chedo ijŏngch'aek."

advantage of loopholes to avoid others. It also gave economic privileges to the local elites and government officials who were the powerholders in the local autonomy system. Whenever there was a movement for reform, opposition would be even stronger, and occasionally, the opposition would even threaten that such measures could bring about a revolt among the yangban class.[31] The yangban ruling class saw themselves as the protectors of the royal family,[32] and they stressed their need for special privileges in order to maintain their ability to control the peasants. Although reform of the tax system faced tremendous difficulties, the yangban had to make some concessions in order to quell the peasant rebellions. Gradually and haltingly, the government implemented reforms that aimed to establish an equitable system. Nonetheless, the yangban would not yield on the issue of the landlord system and large land holdings, which was the economic foundation of the yangban class.

Second, a significant number of scholars argued that peasant rebellions could be mitigated through a reform of the land system that would stabilize the peasant economy. Although they did propose reforms of the tax system, they felt that it was also necessary to reform the land system in order to solve the problems in the agricultural economy at the time. These scholars were fewer in number than those who focused only on tax reform, but their numbers gradually increased during the late Chosŏn period. The peasants wanted land reform, and their views were shared by people ranging from Silhak scholars to rural Confucian students who were all concerned about agriculture and alarmed at the situation in the countryside. For some, their commitment to land reform was firm since they felt that without such reform, it would be impossible to achieve a virtuous monarchy (*wangdo chŏngch'i*) that could give the people stability.[33] Since the differentiation of rural society was affecting not only commoners and the low-born but also the yangban class, scholars began to think seriously about land reform as a solution as the number of "fallen yangban" (*mollak yangban*) was gradually increasing.

Scholars put forth a variety of land reform proposals. Many discussed traditional ideas such as the well-field system (*chŏngjŏnnon*),[34] the equal-field

31. Kim Yong-sop, Ibid., pp. 266-267.

32. *Yŏngjo sillok* (The veritable records of King Yŏngjo), vol. 71, 26th year, 6th month, kyesa, book 43, p. 372.

33. Hong Taeyong, *Tamhŏnsŏ*, Oejip, purok 2, p. 563.

34. The *chŏngjŏn* or well-field system was a program of land reform whose goal was to provide assistance to poor peasants. In order to protect poor peasants, this system proposed that the

system (*kyunjŏnnon*),[35] and the limited-field system (*hanjŏnnon*),[36] while also proposing a reduction of taxes.[37] The objective was to weaken or eliminate large-scale landholding and the feudal landlord system and to establish an economy of independent self-cultivators and autonomous small-scale agriculture. Depending on the proponent, there were differences over the method of achieving this goal (such as confiscation or forced sale) and limits to the amount of land involved. What they all had in common was the goal of stabilizing the peasant economy. Since these land reform proposals appeared in the classics and histories of Confucianism, it was only natural that Confucian scholars adopted and advocated such ideas, with variations according to their degree of social consciousness.

The main types of land reform proposals in the late Chosŏn period were as follows. First, some advocated more radical versions of land reform under a principle of "land for every cultivator" (*kyŏngja yujŏn*). For example, the "village land" (*yŏjŏn*) system aimed to eliminate intermediary exploitation

state distribute state-owned and public land to them. A parcel of land would be divided into a grid with nine plots, and individual farm households would cultivate eight of those plots, living off their harvests. The last plot in the grid would be cultivated collectively, and its harvest would be used to pay taxes to the state. Because the nine-plot grid resembled the shape of the character for "well," this system was called the "well-field" system. After it was originally proposed in ancient China by Mencius, it was continually debated as a form of land reform in pre-modern Korea as well. (ed.)

35. The *kyunjŏn* or equal-field system was a program of land reform whose goal was to provide assistance to poor peasants. It called for the government to stabilize the situation of small-scale farmers by dividing up state-owned and public land into even parcels and distributing them to poor peasants and those without land. This system attempted to overcome the problems of the well-field system which did not take into account the number of able-bodied adults in each household. The equal-field system took into account the number of men and women able to farm and proposed to distribute land equally to both. Land taxation policies based on these ideas were implemented in the Ch'ŏngju region during the Unified Silla Period in the eighth century, but afterwards, the equal-field system served as the theoretical basis for the equal taxation system. (ed.)

36. The *hanjŏn* or limited-field system was a type of land taxation reform. The state would propose to set a maximum limit for landholdings of large landlords in periods when a minority of landlords owned much of the land, creating a large number of poor peasants. From the fourteenth century, during the Koryo period, whenever large landholdings became a problem, a variety of proposals were made to limit land ownership to a maximum ranging from ten to fifty *kyŏl*. It was a gradualist method of achieving equitable land distribution as its proponents believed that the size of landholdings would grow smaller as plots were divided through inheritance. (ed.)

37. Of course, Silhak scholars such as Pan'gye Yu Hyŏngwŏn, Sŏngho Yi Ik, Tamhŏn Hong Taeyong, and Yŏn'am Pak Chiwŏn discussed such ideas, but in general, people who proposed land reform all suggested ideas such as the well-field system, equal-field system, and the limited-field system. Yu Hyŏngwŏn was critical of the proposal to reduce taxes. See Yu Hyŏngwŏn, *Pan'gye surok* (A miscellaneous account of the man from Pan'gye), book 2, land system, vol. 2, p. 14.

by nationalizing all land in the country and then managing agricultural production communally at the village level.[38] Second, others proposed a variation on the well-field system. In this system, commercial agriculture would be introduced, and agricultural production in the country would be divided into six areas of specialization (grains, fruits, vegetables, cloth, forestry products, and livestock). The farmers who were the most productive would be given political offices.[39] Of course, all proposals took into account the development of commerce and industry and of other occupations as a result of the social division of labor.[40]

Some land reform proposals in this period involved utilizing the *tunjŏn* system. Large numbers of *tunjŏn* would be established in all regions of the country with the most skilled farmers in each region put in charge of them. Its proponents aimed to increase agricultural production by using the *tunjŏn* to effect a transition to the well-field system, by improving methods of landlord management and by disseminating advancements in agricultural techniques throughout the country. Another objective was to facilitate social reform by giving political offices to successful managers.[41] Using a different approach, some people advocated the *kyunjak-kyundaejŏn* system in which the state would regulate private landlord management and evenly distribute land to be rented among the cultivators. Its purpose was to contain the differentiation of the peasant class and the landlords' accumulation of tenant

38. Chŏng Sŏkjong, "Tasan Chŏng Yagyong ŭi kyŏngje sasang" (The economic thought of Tasan Chŏng Yagyong), *Yi Haenam paksa hwagap ki'nyŏm sahak nonch'ong*; Sin Yongha, "Tasan Chŏng Yagyong ŭi yŏjŏnje t'oji kaehyŏk sasang" (Chŏng Yagyong's conception of land reform: the yŏjŏn system), *Kyujanggak*, no. 7 (1983); Kim Yong-sop, "18-19 segi ŭi nong'ŏp siljŏng kwa saeroun nong'ŏp kyŏngyŏngnon."

39. Pak Chongkŭn, "Chasan Te Jakuyo no tochi kaikaku shiso no kosatsu" (An examination of Chŏng Yagyong's ideas on land reform), *Chosen gakuho*, no. 28 (1963); Sin Yongha, "Tasan Chŏng Yagyong ŭi chŏngjŏnje t'oji kaehyŏk sasang" (Chŏng Yagyong's conception of land reform: the well-field system), *Kim Ch'ŏljun paksa hwagap ki'nyŏm sahak nonch'ong*, (Seoul: Chisik san'ŏpsa, 1983); Pak Ch'ansŭng, "Chŏng Yagyong ŭi chŏngjŏnjeron koch'al" (An examination of the well-field system proposal of Chŏng Yagyong), *Yŏksa hakbo*, no. 110 (1986); Kim Yong-sop, "18-19 segi ŭi nong'ŏp siljŏng kwa saeroun nong'ŏp kyŏngyŏngnon"; see also Kim Yong-sop, *Chosŏn hugi nong'ŏpsa yŏn'gu* II, revised edition, section IV.

40. Kim Yŏngho, "Chŏng Tasan ŭi chik'ŏpgwan" (Chŏng Yagyong's views on occupations), *Ch'ŏn Kwan'u sŏnsaeng hwallyŏk ki'nyŏm Han'guk sahak nonch'ong*, (Seoul: Chŏng'ŭm munhwasa, 1985); Chŏng Sŏkjong, "Tasan Chŏng Yagyong ŭi kyŏngje sasang."

41. Yu Ponghak, "Sŏ Yugu ŭi hakmun kwa nong'ŏp chŏngch'aeknon" (Sŏ Yugu's scholarship and views on agricultural policy), *Kyujanggak*, no. 9 (1985); Kim Yong-sop, "18-19 segi ŭi nong'ŏp siljŏng kwa saeroun nong'ŏp kyŏngyŏngnon."

farming land.[42] Both of these proposals can be seen as a kind of compromise plan for land reform.

Regardless of the type of proposal, land reform faced significant obstacles. Its impact would be greatest on large landholders and the yangban landlord class, and they were the ones who held political power. The proponents of land reform sought to control the yangban ruling class by strengthening the power of the monarchy. However, kings in this period had little interest in land reform and did not possess the power to overcome the opposition of the yangban class. Although kings did wish to strengthen royal authority, they did not want the royal family's lands to become subject to land reform. Furthermore, Chu Hsi Neo-Confucianism was the dominant ideology in the intellectual world at the time, and the orthodox interpretation of Chu Hsi's views on land policy held that it would be difficult to achieve land reform.[43] Whenever land reform was proposed, Chu Hsi Neo-Confucianists and their followers generally opposed it on the grounds of Chu Hsi's position on land. Their opposition to land reform was virtually absolute since, to them, land ownership was the final line of defense protecting their status interests. As demonstrated by the degree of yangban opposition, the goal of land reform was to establish a land system that represented the interests of the peasants.

In sum, before the opening of the ports in the late nineteenth century, two kinds of proposals aimed to resolve the problems in the agricultural economy. What they had in common was a desire to alleviate peasant rebellions by stabilizing the peasant economy. Despite this shared purpose, there were fundamental differences between the two in their underlying objectives. On the one hand, supporters of tax reform wanted a resolution that would ultimately preserve the economic privileges of the landlord class. On the other hand, proponents of land reform wanted to provide fundamental stability for small-scale agriculture through the elimination of the landlord system. From the perspective of agricultural production, these two proposals reflected the conflict between the large-scale commercial agriculture of the landlords and

---

42. Yi Yungap, "18 segi mal ŭi kyunbyŏngjaknon" (Proposals on *kyunbyŏngjak* [equal cultivation for all who lease land] of the late eighteenth century), *Han'guk saron*, no. 9 (1983).

43. Kim Yong-sop, "Chuja ŭi t'ojiron kwa Chosŏn hugi yuja—chijuje wa sonong kyŏngje ŭi munje" (Chu Hsi's views on land and Confucianists of the late Chosŏn period—the landlord system and the issue of an economy of small-scale agriculture), *Yŏnse nonch'ong*, no. 21 (1985); Kim Yong-sop, *Chosŏn hugi nong'ŏpsa yŏn'gu*, vol. II, revised edition.

the small-scale, independent cultivation of the peasants.[44] In short, they represented differing class interests. Regardless of the kind of reform adopted, tremendous changes would be needed in the economic system and form of the state. No matter how widespread the outbreaks of peasant rebellions became or how strong the demands for land reform grew, the ruling class would never go so far as to allow land reform—as demonstrated by the government's policies to rectify the *samjŏng* and the Taewŏn'gun's internal reforms.

The Opening of the Ports and
the Aggravation of Agricultural Problems

The existing social problems in the agricultural economy became more severe after the opening of Chosŏn's ports. There had been little improvement in the conditions that caused these problems, and the open ports were a new factor in the economy. After the peasant rebellion in 1862, the domestic reforms of the Taewŏn'gun did attempt to address these problems. However, his efforts only aimed for a partial reform of the tax system and did not achieve complete impartiality in the levying and collection of taxes. The feudal economic and taxation systems, which were based on the Chosŏn social status system, continued to exist unchanged. As a result, the same problems in the agricultural economy arose again, and the changes caused by the opening of the ports exacerbated these problems even further. Rural society was now undergoing rapid differentiation and transformation, and the conflict among status groups became more severe than before. The unavoidable consequence of this situation was the Peasants' War in 1894, the later rise of the Hwalbindang, and the continued outbreak of peasant rebellions.

Two factors were behind the worsening problems in the agricultural economy. The first factor was the changes in the economy—namely, the acceleration of differentiation—because of the growth of commerce at the open ports. The second was the spread of the belief in human equality and, concomitantly, the growth of tension between the classes.

First, it was inevitable that the opening of the ports accelerated social differentiation in rural society because of the nature of commerce at the ports. Chosŏn's trade routes suddenly expanded internationally as it began to export

44. Yi Yungap, "18-19 segi Kyŏngbuk chibang ŭi nong'ŏp pyŏndong" (Changes in agriculture in the north Kyŏngsang province region in the eighteenth and nineteenth centuries), *Han'guksa yŏn'gu*, no. 54 (1985).

farm products such as rice, soybeans, and cattle through the open ports. Agricultural production for the market increased rapidly compared to the past, and grain prices rose seemingly on a daily basis. However, since the majority of imported products were manufactured goods such as cotton cloth, only a small number of privileged people in Chosŏn could profit and expand their businesses through such trade. The privileged few were those who were involved in the rice trade in various capacities, such as yangban officials, rice merchants, and yangban landlords (pyŏngjak chiju)[45] and rich landlords (kyŏng'yŏng chiju or chijuhyŏng punong) who were directly involved in production and sold their agricultural goods on the market. In a slightly less advantageous position were the managerial rich peasants (kyŏng'yŏnghyŏng punong).

On the other hand, many small-scale and poor farmers were generally faced with the prospect of ruin as their losses grew from such trade. Domestic cotton traders and those working in the carrying trade faced the same fate.[46] In terms of agricultural production, the prevailing trend was that the comercial activities of the landlords reached a new stage of development. Within the peasant economy, only the managerial rich peasants had positive prospects, and small-scale and poor peasants were growing more and more destitute. In other words, the trend was an acceleration of differentiation that occurred through production for the market.

45. The term pyŏngjak chiju refers to a landlord—usually a yangban—who lent all his land to tenant farmers and just lived off the land rent that they paid. (ed.)

46. Kang Tŏksang (J. Kan Dokusan), "Rishi Chosen kaiko chokugo ni okeru Sen-Ni boeki no tenkai" (The development of Chosŏn-Japan trade immediately after the openings of the ports of Yi Dynasty Chosŏn), Rekishigaku kenkyu, no. 266 (1962); Han Ugŭn, "Migok ŭi kuk'oe yuch'ul" (The international outflow of rice) and "Sŏn'un kwa chŏn'unsa ŭi munje" (The problem of the shipping trade and its government administrators), Han'guk kaehanggi ŭi sang'ŏp yŏn'gu, (Seoul: Ilchogak, 1970); Kajimura Hideki, "Richo makki no mengyo no ryutsu oyobi seisan kozo" (The structure of circulation and production of the cotton industry at the end of the Yi Dynasty), Chosen ni okeru shihonshugi no keisei to tenkai, (Tokyo: Ryukei shosha, 1977); Miyajima Hiroshi, "Chosen Kogo Kaikaku iko no shogyoteki nogyo" (Commercial agriculture in Chosŏn after the Kabo Reforms), Sirin 57, no. 6 (1974); Miyajima Hiroshi, "Tochi chosa jigyo no rekishiteki zentei joken no keisei" (The formation of the historical preconditions of the land survey), Chosenshi kenkyukai ronbunshu, no. 12 (1975); Yoshino Makoto, "Chosen kaikoku ko no kokumotsu yushutsu ni tsuite" (On grain exports after the opening of Chosŏn), Chosenshi kenkyukai ronbunshu, no. 12 (1975); Yoshino Makoto, "Richo makki ni okeru beikoku yushutsu no tenkai to bokokurei" (The development of rice exports at the end of the Yi Dynasty and the act to restrict grain exports), Chosenshi kenkyukai ronbunshu, no. 15 (1978); Yoshino Makoto, "Richo makki ni okeru menseihin yunyu no tenkai" (The development of imports in cotton goods at the end of the Yi Dynasty), Chosen rekishi ronshu, vol. 2 (Tokyo: Ryukei shosha, 1979).

In the mid- to late-nineteenth century, the same patterns of commerce and trade continued year after year, and the volume of trade gradually increased even further. Another important factor was the gradual increase in the number of open ports. As the level of trade increased, its impact on rural society increased proportionately. The richer got richer, and the poor peasant class engaging in small-scale agriculture became more impoverished and fell into ruin. The rice trade was accelerating the concentration of land ownership.

During the period of modernization after the opening of the ports, the safest investment for people with wealth was land. Since rice exports were increasing and the price of rice was rising, anyone with the financial resources to do so bought fields and land. There were instances of high-ranking officials and the wealthy who bought large amounts of farmland all at once in the areas near the open ports.[47] In most cases, people simply bought plots of farmland, one or two at a time, that poor, small-scale peasant cultivators were selling. Over time, they generally chose to invest their rice-trade profits in land, and after twenty to thirty years, they could become large landlords.

As the rice trade grew in the second half of the nineteenth century, the number of people who became large-scale landlords increased significantly. Of course, the increase included many who were landlords before the opening of the ports, but after the opening, many new landlords emerged who skillfully took advantage of the rice trade. Since Japanese merchants and businesses dominated the rice trade, Koreans who had close relations with them were in a better position to profit from the trade. Koreans, however, were not the only ones accumulating land. After the Sino-Japanese War, Japanese also actively bought up land in Chosŏn as the Japanese government began its preparations to take over the country. From the time of the Russo-Japanese War, they established agricultural estates (nongjang) and engaged in commercial agriculture.[48] As a result, from the opening of the ports through the Hanmal

47. Kim Yong-sop, "Kwangmu nyŏngan ŭi yangjŏn-chigye saŏp" (The cadastral survey and land certificate project of the Kwangmu years), Han'guk kŭndae nong'ŏpsa yŏn'gu 2, p. 302 n. 221.

48. Yi Chaemu, "Iwayuru Ni-Kan heigo=kyosen mae ni okeru Nihon teikoku shugi ni yoru Chosen shokuminchika no kisoteki sho shihyo" (The fundamental indices of the colonization of Chosŏn by Japanese imperialism before its occupation or the so-called Japan-Korea annexation), Shakai kagaku kenkyu 9, no. 6 (1957); Asada Kyoji, Nihon teikokushugi to kyushokuminchi jinushisei (Japanese imperialism and the old colonial landlord system) (Tokyo: Ochanomizu shobo, 1968); Pae Yŏngsun, "Hanmal-ilchech'o Ilbon'in taejiju ŭi nongjang kyŏng'yŏng—Sujŏn (Mizuta) nongjang ŭl chungsim uro" (The management of agricultural estates by large-scale Japanese landlords during the late Great Han Empire period and early colonial period), Inmun yŏn'gu, no. 3 (1983); Kim Yong-sop, "Kojongjo wangsil ŭi kyunjŏn sudo munje" (The issue of collecting land

period, the landlord system became more pervasive while the deterioration of the peasant class accelerated.

The extent of the differentiation of rural society can be grasped through an examination of its opposite phenomenon: the prevalence of land accumulation and the growth of landlord management over agriculture. It is possible to examine this issue concretely, using examples provided by recent research. First, the Kim family of Kanghwa Island were small-scale landlords who had been living in this area for about ten generations. Although their fortunes had had their vicissitudes, the size of their holdings increased from 5 *kyŏl*, 77 *pu*, 4 *sok* (393 *turak*) to 12 *kyŏl*, 98 *pu*, 5 *sok* (1086.5 *turak*) between 1876 and 1896.[49]

Second, the Hong family had also lived on Kanghwa Island for over ten generations. Between 1869 and 1898, they increased their landholdings from 3 *kyŏl*, 77 *pu*, 1 *sok* of paddy field to 14 *kyŏl*, 15 *pu*, 1 *sok* of paddy field and 59 *pu*, 2 *sok* of dry fields.[50] Both landlord families were located near the open port of Inch'ŏn, and they were able to accumulate wealth through skillful landlord management that took advantage of opportunities created by the rice trade. Over several years, they had purchased one or two plots of land at a time from peasants who had fallen into hard times.

The Kim family of Kobu County, Chŏlla province was a prototypical example of the rise of a landlord in this period. The Kim family later became a *chaebŏl* (family-owned conglomerate) in the Honam region, and the foundation for its future development was laid in the period from the opening of the ports to the Hanmal period. The founder of the *chaebŏl* family, Kim Yohyŏp, began with a small amount of farmland that he had received from his wife's family. After the opening of the ports, he built up the family's landholdings to the level of a small landlord by utilizing the commercial trade.

rents on kyunjŏn of the royal family during Kojong's reign), *Han'guk kŭndae nong'ŏpsa yŏn'gu*, vol. 2.

49. Kim Yong-sop, "Hanmal-ilcheha ŭi chijuje, sarye 1: Kanghwa Kimssiga ŭi ch'usugi rŭl t'onghaesŏ pon chiju kyŏng'yŏng" (The landlord system in the late Great Han Empire period and colonial period, case study 1: an examination of landlord management through the harvest records of the Kim family of Kanghwa Island), *Tonga munhwa*, no. 11 (1972), reprinted in Kim Yong-sop, *Han'guk kŭnhyŏndae nong'ŏpsa yŏn'gu*.

50. Hong Sung-Chan (Hong Sŏngch'an), "Hanmal-icheha ŭi chijuje yŏn'gu—Kanghwa Hongssiga ŭi chusugi wa changch'aek punsŏk ŭl chungsim ŭro" (A study of the landlord system in the late Great Han Empire and colonial periods—with a focus on an analysis of the harvest records and ledgers of the Hong family of Kanghwa Island), *Han'guksa yŏn'gu*, no. 33 (1981).

His agricultural operations continued to grow, and at the time of his death in 1909, he became a large landlord whose harvest totaled 1,200 *sŏk* of rice.[51]

Kobu County was the region where the 1894 Peasants' War broke out. While the irrationalities of the tax system remained unchanged, the differentiation of rural society (i.e., the accumulation and loss of land) accelerated because of commerce through the open ports. This acceleration led to the intensification of contradictions between the classes in that part of the country. It was in this period and in this area that the Kim family became a large landlord through the accumulation of land.

Similarly, between 1886 and 1916, the Yun family of the Haenam region increased their holdings of farmland from 18 *kyŏl*, 74 *pu*, 5 *sok* to 36 *kyŏl*, 32 *pu*, 3 *sok*.[52] The Yi family of the Naju region (Chŏlla Province) was destitute during the Hanmal period but became a landlord with 25 *chŏngbo* of land by 1915.[53] These and other similar families were enjoying the advantages of the boom in the rice trade, acquiring wealth, and buying up the land of peasants who fell into ruin.

The history of these landlord families reflects both the accumulation of land by yangban officials, landlords, and rice merchants and the loss of land by the peasant class during the period of modernization after the opening of the ports. However, people did not always use normal, legal methods to purchase fields and accumulate land. Even in apparently normal transactions, some cases involved usurious exploitation. There were also instances of exploitation where force or violence was used to obtain land.

A typical example was the problem of the collection of land rent on *kyunjŏn*[54] managed by the royal family. In the fields in North Chŏlla

51. Kim Yong-sop, "Hanmal-ilcheha ŭi chijuje, sarye 4: Kobu Kim ssiga ŭi chiju kyŏng'yŏng kwa chabon chŏnhwan" (The landlord system in the late Great Han Empire period and colonial period, case study 4: the landlord management and capital conversion of the Kim family of Kobu), *Han'guksa yŏn'gu* 19 (1978); reprinted in Kim Yong-sop, *Han'guk kŭnhyŏndae nong'ŏpsa yŏn'gu*.

52. Choi Won-kyu (Ch'oe Wŏn'gyu), "Hanmal-Ilcheha ŭi nong'ŏp kyŏng'yŏng e kwanhan yŏn'gu—Haenam Yun ssiga ŭi sarye" (A study of agricultural management during the Great Han Empire and colonial periods—a case study of the Yun family of Haenam), *Han'guksa yŏn'gu*, nos. 50-51 (1985).

53. Kim Yong-sop, "Hanmal-ilcheha ŭi chijuje, sarye 3: Naju Yi ssiga ŭi sŏngjang kwa kŭ nongjang kyŏng'yŏng" (The landlord system in the late Great Han Empire period and colonial period, case study 3: The development of the Yi family of Naju into a landlord and their management of agricultural estates), *Chindan hakbo*, no. 42 (1976); reprinted in Kim Yong-sop, *Han'guk kŭnhyŏndae nong'ŏpsa yŏn'gu*.

54. The term used is *kyunjŏn sudo*. Though the character today is used in the sense of "gambling," "*to*" refers to the land tax; thus, *sudo* is simply the collection of the land tax. (ed.)

province, the royal family provided the funds for farmers to reclaim land that had become fallow because of consecutive years of floods and drought, and land taxes were to be levied equitably. However, what actually happened was that the land tax was gradually raised, and in the end, the royal family attempted to take ownership rights away from the peasants.[55] There were also cases where large landholdings were obtained through the clearing of new fields. Such land reclamation was an important factor in land accumulation and the differentiation of rural society since it deprived peasants of the opportunity to clear the land themselves and become landowners.

Another trend that emerged with the opening of the ports was the retrenchment and expansion of the landlord system in agricultural production. From the perspective of the landlord class, their response was only natural since they were trying to increase their income from the rice trade. For instance, when the royal family attempted to eliminate *chungdapju* from their palace estate lands, the landlords sought to take their place.[56] Furthermore, landlord families that possessed large landholdings would expel tenant farmers who protested against the land tax and relocate regular tenant farmers to areas near their residences.[57] There were also instances where the landlords or yangban officials assumed control of irrigation and levied a water tax on the tenant-cultivators. Examples included the forced payment of water taxes by a landlord near the Hapdŏk reservoir and the collection of a water tax by the county magistrate (*kunsu*) in the region of the Kobu reservoir.[58] When the landlord class expanded its operations by intensifying its management methods, common peasants, by contrast, would suffer losses.

The flip side of the differentiation of rural society was the rise in tensions between classes and in peasant resistance against the yangban landlord class. The decline of the peasant class and its decreasing landownership were the basis of the growth of the yangban landlord class after the opening of the ports. Yangban landlords had both political and social advantages and still

55. Kim Yong-sop, "Kojongjo wangsil ŭi kyunjŏn sudo munje."

56. Pak Ch'ansŭng, "Hanmal yŏkt'o-tunt'o esŏ ŭi chiju kyŏngyŏng ŭi kanghwa wa hangjo" (The strengthening of landlord management and tax protests in *yŏkt'o* and *tunt'o* during the Great Han Empire period), *Han'guk saron*, no. 9 (1983); Kim Yong-sop, "Hanmal e issŏsŏ ŭi chungdapju wa yŏkdunt'o chijuje" (The landlord system in *yŏkdunt'o* and *chungdapju* during the Great Han Empire period), *Han'guk kŭndae nong'ŏpsa yŏn'gu*, vol. 2.

57. *Kwŏnnong chŏlmok*.

58. Hisama Ken'ichi, "Godoku hyakusho ikki no kenkyu" (A study of peasant uprisings in Hapdŏk county), *Chosen nogyo no kindaiteki yoso* (The modern aspects of Chosŏn's agriculture) (Tokyo: Nishigahara kankokai, 1935); *Chŏn Pongjun kongch'o* (Tonghaknan kirok, vol. 2).

enjoyed special class privileges in the taxation system. Their growth would not have been possible without the sacrifice of commoners, the low-born, and "fallen yangban" who had declined to the status of peasants. It was only natural that the peasant class, whose situation was deteriorating, came to view the rising yangban landlord class as the enemy.

Developments after the opening of the ports contributed to the growth of the social consciousness of the peasantry compared to earlier periods. As disorder in the social status system became more severe in this period, the rise of commoners and the low-born to yangban status became even more frequent.[59] A household cloth tax system (hop'oje) was also implemented in which even the yangban had to bear part of the burden of military service. Amidst these changes, a belief in human equality became widespread as commoners and the low-born rejected the status distinctions that separated them from the yangban.[60] The government officially recognized Catholicism, and Western notions of equality became known. Tonghak ideas of respect for human equality (sain yoch'ŏn) also spread rapidly. As a result, commoners and the low-born began to reject their hierarchical, subordinate relation toward the yangban ruling class, demanding liberation from status distinctions. During the modernization period, peasant attitudes of resistance toward the yangban landlord class became more radical than in the previous period.

The Reform Policies of the Government and the Objectives of the Peasant Movement

As mentioned above, now that Chosŏn had contact with Western states and had been incorporated into their world order, it had to implement systematic reforms that would enable it to deal with the sudden threats to its survival. The challenge facing Chosŏn was to undertake social reform and modernization. Although the focus of reform was a thorough reorganization of the state, it also had to address problems in the agricultural economy that were apparent in Chosŏn. Social contradictions became even more severe than they had been before the opening of the ports, and they were concentrated in problems related to agriculture.

---

59. Sanju sayre.
60. Kim Yong-sop, "Chosŏn hugi ŭi puse chedo ijŏngch'aek," pp. 295-97.

Approaches to reform did not suddenly change with the opening of the ports. Reform efforts in the late nineteenth century were descendants of the traditions of reform from earlier periods. The political leaders of the country remained unchanged, and although Western thought was being introduced, it had not yet replaced the Confucian ideology of the political leadership. Many scholars and officials proposed reforms to resolve the problems in the agricultural economy, based on traditional proposals from before the opening of Chosŏn's ports. As in the previous period, reform proposals can be divided into two general types. The first sought a resolution through a reform of the tax system, and the second argued that it was also necessary to reform the land system.

First, as in the previous period, the government and the ruling class proposed to solve agricultural problems through a reform of the tax system. Tax reform faced considerable difficulties since it was based on—and thus, had developed both direct and indirect intricate connections with—both the feudal social status system and the provincial administration system. In the late Chosŏn period, the government and ruling class did pursue, if slowly, a fundamental agenda of resolving social contradictions through reforms that focused on the tax system. Since this agenda constituted the tradition of policy responses adopted by the Chosŏn state, it was only natural that political leaders turned to that tradition after the opening of the ports. However, a tremendous difference existed between the two periods in the direction of reform. Before the opening of the ports, the objective of reform was only to resolve the social contradictions of the time. Afterwards, reform was seen as necessary to achieve social reform, build a modern state, and develop agricultural commerce and trade through capitalist production.[61]

Beginning with the Kapsin Coup of 1884, the underlying objective of tax system reform was the creation of a modern state.[62] Similar policies were

61. Such ideas can be found in works such as *Kim Okkyun chŏnjip* (The complete works of Kim Okkyun), *Pak Yŏnghyo sangso* (The memorial of Pak Yŏnghyo), and *Yu Kiljun chŏnsŏ* (The complete writings of Yu Kiljun).

62. Kim Sŏkhyŏng, et al., *Kin Gyokukin no kenkyu* (Studies on Kim Okkyun), trans. by Watanabe Manabu, Chapter 6: "Kaikaha no seiko ni tsuite," (Tokyo: Nihon Chosen kenkyujo, 1968); Kang Chaeŏn (J. Kan Jeon), "Kaika shiso-Kaikaha-Kosin seihen" (*Kaehwa* thought, the Kaehwap'a, Kapsin Coup), *Chosen kindaishi kenkyu* (Tokyo: Nihon hyoronsha, 1970); An Pyŏngt'ae (J. An Byonte), "1884nen Kosin seihen no shakai keizaiteki kiso" (The socioeconomic foundation of the Kapsin Coup of 1884), *Chosen kindai keizaisi kenkyu* (Tokyo: Nihon hyoronsha, 1975); Sin Yongha, "Kim Okkyun ŭi kaehwa sasang" (The enlightenment thought of Kim Okkyun), *Tongbang hakji*, nos. 46-47-48 (combined issue, 1985).

adopted again in the Kabo Reforms and the Kwangmu Reforms.[63] The purpose of these policies was to reform the *samjŏng* and to reorganize the state's finances completely. As part of its land policy, the government conducted a cadastral survey to determine land ownership and to issue land certificates (*chigye*). It then recalculated the fertility of fields (*kyŏlbu*) and made monetary payment of taxes mandatory. Despite such efforts, the government was not able to do away with the *kyŏlbu* system, which was the fundamental determinant of tax rates under feudal law, in the cadastral survey. Nonetheless, the survey represented an advance in that it did not use a *kyŏlbu* system in which the meaning of the units was flexible. During the years 1902-1905, it adopted the metric system of the west and changed the *kyŏlbu* system into one based on land area in units of hectares.[64]

During the regency of the Taewongun (1864-1873), the military cloth tax (*kunp'o*) had already been changed to a household cloth (*hop'o*) tax. However, since these changes did not completely do away with status distinctions in the levying of taxes, the Chosŏn state abolished the social status system (under the principle of human equality) and collected household and property taxes from all households. The objective was to abolish the grain loan (*hwan'gok*) system in order to collect all taxes through the land tax and to transfer its rural relief function to the village granary (*sach'ang*) system. Since these reforms had been partially implemented during the Taewŏn'gun's rule, there were now efforts to combine the remaining grain loan storehouses with the new village granaries and to legalize the regulations governing their administration—i.e., the *Sahwan chorye*. All of these steps aimed at eliminating inequalities in the tax system based on social status or occupation and at securing fairness in the levying and payment of taxes. Of course, these measures were not the only reforms attempted of the tax system. The Chosŏn

63. Takjibu saseguk, *Han'guk seje ko* (1909); Mizuta Naomasa, *Richo jidai no zaisei—Chosen zaisei kindaika no katei* (The financial management of the Yi Dynasty—the modernization of Chosŏn's financial system) (Tokyo: Yuho kyokai, 1968); Kim Daejun, *Yijo malyŏp ŭi kukga chaejong e kwanhan yŏn'gu* (Ph.D. diss., Yonsei University, 1973); Kim Insun, "Chosen ni okeru 1894 nen no naisei kaikaku no kenkyu" (A study of the domestic reforms in Chosŏn in 1894), *Kokusai kankeiron kenkyu III* (1968); Pae Yŏngsun, "Hanmal yŏkdunt'o chosa e issŏsŏ ŭi soyugwŏn punjaeng" (Disputes over ownership during the survey of *yŏkdunt'o* in the Hanmal period), *Han'guksa yŏn'gu*, no. 25 (1979); Kim Yong-sop, "Kapsin-Kabo kaehyŏkgi Kaehwap'a ŭi nong'ŏpnon" (The agricultural policies of the Kaehwap'a during the Kapsin and Kabo reform periods) and "Kwangmu nyŏngan ŭi yangjŏn jigye saŏp" (The cadastral survey and land certificate projects during the Kwangmu years), *Han'guk kŭndae nong'ŏpsa yŏn'gu*, Vol. 2.

64. Kim Yong-sop, "Kyŏlbuje ŭi chŏngae kwajŏng" (Changes in the *kyŏlbu* system), *Han'guk chungse nong'ŏpsa yŏn'gu* (Seoul: Chisik san'ŏpsa, 2000), p. 278.

state also tried to revise the entire tax system along the lines of the tax laws of modern Western states.[65]

After the Kapsin Coup, the government's modernization program devoted much effort to the reform of the tax system but had little interest in reform of the land system. The government's response to the land problem was to recognize the existing state of land ownership and simply to put it under a modern property system in an attempt to effect a transition to a capitalist society through the development of landlord capital.[66] For instance, the Kabo Reforms left the landlord system unchanged. In the Kwangmu reforms, the cadastral survey determined ownership rights to the country's land, and the government issued land certificates (*chigye*) to the owners.[67]

The state's adoption of these economic policies was unsurprising since it was trying to reform and modernize society under the leadership of the yang-ban landlord class. Believing that the development of commerce and trade was a shortcut to modernization, the government sought to turn Chosŏn into a mercantile state. These policies were a logical progression of thought given that the landlord class in this period was experiencing tremendous growth through the rice trade. There were some who advocated a reduction of the land tax,[68] but their proposals were never instituted.

The leaders of state reform were opposed to any kind of land reform. Some reformers argued for the necessity of protecting wealth, believing that the poor needed a wealthy class to depend upon in order to survive and that the wealthy would be the central force of capitalist development. Others opposed land reform on the grounds of the sanctity of private property rights in a modern capitalist state. The government also worried that carrying out land reform would anger the wealthy class and cause tremendous disorder by giving peasants a false sense of hope.[69] State reformers in Chosŏn were aware that Europe was in turmoil because social-democratic parties[70] were advocating socioeconomic equality and pushing for systemic reforms.[71] They felt that there had to be a solution to the problems in the agricultural economy other than land reform. As mentioned above, to them, the alternative was to

---

65. *Yu Kiljun chŏnsŏ* VI, *seje ŭi, chaejŏng kaehyŏk*.

66. Kim Yong-sop, "Kapsin-Kabo kaehyŏkgi Kaehwap'a ŭi nong'ŏpnon."

67. Kim Yong-sop, "Kwangmu nyŏngan ŭi yangjŏn jigye saŏp."

68. *Yu Kiljun chŏnsŏ* IV, *chije ŭi* (On the land system).

69. Kim Yong-sop, "Kapsin-Kabo kaehyŏkgi kaehwap'a ŭi nong'ŏpnon."

70. In the *Sŏyu kyŏnmun*, Yu Kiljun used the term "*sahoedang*" or "social party" to refer to social-democratic political parties in Europe.

71. Kim Yong-sop, Ibid.

reform the taxation system and to stimulate the development of agriculture. This approach toward reform was also adopted later by the Independence Club (Tongnip hyŏphoe) and by the enlightenment movements of the late Hanmal period.

A major focus of the pro-landlord program of modernization was to promote agricultural development.[72] There was always the possibility that the government would adopt such measures as its agricultural policy because the ruling class was in control of modernization efforts. Since the government refused to undertake land reform at a time when it seemed urgent, the need arose for an alternative policy that could appease demands for reform. The result was the measures to promote agricultural development.

Government officials firmly believed that agriculture, along with other industries, had to develop in order for commerce to thrive and that, in turn, the development of commerce was necessary to enrich and strengthen the state. The main objectives were to introduce modern Western farming techniques and to increase agricultural production by increasing the total area of land under cultivation. To accomplish the first objective, the government established an agricultural school and hired instructors from England to teach modern agricultural techniques. It also attempted to improve the level of agricultural technology by importing and translating books on agriculture from Japan.[73] To accomplish the second objective, the government raised funds to establish companies that would be in charge of clearing new fields and bringing fallow fields back under cultivation.

Second, the peasants and progressive individuals who shared their views believed that the land system as well as the tax system had to be reformed in order to solve the problems in the agricultural economy and stabilize the peasant economy. The exploitative nature of the tax system made it undeniably difficult for the peasant class to accumulate a surplus and contributed to their decline. However, the more fundamental problem was the feudal land system (i.e., the landlord system) that was oppressing the peasantry. Under the existing land system, it would be difficult to stabilize the peasant economy, even if the tax system were reformed.

---

72. Ibid.

73. Yi Kwangnin, "Nongmu mokch'uk sihŏnjang ŭi sŏlch'i e taehayo" (On the establishment of the agricultural and livestock experimental station) and "An Chongsu ŭi nongjŏng sinp'yŏn" (The *sinpyŏn* of An Chongsu on agricultural policies), *Han'guk kaehwasa yŏn'gu* (Seoul: Ilchogak, 1970).

In numerous peasant rebellions beginning in the late Chosŏn period, the peasants had protested against taxes paid to the state, objecting to the irrationalities of the tax system. They had also protested against the land rent, decrying the landlords' exploitation. Since the former involved a refusal to pay taxes levied by the state, landlords who had to pay taxes would occasionally join the peasants in their protests. But if a rebellion escalated and was directed toward eliminating the source of social contradictions, the struggle would usually develop into a confrontation between landlords and peasants.

The sources of problems were the social status system and the land system. After the opening of the ports, the contradictions became more severe, and rebellions over the land issue intensified as the rice trade facilitated the accumulation of land and accelerated the decline of the peasant class. As a result, peasants and the scholars who represented their interests began to call directly for reform of the land system.[74] Their ideas can be seen as descendants of the land reform theories propounded by Silhak thinkers in the late Chosŏn period, but they also took into account the changed situation that Chosŏn now faced.

The peasant class began to make explicit demands for land reform during the Kabo Peasant War of 1894. Later rebellions also took up land reform as one of their slogans. During the peasant war, peasants demanded the rectification of various unfair taxes and also mentioned land reform, stating that their goal was for "land [to] be divided and cultivated equitably."[75] The peasant war occurred in the same period as the Kabo Reforms. While the Kabo Reforms pursued a modernization program based on the maintenance of the landlord system, the peasant army wanted land reform and openly demanded it. Since the peasants hoped to win the local elites, wealthy, and literate classes to their side,[76] the tax system was their main target when they demanded reform of corrupt administrative practices. However, their ultimate objective and most important goal was land reform, which was a matter of critical importance for their survival. Their demands for land reform con-

---

74. Kim Yong-sop, "Hanmal Kojongjo ŭi t'oji kaehyŏknon" (Proposals for land reform during Kojong's reign) *Han'guk kŭndae nong'ŏpsa yŏn'gu*, vol. 1.

75. O Chiyŏng, *Tonghaksa* (The history of Tonghak) (Kyŏngsŏng (Seoul): Yŏngch'ang sŏgwan, 1940), p. 127.

76. Hwang Hyŏn, *Oha kimun* (Diary of things heard while sitting under a paulownia tree), 2 p'il, Kabo 8 wŏl (August 1894) cho.

tinued in later rebellions; one example was the Hwalbindang's calls for the abolition of private land.[77]

Within the literate class, many in this period shared the views of the peasant class on agricultural issues and were just as passionate about demanding land reform. They felt that in order to defuse potentially revolutionary situations such as the peasant war, it was necessary to stabilize the peasant economy by eliminating the fundamental cause of the rebellions. They believed land reform would be the best method to achieve these goals, and they suggested well-known, traditional ideas such as the well-field, equal-field, and limited-field systems. As a compromise, they also proposed a reduction of taxes. The three land system proposals were intended to put limitations on land ownership. However, their proposals to reduce taxes did not limit land ownership but tried to prevent landlords from buying up land and to return a greater share of the harvest to tenant farmers by legally reducing the land rent.[78] Depending on the extent of the reduction, tax reform represented either a compromise measure or an indirect way to achieve land reform.[79]

The motivations behind demands for land reform varied according to intellectual orientation. Some advocated traditional land reform ideas out of simple recidivism, and others saw them as a method of overcoming the problems of the time. People who had an accurate understanding of current conditions viewed land reform as one part of the reforms necessary for the modernization of the country. In their thinking, a modern society should be based on an economy of independent self-cultivators and autonomous small-scale agriculture. Such a modern society could be established through the development of commerce which would be facilitated by land reform. Their argument was that if reform of the land system (in this case, through a reduction of taxes) could prevent the landlord class from making profits by

---

77. O Sech'ang, "Hwalbindang ko" (An examination of the Hwalbindang), *Sahak yŏn'gu*, no. 21 (1969); Kang Chaeŏn (J. Kan Jeon), "Katsuhinto toso to sono shiso" (The struggles of the Hwalbindang and their thought), *Kindai Chosen no henkaku shiso*, (Tokyo: Nihon hyoronsha, 1973); Pak Ch'ansŭng, "Hwalbindang ŭi hwaldong kwa kŭ sŏnggyŏk" (The activities of the Hwalbindang and their character), *Han'guk hakbo*, no. 35 (1984).

78. Kim Yong-sop, "Hanmal Kojongjo ŭi t'oji kaehyŏknon."

79. An example of the former is the proposal to reduce taxes to one-third of the crop, and examples of the latter are the *sip'ilje* and the *kuilje*, which would have reduced taxes to one-tenth and one-ninth of the crop, respectively. See Kim Yong-sop, "Hanmal Kojongjo ŭi t'oji kaehyŏknon."

accumulating land, the landlords would then naturally convert their wealth into commercial capital.[80]

There were thinkers who continued to discuss land reform in the context of modernization into the years of Japanese rule. Noting that the world had entered the era of republicanism and communism and declared ideals of universal brotherhood, some argued that there was nothing preventing the ruler of a country from dividing and redistributing its land equitably to its citizens.[81] Though these thinkers were aiming to establish a modern society, their proposals for land reform took the form of traditional theories already familiar to them. Their proposals clearly aimed to shift agricultural production to commercial agriculture based on small-scale peasant cultivation.

Both the ruling class and the peasant class shared a desire to resolve social contradictions and problems in the agricultural economy. However, their approaches to reform were completely different. The former focused on strengthening the landlord system and promoting commercial agriculture based on large-scale cultivation under landlord management. By contrast, the latter aimed at the abolition of the landlord system and stabilization and modernization of a peasant economy based on small-scale peasant cultivation. As both approaches partially reflected underlying class interests, conflict between the two was unavoidable and reached its climax with the two opposing reform movements of 1894.[82] In that year, the peasant war was fought to achieve the goals of the peasant reform movement, and the Kabo Reforms were an effort to implement the ideas of the landlord-centered proposal. When the Kaehwap'a (Enlightenment Faction) assumed power in 1894, they needed the cooperation of the peasant army to implement reforms that would establish a modern state, but circumstances made it impossible to do

80. Kim Yong-sop, "Hanmal Kojongjo ŭi t'oji kaehyŏknon"—the opinion of Yi Ki.

81. Ibid.—the opinion of Kim Chedŏk.

82. For studies on the developments of this period from a similar perspective, see the following: Kajimura Hideki, "Richo makki no mengyo no ryutsu oyobi seisan kozo"; Mabuchi Sadanori, "Kogo nomin senso no rekishiteki ichi" (The historical place of the Kabo Peasant War), *Chosen rekishi ronshu*, vol. 2; Mabuchi Sadanori, "Kindai Chosen ni okeru henkaku shutaiteiko shutai no keisei to tenkai" (The formation and development of the leaders of reform and of resistance in early modern Chosŏn), *Rekishigaku kenkyu*, special issue (1975); Cho Kyŏngdal (J. Cho Kyondaru), "Togaku nomin undo to Kogo nomin senso no rekishiteki seikaku" (The historical nature of the Tonghak peasant movement and the Kabo Peasant War), *Chosenshi kenkyukai ronbunshu*, no. 19 (1982); Yi Yungap, "18-19 segi Kyŏngbuk chibang ŭi nong'ŏp pyŏndong" (Changes in agriculture in North Kyŏngsang province in the eighteenth and nineteenth centuries), *Han'guksa yŏn'gu*, no. 53 (1986); Chŏng Ch'angryŏl, Kabo nongmin chonjaeng yŏn'gu (Studies on the Kabo Peasant War) (Ph.D. diss., Yonsei University, 1991).

so. Although it was difficult to mediate among the various status class interests within Chosŏn society, neither the Kabo Reforms nor the peasant war
was simply the result of internal social problems. These two historical events
became opposed to each other both because of the conflict between internal
class interests and because of Chosŏn's changing relations with Japan.

After the Meiji Restoration, Japan embarked on a course of development
to transform the country into a capitalist, imperialist state. In the process, it
became necessary for Japan to consider taking over Chosŏn. There had been
discussions on the so-called *sei-Kan-ron* (conquer Korea policy) before the
opening of the ports. But Japan only started preparations for its takeover after
forcing Chosŏn to open its ports through unequal treaties and beginning to
enjoy huge profits through the commercial trade. During the Kapsin Coup
of 1884, Japan attempted to lay the foundation for its eventual takeover by
establishing a pro-Japanese administration in Chosŏn. When the coup failed
because of the entry of Chinese forces, Japan began to prepare for open war
with Ch'ing China. Meanwhile, the Chosŏn government requested the
Ch'ing army to enter the country because of the outbreak of the peasant war
in 1894, Japan used this request as a pretext to send troops to Chosŏn and
instigated a war with China for control of the country.

Needing a clear pretext to station troops in Chosŏn, Japan pushed for
Chosŏn's independence from its subordinate status to China and forced Chosŏn to undertake internal reforms. Japan ousted the anti-Japanese Min faction
by using its troops to occupy the royal palace and then set up a pro-Japanese
administration with the Kaehwap'a, forcing them to carry out reforms under
Japanese guidance.[83] Japan's goals for the Kabo Reforms were to establish
economic dominance over Chosŏn[84] and, politically, to turn Chosŏn into a

---

83. Tabohashi Kiyoshi, Kindai Ni-Ssen kankei no kenkyu (Research on Japan-Korea relations
in the early modern period), vol. 2 (Keijo (Seoul): Chosen sotokofu chusuin, 1940); Tabohashi
Kiyoshi, "Kindai Chosen ni okeru seijiteki kaikaki" (Political reform in early modern Chosŏn),
Kindai Chosenshi kenkyu (Keijo (Seoul): Chosen sotokofu, 1944); Pak Chonggŭn (J. Boku
Sokon), *Ni-ssin senso to Chosen* (The Sino-Japanese War and Chosŏn), (Tokyo: Aoki shoten,
1982).

84. Cho Kijun, "Yijo malgi ŭi chaejŏng kaehyŏk" (Financial reform of the late Yi Dynasty),
Haksulwŏn nonmunjip, inmun-sahoe kwahak pyŏn 5 (1965); Kang Tŏksang (J. Kan Dokusan),
"Kogo kaikaku ni okeru sinsiki kahei hakko shotei no kenkyu" (A study of the regulations on the
issuance of new currency in the Kabo Reforms), *Chosenshi kenkyukai ronbunshu*, no. 3 (1967);
Kim Chŏnggi, "Kabo kyŏngjanggi Ilbon ŭi tae Chosŏn kyŏngje chŏngch'aek" (Japan's economic
policies toward Chosŏn in the Kabo Reforms period), *Han'guksa yŏn'gu*, no. 47 (1984); Pak
Chonggŭn, *Ni-ssin senso to Chosen* (The Sino-Japanese war and Chosŏn).

dependency[85] or protectorate.[86] Japan could not tolerate the presence of any groups that posed an obstacle to its objectives. They did not hesitate to eliminate any anti-Japanese force, even going so far as to assassinate Queen Min. In terms of its domestic aspects, the Kabo Reforms intended to resolve social contradictions and to establish a modern state; however, the political reforms were carried out with the backing of Japan. Since the reforms were a part of Japan's efforts to take over Chosŏn, the Kaehwap'a administration was unable to escape from the manipulations of Japan.

In contrast to the Kaehwap'a, the peasant army saw Japan as an invader and an enemy. One of the major factors behind the peasant war was Japan's trade with Chosŏn. But the second uprising of the peasant army in September 1894 was an anti-imperial movement as the peasants viewed Japan's recent behavior as acts of aggression—such as its occupation of the royal palace, its role in the change of government, and its coercion of reforms as well as its penetration of the Chosŏn economy. There was no room for compromise between Japan and the peasant army since they stood in opposing positions of aggressor and defender. Just as Japan had to deal with the peasant army in order to take over Chosŏn, the peasant forces felt compelled to respond to Japanese aggressions in order to preserve Chosŏn's sovereignty. This situation made it impossible for the peasant army and the Kaehwap'a administration—with its ties to Japan—to cooperate with each other. The two reform programs were rooted domestically in different sets of class interests, and their positions on international affairs also clashed.

The struggle between the Kaehwap'a administration and the peasant army over the course of reform could not be settled at the level of policy in 1894. In the end, their confrontation unavoidably reached the point of direct conflict. Circumstances were favorable for the government side which was supported by Japan. The government army joined forces with the Japanese army and crushed the peasant army with the cooperation of provincial elites. Seen as a struggle over the path of Korea's modernization, it was a conflict between the landlord system and large-scale commercial agriculture, on the one hand, and peasant-oriented land ownership and small-scale commercial agriculture, on the other.

The result was a victory for landlord forces who were allied with foreign powers, and it is one of the most significant aspects of modern Korean his-

---

85. Nakatsuka Akira, *Ni-ssin senso no kenkyu* (Research on the Sino-Japanese War), Chapter 3 (Tokyo: Aoki shoten, 1968).

86. Pak Chonggŭn (J. Boku Sokon), *Ni-ssin senso to Chosen.*

tory. As a consequence, reform programs representing the interests of the peasantry were defeated, and the country became further settled in the pro-landlord course of modernization. Although peasant movements continued until the end of the Hanmal period, they never regained the strength that they had enjoyed during the peasant war. While there were antagonism and conflicts within the yangban-landlord class over modernization policies (e.g., the reform movement of the Independence Club and the reforms of the Great Han Empire), what they had in common was the fact that their views on modernization were all premised on the maintenance and growth of the land-lord system.

Conclusion

This chapter has examined the two major theories for the solution of problems in the agricultural economy in order to understand the reform policies that emerged in the course of Chosŏn's modernization. These reform proposals first emerged at the end of the feudal era and continued into the modern period after the opening of the ports. The yangban and the landlord class advocated the first course of reform. It proposed to solve problems by reforming only the tax system and was based on the development of the landlord system and large-scale commercial agriculture. The peasant class and progressive yangban supported the second proposal. It advocated reforming the land system as well as the tax system in order to maintain land ownership by the peasantry and to provide stability for small-scale, peasant-based commercial agriculture. Because the former aimed to preserve the class inter-ests of the yangban and landlord classes, I refer to it as the "landlord course" of agricultural modernization. Since the latter attempted to destroy the feudal landlord system in order to stabilize the peasant economy, I call it the "peas-ant course" of agricultural modernization.

Of the two courses, Chosŏn followed a path of modernization after the opening of the ports that only implemented the landlord course of reform. The objective of the Japanese empire was to take over Chosŏn and turn it into a dependency or protectorate. When the Kaehwap'a government devel-oped close relations with Japan, it completely suppressed the peasant course of reform. In short, the Kaehwap'a government was attempting a bourgeois revolution without undertaking land reform. As a result, the reform policies adopted in this period would have to be rethought and revised at a later point in time in order to achieve a true bourgeois revolution.

translated by Michael D. Shin

Index of Terms

chigye 地契 land certificates
chije ŭi 地制議
chijuhyŏng punong 地主型富農
chiju-sijak chŏnjak system 地主時作佃作制 landlord-tenant system
chinp'ye ch'aekja 陳弊冊子
Cho Kyŏngdal 趙景達
chŏlsuje 折受制
Chŏng Yagyong 丁若鏞 (1762-1836; *ho* Tasan, 茶山)
ch'ong'aekje 摠額制 collective responsibility for the payment of taxes
chŏngjŏnnon 井田論 well-field system
chŏnju chŏn'gaekje 田主佃客制
ch'ŏnmin 賤民 low-born
chungdapju 中沓主
Han'guk seje ko 韓國稅制考
hanjŏnnon 限田論 limited-field system
hanmin myŏngjŏn ŭi 限民名田議
hojŏk 戶籍 household registers
hop'obŏp 戶布法 Household Cloth Law
hop'oje 戶布制 household cloth tax system
hwan'gok 還穀 grain loan system
hyŏn 縣 district
Kaehwap'a 開化派 Enlightenment Faction
kuilje 九一制
kun 郡 county
kungjangt'o 宮庄土 palace estate land
kunp'o 軍布稅 military cloth tax
kunsu 郡守 county magistrate
kunyŏkse 軍役稅 military service tax
kuŏngyo 求言敎
Kwŏnnong chŏlmok 勸農節目
kyŏl 結
kyŏlbu 結負
kyŏngja yujŏn 耕者有田 "land for every cultivator"
kyŏng'yŏng chiju 經營地主
kyŏng'yŏnghyŏng punong 經營型富農 managerial rich peasants
kyunjak-kyundaejŏn 均作均貸田

kyunjŏnnon 均田論 equal-field system

Kyun'yŏkbŏp 均役法

min'ŭnso 民隱疏

mollak yangban 沒落兩班 fallen yangban

nobigong 奴婢貢 slave service

nongjŏngso 農政疏

paekgwan jin'ŏn 百官陳言

Pak Chonggŭn 朴宗根

pu 負

pyŏngjak chiju 竝作地主 landlord with multiple landholdings

pyŏngjŏn ŭngbyŏn 兵典 應變

sach'angje 社倉制 village granary system

sahoedang 社會黨

Sahwan chorye 社還條例

sain yoch'ŏn 事人如天 human equality

Samjŏng ijŏng ch'ŏng 三政釐整廳 Office to Rectify the Samjŏng

samjŏng mullan 三政紊亂 disorder of the three systems

Sanju sayre 尙州事例

sei-Kan-ron (J.) 征韓論

seje ŭi, chaejŏng kaehyŏk 稅制議, 財政改革

simu pyŏn 時務篇

sip'ilje 什一制

sok 束

sujogwŏn 收租權 right to collect taxes

Taedongbŏp 大同法

to 賭

Tongnip hyŏphoe 獨立協會 Independence Club

tunjŏn 屯田

turak 斗落

wangdo chŏngch'i 王道政治 rule by the Kingly Way

yangjŏn 量田 cadastral survey

yŏjŏn 閭田 village land (system)

CHAPTER 2

The Independence Club's Conceptions of Nationalism and the Modern State

Chu Chin-Oh
朱鎭五

As the world powers embarked on programs of imperialist aggression, the survival of the Chosŏn dynasty depended on its ability to transform itself into a modern capitalist state and establish a system that could adapt to the new world order it faced. The task involved reforming society and reorganizing the government into a modern nation-state.

Up to now, research on Korea's early modern political thought has mainly focused on the role of the Kaehwap'a (Enlightenment Faction) as the leaders of modern reform efforts.[1] As a result of such work, it is no longer possible to deny that there were forces in Korea in the late nineteenth century that tried to establish a modern state. Although scholars disagree on how to define the Kaehwap'a, they generally agree that it consisted of a group of

---

1. Yi Kwangnin, *Han'guk kaehwasa yŏn'gu* (The history of *kaehwa* in Korea) (Seoul: Ilchogak, 1969); Yi Kwangnin, *Kwahwadang yŏn'gu* (A study of the Enlightenment Party) (Seoul: Ilchogak, 1973); Yi Kwangnin, *Han'guk kaehwa sasang yŏn'gu* (A study of Korea's enlightenment thought), (Seoul: Ilchogak, 1979); Yi Kwangnin, *Han'guk kaehwasa ŭi che-munje* (Issues on the history of enlightenment in Korea) (Seoul: Ilchogak, 1986); Yi Kwangnin, *Kaehwap'a wa kaehwa sasang yŏn'gu* (The Enlightenment Faction and enlightenment thought) (Seoul: Ilchogak, 1989). Kang Cheŏn, *Kankoku kindaishi kenkyu* (Studies on early modern Korean history) (Tokyo: Nihon hyoronsha, 1970); Kang Cheŏn, *Kindai Chosen no henkaku siso* (Early Modern Korea's reform thought), (Tokyo: Nihon hyoronsha, 1977). Sin Yongha, *Han'guk kŭndaesa wa sahoe undong* (Korea's early modern history and social movements) (Seoul: Munhak kwa chisŏngsa, 1980); Sin Yongha, *Han'guk kŭndae sahoe sasangsa yŏn'gu* (The history of social thought in early modern Korea) (Seoul: Ilchisa, 1987); Sin Yongha, *Han'guk kŭndae minjokjuŭi ŭi hyŏngt'ae kwa chŏn'gae* (The form and development of Korea's early modern nationalism) (Seoul: Seoul National University Press, 1987). Young Ick Lew (Yu Yŏng'ik), *Kabo kyŏngjang yŏn'gu* (A study of the Kabo Reforms) (Seoul: Ilchogak, 1990).

government officials who advocated a Western-style modernization. Its members came from a younger generation of officials and *chungin*, but it is important to remember that there were a number of sub-factions within the Kaehwap'a that differed in their thought and politics.

Among these groups, scholars have focused a good deal of attention on the thought and activities of the Independence Club (Tongnip hyŏphoe), which was formed in July 1896 by high-ranking ministers with the support of the royal family and the government.[2] Its original purpose was to build a new gate, Independence Gate, on the former location of Yŏng'ŭn Gate to commemorate the end of Korea's tributary relations with China after the Sino-Japanese War. Around mid-1897, it developed into a movement dedicated to enlightening the people about modern ideas with the formation of a Debating Society, which was organized by younger members of the Club such as Yun Ch'iho (1865-1945). When Russia began to interfere more actively in Chosŏn's internal affairs, it became more political and organized protests against Russia.

The general view of scholars on the Kaehwap'a's reform efforts can be summarized as follows. More than any other political group, the Kaehwap'a had accurate knowledge of world affairs and attempted to respond pragmatically to the changes in Korea's international situation. But the royal

2. The most well-known work is Sin Yongha, *Tongnip hyŏphoe yŏn'gu* (Studies on the Independence Club) (Seoul: Ilchogak, 1976). Articles on the Independence Club include: Ch'oe Chun, "Kojong sidae ŭi k'ŏmyunik'eisyŏn hyŏngt'ae ŭi koch'al" (An examination of forms of communication during Kojong's reign) *Sahak yŏn'gu*, no. 3 (1959); Ch'oe Chun, "Tongnip sinmun p'angwŏn kwa Hanmi kyosŏp" (The *Independent* and Korean-American relations), *Chungangdae nonmunjip*, no. 13 (1969); Pak Sŏnggŭn, "Tongnip hyŏphoe ŭi sasangjŏk yŏn'gu" (A study of the thought of the Independence Club), *Yi Hongsik paksa hoegap kinyŏm Han'guksahak nonch'ong* (Seoul, 1969); Han Hŭngsu, "Tongnip hyŏphoe ŭi ch'ŏngch'i chipdanhwa kwajŏng" (The process of the Independence Club's becoming a political organization), *Sahoe kwahak nonjip*, no. 3 (1970); Yu Yŏngnyŏl, "Tongnip hyŏphoe ŭi mingwŏn undong chŏn'gae kwajŏng" (The development of the Independence Club's people's rights movement), *Sach'ong*, nos. 17-18 (1973); Yu Yŏngnyŏl, "Tongnip hyŏphoe ŭi mingwŏn sasang yŏn'gu" (A study of the Independence Club's conception of people's rights), *Sahak yŏn'gu*, no. 22 (1973); Ch'oe Tŏksu, "Tong-nip hyŏphoe ŭi ch'ŏngch'eron mit oegyoron yŏn'gu" (A study of the Independence Club's con-ception of political systems and diplomacy), *Minjok munhwa yŏn'gu*, no. 13 (1978); Yi Man'gap, "Tongnip sinmun e p'yosi toen kach'i kaenyŏm" (The conception of value as revealed in the *In-dependent*), *Han Ugŭn paksa chŏngnyŏn kinyŏm nonch'ong* (Seoul, 1981); Chang Hajin, "Yun Ch'iho ŭi minjokjuŭi wa kŭndaehwa ŭisik" (Yun Ch'iho's nationalism and conception of modernization), *Inmun yŏn'guso nonmunjip* (Taejŏn: Ch'ungnam University, 1981); Yi Minwŏn, "Tongnip hyŏphoe e taehan yŏlguk kongsa ŭi kansŏp" (The intervention of foreign consuls concerning the Independence Club), *Ch'ŏnggye sahak*, no. 2 (1985).

family and their allies, who were the central power holders, were a reactionary comprador group that colluded with foreign powers to suppress the Kaehwap'a. On the other hand, the masses were ignorant and did not support their efforts. As a result, Korea's modern reforms failed, and the country could not avoid falling under colonial rule.

Studies of the Independence Club have also tended to follow this general framework. However, it is impossible to attain a proper understanding of the Independence Club by examining only the activities and political thought of its most westernized figures. There was a variety of political groups within the Independence Club that differed according to the degree of their adherence to traditional thought and acceptance of Western thought. It is also important to reexamine the relationship between the Independence Club and the government of the Great Han Empire.

Like previous studies, a good portion of this chapter will focus on the thought of two of its younger leaders, Yun Ch'iho and Sŏ Chaep'il (1864-1951). However, it is important to remember that their ideas did not necessarily represent the opinions of the entire Independence Club. Born into a yangban family, Sŏ Chaep'il passed the civil service examination in 1882 and went to Japan in 1883 to study at Toyama Military Academy. Because of his participation in the 1884 Kapsin Coup, he fled into exile to Japan and then went to America in 1885. Through the financial support of an American businessman, he attended Henry Hilman Academy in Pennsylvania; after graduating, he entered Cochran College in Washington, D.C. and eventually finished medical school in 1892. While in college, he became an American citizen and changed his name to Philip Jaisohn. He returned to Korea in 1895 as an advisor to the Privy Council (Chungch'uwŏn). With funds from the government, he launched the bilingual *Tongnip sinmun/The Independent*, the first newspaper to publish in the vernacular, in 1896 and played a leading role in the formation of the Independence Club.[3]

Through the efforts of his father, a military official with ties to the Kaehwap'a, Yun Ch'iho went to Japan in 1881 as a member of a government

---

3. More on the life of Sŏ Chaep'il: In 1894, he married Muriel Armstrong, and they later had two daughters. During the protests against Russian interference, he was fired from his position as advisor and returned to the U.S. He became a businessman in Philadelphia and was a leader of organizations such as The League of the Friends of Korea. But after the Washington Conference of 1921, he stopped many of his political activities. After liberation, he returned to Korea for a short while as an advisor to the U.S. military government but returned to America where he spent the rest of his days.

mission. With the English he learned in Japan, he became the translator for the American consul in Seoul in May 1883. Though he became a member of the Kaehwap'a, he did not participate in the Kapsin Coup of 1884. Nonetheless, he went into exile in China and enrolled in the Anglo-Chinese College in Shanghai, where he converted to Christianity. With the support of American Methodist missionaries, he went to the U.S. in 1888, studying at Vanderbilt University and Emory University. With the formation of a Kaehwap'a administration in 1894, he returned to Chosŏn and served in both the Foreign and Education Ministries. When the Independence Club developed into a political organization, he emerged as one of its leaders. He later became the third chairperson of the Club as well as the second editor of the *Tongnip sinmun*.[4]

The objective of this chapter is to examine the Independence Club's reform program with a focus on its political and social aspects. The first section of this chapter analyzes the intellectual influences on the Independence Club, and the second section focuses on its conception of the modern state. To do so, it is necessary to look at how the Independence Club defined the concept of "independence" (*tongnip*), the most central discourse of this period. I will analyze its program of state-building mainly through its conception of the monarchy and its efforts to turn the Privy Council (Chungch'uwŏn) into a representative assembly. Lastly, I will examine the Independence Club's conception of society and its efforts to support political reforms through cultural programs. Through such an examination, I hope to contribute to a greater understanding of the ideology and activities of modern state building efforts in Korea from the perspective of "internal development" theory.

4. After the dissolution of the Independence Club in 1898, Yun Ch'iho served as a provincial official. From 1906, he devoted himself to educational activities and organizations such as the Taehan chaganghoe (Korean Self-Strengthening Society). In 1912, he was arrested in the so-called "Incident of the 105," and after his release from jail, his activities continued to focus on education, and he gradually became a collaborator with the Japanese. His diary, large sections of which were written in English, is one of the most important sources on the Independence Club and this period in general.

The Development of the Independence Club's Reform Program

SOCIAL DARWINISM AND GRADUAL REFORM

Since the 1870s, politics at the center had been characterized by the conflict between the conservative Min faction, which was centered on the monarchy, and the Kaehwap'a. In the 1880s, the Min faction generally prevailed over the Kaehwap'a, as demonstrated by events such as the Kapsin Coup of 1884. China's defeat in the Sino-Japanese War of 1894-95 was a tremendous shock to the opponents of *kaehwa* reforms. They felt that the outcome of the war represented a victory of Japan's Western-style modernization (*pyŏnbŏpnon*) over China's program of modernization (the *yangmu* reforms). The end of Korea's tributary relations with China meant that the Chinese world order had collapsed and that Korea now had to face the system of Western international law that professed to respect the equality of all countries.

Most people at the time felt that Japan's victory was due to its achievement of "civilization and enlightenment" (*munmyŏng kaehwa*; J. *bunmei kaika*)—i.e., westernization—and that China's defeat was due to its maintenance of old ways and failure to westernize.[5] In their eyes, China became an example of failure, whereas Japan was a model of success. They unquestioningly accepted the views of Young Allen, an American missionary residing in China, who wrote that "the reason for Japan's glory is that it accepted Western ways and received the advice of Westerners whom they hired, and the reason for China's decline is that it did not accept Western ways."[6] They believed that if Korea followed Japan's path, then it would also become a civilized country and could possibly occupy a portion of China like the other powers.[7]

The failure of the Kabo Reforms (1894-96) made people realize that reform had to be accomplished without the assistance of foreign powers and that it should be implemented gradually by first educating the people about the necessity of *kaehwa*. A general consensus emerged that existing ways of thinking in Korea were inadequate to the task of responding to changing conditions. The mood of the times was reflected in the phrase *kubon sinch'am* (literally, "old foundation, new participation") which was one of the

---

5. *Maeil sinmun*, April 29, 1898.
6. *Hwangsŏng sinmun*, September 17, 1898.
7. *The Independent*, August 4, 1896.

slogans of the Great Han Empire.[8] The term *sinch'am* referred to the recognition of the necessity of *pyŏnbŏp* (roughly, "change of system"), and most of the westernizing reforms implemented during the Kabo Reforms period were continued in the Great Han Empire.[9]

Since these ideas formed the intellectual foundation of the Independence Club, it was only natural that some intellectuals tried to explain *kaehwa* by invoking the authority of the Confucian classics. It was an attempt to persuade people with a traditional mindset about the necessity of *kaehwa*. In the *Tae Chosŏn tongnip hyŏphoe hoebo*, an article entitled "Tongnipnon" (Theory of independence) discussed ten items necessary for Korea's self-strengthening and maintenance of its independence.[10] One of the items was "*mu kaehwa*" (implement *kaehwa*).[11] Stating that *kaehwa* involved "the awakening of ignorance and the opening of close-mindedness," the author noted that there were several kinds of *kaehwa* such as "ancient *kaehwa*," the "*kaehwa* of Confucius," and the "*kaehwa* of Kija." The author ultimately defined *kaehwa* as "observing morality and ethics and then, in addition, learning the special skills of other countries." This article clearly shows that there were groups within the Independence Club that tried to understand *kaehwa* through traditional concepts.

On the other hand, Yun Ch'iho had been influenced by Social Darwinism during his student days in America and utilized it to formulate his ideas on reform. He viewed the West as a model for civilization, perhaps more than any of his contemporaries, and felt that it was necessary to pursue "civilization and enlightenment" gradually. Among modern Western forms of thought, Social Darwinism functioned to support capitalism and justify the

---

8. Kim Yongsŏp, *Han'guk kŭndae nong'ŏpsa yŏn'gu* (Studies in Korea's early modern agricultural history) (Seoul: Ilchogak, 1975).

9. To Myŏnhoe, "Kŭndae=chabonjuŭi sahoe kijŏm ŭrusŏ ŭi Kabo kaehyŏk" (The Kabo Reforms as the starting point of modern capitalist society), *Yŏksa wa hyŏnsil*, no. 9 (1993).

10. The main point of the article can be summarized as follows: Although Chosŏn had attained autonomy and independence and stood shoulder to shoulder with the other countries of the world, autonomy would be meaningless unless the ability to maintain independence was lasting. Only by engaging in actual politics could the foundation for independence be secured. The author based his views on a passage from the *I Ching* (Book of Changes).

The ten items that the author discussed were given in classical Chinese and demonstrate that the form of this article was no different from that of the memorials of conservative Confucian students. "Tongnipnon" (Theory of Independence), *Tae Chosŏn Tongnip Hyŏphoe hoebo*, no. 13 (May 31, 1897).

11. It appears that this item was discussed last of the ten items, probably to mitigate the resistance of readers to the idea of *kaehwa*.

pursuit of imperialist expansion.[12] Despite the fact that it often served as the ideology of the powerful, Social Darwinism also appealed to intellectuals of "backward" countries. It is thus necessary to examine the historical significance of Social Darwinism through a brief overview of its spread from the West to Japan and China and finally to Korea.

As is well known, the British social scientist Herbert Spencer was the one who applied Darwin's theories to sociology and developed the theory of Social Darwinism.[13] According to Spencer, the evolution of humanity was a gradual process comparable to ascending a staircase. He felt that advocacy of radical reform was a mistake that over-simplified the origins and consequences of social contradictions. The duty of sociology was to make people realize the boundless complexity of social organisms and to prevent rash reforms by educating them about human social relations.

America was more receptive to the theory of evolution in either its Darwinian or Spencerian form than England, the country of its origin.[14] At the time, the Christian church in the U.S. actively supported American imperialism.[15] In many cases, missionaries were more aggressive than politicians or businessmen in calling for territorial expansion and ignored U.S. diplomatic concerns, calling for the bold use of military force. In the case of Korea, Horace G. Underwood and Horace Allen, who later served as the U.S. consul in Seoul, fit the profile of this kind of missionary. For example, Allen obtained concessions for American capitalists for gold mining in Unsan

12. On Charles Darwin and the influence of his theory of biological evolution on nineteenth century social science, see Arthur L. Caplan and Bruce Jennings, eds., *Darwin, Marx, and Freud: Their Influence on Moral Theory* (New York: Plenum Press, 1984) and David L. Sills, ed., *International Encyclopedia of the Social Sciences* (New York: Macmillan Co. and the Free Press), vol. 14: "Social Darwinism."

13. Recently, it has been remarked that the term "Social Darwinism" may be a misnomer since Spencer's theories had appeared before Darwin published his theory of biological evolution. See Sin Yongha, "Ku Hanmal Han'guk minjokjuŭi wa sahoe chinhwaron" (Korean nationalism and Social Darwinism in the Hanmal period), *Inmun kwahak yŏn'gu*, no. 1 (1995).

14. Richard Hofstadter, *Social Darwinism in American Thought* (Boston: Beacon Press, 1955); Walter LaFeber, *The New Empire: An Interpretation of American Expansion, 1860-1898* (Ithaca: Cornell University Press, 1963); Shimizu Tomohisa, *Amerika teikoku* (The American empire) (Tokyo: Aki shobo, 1968).

15. J.W. Pratt, "The Ideology of American Expansion," *Essays in Honor of William E. Dodd*, Avery Craven, ed., (Chicago: University of Chicago Press, 1935). On page 352 of this chapter, Pratt mentioned a letter written by a missionary sent to China that observed that "all American missionaries here support expansion." See also Alfred Whitney Griswold, *The Far Eastern Policy of the U.S.* (New York: Harcourt, Brace, and Co., (1938) 1964), p. 16.

and for the Seoul-Inchon railway, receiving considerable fees for his services.[16]

Among the three East Asian countries, Japan was the first to be influenced by Social Darwinism. Edward Morse was the person who introduced Darwin's theory of evolution to Japanese intellectuals. He had gone to Japan to do biological research and ended up being appointed a professor of biology at Tokyo Imperial University. His influence played a significant role in the transformation of Japanese intellectuals' ways of thinking, and he also was a strong formative influence on the thinking of Yu Kiljun (1856-1914), another member of the Kaehwap'a.[17] Kato Hiroyuki (1836-1916) and Toyama Shoichi (1848-1900) were among the first intellectuals who attempted to analyze Japanese society through Social Darwinian theories.[18] Fukuzawa Yukichi (1835-1901) appears to have adopted a Social Darwinian view of society at least by the time he wrote *Bunmeiron no gairaku* (Outline of Civilization, 1875). As a result, he abandoned the radical ideology of popular

16. Fred Harvey Harrington, *God, Mammon, and the Japanese: Dr. Horace N. Allen and Korean-American Relations, 1884-1905* (Madison: University of Wisconsin Press, (1944) 1966), pp. 151-176. Underwood also argued, "Thus do commerce and the Church go hand in hand, here as elsewhere, in forwarding His kingdom and spreading abroad the knowledge of the Prince of Peace," and he promoted and even directly sold medicines such as quinine and agricultural implements. Horace Grant Underwood, *The Call of Korea* (New York: Fleming H. Revell, 1908), p. 24; Harrington, ibid., p. 112; "Trade of Korea in 1897," *The Independent*, August 16, 1898.

17. After Morse returned to America, he served for a long time as the director of the Peabody Essex Museum in Salem, Massachusetts and became a prominent authority on Japan.

Yu Kiljun had attended one of Morse's lectures in 1882, and he later visited Morse and decided to study for one year at Governor Dummer Academy in Byfield, Massachusetts through Morse's recommendation. Morse also published an interview with a Korean who appears to have been Yu Kiljun in the May 1897 issue of the journal *Appleton's Popular Science Monthly* (entitled "Korea Interview"). Professor Yi Kwangnin has already written a short introduction on Morse's life and attitudes toward and relationship with Korea, but I am also planning to write a more detailed study of Morse's influence in the near future.

18. After Kato learned about Social Darwinism, his thinking changed considerably. In his 1882 work "Jinken sinsetsu" (A new theory of human rights), he argued that the principles of the competition for existence and survival of the fittest were applicable to society, basing his argument on the theory of natural selection.

Toyama lectured to his students on Social Darwinism through Spencer's work *Principles of Sociology*. Ho Takushu, *Chugoku no kindaika to Meiji ishin* (The modernization of China and the Meiji Restoration) (Kyoto: Dohosha shuppanbu, 1976); Yasuji Ryuichi, *Sinkaron no rekishi* (The history of the theory of evolution) (Tokyo: Iwanami shoten, 1970), pp. 160-62; Nagazumi Akira, ed., *Tonan Ajia no ryugakusei to minzokushugi undo* (Southeast Asian students studying abroad and national movements) (Gan'nando shoten, 1981), pp. 6-9.

rights and became a supporter of monarchy and civilized absolutism.[19] Reflecting the degree of its influence on Japan's intellectual world, the most frequently translated books in Japan in the late nineteenth century were works by Spencer and others on Social Darwinism.[20]

Social Darwinism was introduced to Korea through American missionaries as well as through students who studied in Japan and China. It is generally agreed that the first Korean to study Social Darwinism was Yu Kiljun.[21] He had written a work entitled "Theory of Competition" in 1883,[22] and his *Sŏyu kyŏnmun* (Record of Observations while Traveling in the West) clearly demonstrated the influence of Social Darwinism in his espousal of the "theory of the three stages of the development" of human society (barbarism–semi-civilized–civilized). In the case of Pak Yŏnghyo, there are signs that he had adopted a Social Darwinian worldview in memorials he drafted.[23] However, the influence of Social Darwinism was initially felt in a change in Koreans' perception of international relations. International politics came to be conceived as a struggle for existence, and the sense of crisis about the direction of world affairs increased.[24]

19. Fukuzawa believed that "should we ever attain a perfect civilization, government would become entirely superfluous." In his view, the urgent task facing Japan was the "preservation of the national polity." He did not mean this in the defensive sense of protecting Japan's sovereignty from outside threats. Reflecting a more aggressive worldview, he felt that sovereignty needed to be protected through the emergence of the fittest and most powerful in a world dominated by the principles of the survival of the fittest and the competition for survival. Fukuzawa Yukichi, *Munmyŏngnon ŭi kaeryak* (*Bunmeiron no gairyaku*), translated by Chŏng Myŏnghwan, (Seoul: Hongsŏngsa, 1986), pp. 20–22, 39, 47, 51, 58. (English translation taken from Fukuzawa Yukichi, *An Outline of a Theory of Civilization*, trans. by David A. Dilworth and G. Cameron Hurst (Tokyo: Sophia University, 1973), p. 45)

20. See Ho Takushu, ibid., pp. 182–83.

21. Yi Kwangnin, "*Yu Kiljun ŭi kaehwa sasang*" (Yu Kiljun's conception of *kaehwa*), *Yŏksa hakbo*, no. 75–76 (combined issue), p. 207.

22. "In general, there is nothing among all the things of human existence that did not result from competition, and all things great and small, from the affairs of countries to the affairs of single individuals and families, all progress is a result of competition. If there were no such thing as competition among humans, then how would we gain knowledge, morality, and happiness; if there were no competition among countries, how would they be able to increase and develop their power and prestige, their wealth and strength?" *Yu Kiljun chŏnsŏ* (The complete works of Yu Kiljun), vol. 4 (Seoul: Ilchogak, 1971).

23. See, for example, the section entitled "一日 宇內之形勢" in one of his memorials.

24. There has been a good amount of research on the relationship between Social Darwinism and Korea's enlightenment thought (conceptions of *kaehwa*). The most representative works are: Yi Kwangnin, "Ku Hanmal chinhwaron ŭi suyong kwa yŏnghyang" (The introduction and influence of Social Darwinism at the end of the Chosŏn dynasty), *Serim haksul nonch'ong*, no. 1

Social Darwinism's influence did not remain limited to these matters. Basing their ideas on the theory of social organisms, intellectuals began to emphasize the gradual nature of evolution and the necessity of enlightening people about it. For instance, Yun Ch'iho, like Chinese thinker Yen Fu (1854-1921) and in contrast to Spencer,[25] saw the state as the main force in evolution and stressed the need to increase the power of the state. In the case of China and Korea, although the introduction of Social Darwinism often led to a passive attitude toward imperialism, it performed an important role in making people realize the urgency of self-strengthening reforms. Through Yun Ch'iho, it is possible to trace how this thinking developed into a concrete reform program.

When Yun studied at Vanderbilt University, a Methodist school, and then at Emory University, he was greatly influenced by the ideas of Social Darwinism, whose influence was strong even in Christian circles.[26] It was at this time that he read Josiah Strong's *Our Country* (1885), a book that played a significant role in spreading Social Darwinian ideas among Christians in the U.S.[27] He also read a book titled *Indian Policy* on England's conquest and rule of India, and in his diary, he jotted down the following comments on it:

> I deplore the dominance of the strong over the weak, but if the Indian government had been strong and ably protected its people, would the English have been successful? . . . After England became the ruler [of India], it protected the lives and property of the people as unrest in India

(1977); Sin Ilch'ŏl, *Sin Ch'aeho ŭi yŏksa sasang yŏn'gu* (A study of Sin Ch'aeho's conception of history) (Seoul: Korea University Press, 1980); Sin Yongha, *Sin Ch'aeho ui sahoe sasang yŏn'gu* (The social thought of Sin Ch'aeho) (Seoul: Han'gilsa, 1984); Yi Songhŭi, "Hanmal aeguk kyemong sasang kwa sahoe chinhwaron" (The patriotic enlightenment thought of the Hanmal period and Social Darwinism), *Pusan yŏdae sahak*, no. 2 (1984); Kim Tohyŏng, "Hanmal kyemong undong ŭi chŏngch'iron yŏn'gu" (The enlightenment movements and political theories of the Hanmal period), *Han'guksa yŏn'gu*, no. 54 (1986); Chu Chin-Oh (Chu Chin'o), "Tongnip hyŏphoe ŭi sahoe sasang kwa sahoe chinhwaron" (The social thought of the Independence Club and Social Darwinism), *Son Pogi paksa chŏngnyŏn kinyŏm nonch'ong* (Seoul: Chisik san'ŏpsa, 1988); Sin Yongha, ibid. (1995).

25. Cho Kyŏngnan, "Chinhwaron ŭi Chungugukjŏk suyong kwa yŏksa insik ŭi chŏnhwan—Ŏm Bok, Yang Kyech'o, Chang Pyŏngnin, No Sin ŭl chungsim ŭro" (The introduction of Social Darwinism in China and the transformation in historical thinking: Yen Fu, Liang Ch'i-chao, Chiang Monlin, Lu Hsun) (Ph.D. diss., Sŏngkyungwan University, 1994), pp. 57-59.

26. On Yun Ch'iho's studies in the U.S., see Yu Yŏngnyŏl, *Kaehwagi ŭi Yun Ch'iho yŏn'gu* (Yun Ch'iho during the enlightenment period) (Seoul: Han'gilsa, 1985).

27. *Yun Ch'iho ilgi* (The diary of Yun Ch'iho), December 10, 1889.

was pacified and the threat of foreign trouble receded. [India] is enjoying peace more than in the past as talent is cultivated by providing schools and as learning is encouraged. It truly can be said that England is the savior of India. As the countries of Asia are weak and cannot maintain their power, they fall into the hands of Westerners, and although the political maneuvers of the West are not right, how can Asian countries avoid the error of making the people weak and bringing about foreign invasions?[28]

Yun felt that the internal affairs of a single country or a race of people should not be determined according to the principle of the survival of the fittest, but the principle was applicable to international affairs.[29] It was only natural that he was concerned about the situation of his native land. He wrote:

It has often chilled my most sanguine aspiration—the thought that Corea might not be the "fittest" to "survive." Then what? My business and duty are to contribute my best to make them fit to live. If they cannot be so made after a fair trial, then they are not fit to survive.[30]

As he became more familiar with Social Darwinist ideas, Yun came to see historical development as a three-stage process from barbarism to a semi-civilized state and then to civilization. For him, the term *kaehwa* referred to the complete advancement of human society in terms of both material prosperity and spiritual progress. He felt that Chosŏn had not yet had a "fair trial" to engage in the struggle for existence. What he meant by the term "fair trial" was an opportunity to build a strong, powerful state and achieve "civilization and enlightenment" through Western-style institutions and technology.

Through the influence of Social Darwinism, Yun came to believe in the idea of "Might is Right" as a basic principle of society. The only way for Chosŏn to increase its fitness to survive was to import Western civilization through the spread of Christianity. To accomplish this goal, it was necessary to undertake political reform. He believed that "civilization and enlightenment" should be achieved gradually under a monarchical form of government. He felt that the use of force in coups d'etat in the name of reform, such as the Kapsin Coup and the Kabo Reforms, had had a harmful influence

28. Ibid., May 26, 1889.
29. Ibid., November 27, 1891.
30. Ibid., August 14, 1892.

on Korea's modernization.[31] What was problematic about Yun's ideas was his view that it would be acceptable to carry out reform under the rule of a "civilized country," if it became impossible for Chosŏn to achieve reform on its own and by peaceful means. In his despair over Chosŏn's situation, he even thought that it would be helpful if Chosŏn were taken over by Russia or, preferably, England.[32]

In his editorials in The Independent, Sŏ Chaep'il also tried to explain the term kaehwa using traditional concepts. Noting that the word was "originally coined in China," he interpreted "kaehwa to mean broadening one's ignorant opinions and conducting all affairs practically by approaching them in accordance with reason." More specifically, the character kae referred to public speech and action and hwa to the process of educating "people who are just awakening" so that they attain proper ways of thinking. And "practicality" (silsang) meant "taking only what is genuine and thinking and acting in a fair and honest manner."[33]

Another article in The Independent defined kaehwa as "the genuine advancement of the affairs of people and the understanding of things in accordance with the conditions of the age by making things very convenient and by deep study." The article referred to the kaehwa of the days of Yao and Shun, the legendary kings of ancient China, claiming that this conception of kaehwa was no different than the concept of pyŏnbŏp kaehwa. The author also explained that "getting rid of one's inferior things and adopting the superior things of others is the kaehwa of an individual, and realizing one's deficiencies and adopting the things of others is the kaehwa of the entire country."[34] To Kaehwap'a intellectuals, it was self-evident that a country would prosper if it implemented kaehwa.

On the one hand, intellectuals in the Independence Club viewed the Western powers as fully enlightened nations[35] and Japan as a "somewhat enlightened country."[36] On the other hand, they looked down on China, saying that "the Chosŏn people have nothing to learn from the Chinese because China's state of enlightenment is not even at the level of Chosŏn's."[37] Their

---

31. Ibid., February 26, 1897.
32. Ibid., May 18, 1890.
33. Tongnip sinmun, June 30, 1896.
34. "P'yŏnji" (Letter), ibid., January 20, 1898.
35. "Nonsŏl" (Editorial), ibid., September 24, 1896.
36. "P'yŏnji" (Letter), ibid., January 20, 1898.
37. Ibid., May 21, 1896.

conception of *kaehwa* can also be called "*pyŏnbŏp*" *kaehwa* as they rejected Confucianism. They felt that China was in such a state because it did not study the learning of the West but only studied the Confucian classics.

The changes in their thinking were evident in their views on policy issues. During the time that Kojong was residing at the Russian legation, *The Independent* explained the task of *kaehwa* as the reconciliation of old and new ways, using the following metaphor: When a carpenter fixes an old house, it will easily collapse if the rotted columns are removed before new columns are prepared. The newspaper also criticized those who only decorate the interior of the house and do not think about replacing old columns even though they are decayed. In short, reform of the state had to follow a proper sequence of events and an order of priorities. It was through this logic that *The Independent* criticized the Kabo Reforms; for example, it noted that communication within the country became difficult because the post-horse system was abolished before a modern postal system was established.[38]

KAEHWA AND SILHAK: COMPROMISE OF OLD AND NEW

The *Hwangsŏng sinmun*'s conception of *kaehwa* was also based on the idea of *pyŏnbŏp*.[39] Arguing that the importation of new institutions was urgent, it concluded that Chosŏn would decline into a weak country if new ways were not adopted and old ways were continued. In fact, the newspaper actively supported the introduction of the new, saying that "as it is important to undertake self-strengthening measures, it is essential to abandon the old and follow the new." However, it did not call for the complete replacement of the old by the new; it felt that reform should be achieved through a combination of the old and the new.[40] Its views were fundamentally no different from the Great Han Empire's ideology of *kubon sinch'am* (incorporating the new on the basis of the old).

The *Hwangsŏng sinmun* defined *kaehwa* as the abbreviation of the characters *kaemul sŏngmu, hwamin sŏngsok.*[41] This definition suggests that these intellectuals had an open-minded Confucian perspective on *kaehwa*,

---

38. Ibid., May 23, 1896. Another example was that the soldiers and officers who were stationed in each *pu* and *kun* to prevent thievery and uprisings were removed without an alternate system in place.

39. *Hwangsŏng sinmun*, August 23, 1899.

40. Ibid., April 30, 1904.

41. Roughly translated, this phrase means: "investigating nature to achieve things; enlightening the people to create correct customs."

believing that it "does not just mean dependence and adoration of the West; there was also the *kaehwa* of figures such as Fu Xi, Shen Nong, and Confucius." Their ideas on the classification of *kaehwa*, the great principles (*taedo*) of *kaehwa*, and the distinction between "true" and "false" *kaehwa* were taken virtually word for word from Yu Kiljun's *Sŏyu kyŏnmun*.

There were also differences with Yu Kiljun's ideas. While Yu characterized false *kaehwa* as a "criminal of *kaehwa*" that is no better than the ideas of *chŏksa* (eliminate the heterodox), intellectuals with the *Hwangsŏng sinmun* recognized that since "it takes time to reach actual *kaehwa*," anyone "who works diligently and never rests [can] completely [become] the hero of *kaehwa*." Furthermore, they denounced people who criticized *kaehwa* as "not only criminals of *kaehwa* but also criminals against Fu Hsi, Shen Nung, Chu Hsi, and Confucius." These differences seem to show that the *Hwangsŏng sinmun* clearly supported a more gradual *kaehwa* than Yu Kiljun.

Such thinking led to an emphasis on broadening the people's wisdom (*minji*) and concentrating the strength of the people (*millyŏk*) as the basis of self-strengthening.[42] They asserted that it is necessary to educate the people in new knowledge, new sciences, and, above all, practical fields in order to develop the people's wisdom.[43]

What is striking is that while the intellectuals of the *Hwangsŏng sinmun* advocated the necessity of *kaehwa*, they emphasized that it had a foundation in Silhak thought.[44] They felt that the suppression of Silhak by the authorities, despite a tradition of studies on statecraft (*kyŏngse*), was the main cause of the country's poverty and weakness.[45] They were critical of the view that *kaehwa* could be achieved only by following Western ways, calling it "empty talk." No matter how impressive *kaehwa* was, they felt that it was necessary to find and preserve the systems that were beneficial to Chosŏn, since *kaehwa* was not suited to Chosŏn. In other words, a correct *kaehwa* would be possible only by grafting the modern ways and institutions of the West onto the foundation of Korea's tradition. Seeing Silhak as similar to Western science

42. The expressions "*minji*" and "*millyŏk*" were new terms coined by Yen Fu (see Cho Kyŏngnan, p. 64). The use of these terms demonstrates that Yen Fu's books were widely read in Korea and were influential in Chosŏn society in this period.

43. *Hwangsŏng sinmun*, January 9, 1899. The article in which these views appeared stated the newspaper's agreement with the ideas expressed in the article "Patriotism" (*Aeguknon*) that appeared in the Chinese newspaper, *Ch'ŏngŭibo*.

44. *Hwangsŏng sinmun*, May 18, 1899.

45. *Hwangsŏng sinmun*, May 19, 1902. These views appeared in an article praising the publication of Tasan (Chŏng Yagyong)'s *Mongmin simsŏ* by the publisher Kwangmunsa.

and scholarship, they felt that it could serve as a tradition that could be combined with Western ways. The Great Han Empire's slogan of *kubon sinch'am* was interpreted as being similar in meaning to Chŏng Yagyŏng's ideas of *ko'gŭm chŏlch'ung* (combination of the old and the new) and *sisok ch'amjak* (consideration of the customs of the times).

One of the underlying factors behind the *Hwangsŏng sinmun*'s interest in Silhak was the fact that many of its leading figures, who were called "*sangch'on'in*," belonged to the *chungin* class. The term *sangch'on'in* referred to people who lived in villages north of Seoul. They were also called "*udae saram*" (*udae* people) since they lived in Samch'ŏng-dong at the foot of Inwang Mountain, which was called "*udae*" in pure Korean.[46] Most of the *sangch'on'in* worked as *kyŏm'in* (attendants, subordinates) for powerful families, and they generally used those connections to obtain a position as a clerk (*sŏri*) in a central government office.[47] They were also the leading figures in the printing industry in the late Chosŏn period.[48] Their background gave them the potential for a rapid rise into the elite during the state-led modernization efforts in the Hanmal period and Japan's reordering of Chosŏn's social structure during the occupation period.[49] Along with the social and political emergence of the *sangch'on'in*, another factor was the participation of Chang Chiyŏn (1864-1921) in the *Hwangsŏng sinmun*.[50]

By the time that the Independence Club was formed, intellectuals influenced by Social Darwinism came to believe that it was not possible to achieve leaps in historical development, and they began to pursue gradual reform. Other intellectuals pushed for *pyŏnbŏp kaehwa* based on the ideas of "combining the old and the new."[51]

---

46. Kang Myŏnggwan, "18-19 segi kyŏng'ajŏn kwa yesul hwaldong ŭi yangsang" (Artistic activities and the capital-region *ajŏn* in the eighteenth and nineteenth centuries), *Han'guk kŭndae munhaksa ŭi chaengjŏm* (Seoul: Ch'angjak kwa pip'yŏngsa, 1990), p. 92. Among the principal members of the Independence Club, figures such as Namgung Ŏk, Na Suyŏn, Sin Yongjin, Yŏm Chungmo, Im Chinsu, Kim Tuhyŏn, Chŏng Sŏkgyu, Hong Chaegi can probably be considered *sangch'on'in*. For a more detailed discussion, see Chu Chin-Oh (Chu Chin'o), "19 segi kaehwa kaehyŏknon ŭi kujo wa chŏn'gae" (The structure and development of theories of modern reform in the nineteenth century) (Ph.D. diss., Yonsei University, 1995), pp. 134-37.

47. Chŏng Kyo, *Taehan kye'nyŏnsa*, vol. 1, p. 298. A description of *sangch'on'in* is on p. 205.

48. Kang Myŏnggwan, ibid., pp. 124-33.

49. Cho Sŏng'yun, ibid., pp. 164-67.

50. Chu Chin-Oh, ibid., pp. 169-70.

51. These ideas became more systematized through Chosŏn intellectuals' contact with Chinese ideas on *pyŏnbŏp* which were also based on Social Darwinism.

The Independence Club's
Conception of the Modern State

INDEPENDENCE AND THE BALANCE OF POWERS

The activities of the Independence Club naturally centered on the idea of independence (*tongnip*). They believed that the basis for Chosŏn's independence was its freedom from the yoke of tributary status as a result of China's defeat in the Sino-Japanese War. An editorial in the *Tongnip sinmun* noted:

> Since God regarded Chosŏn with pity, it became an independent country because of the war between Japan and Ch'ing China. Your Highness, the King of Korea, has now become the equal of the kings of all the countries in the world, and because of that, the people of Chosŏn have also become equal with the peoples of all the countries in the world.[52]

They wanted to "notify the world and to convey to future generations Chosŏn's achievement of independence" by building a monument to commemorate it.[53] Building Independence Gate on the former site of Yŏng'ŭn Gate, which was located next to Mohwagwan, would not just cleanse the shame of the past but establish a new foundation for independence.[54] Such sentiments were echoed in the prospectus for the construction of Independence Gate, which stated that its purpose was "to cleanse the disgrace of the past and to build a [new] standard."[55]

Korea first announced its independence to the world at a ceremony at Chongmyo (Royal Shrine) on December 12, 1894 (by the lunar calendar).[56] However, the announcement was not made according to Korea's own will; it was done at the request of Japan. In addition, in article 1 of the Treaty of Shimonoseki, Japan forced China to recognize Korea's independence.[57] The Independence Club expressed their views on these events in the *Tongnip sinmun*:

> In the past, Chosŏn was a tributary state of China, but it was in name only. China did not interfere in Chosŏn's internal affairs, and for several

52. "Nonsŏl," *Tongnip sinmun*, June 21, 1896.
53. "Nonsŏl," *Tongnp sinmun*, July 4, 1896.
54. *Tongnip sinmun*, June 20, 1896.
55. *Tae Chosŏn Tongnip hyŏphoe hoebo*, no. 1, November 30, 1896.
56. *Taehan kye'nyŏnsa*, vol. 1, pp. 101-2.
57. Ibid., pp. 104-5.

hundred years, the Chosŏn government was able to handle all its affairs as it wished. When China recently sent Yuan Shi-k'ai to Chosŏn and involved themselves in the affairs of government, it was done at the request of the Chosŏn government. After the war between Japan and China, it was said that Chosŏn became independent, but in reality, it seems to have become a dependency of Japan.[58]

Although Chosŏn had accepted the suzerainty of China for a long period of time, it actually had been an autonomous country, but China began to interfere in its internal affairs from the time of the Imo Soldiers Riot of 1882. As a result of the Sino-Japanese War, Chosŏn became independent of China, but it was independence in name only.

On the other hand, the *Tongnip sinmun* did not mention the awkward fact that even as the country was declaring its independence, its monarch was residing at the Russian legation because his safety could not be guaranteed in his own palace. In fact, they felt that now was the perfect time to commemorate Chosŏn's independence. The intention of the article quoted above was to refute the recent assertion of "a Japanese newspaper that both Russia and Japan were protecting Chosŏn." Their failure to mention the king's flight to the Russian legation suggests that they felt it did not contradict Chosŏn's status as an independent country.

In its early years, the Independence Club saw Russia as a power that protected, rather than threatened, Chosŏn's independence.[59] The *Tongnip sinmun* welcomed Russia's appointment of Waeber as minister plenipotentiary because they regarded it as a sign of Russia's desire to protect Korea's independence.[60] At the same time, they severely criticized Confucianists' efforts to memorialize the king to return to the royal palace.[61] Russia actively supported the construction of Independence Gate and the publication of *The Independent/Tongnip sinmun*.[62] The Club's conception of independence clearly did not involve escaping from Russian interference.

---

58. *Tongnip sinmun*, May 16, 1896.
59. Russia provided funds for the construction of Independence Gate, and Waeber and his wife also contributed 100 wŏn.
60. "Editorial," *The Independent*, September 1, 1896.
61. *Tongnip sinmun*, February 13, 1897. An editorial defending the king's move to the Russian legation had already appeared on April 23, 1896. Its main target of attack was the ŭibyŏng (righteous army) movement.
62. Yi Kwangnin, ibid., p. 315.

As Russia's policies called for a greater presence in Chosŏn, the *Tongnip sinmun* came to view Russia as the greatest enemy to Chosŏn's independence. When Russia abruptly withdrew its personnel and forces in March 1898, they believed that Chosŏn had finally become a fully independent country. Of course, they knew that Korea had not achieved independence by its own power, nor did they think that it could be maintained permanently under the current situation. But now that independence was achieved—even if in name only, it must be maintained by taking advantage of this opportunity to undertake internal political reform.[63] In their view, what Chosŏn must do was to "abandon old customs and follow its own path," and they warned that if Chosŏn failed, it would become the colony of another power.[64]

The Independence Club felt that the most important way to preserve Chosŏn's independence was to adopt a policy of neutrality. Their plan was to avoid entering into an exclusive alliance with any one power and to give economic opportunities equally to all powers. If Chosŏn divided concessions equally among several countries, their interests would become increasingly tied to that of Chosŏn. The Club expected that those countries would intervene to protect their interests if Korea faced a crisis. As the Minister of Foreign Affairs, Yi Wanyong tried to implement these policies and granted mining and railroad concessions to foreign powers, primarily the United States.

The *Tongnip sinmun* also encouraged the government to grant concessions to foreign powers. They believed that "in establishing relations with other countries, [a country] should not take a one-sided approach like the way a dilettante carries himself or the decisiveness of a man of action, but [it should] develop close and harmonious relations with countries to both the east and the west and develop relations that mutually check and balance each other."[65] They proposed that "the policy that Chosŏn should maintain is to develop good relations with foreign countries so that they do not encroach on Chosŏn—not out of fear but because of their affection for Chosŏn."[66] In order to "develop friendly relations so that Chosŏn is not invaded," it is

63. *Tongnip sinmun*, September 12, 1896.
64. *Tongnip sinmun*, May 28, 1896.
65. "Nonsŏl," *Tongnip sinmun*, January 20, 1898.
66. "Nonsŏl," *Tongnip sinmun*, August 22, 1896.

necessary to implement internal reforms and a foreign policy in accordance with the intentions and principles of the foreign powers.[67]

In the beginning, the leaders of the Independence Club felt that Korea's independence could be preserved only by maintaining a balance of power among the foreign countries involved in Korea. They believed that "no country would occupy [Chosŏn] unless the people of Chosŏn asked another country to occupy it."[68] On the other hand, they opposed anything that would upset the balance of power because they felt that such a disruption would bring about the destruction of Korea. Thinking that "it would be easy for politicians to achieve independence [for Chosŏn] through [a policy of] neutrality,"[69] the Independence Club advocated a diplomacy of neutrality based on the principle of the balance of powers. In their view, the Nishi-Rosen protocol between Japan and Russia meant that the two countries "would protect Korea's independence together." They even felt that "in comparison to other countries that had to shed blood to attain independence, Korea is a fortunate country."[70]

The Independence Club also emphasized the necessity of implementing self-strengthening reforms domestically in order to achieve true independence.[71] They expected that it could be achieved through "civilization and enlightenment" and a policy of "enriching the country and strengthening the military" (puguk kangpyŏng). However, they did not have much interest in building up the military power necessary to protect Chosŏn in case of a breakdown in the balance of powers. The Tongnip sinmun wrote, "In Chosŏn, there is no reason to build a large army and navy to prevent foreign countries from invading. It is sufficient to have a small domestic army and navy to maintain order and suppress rebels such as the Tonghak and righteous armies (ŭibyŏng). But if another country tries to make Chosŏn the dependency of a foreign country, [we] will be prepared."[72] A military was necessary only to prepare for domestic rebellions.

---

67. "Nonsŏl," Tongnip sinmun, December 19, 1896. The newspaper opposed the appointments of Cho Pyŏngsik as Minister of Law and Yi Sejik (aka, Yi Iljik) as head of the criminal division of the Ministry of Law, both of whom were involved in the plot to assassinate Pak Yŏnghyo, because they felt that Chosŏn would be criticized by foreign countries.

68. "Nonsŏl," Tongnip sinmun, May 25, 1897.

69. "Nonsŏl," Tongnip sinmun, January 20, 1898.

70. "The Nissi-Rosen Protocol," The Independent, May 26, 1898.

71. Sin Yongha, ibid., pp. 160-64.

72. Tongnip sinmun, May 25, 1897.

Neutrality is always an option for a country whose independence is threatened. However, while the Independence Club advocated neutrality, in reality it vacillated between Russia and Japan, and by 1898, it sided with Japan. They chose Japan not because of their amicable feelings toward it but in order to maintain a balance of power against Russia.

Since Russia's main focus in this period was Manchuria, Korea was a secondary concern. Despite this fact, the Independence Club adopted an uncompromising anti-Russian stance. As a result, the people had an exaggerated fear of Russia and a favorable view of Japan. An extreme case of such a reaction was the support for a greater East Asian union led by Japan; some right-wing civic groups in Japan proposed such a union in order to counter the threat of the West.[73]

IMPERIAL POWER AND A REPRESENTATIVE ASSEMBLY

Among the leaders of the Independence Club, some felt that an American-style constitutional republic was the most ideal political system in the world,[74] and there were some who wrote editorials in the *Tongnip sinmun/ The Independent* on the divine rights of humans.[75] However, in this period, they felt that the driving force of Social Darwinian evolution was not the people or even the nation but the state and, in particular, the monarchy.[76]

Patriotism and loyalty to the monarch were emphasized in all the patriotic songs published in the *Tongnip sinmun* and in the motto of the Independence Club.[77] All events sponsored by the Independence Club had prayers for and expressions of loyalty to the emperor.[78] Through such rituals, they sought to instill patriotism and love for the country.[79]

To the leaders of the Independence Club, patriotism was a lofty ideal that transcended the family, the clan, social status, and factional affiliation.[80]

73. Chu Chin-Oh, ibid., pp. 177-78.

74. Yun Ch'iho recorded these thoughts as he observed the presidential election during his stay in the U.S. However, during the debates on the State Council in 1898, he noted, "If I ever thought (which I have never done) it possible to have a representative popular assembly in Corea, I give it up now." *Yun Ch'iho ilgi*, May 2, 1898.

75. For example: "All of the people have a certain amount of rights granted by God, and they are rights that no one can take away." *Tongnip sinmun*, March 9, 1897.

76. *Tongnip sinmun*, August 26, 1897. The article was taken from a speech given by Yun Ch'iho during a ceremony in which Christians celebrated the birthday of the emperor in Seoul.

77. Chŏng Kyo, ibid., p. 181.

78. Sin Yongha, ibid., p. 598.

79. "Nonsŏl," *Tongnip sinmun*, June 8, 1897.

80. Sin Yongha, ibid., p. 595.

They felt that "since the country is a relation that is more important than one's parents and is loftier than one's siblings or wife and children, one has a reason to live even if one's parents, siblings, wife and children die, but if one's country perishes, one has no reason to live."[81] Since the monarch, for them, was synonymous with the state, patriotism meant loyalty to the monarch.

During the Great Han Empire period, the political system was restructured into an absolute monarchy. Initially, the Independence Club looked favorably toward efforts to strengthen the monarchy. Editorials in the *Tongnip sinmun* welcomed the adoption of the State Council system (*ŭijŏngbu kwanje*). Moreover, the Club held ceremonies to celebrate events such as the emperor's birthday (called *Mansu sŏngjŏl*), the founding of Chosŏn (*Kaeguk kiwŏnjŏl*), the anniversary of the emperor's coronation (*Kyech'ŏn kiwŏnjŏl*), and the crown prince's birthday (*Ch'ŏnch'ugyŏng-jŏl*)—the first time in the history of the Chosŏn dynasty that these holidays were observed. In return, the royal family granted funds to cover the expenses.

As the power of the Independence Club waned in central politics, opinions on monarchical government became divided. One group pushed for modernization under a monarchical system and focused their efforts on preventing the emperor from appointing anti-reform officials to the State Council. A second group felt that since the emperor was an obstacle to implementing modern reforms, it was necessary to replace the emperor, or, failing that, they would directly recommend officials to be appointed to the State Council.

Yun Ch'iho and Namgung Ŏk were the leaders of the first group.[82] Yun's main objective was to implement gradual, modernizing reforms based on the theories of Social Darwinism. He felt that it would be impossible to achieve modernization without a monarch since no forces existed that could restrict the power of the monarchy. In the case of Japan, which he had visited and viewed as a model for Korea, the monarchy was not an obstacle to modernization; in fact, it became a unifying force for the people. Yun also tried to turn the monarch into a symbol of both the state and modernization through the use of pageantry around the monarch.

---

81. "Nonsŏl," *Tongnip sinmun*, July 31, 1897.
82. Chu Chin-Oh, "19 segi kaehwa kaehyŏknon ŭi kujo wa chŏn'gae."

The clearest result of efforts to strengthen the monarchy was the first article of the six-article *hŏn'ŭi*[83] which stated that it "is necessary to strengthen the absolute authority of the monarch." It expressed their belief that the authority of the monarchy must be strong since the monarch is the central force in modernizing reforms. For the Yun-Namgung group, the goal of the Independence Club was to "establish an eternal and solid foundation by elevating the status of the emperor and hardening the will of the people," and they emphasized that their activities were based on an implicit acceptance of the authority of the emperor. In addition,

> In terms of rights, everyone from the Son of Heaven to the common person has fixed rights. The rights of Your Highness are equal to [those of the leaders of] the six continents and all the countries of the world. If an official, who is a subject of Your Majesty and protects Your Majesty's territory but disrupts its politics and fails to observe the laws, brings harm to Your Majesty and the country, then it is the right of the ministers to denounce and censure that official. There are those who say that if there is an increase of people's rights, then there is a necessary reduction in the authority of the monarchy. Is it possible for the people to be more ignorant? If there is no such debate among the people today, the politics and laws will also deteriorate, and it will be impossible to know what kind of disaster will arise in which region.[84]

At first glance, it appears that they are advocating limits on the power of the emperor to appoint bureaucrats, but it actually came from a belief that the authority of the monarchy would ultimately be strengthened by the open consensus of the people. While the monarch should manage the affairs of the country with absolute authority, that authority was not limitless; however, it ultimately would be strengthened if it were exercised through the consensus and support of the people.

This conception of politics was also apparent in the Yun-Namgung group's proposal for the reorganization of the Privy Council. Their proposal for the introduction of a representative assembly system was a monumental moment in the history of modern political thought in Korea. On the other

---

83. A *hŏn'ŭi* was a document that presented the opinions of officials to the emperor.

84. "Chungch'uwŏn ildŭng ŭigwan Yun Ch'iho tŭng sŏ" (The memorial of Privy Councillor Yun Ch'iho and others), *Sŭngjŏngwŏn ilgi*, Year 2 of Kwangmu, 9th month, 9th day of 1st period (October 23 according to the Western calendar).

hand, in an editorial entitled "A Lower House is Not Urgent," they expressed reluctance to turn political power over to the people:

> [The establishment of] a lower house means giving political power to the
> people. . . . If [the people] are ignorant, they will ruin the government
> whether one person rules or whether several people rule. The fact that a
> monarchy is actually more stable than a democracy in an ignorant world
> is clear from both the past and the present and from all the countries of
> the West. . . . Before [they] imitated Western *kaehwa*, the Japanese were
> one hundred times more civilized than us. But even though Japan began
> to learn about the West and achieved astonishing progress for thirty
> years, they did not establish a national assembly until the 23rd year of
> Meiji (1890), and before they established the Upper and Lower Houses,
> they visited all the countries of the West and studied them deeply.
> However, during the few years that we have had commerce [with other
> countries], all we have learned is how to smoke cigarettes. How can we
> dream of establishing a lower house? It would be proper to think about a
> lower house only after [the country] develops for forty to fifty years by
> educating the people through building schools in all regions, by sending
> students to all the countries of the West, and by improving the
> knowledge of the people.[85]

The Independence Club opposed the creation of a lower house because they
thought that modernization should be carried out through a monarchical
system. Since the people were the object, not the subject, of *kaehwa*, a lower
house would be possible only after the people became completely enlightened
through the exercise of imperial power. Although they did not deny that the
establishment of a lower house (i.e., popular sovereignty) would be achieved
some time in the future, it would be impossible to introduce such a system
in the next forty to fifty years since the people were still ignorant.

On April 3, 1898, the Independence Club held the twenty-fifth meeting
of its Debating Society, and the topic of that day was: "The establishment
of a representative assembly is the most urgent matter in politics." Around
the same time, the *Tongnip sinmun* also published articles on the same topic.
Through these records, it is possible to examine the Independence Club's
conception of a representative assembly and of the relation between the

---

85. "*Haŭiwŏn ŭn kŭpch'i ant'a*" (A Lower House is not Urgent), *Tongnip sinmun*, April 7,
1898.

assembly and the monarch. They planned a political system in which the representative assembly and State Council would be strictly separated. State Councillors (*ŭijŏnggwan*) did not have administrative duties and only had the authority to debate and resolve legislative matters; administrators (*haengjŏnggwan*) only had the administrative authority to implement matters passed by the representative assembly (*ŭihoewŏn*).[86]

In the Independence Club's scheme, representatives were regarded as government officials, and it was the emperor who had the power to appoint them. Matters decided in the assembly could be enacted only after they were presented to the throne and received the emperor's approval. This requirement meant that final authority was in the hands of the emperor. This system did not seek to create a representative organ based on the principle of people's sovereignty. However, in some aspects, it was not meant to be merely an advisory organ for the emperor. The Independence Club did institutionalize some restrictions on the emperor's authority by strictly separating the roles of the cabinet and the representative assembly and by giving the representative assembly legislative authority over all state policy. The purpose of reorganizing the Privy Council into a representative assembly was to create an organ that could act as a balance to the authority of the State Council. Seeing themselves as the spokesmen for the people, the Independence Club proposed that its members occupy half of the seats on the Privy Council.[87] However, not only did the Independence Club lack a nationwide organization, they also had no concrete ideas on how they could reflect the will of the people.

The second group within the Independence Club had different views on political reform. The leaders of this group were former exiles such as Pak Yŏnghyo and former leaders of the Kabo Reforms such as An Kyŏngsu and their followers, and their approach to politics and methods of seizing power were the same ones they had used during the Kapsin Coup and Kabo Reforms. Their plan was to depose Kojong in a coup-d'état and then to use either Prince Ŭihwa, Kojong's second son, or Yi Chunyong, the Taewŏngun's grandson, as a figurehead emperor to seize power for themselves. Their

---

86. *Tongnip sinmun*, April 30, 1898.

87. The Independence Club successfully carried out a protest against the government by organizing the resignation of officials. As a result, from October 7, they held a forum with the new government to discuss plans for the development of the state and the improvement of people's lives. At this meeting, the Independence Club presented two proposals: the reorganization of the Privy Council and the complete abolition of all extralegal taxes.

objective was not simply to change the division of power within a representative assembly but to reorganize government so that reform bureaucrats would monopolize power through the Independence Club's control of both the Privy Council and the cabinet.[88]

In sum, among the leaders of the Independence Club, there were two groups whose opinions differed on the form of monarchical government. The first group strove to establish a strong absolute monarchy in which the leader would govern in union with a reform-minded populace. The second group continued to pursue the reform program of the Kaehwap'a which sought to limit the authority of the monarchy, based on the idea of *kunmin kongch'i* (co-rule by the monarchy and the people), and to establish a dictatorship of reform bureaucrats.

Despite these differences, both groups shared a more modern approach to politics that would begin the reform of the medieval political system and would clearly institutionalize the relation between monarchical authority and people's rights. However, neither group made any concrete proposals for creating a constitution, suggesting that there were still no groups within the Great Han Empire that had a concrete plan for modern political reform.

SOCIAL AND CULTURAL REFORMS

The Independence Club realized that political reform in itself would not be sufficient to overthrow feudalism, establish a modern state, and, in particular, foster nationalism. They proposed a variety of social and cultural reforms that would facilitate the implementation of political reforms. This section will examine the Club's proposals on the social status system, the abolition of feudal customs, and the promotion of patriotism, and to put them in context, it will also be necessary to examine its conception of the masses.

The Independence Club felt that the abolition of status distinctions was important to allow the development of leaders to carry out modern reforms. The *Tongnip sinmun* published many articles that criticized and ridiculed the yangban, and it supported the appointment of officials by merit. Why did the newspaper place so much emphasis on appointing officials "without distinguishing between commoners and yangban"[89] at a time when the social status system had already been legally abolished? On one level, these efforts reflect the fact that despite its legal abolition, people's attitudes about

---

88. For more on this group, see Chu Chin-Oh, ibid., pp. 150-54.
89. *Tongnip sinmun*, September 21, 1898.

hereditary status still had not changed. However, the Independence Club did not mention the yangban system in any of its reform activities, probably because its abolition made it unnecessary to mention.

Among the members of the Independence Club, *chungin* and yangban from less prestigious families tended to be more outspoken on this issue. They were the ones who would receive the most immediate benefit from the abolition of status restrictions. The *Hwangsŏng sinmun*, in which they were the leading figures, contained even stronger critiques of status discrimination in the appointment of officials. It argued that "only by appointing personnel by talent without considering family background or class will it be possible to strengthen the interior and respond to external pressures."[90] The newspaper lamented the "reality that children of the lesser orders have few opportunities for appointment even if their scholarly knowledge is deep, and the nobility gain appointments even if they are lazy, and their knowledge is insufficient."[91]

However, Kaehwap'a intellectuals were not opposed to the social hegemony of scholar-officials (*sadaebu*).[92] Of course, they used the term *sadaebu* to refer not only to traditional yangban who studied the Confucian classics but also to people, such as themselves, who were knowledgeable about the West and had practical administrative skills as well. They also emphasized that discriminatory treatment of military officials had been eliminated and that through individual efforts, they could potentially become provincial governors or even ministers in the government.[93]

The Independence Club held similar views on slavery. It is unclear whether they advocated its complete abolition or just called for the prohibition of the purchase and sale of human beings. At the eighth meeting of the Debating Society of the Independence Club, which was held on October 31, 1897, the topic was "the grave injustice of buying and selling men and women among our people." Editorials in the *Tongnip sinmun* also went no farther than a critique of trafficking in human beings: "though [they] are the children of the country's king and one's fellow countrymen, they regard their brethren as slaves and buy and sell them."[94]

---

90. *Hwangsŏng sinmun*, October 6, 1898.
91. *Hwangsŏng sinmun*, April 9, 1902.
92. *Hwangsŏng sinmun*, December 12, 1901.
93. *Hwangsŏng sinmun*, June 17, 1899.
94. *Tongnip sinmun*, October 15, 1898.

Another part of their reform program was the elimination of harmful feudal customs. A major focus was the promotion of the rights of women, and, as part of that effort, they argued for the necessity of women's education. They also raised issues such as the protection of children, support for love marriages, and the abolition of concubinage, *kisaeng*, shamanism, feng-shui (*p'ungsu*), the custom of early marriage, and the prohibition against women's remarriage.[95] Most of these issues were reforms that they felt had to be implemented in the transition to a modern state and society.

What was problematic about their views was the likelihood that tradition would be completely rejected in the process of modernization. Of course, it is necessary to eliminate feudal customs that are oppressive to the people. However, in any culture, there are customs that cannot be explained purely on scientific and rational grounds. The Independence Club, and in particular the advocates of "civilization and enlightenment," supported a gradual approach to reform, but their ultimate goal was the total westernization of Korean society. They showed very little interest in continuing or searching for the contemporary value of Korean tradition.

Members of the Independence Club felt that Koreans had to adopt Western etiquette, clothing, and even cuisine in order to become modern.

If officials and the people want to receive respect from foreign countries, they should become like the people of enlightened, autonomous, independent countries—[they should] throw away their rice and kimchi and eat beef and bread.[96]

When one interacts with foreigners, it is necessary to know foreign customs to avoid looking like a barbarian to foreigners. . . . Before going to someone's house, do not eat smelly foods such as scallions or garlic. . . . When passing in front of someone, excuse oneself while passing.[97]

It is said it is necessary to adopt all kinds of reforms [*pyŏnbŏp*], and it is urgently necessary to adopt a Western political system. . . . There is a lot that could be said [on this topic], but if East Asia is to reform, the first measure should be to adopt Western forms of dress.[98]

95. Sin Yongha, ibid., pp. 243–47.
96. *Tongnip sinmun*, October 10, 1896.
97. *Tongnip sinmun*, November 14, 1896.
98. *Maeil sinmun*, March 4, 1899.

Of course, these editorials did not represent the opinions of the entire Independence Club. Within the organization, there were groups that were very interested in finding ways to adopt Western culture on a foundation of native tradition. In particular, the *Hwangsŏng sinmun* actively searched for ways to combine tradition with *kaehwa*. The *Maeil sinmun* also severely criticized people who viewed *kaehwa* only as the adoption of Western customs and patterns of life. It appears that these differences were not serious and could have been resolved later internally within the Club.

The Independence Club viewed the masses as still being in a state of ignorance. In their eyes, the masses lacked political consciousness and the ability to rule themselves. At a time when people were worried about the outbreak of popular rebellions—like the French Revolution—if Chosŏn's crisis of sovereignty worsened, their outlook was consistently negative. They felt that there was no possibility of an uprising because the masses lacked patriotic sentiment and conceptions of freedom, popular rights, education, and the development of knowledge. Therefore:

> If officials and the people widen their knowledge and increase their love of their compatriots through newspapers and education, do not wish for any extra rights, and devote themselves to observing the sound laws granted by His Highness, then as wisdom and education naturally increase, people's rights will gradually increase, and the emperor will also pledge to stabilize the conditions of the people and strengthen and enrich the country.[99]

In short, they argued that the masses should follow the lead of the emperor or enlightened people such as themselves. The masses were to be the objects of edification rather than the subjects of education and reform. Since the masses had lived in ignorance for so long and knew little of the affairs of the world, it would be impossible for them to take the initiative in pushing for reform. The Independence Club felt that, at best, the masses could serve as silent sympathizers or followers of self-strengthening reforms efforts under its leadership. In order to turn the masses into "followers," it was necessary to educate them.

> A person who loves the Chosŏn king and the people . . . asked the wisest and most knowledgeable teacher in the world, "What should

99. *Tongnip sinmun,* July 9, 1898.

Chosŏn do?" After sitting silently for awhile, the teacher turned his head to look at the Chosŏn people and said just one word in a thunderous voice. That [word] was "education." It is impossible for the country to develop since the Chosŏn people become the prime minister, head of the army, and merchants with only a little knowledge. The reason that China declined is that it lacked education, and the reason that Japan has prospered is that it has education.[100]

Of course, before this period, Chosŏn had had its own educational system for many centuries. What they meant was that it was necessary to break with traditional education by dedicating themselves to learning Western science.[101] Believing that "whether or not [Chosŏn] joins the ranks of civilized countries like Japan depends on the progress of education,"[102] they first pushed for the training of future administrators of self-strengthening reforms in fields such as industry, law, and foreign languages.[103]

However, the Independence Club did not think that it was right even for people with a modern education to rebel against the existing political system. It was dangerous to undergo political change when the people's abilities were not fully mature. They were opposed to the *ŭibyŏng* movement and the masses' demands for change as manifested in the Kabo Peasants' War of 1894. It was an expression of fear, and what they feared was "threats to the security of the fortress by local rebels" or, in other words, threats to their own lives and property.[104]

100. *Tongnip sinmun*, April 25, 1896.

101. Yun Kŏnch'a, *Chosen kindai kyoiku no siso to koto* (The thought and behavior of Korea's early modern education) (Tokyo: Tokyo University Press, 1982), pp. 107-08.

102. An Ch'angsŏn, "Kyoyuk ŭi kŭpmu" (The urgent task of education), *Tae Chosŏn tongnip hyŏphoe hoebo*, no. 7.

103. The schools that were established at this time were the government-run foreign language school, vocational schools such as Kyŏngsŏng hakdang, and teachers' schools such as Hansŏng sabŏm. There were no schools that taught the humanities or social sciences, and they felt that students who wanted to study such fields could go abroad. For example, during the Kabo Reforms, Yun Ch'iho cancelled plans to establish a college that had been organized by Kim Ch'unhŭi, an official in the Ministry of Education (see *Yun Ch'iho ilgi*, February 14, 1896). Yun's opinion was that "A Korean youth who knows how to handle tools and handle them well is a more desirable citizen than one who may quote Shakespeare or Spencer" (*Yun Ch'iho ilgi*, October 31, 1902). In the above-mentioned article by An Ch'angsŏn, he argued that "most importantly. . . the people should study practical fields and industry."

104. "Nonsŏl," *Tongnip sinmun*, October 24, 1896. In this case, the reason that the Independence Club called for the expansion of the military was not to establish an autonomous national

The Independence Club criticized the popular rebellions that rose up against the oppression of local officials:

> If all the people in a village speak respectfully and with one heart, then no matter how evil an official is, he will not be able to do illegal acts again. . . . However, as what the people of Chosŏn do is stir up rebellions or join the Tonghak party or the righteous armies, they are acting like bandits, rebels, and, thus, criminals according to the law.[105]

When the Club organized mass assemblies, leaders such as Yun Ch'iho, Sŏ Chaep'il, and Yi Wanyong worried about the possibility of "violent behavior by ignorant people" and whether they would spontaneously attack the government on their own.[106]

The focus of the Independence Club was clearly not on increasing popular rights. Although it did stimulate debate on popular rights and the abolition of the social status system, it appears to have been no more than a concession necessary in a bourgeois state to try to mobilize support. The expansion of popular rights was viewed only as a means of strengthening the country's sovereignty.[107] Popular rights necessarily became a subordinate concern to state power as the Independence Club's reforms were mainly concerned with state building rather than the welfare of the masses.

Within an imperialist world order that was ruled by might, it was necessary for a country like Korea to establish a nation-state in order to maintain its sovereignty. One of the urgent tasks facing reformers was to instill a sense of nationalism in people so that they would see themselves as the subjects of history. Although Chosŏn had become independent of the Chinese world order, people still clung to the idea of China as the center of the world.

As part of its effort to promote nationalism, the government developed a national history curriculum and adopted the use of a mixed classical Chinese-

defense force but to suppress the mass movement. See also "Nonsŏl," *Tongnip sinmun*, May 25, 1897.

105. "Nonsŏl," *Tongnip sinmun*, August 12, 1897.

106. *Yun Ch'iho ilgi*, March 10, 1898. In addition, Yun Ch'iho thought that "the people are ignorant, stupid and incapable of raising and maintaining a respectable and orderly insurrection" (*Yun Ch'iho ilgi*, May 1, 1898).

107. These ideas were similar to those of Yen Fu. See James Reeve Pusey, *China and Charles Darwin* (Cambridge: Council on East Asian Studies, 1983), pp. 70-71, and Cho Kyŏngnan, ibid.

vernacular script for official documents during the Kabo Reform period.[108] During the period of the Independence Club, the curriculums of all levels of schools, such as Hansŏng Normal School, had courses in the Korean language and Korean history. The necessity of teaching these subjects stimulated research in both fields.[109]

Increased interest in *han'gŭl* usage and a rise in research on the vernacular from the time of the Kabo Reforms enabled the *Tongnip sinmun*, as well as the newspapers that followed it such as the *Maeil sinmun* and the *Cheguk sinmun*, to be published in the vernacular. The status of *han'gŭl* was elevated from *ŏnmun* (vulgar script) to a *kungmun* (national language). *Han'gŭl* was viewed as the script most suited for an independent country, and the use of *han'gŭl* was emphasized as a way to instill an independent consciousness. Demonstrating the growing interest in *han'gŭl*, the Independence Club's bulletin contained many articles on the standardization of the vernacular grammar in order to facilitate its use.[110] Some intellectuals even began to claim that "the alphabet of Chosŏn is the most superior script in the world."[111]

The promotion of the vernacular was significant because it marked the beginnings of linguistic nationalism in Korea. The term "linguistic nationalism" refers to the belief that language is a major factor in the formation of the modern nation-state. As one of the goals of modern nationalist movements, it takes the form of efforts to promote and standardize the national language. To nationalists, the promotion of a national language was not a practical or intellectual matter. Rather, language was an expression of the national spirit, and as such ideas became more strongly held, language gradually became one of the decisive criteria in the constitution of the nation.[112]

---

108. On December 17, 1894, ordinance 1 on official documents proclaimed in article 14 that "all laws and ordinances will be written in the national language, but it is permissible to append a version in classical Chinese or to use a mixed classical Chinese-vernacular script."

109. Yu Yŏng'ik, ibid., pp. 216-18.

110. Chi Sŏk'yŏng, "Kungmunnon" (On the national language), *Tae Chosŏn tongnip hyŏphoe hoebo*, no. 1; Sin Haeyŏng, "Hanmunja wa kungmunja ŭi son'ik yŏha" (The advantages and disadvantages of classical Chinese and the national language), *Tae Chosŏn tongnip hyŏphoe hoebo*, nos. 16-17. Sin's article was a reprint of a text that was published in *Ch'inmokhoe hoebo*.

111. "Chu Sangho kungmunnon" (Chu Sangho's theory of the national language), *Tongnip sinmun*, April 22, 1897.

112. E. J. Hobsbawm, *Nations and Nationalism since 1780: Programme, Myth, Reality*, translated by Kang Myŏngse, (Seoul: Ch'angjak kwa pip'yŏngsa, 1994), p. 129.

In the West, linguistic nationalism was often used by states to unify their people in regions where various ethnic groups existed and where a multiplicity of languages made communication difficult.[113] In the case of the Korean people, their high degree of racial unity was extremely unusual in world history.[114] In contrast to the West, linguistic nationalism in Korea began as a form of resistance. It emerged as Korean society faced serious external threats and began to organize resistance, on the basis of existing human and social relations, to combat these threats.[115]

An important development in the emergence of linguistic nationalism was the rise of newspapers as a way of reaching the masses. For a newspaper, its choice of a script depended greatly on the type of reader that it targeted. While the main readers for newspapers that published in classical Chinese were older groups such as traditional officials and Confucianists, newspapers that published in the vernacular or a mixed script targeted new social groups. After the Kabo Reforms, the use of *han'gŭl* or a mixed script was no longer problematic. However, efforts to promote the vernacular often did not go beyond calls for its widespread usage. In the intellectual world, the use of classical Chinese was still predominant, and the use of a mixed script was only partially accepted. To promote the exclusive use of *han'gŭl*, it was necessary to publish a newspaper for an audience that shared the ideals of the Independence Club and were in a position to contribute to their dissemination. This audience was composed of groups that had already been using *han'gŭl* before this period and groups that had supported efforts to create a modern state since the emergence of the Kaehwap'a.[116]

The Independence Club's efforts to promote linguistic nationalism through *han'gŭl* had its limits. Despite Yun Ch'iho's support, the Independence Club rejected a proposal to compose its first memorial to the throne in *han'gŭl* in February 1898.[117] Afterwards, most of their memorials were

---

113. Ibid., p. 34.

114. Hobsbawm noted that "China, Korea and Japan...are indeed among the extremely rare examples of historic states composed of a population that is ethnically almost or entirely homogeneous." In the original, this quote can be found in E.J. Hobsbawm, *Nations and Nationalism since 1780: Programme, Myth, Reality* (Cambridge: Cambridge University Press, 1990), p. 66.

115. Chŏng Ch'angnyŏl, "Hanmal pyŏnhyŏk undong ŭi chŏngch'i kyŏngjejŏk sŏnggyŏk" (The political-economic aspects of reform movements in the Hanmal period), *Han'guk minjok-juŭiron* (Seoul: Ch'angjak kwa pip'yŏngsa, 1982), p. 17.

116. Cho Sŏng'yun, "Oesol kwa ŏn'ŏ minjokjuŭi" (Ch'oe Hyŏnbae and linguistic nationalism), *Hyŏnsang kwa insik*, no. 62 (1994), pp. 21-22.

117. *Yun Ch'iho ilgi*, February 20, 1898.

written only in classical Chinese, not even in a mixed script. A similar logic was behind the publication of the *Hwangsŏng sinmun*. In order to enlighten the country in modern thinking, they felt that the future leaders, as well as its first target audience, would come from the privileged classes who were adept in classical Chinese. It was unlikely that they would have voluntarily abandoned the use of classical Chinese, a marker of their social status. It seems clear that the exclusive use of *han'gŭl* did not have the support of the entire Independence Club.

In sum, to achieve the transition to a modern state and overcome threats to the country's sovereignty, the Independence Club proposed social and cultural reforms designed to instill patriotism in the people and thus to unify the strength of the entire nation. For them, the value of patriotism was that it transcended family and clan ties. However, rather than the nation, their emphasis was on the state and the monarch. Such thinking reveals the true meaning of the Independence Club's emphasis on "loyalty to the monarch and love for the country" (*ch'unggun aeguk*).

In late-developing countries that lacked a mature bourgeoisie to serve as the agents of nationalism, nationalism tends to be more conceptual and cultural.[118] As such nationalism is extremely focused on the state, it initially does result in the spread of nationalist sentiment. However, since it ultimately cannot resolve economic inequalities and political discrimination, it also results in the masses becoming marginalized as political actors. Nonetheless, such efforts were of tremendous significance in modern Korean history because they provided an opportunity for the spread of nationalism. The development of nationalist consciousness provided an opening for the later emergence of the people as the subjects of their own history.

Conclusion

The Independence Club pursued a course of autonomous reform through the union of traditional reform ideas and a gradual approach based on the principles of Social Darwinism. Its conception of the modern state can be summarized as follows.

---

118. Pak Hosŏng, "Yuryŏp kŭndae minjok hyŏngsŏng e kwanhan siron" (Contemporary views on the formation of modern nations in Europe), *Yŏksa pip'yŏng*, no. 19 (1992).

The Independence Club emphasized Chosŏn's independence from the Chinese tributary system and advocated its maintenance through self-strengthening reforms. As part of these reforms, they advocated that Chosŏn pursue a diplomacy of neutrality to establish a balance of powers among the foreign countries involved in Chosŏn. Neutrality was seen as necessary for Korea in order to gain time to implement self-strengthening policies. They wanted to establish a political system based on a strong monarchy, and in order to establish a modern nation-state, they emphasized both the central role of the state and a conceptual, cultural form of nationalism.

Most of the reforms proposed by the Independence Club were the same as, or similar to, those implemented by the Great Han Empire. However, a faction within the Independence Club opposed the Great Han Empire and attempted to seize power for themselves, bringing about its dissolution by the government. Through mass assemblies (manmin kongdonghoe) held in March 1898, the Club tried to organize a political movement through mass mobilization and began an effort to drive out high-ranking, conservative officials. Taking advantage of this situation, a faction of the more radical members tried to instigate a coup-d'état against the government but failed because of the opposition of the citizenry and a lack of cooperation by the foreign powers. Kojong dissolved the Independence Club at the end of December 1898, and the Tongnip sinmun ceased publishing a year later. These developments also had a negative effect on the progress of modern reforms in the Great Han Empire period. In short, the members of the Independence Club were not able to assume a leading role in state reform and became marginalized in the course of their power struggle with officials close to the emperor.

In reality, this period was the last chance for the Great Han Empire to find a way to maintain its sovereignty through self-strengthening domestic reforms and an effective foreign policy. Kojong was slow in implementing many aspects of the modern reforms whose goal was to increase imperial authority, seeing them as threats to his power. He was not able to create an optimal situation for the pursuit of modernization and the establishment of an autonomous nation-state through a close union between the Independence Club and the monarchy. Although it was necessary for the monarch to take a central role in reform, the history of this period demonstrates that Kojong was inadequate to the task.[119]

translated by Michael D. Shin

119. For more on this issue, see "Taehan Cheguk 100 chunyŏn chwadam" (A roundtable discussion on the 100th anniversary of the Great Han Empire), *Yŏksa pip'yŏng*, no. 37 (Summer 1997).

Index of Terms

Ch'ŏnch'ugyŏngjŏl 千秋慶節 holiday to celebrate the crown prince's birthday

Chungch'uwŏn 中樞阮 Privy Council

ch'unggun aeguk 忠君愛國 loyalty to the monarch and love for the country

chungin 中人

Fu Xi 伏羲

haengjŏnggwan 行政官 administrators

hŏn'ŭi 獻議六條

Hwangsŏng sinmun 皇城新聞

Kaeguk kiwŏnjŏl 開國紀元 holiday to celebrate the founding of Chosŏn

Kaehwap'a 開化派 Enlightenment Faction

kaemul sŏngmu, hwamin sŏngsok 開物成務 化民成俗

ko'gŭm chŏlch'ung 古今折衝 combination of the old and the new

kubon sinch'am 舊本新參 old foundation, new participation

kungmun 國文 national language

kunmin kongch'i 君民共 co-rule by the monarchy and the people

manmin kongdonghoe 萬民공동회 mass assemblies

Mansu sŏngjŏl 萬壽聖節 holiday to celebrate the emperor's birthday

millyŏk 民力 the strength of the people

minji 民智 people's wisdom

mu kaehwa 務開化 implement *kaehwa*

munmyŏng kaehwa 文明開化 civilization and enlightenment

ŏnmun 諺文 vulgar script

puguk kangpyŏng 富國强兵 enriching the country and strengthening the military

p'ungsu 風水 feng-shui

pyŏnbŏp 變法

sadaebu 士大夫 scholar-officials

sangch'on'in 上村人

Shen Nong 神農

silsang 實狀 practicality

sisok ch'amjak 時俗參酌 consideration of the customs of the times

Sŏyu kyŏnmun 西遊見聞 Record of Observations while Traveling in the West

tongnip 獨立 independence

Tongnip hyŏphoe 獨立協會 Independence Club

Tongnip sinmun/The Independent 독립신문

udae 우대

ŭibyŏng 義兵 righteous armies

ŭihoewŏn 議會阮 representative assembly

ŭijŏngbu kwanje 議政府官制 State Council system

CHAPTER 3

The Legalization of Land Rights under the Great Han Empire

Choi Won-kyu
崔元奎

S tructured into a hierarchical status system, medieval Chosŏn society faced a deepening crisis entering the nineteenth century. Popular uprisings became chronic as conflict between classes intensified because of advances in agricultural production, the extreme economic inequality between classes, and the breakdown of the status system itself. The most significant uprisings were the 1811 Peasant War in P'yŏng'an province and the 1862 peasant uprisings in the three southern provinces. To resolve the crisis, Chosŏn intellectuals at the time proposed two different reform programs: tax reform and land reform.

Proponents of tax reform felt that the crisis was rooted in the unfair, irrational taxation system rather than the severe inequalities of land ownership. The tax system, in which tax burdens varied according to social status, became unstable as the status system began to break down. Inequality in taxes had worsened with the ascension of some members of lower status groups to the tax-exempt ruling class, shifting their former tax burdens to a shrinking pool of lower status taxpayers. Peasants protested their increased tax payments, demanding that the government resolve this crisis, and it became clear that the government could no longer function under the existing tax system. Under the principle of "equal levying and equal payment" of taxes, the ruling class proposed a reform of the so-called *samjŏng* (three [tax] systems)— land surveys for land tax system (*chŏnjŏng*), a household cloth tax (*hop'oje*) for the military tax system (*kunjŏng*), and *sach'ang* for the grain loan system (*hwanjŏng*).[1] Their reforms proposed either to levy taxes primarily on land, the main source of wealth, by accurately measuring its productivity or to impose taxes on all households regardless of social status.

Proponents of land reform, however, felt that the main cause of problems was not simply the unequal tax system but also the landlord system. The landlord system was becoming more widespread and entrenched because of the increasing impoverishment of self-cultivators and other elements of the peasant class. The objective of land reform was to establish a self-sustaining economy based on small-scale agriculture by abolishing or, at least, by weakening the landlord system. There were two approaches to land reform—one that focused on administrative measures such as tax reduction and the other focusing on methods such as the well-field (*chŏngjŏnnon*), equal-field (*kyunjŏnnon*), limited-ownership (*hanjŏnnon*), and the village-land (*yŏjŏnnon*) systems. Proposals on the latter either called for the land to be returned to government ownership or advocated establishing a maximum limit on land ownership. The former advocated placing restrictions on the rate of land rent rather than limiting land ownership.

Proposals on land rent reduction were also divided into two positions. The pro-landlord position advocated setting the legal rate of land rent at the lowest possible level according to existing customary practices in order to preserve the landlord system. The pro-peasant position focused on stabilizing the peasant economy by fixing land rents at the lowest possible rate, with the ultimate objective of eliminating the landlord system. Despite the different objectives of these two positions, what they had in common was the attempt to find a solution by adjusting rates of land rent and commodifying cultivation rights without affecting the landlords' ownership of land.[2]

---

1. For overviews of existing research on this topic, see: Kŭndaesa yŏn'guhoe, *Han'guk chungse sahoe haech'egi ŭi che munje* (Problems in the period of the breakdown of Korean feudal society), vol. 1+2 (Seoul: Han'ul, 1987) and Han'guk yŏksa yŏn'guhoe, *Han'guk yŏksa immunchungse p'yŏn* (Introduction to Korean history—the feudal period) 2 (Seoul, P'ulbit, 1995). Definitions of these terms and systems can be found in the relevant sections in the *Han'guk chŏngsin munhwa yŏn'guwŏn, Han'guk minjok munhwa taebaekhwa sajŏn* (Encyclopedia of Korean national culture) (Seoul: Han'guk chŏngsin munhwa yŏn'guwŏn, 1991).

2. For more on theories of land reform, see: Kim Yong-sop (Kim Yongsŏp), *Han'guk kŭndae nong'ŏp sa yŏn'gu* (Studies on the history of agriculture in modern Korea), vol. 1+2 (Seoul: Ilchogak, 1988); Kim Yong-sop, *Han'guk kŭnhyŏndae nong'ŏp sa yŏn'gu—Hanmal Ilche ha ŭi chiju che wa nong'ŏp munje* (Studies on the history of agriculture in modern and contemporary Korea—the landlord system and agricultural problems during the Hanmal and Japanese occupation periods) (Seoul: Ilchogak, 1992); Ch'oe Wŏngyu, "19 segi yangjŏnnon ŭi ch'ui wa songgyŏk" (The nature of and changes in land survey theories in the nineteenth century),

Although the differences in opinion over agricultural and land policies reflected the differing political economic bases of their supporters, they were in agreement on the need for a cadastral survey and reform of land survey methods in order to achieve their goals. One of the main targets of reform was the *kyŏlbu* system (*kyŏlbuje*), a land measurement system whose units had been used in all previous land surveys. As will be explained below, the units *kyŏl* and *pu* were based on crop output rather than land area; as a result, parcels of differing areas could have the same measurements in *kyŏl* and *pu* depending on their degrees of fertility. The system was devised to enable the government to collect taxes fairly and to make prebendal grants of lands to officials in an equitable manner as remuneration for their service. It can be regarded as the method of land management suited to a self-sufficient agricultural economy.

The numerous limitations of the *kyŏlbu* system became apparent with the development of a commercial monetary economy and private land-ownership as a modern sense of exclusive property rights emerged. The changes in the economy stimulated the commodification of land, making absolute area a more suitable unit of measurement. Reformists at the time recommended that the state measure all land according to area rather than crop output. Silhak scholars had advocated land reform from the late Chosŏn period until the advent of the Great Han Empire. In contrast, the Kaehwap'a (Enlightenment Faction) reformers in the Hanmal period wanted to maintain the existing state of private land ownership and implement only a modern land tax system in order to establish a modern state. Whether the target of reform was the land system or the taxation system, a cadastral survey based on measuring land area would enable the state to regulate and manage land in a way that would facilitate the implementation of reforms. Both Silhak thinkers and the Kaehwap'a agreed on the necessity of a cadastral survey according to a new land measurement system.

Reform was all the more urgent because of the existing, customary practice of conducting land transactions at the village level. This system had reached the point where it could no longer handle a land market that expanded into a nationwide market based on private property rights. As a consequence, problems arose such as fraud in land transactions and illegal black market transactions with foreigners. The root of these problems was the gap between the institutional order and changing reality. Only the introduction

Chungsan Chŏng Tŏkgi paksa hwagap ki'nyŏm Han'guk sahak nonch'ong (Seoul: Kyŏng'in munhwasa, 1996).

of a system of capitalist land rights could solve these problems by enabling the administration of land in a manner consistent with the recognition of exclusive property rights. In this a system, the state would keep records of all aspects related to land such as its location, shape, size, classification, and status of ownership and tenancy.[3]

The Great Han Empire selectively adopted measures from various reform proposals to form policies suited to its needs and undertook a cadastral survey to establish a state-regulated system of land rights.[4] The objective of this chapter is to examine the details and significance of the cadastral survey within the context of the historical changes mentioned above. The first part will cover the land survey itself, and the second will analyze the issuance of *kwan'gye* (official land deeds). This chapter also hopes to lay the groundwork for an examination of the similarities and differences between the Great Han Empire's cadastral survey and the "modern" one conducted by the Japanese in the 1910s.

The Yangji Amun Cadastral Survey

INVESTIGATION OF LAND RIGHTS

After King Kojong proclaimed the establishment of the Great Han Empire in 1897, the government initiated a land survey in June 1898 to

---

3. The plunder of land under Japanese colonialism is discussed in: Yi Chaemu, "Iwayuru *Nikkan heigo = kyosen* mae ni okeru Nihon honteikoku shugi niyoru Chosen shokuminchika no kisoteki shoshihyo" (The so-called Japan-Korea annexation=occupation: the basic objectives for colonizing Korea by Japanese imperialism), *Shakaigaku kenkyu* 9-6 (Tokyo, 1958); Kim Yong-sop, "Kojong cho wangsil ŭi kyunjŏn sudo munje" (The problem of water supply for the *kyunjŏn* of the royal family during the reign of King Kojong), *Han'guk kŭndae nong'ŏpsa yŏn'gu*, vol. 2 (Seoul: Ilchogak, 1988); Ch'oe Wŏngyu, "1900 nyŏndae Ilche ŭi t'ojigwŏn ch'imt'al kwa kŭ kwalli kigu," (The seizure of land rights and the (land) management system of the Japanese empire in the 1900s), *Pudae sahak* 19 (1995).
4. Studies on the Great Han Empire's cadastral survey include: Kim Yong-sop, "Kwangmu nyŏn'gan ŭi yangjŏn chigye saŏp (Land deeds and land survey operations in the Kwangmu years)" *Han'guk kŭndae nong'ŏp sa yŏn'gu*, vol. 2 (Seoul: Ilchogak, 1988); Kim Hongsik et al., *Taehan Chegukgi ŭi t'oji chedo* (The land system of the Great Han Empire) (Seoul: Minŭmsa, 1990); Miyajima Hiroshi, *Chosen tochi chosa shigyoshi no kenkyu* (Research on the history of the Chosŏn cadastral survey operations) (Tokyo: Tokyo University, Toyo Bunka Kenkyujo, 1991); Han'guk yŏksa yŏn'guhoe t'oji taejangban, *Taehan Cheguk ŭi t'oji chosa saŏp* (The cadastral survey of the Great Han Empire) (Seoul: Minŭmsa, 1995).

facilitate political reform.[5] The goal of the survey was to determine the topography and economic resources of the entire country by investigating the shape, value, and ownership status of arable land, woodlands, rivers and lakes, coastal areas, homes, and roads. By recognizing the legality of ownership, the state wanted to establish a system of direct management over land. These measures were meant to solve the problems caused by the shortcomings of the traditional legal order—the frequent forgery of documents to sell land secretly and the black market sale of land to foreigners. Another objective was to facilitate the reform of the land tax system.[6]

In July 1898, the Great Han Empire established the Yangji amun (Bureau of Land Survey) as the government organ in charge of the cadastral survey. The main personnel of the Yangji amun consisted of three directors (*ch'ongjae*), three deputy directors (*puch'ongjae*), three archivists (*kisawŏn*), and six head clerks (*chuim sŏgi*), and it undertook three general tasks: cadastral surveys, investigation of land rights, and issuance of *kwan'gye*.[7] It targeted all sources of productive value beginning with paddy and dry fields.[8] Although the scope of its work originally included woodlands, rivers, and lakes, it never carried out surveys of those areas.[9]

In determining land rights, the Yangji amun distinguished between rights of ownership (*soyugwŏn*) and rights of cultivation (*kyŏngjakgwŏn*). In land registers (*yang'an*), the current owner was indicated by the term *siju*, and the current, actual cultivator of the land was listed as the *sijak*. The old land registers had only covered rights of ownership, and it recorded information according to the following system. First, land was divided into those

5. "T'oji ch'ŭgnyang e kwanhan sagŏn" (Incidents related to land surveying), *Kŏrae chon'an* (*Nongsanggongbu kŏraejon tang*) 3, June 22, 1899.

6. Black market purchases of land by foreigners was so severe a problem that it was mentioned frequently in contemporary documents such as the *Hwangsŏng sinmun*. It was one of the problems that the Great Han Empire urgently needed to address. For research on this subject, see footnote 3. Black market sales of residences were also a problem, particularly in Seoul. This issue has been examined in: Wang Hyŏnjong, "Taehan Chegukki Hansŏngbu ŭi t'oji kaok chosa wa woegug'in t'oji ch'imt'al taech'aek" (Survey of residences within Seoul prefecture during the Great Han Period and the Policies on Foreign Seizure of Land), *Sŏulhak yŏn'gu* 10 (1998).

7. Although the official land deeds were issued by the Chigye amun, it appeared that the Yangji amun conducted the cadastral survey. "Chigwŏn kaeryang," *Hwangsŏng sinmun*, Sept. 3, 1898; "Nongbu sinjŏng," *Hwangsŏng sinmun*, Aug. 10, 1898.

8. *Chŭngbo munhŏn pigo* (Notes to supplementary documents), chŏnbugo (Land Tax Report), vol. 2.

9. "Chigye amun chigwŏn kŭp ch'ŏmu kyujŏng (kaejŏngnyŏng)" (Personnel and operational regulations of the *Chigye amun* (revised ordinances)) and "Chigye kamni ŭnghaeng samok" (Management of land deeds and related items), article 31.

with owners (*yujujŏn*) and those without (*mujujŏn*). In the case of *yujujŏn*, the land register recorded the current owner (*kŭmju*) and the former owner at the time of the previous survey (*kuju*), indicating changes in ownership rights. The *kumju* were further distinguished into those who cultivated their own land (*kiju*) and those who did not (*chinju*).[10]

In the old *yang'an*, the "owner" (*chu*) was not necessarily the person who was legally granted ownership rights by the state but was just the current holder of the land at the time of the land survey. The owner listed in the *yang'an* was simply the one who had claimed rights of ownership before the time of the survey. If a document predating the *yang'an* established a prior right to the property, then the rights of the owner in this document prevailed over that of the owner listed in the land register.[11] The *yang'an* was only one among many types of legally valid documents. Another characteristic of the old *yang'an* was that they did not require owners to use their legal names as recorded in household registers (*hojŏk*).[12] There were many instances where owners used a nickname, names of their slaves, or various other names. In addition, land registers recorded the owner's occupation, thus indicating his social status.

For the cadastral survey, the Yangji amun made landowners erect a wooden marker on their land bearing their names, and the name had to be recorded in the presence of the landowner himself, the local magistrate (*myŏnjang*), or a land appraiser (*chisimin*) whose duty was to guide officials through the farmland. But the practice of using fake or alternate names continued as before, since there was no requirement to use legal names, just as in the past. Although requiring owners to use their legal names was necessary in order for the state to manage land rights effectively, the Yangji amun delayed

10. For more on *yang'an*, see: Kim Yong-sop, "Yangan ŭi yŏn'gu" (Studies on land registers), *Chosŏn hugi nong'ŏpsa yŏn'gu 1* (Studies on the agricultural history of the late Chosŏn period, vol. 1) (Seoul: Ilchogak, 1970); Pak Pyŏngho, "Soyugwŏn ŭi kwannyŏmsŏng kwa hyŏnsilsŏng" (The theories and reality of ownership rights), *Chŏnt'ongjŏk pŏp ch'egye wa pŏb ŭisik* (The traditional legal system and legal thought) (Seoul: Seoul National University Press, 1972); Yi Yŏnghun, *Chosŏn hugi sahoe kyŏngjesa* (The socioeconomic history of the late Chosŏn period) (Seoul: Han'gilsa, 1988); Miyajima Hiroshi, ibid.

11. *Sok taejŏn* (Legal code supplement), Hojŏn yangjŏn an (Household law, article on cadastral surveys), and *Sinbo sugyo chimnok* (Recent additions to the legal compendium), Chosŏn Ch'ongdokbu Chungch'uwŏn p'an (1943), pp. 303-04.

12. O Pyŏng'il, "Yangjŏn chorye" (Regulations for cadastral surveys), *Chŏn'an sik* (Chungch'uwŏn), March 10, 1899. See also *Sabŏp rŭmbo 2*, no. 42, June 15, 1904, "P'yŏngniwŏn kŏmsa Hong Chong'ŏk ŭi Pŏpbu Taesin Yi Chiyong e taehan pogoso" (Report on Minister of Law Yi Chiyong by Hong Chong'ŏk, Inspector of the P'yŏngniwŏn).

addressing this problem until the issuance of *kwan'gye*. However, unlike the old *yang'an*, the new *yang'an* gave the surnames for all the owners but did not list their social status—an indication of the changes going on in society at the time.

One new feature of the Yangji amun's *yang'an* was that, unlike the past, they listed the holders of the rights of cultivation, listing them as *sijak*. There were two main reasons for listing the *sijak*. First, it can be seen as a measure designed to unify the two ledgers of the existing bookkeeping system into a single new *yang'an*. While the central government kept *yang'an* to record land ownership, provincial administrators used *kitki* for the purposes of collecting the land tax. The existing *yang'an* were used by the central government to determine the total amount of taxes to be levied, but they only recorded ownership at the time of the land survey and did not include subsequent changes. The *kitki* were ledgers for tax collection created by the provincial government by revising and supplementing the information in the *yang'an*; they contained a list of the actual taxpayers. The dual bookkeeping system was a reflection of the two-tiered administrative structure of the Chosŏn state.

The adoption of the new *yang'an* also clearly had the purpose of enabling the Great Han Empire to gain direct control over land rights and to stabilize state finances. During the cadastral survey, the Yangji amun investigated the *siju* and *sijak*, the two holders of land rights, as well as the *kyŏlho* (households) and *kyŏlmyŏng* (individuals) who actually bore the tax burden. But when the land registers were finalized, they recorded only the *siju* and *sijak* and left out those *kyŏlho* and *kyŏlmyŏng* who were not *siju* or *sijak*.[13] This measure can be seen as an effort by the Great Han Empire to bestow different kinds of land rights to the *siju* and *sijak* and to make them responsible for the payment of taxes.[14]

Second, the recording of *sijak* in the *yang'an* demonstrated that the state recognized cultivation rights, along with ownership rights, as a full "real right" (*mulgwŏn*). The importance placed on cultivation rights can be demonstrated in the *yang'an* of Onyang in the northern part of South

13. For a detailed analysis of this process, see Yi Seyŏng and Ch'oe Yun'o, "Kwangmu yangan kwa siju ŭi silsang" (The status of *siju* in the Kwangmu land registers), *Taehan Chegukgi ŭi t'oji chedo*.

14. See Choi Won-kyu (Ch'oe Wŏn'gyu), "Taehan Chegukki yangjŏn kwa kwan'gye palgŭp saŏp" (Cadastral surveys and the issuing of land deeds during the Great Han Empire), *Taehan Chegukgi ŭi t'oji chedo*.

Ch'ungch'ŏng province, the region where the first cadastral surveys were conducted. Although most of the landlords in this area paid their own taxes, the survey also covered the *sijak*. If the payment of the land tax were the only concern, it would have been easier simply to record only the landowners since landlords had been traditionally responsible for paying taxes, and it would have been unnecessary to record the *sijak*. However, the insistence on listing the *sijak* in the *yang'an* seems to have come from a desire to guarantee the legal status of cultivation rights even for those who did not legally bear any tax burden. Just as the *siju* was the holder of ownership rights, the *sijak* likewise became the holder of cultivation rights.

Despite the fact that the 1894 Peasant War ended in a victory for the ruling landlord class, the government's attempt to legalize cultivation rights (i.e., tenancy rights) seems to have been a response to current political conditions. After the war, the tensions between the landlords and the peasantry could not be quelled without making concessions to the peasant class, and in fact, tensions at the time were actually escalating. As the encroachments of the foreign powers grew more serious, the ruling class considered a variety of solutions, one of which was the survey of *sijak*.[15] For them, the most urgent task was to overcome the national crisis while protecting the legal rights of existing landowners (i.e., the *siju*). To address these problems, domestic harmony was essential, and to achieve it, it was necessary to reduce the tension between the classes. The legalization of cultivation rights was an effort at compromise that sought the cooperation of the peasant class with whom the ruling landlord class was in conflict. In return for the legalization of these rights, the state demanded that the cultivators themselves assume responsibility for paying taxes.

LAND SURVEYING

To introduce modern methods of land surveying into Korea, the Yangji amun hired an American surveyor, Raymond Edward Leo Krumm, as head

---

15. The protection of cultivation rights also had the purpose of preventing the plunder of land by foreigners under the pretext of holding occupation rights. During the Kabo Reforms, it was declared that the "land, forests, and mines of the country could not be owned, bought or sold by the people of this bureau." *Pŏbgyuryu p'yŏn* (Volume on laws and regulations), Bureau of Cabinet Records, 1st year of Kŏnyang. In "Legal regulation no. 1: Regulations on mortgages and pawn shops," promulgated on Nov. 5, 1898, the state prohibited people from mortgaging any of their movable or immovable property to foreigners. *Choch'ik pŏbnyul* (Royal edicts and laws), Legal Regulation no. 1, November 5, 1898 (Seoul: Seoul National University Library, 1991), p.59.

engineer in 1898. He was put in charge of all surveying work, the training of apprentices, and the survey of the Seoul region.[16] However, these plans were suspended because of concerns about feasibility such as their high cost and the unproven effectiveness of Western land survey methods in Korea.[17] Instead, the Yangji amun used the traditional surveying methods but implemented qualitative improvements that took into account recent economic changes.[18]

The *kyŏlbu* system and the *chaho chibŏn* (character and numbering) system were two of the traditional methods used in surveying. The term *chaho chibŏn* referred to the series of characters and numbers assigned to plots of land according to the order they were surveyed. In the cadastral surveys, *chaho* were taken from the *Thousand Character Classic*, and each character was a unit that generally represented five *kyŏl* of land. For example, the character "*ch'ŏn*" (heaven) was the first character assigned to a plot, but if its area exceeded five *kyŏl*, then the next character "*chi*" (land) was used. According to this method, all of the characters would be used when a plot of land reached five thousand *kyŏl*. If the area exceeded five thousand *kyŏl*, characters were taken again from the beginning of the *Thousand Character Classic*, and each subsequent series of characters would have a number written above, beginning with "2," then "3," and so on. In addition, individual plots of land within a single *chaho* were also assigned numbers in the order they were surveyed.

In the *kyŏlbu* system, the breakdown of units was as follows: 1 *kyŏl* = 100 *pu*, 1 *pu* = 10 *sok*, and 1 *sok* = 10 *p'a*, and 10,000 *yangjŏn ch'ŏk* (the length of a *ch'ŏk* used in cadastral surveys) was taken to be equal to 1 *kyŏl*. Plots of land were classified into one of six grades based on crop output, and each grade had a range of 15 *pu*. In this system, plots of land of the same

---

16. "Ch'ikryŏng che 25 cho Yangji amun chigwŏn kŭp ch'ŏmu kyujŏng" (Imperial ordinance no. 25, Personnel and operational regulations of the Yangji amun), articles 9, 11, 16 published in *Ku Han'guk kwanbo* no. 996, July 8, 1898; "Tae Han'guk chŏngbu eshŏ Miguk yangji kisa kogyŏm ŭl pon'guk yangji kisa ro kobing hanŭn hapdong" (The joint appointment of American and Korean land surveyors by the government of Korea)" vol. 1, 2, 3, of *Woebu Yangji amun naegŏmun*. See also "Imperial ordinance no. 25, Personnel and operational regulations of the Yangji amun," article 17 (published in "*Yangji kaesi*" (Commencement of land surveying), *Hwangsŏng sinmun*, April 1, 1899).

17. For more on the historical context, see Kim Yong-sop, "Kwangmu nyŏn'gan ŭi yangjŏn chigye saŏp (Land deeds and land survey operations during the Kwangmu years)," *Han'guk kŭndae nong'ŏpsa yŏn'gu*, vol. 2, pp. 515–28.

18. The principles of the Yangji amun's cadastral survey were mainly taken from "Yangjŏn samok" (Items on the cadastral survey), *Chŭngbo munhŏn pigo*, chŏnbugo 2.

area could differ in terms of *kyŏlbu*, meaning that the amount of taxes levied would be different because of differences in the grade of land. The Great Han Empire's cadastral survey introduced three innovations in land surveying. First, in order to reduce the number of omitted agricultural fields within an administrative area, the Yangji amun had officials make maps called *ŏrin toch'aek* (literally "fish-scale map book"). They were a type of cadastral map in which the location of all plots of land was drawn in a pattern resembling fish scales.[19] It seems that the Yangji amun also intended these "fish-scale" maps to address the problem of grading land—the criteria for tax collection. While the old *yang'an* had a fairly high proportion of fallow or barren land (*chinjŏn*) and *mujujŏn*, there was hardly any in the Yangji amun's *yang'an*. The reason seems to have been rooted in the differences in the objectives of the government in conducting the surveys.

It appears that the Yangji amun wanted to facilitate the complete elimination of *mujujŏn* through the legalization of the ownership rights of all cultivated land. The purpose of adopting new surveying methods was to determine and record even the ownership of arable land that would have been categorized as either *chinjŏn* or *mujujŏn* in the past. The general trend at the time was toward the conversion of *mujujŏn* into *yujujŏn*, and in this period, the conversion occurred on a wide scale. The extent of this change was demonstrated in the government's measures toward *tŭngoejŏn*, lands such as *hwasok* (land destroyed by fire and cultivated irregularly because of its low fertility) or *sokhang* (abandoned land) that were considered so inferior that they were not included in earlier *yang'an* and not subject to tax collection. As part of its response to the problems facing Korea, the Yangji amun elevated the grade of existing *tŭngoejŏn*, enabling them to be recorded in *yang'an*.[20]

Second, the Yangji amun introduced the use of cadastral maps (*chŏndap tohyŏngdo*) that utilized a more diverse set of geometric shapes to depict paddy and dry fields. Existing field shapes had been restricted to a very simple set of five geometric figures that had been established in 1444 (Sejong

---

19. *Sago rŭmbo* 2, no. 42, June 15, 1904, "P'yŏngniwŏn kŏmsa Hong Chong'ŏk ŭi Pŏpbu Taesin Yi Chiyong e taehan pogoso" (Report on Minister of Law Yi Chiyong by Hong Chong'ŏk, Inspector of the P'yŏngniwŏn); Yi Ki, *Haehak yusŏ* (Writings of the late Yi Ki) vol. 2, Kŭpmu p'alcheŭi chŏnje 5, pp. 52-3.

20. It seems that *sokjŏn* did not appear in the Yangji amun's *yang'an* not because they were treated as *tŭngoejŏn* but rather because they were upgraded and registered as grade six land. Since *hwajŏn* (fire fields), the lowest grade of land, was not assigned a number according to the *chaho chibŏn* system and was listed separately, it is reasonable to conclude that all grades of land above *hwajŏn* were officially recorded in the *yang'an*.

26): square (called *panghyŏng*, #1), rectangle (*chikhyŏng*, #2), trapezoid (*chehyŏng*, #3), isosceles triangle (*kyuhyŏng*, #4), and right triangle (*kugohyŏng*, #5).[21] As the concept of private property spread, the number of shapes was increased in order to depict the actual appearance of fields more accurately. In the regulations for the 1820 land survey during Sunjo's reign (1800-1834), additional shapes were adopted such as the irregular quadrilateral (*sabuldŭnghyŏng*), eyebrow (*mihyŏng*), bull's horn (*ugakhyŏng*), circle (*wonhyŏng*), bow and arrow (*hosihyŏng*), pentagon, hexagon, snake (*sahyŏng*), and large drum (*taegop'ahyŏng*).[22] Following these developments, the Yangji amun used a total of ten geometric shapes, adding five new shapes in addition to the five original ones: circle (#6), oval (#7), bow and arrow (#8), triangle (#9), and eyebrow (#10). Plots of land that did not correspond to any of these shapes were simply classified as polygons (*pyŏnhyŏng*). In practice, however, *yang'an* used not only equilateral and nonequilateral shapes but also polygons of more than five sides and even figures that were a combination of shapes.[23]

Another important change to cadastral maps was the addition of new items to the *chŏndap tohyŏngdo*. The maps were supposed to be pictorial depictions of the shape of the farmland, and on each side of the drawing were written its length and *sap'yo* to make it easy to visualize the shape and location of the fields. *Sap'yo* was the traditional method of depicting the location of land in the Chosŏn period. It marked the boundaries of a parcel of land by indicating the topographical and geographical features bordering the land on the north, south, east, and west.

In pre-modern times, the boundaries of fields generally conformed to the natural features of the land because of technological limitations. It was very difficult to depict the actual shape of fields with just a few abstract geometric terms since the natural contours of the land were diverse and often irregular. In cases where the shape of a field changed greatly over time or where it was a combination of two or more geometric figures, depicting its true shape was

---

21. "Chŏnje sangjŏngso chunsu chohoek" (Prescriptions for the preparation and implementation of a land system), *Kyŏngsang chwado kyunjŏnsa yangjŏn sachŏlmok* (Articles of the cadastral survey submitted by the Director of Land Survey for Left Kyŏngsang Province).

22. *Yangjŏn samok*, (heading: "*Kaeryangnok* [Record of re-survey], January 1820").

23. *Chŭngbo munhŏn pigo*, chŏnbugo 2, vol. 2, p. 645. This section also appeared exactly the same in article 17 of "Chigye kamni ŭnghaeng samok" except for the omission of the trapezoid shape. Just before the beginning of the Yangji amun's cadastral survey, O Pyŏng'il discussed a variety of field shapes. See his "Yangjŏn sik" (Methods of cadastral surveys), *Chŏn'ansik* (Chungch'uwŏn).

impossible without an actual drawing of the field. To solve this problem, the use of *chŏndap tohyŏngdo* was necessary. Recording the original shape of the land at the time of the survey in ledgers was essential in resolving disputes over land and in facilitating the implementation of the state's land development policies. If the purpose of the Great Han Empire's cadastral survey had simply been to resolve problems in the land tax system, then there would have been no need to devote so much time and resources to making the cadastral maps. These problems could have been overcome using existing surveying methods.

In addition, the new *yang'an* even recorded the number of *chwa* and *yŏl*, which were the basic counting units for individual plots of land as well as the units indicating the minimal area necessary for cultivation for dry fields and paddy fields, respectively. The use of these units can be seen as part of an effort to create a detailed picture of the actual appearance of land. The cadastral survey introduced several new methods with the purpose of changing methods of land surveying from those based on crop output to those based on area.

Third, the Yangji amun also considered different methods of recording the dimensions of land in order to describe its actual shape more accurately. Its *yang'an* contained a new section for entering the actual area of a plot of land measured in *ch'ŏk*. In the past, fields were reduced to simplified shapes, and only their length and width in *yangjŏn ch'ŏk* were recorded. In contrast, the new *yang'an* included the length of all sides that appeared in the *chŏndap tohyŏngdo* and recorded the actual area. This method enabled a more accurate calculation of the shape and area of land than before.

In previous cadastral surveys, the grade of the land was determined after the absolute area was calculated in *yangjŏn ch'ŏk*, and then the quantity of *kyŏlbu*, which represented the amount of tax to be collected, was fixed based on the land grade. However, because the land grade was determined by crop production, it was not a fixed, permanent value but could change over time. In fact, the breakdown of the land tax system (*chŏnjŏng mullan*)—one of the *samjŏng*—stemmed from discrepancies between the land grade and the actual crop output. The Yangji amun did not deviate much from existing procedures in that it also calculated the absolute area based on the area in units of *yangjŏn ch'ŏk* and then set the quantity of *kyŏlbu* after determining the land grade.[24] The *kyŏlbu* system and the existing *yang'an*, which contained only

24. In Yong'in county, many problems, including protests by villagers, arose because the Yangji amun's cadastral survey overestimated the land grade, i.e., the number of *kyŏlbu*. The Chigye amun resurveyed the land and made new *yang'an* that resulted in a 30% reduction of the

simplified estimates of land area, were useful for levying land taxes according to crop output. However, they were inadequate for the state's efforts to legalize land ownership rights and set up a system of land management.[25] The state would be able to exert control over land rights only if both the shape and the area of the land were accurately measured and recorded in the official ledgers. The Yangji amun implemented improvements to existing methods of land surveying to resolve some of the problems with the *kyŏlbu* system— by using a cadastral map and more accurate geometric figures to depict the shape of fields and by recording the exact length of each side of a field.

Besides the changes in surveying methods, the method of calculating the land tax also differed from that of the past. Up to that time, the land grade was based only on grain yields, but the Yangji amun also took into consideration land prices and natural factors such as fertility, availability of water sources, and location. One major factor behind the change was a change in the determination of land value. Before, land prices had been based only on crop output, but other socioeconomic factors, such as access to transportation, became important determinants of land value in this period. It seems evident that the state was trying to implement the basic measures necessary to reform the land tax system in a way that would take these changes into account.[26] The government of the Great Han Empire adopted a system of measurement based on actual land areas, and it was also making preparations to abolish the existing system of levying land taxes on entire communities and to replace it with a system of levying taxes on individual plots of farmland.

kyŏlbu. Yi Yŏngho, "Taehan Cheguk sigi t'oji chedo wa nongminch'ŭng punhwa ŭi yangsang" (The land system of the Great Han Empire and the differentiation of the peasant class), *Han'guksa yŏn'gu*, no. 69 (1990).

25. *Chŭngbo munhŏn pigo*, chŏnbugo 2, vol. 2, p. 645. Beginning with Chŏng Yagyong, all intellectuals who advocated the establishment of a state system of land management mentioned the problems with the *kyŏlbu* system and called for the introduction of a measuring system based on units of area. Kim Yong-sop, "Tasan kwa P'ungsŏk yangjŏnnon" (Tasan's and P'ung-sok's views on cadastral surveys), and "Kwangmu yŏn'gan ŭi yangjŏn chigye saŏp" in *Han'guk kŭndae nong'ŏpsa yŏn'gu*, vol. 2.

26. Of course, in determining the land grade, the Yangji amun took into account the comments of *chisimin* and the grade recorded in the old *yang'an*, seeking a gradual transformation rather than a rapid change. "Chigye kamni ŭnghaeng samok," article 29.

The Chigye Amun's Cadastral Survey
and the Issuance of Land Deeds

CADASTRAL SURVEY

(1) Investigation of Ownership Rights

The Great Han Empire temporarily suspended the cadastral survey in 1901 because of severe weather conditions, and it was resumed in 1902 with the establishment of the Chigye amun (Bureau of Land Deeds), into which the Yangji amun was incorporated. The government announced the "Personnel and Operational Regulations of the Chigye amun" (*Chigye amun chigwŏn kŭp ch'ŏmu kyujŏng*) on October 22, 1902, and the Chigye amun was charged with carrying out the issuance of *kwan'gye* (land deeds) in Seoul and in every county of the country's thirteen provinces. Its duties were divided into two tasks. The first task was to conduct a cadastral survey to create *yang'an*, and the second was to issue new *kwan'gye* and to collect existing sales documents to remove them from circulation. These regulations were revised and reissued on November 11, 1902.[27]

The central office of the Chigye amun had a director and deputy director, and under them were the departments of Records, General Affairs, and Accounting as well as other offices. A Superintendent of Land Deeds (*chigye kamni*) was dispatched to each province to oversee the distribution of deeds, and the provincial governors (*kwanch'alsa*) were appointed as Directors of Land Deeds (*chigye kamdok*).[28] The organization was a centralized hierarchy with the Chigye amun at the top followed by the superintendent and then a government official working under a local committee. The head clerk in each county was also assigned to assist in this work.[29]

Because problems with land transactions such as forgery and black market sales were steadily growing worse, the Chigye amun made some changes to the survey methods of the Yangji amun in order to address these problems first. In a cadastral survey, it was usual for land measurements to be conducted in conjunction with the investigation of land rights. However, the Chigye amun decided that the issuing of *kwan'gye* was the most urgent task, and it undertook a cadastral survey that focused on the items necessary for this task.

---

27. "Chigye amun chigwŏn kŭp ch'ŏmu kyujŏng," articles 1, 17.
28. Ibid., article 12; ibid., (revised ordinances), article 6.
29. Ibid., articles 4, 6.

The Chigye amun's cadastral survey targeted all forms of immovable property. Forests, rivers, and lakes were surveyed only when necessary, but in those instances, their boundaries and measurements were recorded in detail.[30] In its investigation of residences, the survey sought information on the type of roof (thatched or tile), the number of rooms, and the name of the head of the household.[31] Whereas both residences and residential land appeared in the Yangji amun's yang'an, the Chigye amun listed only farmland in its yang'an, and residences were recorded in a separate ledger called kasaan (residential ledger). To facilitate control of rural areas, the Chosŏn state had organized households into groups of five called t'ong, and the kasaan recorded information about each of the households in a t'ong in sequence. Residential land was no longer classified together with farmland and now was treated under a separate category. This distinction was necessary because there were cases where the owner of a residence and the owner of the land it was built on were different.[32] Even under common law, ownership of residences and residential land were regarded as separate matters.[33]

The Chigye amun focused its efforts on issuing official land deeds based on the information provided in the yang'an. It restricted eligibility to the siju, and its cadastral survey also recorded information on only the siju and not the sijak. Nonetheless, the Great Han Empire's policy was not the complete abolition of cultivation rights. It could not afford to ignore the policies of the Yangji amun nor the calls for reform of the land system whose

---

30. Ibid., articles 27, 31. Chŭngbo munhŏn pigo, chŏnbugo 2, p. 645, article 5.

31. Kwan'gye were not issued in foreign settlements and in Seoul, which had already been using their own deeds for residences, land, and inherited land. "Chigye amun chigwŏn kŭp ch'ŏmu kyujŏng (kaejŏngnyŏng)," (revised ordinances), articles 1, 10.

32. When residences were recorded in a separate ledger, the method of recording residential land also changed. In the Yangji amun's yang'an, residential sites were all noted under the column for the siju, but in the Chigye amun's land survey, there were differences according to region. For example, in P'yŏnghae County in Kangwŏn province and in the Suwŏn and Yongin regions of Kyŏnggi province, residential sites were not indicated in the yang'an, but in Kansŏng county, they were recorded in the section on field shapes.

33. Residential deeds (kagwŏn) were called kagye, and they were issued at the Office of the Superintendent (Kamnisŏ) in places such as the open ports and market areas. These deeds were first issued in Seoul in 1893, and after the form underwent a revision in December 1905, the Ministry of the Interior passed new regulations in May 1906. The first form used for residential deeds can be found in Chosŏn Ch'ongdokbu Chungch'uwŏn, Chosŏn chŏnje ko (A study of the land system of Chosŏn) (Kyŏngsŏng, 1940), p. 406.

goal was the legalization of cultivation rights. The Great Han Empire later passed a separate law to implement its policy on the *sijak*.[34]

The Yangji amun and the Chigye amun used different methods of determining the ownership and the grade of land. First, the kinds of land that appeared in their *yang'an* were different. The *yang'an* of the Chigye amun had a greater amount of *chinjŏn* (fallow land) compared to those of the Yangji amun, and among the *chinjŏn*, a significant amount had no owner (*muju chinjŏn*). The difference seems to have resulted from the fact that the two cadastral surveys used different standards in determining the type of land and the land grade. The Yangji amun's policy on *chinjŏn* was to elevate their land grades; as a result, land taxes became so burdensome that popular uprisings even erupted in protest.[35]

Aware of these problems, the Chigye amun took a different approach to *sokjŏn*, farmland which alternated between years of cultivation and fallow years, with the exception of *hwasokjŏn*, a type of *hwajŏn* that was even more infertile. It classified *sokjŏn* as grade six land but recorded it in *yang'an* as a type of *chinjŏn*. The Chigye amun classified *chinjŏn* with a clear owner as *yuju chinjŏn*, but in contrast with the Yangji amun's cadastral survey, there was also a significant amount of *muju chinjŏn*. Although the quantity of *muju chinjŏn* partly reflected actual conditions, the majority of that land was either *ŭnnugyŏl* (hidden lands),[36] which was used for tax evasion, or fields that had been abandoned by their owners.[37] In the *yang'an*, *ŭnnugyŏl* was initially recorded as *mujujŏn* and abandoned land as state land, but there

34. For more details, see Choi Won-kyu, "Taehan Cheguk kwa Ilche ŭi t'ojigwŏnbŏp chejŏng kwajŏng kwa kŭ chihyang" (The passage and objectives of the land rights law of the Great Han Empire and Japan), *Tongbang hakji*, no. 94 (1996).

35. See Yi Yŏngho, "Taehan Cheguk sigi t'oji chedo wa nongminch'ŭng punhwa ŭi yangsang."

36. The category of *ŭnnugyŏl* included both cases where cultivated land was exempted from taxes because of natural disaster and cases in which newly reclaimed land was not registered in any ledger and did not submit any taxes to the central government. Normally, the taxes collected on this land were used as a source of revenue for the provincial governor or the local government office, but there were cases where the land was never investigated, and taxes were not paid.

37. The difference between pre-modern and modern conceptions of land ownership was that in the pre-modern period, the status of cultivation was an important criterion for determining ownership. Thus, it is doubtful that the pre-modern period had a fully developed conception of exclusive property rights. For instance, *chinjŏn* that resulted when peasants abandoned the land was considered to be ownerless (*muju*), and laws regarded people who reclaimed the land as the landowners. The notion of ownership as an exclusive right to land became established and was protected by law after the beginning of the modern period.

probably were cases where they were restored to their original designations after a final inspection when the *kwan'gye* were issued.

Through its investigation of ownership rights, the Chigye amun collected information on private, state-owned, and public lands. It was illegal for government offices to sell public land under their jurisdiction such as the land belonging to royal tombs, palace parks, cemeteries, palaces, schools, stations, military bases, and temples. The Chigye amun investigated whether any public land had come under private ownership and ordered such land to be returned to the state.[38] The methods used to investigate state and public land were different from those used for privately owned land. In these cases, the Chigye amun recorded information not only on the government office that was the *siju* but also on the *sijak*. According to regulations established by the Kabo Reforms (1894-1896), the Chigye amun assigned land grades to all public land, according to the same criteria as those used for private land, and collected information on its *sijak* who directly bore the tax burden.[39]

However, the *siju* listed in the Chigye amun's *yang'an* were, in general, just the current landholders at the time of the cadastral survey; they had not been subject to any inspection that certified them as the legal owners. Thus, it was possible that the listed *siju* was not the actual landowner. The Chigye amun attempted to solve this problem through its procedures for distributing *kwan'gye* as will be explained below.

(2) Land Surveying

The Chigye amun felt that its main task was the rapid distribution of *kwan'gye*, and its plan for land surveying utilized, where useful, the methods and results of previous cadastral surveys. It made use of existing land registers and ledgers such as the *chillak sŏngch'aek*, which recorded information on *chinjŏn* and farmland that had become uncultivable because it was covered by something such as sand.[40] Its cadastral survey also took into account the problems that arose during the Yangji amun's land surveys. The Chigye amun adopted many of the Yangji amun's methods such as its system of

---

38. "Chigye amun chigwŏn kŭp ch'ŏmu kyujŏng," articles 11, 24.

39. Ibid., article 25. When the Chigye amun conducted a survey of tenants (*chag'in*) on state and public land, it could have listed both the tenant-cultivator and the *chungdapju*, a kind of agent who rented land from landowners and leased it to others. However, the tenant recorded on the Chigye amun's *yang'an* had the responsibility of paying the land tax whether he was the actual tenant-cultivator or a *chungdapju*. Of course, for state or public land, there were occasional cases where no cultivator was recorded.

40. The expression *kujin muju* found in the *Kangwŏndo Kansŏnggun yang'an* (Land register of Kansŏng County, Kangwŏn province) was a term for such land.

determining land types, method of entering the *kyŏlbu*, the use of *chŏndap tohyŏngdo*, and the *chaho chibŏn* system. However, it modified some of these methods in order to facilitate the issuing of *kwan'gye*. As a result, the following differences existed between the *yang'an* of the Yangji amun and the Chigye amun.

First, the *yang'an* of the Chigye amun recorded only the shape of the rice fields just like earlier *yang'an* but unlike those of the Yangji amun, which used the *chŏndap tohyŏngdo*. Diagrams of the fields were taken from the set of ten geometric shapes, and in cases where none of them were suitable, the exact shape of the field was supposed to be drawn.[41] However, in the Chigye amun's *yang'an*, most of the fields were depicted as rectangles, and the use of other shapes was rare. It also simplified the method of measuring the boundaries of fields by only recording their approximate length and width. In its *yang'an*, the discrepancy between the actual shape of the land and its depiction was greater than that for the Yangji amun's *yang'an*.[42] Though there must have been numerous inaccuracies in the measurements, these modifications allowed the work to proceed quickly.

Second, there were differences in the *chaho chibŏn* system—i.e., in the way characters and numbers were assigned to plots of land. The Yangji amun had emphasized accurate depiction of the shape of fields, dividing land into individual plots according to their shape and assigning each a *chaho chibŏn*. Land within a *chibŏn* was indicated by the term *naebun*, and the shape of each section of the land was drawn in the cadastral map. By contrast, while the Chigye amun did try to take the natural shape of the land into consideration, it combined, whenever possible, plots belonging to the same owner and assigned them a single *chibŏn*. Thus, it could be said that the surveying methods of the Yangji amun focused on the land while those of the Chigye amun emphasized the landowner.

Third, the Chigye amun expanded the use of a measuring system based on absolute area in order to solve some of the problems involved in land surveying. Until this period, *yangjŏn ch'ŏk* had been used to record the absolute area of land. However, it was unsuitable for use in land deeds used among the people because it was a unit used only by the government and was not in common use in the countryside. In documents such as harvest journals, the units of area actually used by the people were *yŏl* and *chwa*; i.e.,

41. "Chigye amun chigwŏn kŭp ch'ŏmu kyujŏng," article 17.

42. *Chinch'ŏn kun sasongnok* (Records of the settlement of disputes in Chinch'ŏn County), book 8, August 1, 1903 in *Chosŏn chŏnje ko*, p. 441.

baemi (the pure vernacular term for a single paddy field). The Chigye amun adopted these units, as well as the *turak-ilgyŏng* system, for use in its *yang'an*.

In rural areas, a variety of units had been in customary usage such as those based on the amount of seed used in planting, sections of farmland, and the amount of labor inputs.[43] The government had used the *kyŏlbu* system as its official units of measurement from the Unified Silla period to the end of the Chosŏn period. The *turak* had always been a secondary unit of measurement, and the first record of its use was in *Kŭmyang chamnok* written by Kang Hŭimaeng in 1483. The *turak*, which was based on the amount of seed used, was a traditional unit used to measure the area of paddy and dry fields, and it was the Chinese character expression for the vernacular term *majigi*. The term *majigi* was derived from the word *maljitgi* with the final consonants removed from the first two characters. One *turak* represented the size of land that could be sown using one gourd of seed. The term *turak* was a combination of two characters: *tu*, which meant "to count," and *rak*, from the term *nakjong* which meant "dropping seeds." The use of *turak* had emerged with the development of rice transplantation, but the government did not adopt it as an official unit of measurement until the mid-nineteenth century.[44]

43. Examples of the usage of these units can be found in landowners' *ch'usugi* (harvest journals). Kim Yong-sop, "Kanghwa Kim ssi ka ŭi chiju kyŏng'yŏng kwa kŭ sŏngsoe" (The successes and failures of the agricultural management of the Kanghwa Kim family), *Han'guk kŭnhyŏndae nong'ŏpsa yŏn'gu*. See footnotes 2 and 87.

Units of labor input were based on the amount of labor needed to plow for a day and included terms such as *hanch'am kari* and *hannajŏl kari* (plowing for half a day). These units were used to record the area of dry fields in regions of Kyŏnggi, Kangwŏn, and North Ch'ungch'ŏng provinces, where the area of dry fields was greater than that of paddy fields. The unit based on sections of farmland was called *paemi*, a pure vernacular term that was written as *yami* in Chinese characters according to *idu* transcription system. Units of *paemi* were generally used when calculating the area upland paddy fields that were organized in a pattern resembling a ladder. In recent decades, the use of these units has declined as the government undertook a reorganization of farmland in the country.

44. For paddy fields, the output and the amount of seeds used in sowing remained relatively constant; however, for dry fields, the size of the land and the number of seeds in a *hanmal* (18.039 liter) differed greatly according to the type of grain. However, in actuality, the term *majigi* represented a specific area and did not differ according to the type of grain. The area of a *turak* differed according to the region of the country, but in 75% of the country, 200 *p'yŏng* of paddy field was taken to be one *majigi* (1 *p'yŏng* = 3.3058 square meters). For dry fields, there were fifteen variations around the country for the number of *p'yŏng* per *turak*. In 43% of the country, 200 *p'yŏng* was equal to one *majigi*, and in 24% of the country, the ratio was 100 *p'yŏng* per *majigi*.

The introduction of the units *yŏl* and *chwa* had already begun during the Yangji amun's cadastral survey. By also adding the *turak-ilgyŏng* system, the Chigye amun achieved a partial solution of problems arising in *yang'an* without a cadastral map.[45] Although there were regional variations in the areas designated by the terms *turak* and *ilgyŏng*,[46] the Chigye amun created a new *turak-ilgyŏng* system in which the dimensions used in Kyŏnggi province were set as the standard units. In this system, 1 *turak* = 500 *ch'ŏk* and 1 *kakgyŏng* = 125 *ch'ŏk*, while 1 *ilgyŏng* = 4 *sigyŏng* = 32 *kakgyŏng* = 4000 *ch'ŏk*. The area of individual plots of land in units of *yangjŏn ch'ŏk* was recorded in the *yang'an* after being converted into *turak* and *ilgyŏng* units.[47] Most of the land was recorded without distinguishing between cultivated and fallow land, except for cases where there was no recipient for the *kwan'gye*, such as *chinjŏn* without an owner.

The Chigye amun developed a measurement system based on units of absolute area to be used in conjunction with the *kyŏlbu* system because of the need to know the absolute area of land in order to determine ownership rights. The *kyŏlbu* system continued to be used as the basic units of the land tax system in which taxes were assessed on communities rather than individuals, but its importance was greatly diminished. Consideration of land price, as well as crop productivity, in determining land grade was a preparatory step for the conversion to a land tax system based on land value.[48]

The "Regulations for Measurement" (*Toryanghyŏng kyuch'ik*), enacted in July 1903, clearly demonstrate the movement towards the adoption of a

In the nineteenth century, there were slight differences in usage according to the *yang'an* since regions would follow local practices in the definition of *turak*. The standardization of *turak* as a unit of absolute area was accomplished during the cadastral survey of the Kwangmu years, which is the topic of this chapter, but the Great Han Empire adopted the metric system as its official units of measurement. Under Japanese rule, units of measurement were changed again with the Ch'ŏkgwanbŏp (Law for Standardizing Measurements), and in 1960, the government reinstated the metric system as its official units of measurement. Kim T'aeyŏng, "Kyŏlbubŏp," *Han'guk minjok munhwa taebaekhwa sajŏn*, vol. 1, pp. 816-17; Kim Yŏngjin, "Majigi," ibid., vol. 7, pp. 583-84.

45. See *Ch'ungch'ŏng namdo Asan kun yang'an ibuk sambuk nammyŏn hyŏnnae myŏn* (Land register of South Ch'ungch'ŏng province, Asan county).

46. Ministry of Agriculture and Commerce of Japan, *Han'guk nongsan chosa pogo* (Report on the survey of Korean agricultural production), (Kyŏnggi Ch'unch'ŏng Kangwŏn p'yŏn), 1906, pp. 294-98.

47. The *turak* system did not simply follow existing local practices but was a system of absolute area that was adopted from customary practices. For a detailed discussion, see Miyajima Hiroshi, *Chosen tochi chosa chigyoshi no kenkyu*, pp. 264-74.

48. "Chigye amun chigwŏn kŭp ch'ŏmu kyujŏng," article 18.

system based on absolute area. According to these regulations, 1 *yangjŏn ch'ŏk* was equal to 5 *chuch'ŏk*, with 1 *chuch'ŏk* = 20 centimeters and 1 *yangjŏn ch'ŏk* = 1 meter.[49] The units of area were defined as follows: 1 *p'a* = 1 square meter, 1 *pu* = 1 acre, 1 *kyŏl* = 1 hectare. The land grading system also underwent changes in this period. The area of "grade one" land was converted into meters and adopted as the standard unit of area. All other land grades were defined in proportion to this standard. In the process, *kyŏl* and *pu* were converted into units of area. In these regulations, there was no mention of land grades, and they claimed that the new regulations were established by combining aspects of both the old and new systems in order to facilitate commerce and trade and to promote the public interest.[50] It seems that *kyŏl* and *pu* became units of absolute area and now only referred to the amount of taxes to be paid per unit area.[51]

In sum, the surveying methods of the Chigye amun fell short in some aspects of being a truly modern cadastral survey. They were a reflection of the situation of the Great Han Empire, which was trying to establish a state system of land management by investigating ownership rights and issuing land deeds.[52]

THE ISSUANCE OF *KWAN'GYE*

In earlier times, land deeds had been called by a variety of names such as *kyegwŏn, chigwŏn, konggwŏn,* and *sagwŏn,* and people from all social

---

49. From 1444 (26th year of Sejong's reign), the *yangjŏn ch'ŏk* was set to be equal to 4.775 *chuch'ŏk,* but from Injo's reign (1623-1649), it was defined as the *yangjŏn ch'ŏk* used in the 1634 cadastral survey (*Kapmu yangjŏn*), which was equal to 4.9996 *ch'ŏk.* The length of a *chuch'ŏk* continually changed: from 1444, it was 20.81 cm; from Injo's reign, 21.79 cm; in the Hanmal period, 20.48 cm; and in 1903, 20 cm. Pak Hŭngsu, "Yijo ch'ŏkdo e kwanhan yŏn'gu (Research on the *ch'ŏk* system of the Yi Dynasty," *Taedong munhwa yŏn'gu,* no. 4 (1967) and "Yijo ch'ŏkdo kijun ŭrosŏ ŭi hyŏnsup'yo ŭi kach'i" (The value of *hyŏnsu* markers as standards for the *ch'ŏk* system of the Yi Dynasty), *Kwahak kisul yŏn'gu,* no. 3 (1975). See also Kim Chaejin, "Chŏn'gyŏlje yŏn'gu" (Research on the Land Measurement System), *Kyŏngbukdae nonmunjip,* nos. 2+3; *Chosŏn chŏnje ko,* pp. 276-79.

50. *Ku Han'guk kwanbo* (*hooe*), March 29, 1902, p. 976.

51. The Regulations of Measurement (*Toryanghyŏng kyuch'ik*) were to be implemented depending on the situation in each province. The government decided to enforce the "Law of Measurement" (*Toryanghyŏngbŏp*), which was promulgated on March 21, 1905, in all regions of the country. *Ku Han'guk kwanbo,* Appendix, March 29, 1905, vol. 14, pp. 307-18.

52. The government's views were similar to those of Japanese officials such as Ito Hirobumi who attempted to implement various land laws during the last years of the Great Han Empire period without undertaking a land survey. Their plan was to legalize land ownership rights first and to handle problems of surveying as they arose. Ch'oe Wŏngyu, "Taehan Cheguk kwa Ilche ŭi t'ojigwŏnbŏp chejŏng kwajŏng kwa kŭ chihyang."

classes had often called for the establishment of an official state-run system to manage them. As problems over land rights increasingly erupted at the end of the nineteenth century, the government could no longer delay implementing a land deed system. Forged documents were circulating in increasing quantities, and the corrupt practice of secretly selling others' land became so severe that losses were tremendous for both the state and the people. Finally, in the latter half of 1900, the Privy Council (*Chungch'uwŏn*) began official discussions on the necessity of issuing *kwan'gye* to solve these problems.[53] The Chosŏn state had experience in establishing such systems before such as the existing *ib'an* (estate registration) system, the *chigye* (land deed) system for foreign settlements, and the *kagye* (residential deed) system for Seoul prefecture.[54] Based on this experience and prevailing public sentiment, the government adopted a policy of issuing *kwan'gye* and established the Chigye amun to carry it out.[55]

After deciding the order of the provinces in which it would issue *kwan'gye*, the Chigye amun began its operations by announcing through government bulletins and other public channels that all eligible people had to take their *kugwŏn* to the local county office and receive a *kwan'gye* within a specified period of time.[56] The issuing of *kwan'gye* began in Kangwŏn province on March 11, 1902.[57] For administrative purposes, the province was divided into east and west regions (called *Yŏngdong* and *Yŏngsŏ*, respectively), and work commenced in Uljin in the east and in Ch'unch'ŏn in the west. Local officials began issuing *kwan'gye* in Chiksan county in South Ch'ungch'ŏng province from November 12, 1903, just as the cadastral survey in that region was completed.

---

53. "Chungch'uwŏn Ŭigwan Kim Chunghwan sangso" (Memorial by Privy Councillor Kim Chunghwan), *Ilsŏngnok*, Sept. 1,1901 (Oct. 12 by the solar calendar).

54. On the land deed system in foreign settlements, see Wada Ichiro, *Chosen tochi chizei seido yobi chosa hokokusho* (Report on the survey of the Chosŏn land tax system) (Keijo: Chosen sotokufu, 1920). On the issuing of residential deeds in Seoul, see Asao Takekame, *Chosen dense ko*, (A Study of the Chosŏn Land Tax System) (1940), and Wang Hyŏnjong, "Taehan Chegukki Hansŏngbu ŭi t'oji kaok chosa wa woegug'in t'oji ch'imt'al taech'aek."

55. "Hyŏk Yangji amun inch'ul chigye pal'gŭp ujont'o siju sŏnsigikun," (The first experimental issuing of land deeds in a county by the reformed Chigye amun for land acquired as royal stipends) in *Chŏngbo munhŏn pigo*, chŏnbugo 2, vol. 2, p. 645.

56. *Ku Han'guk kwanbo*, no. 2288, August 26,1902, vol. 11, p. 784. The *kugwŏn* was an older form of ownership document that was widely used at the time.

57. "Chigye amun ch'ongjae sŏri puch'ongjae Yi Yong'ik kŭnju Kwangmu 6 nyŏn 3 wŏl 11 il," Ibid., no. 2147, March 14, 1902, vol. 11, p. 228.

(1) Land Deeds and Their Significance

Kwan'gye were to be issued for all forms of real estate.[58] The Chigye amun targeted not only the private property of all the country's citizens but even property belonging to state organs and government offices including the royal family's.[59] Since Japan revised its emigration laws and increasing numbers of Japanese came to Korea and bought land on the black market, the government of the Great Han Empire also wanted to address this problem through the implementation of its land deed policy.[60]

International treaties set limits on the amount of property that foreigners could own, and domestic law was revised accordingly. During the Kabo Reforms, regulations prohibiting the possession or occupation of land by foreigners were expressly stipulated by law, and in 1900, regulations were further toughened to allow black market transactions to be punished as treason.[61] Nevertheless, Japanese continued to purchase land on the black market by taking advantage of customary transaction practices. As shown in Table 1 (p. 123), which lists statistics compiled by the government in 1904, black market activity was significant in North Chŏlla province, and the Japanese later used the land that they secretly bought to become large landowners.[62] To overcome this crisis, the Great Han Empire searched for suitable institutional mechanisms at the state level.

Even though *yang'an* were the principal source of information for issuing *kwan'gye*, they were not always issued to the person listed in the *yang'an*. They were issued only after completing a procedure to confirm the owner of the land. Since *yang'an* were made through on-site inspections, a separate procedure was needed to determine ownership conclusively because of the

---

58. "Chigye amun chigwŏn kŭp ch'ŏmu kyujŏng" and "Chigye amun chigwŏn kŭp ch'ŏmu kyujŏng (kaejŏngnyŏng)" (revised ordinances), article 1. "Chŏndap sallim ch'ŏnt'aek kasa kwan'gye sech'ik" (Detailed regulations for *kwan'gye* of Agricultural Lands, Forests, Rivers, Lakes, and Residences), article 1.

59. "Chigye kamni ŭnghaeng samok," article 11; "Chigye amun chigwŏn kŭp ch'ŏmu kyujŏng (kaejŏngnyŏng)" (revised ordinances), article 10. Land deeds were not issued for property owned by foreigners.

60. Ch'oe Wŏngyu, "1900 nyŏndae Ilche ŭi t'ojigwŏn ch'imt'al kwa kŭ kwalli kigu."

61. "Ŭiroe woeguk ch'ison kukch'eja ch'ŏdannye kaejŏng kŏn" (Revised measure on legally punishing people whose dependency on foreign countries harms Korea) in *Ku Han'guk kwanbo*, no. 1562, May 1, 1900, vol. 8, p. 430.

62. See footnote 3.

possibility that the *siju* in a *yang'an* was recorded erroneously or listed under a false name.[63]

The method of confirming ownership differed according to the documents available. First, in the most common case, the *siju* listed in the land register also was in possession of the *kugwŏn*, the ownership document in general usage at the time. There was little problem in obtaining legal recognition of ownership since the name on the *yang'an* was the same as the one on the *kugwŏn*.[64] The Chigye amun simply issued the *kwan'gye* after confirming the names on the two documents.[65]

Second, there were cases where the two documents could not conclusively determine ownership because the owner was not listed as the *siju* in the *yang'an*[66] or because the owner did not possess the *kugwŏn*. *Kugwŏn* did not exist for ownerless (*muju*) land or reclaimed land that would not have been the object of a transaction. There were also instances where the *kugwŏn* no longer existed because it was lost or destroyed in a fire or flood.

Third, two sets of documents sometimes existed for the same piece of land. It was necessary to employ a different method of determining ownership when two or more people were technically eligible to receive the land deed because of a forged document or because one person had sharecropping rights (*tojigwŏn*) that could be used to claim ownership.[67] In the second and third cases, the Chigye amun would issue *kwan'gye* when the actual owner of the land in question received official documents from the local county office that verified his or her ownership.[68] Official documents that could be

---

63. The cadastral survey conducted by the Japanese in Korea in the 1910s differed from the Chigye amun's issuing of *kwan'gye*. The Japanese made *t'oji chosabu* after determining ownership of land based on on-site inspections and notification by landowners. When the holder of property rights was determined after the results of the cadastral survey were made official, the authorities then made *t'oji taejang* based on this information. In addition, the Japanese implemented a property registration system to regulate property rights by having owners apply to register their property and have it recorded in *t'ŭnggibu*. See Government-General of Chosŏn, "Pudongsan tŭnggi chedo" (Real estate registration system), *Chosŏn hwibo* (Sept. 1916); Sin Yongha, *Chosŏn t'oji chosa saŏp yŏn'gu* (Research on the Chosŏn cadastral survey) (Seoul: Chisik san'ŏpsa, 1982).

64. On the legal authority of *maemae mungi*, see Pak Pyŏngho, *Han'guk pŏpjesa ko* (A study of Korean legal history) (Seoul: Pŏmmunsa, 1974).

65. "Chigye kamni ŭnghaeng samok," article 8.

66. Judging from extant *yang'an*, they did not include forests, general cultivated land, or other low-fertility land that was occasionally left fallow. In addition, there was *ŭnnugyŏl* that was omitted from the *yang'an*, and there was probably land that had not yet been surveyed.

67. Ibid., article 8.

68. Ibid., article 8.

used included documents filed at a government office, *ib'an* documents, *kitki*, and *haengsimch'aek* (another name for the old *yang'an* that were made at the *kun* and *hyŏn* levels before the Yangji amun's cadastral survey).[69]

Through the issuing of *kwan'gye*, the Chigye amun also carried out a policy of collecting all *kugwŏn* and removing them from circulation.[70] This policy had two purposes. The first was to eliminate the possibility of confusion caused by the existence of two separate documents for land ownership, the *kwan'gye* and the *kugwŏn*. The difference between the two documents was that *kwan'gye* were issued by the government and *kugwŏn* were used by the common people. However, since both had equivalent legal authority as sales contracts and evidence of ownership, it was necessary to revoke the legal status of *kugwŏn* in the process of issuing *kwan'gye*.[71] The second purpose was to abolish existing ownership rights and bestow upon owners a new kind of legal claim to their land. Unlike *yang'an*, *kwan'gye* had the effect of "original acquisition" (*wŏnsi ch'widŭk*), treating the land as if had never been owned before.[72]

The Chigye amun needed to resolve some procedural issues in order to invest *kwan'gye* with legal authority and to expedite the completion of its work. First, only one name could appear as the owner on the *kwan'gye*, and it had to be the legal name. Even if the person who received the *kwan'gye* was the owner himself, problems such as fraud could still arise if the person used a fake or alternative name on the deed. Thus, a modernizing state had to adopt a modern household registration law in order to create the institutions necessary for a system of legalized names. For these reasons, the Chigye amun prohibited people from changing or assuming names when applying for a *kwan'gye*. If a violation occurred, it stipulated that the violator would be punished and his land confiscated.[73]

---

69. Once a *yang'an* was made, it was impossible to record any changes to the land rights. Therefore, when land taxes were assessed, they often did not accurately reflect actual conditions. For this reason, authorities kept a separate ledger, called a "*kitki*," to enable adjustments to the land tax. These ledgers contained information on all plots of land that were owned or rented by actual taxpayers. See Pŏbjŏn chosabu, *T'oji chosa ch'amgosŏ* (Reference book on cadastral surveys), (1909).

70. See the related sections in "Chigye kamni ŭnghaeng samok," and "Chŏndap sallim ch'ŏnt'aek kasa kwan'gye sech'ik."

71. "Chigye kamni ŭnghaeng samok," article 8.

72. "Chigye amun chigwŏn kŭp ch'ŏmu kyujŏng (kaejŏngnyŏng)," article 13; "Chigye kamni ŭnghaeng samok," article 8; "Chŏndap sallim ch'ŏnt'aek kasa kwan'gye sech'ik," article 1.

73. "Chigye kamni ŭnghaeng samok," article 9 and "Chŏndap sallim ch'ŏnt'aek kasa kwan'gye sech'ik," article 4. The Great Han Empire implemented a modern household registration system.

Second, the Chigye amun made the landowner himself responsible for applying for a *kwan'gye*. If it had been optional and left to the landowner's choice, it would have been impossible to achieve the goal of establishing a property management system at the state level because of difficulties in conducting inspections to confirm legal ownership. If the Chigye amun discovered that a landowner did not apply for a *kwan'gye*, the state would seize the property in question.[74] The state seems to have been aware of the shortcomings of *yang'an* and adopted these regulations because it wanted to complete the cadastral survey through the issuing of *kwan'gye*.

Another objective behind the issuance of *kwan'gye* was to determine the ownership of not just property listed in *yang'an* but all property within the country's borders. The state's intentions were evident in its policy of confiscating land belonging to owners who did not apply for a *kwan'gye* and in its efforts to track down state land that had been privatized by exploiting loopholes in existing laws.[75] In the process, the state also worked to classify all property into either private land or state-owned public land.

In the end, the Chigye amun imposed exclusive property rights on all land under the principle of one owner per parcel of land, and it consolidated the land of the country into a government-run system that regulated property rights. These rights could not be violated for any reason; they bestowed the status of an "original acquisition" on all land and were no different from the definition of property rights used in Japan's cadastral survey in the 1910s.[76] In actuality, the Chigye amun simply investigated and legalized existing property rights, but since it legally established "new" property rights that constituted a "break" with the old, its work also intended to eliminate any disputes over ownership that had persisted up to this time.

(2) The Form and Function of the Kwan'gye

While one function of *kwan'gye* was to certify ownership and to serve as proof of sale or purchase, another function that they had to fulfill was to

---

The household registration law was designed to create a system of legal names, and its next goal was to establish congruence between the names in the household registers and those in the *yang'an*.

74. "Chŏndap sallim ch'ŏnt'aek kasa kwan'gye sech'ik," article 3; "Chigye kamni ŭnghaeng samok," article 8. In the initial regulations, it was stipulated that the government would seize only 4/10ths of the property; however, it adopted tougher measures for the *kwan'gye*, reflecting the sense of crisis at the time. Requiring landowners to obtain a *kwan'gye* suggests that the issuing of land deeds was meant to be a process of determining ownership.

75. "Chigye kamni ŭnghaeng samok," article 24.

76. For more on this topic, see Hayakawa Yasuji, *Chosen hudosan toki no enkaku* (The history of real estate registration in Chosŏn) (1921).

keep track of changes in ownership that occurred after they had been issued. Land deeds had to record current and past ownership so that a third party could always ascertain that information. The government of the Great Han Empire attempted to address this need through the introduction of the *kwan'gye* system.

After the establishment of the Chigye amun, the *kwan'gye* document went through two stages of development before it was finalized. At first, the Chigye amun created two forms: the "Great Han Agricultural Land Deed" (*Taehan chŏnt'o chigye*) as proof of ownership and the "Great Han Agricultural Farmland Transaction Certificate" (*Taehan chŏnt'o maemae chŭng-gwŏn*) for use in transactions.[77] However, several problems arose. Foreign ownership was not explicitly prohibited, and *kwan'gye* were not issued for residences, forests, rivers, and lakes—only for farmland. Despite the new registration system, it was still impossible to get information on the past owners of a parcel of land.[78] Because of these problems, the government revised the "Personnel and Operational Regulations of the Chigye amun" in November 1902 and combined the two documents into a revised one called the "Official Land Deed for Farmland of the Great Han Empire" (*Taehan Cheguk chŏndap kwan'gye*).

The government issued the revised *kwan'gye* not only for agricultural land but also for all kinds of property including woodland, rivers, and lakes. The use of term *kwan'gye* (official deed) was an assertion of the state's authority over the country's land. The *Taehan Cheguk chŏndap kwan'gye* recorded the names and addresses of the previous owner who sold the land and the guarantor; it served as an ownership document that listed all past owners and as a record of all transactions involving the land. In this regard, *kwan'gye* performed the same functions as earlier transaction records. The difference was that it was made specifically to prevent problems such as black marketing and fraud by enabling the state to manage land rights.

The main features of *kwan'gye* were as follows. First, the method of recording the buyer's name was different in *kwan'gye* than in *maemae mungi* (transaction records) which were private documents. In order to guarantee a third party's right to challenge a sale, it was illegal for the parties involved to use alternative names or to engage in private transactions that were not reported to local authorities. Second, the *kwan'gye* used the same units of measurement as *maemae mungi*: *kyŏlbu* and *turak*. While the *kyŏlbu* units

77. "Chigye amun chigwŏn kŭp ch'ŏmu kyujŏng," articles 13, 21, 22.
78. Choi Won-kyu, "Taehan Chegukki yangjŏn kwa kwan'gye palgŭp saŏp."

used in both documents were identical to those used in *yang'an*, the units of *turak* were different. *Maemae mungi* used the unit in usage among the common people, and the *turak* used in *kwan'gye* was a unit of absolute area as it was in the Chigye amun's *yang'an*. Third, although *maemae mungi* contained similar information as *yang'an*, it did not include detailed information on the location and shape of the land so that a third party could ascertain it easily. On the other hand, *kwan'gye* contained exactly the same information as *yang'an*, making it possible for the two to update each other.

The data in *kwan'gye* came from the new *yang'an* made during the recent cadastral survey, but *maemae mungi* were based on the old *yang'an*. Since the criteria used for the two documents were different, the Chigye amun issued *kwan'gye* only after comparing and verifying the information in the *maemae mungi* with that in the new *yang'an*. Any discrepancies between the two were resolved by resurveying the land.[79]

The Chigye amun also issued *kwangye* for residences, and the *kasa kwan'gye* contained exactly the same information as the *kasaan* (residential ledger).[80] They recorded information such as the type of roof, number of rooms, sale price, and the names of the seller and the guarantor. In these *kwan'gye*, the location of buildings was indicated not by the *chaho chibŏn* system but by their *t'ongho*; i.e., their number according to the five-household system.

As can be seen in Figure 2 (p. 121), all *kwan'gye* had three identical sections; one was given to the landowner, and the other two were filed at the Chigye amun and the local government office. When there was a change in ownership, the *kwan'gye* had to be returned, and a new one was issued.[81] If the old *kwan'gye* was not exchanged after a transaction, the state would seize the land involved.[82] Laws prohibited the sale of property without a *kwan'gye*, and only one *kwan'gye* was supposed to exist for each unit of property.

A comparison of *yang'an* and *kwan'gye* with the documents made during the Japanese cadastral survey in Korea in the 1910s suggests that the

79. "Chigye kamni ŭnghaeng samok," article 8.
80. A few of the residential deeds (*kasa kwan'gye*) are still in existence and are located in archives such as the Changt'omunjŏk of the Kyujanggak (Documents of Agricultural Estates of the Palace Library) and in the Komunsŏ of the Kungnip tosŏgwan (Rare Manuscript section in the National Library). The "Chŏndap sallim ch'ŏnt'aek kasa kwan'gye sech'ik" was printed on the back of the *kwan'gye*—but only the relevant sections for each type of *kwan'gye* (i.e., whether it was for agricultural land, forests, residences, etc.).
81. "Chŏndap sallim ch'ŏnt'aek kasa kwan'gye sech'ik," article 2.
82. Ibid.

two sets of documents had many similarities. The *silji chosabu* performed the function of the *yang'an*, and the *t'oji tŭnggibu* was similar to the *kwan'gye* filed at the Chigye amun. The *t'oji taejang* fulfilled the function that the *yang'an* and the *kwan'gye* filed at the provincial government office handled together. In addition, the *tŭnggi chŭngsŏ* performed a similar role as the *kwan'gye* issued to individuals.

Although the Great Han Empire's documents were different from the *t'oji taejang* and *pudongsan tŭnggibu* used during the colonial period, they shared the common objective of enabling the state to keep track of past ownership of all property. By its very nature, *yang'an* did not allow for changes in the *siju*'s name when land was sold, making it impossible to keep track of changes in ownership. However, it was possible with *kwan'gye* since one existed for each plot of land. The *kwan'gye* sent to government offices were collected in one place at the *myŏn* (subcounty) or *tong* (village) level and were filed according to their *chaho*. Similar to the later *t'oji tŭnggibu*, the filing system of *kwan'gye* made it easy to determine the authenticity of ownership when land was sold or used as collateral for a loan.[83]

The issuance of *kwan'gye* was also important to state finances. First, the state charged registration fees for all transactions involving property, seeking to use the fees as an important source of revenue. The two parties each paid half of the fee which was set at 1/100 of the original property value. The local government office was responsible for collecting the fees and then sent them to the Chigye amun. Considering the fact that land sales were active and land prices were continually rising at the time, it is likely that the *kwan'gye* system produced a significant amount of revenue for the government.[84]

Second, the issuing of *kwan'gye* was also a preparatory step toward the establishment of a new land tax system. The *kyŏlbu* system was not abolished and still used to levy taxes. However, the state began to require that the sale price for every transaction be recorded on *kwan'gye*. Since land price became a factor in the calculation of land tax, it seems clear that the state was making preparations for a conversion to a land tax system based on land value.

Kwan'gye had to be used for any change in land rights such as a transfer of ownership or the use of land as collateral for a loan. For the former, the old

83. This fact can be confirmed by looking at the *Kwangye ch'ŏl* (File of *kwan'gye*) for Chŏngdong myŏn, Kangnŭng County, Kangwŏn Province located in the National Library.

84. "Chŏndap sallim ch'ŏnt'aek kasa kwan'gye sech'ik," articles 7, 8. Paper and printing fees were charged separately.

kwan'gye had to be returned, and a new one was issued. For the latter, it was necessary to receive a permit from the government. The state prohibited the customary practice of conducting transactions through the exchange of personal documents, and the punishment for violations was the confiscation of the property involved.[85]

Another objective of the *kwan'gye* system was to implement mechanisms that would prevent foreigners from purchasing land on the black market. At the time, foreigners took advantage of loopholes in existing transaction customs by using personal documents with other people's names or even without a name at all to acquire property. Even if foreigners continued to purchase land on the black market, they would not have been able to exercise any rights to the land since their ownership was not legally recognized by the state. With the introduction of the *kwan'gye* system, laws prohibiting foreign ownership of land, which had existed in name only, now were enforceable in reality.

To sum up, the issuing of *kwan'gye* enabled the state to assert its authority over land rights in the country. It signified a transition in the state's method of controlling land from an indirect system that worked through local communities to a direct system of control over individual plots of land. In relation to state finances, the state's objective seems to have been to abolish the existing land tax system which levied taxes on communities and to introduce a system based on absolute area and land value which would enable the state to levy land taxes directly on landowners. In this sense, it could be said that the issuing of *kwan'gye* aimed at the establishment of a modern land tax system and state management of modern land rights.

Conclusion

The Great Han Empire conducted a cadastral survey to lay the foundation for a political reform whose ultimate goal was the establishment of a modern state. More specifically, its objective was to create the modern institutions necessary for state management of land rights, and this task involved the following features. First, the topographical features of the land were mapped and recorded in ledgers. Second, the state wanted to establish a land tax system based on land value in which taxes were levied directly on individual

---

85. Ibid., articles 2, 3.

landowners. Third, the cadastral survey aimed to legalize land rights by defining the different kinds of land rights and determining the ownership of all land in the country.

Of these three aspects, the focus of this study has been on the third one. The basic principle of the Great Han Empire's cadastral survey was to recognize existing ownership rights in order to pursue a landlord-oriented reform. Nonetheless, it did not give all legal advantages to ownership. At a time when foreign encroachments were growing even more serious, the government was concerned with promoting unity among the people. To do so, it recognized the cultivation (tenancy) rights of the peasantry as a full legal right, though they were made subordinate to ownership rights. The land tax system was revised according to these changes, and the landlord and the cultivator were made equally responsible for the payment of taxes.

Although *kwan'gye* legally recognized the ownership rights of landlords, this did not mean that cultivation rights were reduced to a simple contractual leasing relation. Judging from the Yangji amun's cadastral survey and the Great Han Empire's Property Jurisdiction Law (Pudongsangwŏn sogwanbŏp), it appears that the Chigye amun also continued to regard cultivation rights as a "real right."[86] The government's position appears to have been in line with the prevailing opinion on land rights at the time. The level of land rent, which reflected the status of cultivation rights, is an issue that needs to be examined separately. However, because the status of cultivation rights as a "real right" restricted the landlords' ability to revoke or transfer them at will, the probability was greater that land rents would fall rather than rise.

The cadastral survey involved a combination of Western technology and methods with traditional reform proposals. It was also a response to several of the problems faced by Korean society at the time. Its goal was to create an institutional mechanism that would prevent the illicit land sales and fraud that became frequent with the expansion of the commodification of land. The government also wanted to prevent black market sales of land that occurred because foreigners circumvented laws against foreign landownership. It attempted to solve these problems by conducting a cadastral survey that used qualitatively different methods from those of the past; however, around the time of the Russo-Japanese War, Japan halted these efforts through its increasing influence over Korea's domestic affairs.

---

86. On the Property Jurisdiction Law, see footnote 36.

After the conclusion of the Convention of 1905 between Chosŏn and Japan, the Great Han Empire was placed under the rule of Japan's Residency-General, and it faced even greater difficulties in pursuing its reforms. As it tried to resist Japanese interference, it continued to implement reforms within its limited range of action. One such effort was the Property Jurisdiction Law, which was passed in 1906. Japan repealed the law when it became an impediment to its designs for Korea, and it passed its own series of land laws including the Regulations on the Verification of Land and Residences (T'oji kaok chŭngmyŏng kyuch'ik).

Though both the Great Han Empire's and Japan's laws were modern land laws, they were different in substance. On the one hand, Japan's fundamental goal was to promote the development of Japanese capitalism through the maintenance of the landlord system in Korea. In order to establish control over rural areas, it conducted a cadastral survey in the 1910s that bestowed absolute legal protection to existing ownership rights and levied land taxes directly on landowners. On the other hand, the goal of the Great Han Empire's land laws was to confer exclusive ownership rights to landowners while, at the same time, recognizing cultivation rights as a full "real right"—showing clear differences with Japanese law. As Japan extended its control over Korea, it terminated reforms enacted by the Great Han Empire that ran counter to its interests. It also reorganized Korean society by strengthening the landlord system and establishing a legal system based on absolute rights of ownership that served its needs. Japan began to implement these goals with the cadastral survey that commenced in 1910.

The tools and surveying methods used by the Japanese in their cadastral survey were completely modern and systematized. By contrast, the Great Han Empire's cadastral survey not only was not as modern but also was interrupted before it could be completed. For these reasons, later scholars have judged the Great Han Empire's cadastral survey negatively, saying that it was generally inferior to Japan's cadastral survey in matters of form such as its standards and its level of completion. However, both surveys were similar in their objective of transforming the pre-modern legal order into a modern legal system. The fundamental difference was that while Japan tried to establish control over Korean society through the maintenance of a powerful landlord system, the Great Han Empire attempted to protect the rights of the peasantry by granting full "real right" status to cultivation rights.

translated by Min Suh Son

TABLE 1

BREAKDOWN BY COUNTY OF BLACK MARKET TRANSACTIONS
AND LAND SALES IN NORTH CHŎLLA PROVINCE
(units of area in *turak*)

County	Private Land	*Kyunjŏn*[87]	Total Amount of Land	Number of Japanese	Number of Sellers
Kobu	326.0		326.0	2	4
Kŭmje	68.0	1,098.0	1,166.0	2	37
Mangyŏng	530.0		530.0	1	53
Puan	186.0		186.0	1	22
Okgu	2,598.0	1,328.9	3,926.9	28	414
Yong'an	144.0		144.0	1	2
Iksan	367.0		367.0	2	40
Chŏnju	1,407.5	3,703.0	5,110.5	3	277
Hamyŏl	50.0		50.0	1	3
Imp'a		3,687.0	3,687.0	11	340
Total	5,676.5	9,816.9	15,493.4	52	1,193

SOURCE: *Chŏlla pukto sib'il kun kongsari sannok woein chammae sŏngch'aek*, 1904.

87. The term *kyunjŏn* here does not mean the *kyunjŏn* mentioned earlier in the "equal field" system of land reform. In this instance, *kyunjŏn* refers to infertile land that was redistributed by the government for private ownership and then subjected to taxes. Because this land could not be cultivated, the owner paid taxes but produced no crop, making it an unprofitable property that was, as a consequence, particularly likely to be sold in the black market to the Japanese.

FIGURE 1

KASA KWAN'GYE OF THE GREAT HAN EMPIRE

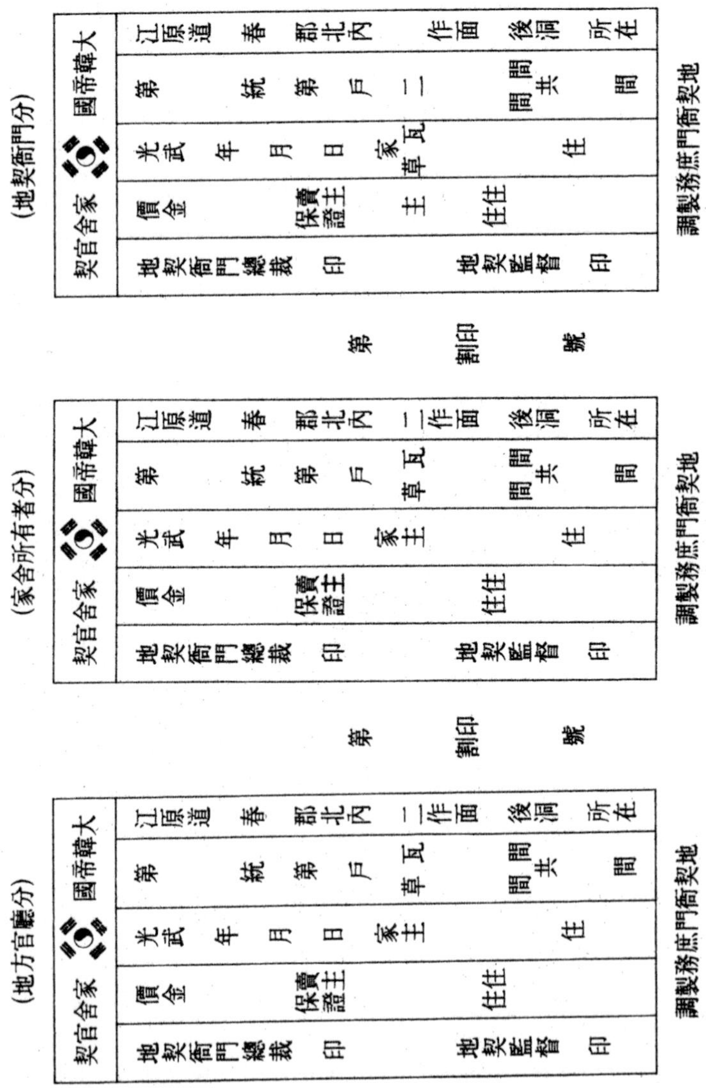

(地契衙門分)

大韓帝國　契合舍家

江原道　春川郡　北內面　後洞　所在
第　統　第　戶　二　作　間　間共　間

光武　年　月　日　家瓦　草　住

價金　保證　賣主　主　住住

地契衙門總裁　印　地契監督　印

調製務所門衙契地

第　割印　號

(家舍所有者分)

大韓帝國　契合舍家

江原道　春川郡　北內面　一作　後洞　所在
第　統　第　戶　草瓦　間間共　間

光武　年　月　日　家主

價金　保證　賣主　住住

地契衙門總裁　印　地契監督　印

調製務所門衙契地

第　割印　號

(地方官廳分)

大韓帝國　契合舍家

江原道　春川郡　北內面　一作　後洞　所在
第　統　第　戶　草瓦　間間共　間

光武　年　月　日　家主

價金　保證　賣主　住住

地契衙門總裁　印　地契監督　印

調製務所門衙契地

FIGURE 2

CHŎNDAP KWAN'GYE OF THE GREAT HAN EMPIRE

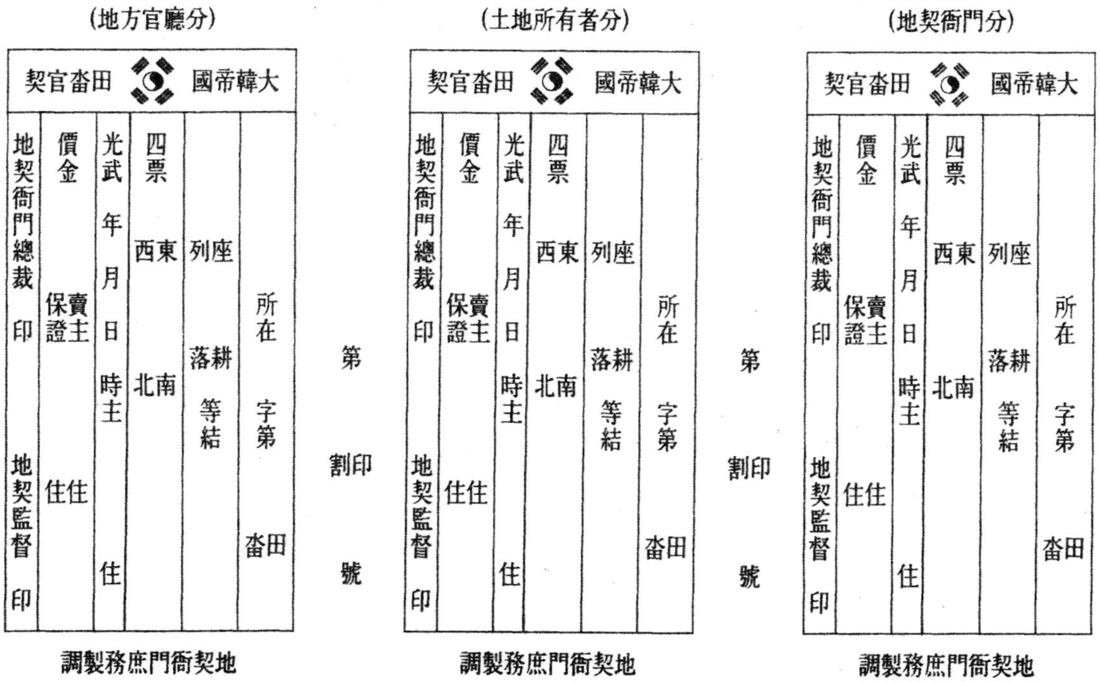

Index of Terms

kasaan 家舍案 residential ledger

kasa kwangye 家舍官契

kiju 起主 those who cultivated their own land

kitki 衿記

Kŏrae chon'an 去來存案

kugohyŏng 句股形 right triangle

kujin muju 舊陳無主

kuju 舊主 former owner at the time of the previous survey

kŭmju 今主 current owner

kunjŏng 軍政 military tax system

kwan'ge 官契 official land deeds

kyŏl 結

kyŏlbuje 結負制 *kyŏlbu* system

kyŏlho 結戶 households

kyŏlmyŏng 結名 individuals

kyuhyŏng 圭形 isosceles triangle

kyunjŏnnon 均田論 equal field system

maemae mungi 賣買文記 transaction records

majigi 마지기

maljitgi 말짓기

mihyŏng 眉形 eyebrow

mulgwŏn 物權 real right

myŏn 面 subcounty

naebun 內分 land within a *chibŏn*

nakjong 洛種 dropping seeds

ŏrin toch'aek 漁鱗圖冊 (literally) fish-scale map book

p'a 把 1 *sok* = 10 *p'a*

panghyŏng 方形 square

pu 負

Pudongsangwŏn sogwanbŏp 不動産權所管法 Property Jurisdiction Law

pyŏnhyŏng 邊形 polygon

sabuldŭnghyŏng 四不等形 irregular quadrilateral

sahyŏng 蛇形 snake

samjŏng 三政 the three (tax) systems

sap'yo 四標

sijak 時作 actual cultivator of the land

siju 時主 current owner

sok 束 1 *pu* = 10 *sok*

sokhang 續降 abandoned land

sokjŏn 續田 farmland which alternated fallow years between years of cultivation

Sok taejŏn 續大典 Legal code supplement

taegop'ahyŏng 大鼓跛形

Taehan cheguk chŏndap kwangye 大韓帝國田畓官契 Official Farmland Deed for Farmland of the Great Han Empire

Taehan chŏnt'o chigye 大韓田土地契 Great Han Agricultural Land Deed

Taehan chŏnt'o maemae chŭnggwŏn 大韓田土賣買證券 Great Han Agricultural Farmland Transaction Certificate

tojigwŏn 賭地權 sharecropping rights

t'oji kaok chŭngmyŏng kyuch'ik 土地家屋證明規則 Regulations on the Verification of Land and Residences

tong 洞 village

t'ongho 統號 number according to the five-household system

tŭngoejŏn 等外田

ugakhyŏng 牛角形 bull's horn

ŭnnugyŏl 은누결 hidden lands

wonhyŏng 圓形 circle

wŏnsi ch'widŭk 原始取得 original acquisition

yami 夜味

yang'an 量案 land registers

Yangji amun 量地衙門 Bureau of Land Survey

yangjŏn ch'ŏk 量田尺 the length of a *ch'ŏk* used in cadastral surveys

yŏjŏnnon 閭田論 village-land system

PART II

LANDLORDS AND PEASANTS

The Landlord System and the Agricultural Economy during the Japanese Occupation Period

Kim Yong-sop
金容燮

During the Japanese occupation period, particularly in the 1920s and 1930s, problems in the agricultural economy in Korea became even more severe than they had been in the Hanmal period. Demanding a resolution of these problems, the peasant movement underwent a qualitative transformation and reached a new stage of development. Japanese capitalism, which had reached the stage of monopoly capitalism, gained complete control over Korean agricultural and economic institutions. The Japanese achieved a partial solution of the agricultural problems that had persisted from the end of the Chosŏn period—but only as far as was necessary to control and exploit Korea. At the same time, they intensified their exploitation of the peasantry by promoting the rational management methods of capitalist modernization.

Japan's partial solution focused on a reform of the existing feudal system of taxation, particularly the land tax, by establishing a modern land tax system after the cadastral survey. However, these reforms were not sufficient to resolve the social contradictions caused by the agricultural problems of the time because policies did not address the issues of land distribution or the unequal distribution of income between landlords and tenant farmers. Because of the needs of Japanese capitalism, the Japanese instead tried to utilize the landlord class to support their rule in Korea by strengthening the existing landlord system. This system enabled the unrelenting exploitation of the Korean peasantry.

In short, problems in the agricultural economy under Japanese rule were rooted in the growth of the landlord system, which served as one pillar of Japanese capitalism, and the intensification of landlord management. These problems were manifested in the accumulation of land by the landlord-capitalist class, in the resulting differentiation of the peasant class, and in the struggle against the large landlord and capitalist class by the peasant masses. These masses were composed of impoverished peasants, tenant farmers, and owner-cultivators who were in danger of falling into destitution. It could be said that these problems ultimately became focused in the class antagonism between landlords and tenants. The peasant movement was not simply concerned with economic issues but also engaged in an anti-imperial, anti-Japanese political struggle that was connected with the national liberation movement. Problems in agriculture during this period were not simply economic or class issues but also issues of national and political significance.

To understand Korean agriculture in the occupation period, it is important to examine the relation of the landlord system with Japanese capitalism and imperialism. In addition, the peasant movement should not be seen as a development purely within rural society but should be understood in relation to the basic changes in Korean society that were driving toward the establishment of a new state. Based on case studies of changes in the landlord system from the Hanmal period to the occupation period, this chapter attempts to provide a comprehensive overview of the general nature and characteristics of the landlord system and the aims of the peasant movement.

Japan's Agricultural Policies toward Korea and the Landlord System

The problems in the agricultural economy were concentrated, above all, in issues related to land. The main cause was the accumulation of land by the landlord-capitalist class which became prevalent at the time because of both the expansion of the landlord system since the Hanmal period and Japan's agricultural policies toward Korea after 1910. Although the landlord system had expanded during the Hanmal period, this expansion became even more evident after 1910. The reason was that in order to exploit Korean agriculture, Japan's policies facilitated the expansion of the landlord system through land accumulation.

The key feature of Japan's agricultural policies was the central importance of the landlord system and the landlord class.[1] Since the landlord system was one of the foundations of Japanese imperialism, Japan naturally wanted to protect the interests of the Japanese landlord class, to control Korean agriculture through this landlord system, and to exploit the fruits of agricultural production. Its policies focused on the landlord-capitalist class who collected land rent, rather than on the peasants who were the actual producers. In fact, the policies served the interests of the Japanese landlord and capitalist class and not those of the Korean landlord class. The problems in the agricultural economy were fundamentally rooted in Japan's agricultural policies and, accordingly, in the economic system and agricultural institutions which carried out those policies.

The Government-General based its agricultural policies on information gathered from the various surveys conducted during the Hanmal period. The policies were developed in stages in conjunction with Japan's overall economic policy for the exploitation of Korea.

The first stage was the period of the establishment of the exploitative agricultural policies in the 1910s. It was during this period that the Government-General promulgated the Company Law (*Hoesaryŏng*) and conducted the cadastral survey (*t'oji chosa saŏp*). The Company Law was a licensing law[2] that required the permission of the Government-General to establish a company for commercial activities.[3] The objective was to give Japan control over the commercial and industrial activities of Koreans and to enable the Japanese to have a monopoly over business activities within Korea. The Company Law was an anti-capitalist law that went against the capitalist principle of freedom of enterprise, and Japan enacted it because the basic principle of colonial rule by capitalist countries is to secure commodity markets and raw materials from the occupied land.

---

1. Kim Yong-sop (Kim Yongsŏp), "Ilche ŭi ch'ogi nong'ŏp singminch'ek kwa chijuje" (The agricultural policies of the early colonial period and the landlord system), *Han'guk kŭndae nong'ŏpsa yŏn'gu: Hanmal-Ilcheha ŭi chijuje wa nong'ŏp munje* (Seoul: Ilchogak, 1992).

2. Paek Nam'un, "Chosen keizai no gendankairon" (The present stage of the Chosŏn economy), *Shiso iho*, no. 17 (1938).

3. Chosŏn Ch'ongdokbu (Government-General of Korea), *Chosen horei shuran* (Laws and ordinances of Korea) (1932) vol. 16, chapter 2, "Commerce, Company Law" (December 1910, *Seirei* (Laws and institutions) number 13, revised 1918). "*Article 1.* The establishment of companies requires the permission of the Governor-General." See Son Chŏngmok, "Hoesaryŏng yŏn'gu" (An examination of the Company Law), *Han'guksa yŏn'gu*, no. 45 (1984).

However, Japan's agricultural policies were different from its policies on commerce and industry. Japan created legal and institutional apparatuses to protect land ownership and accumulation by the landlord and capitalist class, and it placed no restrictions on land ownership or accumulation by Koreans, allowing the existing situation to continue. It adopted these policies because the Japanese needed a social class that would collaborate with them politically and socially in order to rule the Korean people and to turn Korea into a major food supplier.

One apparatus was the cadastral survey, and its purpose was to draw up cadastral maps by exactly measuring all the land in the country, to create land registers by determining land ownership, and to enable cash payments of taxes by recalculating land values.[4] As a result of the survey, both Japanese and Korean landlords and capitalists, who wanted to increase their landholdings, were able to acquire exact statistics on farmland and to purchase it in a systematic manner. They could then accumulate land and operate their farms under more favorable conditions.[5] Since the price of rice continued to rise in this period, the landlord-capitalist class was continually able to enjoy high returns on its investments in land. Consequently, Japanese capital surged into Korea, and land investment and accumulation became prevalent as an extremely attractive business.[6] Land accumulation underwent such a surge that, as will be explained below, the number of Japanese with multiple landholdings reached about 40,000 by the beginning of the 1920s.

The cadastral survey brought about a change from the existing feudal tax system (the *kyŏlbu* system) into a modern monetary tax system. In the process, Japan subsumed the tax system, which was designed to exploit Korean

4. *Chosen horei shuran*, volume 16, Chapter 1, Land, Land Survey Ordinance (August 1912, revision 2); Chosŏn Ch'ongdokbu, Rinji tochi chosa kyoku, *Chosen tochi chosa jigyo hokokusho* (Report on the cadastral survey) (1918); Wada Ichiro. *Chosen no tochi seido oyobi chizei seido chosa hokokusho* (A study of land system and land tax in Korea) (1920); Sin Yongha, *Chosŏn t'oji chosa saŏp yŏn'gu* (A study of the cadastral survey in Korea) (Seoul: Han'guk yŏn'guwŏn, 1979). See Miyajima Hiroshi, *Chosen tochi chosa jigyoshi no kenkyu* (Studies on the history of the cadastral survey in Korea) (Tokyo: Kyuko shoin, 1991).

5. Sŏn'u Chŏn, *Chosŏn ŭi t'oji kyŏmbyŏng kwa kŭ taech'aek* (Land accumulation in Korea and responses to it) (Kyŏngsŏng: Chosŏn tosŏ chusik hoesa, 1923), pp. 5–8. This published volume is a collection of articles that appeared in the *Tonga Ilbo* (Nov. 24, 1992–Feb. 11, 1923) under the same name. In the section entitled "II. The causes of land accumulation," there is an item, "1. The land survey and opposing influences." The situation of land purchases and investment after the conclusion of the cadastral survey is given in Table 1 (p. 164).

6. Sŏn'u Chŏn (1923), see in Part II the section: "2. Increase in rice prices and the rise of landlord earnings (investment earnings from land)." The increase of rice prices is shown in Table 2 (p. 164).

agriculture and the peasantry, under Japan's capitalist institutions, enabling its efficient management.[7] However efficient this arrangement may have been, the tax system itself was extremely irrational, and the amount of taxes levied, which was already excessive, continually increased. Since many Korean peasants went bankrupt because of the heavy burden of taxes and fees, Japanese landlords and capitalists were able to buy up their land easily.[8]

In this period, Japanese landlords and capitalists invested in agriculture as well as in commerce and industry, aggressively engaging in land accumulation in order to manage their investments as an enterprise (*nongjang* management). Since laws restricted Koreans from engaging in commerce and Industry, their investment opportunities were naturally limited to land. Land accumulation for the purpose of landlord management also became prevalent among Koreans.[9]

The second stage in the development of the Government-General's agricultural policies was the period of the intensification of the exploitative agricultural policies in the 1920s. It was during this period that the Japanese consolidated the financial system in Korea and implemented the Program to Increase Rice Production (PIRP, Chosŏn sanmi chŭngsik kyehoek). The consolidation of the financial system created a pyramidal structure that was both centralized and reached rural localities. The Industrial Bank of Chosŏn (IBC, Chosŏn siksan ŭnhaeng) was established in 1918 by a special law allowing a merger of agricultural and industrial banks that were managed by

---

7. Kim Hanju, "Chosŏn chiseryŏng yŏn'gu" (An examination of the Korean Land Tax Ordinance), *Haksul*, no. 1 (1946); Im Pyŏngyun, *Shokuminchi ni okeru shogyoteki nogyo no tenkai* (The development of commercial agriculture in the colony) (Tokyo: Tokyo University Press, 1971); Pae Yŏngsun. "Hanmal ilche ch'ogi ŭi t'oji chosa wa chise kaejŏng e kwanhan yŏn'gu" (An examination of the cadastral land survey and land tax reform in late Chosŏn and early colonial years) (Ph.D. diss., Seoul National University, 1987).

8. Pak Hŏn'u, "Nongch'on p'ip'ye ŭi wŏn'in" (The origins of rural poverty), *Sinmin* no. 49 (May 1929); Kim Up'yŏng, "Chosŏn chose ŭi ch'use wa Chosŏnin ŭi pudam" (Changes in Korean taxes and the burdens of the Korean people), *Tonggwang*, no. 30 (February 1932); Kim Up'yŏng, "Chosŏnin kwa pin" (The Korean people and poverty), *Tonga ilbo*, June 5, 1927. Chosŏn sajŏng chosa yŏn'guhoe, "Chosŏn hyŏnhaeng seje kŭp pudam chosa (The current tax system of Chosŏn and a survey of charges), *Tongbang pyŏngnon*, no. 1 (April 1932); Yi Yŏsŏng and Kim Seyong, *Sutja Chosŏn yŏn'gu* (A statistical study of Chosŏn) 3, chapter 2, "Chosŏn chose chedo ŭi haebu" (An analysis of the Chosŏn tax system, 1932); Yang Kapsŏk, "Chosŏn ŭi kŭm'yung chabon kwa nongch'on kyŏngje wa ŭi kwangye" (Chosŏn financial capital and its relation to the rural economy), *Sindonga*, no. 40 (February 1935).

9. Yi Kakjong, "Chosŏn ŭi nongch'on munje wa ki taech'aek" (The rural problems in Korea and responses to it), *Sinmin*, no. 8 (1925).

Koreans and had been established in all regions of the country. The exception was the Bank of Chosŏn, which served as the central bank.

The various financial cooperatives, which provided financial services to people engaged in agriculture in all regions of the country, were merged into a single, centralized organization, the Chosŏn Association of Financial Cooperatives (Chosŏn kŭm'yung chohap hyŏphoe, 1928), which later became the Chosŏn Federation of Financial Cooperatives (Chosŏn kŭm'yung chohap yŏnhaphoe) in 1933. The Chosŏn Savings Bank (Chosŏn chŏch'uk ŭnhaeng) was established in 1929 to provide financial services to the working classes by taking over and expanding the savings deposit business of the IBC. These banks did not conduct business only through central offices in Seoul; they expanded their business by establishing branches (extractive institutions for exploitation) in all regions of the country.[10] Special companies like the Oriental Development Company (ODC, Tongyang ch'ŏksik chusik hoesa) had finance departments that also functioned as financial institutions.

Although several banks such as Chosŏn Commercial Bank (Chosŏn sang'ŏp ŭnhaeng) and Hanil Bank were still financed by Korean capital in this period, their level of capitalization was quite low.[11] Japanese capital and financial institutions dominated the entire Korean economy.[12] As these extractive organizations expanded, Korean farmland and the peasantry came increasingly under the control of Japanese financial capital and, inevitably, became owned by it.[13] While landlords and capitalists utilized finance capital to increase their opportunities for profit, the petty, poor peasants bore the debts from the high-interest loans of the landlords and capitalists, becoming easy targets of exploitation.[14] It became quite a simple matter for Japanese

10. See Ko Sŭngje, *Han'guk kŭm'yungsa yŏn'gu* (A study of the financial history of Korea) (Seoul: Ilchosa, 1970), chapters 3-6.

11. *Sutja Chosŏn yŏn'gu* (1932), vol. 2, chapter 1, "Chosŏn nae kŭm'yung chabon" (Finance capital in Korea), pp. 15-20; Ko Sungje, ibid., chapters 11-17.

12. No Tonggyu, "Chosŏn nong'ŏp ŭi hyŏnsang kŏp changnae" (The present state and future of Chosŏn agriculture), *Sindonga*, no. 15 (January 1933); Pak Mungyu, "Chosŏn nongch'on kwa kŭmyung kigwan ŭi kwangye—t'ŭkhi kŭmyung chohap e taehayŏ" (The relationship between rural Chosŏn and financial institutions—with a focus on financial cooperatives), *Sindonga*, no. 28 (February 1934); Yang Kapsŏk, ibid.

13. *Sutja Chosŏn yŏn'gu* (1931). On page 10, there is a quote from Mikami Hideo's *Minzoku mondai* (National Problems), saying that Japanese finance capitalists possessed approximately 62% of Korean land.

14. Chosŏn Ch'ongdokbu, *Chosen no kosaku kanko* (Tenancy customs in Chosŏn), vol. 2, chapter 16 "The situation of landlords and tenants," (1932). No Tonggyu, "Chosŏn nong'ga kyŏngje silsang chosa haebu" (A survey and analysis of the true state of the rural household

financial institutions, landlords, and capitalists to take the land of the destitute Korean peasantry.

The Program to Increase Rice Production was a state effort to bring about substantial increases in rice production in Korea in order to secure a supply of rice to satisfy Japan's increasing demand.[15] It involved projects such as land improvement, the construction of irrigation facilities, the spread of improved seed varieties, improvements in farming tools, and the use of chem.ical fertilizers. The program was an example of the depredatory nature of Japanese imperialism, as can be shown by an examination of its sources of funding.

Funding for the program came mainly from low-interest loans (an average of 7.4%) from the state (Bureau of the Budget) and financial institutions such as the ODC and the IBC. It was supplemented by subsidies from the Government-General and procurement funds from businessmen involved in the project.[16] Particularly in the cases of land improvement and irrigation works, financing was secured through the authority of government organs and was backed by the coercive force of legal ordinances. For instance, the Government-General enacted the Chosŏn Land Improvement Law (Chosŏn t'oji kaeryangryŏng) in 1927[17] and established agencies such as the ODC's

economy in Korea), *Tongbang pyŏngnon* (July-August 1932), special supplemental issue on the Chosŏn rural situation. See Pak Mungyu, ibid. (1934). (men-tioned in footnote 12)

15. See Yanaihara Tadao, "Chosen sanbei zoshoku keikaku ni tuite" (The Program to Increase Rice Production in Korea), *Nogyo keizai kenkyu* 2-1 (1926); Kondo Yasuo, "Tosi—shokuminchi nogyo no sihai," *Nogyo keizairon* (Tokyo: Asano shoten, 1932) (This article was republished in the book *Chosen keizai no siteki dansho* under a different title, "Nihon teikokushugi no Chosen sanbei zoshoku keikaku" (The Japanese imperialist Program to Increase Rice Production in Chosŏn, 1987)); Ouchi Takeji, "Chosen ni okeru beikoku seisan" (Rice production in Korea), *Chosen keizai no kenkyu* 3 (1938); In Chŏngsik (In Teishoku), "Chosen sanbei zoshoku no kikoteki tokucho" (The structural characteristics of the Program to Increase Rice Production in Chosŏn), *Chosen no nogyo kiko* (Tokyo: Hakuyosha, 1940); Kawai Kazumu, *Chosen ni okeru sanbei zoshoku keikaku* (The Program to Increase Rice Production in Chosŏn) (Tokyo: Miraisha, 1986); Pak Yŏnggu, "Iljeha 'Sanmi chŭngsik kyehoek' ŭi kyŏngjesajŏk yŏn'gu" (An economic history of the 'Program to Increase Rice Production' during the occupation period) (Ph.D. diss., Yonsei University, 1991).

16. Chosŏn Ch'ongdokbu, Norinkyoku, *Chosen sanbei zoshoku keikaku yoko* (Outline of the Program to Increase Rice Production in Chosŏn) (1926), pp. 9-11, 17, 21; Ibid., *Chosen sanbei zoshoku keikaku no jiseki* (The actual results of the Program to Increase Rice Production) (1928), pp. 4-9.

17. *Chosen horei shuran*, volume 10, article 1, "Tochi, Chosen tochi kairyomei" (Land: the Land Improvement Ordinance of Chosŏn) Regulation No. 16 (December 28, 1927). See Chosŏn Ch'ongdokbu Norinkyoku, *Chosen tochi kairyo kankei reiki* (Regulations on land improvement in Chosŏn), part 1, "Tochi kairyo" (Land Improvements) (1934). See also Yi Aesuk,

Bureau of Land Improvement and the IBC's Chosŏn Land Improvement Company (Chosŏn t'oji kaeryang chusikhoesa) to implement the program. The PIRP was a top-down state program in which the needs of Japanese imperialism and capitalism coincided; as a result, Japan was able to achieve its goal of extracting huge quantities of the rice produced.

From its conception, the PIRP was not meant to benefit the Korean peasantry and did not consider the general interests of the Korean populace. Its most striking aspect was that rather than functioning as a state welfare program for the development of Korean agriculture or for the economic improvement of the Korean peasant, it was more of a business venture or predatory activity undertaken by large and small-scale Japanese capitalists in pursuit of large profits. With the implementation of the program, speculative capital flowed into Korea from Japan and led to a boom in land investment and land accumulation. The trend of land accumulation remained unchanged from the previous stage; as will be explained below, when the PIRP was discontinued, the number of landlords with multiple holdings exceeded 100,000.

Obviously, a program run by and for landlords and capitalists could not avoid running into problems. In all regions of the country, Korean agriculture came directly under the control of Japanese finance capital and speculative capital, creating a tense situation.[18] This was true whether irrigation works or only necessary agricultural improvements were being undertaken and regardless of the scale of individual operations (whether landlords or peasants). Especially in areas implementing irrigation improvements, large numbers of farmers went bankrupt, including tenants, owner-cultivators, and even small- to medium-scale landlords. They suffered from the heavy burdens of cooperative fees (*chohapbi*) and irrigation taxes (*suse*) that were used to cover the expenses and interest required for the improvements. It became extremely easy for large-scale Japanese landlords and capitalists (i.e., companies) to buy up their land.[19] Despite the program's purported intention of increasing rice

"Ilcheha suri chohap ŭi sŏllip kwa unyŏng" (The establishment and operation of irrigation cooperatives during the occupation period), *Han'guksa yŏn'gu*, nos. 50-51 (1985).

18. Kondo Yasuo, ibid. (1932).

19. Min Pyŏngdŏk, "Chosŏn nong'ŏp ŭi kaegwan" (An overview of Chosŏn agriculture), *Chosŏn chi kwang*, no. 64 (February 1927); Pak Insu, "Ponggŏn yuje wa kŭm'yung chabon ŭi yahab" (The conspiracy between the feudal hereditary system and financial capital), *Sinhŭng*, no. 4 (January 1931); Yi Hun'gu, "Nongch'on chungsan kyegŭp ŭi mollak kwa kŭ taech'aek" (The failure of the rural middle class and responses to this situation), *Tongbang pyŏngnon* (July 1932), p. 8, special supplemental issue on the Chosŏn rural situation; Yi Hun'gu, "Suri chohap ŭi wigi— Chosŏn nongch'on ŭi amchong" (The crisis of irrigation unions—The cancer of rural Korea), *Tonggwang*, no. 30 (February 1932); Han Changkyŏng, "Suri chohap kwa t'oji kyŏmbyŏng"

production, irrigation projects and land improvements actually ended up functioning as a catalyst for land accumulation.[20]

Furthermore, the PIRP undermined many existing agricultural practices and the traditional system of production in Korea. Passed down and developed over thousands of years, these practices could have been useful even in modern agriculture if they had been preserved. The program required the use of Japanese rice plants, improved Japanese farming tools, and Japanese chemical fertilizers (i.e., forced capital investment). Despite its grand-sounding title, the PIRP actually brought about a relative stagnation in agricultural productivity as compared to periods before and after the program.[21]

It was unrealistic to expect peasants to make an effort to increase their productivity at a time when the Japanese were causing Korean peasants to fall into ruin by buying up their land and turning them into tenant farmers or propertyless peasants. The PIRP required a large capital investment, but it was unreasonable to demand such an investment from destitute peasants barely able to eke out a living. They even lacked any legal protection for their tenancy rights.[22] In sum, the PIRP was an effort to exploit rice production by reorganizing and controlling Korean agriculture and farmland under Japanese institutions while Japanese capitalism undermined traditional Korean agricultural practices and seized Korean farmland.

In the 1930s, during the latter part of the second stage, the agricultural depression of world capitalism compounded the effects of the chronic

(Irrigation unions and land accumulation), *Tongbang pyŏngnon* (July-August 1932); Kim Chin'guk, "1931 nyŏn ŭi nongmin undong kae'gwan" (An overview of the peasant movement in 1931), *Chosŏn ilbo* (January 1932); Pae Sŏngnyong, *Chosŏn kyŏngje ŭi hyŏnjae wa changnae* (The present and future of the Korean economy) (Seoul: Hansŏng tosŏ chusikhoesa, 1933), pp. 16-18, 28-29; Chang Hyŏnch'il, "Chosŏn suri chohap kwa chungnong kyegŭp" (Korean irrigation cooperatives and the agricultural middle class), *Sindonga* no. 40 (February 1935); Kondo Yasuo, ibid. (1932). See also Tohata Seichi and Okawa Kazushi, *Chosen beikoku keizairon* (Theories on the Korean rice economy) (Tokyo: Nihon gakujutsu shinkokai, 1935), pp. 81-82; Yi Kyŏngnan, "Ilcheha suri chohap kwa nongjang chijuje" (Irrigation unions and *nongjang* landlords), *Hangnim* nos. 12-13 (combined issue, 1991).

20. Hisama Ken'ichi, *Chosen nogyo no kindaiteki yoso* (The modern aspects of Korean agriculture) (Tokyo: Nishigahara kankokai, 1935), p. 22.

21. In Chŏngsik, *Chosen no nogyo kiko bunseki* (An analysis of the structure of Chosŏn agriculture) (Tokyo: Hakuyosha, 1937), pp. 225-31; Chŏn Sŏkdam (Zen Shakutan) and Ch'oe Yungyu (Sai Junkei), *Chosen kindai shakai keizaishi* (The socioeconomic history of early modern Chosŏn (Tokyo: Ryukei shosha, 1978), pp. 201-06; Chŏng Munjŏng, "Sanmi chŭngsik kyehoek kwa nong'ŏp saengsanryŏk chŏngch'e e kwanhan yŏn'gu" (A study of the Program to Increase Rice Production and the stagnation of agricultural productivity) in Chang Siwŏn, et al., *Han'guk kŭndae nongch'on sahoe wa nongmin undong* (Seoul: Yŏlŭmsa, 1988); Pak Yonggu, ibid.

22. No Tonggyu, ibid. (1933). See footnote 12.

economic recession of Japanese capitalism, ruining many peasants through the serious damage inflicted on Japanese and Korean agriculture by a crash in grain prices.[23] Japan adopted an inflationary policy to overcome the crisis, but since this led to a large gap in prices between farm products and manufactured goods,[24] the policy was unable to reverse the decline of the peasant class. Through this policy, Japan shifted the negative effects of the depression to Korea, which was under its domination; in turn, the large landlord-capitalist class in Korea shifted the burden to small- to medium-scale landowners and tenant farmers. Because these conditions often forced Korean peasants to run into deficit and because they also had to pay myriad taxes and fees, they accumulated debts, and many were driven into bankruptcy. Estimates on total debt range from 500 to 800 million yen.[25] During the time of the Japanese occupation and the years of the PIRP and economic depression, it was not surprising that many small-scale, poor Korean peasants went bankrupt,

23. Ch'oe Sanghae, "Segyejŏk kyŏngje konghwang kwa Chosŏn ŭi nong'ŏp konghwang ŭi chonmang" (Observations on the global economic depression and the agricultural depression in Korea), *Tonggwang*, no. 21 (May 1931); Aengdo wŏn'in, "Chosŏn nongch'on ŭn ŏdero kana—t'ŭkhi konghwang kwa t'oji ŭi hyangbang e taehayŏ" (Where is rural society in Chosŏn going? —with a focus on the direction of the recession and land), *Sinmin*, no. 65 (March 1931); Ma O, "Nong'ŏp konghwang kwa nongmin ŭi mollak kwajŏng" (The agricultural recession and the decline of the peasantry), *Tonggwang*, no. 20 (April 1931); No Tonggyu, ibid. (1933); Yi P'yŏng, "Inp'urreishun kwa Chosŏn e mich'i nŭn yŏnghyang" (Inflation and its effect on Chosŏn), *Chungmyŏng*, no. 3 (1933);

"Chungnongch'ung ŭi mollak—sesam sŭroun pur'an" (The failure of the agricultural middle class—Renewed anxieties) *Chosŏn ilbo* (editorial) November 20, 1930; "Hyŏng'ŏn halsu ŏpnŭn ch'amsang—nongmin dŭr'ŭn ŏdero" (A sad spectacle impossible to describe—What is happening to the peasants?), *Chosŏn ilbo* (editorial), December 4, 1930.

24. Pae Sŏngnyong, "Inp'urreishun chŏngch'ek kwa Chosŏn nongmin" (Inflation policy and Chosŏn peasants), *Singyedan*, no. 1 (October 1932); Yi P'yŏng, ibid. (1933); "Chosŏn nongmin munje wa nong'ŏp munje" (The problems of Chosŏn peasants and the agricultural situation), *Chosŏn ilbo* (editorial), January 11, 1933.

25. See Chosŏn Ch'ongdokbu, Norinkyoku, *Chosen ni okeru kosaku ni kansuru sanko jiko tekiyo* (A summary of reference items on tenancy in Chosŏn) (1934), p. 73, and *Sojaknong ŭi puch'ae sanghwang* (The debt situation of tenants) (1930 survey); Yi Kwan'gu, "Nongch'on kyŏngje mollak ŭi p'yŏn'yŏng" (The signs of rural economic failure), *Hyŏndae p'yŏngnon*, no. 6 (January 1927); Sŏ Ch'un, "Nong'ga puch'e 5 ŏk wŏn—Chosŏn nongch'on ŭn ŏdŭiro kana" (The 500 million won debt of farming households—what is happening to rural society in Chosŏn?), *Sindonga*, no. 1 (November 1931); No Tonggyu, ibid. (1932, 1933); Sŏng In'gwa, "Chosŏn nongga ŭi p'ip'ye sanghwang" (The impoverishment of Korean farming households), *Sindonga* (January 1934); Im Pongsun, "Chosŏn nongmin ŭi puch'e aek" (The amount of debt of Korean peasants), *Sindonga* (December 1934); Takahashi Kamekichi, *Gendai Chosen keizairon* (Theories of the modern Chosŏn economy) (Tokyo: Chikura shobo, 1935), pp. 218-26; "Chosŏn ŭi nongmin munje" (Problems concerning the peasantry of Korea), *Chosŏn Ilbo* (editorial), June 6, 1926.

but even small- to medium-scale landlords rapidly fell into destitution. As a result, large landlords and capitalists easily bought up their land.[26]

The third stage in the development of Japan's agricultural policies began in the 1930s; this was the period when agricultural exploitation operated under a control economy. As will be discussed in section 4 of this chapter, Japan's agricultural policies in this stage were a response to the failure of its exploitative policies. That is, they were a response to the outbreak of Korean peasant resistance (i.e., tenancy disputes and the peasant movement) against the agricultural policies that Japan had enacted in Korea up to this point. However, the objective of these policies was not to achieve a fundamental solution of the problems in the agricultural economy for the sake of the peasantry. Rather, it became necessary to change and regulate the landlord system to a limited extent because of the need to placate the angered peasants and protect the interests of the Japanese imperial state (i.e., as a defense against socialism). Since these policies were unable to stop the impoverishment of the peasantry and the destruction of rural villages, the decline and differentiation of the peasant class, due to the accumulation of land by large-scale landholders, remained unchanged from the previous stage.[27]

Even just based on statistics collected by the Japanese authorities, it is possible to trace the general trends in land accumulation and in the decline and differentiation of the peasant class during these stages.

First, over the course of the 1910s and 1920s, land accumulation by Japanese capitalist institutions gradually became more severe, and the traditional rural order ultimately reached the verge of complete upheaval. This trend can be demonstrated by the growth in the number of landlords engaged in amassing land. According to Table 3 (p. 165), in just fifteen years from 1917 to 1932, the number of Type A landlords (*chiju kap*) more than doubled from 15,485 to 32,890. In the ten years from 1917 to 1927, the number of Type B landlords (*chiju ŭl*) increased almost 50% from 57,713 to 84,359. However, since Table 3 only has data from 1917, the size of the

---

26. See Table 3 in this chapter (p. 165) and the column "Type A Landlord" in the "Chart of Farm Household Figures for Landlords, Owner-cultivators, Semi-tenants, and Tenants" on page 10 of Chosŏn Ch'ongdokbu Norinkyoku, *Chosen ni okeru kosaku ni kansuru sanko jiko tekiyo* (1932); "Yŏnnyŏn kyŏkgam toi'nŭn Chŏnbuk Chosŏn'in soyuji (chiju)" (The yearly decline of land owned by Chosŏn people in North Chŏlla province), *Chung'oe ilbo*, November 14, 1928; "Nongji soyu e nata'nan Kyŏngbuk chiju mollaksang" (The decline of landlords in North Kyŏngsang province as seen in (changes in) agricultural land ownership), *Chosŏn chungang ilbo*, July 11, 1935.

27. See Table 6 in this chapter (p. 167).

increase would be even greater if data from 1910 were taken into account, as land accumulation had been prevalent since the Hanmal period. Not all landlords were able to take part in the boom in land accumulation, and regardless of the scale of their landholdings, the landowners able to engage in accumulation were mainly the small number of individuals who either had connections in the Japanese occupation government or were knowledgeable about politics and finance. If statistics only recorded the number of landlords who were actively involved in land accumulation, then the rate of increase would be even greater.

Second, anyone with sufficient financial resources, whether Japanese or Korean, could engage in land accumulation. However, because of the political and economic situation of the time, the Japanese landlord–capitalist class was the main force in land accumulation.[28] Beginning in the 1910s (the stage of the cadastral survey), capital for their land purchases surged into Korea like a flood surging into an unprotected land.[29]

The trends in Japanese landownership in Korea can be seen clearly in Table 4 (p. 166). The table is a compilation of the number of tax-paying landowners, as determined by the territorial principle (sokjijuŭi) at the county and pro-vincial levels. According to these statistics, the number of Japanese taxpayers (i.e., landowners) gradually increased over time. In the Hanmal period, only a few Japanese owned land, but the number of landowners reached 44,378 in 1921 and surpassed 100,000 by 1933. Of course, despite this increase, the number of Japanese landowners never exceeded that of Korean landowners. Nonetheless, the increase was truly astounding, considering the fact that the Japanese had been legally prohibited from owning land in Korea before the occupation. In 1909, the amount of land bought by Japanese was estimated at around 60,000 chŏngbo (including both residential land and cultivated land);[30] by the 1930s, the amount of cultivated land alone exceeded 600,000 chŏngbo.[31]

---

28. See Sŏn'u Chŏn, ibid. (1923), Causes of Land Accumulation 4, "Land Purchases by the Japanese and the Foreign Migration of Chosŏn Peasants." This part was deleted from the book in its entirety but can be found in the original Tonga ilbo serialization (December 21-24, 1922).

29. Kondo Yasuo, ibid.

30. In Chŏngsik, "Nongch'on chabonchehwa ŭi che hyŏng kwa Chosŏn t'oji chosa saop ŭi ŭiŭi" (The diverse forms of rural capital transformation and the significance of the Chosŏn land survey), Pip'an (September 1936).

31. Paek Nam'un, ibid.; Chin Yŏngch'ŏl, "Oerae chabonjuŭi ŭi Chosŏn aneso ŭi paljŏn" (The development of foreign capitalism in Chosŏn), Hyesŏng 1, no. 5 (May 1931).

As can be seen in Table 5 (p. 167), among large landlords with over 30 *chŏngbo* of land, the average area of land per person was three times greater for Japa-nese landlords than it was for Korean landlords. Among ultra-large landlords (*ch'ogŏdae chiju*) with over 500 *chŏngbo* of land, the number of Japanese landlords was far greater than the number of Korean landlords.

With the mid-1920s as a turning point, the number of Korean landlords gradually declined at all levels of landownership (first among the large landlords and later among the petty landowners), while that of Japanese landlords continued to increase (see Table 4). These trends are better illustrated in Table 6 (p. 167), which estimates changes in the number of large landlords. According to this table, the number of large-scale Korean landlords increased until the mid-1920s but gradually decreased thereafter, while the number of Japanese large landlords continually increased. Judging from these trends, it seems clear that the decisive factor behind the boom in land accumulation was the purchase of land by the Japanese.

Third, land accumulation by Japanese landlords and capitalists was so widespread and occurred on such a large scale within such a short period of time that it was without historical precedent. It resulted in a correspondingly severe differentiation of traditional rural society. Differentiation involved, on the one hand, the sudden decline of owner-cultivators—the middle-class of Korean rural society—and a portion of the landlord class, i.e., the economic ruling class (both landlord A and B). On the other hand, there was simultaneously a tremendous increase in the number of tenant farmers whose existence was a manifestation of rural poverty.[32] In addition, the numbers of

32. Yi Hun'gu, "Nongch'on kyŏngje ŭi wigi" (The crisis of the rural economy), *Chosŏn ilbo*, January 1, 1925; Kwang U, "Chosŏn e issŏsŏ ŭi t'oji munje" (The land problems of Korea), *Kyegŭp t'ujaeng* (January 1930). According to Kim Hoyong, this study was published in Japanese (Nodongja sobang, 1930), and can also be found in Pak Kyŏngsik, ed., *Chosen mondai siryososho* (Documents on the Korean problem) (Seoul: Han'gukhak chinhŭngwŏn, (1982) 1987), vol. 7. See also Pae Sŏngnyong, "Nongch'on munje kangjwa—nongch'on ŭi kyegŭpsang" (A lecture on rural problems—The class aspect of the countryside), *Chosŏn ilbo*, March 30–April 10, 1930; Pak Mun'gyu, "Nongch'on sahoe punhwa ŭi kichŏm urosŏ ŭi t'oji chosa saŏp e taehayŏ" in Keijo Teikoku Daigaku Hobungakkai, ed., *Chosŏn sahoe kyŏngjesa yŏn'gu* (Tokyo: Tokoshoin, 1933). After liberation, this study was retitled "T'oji chosa saop ŭi t'ŭkjil—Pan bonggŏnjŏk t'oji soyuje ŭi ch'angch'ul kwajŏng e kwanhan punsŏk" (The characteristics of the land survey—An analysis of the creation of the semi-feudal land system) and included in *Chosŏn t'oji munje nongo* (A study of land problems in Chosŏn) (1946). See also Kang Mangil, *Ilche sidae pinmin saenghwalsa yŏn'gu* (A history of the life of the poor in the colonial period) (Seoul: Ch'angjak kwa pip'yŏngsa, 1987), chapter 1, "Nongch'on pinmin ŭi saenghwal" (The life of the rural poor); Kang T'aehun, "Ilcheha Chosŏn ŭi nongminch'ŭng punhae e kwanhan yŏn'gu" (An examination of rural class differentiation in colonial Chosŏn) in *Han'guk kŭndae nongch'on sahoe wa nongmin undong*.

slash-and-burn farmers (*hwajŏnmin*) and agricultural wage-laborers grew to the point where they became statistically relevant.[33]

In 1917, owner-cultivators amounted to less than 20% of all farm households, and after peaking in 1922, their numbers began to decrease even more (see Table 3). From 1923, the Government-General attempted to raise the percentage of owner-cultivators by including Type B landlords in the category of "owner-cultivator," but it was impossible to stop the overall trend of decline. In addition, semi-tenants (*cha-sojaknong*) accounted for 40.2% of all farm households in 1917, but thereafter, their percentage continually decreased until it was only 23.8% in 1939. The decrease in the numbers of both owner-cultivators and semi-tenants meant that many of them had become landless, reduced to the status of tenant farmers. Accordingly, between 1917 and 1939, the percentage of tenants increased from 37.4% to 52.4%, and other landless peasants were forced to become slash-and-burn farmers or agricultural wage-laborers.

Based only on the data in Table 3, it might be possible to conclude that the differentiation of the peasant class was not a significant problem in this period. Since the number of agricultural laborers was still not large, there appeared to be other opportunities to make a living in rural areas. This table, however, does not accurately reflect the nature of the differentiation of rural society. At the time, industry in Korea had not developed to the point that it could absorb all the excess rural population, and it was not until the late 1930s that Japan implemented industrial policies that made such development possible. Even if many peasants went bankrupt and lost their land, they remained either in the agricultural community or in the towns and so cannot be included in the laborer class. The excess agricultural population was not even partially absorbed into urban wage-laborers or industrial workers until the implementation of industrialization policies in the latter half of the 1930s.[34]

33. Chosŏn Ch'ongdokbu Norinkyoku, *Chosen nochi nenpo* (Annual report of Korean agricultural lands) (1940), p. 139, see the table of the "Number of tenant households in regards to the number of farm households for all of Chosŏn" and Table 3 of this chapter; see Kang Mangil, ibid., chapter 2 "Hwajŏnmin ŭi saenghwal" (The life of slash-and-burn farmers).

34. Yi Hun'gu, "Nongch'on ingu tosi chipjung ŭi wŏnin" (The origins of the urban concentration of rural peasants), *Chogwang*, no. 30 (April 1938); Tadahisa Koji, "Chosen in okeru nomin rison" (Korean peasants leaving their villages), *Shokugin chosa geppo* (Monthly report of the Industrial Bank of Chosŏn) 34 (1941); Tadahisa Koji, "Senjika Chosen no rodomondai" (The labor problems of wartime Chosŏn), *Shokugin chosa geppo* 38 (1931); An Pyŏngjik, "Nihon Chisso ni okeru Chosenjin rodosha kaikyu no seicho ni kansuru kenkyu" (An examination of the development of the Chosŏn laborers class at Japan Nitrogenous Fertilizer Company," *Chosenshi*

The majority of dispossessed peasants could not find work in Korea, with the exception of those who became slash-and-burn farmers in the mountains or highland areas. The only way for them to survive was to migrate to Japan, Manchuria, or Siberia, and indeed, the number of emigrants increased more and more each year. From 1922 to 1942, the number of emigrants to Manchuria increased from 650,000 (around 103,000 households) to 1,560,000,[35] and there were approximately 960,000 emigrants to Japan in 1919.[36] Although the migrants were certainly not all dispossessed peasants, the majority were peasants who had lost their land and were driven out of rural villages. If the number of emigrants is taken into account along with the data from Table 3, then the differentiation of the peasant class was indeed a serious problem in this period. In short, Japan's agricultural policies drove Korean peasants off their land and out of the country, while enabling Japanese landlords and capitalists to buy up their land. It is in these developments that the causes of the problems in the agricultural economy can be found.

The Characteristics of the Landlord System and the Rural Crisis

Although land accumulation by the landlord-capitalist class was one factor behind the problems in the agricultural economy, it was not enough, in and of itself, to cause these difficulties. The severity of the land problem was intensified because the management methods of agricultural businesses facilitated the thorough exploitation of the Korean peasantry. These methods were an integral aspect of land accumulation. Through their exploitative management practices, landlords and capitalists brought about the failure and differentiation of the Korean peasantry. As a result, they increased their landholdings even more by buying up the land of bankrupt peasants. Ultimately, the root of the problems in the agricultural economy lay in the contradictory

kenkyukai ronbunshu 25 (1988); Yu Sŭngnyŏl, "Ilche ŭi Chosŏn kwang'ŏp chibae wa nodong kyekŭp ŭi sŏngjang" (Japan's control of Korea's mining and the development of the labor class), *Han'guk saron*, no. 23 (1990).

35. Ko Sŭngje, *Han'guk i'minsa yŏn'gu* (A study of the history of immigration in Korea) (Seoul: Changmungak, 1973), pp. 91, 100; Tadahisa Koji, "Senjika Chosen no rodomondai" (The labor problems of wartime Chosŏn), *Shokugin chosa geppo* 38 (1931).

36. Ko Sŭngje, ibid., pp. 237, 282; Kang Hundŏk, "Ilcheha kungnae sojak chaeng'ŭi wa haeoe iju nongmin" (Domestic peasant disputes in the colonial period and peasants immigrating overseas), *Han'guksa yŏn'gu*, no. 45 (1984).

relationship between the landlord-capitalist class and the peasant producers which was mediated by these management methods. Agricultural businesses were managed through the landlord-tenant system, and the contradictions of this system ultimately led to the rise of the peasant movement, which took the form of tenancy disputes.

The fact that large landholders adopted the landlord-tenant system to manage their businesses was closely related to the characteristics of Japanese capitalism. In fact, the landlord system was an embodiment of the very nature of Japanese capitalism. This economic system conveniently facilitated Japan's goal of achieving the greatest efficiency in exploiting Korean agriculture and the peasantry. Its purpose certainly was not to dismantle the feudal landlord system through an agricultural revolution nor, consequently, to stabilize the peasant economy.

As Japan reached the stage of monopoly capitalism in the 1920s and the stage of national monopoly capitalism in the 1930s, all economic institutions came to abide by capitalist principles.[37] Despite such changes, agricultural production in Japan did not resemble that of Western capitalist states. In Western countries, the social structure of agriculture generally consisted of landlords at the top followed by capitalist agricultural entrepreneurs (tenants) and then agricultural workers at the bottom, or, alternatively, landlords followed by capitalists and then agricultural workers. In contrast, Japan preserved the agricultural practices and relations of production of the Chosŏn period's feudal mode of production and transplanted its landlord system to Korea. The result was a structure that consisted of landlords at the top and tenant farmers at the bottom, or landlords followed by capitalists and then tenant farmers.[38]

In order to occupy Korea and exploit its agriculture and peasantry, Japan maintained the old feudal relations of production and agricultural customs as the basis of agricultural production. At the same time, Japan took control of all the institutions of Korean agriculture through the operation of monopoly and finance capital.[39]

---

37. Kajinishi Mitsuhaya, et al., *Nihon shihonshugi no botsuraku* (The decline of Japanese capitalism) I-IV (Tokyo: Tokyo Daigaku Shuppankai, 1975); Yamazaki Ryuzo, et al., *Ryotaisen kanki no Nihon shihonshugi* (Japanese capitalism in the interwar period), vols. 1-2 (Tokyo: Otsuki shoten, 1978).

38. See Asada Kyoji, *Nihon teikokushugi to kyu shokuminchi jinushisei* (Japanese imperialism and colonial landlordism) (Tokyo: Ochanomizuo shobo, 1968), chapters 1, 3.

39. Pak Insu, "Ponggŏn yuje wa kŭm'yung chabon kwa ŭi yahap" (The conspiracy between the feudal remnants and financial capital), *Sinhŭng*, no. 4 (January 1931); Pak Mun'gyu, ibid.; Pak Mun'gyu, "Chosŏn nongch'on kigu ŭi t'ong'gyejŏk haesŏl" (A statistical explanation of the

What were the reasons that the landlord-tenant system became the central factor in problems in the agricultural economy during this period? What were its characteristics as an economic system? What irrationalities were inherent in it? There is no need to go over the details of the landlord-tenant system since it has already been discussed above and since there are many primary sources and much research on the topic. However, since problems in the agricultural economy led to the rise of the peasant movement and tenancy disputes over the landlord-tenant system, it is necessary to point out at least some of the major economic aspects of this system in order to understand the roots of the movement.

First, the landlord-tenant system in this period was a pro-landlord system based upon the principles of freedom of contract and of private land ownership as practiced in Japan. Since the rights of landowners were inalienable, the state could not encroach upon these rights. Landowners were free to lease their land to tenant farmers in accordance with the relevant sections in the civil law, and the provisions of this law also gave legal protection to their methods of managing their farms and *nongjang*.[40] Considering the fact that 80% of the population were peasants and that 70-80% of all peasants were tenant farmers, it would have been logical to have legal provisions—such as a "Tenancy Law"—that protected the livelihood of tenants. The Government-General, however, showed no such concern until the enactment of the Chosŏn Agricultural Lands Ordinance (Chosŏn nongjiryŏng; aka, Tenancy Law) in 1934. Not only did Japan ignore the interests of Korean peasants, but it did not even provide legal protection for its own peasantry.[41] Since the legal system of capitalist countries is usually designed to serve the interests of owners, the state's primary concern was the interests of landlords. In such a

---

Korean rural structure), *Sinhŭng*, no. 9 (May 1935); Pak Mun'gyu, "Chosŏn nong'ŏp saengsan kwangye go—Panbonggŏnjŏk t'oji soyuje - pan-nongnojejŏk yŏngse kyŏngjak kigu e kwanhan punsŏk" (The relations of production of Korean agriculture—an analysis of the semi-feudal land ownership system and the semi-serfdom system of the petty cultivation structure) (1936 manuscript, published in 1946 in *Inmin kwahak* and *Chosŏn t'oji munje non'go*); Paek Nam'un, ibid. (1938); No Tonggyu, ibid. See footnote 12; In Chŏngsik, "Chosŏn nongch'on kyŏngje ŭi yŏn'gu" (A study of the Korean rural economy), *Chungang* (February–September 1936).

40. Sawamura Yasushi, *Nogyo tochi seisakuron* (On agricultural land policies) (Tokyo: Yokendo, 1933), p. 1; Sawamura Yasushi, *Kosakuho to jisakuno soteiho* (The Tenancy Law and the Law to Promote Self-Cultivation) (Tokyo: Kaizosha, 1927), p. 563.

41. See Kondo Yasuo, *Nihon nogyoron* (Theories on Japanese agriculture), vol. 1, Chapter 1, section 4, "The Development of the Agricultural Lands Law—solution from above" (Tokyo: Ochanomizu shobo, 1970). In Japan, after the failure to pass the Tenancy Law in 1931, elements of this law were enacted in the Agricultural Lands Arbitration Ordinance of 1938.

situation, it was difficult to expect the state to provide legal protection for tenant farmers.

Second, although the landlord-tenant system was not a formal legalized institution, its customs were as binding as the force of law and as widespread as a formal economic institution. This system had developed over time from the agricultural practices and customs of the feudal landlord system which, in turn, was based on the long-standing tradition of *pyŏngjak pansu* under which the tenant gave half the harvest to the landlord. The transformation of these traditional customs into a lessor-lessee relationship under a modern civil code gave legal protection to the landlord-tenant system.[42] Other factors in this transformation were the rational, exploitative economic logic of capitalism and the avarice of landlords and capitalists. As examined above, the rights that tenants had traditionally enjoyed (e.g., tenancy tenure, tenancy rates) were gradually eroded, while the rights of landlords under Japanese capitalism became greatly strengthened.

Japan had initially taken a flexible approach to landlord management in Korea, following traditional agricultural practices. However, as it tightened its rule over Korea, Japan increased its exploitation of the peasantry and its pursuit of profit by employing stricter methods of landlord management. As feudal agricultural practices came to operate under capitalist management principles, the landlord-tenant system effectively functioned as an institution that greatly increased the landlords' and capitalists' exploitation of the peasantry in comparison with the past.

Third, in capitalist societies, tenant farmers were generally viewed, in terms of social status, as either entrepreneurial farmers or capitalist tenants who operated as independent agricultural producers. However, in Korea, it was difficult for tenant farmers to attain such status under the tenant-landlord system. There were entrepreneurial tenants who managed their farmland by using agricultural workers or wage laborers,[43] but they were few in number.

---

42. See Yoshida Masahiro, *Chosen ni okeru kosaku ni kansuru kihon hoki no kaisetu* (A commentary on the basic laws concerning tenants in Korea) (Kyŏngsŏng-bu: Chosen Nosei Kenkyu Doshikai, 1934), "Regulations Regarding Tenancy in the Second Civil Law" in Appendix 1.

43. Pak Sŏngryŏng, "Nongch'on munje kangjwa—nongch'on ŭi kyegŭpsang" (A lecture on rural issues—the class situation of rural society), *Chosŏn ilbo*, March 30–April 10, 1930; No Tonggyu, ibid., (1932, 1933). See footnotes 12 and 14; Yi Kakjong, "Chosŏn ŭi nongch'on munje wa ki taech'aek" (The rural problems of Korea and responses to it), *Sinmin*, no. 8 (1925); Ono Tamotsu, "Chosen noson no jittaiteki kenkyu" (A study of the actual condition of rural Chosŏn), *Ronso* 4 (Daido gakuin, 1941), pp. 268-71.

The vast majority of tenant farmers either was engaged in subsistence agriculture or had fallen to the status of agricultural laborers.

In general, agricultural production in a capitalist economy involves three or four factors: land, management (business), labor, and/or capital. Each factor receives a share of the product in proportion to the amount each contributed to production. Tenant farmers, as agricultural producers, usually contributed labor and a portion of the agricultural capital. However, since they had to pay high tenancy fees and bear other financial burdens, their compensation was not equivalent to that of an entrepreneurial farmer; instead, they were compensated only for their labor or even less.[44] Of course, the situation was generally the same under both Korean and Japanese landlords, but the latter case tended to be more severe. In the case of Japanese landlords, owners of the *nongjang* would invest in land, run the business directly, and put up much of the agricultural capital. Because the landlord collected high tenancy fees in return for these expenditures, tenants received, at most, only compensation for their labor.

Historians have engaged in a lively debate on the social status of tenant farmers during the occupation period. Scholars who have taken a theoretical approach to the issue have been quick to conclude that tenant farmers were agricultural laborers or belonged to a comparable class rather than independent agricultural producers. They have put forth the following arguments on the nature of the landlord system:

1. Tenant farmers must be seen as agricultural laborers.[45]
2. The nature of tenancy is that of a "labor tenant system."[46]
3. As feudal agriculture developed into a capitalist system, "small farmers were being transformed into wage laborers."[47]

44. Yi Hun'gu, "Sojak munje ŭi kyŏngjehakjŏk il koch'al" (An economic study of the tenancy problem), *Chosŏn ilbo*, August 19–September 13, 1927; SY, "Sojak undong ŭi kuich'akjŏm" (The outcome of the tenant movement), *Kaebyŏk* (January 1926); Kwang U, ibid; Pak Mun'gyu, ibid. (see footnote 32); Pak Yongnae, "Chosŏn sojak munje wa nongjiryŏng ŭi silsi" (The tenancy problem in Chosŏn and the implementation of the Agricultural Lands Ordinance), *Chosŏn ilbo*, January 1-2, 1935; Ono Tamotsu, ibid., p. 215.
45. Yi Sŏnghwan, "Kia sŏnsang karonohin Chosŏn ŭi nong'ŏp nodongja munje" (The problem of starving agricultural laborers in Chosŏn), *Kaebyŏk*, no. 62 (August 1925).
46. Asakura Noboru, "Chosen no kosaku mondai to sono taisaku" (The tenancy problem of Chosŏn and its solution), *Nogyo keizai kenkyu* 7-2 (1931).
47. Tsumagari Kuranajo, "Chosen ni okeru kosaku mondai no hatten katei" (The development of the tenancy problem in Chosŏn), *Chosen keizai no kenkyu*, Funada Kyoji, ed. (Tokyo: Toko shoin, 1929).

Scholars have also proposed a variety of theories on the tenancy system in Japanese-owned *nongjang*:

1. It was a special kind of semi-employment agricultural system.[48]
2. Although tenants appeared to be entrepreneurs, they were actually agricultural laborers.[49]
3. Similar to the sharecropper system in plantations in the U.S., it was a profit-sharing system similar to an employment contract system.[50]
4. The nature of landlord-tenant relations in *nongjang* were actually closer to an employer-employee relationship based on a contract.[51]
5. Tenants were agricultural laborers whose wages were not fixed.[52]

Nonetheless, Japanese landlords and capitalists refrained from operating their *nongjang* only with agricultural laborers and persisted in using tenant farmers. Employing tenants was more efficient in exploiting the labor needed to run the *nongjang*,[53] and it also enabled landlords and capitalists to shift most of the responsibility and risks of capital expenditure to the tenants.[54] Despite differences in each province, the occupation government's position toward tenants was the same throughout the country. Through the Agricultural Lands Ordinance (1934), the government adopted a policy of preventing the decline of tenants to the status of agricultural laborers.[55] By allowing tenants to maintain the appearance of being independent agricultural

---

48. Kwang U, ibid.

49. Hisama Ken'ichi, *Chosen nosei no kadai* (The tasks of agricultural administration in Chosŏn) (Tokyo: Selbido, 1943), pp. 327-29. It resembles the expression found in Kim Yŏngjin, "Ilch'ŏnman sojak'in ŭl taehayo" (Regarding 10,000 tenants), *Sinmin*, no. 12 (April 1926). Such views have also been advanced about the tenant-landlord system in Japan. See Oki Masamu, "Jinushi wa nogyosha desu ka" (Are landlords farmers?), *Nogyo to keizai* 1-2 (1934).

50. Sawamura Yasushi, *Nogyo seisaku* (Agricultural policy), vol. 1 (1932), pp. 204-08, 283; Sawamura Yasushi, *Kosakuho to jisakuno soteiho*, pp. 528-31.

51. Miyoshi Toyotaro, "Nogyo keieisha no giseiteki kairyo jigyo ni tokyaku no rikai wo motomu" (Asking for the understanding of the authorities in the sacrificial improvement activities of the agricultural managers), *Chosen nokaiho* (Bulletin of the Agricultural Association of Chosŏn) 4-2 (1930).

52. Tohata Seiichi, *Nihon nogyo no tenkai katei* (The development of Japanese agriculture) (Tokyo: Iwanami shoten, 1936) (revised edition), p. 68.

53. Sawamura Yasushi (1927), p. 531; Oki Masamu, ibid.

54. Kang Yŏnt'aek, "Chosen nogyo ni okeru seisan shisutemu no bunka" (The division of production systems in Korean agriculture) *Nogyo keizai kenkyu* 15-3 (1939).

55. Article 2 of Chosŏn nongjiryong (Chosŏn Agricultural Lands Ordinance) did not recognize contracts for practices such as employment farming and contract farming. See section 4 of this chapter.

producers, the Japanese authorities tried, out of political considerations, to counter criticism from society about their exploitative agricultural policies.[56]

Fourth, another characteristic of the landlord-tenant system under Japanese capitalism was that the economic situation of tenant farmers was truly desperate as they were mainly engaged in extremely small-scale, petty agriculture. Under this system, it is not surprising that tenants faced such dire circumstances. The severity of their situation was even more evident in the size of the landholdings they cultivated. As indicated in Table 7 (p. 168), there were some tenants who operated medium- and large-scale farms. However, because of a surplus rural population and the lack of urban industries to absorb it, the great majority of tenant farmers in this period was engaged in either small-scale agriculture (less than one *chŏngbo* of paddy and fields) or subsistence agriculture (less than three *tanbo*). More specifically, about 60.5% of all semi-tenants were at that level, as were 67% of all tenants. With such small landholdings, it would have been difficult to support their households even if they had been able to keep the entire harvest. The number of peasants who emigrated to Manchuria or Japan continued to grow, and later, the number of peasants migrating to cities also increased. Nevertheless, the problem of extremely small-scale, subsistence farming remained unresolved.

During the occupation period, subsistence farmers had to pay excessively high tenancy fees, and landlords also shifted the burden of fertilizer costs and various taxes and fees to the peasants. It was common for peasants to be running deficits, but even if they were able to avoid deficits, they would not have enough surplus left to maintain their households.[57] In the spring, they faced poverty and starvation since their food supplies would have already run out.[58] Being a tenant farmer in this period was synonymous with being

56. Yoshida Masahiro, ibid., p. 16.

57. See 'Noka no yojo' (The surplus of farm households) of the clauses for tenants, semi-tenants in Chosen nokai (Agricultural Association of Chosŏn), *Noka keizai chosa* (Economic survey of farm households), (Kyonggi, South Chŏlla, South Kyŏngsang, South P'yŏng'an, and South Hamgyŏng Provinces in 1930-32); Kim Yongbok, "Sojakin ŭi kobaek" (The confession of tenants), *Sinmin*, no. 12 (April 1926); Cho Minhyŏng, *Chosŏn nongch'on kuchech'aek* (Aid policies for rural Chosŏn) (1930), see the appendix, "Sojaknong tojak 1,2 chŏngbo suji kaesan" (Estimated income and expenditures for rice-farming tenants with 1 to 2 chongbo (of land)); In Chŏngsik, "Chosen nomin seikatsu no jokyo" (The situation of Korean peasant life), *Chosa geppo* (Monthly survey report) (1940), issue 3-4; Himeno Minoru, ed., *Chosen keizai zuhyo* (Statistical graphs and charts on the Chosŏn economy) (Kyŏngsŏng: Chosen Tokei Kyokai, 1940), pp. 175-77; Takahashi Kamekichi, ibid., p. 228.

58. See Chosŏn Ch'ongdokbu, *Chosen no sosaku kanko* (Tenancy customs in Korea) (1932), second volume, chapter 12, "Chajaknong kŭp sojaknong chung ŭi ch'un'gungmin kŭp imgŭm nodong ŭl haengha nŭn sojaknong hosu" (The number of tenant households suffering hardship

destitute and hungry. In newspapers and journals, criticism of high tenancy fees, the landlords' transfer of various taxes and fees to the peasants, and the feudal forced labor system appeared continually. However, it was difficult to restrain these forms of exploitation since there was fierce competition for land among tenants. Tenants had no choice but to submit to the exploitation resulting from the imposition of starvation rents by the landlord class and the burden of various other financial obligations.

Because of these kinds of exploitation, tenant farmers had to work as wage-laborers on other people's farms in order to support their families. But even that extra work was not enough to solve their difficulties. Despite the heavy work involved, wages for agricultural laborers were very low compared to those for the average urban worker.[59] Suffering from the burden of high rents, tenants relied on high-interest loans to overcome their financial problems. They ended up accumulating debts and became trapped in a state of continual exploitation in which they virtually became in-dentured slaves. Not surprisingly, intellectuals in this period regarded tenant farmers engaged in subsistence agriculture as "a kind of serf"[60] or a "serf with freedom in name only."[61] One intellectual called the landlord-tenant system a "system of rural slavery disguised as capitalism."[62]

In sum, the landlord-tenant system made it difficult for tenants to survive under the economy of the occupation period. As the countryside

and becoming wage labor, among owner-cultivators and tenants) and Chosŏn Ch'ongdokbu Norinkyoku, *Chosen ni okeru kosaku ni kansuru sanko jiko tekiyo* (1932), p. 24, table, "Ch'ungye sikryang tangyonggi e saenghwal kungbip han nongga hosu" (The number of destitute farm households during the spring non-harvest season) (1930 survey). According to these sources, 18.4% of owner-cultivators, 37.5% of semi-tenants, 68.1% of tenants were short of food and destitute. Reports on social problems related to this situation appeared numerous times at the time in several newspapers.

59. Il kija (anonymous reporter), "Nongch'on kwa nodong munje" (The problems of rural society and labor), *Kongje*, no. 7 (April 1921); Yu Chinhŭi, "Sojak undong kwa kŭ naeyong kŏmkyu" (An examination of tenant movements and their details) *Tonga ilbo*, March 25, 1925; Sŏn'u Chŏn, "Nongmin ŭi tosi ichŏn kwa nong'ŏp nodong ŭi pulli ŭi che wŏn'in" (The migration of peasants to the cities and various origins of the disadvantageous situation of agricultural labor) *Kaebyŏk*, no. 26 (August 1922); Kim Yŏngjin, "Il ch'ŏnman sojakin ŭl taehayŏ" (Regarding 10,000 tenants), *Sinmin*, no. 12 (April 1926). See also *Sutja Chosŏn yŏn'gu* (1932), vol. 2, chapter 4, "Chosŏn nodongja hyonhwang" (The present position of Korean workers), section 4, "Chosŏn nodongja ŭi imgum" (The wages of Korean laborers).

60. Il kija (anonymous reporter), "Nongch'on kwa nodong munje."

61. Yi Sunt'ak, "Nodong undong kwa sojak undong ŭi hyŏpdong" (Cooperation between the labor movement and the tenant movement), *Kaebyŏk* (May 1924).

62. Pak Shimgyŏng, "Chosŏn nongch'on munje ŭi hyŏnje wa changnae" (The present and future of the Korean rural problems), *Chosŏn chi kwang*, no. 81 (November-December 1928).

became impoverished, large numbers of tenant farmers constantly faced starvation. Many ended up migrating to Japan, Manchuria, China, or Siberia, and those who did not were reduced to becoming slash-and-burn farmers (see Table 3). Even if some tenants managed to avoid falling into such circumstances, it was still difficult for them to become stable and independent agricultural producers. Many of them had already become de facto wage-tenants or destitute agricultural laborers who were under the domination of the landlord-capitalist class. They were being turned into indentured slaves, suffering from high-interest debts, who found themselves in a situation where it seemed impossible to regain their lost status.

The Consequence of the Agrarian Crisis: The Peasant Movement

The problems in the agricultural economy during the occupation period ultimately resulted in the rise of the peasant movement. In order to survive under these economic conditions, tenant farmers had to rebel against the landlord-capitalist class and engage in active struggle. Because the landlord-capitalist class, which was responsible for creating these conditions, was economically powerful and backed by the state, the movement had to employ effective methods of resistance and engage in continual struggle over a long period of time in order to achieve its goals. In fact, this was the way the movement of tenant farmers developed in Korea. As the movement emerged during the 1920s and 1930s, it engaged in a series of tenancy disputes by the peasants. As Table 8 shows (p. 168), the outbreak of tenancy disputes was quite frequent. There is not enough space here to discuss the development of tenancy disputes in detail. However, to achieve a better understanding of the nature of the landlord system, it is necessary to go over at least the main points of the intellectual background of the movement as well as its demands, organizations, aims, and ideology.

The intellectual influences on the peasant movement are generally regarded as coming from two main sources: economic and class thought, on the one hand, and nationalist and political thought, on the other. Some scholars have emphasized only one of the two kinds of thought, but starting from the 1920s and 1930s, scholarship on the movement has generally treated both.[63]

63. Paek Nam'un, "Chosen keizai no gendankairon." According to Paek, the social problems of the colonial period were determined politically nationalistic conflict, and socioeconomically, by

Scholarship on economic and class thought has argued that tenants developed an antagonistic class consciousness toward landlords because they felt that their miserable economic situation was caused by land accumulation and the resulting exploitation by the Japanese landlord-capitalist class.[64] In reality, the development of this class consciousness was already widespread by the end of the feudal period. As socialist thought—the so-called "new thought" (sin sasang)—was introduced into Korea in the 1920s, it influenced the labor class both consciously and unconsciously as well as in direct and indirect ways, since it had a large influence on Korean political and social movements. In the process, existing forms of class consciousness came to be expressed through the new socialist thought. Because of their dire economic situation, it was natural that tenant farmers would engage in a peasant movement under the influence and leadership of this new form of social thought.

On the influence of nationalist and political thought, both observers at the time and later scholars noted that the exploited Korean peasantry and

capitalistic and class conflict. See also Yi Sŏnghwan, "Chosŏn nongmin undong ŭi chŏngse" (The state of peasant movements in Chosŏn), Chosŏn ilbo, January 1, 1928. According to Yi, the goals of the peasant movement organizations can be generally categorized as follows:

1. Aiming for support and improvement in tenancy conditions from the landlords.
2. Aiming for friendship with and education of the peasants and improvements in rural customs.
3. Embracing the entire peasant class to solve the urgent national problems.
4. Aiming for economic improvement through agricultural reform and credit, consumer, and sales cooperatives.

Among those, it was indicated that goals 1 and 3 had the most support, and the significance of the peasant movement was viewed as follows:

"We can see the direction in which the Korean peasant movement is advancing and developing. Namely, the former (goal 1) is comparatively class-oriented and engaged in struggle. Because the scope of the struggle is largely limited to the economic sphere, it is doubtful whether the distinctiveness of Korea in the purpose and the means (special areas being a separate problem) can be fully grasped. However, the latter (goal 3) is not only the acquisition of immediate, economic gain. . . excluding special areas, there are many cases where the Korean peasant movement can join with the latter. In any case, the struggle. . . advancing as a political struggle that is separate from the economic struggle is also necessary. That there is, in Korea, the advance of a political struggle by peasants to resolve the urgent national problems is of particular importance."

According to Kobayakawa Kuro, ed., Chosen nogyo hattatsushi (The history of Korean agricultural development, Seisakuhen (policy volume) (Kyŏngsŏng: Chosen Nokai, 1944), p. 531), those economic conditions were suddenly changed by World War I and the tenancy disputes were no longer simple economic disputes but merged with the ideological and nationalist struggle. While becoming extremely complex and rancorous, the disputes became the frontline of the struggle.

64. Chosŏn Ch'ongdokbu, "Chosen no gunshu" (The Chosŏn masses), Chosa shiryo 16 (1926), p. 15; Asakura Noboru, "Chosen no sosaku mondai to sono taisaku" (The tenancy problems of Korea and countermeasures), Nogyo keizai kenkyu 7-2 (1931); Yi Hun'gu, "Nongch'on chungsan kyegup ŭi mollak kwa kŭ taechaek."

tenant farmers developed a nationalist consciousness and an intense hatred toward the Japanese landlord-capitalist class as well as toward Japanese imperialism.[65] These sentiments developed because it was Japanese capitalist institutions that occupied Korea, dominated Korean agriculture, and exploited the Korean peasantry. Furthermore, within the landlord-capitalist class, the Japanese were the main group bringing about the decline of the tenant farmer class. Because nationalist sentiment lay just under the surface of their everyday lives, the peasants needed only some sort of stimulus to trigger the emergence of a peasant movement that would engage in national political struggle. The necessary stimulus was provided in the 1920s when Japan's discriminatory agricultural policies and exploitation of the peasantry reached their peak. At the same time, the socialist national liberation movement and the so-called "Culture Movement" encouraged peasants to get involved in efforts to create a "new society" that were, in reality, political movements. These movements began to emerge gradually around 1920 both within Korea and abroad.[66]

The influence of these two kinds of thought on the peasant movement was obviously not the same in all periods and in all regions of the country. Nonetheless, peasant movements came increasingly under their influence in several regions. As these movements underwent growth and development, the

65. "Chosŏn nongmin undong ŭi chŏngch'ijŏk kyŏnghyang" (The political tendencies of the Chosŏn peasant movement), *Chosŏn ilbo* (editorial), March 24-26, 1925; Sawamura Yasushi, *Nogyo seisaku*, vol. 1, pp. 281, 283; Kim Kisŭng, "Pae Sŏngryong ŭi chongch'i-kyŏngje sasang yŏn'gu" (A study of the political and economic thought of Pae Sŏngryong) (Ph.D. diss., Korea University, 1991), p. 85.

66. The Korean Socialist Party (*Hanin sahoedang*) (1918-1921) and the Koryŏ Communist Party (*Koryŏ kongsandang*) (1921-1922) were established, respectively, in the Soviet Union and China. Their party regulations, manifestoes, and platforms were disseminated to domestic activists, and within Korea, various newspapers and magazines published articles introducing socialist thought (Kim Chŏngmyŏng, ed., *Chosŏn tongnip undong* (The Korean independence movement) (Kyŏngsŏng: Wŏnsŏbang, 1967) 5, Part 7, "Basic documents regarding the Korean communist movement;" principles of the Korean Socialist Party (1920), the manifesto, party platform, and party regulations of the Korean Communist Party (1921)). For example, studies by Japanese socialist thinkers on the peasant movement were translated and spread to the general public (e.g., Sano Manabu, "Sahoejuŭi wa minjok undong" (Socialism and national movements), *Tonga ilbo*, July 4-12, 1923; "Sahoejuŭi wa nong'ŏp munje" (Socialism and agricultural problems), *Tonga ilbo*, August 30-September 9, 1923; "Sahoejuŭi wa nongmin munje" (Socialism and peasant problems), *Tonga ilbo*, November 8-14, 1923; "Sahoejuŭi wa nongmin undong" (Socialism and peasant movements), *Sasang undong* 3-2, 1996). However, it probably took a long time for documents and works from abroad to reach domestic intellectuals and then to be spread among the masses. For an overview of the ideology of the socialist movement, see Kim Myŏng-gu, "1920 nyŏndae chŏnban'gi sahoe undong i'nyŏm e issŏsŏ ŭi nongmin undongron" (Peasant movement theory in the social movement ideology of the early 1920s), *Han'guk kŭndae nongch'on sahoe wa nongmin undong.*

two kinds of thought became combined into a single ideology, and these changes elevated the peasant movement from an economic struggle focusing on tenant disputes into an anti-imperial, anti-feudal political movement whose objective was "national liberation" and "national revolution." The transformation of the peasant movement was closely related to the socialists' strategy for the national liberation movement. The Korean Communist Party (KCP), the vanguard party of socialism, was established within Korea and set strategy for the liberation movement together with the Communist International (Comintern).[67] Influenced and guided by the KCP and Comintern, the peasant movement completely followed their strategy in the late 1920s and early 1930s.

Tenancy disputes reach their peak as a form of peasant resistance when they become a political movement, and this is what gradually happened in Korea during this period. Though the factors behind the emergence of tenancy disputes were related to issues of great significance, they usually began with relatively modest demands such as the rectification of the irrationalities and contradictions in the landlord-tenant system, which was the context for these disputes. The demands and slogans of tenants focused on four central issues (among others):

1. the deprivation of tenant rights (*sojakgwŏn*) (the tenants' right of cultivation)—i.e., the [arbitrary] change of tenants
2. high tenancy fees
3. the landlords' transfer of the payment of taxes and fees to their tenants
4. intermediary exploitation by the agents of the landlords[68]

Point 1 called for the stabilization of tenancy rights for tenant farmers, and point 2 referred to a demand that the high tenancy fees be lowered to

---

67. See Chosŏn Ch'ongdokbu, *Kyosanshugi undo ni kansuru bunkenshu* (Collected documents on the communist movement) (1936), and Kim Chŏngmyŏng, ibid. (1967). Among the basic documents of the Chosŏn communist movement, see "Theses on National and Colonial Problems" (the Lenin theses), and the "General Theses on Eastern Problems." See also the "Chosŏn kongsandang sŏn'ŏnsŏ" (Manifesto of the Korean Communist Party) in "Interrogation of Ku Yŏnhŭm, an official of the Communist Party" in Kajimura Hideki and Kang Tŏksang, eds., "Kyosanshugi undo" (The communist movement), *Gendaishi shiryo 29* (Documents of modern history), *Chosen* 5 (Tokyo: Misuzu shobo, 1972), pp. 419-22.

68. Chosŏn Ch'ongdokbu, *Chosa siryo* (Survey materials of the Government-General of Chosŏn) 26, *Chosen no kosaku kanshu* (1929), p. 60; Chosŏn Ch'ongdokbu, *Chosen ni okeru kosaku ni kansuru sanko jiko tekiyo*, pp. 83-87; Chosŏn Ch'ongdokbu, *Chosen nochi nenpo* (Yearbook of Chosŏn Agriculture) 1, pp. 20-24.

30-40% of the harvest and that estimated fees be decreased in years of a bad harvest. Points 3 and 4 expressed a demand for the elimination of indirect methods of exploitation by the landlord class and of intermediary exploitation by employees of the landlord (e.g., *saŭm*) which occurred under various guises.[69]

However, as the peasant movement grew, the slogans and demands of the peasants went beyond these issues and became more radical. In the 1930s, the leaders of the peasant movement directed its aims toward the anti-imperialist, anti-feudal program of "Chosŏn Revolution" (*Chosŏn hyŏkmyŏngnon*). The movement even proposed a program of land revolution and the abolition of the landlord system, advocating a radical peasant revolution.[70]

The development of the peasant movement during the 1920s and 1930s can be seen more clearly through an examination of the organizations of the movement and the ideology that determined its aims. In general, tenant farmer unions (*sojakin chohap*) or peasant unions (*nongmin chohap*) organized tenancy disputes, but they did not emerge in all regions of the country, arising mainly in advanced areas where modern social thought was relatively widespread. Over the course of several stages, the peasant movement clearly underwent a qualitative change through a deepening of the theoretical understanding of ideology and social revolution by the intellectuals who were the leaders of the national liberation movement.

69. These aspects had already appeared in the tenancy disputes in the Sunch'on and Kwangju regions in 1923—which can be seen as the initial stage of the peasant movement. See Hŏ Changman, *1920 nyondae ŭi nongmin undong ŭi paljŏn* (The development of the peasant movement in the 1920s), (Pyongyang: Chosŏn nodongdang ch'ulp'ansa, 1962), pp. 56-60; Kanamori Josaku, "Chosen nomin undo kumiai undosi—1920 nendai no Chinju·Sunch'on wo chushin to shite" (The history of the associations of the Chosŏn peasant movement—centered on Chinju and Sunch'ŏn in the 1920's), *Chosen shiso*, nos. 5-6 (1982).

70. Kajimura Hideki and Kang Tŏksang (1965), "Chosen shakai undo ryakushi koosu" (A short history course of the Korean social movement), ibid., p. 168; Kim Chŏngmyŏng (1967), "Chosŏn e issŏsŏ ŭi nongmin undong ŭi ch'use" (The transition of the peasant movement in Korea), ibid., p. 408; Asada Kyoji, "Chosen ni okeru konichi nomin undo no tenkai katei" (The developmental of the anti-Japanese peasant movement in Korea), *Nihon teikokushugi ka no minzoku kaiho undo* (National liberation movements under Japanese imperialism) (Tokyo: Miraisha, 1973); Sin Chubaek, "1930 nyŏndae Hamgyŏngdo chibang ŭi hyŏngmyŏngjŏk nongmin chohap undong yŏn'gu" (A study of the revolutionary peasant union movement in the Hamgyŏng region during the 1930's) (M.A. thesis, Songgyunkwan University, 1989); Chi Sugŏl. *Ilcheha nongmin chohap undong yŏn'gu: 1930 nyŏndae hyŏngmyŏngjŏk nongmin chohap undong* (A study of the peasant union movement in under Japanese rule: the revolutionary peasant movement in the 1930s) (Seoul: Yŏksa pip'yŏngsa, 1993).

The first stage was the period of the Korean Workers Mutual Aid Association (Chosŏn nodong kongjehoe, WMAA), which was formed in 1920 and guided and promoted the tenants' struggle against large landlords. With a membership consisting of both nationalists and socialists, the WMAA was a labor organization whose purpose was to defend the interests of the proletariat class which included both workers and tenant farmers.[71] It established branch associations throughout the country and organized labor and peasant movements.

In particular, the WMAA provided guidance to peasant and tenant movements through writings such as treatises on tenant farmer unions and articles urging tenants to unite.[72] It also engaged in theoretical struggle to argue systematically for the necessity of such a movement. The WMAA argued that the struggle against the landlords should not take the form of individual efforts by farmers but should be an organized movement that would gain strength by uniting all peasants in organizations such as tenant farmers unions. It also proposed that peasants should push for demands such as a decrease in the high tenancy fees and the legalization of tenancy rights (cultivation rights) in order to reform the irrational tenancy system.[73] In the early 1920s, there were many cases where peasant movements were organized both directly and indirectly under the guidance of the WMAA and the leadership of its members.

Although the peasant movement had anti-landlord and anti-capitalist aspects, it was difficult for the movements guided by the WMAA to organize under a single ideology and, at the same time, maintain horizontal solidarity throughout the country. The difficulties arose because of the simplicity of their strategy and the moderate political tendencies of the labor-peasant organizations that led them. Socialists were dissatisfied with this movement because they wanted to turn it into a thoroughly class-based economic movement. They felt that the movement would be more effective if it were to engage in a class struggle against large landlords and the capitalist class under a single ideology and with the leadership of a single organization.

71. Sin Yongha, "Chosŏn nodong kongjehoe ŭi ch'angnip kwa nodong undong" (The labor movement and the establishment of the Chosŏn Workers Mutual Aid Association), *Han'guk kŭndae sahoesa yŏn'gu* (Seoul: Ilchisa, 1987).

72. Sin Paek'u, "Sojak'in chohapnon" (Theory of tenant association), *Kongje*, no. 2 (1920); "Sojak'in munje e taehayŏ—Nodong kongjehoe ŭi sŏn'ŏn" (On the tenancy problem—the declaration of the Korean Workers Mutual Aid Association), *Tonga ilbo*, July 31-August 3, 1922.

73. Yu Chinhŭi, "Sojak undong kwa kŭ naeyong kŭmkyu" (An examination of the tenant movement and its contents) *Tonga ilbo*, March 21-29, 1921.

The second stage was the period of the leadership of the Chosŏn Worker-Peasant League (Chosŏn nonong ch'ong tongmaeng), which was formed in 1924. Socialist activists, who were dissatisfied with the WMAA, believed that more efficient leadership organs were necessary in order for the peasant movement to be more effective. Their thinking was shaped by their experiences in tenancy disputes in all regions of the country, and they were convinced of the necessity for a union of all tenant unions. Their efforts led to the creation of the Chosŏn Worker-Peasant League as the leadership organization of the labor and peasant movements.[74] As a result, the peasant movement came to operate, directly and indirectly, under the League's leadership and influence.

The membership of the Chosŏn Worker-Peasant League was composed of socialists from various factions. Since they all were followers of Marxism-Leninism, the League was able to become an organization that pursued a single ideology, and thus, the peasant movement under its leadership could also become unified. They proclaimed their political views and objectives in the following platform:

1. We take as our goal the realization of a completely new society through the liberation of the labor-peasant class.

2. We promise to engage in a total struggle against the capitalist class through the power of solidarity until we achieve final victory.

3. We seek the promotion of welfare and economic improvement in accordance with the present conditions of the labor-peasant class.[75]

Their objective was to build a new society—i.e., a socialist society—in Korea by instilling class consciousness in the labor-peasant class and by organizing a class struggle against landlords and capitalists through the united strength of a labor-peasant class armed with that class consciousness. Their views were not unreasonable, considering the problems faced by the labor-peasant class at the time. The traditional agricultural system was being destroyed by Japan's domination of Korean agriculture, and farmers were

74. On the history of the Chosŏn Worker-Peasant League, see Hŏ Changman, ibid.; Kim Chunyŏp and Kim Ch'angsun, *Han'guk kongsanjuŭi undongsa* (The history of the Korean communist movement), vol. 2 (Seoul: Kodae Aseamunje yŏn'guso, 1969), pp. 57-100.

75. Kyokido keisatsubu (Kyonggi provincial police headquarters), *Chian gaikyo* (The general situation of public peace), p. 12; Kim Chŏngmyŏng (1967), "Chosŏn e issŏsŏ ŭi nongmin undong ŭi ch'use" (Changes in the Chosŏn peasant movement), ibid., p. 406; Han Honggu and Yi Chaehwa, eds., *Han'guk minjok haebang undongsa charyojip* (Documents of the history of the Korean national liberation movement) 2, p. 196.

going bankrupt, with many ending up migrating to Japan, Manchuria, and Siberia. In the mid-1920s, as the increased exploitation of the peasantry by the landlord-capitalist class came into conflict with the anti-landlord, anti-capitalist ideology of the Worker-Peasant League, there was a violent outbreak of tenancy disputes and peasant uprisings in all regions of the country. Just to name a few incidents, there were tenancy disputes in the Andong region; on the islands south of Cholla province such as Amt'ae and Chaŭn; in the ODC's *nongjang* in the Chaeryŏng region; and in the Yiyŏpsa Nongjang in Okgu.[76]

In the third stage of development, the peasant movement operated within the strategy set by the national liberation movement which was led by the Korean Communist Party (KCP) and the General League of Chosŏn Peasants. The KCP was formed in 1925 as the vanguard party of the socialist movement and promulgated its "Manifesto" the following year.[77] Also in 1925, the Chosŏn Worker-Peasant League split into the General League of Chosŏn Workers (Chosŏn nodong ch'ong tongmaeng) and the General League of Chosŏn Peasants (Chosŏn nongmin ch'ong tongmaeng) (1925-1927) to further the growth of both the labor and the peasant movements. Viewed as an illegal organization by the Japanese authorities, the KCP was a target of suppression and was forcibly dissolved several times. The leaders of the peasant league were also implicated in these incidents and repeatedly arrested, making it virtually impossible for them to lead the peasant movement directly. However, since the KCP had already explicated its policies on the peasant movement in its "Manifesto" and through party platforms and pronouncements, the party was generally able to provide guidance to the peasant movement, though only gradually. As a result, the peasant movement underwent significant changes in the succeeding years.

The changes in the peasant movement were related, above all, to changes in the mindset and strategy of communists and the Korean Communist Party.

76. See Kang Chŏngsuk, "Ilcheha Andong chibang nongmin undong e kwanhan yŏn'gu" (A study of peasant movements in the Andong region under Japanese rule) in *Han'guk kŭndae nongch'on sahoe wa nongmin undong*. Yamato Kazuaki, "Chosen nomin undo no tenkanten— 1925 nen Cholla nando Tadohae chiyok no kosaku sogi bunseki" (The turning point of the Korean peasant movement—an analysis of the 1925 tenant strike in the Tadohae Region in South Cholla province), *Rekishi hyoron*, no. 413 (1983); Hŏ Changman, ibid. (1962); Asada Kyoji, *Nihon teikokushugi ka no minzoku kakumei undo*, pp. 198-237; Cho Tonggŏl, *Ilcheha Han'guk nongmin undongsa* (History of the peasant movement in Korea under Japanese rule) (Seoul: Han'gilsa, 1979).

77. Kajimura Hideki and Kang Tŏksang, "Ku Yŏnhŭm shucho" (Interrogation of Ku Yŏnhŭm), ibid., p. 419.

Going beyond the economism of the past, they believed that it was necessary to engage in a political struggle to liberate Korea completely from the oppression of Japanese imperialism. In other words, a social revolution also had to be, at the same time, a national revolution. To achieve these ambitious goals, they felt that it was essential to oppose the enemy by building a united revolutionary front that was supported by the entire strength of the nation. The struggle would be effective and victorious if the labor-peasant class, which comprised 87% of the population and whose revolutionary consciousness was the most developed, stood at the forefront of the struggle for liberation.

The party felt that it was necessary to reorganize peasant organizations into peasant unions and to conduct the movement through these unions in order to enable the peasants to engage in struggle.[78] In the process, large numbers of new peasant unions replaced the former tenant unions in the late 1920s. There were calls for the peasant movement to be placed under the leadership of the Worker-Peasant League, and it also became clear that it was necessary to establish organizations to engage in an economic struggle in order to widen the scope of the political struggle.[79] Thus, the peasant movement developed into a movement that pursued the twin ideals of national liberation and national revolution.

However, during this stage, the movement ran into many problems trying to pursue the course set by its leaders. The party found it difficult to establish an organizational base within the worker-peasant class or even to establish roots in that class since the party leadership was mainly composed of intellectuals and students.[80] It was also difficult for the KCP to function as a vanguard party while it was repeatedly being disbanded and rebuilt because of Japanese suppression. Since the KCP was pursuing a united front strategy with radical nationalists through the formation of the Sin'ganhoe in 1927, it faced additional difficulties in reconciling these policies with the pursuit of national revolution, i.e., a social revolution.

The fourth stage was the period of the "revolutionary" peasant union movement which lasted from the end of the 1920s through the first half of the 1930s. In this period, while socialists failed to establish a vanguard party in Korea, the leaders of the peasant movement established new peasant unions

---

78. Kajimura Hideki and Kang Tŏksang, ibid., pp. 419-22; Kim Myŏnggu, ibid.

79. *Taisho shimbun* (Taisho newspaper) no. 13. One example is the article on page 2 of the March 29, 1928 issue.

80. Kajimura Hideki and Kang Tŏksang (1965), "Komintanu ketteisho" (Resolution of the Comintern), p. 119; Kim Chunyŏp and Kim Ch'angsun, ibid., vol. 3, appendix, p. 361.

throughout the country with results varying according to region.[81] The shifts in the peasant movement stemmed from both internal and external factors. The main internal factor was the KCP's response to the effects of political oppresssion and economic depression in Korea. The KCP's original plan for the peasant movement was to unite its vanguard party, which would provide leadership, with the front-line organizations of the peasant unions so that the movement would operate as a part of the national liberation movement. However, the prospects for establishing a vanguard party were not promising. Because of the agricultural recession of the Japanese and world capitalist economies, the burden that the peasants bore became excessive, accelerating their impoverishment. Since the leaders of peasant movements and regional vanguard parties had to conduct their activities together in all regions, it became necessary for the regional peasant unions to take charge of the peasant movement while simultaneously taking on the role of a vanguard party for the KCP.[82]

The main external factors were the policies of the Comintern and Profintern (aka, Red International of Labor Unions) on Korea. At its Sixth Congress, the Comintern adopted various theses on "the revolutionary movement in colonial and semi-colonial regions,"[83] and on the Korean question, it adopted the so-called "December Theses," whose objective was to promote the formation of a revolutionary vanguard among workers and peasants. The December Theses instructed that if the bourgeois class became closely integrated with Japanese capitalism, the national liberation movement should not remain a simple anti-imperial, anti-feudal movement but must develop simultaneously into a class struggle of the labor-peasant class against the national bourgeoisie.[84] In its "September Theses," the Profintern issued a directive that it was necessary to organize new labor and peasant unions to oppose the moderate political tendencies of the national bourgeoisie and to

---

81. See footnote 70.

82. There are vivid descriptions of this situation in "Nongmin chohap chaegŏn undong kwa nongmin munje" (The movement for the reconstruction of the Agricultural Association and the peasant problem), *Shiso iho* 17, (1938), which examined the peasant association of the Myŏngch'ŏn region and utilized the guiding documents of the movement.

83. Chosŏn Ch'ongdokbu, *Kyosanshugi undo ni kansuru bunkenshu* (Analysis of the communist movement), pp. 153-215; Murata Yoichi, trans. and ed., *Kominutanu shiryoshu* (Documents of the Comintern), vol. 4, pp. 414-49; Kim Chŏngmyŏng, ibid., pp. 701-39.

84. Chosŏn Ch'ongdokbu, *Kyosanshugi undo ni kansuru bunkenshu* (1936), pp. 536-48; Murata Yoichi, trans. and ed., *Kominterun shiryoshu*, vol. 4 (Tokyo: Otsuki shoten, 1981), pp. 487-95; Kim Chunyŏp and Kim Ch'angsun, ibid. vol. 3, appendix, pp. 388-93; Kim Chŏngmyŏng, ibid., pp. 740-47.

use those organizations to engage in "revolutionary" labor union and "revolutionary" peasant union movements.[85] Regardless of whether they were moderate or radical in their politics, many of the national bourgeoisie became closely tied to Japan and became collaborators in Japan's domination of Korean agriculture, its exploitation of the Korean peasantry, and the maintenance of its system of rule. It was natural that the peasant union movement in this period developed revolutionary tendencies.

Although peasant unions arose in all regions of the country, they were particularly active in Hamgyŏng province.[86] Many peasant unions in this province engaged in a fierce struggle not just through tenancy disputes related to the landlord-tenant system but also against Japan's exploitation of the peasantry and the everyday administrative policies that sought to control the Korean people. Peasant movements began to adopt revolutionary slogans such as the following:

All the masses of poor peasants, starving farmers, and seasonal laborers! Let's oppose the imperialist wars and overthrow the murderous Japanese thugs for the complete liberation of the Chosŏn people. Let's rise up together with the workers and peasants of the countries of the world. . . and fight. . . to establish a soviet government [that stands] for bread, freedom, and peace.[87]

85. Chosŏn Ch'ongdokbu, *Kyosanshugi undo ni kansuru bunkenshu* (1936), pp. 548-56; Murata Yoichi, trans. and ed., *Kominterun shiryoshu*, vol. 4, pp. 471-76; Kim Chunyŏp and Kim Ch'angsun, ibid., vol. 3, appendix, pp. 388-93; Kim Chŏngmyŏng, ibid., pp. 766-71.

86. Chosŏn Ch'ongdokbu Keimukyoku, "The peasant movement within the socialist movement," *Chosen no chianjokyo* (The state of public security in Chosŏn, 1930), p. 28; Kim Chŏngmyŏng, "Chosŏn e issŏsŏ ŭi nongmin undong ŭi ch'use" (The transition of the peasant movement in Korea), ibid., p. 408; Hida Yuichi, *Nitteika no Chosen nomin undo* (The Chosŏn peasant movement under Japanese imperialism) (Tokyo: Miraisha, 1991); Tachigi Masahito, "Shokuminjika Chosen ni okeru chiho minshu undo no tenkai—Hamkyong namdo Hongwon gun no jirei o chushin to shite" (Development of regional minjung movements in colonial Chosŏn—A case study of Hongwon county in South Hamgyŏng province), *Chosenshi kenkyukai ronbunshu*, no. 20 (1983); Asadi Kyoji, ibid.; Sin Chubaek, ibid.; and Chi Sugŏl, ibid. (see footnote 70). See also Yi Chunsik, "Ilche ch'imnyakgi Chŏngp'yŏng chibang ŭi nongmin undong e taehan yŏn'gu" (A study of peasant movements in the Chŏngp'yŏng region under Japanese imperialism), *Ilcheha ŭi sahoe undong kwa nongch'on sahoe*, Han'guk sahoesa yŏn'guhoe, ed. (Seoul: Munhak kwa chisŏngsa, 1990); Yi Chongmin, "1930 nyŏndae ch'oban nongmin chohap ŭi nongmin sŏnggyŏk yŏn'gu" (A study of the characteristics of peasant unions in the early 1930s) (M.A. thesis, Yonsei University, 1989).

87. Quoted in the "Judgment" (*Pan'gyŏl*) on the Second Chŏngp'yŏng farmers' union incident; see also Yi Chunsik, ibid., p. 270.

All the oppressed people in Chosŏn. . . in the countryside, in factories, and in all places of oppression. . . let's shout the slogans of "Overthrow Imperialism," "Hurrah for the Liberation of the Weak Nations of the World," and "Hurrah for the Liberation of the Chosŏn People."[88]

Peasant unions also adopted revolutionary platforms, calling for the "confiscation of all land and its free distribution to the peasants."[89] They believed that "the Chosŏn revolution must be a bourgeois democratic revolution whose goals were the destruction of feudal remnants, a fundamental reform of the relations of the agricultural system, and a land revolution to overcome the state of capitalist slavery."[90] As a result, the peasant movement began to engage in direct battles with the police. Having already gone beyond an economic struggle, the peasant movement in Hamgyŏng province developed into a political struggle; it also became a revolutionary movement whose objective was the overthrow of Japanese imperialism.

In this stage, the peasant movement underwent tremendous development in comparison with earlier tenancy disputes. Tenancy disputes in the first half of the 1920s did not go beyond an economic struggle. Although its leaders in the latter half of the 1920s conceived of the movement as a revolutionary struggle that was part of the national liberation movement, such thinking was not fully reflected in the movement itself. But by the fourth stage, the peasant movement was clearly calling for a bour-geois democratic revolution that aimed to overthrow the Japanese empire and to achieve national liberation and socialism. These changes represented the ideological culmination of the peasant movement, demonstrating the substantial qualitative development that it had undergone during the occupation period. Of course, such development did not mean that these views were shared by the entire peasant class. However, it is undeniable that these changes reflected the general direction of the peasant movement in this period. Consequently, the trends of peasant movement in Hamgyŏng province were not unique to the region

88. Kotohoin kensakyoku (Inspectorate of the High Court), "Sochon nomin kumiai kyogikai jiken" (The Tanch'ŏn peasant union meeting incident), *Shiso geppo* 3-8 (1933); Yi Chongmin, ibid., p. 73.

89. Kotohoin kensakyoku, "Chosen Kongch'ong sanken Hamju heiya iinkai soshiki junbi iinkai jiken," (Incident of the Committee for Preparing the Establishment of the Hanju Plains Committee for the Reconstructuion of the Young People's League of the Communist Party), Hamju heiya nomin kumiai soshiki junbi iinkai kodokoryu, *Shiso iho* 11 (1937), p. 267.

90. Kotohoin kensakyoku, "Nongmin chohap chaegon undong kwa nongmin munje" (The peasant problem and the movement to reconstruct the peasant unions), *Shiso iho* 17 (1938).

but reflected the direction of the movement across the entire country, clearly showing its aims and objectives.

Conclusion

This chapter has examined the origins of the problems in the agricultural economy during the Japanese occupation period and the aims of the peasant movement that attempted to resolve them. The objective was to clarify the actual workings of the landlord system in this period and to contribute to an understanding of the agricultural systems that were established after liberation. In this section, I will conclude by summarizing and synthesizing the main points of my analysis.

The origins of the agrarian crisis were related to Japan's dominance over the Korean economy and its implementation of exploitative agricultural policies. From the 1910s to the 1930s, Japan seized control over the economy and agriculture in Korea through the introduction of finance capital by establishing financial institutions such as the Bank of Chosŏn, the Industrial Bank of Chosŏn, the system of financial cooperatives, and the Chosŏn Savings Bank. In the 1910s, Japan implemented its exploitative policies through the Company Law and the cadastral survey. In the 1920s, these policies were intensified through the implementation of the Program to Increase Rice Production. Within the short span of ten to twenty years, capital investment by Japanese landlords and capitalists surged into Korea, and much of that capital was used to invest in and accumulate land.

Up to the Hanmal period, only a small number of people had purchased land and set up *nongjang*, but during the occupation period, the number of people buying land exceeded 100,000 as *nongjang* were established solely for the purpose of exploitation. Some people bought only a small parcel of *taet'o*, but in most cases, people and companies bought land ranging from several *chŏngbo* to tens of thousands of *chŏngbo* in size, thereby becoming small to medium landlords or even large landowners. Land accumulation was also prevalent among Korean landlords and capitalists because of the same factors. As a result, small to medium Korean landowners and peasants became either petty landowners or landless peasants, and many of them then became tenant farmers for both Japanese and Korean landlords. The ones who became tenants were actually fortunate, since tens and even hundreds of thousands of peasants were forced from their land and migrated to places such as Manchuria, Japan, and Siberia.

One of the main characaeristics of the landlord system under Japanese rule was that the rights of landlords—that is, their control over tenant farmers—became greatly strengthened compared to the Hanmal period. At first, Japanese bought land illegally and took a flexible approach to managing their farms, following the customs of Korea's traditional landlord system. However, as Japan gradually intensified its exploitative agricultural policies, it gained complete institutional control over the Korean economy and, while preserving traditional agricultural practices, promoted the growth of the landlord system under the name of capitalist management or rational management. Korean landlords also adopted the same approach to management and agricultural business. As one would expect, tenant fees rose, and the burden of various taxes and fees such as irrigation fees, water taxes, fertilizer and seed costs was completely shifted to the peasants. Peasants were also forced to do various kinds of labor. It became difficult for tenant farmers to support their households with the income from their rented lands, so they had to take out loans from landlords or usurious moneylenders in order to survive.

Japanese landlords often emphasized their differences with absentee Korean landlords, bragging that they were making a large contribution to the improvement of agricultural production in Korea by developing the farmland and managing *nongjang* directly as capitalist agricultural entrepreneurs. However, since the tenancy system did not achieve a complete break from the feudal landlord system, *nongjang* actually operated according to the most backward methods of capitalist agricultural management. In the name of capitalist management, tenant farmers were exploited and dominated more viciously than in any other period. Since the *nongjang*-landlord system was extremely irrational, landlords tried to justify it by claiming that it used capitalist, rational management methods. However, the relations of production were not structured into a hierarchy of landlords-capitalists-laborers nor a hierarchy of landlords/capitalists-workers. Tenants were not allowed to act as entrepreneurial farmers, and agricultural production did not involve the direct management of capitalists in which *nongjang* owners (i.e., landlords) would hire agricultural laborers and manage their operations them-selves. While the *nongjang* land system appeared to define tenants as entrepreneurial farmers, it was in reality a system in which the tenant farmers were controlled and exploited as "hired tenants" who were comparable to laborers. This system developed because of its advantages in managing *nongjang*.

Since it was difficult for tenant farmers to survive under this landlord system, they engaged by necessity in a struggle for survival against the land-lord-capitalist class. This struggle took place in the 1920s and 30s, the period of tenancy disputes and the rise of the peasant movement. As is well known, the struggle was not just a simple economic movement but became politicized, developing into a movement for national liberation and revolution.

Originating in Japan's excessive exploitation of Korean agriculture and the peasantry, the rise of the peasant movement clearly signified the failure of Japan's exploitative agricultural policies. It also revealed the systemic limits of Japanese capitalism, one of whose foundations was landlord capital. It was necessary to devise a plan or policy to solve the problems in the agricultural economy by any means possible. However, it was difficult to agree on a single plan or policy since a solution involved issues in which the interests of Japan and Korea and of landlords and peasants were fundamentally in conflict. The intensification of the conflict between the landlord and peasants in the countryside and the disagreement over the method of solving problems in the agricultural economy became the internal cause of the ideological and systemic conflicts in Korean society after liberation.

translated by Howard Kahm

TABLE 1

Year	Number of Transactions	Number of Individuals	Purchase Price (*wŏn*)
1917	173,963	343,155	16,219,668
1920	271,790	556,922	110,040,235

TABLE 2

THE WHOLESALE MARKET PRICE PER *SŎK* FOR EACH TYPE OF UNPOLISHED RICE
(The average market price in twenty-one markets across the country)

Year	High-grade	Medium-grade	Low-grade	Average
1915	9.51	9.09	8.90	9.17
1916	11.58	11.16	10.74	11.16
1917	16.52	16.12	15.69	16.11
1918	26.79	26.08	25.54	26.14
1919	39.47	38.36	37.63	38.49
1920	37.10	36.14	35.48	36.24

TABLE 3
TRENDS IN LAND ACCUMULATION AND THE DIFFERENTIATION OF THE PEASANT CLASS

Year	Type A Landlords	Type B Landlords	Independent cultivators	Semi-Tenants	Tenants	Slash-and-burn farmers	Agricultural laborers	Total
1917	15,485	57,713	517,996	1,061,438	989,362			2,641,994
1922	17,157	81,926	534,907	971,877	1,106,598			2,712,465
1927	20,737	84,359	519,389	909,843	1,217,889	29,131		2,781,348
1932	32,890	71,923	476,351	742,961	1,546,456	60,407		2,931,088
1933			545,502	724,741	1,563,056	82,277	93,984	3,009,560
1939			539,629	719,232	1,583,358	69,280	111,634	3,023,133

PERCENTAGES OF THE ABOVE

Year	Type A Landlords	Type B Landlords	Independent cultivators	Semi-Tenants	Tenants	Slash-and-burn farmers	Agricultural laborers	Total
1917	0.6	2.2	19.6	40.2	37.4			100.00
1922	0.6	3.1	19.7	35.8	40.8			100.00
1927	0.8	3.0	18.7	32.7	43.8	1.0		100.00
1932	1.1	2.4	16.3	25.4	52.7	2.1		100.00
1933			18.1	24.1	52.0	2.7	3.1	100.00
1939			17.8	23.8	52.4	2.4	3.7	100.00

SOURCE: Chosŏn Ch'ongdokbu nongnimbu, *Chosŏn nongji yŏnbo* (Annual report on Korean agricultural lands), p. 139.

TABLE 4

NUMBER OF PAYERS OF THE LAND TAX, ACCORDING TO LAND AREA

		1921	1922	1927	1928	1933	1934	1936
200 + *chŏngbo*	Japanese	169	176	192	178	192	190	181
	Korean	66	62	45	47	43	44	49
100 + *chŏngbo*	Japanese	321	304	361	357	406	412	380
	Korean	360	265	290	319	308	422	336
50 + *chŏngbo*	Japanese	519	529	683	671	766	755	749
	Korean	1,650	1,361	1,617	1,630	1,581	1,739	1,571
20 + *chŏngbo*	Japanese	1,420	1,533	2,335	2,220	2,579	2,529	2,958
	Korean	14,438	12,167	15,346	15,228	13,380	13,549	12,701
10 + *chŏngbo*	Japanese	1,544	1,734	2,403	2,463	3,400	3,367	3,504
	Korean	29,646	30,358	31,958	32,211	30,464	29,993	30,332
5 + *chŏngbo*	Japanese	2,555	3,036	4,454	4,772	6,541	6,496	6,901
	Korean	111,328	111,021	118,229	120,076	108,871	104,880	106,162
1 + *chŏngbo*	Japanese	11,532	12,875	18,767	20,003	28,009	28,175	27,313
	Korean	968,116	980,048	1,024,771	1,030,113	980,212	933,459	922,026
< 1 *chŏngbo*	Japanese	26,318	28,752	36,727	37,822	66,038	65,174	64,312
	Korean	2,292,936	2,336,165	2,609,834	2,621,784	2,971,844	2,257,086	2,595,898
Total	Japanese	44,378	48,939	65,922	68,486	107,931	107,098	106,298
	Korean	3,418,540	3,471,447	3,802,090	3,821,408	4,106,703	3,651,172	3,669,075

SOURCE: Chosŏn nonghoe, *Chosŏn nong'ŏp paldalsa* (The History of Agricultural Development in Chosŏn), Volume on development (1944). Taken from Appendix, Table 4.

TABLE 5a

LAND OWNERSHIP ACCORDING TO NATIONALITY,
LANDLORDS WITH OVER THIRTY *CHŎNGBO* OF LAND (LATE 1930S)

	Number of Landlords	Area of Land Owned (*chŏngbo*)	Average Area of Land Owned Per Landlord (*chŏngbo*)
Korean	4,162	340,970	81.92
Japanese	870	216,704	249.08
Total	5,032	557,674	

TABLE 5b

BREAKDOWN OF TABLE 5A

	Korean	Japanese
30~50 *chŏngbo*	1,921	290
50~100 *chŏngbo*	1,439	270
100~300 *chŏngbo*	760	197
300~500 *chŏngbo*		49
500~1,000 *chŏngbo*	32	27
> 1,000 *chŏngbo*	10	37
Total	4,162	870

SOURCE: Paek Nam'un, "Chosen keizai no gendankairon"
(On the present stage of the Chosŏn economy), *Shiso iho* 17 (1938).

TABLE 6

CHANGES IN THE NUMBER OF LARGE LANDOWNERS
WITH MORE THAN FIFTY *CHŎNGBO* OF LAND (ESTIMATED)

		1910–13	1925–27	1930	1936	1942
100+ *chungbo*	Japanese	79	201	301	321+	567
	Korean	314	968	800	659+	488
50+ *chungbo*	Japanese	35	129	251		642
	Korean	1,471	1,483	1,438		1,351

SOURCE: Chang Siwŏn, *Ilcheha taechiju ŭi chonjae hyŏngt'ae e kwanhan yŏn'gu*
(An examination of the modes of existence of the large landlords under Japanese rule),
(Ph.D. dissertation, Seoul National University, 1989), p. 60.

TABLE 7

THE NUMBER OF HOUSEHOLDS BASED ON SCALE OF AGRICULTURE
(1923 Survey)

	Landlord	Owner-cultivator	Semi-tenant	Tenant	Pauper (窮民)	Total
Large	6,866	94,453	98,628	88,226		
Medium	22,994	179,016	263,747	233,029		
Small	39,455	172,390	329,431	354,399		
Petty (細)	52,670	107,819	225,605	298,084		
Total	121,985	553,678	917,311	973,738	162,209	2,728,921

survey criteria:
1. Landlords: large = >20 *chŏngbo*; medium = >5 *chŏngbo*; small = >1 *chŏngbo*; petty = <1 *chŏngbo*.
2. Owner-cultivators and Tenants: large = >3 *chŏngbo*; medium = >1 *chŏngbo*; small: >3 *tanbo*; petty = <3 *tanbo*.
3. Paupers: those who have fallen into poverty and work as laborers for another farm household.

SOURCE: Chosŏn Ch'ongdokbu nongnimguk (Bureau of Agriculture and Forestry, Government-General of Korea), *Chosen ni okeru kosaku ni kansuru sanko jiko tekiyo* (A summary of reference items on tenancy in Chosŏn, 1932), p. 22.

TABLE 8

OUTBREAK OF TENANCY DISPUTES

Year	Number of Outbreaks	Year	Number of Outbreaks
1920	15	1930	726
1921	27	1931	667
1922	24	1932	300
1923	176	1933	1,975
1924	164	1934	7,544
1925	204	1935	25,834
1926	198	1936	29,975
1927	275	1937	31,799
1928	1,590	1938	22,596
1929	423	1939	16,452

SOURCE: Bureau of Agriculture and Forestry, Government-General of Korea, *Chosŏn nongji yŏnbo I* (Yearbook of Chosŏn Farmland, 1940), pp. 5-6.

Index of Terms

cha-sojaknong 自小作農 semi-tenants

chiju kap 地主甲 Type A landlords

chiju ŭl 地主乙 Type B landlords

ch'ogŏdae chiju 초거대지주 ultra-large landlords

chohapbi 組合費 cooperative fees

Chosŏn chŏch'uk ŭnhaeng 朝鮮貯蓄銀行 Chosŏn Savings Bank

Chosŏn hyŏkmyŏngnon 朝鮮革命論 Chosŏn Revolution

Chosŏn kŭm'yung chohap hyŏphoe 朝鮮金融組合協會 Chosŏn Association of Financial Cooperatives

Chosŏn kŭm'yung chohap yŏnhaphoe 朝鮮金融組合聯合會 Chosŏn Federation of Financial Cooperatives

Chosŏn nodong ch'ong tongmaeng 朝鮮勞動總同盟 General League of Chosŏn Workers

Chosŏn nodong kongjehoe 朝鮮勞動共濟會 Korean Workers Mutual Aid Association

Chosŏn nongjiryŏng 朝鮮農地令 Chosŏn Agricultural Lands Ordinance; aka, Tenancy Law

Chosŏn nongmin ch'ong tongmaeng 朝鮮農民總同盟 General League of Chosŏn Peasants

Chosŏn nonong ch'ong tongmaeng 朝鮮勞農總同盟 Chosŏn Worker-Peasant League

Chosŏn sang'ŏp ŭnhaeng 朝鮮商業銀行 Chosŏn Commercial Bank

Chosŏn sanmi chŭngsik kyehoek 朝鮮産米增殖計劃 Program to Increase Rice Production (PIRP)

Chosŏn siksan ŭnhaeng 朝鮮殖産銀行 Industrial Bank of Chosŏn

Chosŏn t'oji kaeryang chusikhoesa 朝鮮土地改良株式會社 Chosŏn Land Improvement Company

Chosŏn t'oji kaeryangryŏng 朝鮮土地改良令 Chosŏn Land Improvement Law

hoesaryŏng 會社令 Company Law

nongmin chohap 農民組合 peasant unions

pyŏngjak pansu 竝作半收 system under which the tenant gave half the harvest to the landlord

saŭm 舍音 employees of the landlord

Sin'ganhoe 新幹會

sojakgwŏn 小作權 tenant rights

sojakin chohap 小作人組合 tenant farmer unions
sokjijuŭi 屬地主義 territorial principle
suse 水稅 irrigation taxes
t'oji chosa saŏp 土地調査事業 cadastral survey
Tongyang ch'ŏksik chusik hoesa 東洋拓殖株式會社 Oriental
Development Company (ODC)

CHAPTER 5

The Emergence of New Types of Landlords in the Occupation Period

Hong Sung-Chan
洪性讚

The landlord system in Chosŏn underwent tremendous quantitative growth and various qualitative changes from the Hanmal period to the end of the Japanese occupation period. During the late Chosŏn and Hanmal periods, the government suppressed the peasants' demands for reform and pursued agricultural reforms and a modernization policy based on the maintenance of the landlord system that served the landlords' interests. After its takeover of Korea, Japan similarly pursued a policy of maximizing its exploitation of Korean agriculture by incorporating it into its capitalist economy and "developing its sources of profit."[1] Over the years, much research and numerous case studies have been done on the growth and transformation of the landlord system in this period.[2] Recently, there have also been long-range

---

1. Kim Yong-sop (Kim Yongsŏp), "Kŭndaehwa kwajŏng'esŏ ŭi nong'ŏp kaehyŏk ŭi tu panghyang" (The two paths of agricultural reform in Korea's modernization), *Han'guk chabonju ŭi sŏnggyŏk nonjaeng* (Seoul: Taewangsa, 1988); Kim Yong-sop, *Han'guk kŭnhyŏndae nong'ŏpsa yŏn'gu: Hanmal Ilcheha ŭi chijuje wa nongŏp munje* (revised edition) (Seoul: Chisik sanŏpsa, 2000).

2. For a summary of the studies on this subject, see Chang Siwŏn, "Iljeha taejiju'ŭi chonjae hyŏngt'ae e kwanhan yŏn'gu" (Study on the modes of existence of the large landlords in the Japanese colonial era) (Ph.D. diss., Seoul National University, 1989); Pak Ch'ŏnu, "Iljeha chijuje wa nongmin undong" (The landlord system in the Japanese colonial period and the peasant movement), *Han'guk chabonjuŭiron* (Seoul: Hanul ak'ademi, 1990); Nakamura Fukuji, "Chosen jinushisei kenkyu no aratana doko—Kankoku ni okeru jinushi keiei no jirei kenkyu no shokai wo chushin ni," (New trends in research on the landlord system in Korea—centering around the study of examples of landlord management in Korea), *Nihon jinushisei to kindai sonraku* (Tokyo: Sofusha, 1994); Chŏng Yŏnt'ae, "Ilje ŭi singmin nongjŏng kwa nong'ŏp ŭi pyŏnhwa" (Japanese

studies that cover the entire period from the late Chosŏn to the Liberation period. One landmark study has done an in-depth analysis of the landlord system and agricultural economy during those periods; it has illuminated the agricultural factors and rural origins of the differing agricultural systems that were formed in North and South Korea after the division of the country.[3]

Because of such scholarship, it is now possible to revise the view of Korean agriculture originally proposed by Japanese scholars in the 1930s. They emphasized a dichotomy between active, entrepreneurial Japanese landlords and passive, absentee Korean landlords such as the stereotypical avaricious, parasitic landlords that appeared in agrarian novels of the time.[4] It is true that there did exist passive, rent-seeking landlords who did not even know the location of all their landholdings. Having no interest in land or agricultural improvements, they would hire a supervisor or manager (*marŭm* or *nonggam*) to tend to their land and were content to exploit their tenants through high tenant fees and usurious loans as they had in the past.[5] On the other hand, an increasing number of landlords actively took advantage of Japan's capitalist agricultural policies and economic institutions to transform their farms and engage in new forms of landlord management such as *nongjang* (agricultural estates), agricultural trusts (*sint'ak chijuje*), and capitalist agricultural entrepreneurship.[6]

The purpose of this chapter is to review the existing scholarship on the landlord system in order to examine the types of landlords that emerged during the occupation period. More specifically, it will focus on three issues: how formerly static landlords utilized Japanese finance capital after the Japanese takeover; how, in this process, existing methods of landlord management changed, and finally how these landowners widened their political and social networks in order to preserve and expand their interests. In other words,

---

colonial agricultural politics and changes in agriculture), *Han'guk yŏksa ipmun III* (Seoul: P'ulpit, 1996).

3. Kim Yong-sop, ibid.

4. For examinations of portrayals of colonial landlords in literature, see Sin Ch'unho, "Han'guk nongmin sosŏl yŏn'gu" (An examination of Korean agrarian novels) (Ph.D. diss., Koryŏ University, 1980); Cho Namch'ŏl, "Iljeha Han'guk nongmin sosŏl yŏn'gu" (An examination of Korean agrarian novels under Japanese rule) (Ph.D. diss., Yonsei University, 1985); Cho Chŏngnae, "1940 nyŏndae ch'ogi Han'guk nongmin sosŏl yŏn'gu" (An examination of Korean agricultural novels from the early 1940s) (Ph.D. diss., Yonsei University, 1987).

5. Hisama Ken'ichi, "Jinushiteki shokuno no chosei," (Adjustments in the function of landlords) *Chosen nosei no kadai* (Tokyo: Seibido, 1943), p. 337; Hishimoto Chŏji, *Chosen mai no kenkyu* (Tokyo: Chikura shobo, 1938), pp. 92–93.

6. Kim Yong-sop, ibid., pp. 2–3.

the objective is to provide a typology of landlords with a focus on the new kinds of landlords who innovated their management methods and actively adapted themselves to the new agricultural conditions under Japanese rule.

There are two reasons for limiting my focus to these types of landlords. First, though they did not constitute a majority of the total number of land-lords, they were the type of landlord that the Japanese consistently sought to promote through its agricultural and landlord policies. Second, although the degree of change differed among landlords, these were the changes that they themselves wanted to implement. One of the important tasks of modern Korean historiography is to determine the nature of changes in the landlord system and the landlord class during Japanese rule. It is especially important to examine trends in new forms of the landlord system and new types of landlords because they were the first to adapt to the new agricultural con-ditions and played a central role in changes in the landlord class after Japan's takeover. This chapter is intended to contribute in a small way to stimulating further research on this topic.

Landlords and Finance Capital

The landlord system underwent many changes in the late Chosŏn and the Hanmal periods. There emerged new kinds of farmers such as commer-cial landlords (*kyŏngyŏng chiju*), managerial rich peasants (*kyŏngyŏnghyŏng punong*), and *chungdapju*, and their emergence brought about a change in the traditional relationship between landlords and tenant farmers.[7] When agricultural conditions changed dramatically under Japanese rule, the landlord system underwent yet another transformation. The most significant eco-nomic change faced by the landlord class was Japan's establishment of a network of large-scale financial institutions in Korea. Reaching the stage of finance capitalism in the 1920s and the stage of state monopoly capitalism in the 1930s, Japan maximized its exploitation of Korea by utilizing large amounts of capital to develop Korean agriculture. In short, Japan exploited Korea through capitalist institutions that regulated and manipulated capital flows. Immediately after its occupation began, Japan embarked on building a financial system in order to create a more efficient way to raise and distribute

---

7. Kim Yong-sop, *Chosŏn hugi nongŏpsa yŏn'gu I*, revised edition (Seoul: Chisik san'ŏpsa, 1995); *Chosŏn hugi nongŏpsa yŏn'gu II*, revised edition (Seoul: Ilchogak, 1990); *Han'guk kŭndae nongŏpsa yŏn'gu II*, revised edition (Seoul: Ilchogak, 1984); ibid.

funds for colonial development. It sought to deepen the penetration of financial institutions into the Korean economy by creating a centralized, hierarchical system. At the apex was the Bank of Japan followed by the Bank of Chosŏn (Chosŏn Ŭnhaeng) and the Industrial Bank of Chosŏn (IBC, Chosŏn Siksan Ŭnhaeng) and finally general banks and financial cooperatives. Japan also established a direct financial market by opening the Kyŏngsŏng Stock Exchange (Kyŏngsŏng Chusik Hyŏnmul Chwiin Sijang), which was the equivalent of today's stock exchanges.

Another important change after the takeover was that it was now possible for Japanese financiers and capitalists to make large-scale investments in Korean land and agriculture by using land as collateral. Such investments were made possible by the cadastral survey that was conducted in the 1910s. The Japanese occupation government guaranteed the inviolability and unlimited protection of land ownership under a modern legal system, implementing a real estate registration system. As a result, Japan created the legal and institutional apparatus necessary for the landlord class to utilize finance capital. The close relation between landlords and finance capital was demonstrated in the 1920s when Japan conducted large-scale land improvements and irrigation projects through the Program to Increase Rice Production (PIRP, Chosŏn sanmi chŭngsik kyehoek), which necessitated a massive influx of finance capital into Korea.

The landlord class came under the domination of finance capital as it adjusted to its central role in the economy. Just as it is difficult to imagine any sizable company today that does not use bank loans, landlords with sizable holdings regularly borrowed money from banks and financial cooperatives, using their lands and grain as collateral. Many landlords also opened current accounts with banks and issued checks in their daily transactions. Funds from bank loans came to be circulated in a system in which large landlords obtained funds from the IBC, the Oriental Development Company (ODC, Tongyang ch'ŏksik hoesa), and general banks, while small and medium landlords mainly utilized general banks and financial cooperatives. Landlords took out loans from financial institutions to expand their landholdings by purchasing and reclaiming new lands and to increase production by improving their land, seed quality, farm tools and equipment, and fertilization methods. They increased their profits by waiting until prices rose before shipping their grain, and some even transformed themselves into bourgeoisie by investing their bank loans in non-agricultural businesses. To obtain funds for their activities, landlords frequently took out long- and short-term loans from banks either on credit or by mortgaging their lands and grain.[8]

Some of the landlords who engaged in such financial maneuverings later became prominent businessmen in South Korea. For example, Yi Pyŏng-ch'ŏl, the son of a landlord and the future founder of the Samsung conglomerate, was also operating grain-selling, transport, and refinery businesses in 1936. He used the Masan (South Kyŏngsang province) branch of the IBC as if it were his own private coffer, becoming a large landowner with two million *p'yŏng* of land within just two to three years.[9] Kim Yŏnsu, a large landlord who was the most prominent of the Korean bourgeoisie, received a large loan with the help of the Government-General and undertook large-scale land reclamation projects in Sonbul (South Chŏlla) and Haeri (North Chŏlla) Counties.[10] A large landlord in Tongbok (South Chŏlla), O Kŏngi took out short term loans to ship grain but would delay the shipping date until the pre-harvest period, when rice prices would reach their highest levels.[11] The Cho family, a large landlord from Koksŏng (South Chŏlla), borrowed money from the IBC to go into the gold-mining business.[12] Similarly, other landlords such as the Mun family from Amt'ae, the Yi family from Posŏng, and the Yun family from Haenam, also depended on long- and short-term bank loans to operate their farms and businesses.[13] The use of bank capital

8. Hong Sung-Chan, "Iljeha kiŏpgajŏk nongjanghyŏng chijuje ŭi yŏksajŏk sŏnggyŏk" (The historical characteristics of the entrepreneurial *nongjang* style landlord system under Japanese rule), *Tongbang hakji*, no. 63, 1989.

9. Yi Pyŏngch'ŏl, *Hoam chajŏn* (Seoul: Chung'ang ilbosa, 1986), chapters 2+3.

10. Kim Sanghyŏng, *Sudang Kim Yŏnsu* (Seoul: Sudang kinyŏmsaŏp'hŏe, 1971); Kim Sang-hong, *Samyang oshimnyŏn* (Seoul: Chusik hŏesa samyangsa, 1974). See also Carter J. Eckert, *Offspring of Empire: The Koch'ang Kims and the Colonial Origins of Korean Capitalism, 1876-1945* (Seattle and London: University of Washington Press, 1991).

11. Hong Sung-Chan, *Han'guk kŭndae nongch'onsahŏe ŭi pyŏndong kwa chijuch'ŭng* (Seoul: Chisik sanŏpsa, 1992), pp. 246-49.

12. Hong Sung-Chan, "Hanmal iljeha ŭi chijuje yŏn'gu: Koksŏng Cho ssigaŭi chijuro ŭi songjang kwa pyŏndong" (An examination of the landlord system in the late Chosŏn and Japanese occupation periods: the development and changes of Koksŏng Cho family as a landlord), *Tongbang hakji*, no. 49 (1985).

13. Pak Ch'ŏnu, "Hanmal iljeha ŭi chijuje yŏn'gu: Amt'aedo Mun ssiga'ŭi chijuro ŭi sŏngjang kwa kŭ pyŏndong" (An examination of the landlord system in the late Chosŏn and colonial periods: the development and changes of the Amt'ae Island Mun Family) (MA thesis, Yonsei University, 1983); Hong Sung-Chan, "Hanmal iljeha ŭi chijuje yŏn'gu: 50 chŏngbo chiju Posŏng Yissiga ŭi chiju kyŏngyŏng sarye" (An examination of the landlord system in the late Chosŏn and colonial periods: a case study of the Posŏng Yi Family's land management), *Tongbang hakji*, no. 56 (1986); Choi Won-kyu (Ch'ŏe Won'gyu), "Hanmal iljeha nongŏp kyŏngyŏng e kwanhan yŏn'gu: Haenam Yunssiga ŭi sarye" (An examination of agricultural management in the late

was even more widespread among Japanese landlords and agricultural companies. The Ungbon Nongjang regularly borrowed large sums of money from the Bank of Chosŏn, the IBC, and the financial cooperative in Okgu.[14] Chosŏn Kaech'ŏk Company took out large loans from the IBC, while Puri Hŭngŏp issued company bonds that were bought up by the IBC.[15]

The relationship between banks and landlords went beyond that of lender and borrower and developed into one of close symbiosis. Landlords actively participated in the establishment of general banks, founding banks and serving as shareholders and executives.[16] Most of the twenty-four founding members of Honam Bank in Kwangju, established in August 1920, were wealthy local landlords. For example, Chŏng Sut'ae, a large landlord in Koksŏng, played a decisive role in procuring funds for its initial capitalization and became one of its executives, though he was not one of the founding members.[17] Landlords were also actively involved in banks such as Hosŏ Bank of Yesan (South Ch'ungch'ŏng), Samnam Bank of Chŏnju (North Chŏlla), and Kyŏngil Bank of Taegu (North Kyŏngsang). Tomita Gisaku, a large landlord in Chinamp'o (South P'yŏng'an), was the leading figure in the establishment of Samhwa and P'yŏngyang Banks. Kim Yŏnsu took over Haedong Bank when it fell into difficulties, while another large landlord, Min Yŏnghwi, took over Hanil Bank under similar circumstances. It was also

Chosŏn and Japanese colonial periods: a case study of the Haenam Yun family), *Han'guksa yŏn'gu*, nos. 50-51 (combined issue, 1986).

14. Chu Pong'gyu and So Sunyŏl, *Kŭndae chiyŏk nongŏpsa yŏn'gu* (Seoul: Seoul National University Press, 1996), pp. 181–89.

15. Hong Sung-Chan, "Iljeha kŭmyungjabon ŭi nonggiŏp chibae: Purihŭngŏp ŭi kyŏngyŏng pyŏndong kwa Chosŏn siksan ŭnhaeng" (The control of agricultural enterprises by finance capital during the Japanese occupation period: the IBC of Chosŏn and changes in Purihŭng'ŏp's management), *Tongbang hakji*, no. 65 (1990a).

16. Ko Sŭngjae, *Han'guk kŭm'yungsa yŏn'gu* (Seoul: 1970); Kim Sŏngbo, "Iljeha Chosŏnin chiju ŭi chabon chŏnhwan sarye," (A case study of capital conversion by Chosŏn landlords during the colonial period), *Han'guksa yŏn'gu*, no. 76 (1992); Yun Sŏkbŏm, Hong Sung-Chan, U Taehyŏng, and Kim Tong'uk, *Han'guk kŭndae kŭm'yungsa yŏn'gu* (Seoul: Segyŏngsa, 1996); Hong Sung-Chan, "Iljeha p'yŏngyang chiyŏk Ilbonin ŭi ŭnhaeng sŏlip kwa kyŏngyŏng: Samhwa, P'yŏngyang, Taedong ŭnhaeng ŭi sarye rŭl chungsim ŭro," (The establishment and management of banks by the Japanese in the Pyongyang region during the colonial period—focusing on case studies of the Samhwa, Pyongyang, Taedong Banks), *Yun Kijung kyosu chŏng'nyŏn ki'nyŏm nonmunjip* (Seoul: Taehan kyo'gwasŏ chusikhŏesa, 1997).

17. Hong Sung-Chan, "Hanmal Ilcheha Chŏnnam chiyŏk Han'guk'in ŭi ŭnhaeng sŏllip kwa kyŏngyŏng: Kwangju nonggong ŭnhaeng-Honam ŭnhaeng ŭi sarye rŭl chungsim ŭro" (The establishment and operation of banks by Koreans in South Chŏlla Province in the Hanmal period and under Japanese rule: a case study of the Kwangju Agriculture and Industry Bank and the Honam Bank), *Sŏnggok nonch'ong*, no. 30 (1999).

mainly large landlords who set up financial cooperatives in both rural and urban areas and served as their trustees or on their board of directors.

In many cases, banks did more than just loan money to landlords. In 1925, Hansŏng Bank became one of the founding shareholders (owning 5% of the total amount of stock) of Kyŏngsŏng Hŭngsan, an agricultural company with a capitalization of 500,000 yen. In 1929, the bank gained ownership of the company by acquiring 61.4% of its stock, and it even took over management of the company, assigning its own directors and regulators to serve as the company's president and board of directors.[18] When Puri Hŭngŏp and Chosŏn Kaech'ŏk Company experienced difficulties, the IBC, which was the main bondholder for both companies, also dispatched its personnel to take over their operations. In the early 1930s, the IBC established an agricultural company, Sŏng'ŏpsa, as a subsidiary to manage the farmland it acquired, providing all the capital and the company's board of directors. As large landlords went bankrupt one after another during the Great Depression, the IBC acquired their lands as payment for their mortgages. Through the Sŏng'ŏpsa, the IBC acquired and merged Puri Hŭngŏp and Chosŏn Kaech'ŏk Company, the two biggest agricultural companies in Korea at the time.[19] The IBC occupied a dominant position in Korean agriculture as the parent company of a massive financial concern that controlled subsidiaries such as Sŏng'ŏpsa and sub-subsidiaries such as Puri Hŭngŏp and Chosŏn Kaech'ŏk Company.

By borrowing money to expand their landholdings and to divert their capital into new businesses, landlords during the occupation period gained a tremendous opportunity to accumulate capital in a financial market where there was a severe gap between official and private interest rates. Such opportunities also came with grave risks. If a landlord were successful in business using large loans from banks, he would gain the financial leverage to make large profits and to expand his business. If he were not successful, his financial situation would worsen because of the pressure of repaying the principal and interest, making it impossible to avoid downsizing or even bankruptcy. The potential for instability and crisis could also be aggravated

18. Nakamura Sukeyoshi, ed., *Chosen ginko kaisha kumiai yoroku* (General list of banks, companies, and cooperatives in Chosŏn) (Keijo: Toa keizai jihosha, 1925), p. 63; Nakamura Sukeiyoshi, *Chosen ginko kaisha kumiai yoroku* (Keijo: Toa keizai jihosha, 1929), p. 55.

19. Hong Sung-Chan, "Iljeha kŭm'yung chabon ŭi nonggŏp chibae: Chosŏn siksan ŭnhaeng ŭi Sŏngŏpsa sŏllip kwa kŭ unyŏng" (The control of agricultural enterprises by finance capital during the Japanese occupation period: the establishment and management of the Sŏng'ŏp Company by the IBC of Chosŏn), *Tongbang hakji*, no. 68 (1990).

by events such as sudden economic downturns, a drop in rice prices, reduced production due to a poor harvest, tenant disputes, delays in reclamation projects, changes in the government's economic policies, rising interest rates, or a loan freeze.

Many landlords and companies did in fact suffer sudden reversals of fortune, particularly during the 1930s and 1940s. For example, Yi Pyŏngch'ŏl, who had quickly become a large landlord between 1936-37 through money borrowed from the IBC, just as rapidly went bankrupt from the burden of repaying the principal when the IBC suddenly stopped issuing loans because of the passage of the "Emergency Fund Regulation Law" after the outbreak of the Sino-Japanese War in 1937. In April 1933, Amyŏng Nongjang in T'ongch'ŏn County (Kangwŏn province) was taken over by the IBC because of problems repaying its approximately 100,000 yen in loans from the IBC and because of the fall in rice prices during the Great Depression. In the winter of 1930, Ch'ŏnsang Dongjok turned over the Ch'ŏnjwa Nongjang in Ongjin County (Hwanghae province) to the IBC, its main lender, as repayment for its loans. Likewise, Hajŏnjo, a joint-stock company which reclaimed 207 *chŏngbo* of state-owned land in 1917 and managed it for twenty years, relinquished its *nongjang* in Puan County (North Chŏlla province) to the IBC in 1937 when it faced insurmountable financial problems.[20] The Yi family of Naju (South Chŏlla), who had around 100,000 yen in loans from the IBC in the early 1940s, eventually sold some of its farmland and reorganized its operations in order to get some relief from loan repayments.[21] Twenty *chŏngbo* of farmland, which Hansŏng Bank acquired in 1932 as repayment for a loan and which it hired Chwadŭng Nongjang to run, originally belonged to a landlord who went bankrupt during the Great Depression.[22] Chosŏn Kaech'ŏk Company, which had been carrying out large-scale reclamation projects with loans from the IBC, accumulated debts because of delays in reclamation work resulting from flawed designs, and it then came under the control of the IBC capital and personnel. The IBC acquired Puri Hŭng'ŏp, another large-scale land reclamation company with large debts to

---

20. Hong Sung-Chan, ibid.; Hong Sung-Chan, "Haebang chikhu ŭi nongjang chaju kwalli undong kwa kŭ kwigyŏl: Hwanghaedo Ongjingun Sŏngŏpsa Malyŏng nongjang ŭi sarye" (The self-management movement of *nongjang* and its results in the immediate post-liberation period: a case study of the Malyŏng *nongjang* of Sŏng'ŏp Company in Ongjin County, Hwanghae Province), *Tongbang hakji*, no. 70 (1991).

21. Kim Yong-sop, ibid. (2000), pp. 157-58.

22. Kim Kyusŭng, "Noji kairyŏ no senkusha Satō nojo no bekken" (A glance at Chwadŭng *nongjang*, a pioneer in agricultural improvement), *Chosen nokaiho*, 7, no. 11 (1933).

the bank, as a subsidiary when it could not overcome the pressures of a drop in rice prices, tenant disputes, and interest payments.[23] Similarly, the Cho family of Koksŏng, who borrowed from the IBC and financial cooperatives to expand into gold mining, downsized its agricultural operations when it failed in its new business because of falling gold prices and a change in policies on gold production.

For landlords, utilization of bank capital was the key that made the difference between growth and decline in their agricultural businesses and between bankruptcy or expansion into non-agricultural businesses. Behind the daily drama of the successes and failures of landlords, there was a colonial network of banks and financial cooperatives with the Bank of Japan at the apex. During the occupation period, landlords constantly faced the threat of decline or bankruptcy even as they had opportunities for growth and expansion. It was no longer possible for them to continue to be passive landlords who had no interest in improving their businesses and lived comfortably off exploitative tenant fees as in the past. As long as they borrowed from banks and as long as they fell under the control of finance capital, they were compelled to take an active role in changing their agricultural businesses in order to survive. This trend became stronger the more that finance capital established control over landlords and the greater the scale of their agricultural holdings.

Transformation of Agricultural Management

As Korean agriculture came completely under the domination of finance capital and state monopoly capital, farmland became just one of the forms of property that landlords owned. They had constant opportunities to invest in non-agricultural industries and would invest in banks, railroads, or gold mines if there were a boom in that area. Some even moved into "seasonal" industries such as military procurement when profits were high. There were many landlords whose investments in non-agricultural businesses exceeded

---

23. Hong Sung-Chan, ibid. (1990a, 1990b); Hong Sung-Chan, "Iljeha kŭm'yung chabon ŭi nonggiŏp chibae: Chosŏn kaech'ŏk ŭi kyŏngyŏng pyŏndong kwa Chosŏn siksan ŭnhaeng," (The control of agricultural enterprises by finance capital during the Japanese occupation period: the IBC of Chosŏn and changes in management methods at Chosŏn Kaech'ŏk Company), *Kuksagwan nonch'ong*, no. 36 (1992).

their investments in land.[24] In this period, many people also made fortunes in non-agricultural businesses through capitalist methods and then used that capital to become large landlords. Pursuing sources of high profits, landlords had the freedom to build up or diversify their assets, and it became common for landlords to develop into bourgeoisie and vice versa. If landlords left large amounts of capital locked up in farmland, they would be un-able to invest in other areas, effectively paying high opportunity costs. Landlords had to take an active role in operating their farms and to decide what kind of labor to employ—either tenant farmers or wage laborers. They also had to be actively involved in all aspects of production, distribution, and marketing and run all their operations according to scientific methods and rational planning. This situation was all the more true for landlords who were highly dependent on financial institutions and had more problems repaying the principal and interest on their loans. As the landlord system adapted to changes in agriculture after the Japanese takeover and became incorporated into the Japanese economy, it changed and diversified into many different forms.

However, not all colonial landlords followed the trends of the time and adopted new methods of management. As mentioned above, many landlords were absentee landlords who did not even know the location of their own tenants. They were passive landlords who had no interest in land or agricultural improvements and simply hired *marŭm* or managers to collect tenancy fees that were fixed every year.[25] Significant numbers of landlords lost all their land when they failed to adapt to the changing circumstances, and the decline of these landlords grew even more severe as Japan's agricultural policies became more exploitative and as the economic recession lengthened. Landlords in this period had to adopt new business practices by entering into Japan's network of financial control and by developing close ties with Japan's capitalist agricultural policies and agricultural institutions. Such were the inexorable pressures put on landlords at the time, and in fact, many landlords

24. These landlords were also called "bourgeois landlords." Chang Siwŏn, ibid. Chang calculated the amount of extra-agricultural investment by uniformly multiplying fifty yen of nominal capital for each stock owned by a landlord; however, one could set up a company on the condition of submitting just one-fourth of the total nominal capital at the time. Therefore, the amount should be calculated by multiplying the actual paid capital per each stock (rather than fifty yen), which differed from company to company.

25. On the modes of existence of the old-style, static landlords, see Hisama Ken'ichi, ibid.; Hishimoto Choji, ibid.; Tohata Seiichi and Okawa Kazushi, *Beikoku keizai no kenkyu* (An examination of the rice economy) (Tokyo: Yuhikaku, 1939), pp. 301-02.

did attempt such changes.[26] More specifically, there were three new forms of the landlord system: *nongjang*, agricultural trust companies, and capitalist entrepreneurial agriculture.

NONGJANG (AGRICULTURAL ESTATES)

The most common type of new landlord system was the *nongjang*. *Nongjang* owners used tenants to cultivate the land, but unlike absentee landlords, they took a direct role in management and effectively turned the tenants into wage laborers, by taking complete control over the whole process of production, distribution, and marketing. These *nongjang* owners have been called "active, entrepreneurial landlords."[27]

These landlords actively looked for ways to increase their production such as the thorough introduction of scientific agricultural management methods. For example, taking over farmland owned by the IBC in late 1937, Sŏngŏpsa opened a branch in Puan (North Chŏlla province) in late January 1938 and requested a soil analysis from the Government-General's agricultural testing facility in Suwŏn. Similarly, in May 1938, Sŏngŏpsa's *nongjang* in Yŏngbuk commissioned an analysis of soil fertility from a research institute, which included an analysis of the soil layers, soil sifting, and chemical composition, and received a report on six items where agricultural techniques could be improved.[28] In short, the company took a scientific approach to researching the types of fertilizer and methods of weeding, cultivation, and fertilizer-mixing that were appropriate for the quality of its land. Carrying out meteorological analyses, the company measured the temperature, average rainfall, humidity, duration of sunshine, evaporation rate, and wind speed and direction. They also gathered long-range meteorological data to use in their long-term planning.[29]

Nongjang owners also worked together with scholars. They read research by agricultural scientists on topics such as the prevention and extermination of insects, the application of manure and green manure, animal husbandry, water drainage methods, and new varieties of seeds. They often hired agricultural scientists and specialists in various capacities, and they consulted

26. Kim Yong-sop, ibid. (1992), p. 3.

27. Hisama Ken'ichi, ibid.

28. Hong Sung-Chan, ibid. (1990b).

29. Ohashi Seisaburo, ed., *Chosen sangyŏ shishin* (Keijo: Kaihatsusha, 1915); Kim Sanghong, ibid.; Hong Sung-Chan, ibid. (1993); Yi Kyusu, "Nihonjin jinushi no tochi shuseki katei to Gunsan noji kumiai," (Land accumulation by Japanese landlords and the Kunsan Agricultural Association), *Hitotsubashi ronso* 116, no. 2 (1996).

engineers when they built irrigation facilities.[30] Agricultural companies allocated funds for research in their budgets and conducted various experiments in their testing bureaus.[31] Landlords and companies would also hire graduates of agricultural schools and send them to participate in various lectures and workshops. Large landlords, such as O Kŏn'gi, would experiment with growing different kinds of vegetables in a greenhouse.

Landlords and agricultural companies devoted much effort to selecting and managing tenant farmers. First, they selected their tenant farmers in a manner that was equally or, in some ways, even more rigorous than that of any modern business. In the 1930s, O Kŏn'gi of Tongbok required prospective tenant farmers to fill out a tenancy application and *Chosa sahang*, the equivalent of a resumé, on which he based his decisions. The criteria covered five areas: the land, sources of income, tenancy fee, characteristics of the tenant farmer, and references. To judge a tenant farmer, employers examined personal characteristics (e.g., health, age, occupation, personality, education, credit), family situation (e.g., gender composition, number of able workers and dependents), farmland (amounts of owned and/or tenant land), food and capital expenditures (e.g., annual consumption of rice, barley, and capital, minimum rate for self-sufficiency, deficits), and other factors such as residence, secondary sources of income, debts, livestock, and farm equipment. When examining land, employers required information on location, fertility, and availability of irrigation.[32] They took a scientific, rational approach to determining what types of tenants were suited for which kinds of land.

Landlords would also take the drastic step of dismissing their current tenants. In June 1931, the Hong family, a landlord family from Ŭnyul County (Hwanghae province), fired all their existing tenant farmers as part of an effort to rationalize their operations. They replaced them with new tenants from productive, docile families with little debt and at least two able-bodied laborers per family, and gave them sixteen *turak* (about one *chŏngbo*) of

---

30. Hong Sung-Chan, ibid. (1990b).

31. For instance, in December 1942, Chosŏn Kaech'ŏk Company conducted experiments in the effectiveness of human fertilizer in devalued land, the construction of levees in parched land areas, methods of prevention for rice-plant fever, new varieties of seed, concentrated planting of trees, and methods of constructing culverts for drainage in all of its *nongjang*. Hong Sung-Chan, ibid. (1993), p. 830.

32. Hong Sung-Chan, *Han'guk kŭndae nongch'on sahŏe ŭi pyŏndong kwa chijuch'ŭng*, pp. 186-90.

paddy field to cultivate.[33] In the case of Sannohe Kunimasu, a large landlord from Kimhae (South Kyŏngsang), his primary objective concerning tenant farmers was "the elimination of lazy tenants."[34] The local branch of Sŏngŏpsa, the agricultural company that was mentioned earlier, also fired most of the existing tenant farmers when it took over farmland in the Puan region. Dismissals of tenant farmers were more common in cases where a new landlord inherited the tenants from the land of a bankrupt landlord. In this sense, tenant dismissals were similar to the massive layoffs of personnel that occur today when a failed company is taken over by another company in a merger. By firing tenant farmers, landlords were looking for a way to improve productivity by giving reliable tenant farmers more than the standard share of land.[35]

Tenant farmers were subject to strict supervision in all aspects of cultivation. Tilling, sowing, transplanting, harvesting, drying, threshing, refining, and packing all had to be done using pre-determined seed varieties, according to fixed methods and in designated locations. Fertilizer also had to be mixed according to a fixed composition of ingredients and applied a set number of times on specified days. In order to coordinate these activities, landlords drew up daily cultivation schedules based on personal experience, meteorological data, and the annual cultivation plans submitted by each *nongjang*. Each *nongjang* made seasonal, monthly, and daily work schedules based on the cultivation schedule issued by the main office of the company.[36] The Chosŏn Kaech'ŏk Company received progress reports from its *nongjang* and branch offices every ten days in normal periods or every two to three days during busy months. By publishing them as a *Sunbo* (ten-day report), it kept a close eye on its *nongjang* and encouraged competition among them.

---

33. O Wonsŏk, "Inritsu jinushi Hong Kwang'ui shi no kosakunin kumiai jokyo," (The situation of the tenant farmer union for a ŭnyul landlord Mr. Hong Kwang'ui) *Chosen nokaiho*, 7, no. 10 (1933).

34. The landlord moved the tenant rights and decreased or increased tenant farming area of each tenant farmer according to the records of agricultural improvement, public service, transplantation of wet fields, weeding, extraction of millet. Pak Sokdong, "Kagayaku Rokuzan nojo" (Noksan Nongjang), *Chosen nokaiho*, 7, no. 10 (1933).

35. Landlords would dismiss tenant farmers when they acquired new land or when they consolidated their tenant farmland in one place and turned it into a *nongjang*. See Kim Sanghong, ibid.; In Chŏngsik, *Chosen no nogyo kiko* (Tokyo: Hakuyosha, 1940), p. 302.

36. Hong Sung-Chan, ibid. (1990b); Saito Hisatarŏ, "Chosen ni okeru nogyo shido ni tsuite," (On agricultural instruction in Chosŏn), *Chosen nokaiho*, 9, no. 1 (1935); Tansho Teruyoshi, "Chosen ni okeru noji keiei," (Management of farmland in Chosŏn), *Chosen nokaiho*, 3, no. 2 (1929).

Based on the progress in cultivation, the company would set up "special reinforcement periods" or order group work to be done in a certain *nongjang*, and on those days, it kept a record of daily attendance.

Landlords established offices and hired graduates of colleges, professional schools, or agricultural schools to staff them. Large landlords would set up a pyramidal organizational structure with a central office, branch offices, and local offices. For example, the Cheryŏng *nongjang* of the ODC had an organization that linked the main office, branches, individual *nongjang* (i.e., office), tenant farmer unions in fifteen districts, and six-person groups of tenant farmers under a collective responsibility system. Likewise, the Chosŏn Kaech'ŏk Company had an organizational structure connecting the following offices: main office—local office—*nongjang*, Research Bureau, Forestry Bureau—local and county/district offices.[37] The main offices of these companies had strict, centralized control over lower-level offices. Taking the previous year's results into consideration, the main office calculated and implemented its budget, and it also coordinated high-volume purchases of commodities needed by all of its *nongjang* in order to reduce expenses.

Large-scale *nongjang* arranged parcels of farmland in even-sided squares formed by roads and irrigation paths (main and local water lines), with an office, storehouses, and tenant farmers' houses concentrated at the center.[38] During the busy season, daily working hours were signaled with a siren or a bell, and there was a billboard for official announcements in front of the office. All kinds of equipment and ledgers, such as telephones and safes, were kept in the office, and on its walls hung the *nongjang*'s motto[39] as well as various charts showing the progress of work.

Landlords and companies implemented a diverse incentive system for employees and tenant farmers. For instance, Ungbon Nongjang, whose employees were mostly college graduates, held a competition each year to promote increased productivity; it commended the top employees and gave them monetary prizes for the increased harvest.[40] Ch'ŏn'gi Nongjang

---

37. Kim Yong-sop, ibid. (2000), pp. 289-91; Hong Sung-Chan, ibid. (1993).

38. Chŏe Wŏn'gyu, "1920-30 nyŏndae Ilje ŭi Han'guk nong'ŏp singminch'aek kwa Ilbon'in chajak nongch'on kŏnsŏl saŏp: Puri nongch'on sarye" (Japanese colonial agricultural policies in Chosŏn in the 1920s to 1930s and the establishment of Japanese self-sufficient farming villages—a case study of the Puri farming village), *Tongbang hakji*, no. 82 (1993).

39. For more on the "constitution" (場憲) of Yŏngbuk Nongjang and the "*nongjang* motto" (農場銘) of the Chosŏn Kaech'ŏk Company, see "An account of a visit to the exemplary Yŏngbuk Nongjang." Kim Kyusŭng, *Chosen nokaiho* 8, no. 2 (1934); Hong Sung-Chan, ibid. (1993).

40. Chu Ponggyu and So Sunyŏl, ibid., pp. 165-67.

sponsored crop fairs and promoted competition among tenant farmers by giving awards to the most productive tenant farmers and tenant farmer unions.[41]

Landlords were also actively involved in the marketing of rice. Those who had large quantities of rice to sell refined the rice themselves and then transported and stored it at export ports before shipping it to Japan. To do so, they had to own their own rice-processing facilities, trucks, and ships. Large-scale transactions in rice were conducted through grain sellers in places like Inchon, Osaka, Kobe, and Tokyo. Since quality control and standardization of products were necessary for such transactions, rice went through strict quality inspections, and most companies shipped rice with their logos stamped on the rice bags. In addition, landlords sold rice not only in over-the-counter transactions but also in the futures market to engage in hedging.[42]

It was absolutely crucial for landlords to collect information in order to be able to estimate the price of rice accurately. They subscribed to a number of newspapers and magazines as well as trade papers such as the *Mibi ilbo*. They set the shipping and selling dates for rice based on information on grain prices collected from grain exchanges in Korea and abroad. To maximize their profits, they would postpone shipping until the pre-harvest period, and if the interval was long, they borrowed money from banks to tide them over, using the stored grain as collateral. Since landlords had to insure all their stored grain, many of them even decided to do it themselves by opening a private branch of an insurance company.[43]

---

41. So Sunyŏl, "Shokuminchi koki Chosen jinushisei no kenkyu—Zenra hokudo o chushin ni," (An examination of the landlord system in Chosŏn during the late colonial period—focusing on North Chŏlla Province), *Kyoto Daigaku daigakuin kenkyuka hakase gakui ronbun*, 1994, pp. 116-17. Noksan Nongjang also held a "work competition" (勞力競進會) every year. See Pak Sŏkdong, ibid.

42. Most of the landlords who sold grain at the Grain Exchange collected their tenancy rents in the fall and stored their grains until the spring or summer of next year. They insured a percentage of the grains at the same market in case grain prices crashed. However, it was difficult to take advantage of this without previous experience, and sometimes, speculation led to losses of large sums of money. Hishimoto Choji, ibid., pp. 471-72.

43. Hong Sung-Chan, *Han'guk kŭndae nongch'on sahŏe ŭi pyŏndong kwa chijuch'ŭng*, p. 255. In an advertisement in March 1920, Nikka Life Insurance Company included a list of twenty policyholders who signed contracts as businessmen in the region of the Taegu branch of the IBC of Chosŏn (only those with the minimum liability of 2,500 won). Among them, three were categorized as a landlord or a large landlord, four as grain merchants as well as landlords, and thirteen as grain merchants. In short, policyholders in the area who signed the contracts as

During the occupation period, owners of *nongjang* completely reorganized their agricultural operations into organizations for exploitation, attempting to maximize their profits by managing their farmland according to rational, scientific methods. On the other hand, tenant farmers, although still tenants in name, were in reality no different from wage laborers whose form of existence alternated between being tenant farmers and a proletariat.[44] Tenant farmers had almost completely lost their autonomy in handling production, distribution, and marketing. They no longer constituted the majority of landowners, nor did they have control of the management of their land.

AGRICULTURAL TRUSTS

Another new type of landlord system that appeared during the occupation period was the agricultural trust system.[45] In this system, landlords went beyond using tenants to cultivate the land and turned over complete control of hiring tenants and cultivation to another landlord or company, agreeing to divide the profits. These cases usually involved passive landlords who were not knowledgeable of local conditions, had little direct experience with agricultural management, were tired of the repeated tenant disputes, and needed to implement drastic changes in their traditional management practices.[46] Although this system was similar to the *chungdapju* system during the

businessmen were all landlords and/or grain merchants. See *Maeil sinbo*, March 9, 1920, "Advertisement" section.

44. Kim Yong-sop, ibid. (2000), p. 475 and Hong Sung-Chan, ibid. (1989). See also Yamada Tatsuo, "Zenrahokudo ni okeru nogyo keiei no shoso" (An overview of agricultural management in North Chŏlla Province), *Nogyo to keizai* 8, no. 8, p. 65, "Since they had almost no autonomy to plan the entire process of cultivation themselves and had to cultivate according to the landlords' plans, their status fell to that of wage laborers."

45. Kim Yong-sop, "Chosŏn sint'ak ŭi nongjang kyŏngyŏng kwa chijuje pyŏndong" (Changes in the landlord system and the management of *nongjang* by Chosŏn Trust Company), ibid.; Hong Sŏngch'an, ibid. (1989).

46. In January 1937, the foundation of Chinmyŏng Academy decided to entrust the management of their farmland to the Chosŏn Trust Company, and the following quote provides a good example of this kind of situation.

Since the land of our school originally belonged to the royal palace, tenant farmers are used to the customary practices of tenants on royal lands, as if received by heredity. For many years, the foundation of this school has attempted to reform this situation and has achieved some improvements, but there are still some difficulties in managing cultivation. Since the rectification of these bad practices is urgent, it is necessary to plan large-scale innovations and to change our approach completely.

Chinmyŏng yŏja chunggodŭng hakkyo, *Chinmyŏng 75 nyŏnsa* (Seoul, 1980), p. 147.

late Chosŏn and Hanmal periods,[47] the difference was that in the new system, the trustee assumed full responsibility for the farmland and directly controlled and planned all aspects of cultivation. This type of work was also handled by agricultural companies during the occupation period under the name "real estate trust business."[48]

In this system, there were three ways of dividing profits between a landlord and a trustee. First, there was the fixed-rate system in which the remainder of the income from tenants after expenses were paid was divided according to a predetermined ratio. Such farmland was called *pot'ong kwalliji* (general managed land), and the trustee generally received twenty percent of tenant fees. Second, there was the fixed-sum system in which after expenses were taken care of, the contractor paid the landlord a pre-determined *sint'akjiryo* (land trust fee), regardless of the quality of the harvest, and kept the remainder of the profit. This kind of farmland was called *insu kwalliji* (subcontracted managed land). In the third method, the landlord kept all of the income after expenses were paid and gave the trustee only a fixed fee. If the business did well, the trustee would receive a special bonus.

Agricultural trusts were widespread during the occupation period. For example, as early as 1906, Puri Hŭngŏp began to manage large amounts of land as a trust.[49] In 1910, a number of the members of the Kunsan Agricultural Cooperative entrusted the purchase and management of their farmland to other members, who had more specialized knowledge and experience in management, and only received a fixed land rent in return.[50] In a 1929 survey conducted by the Japanese, the *kwalliji* (managed land) of Japanese agricultural managers (of more than 30 *chŏngbo*) was operated as an agricultural trust.[51] Additional examples include the farmland in Kanghwa that Chinmyŏng Girls' Academy entrusted to Chosŏn Sint'ak (Chosŏn Trust

47. Kim Yong-sop, "Hanmal'e itsŏsŏ ŭi chungdapju wa yŏk'ddun't'o chijuje" (*Chungdapju* and the landlord system in *yŏkdunt'o* in the Hanmal period), ibid. (1984).

48. "Chŏllabukdo nongsa hŏesa chŏnggwan mit sojak kyeyaksŏ" (The regulations for agricultural companies and tenancy contracts in North Chŏlla Province), *Chŏlla munhwa nonch'ong* 1 (1986).

49. In May 1921, Puri Hŭngŏp managed 1,443 *chŏngbo* of its own land along with 5,400 *chŏngbo* of entrusted land, which was almost four times the amount of its own land. In July 1929, the company's Chŏnbuk *nongjang* was managing 1,298 *chŏngbo* of its own land as well as 1406 *chŏngbo* of entrusted land, while Sŏson Farm of the same company was managing 4,290 *chŏngbo* of its own land along with 3,328 *chŏngbo* of entrusted land.

50. Yi Kyusu, ibid. (1996).

51. Chosŏn Ch'ongdokbu siksan'guk, *Chosen no nogyo* (Keijo: Chosŏn ch'ongdokbu, 1930), pp. 177-206.

Company) in January 1937[52] and the farmland that the Yi family in Naju (Chŏlla province) also hired the same company to operate in 1940.[53]

In the agricultural trust system, the landowner was not involved in the cultivation and management of the land; the trustee assumed full responsibility over agricultural operations. The relations among the landlord, trustee, and tenant farmer exactly paralleled the class relations among landlords, agricultural capitalists, and laborers. In the case of *insu kwalliji*, the tenant farmer paid a tenant fee to the trustee, and then the trustee paid part of that amount to the landlord as the "land trust fee." Accordingly, the tenant farmer's share constituted wages or the portion of necessary labor, and the tenant fee paid to the trustee was not land rent but represented the amount of surplus value. The trustee paid a portion of the surplus value to the landlord as land rent (land trust fee) and kept the rest as profit. Trustees could maximize their profits only by paying lower land rents to the landlord or by giving a lower share of the harvest to the tenants. If the profits were below the general average rate of profit, they would abandon the agricultural trust business. In short, they behaved like agricultural capitalists. In order to secure not just average profits but also a greater extra profit, trustees sought to increase the quantity of both absolute and relative surplus value. Such efforts ultimately led to a strict control over the management of tenant farmers.

During the occupation period, there were landlords who cultivated both their own land and trust land, and they employed the same methods to manage the two different kinds of land. After being hired to operate the Yŏngbuk Nongjang in the early 1930s, Chwadŭng Nongjang stationed two full time employees in each of the two districts of the *nongjang* and chose village leaders to serve as their assistants. During the harvest, it hired about fifteen temporary workers for approximately three months. Employing the methods that they had been using in their own *nongjang*, Chwadŭng Nongjang achieved a remarkable increase in production by requiring tenant farmers to begin work early, to increase production of manure for fertilizer, to conserve water, and to adopt new types of seeds. The *nongjang* also forced women to work and required tenants to do shallow seeding and dense planting and to eliminate millet and weeds.[54] When Chwadŭng Nongjang was contracted to oversee twenty *chŏngbo* of farmland from Hansŏng Bank in 1932, the *nongjang* again achieved positive results by managing tenant farm-

---

52. *Chinmyŏng 75 nyŏnsa*, p. 147.
53. Kim Yong-sop, ibid. (2000), p. 158.
54. Kim Kyusŭng, ibid. (1934).

ers with the same methods used on its own lands.[55] Just as landlords managed their own land and trust land using the same methods, tenant farmers simply farmed the land according to the landlord's directions and only had to pay the tenant fee. It mattered little to them whether the land they cultivated belonged to the landlord or was entrusted to a different landlord.[56]

AGRICULTURAL ENTREPRENEURS

During the occupation period, some landlords used capitalist methods to manage their lands by hiring wage laborers rather than contracting tenant farmers. They were capitalist agricultural entrepreneurs who adapted the methods of the managerial landlords and managerial rich peasants of the late Chosŏn period to the agricultural conditions of their time. Two good examples of this type of landlord are the Yi family of Naju and the Yu family of Kurye (North Chŏlla). They used tenants to cultivate a part of their farmland and directly managed the remaining land, hiring *marŭm* and those living outside of their property to cultivate it under their planning and supervision.[57] In order to maintain an available pool of cheap labor, the Yi family rented houses outside of the tenant farmers' area to workers in return for their labor and directly managed their own land. The Maeha Nongjang, which Kim Yŏnsu established in Manchuria in 1938, was a more advanced form of this type of landlord system. Unlike the Yi family, Kim Yŏnsu managed his *nongjang* as a completely self-cultivating *nongjang* by employing as laborers the "young countrymen who wandered around the continent all alone."[58]

55. Kim Kyusŭng, ibid. (1933).

56. Tenancy disputes in trust land did not occur between the landlord, who hired an agricultural trust, and the tenant farmers, but they were instances of class conflict between the trustee and the tenant farmers. Therefore such disputes had the characteristics of labor disputes waged by laborers (=tenant farmers) against agricultural capitalist (=trust company). Hong Sung-Chan, ibid. (1989).

57. Kim Yong-sop, "Naju Yi ss'iga ŭi chiju kyŏngyŏng ŭi sŏngjang kwa pyŏndong" (The development and changes in landlord management methods of the Naju Yi Family), ibid. (2000); Yi Chongbŏm, "20 segi ch'o chayŏng (so)jiju ŭi nong'ŏp kyŏngyŏng kwa nongmin saenghwal— Kurye kun T'oji myŏn Omi dong sarye" (The agricultural management methods of (small) self-cultivating landlords in the early twentieth century—a case study of Omi Village, T'oji Subcounty in Kurye County), *Hangnim*, no. 16 (1994).

58. Each hired farmer was paid approximately 155 yen each season on the condition that he cultivated 1.5 *chŏngbo* of land of high fertility and 1 *chŏngbo* of barren land. They were also required to make straw bags and straw ropes after harvest; each bag was valued at 35 *chŏn* (錢) and 25 *chŏn* for 1 *kwan* (貫) (7.5 pounds) of straw rope. Half of these amounts was distributed as wages. Kim Sanghong, ibid., pp. 143-44.

As mentioned above, although many landlords were content to follow traditional, static methods of management, a significant number adapted to the changing conditions of the times and, in general, transformed into one of the three new types of landlord. Did these new types of landlord have prospects for growth or for decline in this period? It seems that prospects for growth were greater for the following two reasons.

First, Japan's agricultural policies were conducive to growth. From the beginning of its occupation, as is well known, Japan implemented various policies to transform static landlords into a new type of landlord.[59] Similarly, in 1944, toward the end of its rule, Japan implemented a communal responsibility system for agricultural production, assigning production quotas to each village, and placed primary responsibility for production on the landlords rather than the peasants. Around the same time, the Japanese also announced guidelines for the "promotion of landlord activity" and a list of measures directed against lazy farmers. In order to promote increased production by landlords, the former measure encouraged absentee landlords, particularly those who owned farmland within the district of an irrigation cooperative, to return to farming and made it a duty for them to supervise farmers, implement land improvements, hire agricultural instructors, and build up facilities to handle the increased production. The latter was a measure that gave landlords the right to dismiss disobedient tenant farmers arbitrarily. In order to provide institutional support for these measures, the Japanese government revised the Emergency Farmland Management Ordinance and prohibited the lease or sale of farmland to unproductive farmers or absentee landlords who had no interest in cultivation. The Japanese no longer used indirect incentives, such as granting subsidies or providing low interest financing, but adopted legal, institutional, and administrative means of coercion to transform landlords into *nongjang* landlords or active, entrepreneurial landlords.[60]

At the state level, Japan also pursued a policy of promoting the agricultural trust system by attempting to entrust the management of the land of static landlords to landlords who had specialized knowledge of and experience in agricultural management. Japan established Chosŏn Sint'ak as a quasi-governmental company to take over the management of the lands of unproductive landlords; its purpose was to provide relief to small and medium

---

59. Hisama Ken'ichi, "Jinushiteki shokuno no chosei," ibid. (1943).

60. Hong Sung-Chan, ibid. (1989); U Taehyŏng, *Han'guk kŭndae nong'ŏpsa ŭi kujo* (Seoul: Han'guk yŏn'guwŏn, 2001), pp. 171-75.

landlords who faced grave difficulties in the early 1930s because of the Great Depression.[61] In 1944, Japan promulgated a set of guidelines for the implementation of an agricultural land management system, announcing its intention to transfer forcibly the land of absentee landlords, who did not comply with the government's policy to increase production, to trust companies or cooperatives such as *nongjang*, irrigation cooperatives, and land management unions. The guidelines specified that "all lands belonging to absentee landlords, regardless of their size, will be managed by a trust cooperative" and that the trust institution, such as an irrigation cooperative, in charge of cultivation will be paid a "management fee of twenty percent" of the income from the land.[62] The Japanese originally had tried to encourage landlords to transform themselves into innovative agricultural entrepreneurs, but in cases where such transformation was impossible, the state's policy was to force unproductive landlords to entrust their land to entrepreneurial landlords.

Second, the landlords themselves adapted to the changing economic and political conditions and actively adopted new methods of agricultural management during the occupation period. Even with the same land and tenant farmers, productivity and profitability would vary depending on the way the landlord organized and managed his land and businesses. A clear example of the impact of such a change was the case of Kim Kyusŭng, who worked at Kyŏngsŏng Hŭngsan where he gained experience and training in agricultural management. In 1932, he was hired to manage twenty-two *chŏngbo* of farmland in the district of the Tong'in Irrigation Cooperative (Tong'in Suri Chohap). He implemented management reforms by stationing a full-time employee on the land and dispatching two additional temporary harvest workers. A year later, he increased the income from the sale of the rice cultivated by the tenant farmers (minus fertilizer costs, irrigation taxes, land taxes, Agriculture Association (Nonghoe) fees, and management fees) by five times over the previous year, and he received a special bonus from the landlord in addition to his management fee.[63]

These changes in business practices became even more widespread with the generational change from owners with a classical Chinese education to

61. Kim Yong-sop, "Chosŏn sint'ak ŭi nongjang kyŏngyŏng kwa chijuje pyŏndong," ibid. (2000).

62. Hong Sung-Chan, ibid. (1989).

63. Kim Kyusŭng, ibid. (1934), pp. 73–74. Chwadŭng Nongjang mentioned in footnotes 54 and 55 is also a similar case.

those who were more fluent in Japanese. In short, it was a shift to a generation familiar with the new changes brought about by Japanese capitalism. For example, the son of the Yun family in Haenam studied economics at Hosei University in Tokyo in the 1920s, and when his generation took over the family's operations, they actively embarked on reorganizing the family farms into a *nongjang* system. Taking out large loans from the IBC in the 1920s and 1930s, they established two *nongjang* that engaged in land reclamation and, in the same period, greatly intensified their regulation of their tenant farmers.[64] O Kŏn'gi of Tongbok, who returned to Chosŏn in the 1920s after studying at Tokyo Myŏngyo Middle School and other schools in Japan, took over his father's business and established Tonggo Nongjang, transforming the family's operations into a *nongjang* system.[65]

A large landlord in Muan (South Chŏlla province), Hyŏn Chunho studied at Meiji University in Japan and took over his family's business after he returned. He was one of the leading figures in the establishment of Honam Bank in 1920 and established Hakp'a Nongjang in the 1930s.[66] Similarly, Kim Yŏnsu, who was from a large landlord family, studied economics at Kyoto Imperial University and took over the family's farms after his return in the early 1920s. He reorganized agricultural operations into a *nongjang* by gathering all the family's tenant land in one location and by getting rid of the existing tenant farmers. In addition, he established new farms to conduct large-scale land reclamation projects and even expanded business to Man-churia, where he opened several *nongjang* that used both tenant farmers and wage labor.[67] The Mun family in Amt'ae Island was a similar example of a family who changed their methods of agricultural management as a result of a generational change.[68] In short, adapting to the trends of the time, landlords took advantage of the agricultural policies of the Japanese and transformed their agricultural and business practices as they developed close ties with the institutions of Japanese capitalism.

---

64. Choi Won-kyu, ibid. (1986).

65. Hong Sung-Chan, *Han'guk kŭndae nongch'on sahŏe ŭi pyŏndong kwa chijuch'ŭng*, pp. 176-77.

66. Son Chŏng'yŏn, *Musong Hyŏn Chunho* (Kwangju: Chŏn'nam maeil sinmunsa, 1977); Hong Sung-Chan, ibid. (1999).

67. Kim Sanghong, ibid.; Kim Yong-sop, "Kobu Kim ss'iga ŭi chiju kyŏngyŏng kwa chabon chŏnhwan" (The landlord management of the Kim family of Kobu and their capital conversion), ibid. (2000).

68. Pak Ch'ŏnu, ibid. (1985).

Expansion of Political and Social Networks

During the occupation period, the most important concern for landlords was the maintenance of and increase in their wealth, i.e., a strong need for protection. A good example of the landlords' mindset was an aphorism written on the cover of the "Harvest Journal" from the 1910s of the Chŏng Il'u family, a large landlord in Koksŏng (South Chŏlla province): "An old saying goes, 'It is difficult to begin an undertaking,' but the most difficult is to maintain it and bring it to completion." However, it was not always easy for landlords to find a means of protecting their interests.

Above all, protection required close relations with government officials and institutions. In this period, the landlord system became incorporated into Japan's capitalist economy; at the time, the Japanese economy was reaching the stages of finance capitalism and state monopoly capitalism. In order to maintain and expand their businesses, landlords needed a firm grasp of the workings of finance and state monopoly capitalism as well as the information, daring, entrepreneurial spirit, and experience necessary to utilize such knowledge. In particular, it was absolutely necessary to develop close ties with financial institutions that carried out Government-General policy such as the Bank of Chosŏn, the IBC, the ODC, and financial cooperatives since they controlled access to capital. To develop such relations, it was crucial to have the support and protection of the authorities and close relations with government officials who controlled the finance institutions and had a monopoly on all information regarding development.

Landlords constantly faced intensified class conflict in the form of tenancy disputes. Although tenancy disputes against small and medium landlords were frequent, they did not have much social impact since they were small in scale and generally did not develop into public protests. On the other hand, tenant disputes against large landlords were accompanied by large-scale demonstrations and lasted longer, leading to more significant social repercussions. Large-scale disputes primarily occurred in the fall as tenant farmers protested by refusing to harvest the rice, leaving the plants standing in the paddy fields. These were known as the "autumn struggle" (*ch'ut'u*). For example, a tenant dispute in Ungbon Nongjang in the 1930s began when the tenant farmers collectively decided to return the landlords' "Notice of Tenant Fee Payment" to protest the higher-than-expected tenant fees demanded.[69] In the spring, protests occurred when farmers refused to transplant the young rice seedlings, leaving them in their seedbeds. These were naturally called the "spring struggle" (*ch'unt'u*). A lengthy strike was a serious threat to both landlords and tenants alike. Tenant farmers were threatened with the loss of their livelihood, and landlords faced a crisis because of the possible interruption of their cash flow.

Similar to labor disputes today, the two sides engaged in lengthy negotiations, gathering data on issues such as living expenses and productivity and exchanging several proposals and lists of demands.[70] The proposals were so complicated that only the participants involved could understand which proposal was advantageous to their side. Sometimes, the tenant farmers would divide into hard-line and moderate factions when deciding whether or not to accept a proposal. For example, when the tenant dispute at Sŏsŏn Nongjang of Puri Hŭngŏp became protracted, the initial conflict between the landlord and the tenant farmers developed into a conflict among the tenant farmers themselves.

A protracted struggle naturally led to the involvement of outside forces. Civic groups dispatched survey teams and issued statements of support for the tenants; landlords joined with other nearby landlords and prepared their response in meetings with the police and local government officials. In order to cope with tenancy disputes and other forms of class conflict, landlords had to cultivate close ties with government officials who controlled the police and had information on local affairs. These connections were even more necessary for the new types of landlords, because they were expanding the scale of their businesses by increasing their investments in agriculture through a constant influx of bank capital. They were also intensifying the use of tenant farmers as labor as they became directly involved in all aspects of production, distribution, and marketing.

In order to protect their interests, landlords actively utilized blood relations, regional ties, alumni networks, and marital ties to expand their networks of political and social connections. First of all, they constructed a network of blood relations by playing a leading role in strengthening clan unity.

69. Hong Sung-Chan, ibid. (1989).

70. Chu Pong'gyu and So Sunyŏl, ibid., pp. 258-59, 266-74; Kim Yong-sop, ibid. (2000), pp. 309-14; Hong Sung-Chan, ibid. (1990a); Yi Kyusu, "Kindai Chosen ni okeru shokuminchi jinushisei to nōmin undō" (The colonial landlord system and the peasant movement in early modern Chosŏn), *Hitotsubashi Daigaku daigakuin shakaigaku kenkyuka hakase gakui ronbun* (1994), pp. 205-06.

For instance, they would take an active role in the clan association or publish genealogies and the collected works of their ancestors.[71] Landlords also built networks of marital ties through intermarriage with prominent local families in all regions of the country.[72] They organized the publication of local gazettes with other nearby landlords and local elites and gave their support to the establishment of schools for the children in the area. They reinforced their close ties with local elites and government officials by working as the chairman or by serving on the board of directors or as trustees of all kinds of government and public organizations, such as agricultural associations, landlord associations, fire fighting guilds, school cooperatives, the Red Cross, and military support leagues as well as cooperatives for irrigation, forestry, sericulture, silk-worm cultivation, and financial credit.[73]

The landlords took special care to maintain close relationships with employees of financial institutions and government officials in both Chosŏn and other countries. They widened their network of connections by sending out greeting cards and gifts during the year-end holidays. When there was a change in personnel, they threw farewell or welcoming banquets and also sent congratulations by phone or telegraph. Landlords also attended the various social gatherings held by the Government-General and by offices at the provincial and district levels.[74] They also cultivated a network of ties with important figures in non-agricultural industries by becoming shareholders or by serving on the board of directors of banks, financial institutions, and industrial companies and commercial enterprises. They were able to strengthen connections with figures in non-agricultural businesses and to obtain

71. Hong Sung-Chan, ibid. (1981); Hong Sung-Chan, "Hanmal iljech'o hyang'nich'ŭng ŭi pyŏndong kwa munmyŏng kaehwaron: Posŏng kunsu O Chaeyŏng ŭi sarye rŭl chungsim ŭro" (Changes in the *hyangni* class and their conception of civilization and enlightenment in the Hanmal and Japanese occupation periods: a case study of O Chaeyŏng, county magistrate of Posŏng), *Han'guksa yŏn'gu*, no. 90 (1995).

72. Hong Sung-Chan, *Han'guk kŭndae nongch'on sahŏe ŭi pyŏndong kwa chijuch'ŭng*, p. 60.

73. Hong Sung-Chan, ibid. (1992), part I, chapter 2. O Kŏn'gi of Tongbok spent approximately 10,000 yen on various kinds of quasi taxes, such as "contributions" and "donations" (i.e., 寄附金, 慰勞金, 贊助金) from March 1939 to February 1940, which exceeded the amount of roughly 9,000 wŏn of official taxes he paid; Chi Sugŏl, "Iljeha Kongju chiyŏk yuji chipdan ŭi toch'ŏng ijŏn pandae undong (1930.11-1932.10)" (The local elites' movement against the relocation of the provincial office in the Kongju region under Japanese rule (November 1930-October 1932)), *Yŏksa wa hyŏnsil*, no. 20 (1996), p. 226.

74. Hong Sung-Chan, "Hanmal ilje hyang'nich'ŭng ŭi pyŏndong kwa munmyŏng kaehwaron: Posŏng kunsu O Chaeyŏng ŭi sarye rŭl chungshim ŭro." Landlords wore only acceptable clothing, such as tuxedos, to parties and attached entrance passes to their outfits. They dressed in bow ties and silk hats and went to these parties in their own cars.

necessary information by attending shareholder meetings not only when they served on a company's board of directors as a major stockholder but also even if they held only a token amount of shares.

Landlords also sought direct access to political power. They ran for local government posts or became involved in politics by becoming sponsors of or serving as election committee members for politicians. Just as entrepreneurs today use their businesses to run for office, landlords used their agricultural businesses, which penetrated into various levels of local society by linking landlords, employees of *nongjang*, and elites at the *kun* (county), *myŏn* (township), *ri* (natural village), and *tong* levels, to serve as their campaign organizations.[75] As local elites and the leaders of public opinion, they were able to forge ties with central politics by cultivating relations with influential figures in political and financial circles in Seoul. It was easier for landlords to expand their connections through regional or school ties if, for example, someone from their hometown or an alumni friend from their school days in Japan became a successful political or financial figure in Seoul with country-wide prominence.[76]

The need for landlords to develop ties with influential figures became greater, the larger the scale of their business, the greater their dependency on banks and other financial institutions, the more they adopted new forms of agricultural management, the more they needed sources of information, and the faster a generational change occurred to owners educated in Japanese rather than classical Chinese. One example was the Yi family of Posŏng, one of the most prominent aristocratic families in the southwestern Honam region (Chŏlla province). Interestingly, during the Hanmal and early occupation periods, they had been supporters of the anti-Japanese, anti-Western ideas of *ch'ŏksa* (eliminate heterodoxy). When they accumulated a large amount of debt to the IBC and other banks during the Great Depression, the

---

75. Hong Sung-Chan, *Han'guk kŭndae nongch'on sahŏe ŭi pyŏndong kwa chijuch'ŭng*, part I, chapter 1.; Chi Sugŏl, "1930 nyŏndae huban'gi Chosŏnin taejijuch'ŭng ŭi chŏngch'ijŏk tong-hyang" (The political activities and tendencies of the large Chosŏn landlords in the second half of the 1930s), *Yŏksa hakbo*, no. 122 (1989); also see Im Taesik, "1930 nyŏndae mal Kyŏnggi chiyŏk Chosŏnin taejiju ŭi nong'ŏe t'uja wa chibang ŭihŏe ch'am'yŏ" (Non-agricultural investment by large Chosŏn landlords and their participation in local politics in Kyŏnggi province in the late 1930s), *Han'guk saron*, no. 34 (1995).

76. There were many landlords who set up scholarship foundations and supported promising youths. This in fact brought about the effect of devising long-term countermeasure to expand the net of connection for these landlords. See Kim Sanghyŏng, ibid.; Son Chŏng'yŏn, ibid., pp. 177-79; Yi Tong'uk, *Kyech'o Pang Ŭngmo* (Seoul: Pang Ilyŏng munhwajaedan, 1996), pp. 247-57; Hong Sung-Chan, *Han'guk kŭndae nongch'on sahŏe ŭi pyŏndong kwa chijuch'ŭng*, p. 267.

family reorganized their farms into *nongjang* in the early 1930s, and one member was elected to the local council in Poknae township in 1931. In succeeding years, various family members served on several local committees such as the Posŏng County Educational Council, the board of trustees of Posŏng County School, the school board of Poknae Public Normal School, the Poknae Regional Council of the Imperial Aviation Association, and the South Chŏlla Province Agricultural Promotional Association.[77]

Another example was O Kŏn'gi, a large landlord in Tongbok. After his return from studying in Japan, he acquired farmland and reorganized it into a *nongjang* and managed it by utilizing large loans from banks such as the IBC and Honam Bank. He also sought to expand his connections by serving on local committees including the local town council, the board of trustees of the County Agricultural Association, and the county's tenancy committee. He also served on the school board of the local normal school, the booster committee of Kwangju Girls' High School, the Income Survey Committee of the Kwangju Tax Office, the Hwasun branch of the Chosŏn Fire Committee, the Hwasun branch of the Tuberculosis Prevention Committee, and the Sericulture Association of South Chŏlla Province. In 1937 he was elected to the Provincial Assembly of South Chŏlla province, and, in the late colonial period, he became the mayor of Tongbok Township.[78] As these examples show, all types of landlords actively engaged in expanding their political and social connections by participating in various large and small organizations—not just the largest landlords like Kim Yŏnsu or Tomita Gisaku, who were known throughout the country, but even relatively unknown provincial landlords like the Yi family of Posŏng (Yi Yong'ŭi) or the O family of Tongbok (O Kŏn'gi).

During the occupation period, landlords obtained special privileges, such as loans and access to information by using their familial, regional, alumni, and marital connections to "lobby" financial institutions and government offices.[79] They formed pressure groups by developing ties with the economic networks that developed around the landlord system—i.e, banks, grain mer-

77. Hong Sung-Chan, "Hanmal iljeha ŭi chijuje yŏn'gu: 50 chŏngbo chiju Posŏng Yissiga ŭi chiju kyŏngyŏng sarye."

78. Hong Sung-Chan, *Han'guk kŭndae nongch'on sahŏe ŭi pyŏndong kwa chijuch'ŭng*, p. 264.

79. One of the secrets behind the accumulation of wealth for the large landlord Kim Kapsun of Kongju was his "social networks" and his "lobbying" efforts; in other words, obtaining information regarding development before others through illegal business dealings. See Chi Sugŏl, ibid. (1996), p. 226.

chants, rice-polishing merchants, grain-warehouse owners, grain exchanges, and the Chosŏn Agricultural Association (Chosŏn Nonghoe). Through these groups, they promoted and defended their interests to the Japanese government, the Diet, and mass media.[80] Of course, even the Japanese government could not easily ignore their demands; in the process, the landlords' political views became changed, amounting to an acceptance of Japanese rule in Chosŏn.

Conclusion

From the late Chosŏn period through the Hanmal and occupation periods, there was constant tension and conflict between landlord-oriented and peasant-oriented programs of modernization. After Liberation, two different economic systems were established in North and South Korea, and the divided countries implemented differing programs of agricultural land reform. Two separate agricultural systems were created in the north and the south as left- and right-wing political groups could not reach a suitable compromise between the two programs.[81]

In such circumstances, all landlords underwent major changes regardless of their style of management. However, the new types of landlord who had actively adapted to the changes in the agricultural economy during the occupation period were relatively successful in adapting, once more, to the new economic conditions in South Korea after Liberation. As they frequented banks, they became familiar with the workings of the Japanese economy. As they became the leading force in landownership and commercial agriculture and reorganized the landlord system into a business enterprise, they acquired entrepreneurial managerial methods. Landlords had the ability to diversify their assets and a deep understanding of the workings of capitalist enterprise by serving as shareholders and executives of companies in non-agricultural

---

80. The Organization for the Protection of Chosŏn Rice (鮮米擁護期成會) was formed in July of 1932 to cope with the Japanese movement to limit import of Chosŏn rice during the Great Depression era. Its sponsors were executives from the Bank of Chosŏn, the IBC of Chosŏn, Chosŏn Grain Storage Company, the ODC, Chosŏn Land Improvement Company, Agricultural Association of Chosŏn and Puri Hŭng'ŏp, as well as the major grain merchants of Chosŏn. Chŏn Kangsu, "Nong'ŏp konghwanggi ŭi migok-mi'ga chŏngch'aek e kwanhan yŏn'gu" (An examination of policies toward grain and grain prices during the agricultural depression period), *Kyŏngje sahak*, no. 13 (1989), p. 156.

81. Kim Yong-sop, ibid. (2000), pp. 478–85.

industries. Because of their high level of education, the transition after 1945 from a generation educated in Japanese language to one conversant in English was relatively smooth. Because of their efforts to expand their political and social connections during the occupation period, they had various personal networks they could mobilize when necessary. Since they gained familiarity with politics from their participation in various kinds of elections, they were able to adapt rapidly to the election system established in the south after Liberation.

In the political and social chaos brought about by Liberation, division, and the Korean War, it was difficult for landlords from the occupation period to transform themselves into capitalists after Liberation. However, the new types of landlords were relatively successful in achieving that transformation.[82] Compared to other classes, they adapted rapidly to the post-Liberation election culture and produced a large number of politicians. One example was the Yi family of Posŏng, a large landlord family that had worked on campaigns for candidates during the 1933 elections for the South Chŏlla Provincial Assembly. After Liberation, one member of the family served on the constitutional committee (Yi Chŏngnae), and another became a prominent member of the opposition party (Yi Chungjae). Similarly, Yun Chŏnghyŏn, member of a large landlord family from Haenam, became a representative in the National Assembly after Liberation. During the occupation period, Chŏng Sut'ae and Chŏng Kyut'ae, two members of the Chŏng family of Koksŏng, were elected to the South Chŏlla Provincial Assembly, and after the founding of the Republic of Korea, Chŏng Naehyŏk served as the Vice-Speaker of the National Assembly.

translated by Kelly Y. Jeong

---

82. Yi Chisu, "Haebang hu nongji kaehyŏk kwa chijuch'ŭng ŭi chabon chŏnhwan munje," (The post-liberation land reform and the issue of capital conversion by the landlord class) (MA thesis, Yonsei University, 1994). In their response to the land reform, some landlords established a number of schools in all regions of the country.

Index of Terms

nonggam 農監 supervisor or manager
Nonghoe 農會 Agriculture Association
pot'ong kwalliji 普通管理地 general managed land
Puri hŭngŏp 不二興業
P'yŏngyang ŭnhaeng 平壤銀行 Pyongyang Bank
ri 里 natural village
Samhwa ŭnhaeng 三和銀行 Samhwa Bank
Samnam ŭnhaeng 三南銀行 Samnam Bank
sint'ak chijuje 信託地主制 agricultural trusts
sint'akjiryo 信託地料 land trust fee
Sŏng'ŏpsa 成業社
sunbo 旬報 ten-day report
Tong'in suri chohap 同仁水利組合 Tong'in Irrigation Cooperative
Tongyang ch'ŏksik hoesa 東洋拓殖會社 Oriental Development Company
Ungbon nongjang 熊本農場
Yi Pyŏngch'ŏl 李秉喆
Yŏngbuk nongjang 永北農場

CHAPTER 6

The Decision-Making Process and Implementation of the North Korean Land Reform

Kim Seong-bo
金聖甫

In March 1946, North Korea carried out one of the most rapid and radical land reforms in world history. Within a single month, all land that had been cultivated by tenant farmers was seized from their landlords. 29,683 households with more than five *chŏngbo* of land were classified as belonging to the landlord class. Both their land and their assets were seized, and they were forced to move to another *kun* (county). The amount of confiscated land totaled 1,008,178 *chŏngbo* which was approximately 55.4% of the 1,820,098 *chŏngbo* of total farmland in North Korea (1 *chŏngbo* = approximately 1 hectare or 2.45 acres). The confiscated land was distributed to the peasants, beginning with landless farmers, and 724,522 peasant households received parcels of land. Land distributed through the land reform could not be sold or leased, and the state came to exercise complete administrative control over the land.

Existing scholarship has generally explained the enactment of such a radical land reform in North Korea through external factors such as the direct implementation by the Soviet Union of its own model in order to "Sovietize" the North and establish a separate government there. The importation of the Soviet model has been understood as a policy that was imposed from above by the Soviet Military Government and the Korean Communist Party (KCP) and lacked mass initiative.[1]

As will be discussed below, it is undeniable that the Soviet Union had a large influence on the North Korean land reform and on the formation of the North Korean regime after liberation. However, external factors or the effects of coercive power from above are not sufficient to provide answers to the following two questions. First, why did North Korea carry out a radical land reform while Eastern European countries occupied by the Soviet Army implemented a moderate land reform that compensated landlords and placed limits on the total amount of land involved? The fact of Korea's division cannot adequately explain the difference since land reform was carried out on a limited basis in East Germany, another divided country. Second, why has the North Korean system retained such a high degree of internal unity despite the collapse of the Soviet Union and Eastern Europe?

To answer these questions, it is necessary to look at the internal dynamics of North Korea as well as the concrete steps taken in the process of land reform. The main issues are: What were the general policies of the Soviet occupation forces in post-World War II North Korea, how did they culminate in a radical land reform, and what was the relation of these policies to the internal structure of North Korean society? It is also important to analyze how the land reform contributed to the internal unity of the North Korean regime.

Another objective of this chapter is to overcome the limitations of the opposite trend in research on North Korea which has deemphasized the "Sovietization model." What these studies have in common is that they all ignore aspects of the actual history of North Korea. For instance, there is research from North Korea itself that completely neglects the Soviet influence on the land reform.[2] Some studies speculate that Soviet influence was not significant because Korea still would have undergone a socialist revolution if it had not been occupied by the U.S. and Soviet Union after liberation.[3] Furthermore, if an internally-driven, spontaneous land reform had been

1. Joseph Man-Kyung Ha, "Politics of Korean Peasantry: A Study of Land Reform and Collectivization with Reference to Sino-Soviet Experiences" (Ph.D. diss., Columbia University, 1971).

2. Son Chŏnhu, *Uri nara t'oji kaehyŏksa* (History of Land Reform in Our Country) (Pyongyang: Science Encyclopedia Press, 1983); Kim Sŭngjun, *Uri nara esŏ ŭi nongch'on munje haegyŏl ŭi ryŏksajŏk kyŏnghŏm* (The Historical Experience of Resolving the Village Problem in Our Country) (Pyongyang: Korean Worker's Party Press, 1965).

3. Kang Chŏnggu, *Chwajŏl toen sahoe hyŏkmyŏng—Mi kunjŏng ha ŭi Namhan-P'illip'in kwa Pukhan yŏn'gu* (Social Revolution Denied—South Korea and the Philippines under American Military Government) (Seoul: Yŏlŭmsa, 1989).

implemented in the North, the reform would have been conducted with a great amount of flexibility, and the North Korean state would have gained mass support. In actuality, the land reform was implemented with little flexibility because the imperatives of state apparatuses were of even greater importance than mass initiative.

The main objective of this chapter is to undertake a comprehensive examination of both external and internal factors, as well as the dynamics of both central politics and rural society, in North Korea's land reform. [4] Through an analysis of the radicalization of the land reform and the responses of landlords and peasants, this chapter seeks to understand the unique aspects of the land reform and its consequences on the formation of the North Korean state within the context of the conflicts between the U.S. and Soviet Union, between capitalist groups and socialist forces, and between landlords and peasants.

Politics at the Center: The Transition from a Moderate Line to a Radical Line

According to existing available sources, it was the socialists—and among them the communists—who were the first to argue for the necessity of land reform and present a plan for it. Those involved in the land reform were mainly active in Seoul and in South Hamgyŏng province, the center of the Red Peasant Union movement during the colonial period.

In Seoul, the Korean Communist Party was reestablished under the leadership of Pak Hŏnyŏng (1900-1956), and it promulgated its "August Theses" in 1945 which included a program for the nationalization of land. In its "Resolution on the Land Question" of October 3, 1945, the KCP Central Committee clarified the party's position, calling for the land to be appropriated without compensation, nationalized, and then distributed for free on the basis of the "labor power" (*nodongnyŏk*) and size of each farm household.

---

4. Attempts to explaining post-liberation Korean contemporary history through examining together external and internal forces, central politics, and the tendencies of mass society, have already yielded important results. Bruce Cumings, *The Origins of the Korean War*, two volumes (Princeton: Princeton University Press, 1981, 1990); Pak Myŏngnim, *Han'guk chŏnjaeng ŭi palbal kwa kiwŏn* (The outbreak and origins of the Korean War), two volumes (Seoul: Nanam Press, 1996). The nationalist side of Kim Il Sung and the special characteristics of the North Korean system are examined in Charles K. Armstrong, "State and Social Transformation in North Korea, 1945-1950" (Ph.D. diss., University of Chicago, 1994).

The fate of the land belonging to small and medium landlords would be decided in relation to their "capacity" (*yŏngnyang*). A more detailed explanation of this resolution was included in the "Commentary on the Resolution on the Land Question." The ultimate goal of the land reform was to confiscate all "land exceeding ten *chŏngbo*" owned by large landlords and to seize the land of small and medium landlords that exceeded what the family could cultivate by itself. In the new land ownership system, confiscated land would be distributed to the peasants, but the state would have administrative and legal rights to the property.[5]

The initial steps toward land reform in the North were similar to the land reform proposals put forth by the KCP Central Committee in the South. After liberation, an organized peasant movement led by communists emerged first in Hamgyŏng province—more specifically, in South Hamgyŏng. In this region, the movement adopted a land reform policy that "would not distinguish among groups such as Japanese collaborators, national traitors, and other landlords who can join in the establishment of people's democracy (*inmin minjujuŭi*) and [that] would seize all their land and abolish tenancy completely."[6] In P'yŏng'an province, the initial land reform proposal was also quite radical. On September 13, 1945, the South P'yŏng'an Provincial Committee of the KCP adopted a land policy that called for the confiscation of the land of large landlords.[7] However, the strong demands for land reform by domestic socialists and the peasantry were blocked. The power that blocked these demands was not the right wing or the U.S. military government, but the Soviet Union (Army) itself.

5. "'T'oji munje e taehan kyŏlŭi' haesŏl" (Explanation of the 'Resolution on the land question), October 1945, pp. 6-7.

6. *Olt'a* (organ of the North Korean Communist Party, South Hamgyŏng Party Bureau), January 1, 1946.

7. The text of the September 13 decision on land reform of the KCP South P'yŏng'an Committee has not yet been made public. However, the September 25 meeting of the South P'yŏng'an Enlarged Committee, which included "corrections" of thirteen prior decisions considered "extreme left," outlined the general aspects of the land reform decision. "Their error was in failing to correctly understand the relation of the land reform to the international question and defense against the danger of imperialist invasion. Thus, confiscation of land from major landlords was clearly an extreme left offense." Korean Communist Party, South P'yŏng'an Provincial Committee, "Report of the First Meeting of the South P'yŏng'an Representatives of the Korean Communist Party," December 26, 1945. Hallim University Asian Culture Research Center, eds., *Chosŏn kongsandang mungŏn charyojip (1945-46)* (Korean Communist Party documents (1945-46)) (Ch'unch'ŏn: Hallim University Press, 1993), p. 65.

In August 1945, immediately after liberation, both the Soviets and Korean communists thought that the division of the peninsula would be temporary, and they did not have any plans to carry out a radical land reform in order to "communize" the North. Their basic position was to prepare for the possibility of a unified government in accordance with Allied agreements while establishing a "provisional governing body" in the North that would be friendly toward the Soviet Union or, at least, not opposed to it. Their program for socioeconomic reform was limited to eliminating pro-Japanese collaborators and the far right who were obstacles to the establishment of such a body. On land reform, their platform called only for the confiscation of land from Japanese imperialists and pro-Japanese collaborators and for the distribution of this land to the peasants. This is not to deny that the ultimate goal of the Soviets and the socialists was to "communize" the Korean peninsula. In a situation where they had to cooperate with the U.S. and bourgeois nationalist forces, the Soviets were aware of their limitations and did not set ambitious goals.

The first indication of a change in policy became apparent in Pyongyang, the center of the northern region, where the Soviet 25th Army Command was stationed. On September 25, the South P'yŏng'an Provincial branch of the KCP passed a "Platform" and a resolution "On the Political Line," which included decisions on the land question. First, "On the Political Line" declared:

> Of course, the Korean Revolution is at the stage of bourgeois revolution. In Korea, Japanese imperialism must be thoroughly purged, and a land revolution must be undertaken that will distribute land to the peasants by confiscating land from all landlords. However, international conditions at the current time will [only] allow Korea to purge Japanese imperialist elements thoroughly. . . .
>
> 3. Recognition of private property and private ownership of land. In the past, we thought that only the land of large-scale landlords would be confiscated because our understanding of international conditions was weak. The most correct political line is for us to purge pro-Japanese elements. [To establish] a grand national union of non-pro-Japanese [groups] would also be a correct [line]. Thus, it is necessary to recognize the private property and private landholdings of the non-collaborators.

Therefore, we annul the section in the platform on land that calls for the limited confiscation of land from large-scale landlords.[8]

In addition, the following was resolved in the "Platform:"

8. All land belonging to Japanese imperialists, pro-Japanese Koreans, and reactionary landlords will be seized and nationalized, and this land will be distributed freely to the peasants.

9. The land of the Oriental Development Company and other Japanese-owned land will be seized without compensation and nationalized. Such land will be distributed to poor farmers according to their ability, but for this year, tenancy fees will be calculated according to the "3-7 system."

10. Confiscated production facilities will be nationalized and managed by workers, and confiscated land will be distributed freely to the peasants according to their ability.[9]

While the South P'yŏng'an Provincial branch of the KCP saw land revolution as a fundamental objective, they limited the scope of land confiscation to pro-Japanese landlords, taking into consideration the current international situation. That is, they took into account the fact that Korea had been liberated by the U.S. and Soviet armies and the necessity of continued cooperation between the U.S. and the Soviet Union. These documents also clearly reveal that they did not openly call for the confiscation of land from large landlords because of their policy for the respect of "private property."

Around the time of the October 3 resolution on the land question by the KCP Central Committee, preparatory meetings were beginning in Pyongyang for the opening of the "Korean Communist Party Five-Province Party Members and Enthusiasts Conference." After a series of meetings that began on October 1, the conference was formally opened on October 13. The preparatory meetings deliberated on matters such as the KCP Central Committee's land reform proposals and became the occasion for these proposals to be revised in consultation with the Soviet Military Government and other groups.

At the preparatory meetings and the official conference, issues such as land reform became a point of debate as a variety of opinions emerged.[10] At

---

8. Korean Workers' Investigation Center, *Orŭn nosŏn ŭl wihayŏ* (For the correct line) (Seoul: Uri munhwasa, November 1945), p. 28.

9. *Orŭn nosŏn ŭl wihayŏ*, p. 29.

the conference, the land reform proposal was criticized for targeting large landlords for the compulsory seizure of land, and the general consensus was for the confiscation of land only from Japanese imperialists and pro-Japanese landlords. This conference criticized the KCP's anti-feudal land reform policy and decided to support a land reform on only anti-imperialist grounds.

What was the Kim Il Sung faction's position on land reform? The faction opposed the domestic socialists' plan to seize the land of large landlords and proposed to confiscate only the land of pro-Japanese landlords. Kim Il Sung's "On the Grand Unity of the Nation," which was based on a speech he gave in October 1945, demonstrates that he was not acting simply according to the dictates of the Soviet Union. In this speech, he refers more to the policies of the Chinese Communist Party (CCP) rather than those of the Soviet Communist Party. Kim noted that the CCP's land reform proposal was based on the principle of "land to the tiller" that was advocated in the "Three People's Principles." He also pointed out that "the phrase 'land to the tiller' was the phrase of Sun Yat-sen, and comrade Mao Zedong also adopted it."[11] It was also around this time that Kim adopted Mao's position that the land of the landlords should be distributed and turned over to the ownership of the peasants in accordance with the principles of "land to the tiller" and "equal land rights" under Mao's theory of "New Democracy." The idea of "land to the tiller" is, in fact, not unique to China but is an element of traditional thinking on land ownership and land reform in Korea as well, which is also part of the Confucian cultural sphere.

However, Kim Il Sung (1912-1994) asserted that now was not proper time for slogans such as "land to the tiller" or "seize land and give it to the peasants" and that "confiscating the land from the running dogs of the Japanese and giving it to the peasants is the most correct slogan."[12] It was part of his effort to create a united national front that included nationalist and capitalist groups by limiting confiscation to the land of Japanese collaborators and leaving untouched the lands of ordinary landlords. The limitation of the scope of the land confiscation was in accord with the platform of the Fatherland Restoration Society (Choguk kwangbokhoe), which had been founded in Northeast China and adopted the Seventh Congress of the Comintern's

10. *Orŭn nosŏn ŭl wihayŏ*, p. 46; author unknown, "On Political Conditions in Korea," July 22, 1947, RTsKhIDNI, Fond 17, Opis 128, Delo 1119, pp. 216-19.

11. Kim Il Sung, *Minjok taedongdangyŏre taehayŏ* (On the grand unity of the nation) (Tianjin: Korean Communist Party, Tianjin City Committee, March 1946), p. 6.

12. Kim Il Sung, *Minjok taedongdangyŏre taehayŏ*, p. 13.

policies on both popular and united fronts. Furthermore, as Kim mentioned in "On the Grand Unity of the Nation," the CCP had "abandoned its position on the confiscation of landlord land" during the second united front and shifted to a policy of seizing the land only of those who had cooperated with Japan.[13]

Developed through his own experiences, Kim Il Sung's views on state building were in line with the policies promoted by the Soviet occupation forces. Unlike the domestic communists, Kim was able to pursue a moderate line initially. However, actual events unfolded in a different direction. After the London Conference of Foreign Ministers in September-October 1945, cooperation between the U.S. and the Soviet Union gradually broke down on Japan and other Northeast Asian issues.[14] The Soviets became concerned that the U.S. was creating a de facto separate regime in south Korea because of developments such as the formation of the Korean Democratic Party (KDP) in September 1945, the U.S. military government's support of the KDP, and the consolidation of the Right after the return of Syngman Rhee and the remaining members of the Korean Provisional Government. The lack of support for reform within North Korea itself and the anti-communist Sinŭiju Incident of November 1945 created a sense of crisis among the Soviets that it would be impossible to create a stable base of support in the North as long as the large landlord class was not eliminated from rural society.

North Korea's land reform has often been viewed as a sudden response to the formation of the U.S.-Soviet Joint Commission which was agreed upon at the Moscow Foreign Ministers' Conference. However, such views represent only how the land reform looked to outsiders. By November 1945, both the Northern Bureau of the KCP and the Soviet occupation forces had already discarded the earlier course of confiscating only the land of pro-Japanese landlords and were preparing a more fundamental land reform that would, at the very least, seize the land of all large landlords.

In November 1945, Lebedev proposed to his superiors that a land reform should be conducted before the spring planting in 1946 and involve the

13. Kim Il Sung, *Ibid.*, p. 5.
14. Kim Seong-bo, "Soryŏn ŭi taehan chŏngch'aek kwa Pukhan esŏ ŭi pundan chilsŏ hyŏngsŏng, 1945-1946" (Soviet policy toward Korea and the formation of the division system in North Korea, 1945-1946) in *Yŏksa munje yŏn'guso*, ed. *Pundan osimnyŏn kwa t'ongil sidaeui kwaje* (Seoul: Yŏksa pip'yŏngsa, 1995); Yi Chŏngsik, "Naengjŏn ŭi chŏngae kwajŏng kwa Hanbando pundan ŭi koch'akhwa—Sŭt'allin ŭi Hanpando chŏngch'aek, 1945" (The Development of the Cold War and Solidification of Division on the Korean Peninsula—Stalin's Korea Policy, 1945) in Yu Yŏng'ik, ed. *Sujŏngjuŭi wa Hanguk hyŏndaesa* (Seoul: Yonsei University Press, 1998).

seizure of land belonging to large landlords in North Korea. After a survey of rural areas by Soviet and Korean experts, a new reform plan was prepared that expanded the scope of land seizures. The "Shikin Report," which was drafted around this time, clearly shows the sentiments of people in North Korea as agreements were being reached at the Moscow Conference.

Plans for the Soviet Military Government's land reform became more concrete at the end of 1945. As the Allies opened the Moscow Conference to decide the Korean question in December 1945, the Soviet side became extremely concerned about developments in Korea. In the January 1, 1946 "Bulletin" of the Information Bureau of the CPSU Central Committee, a report on "Conditions in Korea after the Japanese Surrender" noted that even before agreements on a trusteeship policy could be reached, the U.S. was already preparing for a division of the country in the southern part of Korea. The report concluded that "two de facto regimes have been established in the two occupation zones in Korea . . . in the Soviet occupation zone, a democratic regime in the form of people's committees and, in the American occupation zone, a reactionary regime in the form of a military government supported by reactionary forces" had emerged. The conclusion added:

> In South Korea, the U.S. occupation authorities are using bourgeois democratic parties and reactionary bourgeois landlord organizations to build a system that will preserve the U.S.'s political and economic influence in Korea, out of fear of Soviet influence and the development of democratic struggle of the popular masses.

In short, by the end of 1945, the Information Bureau of the CPSU had concluded that "two de facto regimes" had already emerged in North and South Korea.[15]

Soviet concerns were not completely unfounded. When strong resistance arose in the South against the trusteeship policy at the end of October 1945 after it became known, the U.S. Army Military Government in Korea (USAMGIK) itself reversed its position on joint trusteeship over North and South Korea. The U.S. military government asked Washington for a concrete plan to establish a regime first in the south. Outlined by William R. Langdon of the State Department, the "Langdon Plan" proposed the

---

15. Information Bureau, Central Committee, Communist Party of the Soviet Union, "Conditions in Korea after the Japanese Surrender," *Bylleten*, no. 1 (Serial Number 25), 1 January 1946, RTsKhIDHI, Fond 17, Opis 128, Delo 94, p. 16.

establishment of a Governing Commission that would be part of the USAMGIK's plan for an interim government. He proposed to the Secretary of State 1) that the USAMGIK form a council within the military government centered on Kim Ku to organize a Governing Commission; 2) that the Governing Commission be integrated with the Military Government, with the Military Government handed over to an organization of Koreans; 3) that the Governing Commission succeed the military government as an interim government; and 4) that the Governing Commission hold elections for a head of state who would then form a government.[16]

In the document "Inquiry—Report on Political Conditions in North Korea" which was sent to Vice-Chairman Lozovskii of the Soviet Commissariat for Foreign Affairs (Foreign Ministry) on December 25, 1945, General Shikin of the Soviet High Command expressed concern about the progress of reform in North Korea and proposed that it is necessary to undertake a more radical reform. Conveying his misgivings about the situation in Korea, he stated that the implementation of "bourgeois democratic reform" was proceeding extremely slowly and that, as a result, "a lasting economic and political base, that could maintain the national interest even after the withdrawal of military forces, is not being established in Korea." He also noted that the development of "national leaders" was not going well, and Cho Mansik's (1883–?) attitude toward the Soviet Union was unreliable. In conclusion, Shikin proposed the following three points:

- In order to reconstruct the North Korean economy rapidly and train national cadres, it is necessary to concentrate authority in North Korea and put it in the hands of Korean democratic activists.
- The domination of land by large landlords has become an obstacle to the development of the struggle for people's democracy. We cautiously assert the necessity for agricultural reform to be carried out in the near future.
- It is necessary that civilian organs under the 25th Army Command complete and strengthen the organization of skilled cadres who can effectively organize the economic and political life of North Korea. The Military Council of military districts and the army must be

---

16. Chŏng Yong'uk, "1942-47 nyŏn Miguk ŭi taehan chŏngch'aek kwa kwado chŏngbu hyŏngt'ae kusŏng" (American policy toward Korea and its plans for a provisional government, 1942-47) (Ph.D. diss., Department of Korean History, Seoul National University, 1996), p. 79. Langdon was appointed advisor to USAMGIK in December 1945.

more attentive to the problems of selecting and preparing new democratic cadres who will be friendly to the Soviet Union and will effectively secure the strengthening of our political position in Korea.[17]

It seems that Shikin wrote this report under the assumption that the Soviet army would soon be able to withdraw from Korea. He felt that the "bourgeois democratic reconstruction" for maintaining the Soviet Union's national interest was proceeding slowly, and he envisioned a policy that called for the realization of three goals: the training of democratic national cadres, the concentration of power and its subsequent transfer to the Koreans, and land reform. Interestingly, there was a plan to concentrate power in the North and transfer it to Koreans by establishing a power base by reorganizing the people's committees through elections. Even under the Soviet military government, Koreans were able to maintain their own self-governing organs, but the transfer of power to the Koreans was part of the Soviet Union's plan to create a strong political and social base in North Korea that would not conflict with Soviet interests. Significantly, this plan also involved a land reform that would undermine the domination of land ownership by all large landlords and not just Japanese and pro-Japanese Korean landlords. It seems clear that both the creation of the North Korean Provisional People's Committee and the land reform, which were carried out in February and March 1946 respectively, were already being discussed internally within the Soviet Far Eastern Army at the end of 1945.

Rather than to establish separate states, the Soviets' primary goal was clearly to create a base of support in the North that would be friendly to Soviet interests before the imminent establishment of a unified government. However, the various measures in the Soviet plans would have appeared to the U.S. and Koreans as an effort to create a separate government, and in fact, things were moving in that direction. Nonetheless, the Soviet army's proposal did not directly influence the agreements on the Korean question reached by the Soviet Union and the United States at the Moscow Foreign Ministers' Conference in December 1945. Even as the division was becoming a reality in the Korean peninsula, the Soviet Foreign Ministry, which was in charge of all the country's foreign affairs, still approached the Korean problem based on a policy of international cooperation with the U.S. Still, it thought that it would be difficult to pursue Soviet interests on the Korean

17. I. V. Shikin, "On Political Conditions in North Korea," 25 December 1945, AVPRF, Fond 013, Opis 7, Papka 4, Por. 46, pp. 12-13.

peninsula under a trusteeship in which the Soviet Union would be only one of the four powers involved.

Tensions between the U.S. and Soviet Union in Korea and left-right conflict among Koreans were already becoming severe even before the trusteeship crisis erupted in early 1946. It was within this context that discussions on land reform began to move in a more radical direction. The increasing differences and growing mutual distrust between North and South Korea pushed both sides to extremes. However, Moscow was still able to contain domestic radicalism in North Korea. Elections for the people's committees in late 1945 were cancelled, and the land survey of January 2, 1946 was not conducted properly. Moscow still felt that it was important to respect agreements with the U.S. and tried as much as possible not to antagonize the United States. The Moscow accords were the result of these efforts.

What disrupted this situation was forces within the Korean peninsula— in particular, the activities of the right wing. The opposition to trusteeship by the Right was a clear rejection of U.S.-Soviet agreements which called for the establishment of a unified government. While socioeconomic factors made land reform inevitable, it was political circumstances rather than socioeconomic conditions that led the land reform to take a more radical form. Some scholars have thought that the reasons for the radicalism of North Ko-rea's land reform lay in socioeconomic conditions, arguing that an excess ru-ral population and the widespread existence of petty landlords necessitated the seizure of even land belonging to petty landlords. However, the radical nature of the land reform lay not in the scope of land seizure but in the method of compensation. In fact, South Korean land reform was similar to that of the North in that both involved the confiscation of all land cultivated by tenant farmers. However, South Korea implemented a moderate land reform in which peasants paid for the land they received to compensate the landlords.

Who, then, was responsible for the radicalization of the land reform in the North? When the Cho Mansik group did not actively support the Moscow accords during the 1946 trusteeship crisis, the role of bourgeois nationalist forces within the North Korean power structure became further reduced. When the North Korean Provisional People's Committee (NKPPC) was launched on February 8, 1946, serious discussions began on the land reform issue. It clarified its position on land reform in Article Two, Paragraph Two of the Resolution of the NKPPC:

Strive as rapidly as possible to prepare the basis for a land reform in which land will be freely distributed to the peasants by reorganizing the land and forests confiscated from Japanese invaders and pro-Japanese reactionaries, by nationalizing the land and forests of large-scale landlords through appropriate means, and by abolishing the semi-tenancy system.[18]

At the time, the plan for land reform was to appropriate land from large landlords, to nationalize that land, and then to distribute it to peasants for free. The three main principles of the plan—nationalization of land, the abolishment of tenancy, and the free distribution of land—were reiterated in a statement by the chairman of the NKPPC released on February 18.[19]

Plans for land reform became explicitly radical at the same time that the NKPPC was launched. The Northern Branch of the Korean Communist Party then began to investigate what kind of land reform the peasants desired. It reached an important decision at the Fourth Enlarged Executive Committee Meeting which opened on February 15. At this meeting, the Committee resolved "to strive to handle the land issue according to the opinions and demands of the peasant masses by diligently collecting their opinions on the land [issue]."[20] Immediately afterwards, from February 18, petitions on land reform from peasants were collected in all regions in the North. The Northern Branch of the KCP was trying to maintain the momentum for land reform by joining forces with peasant radicalism.

The Rise of Peasant Radicalism and the Establishment of the Land Reform Law

In February 1946, the Soviet Union and the Korean Communist Party made a fundamental shift in their policies. They had initially focused on forming a pro-Soviet regime through a left-right coalition with bourgeois nationalist forces, but now they wanted to create a stable regime centered on

18. Korean Central News Agency, *Chosŏn chung'ang nyŏn'gam* (Korean Central Yearbook) (Pyongyang: Korean Central News Agency, 1950), pp. 37-38.

19. "We must nationalize the property, forests, etc. of Japanese imperialists, national traitors, and Korean big landlords, distribute the land freely to the peasants, and eliminate the tenancy system." *Chosŏn sinmun*, February 2, 1946.

20. *Tang ŭi chŏngch'i nosŏn kwa chŏngdang saŏp ch'onggyŏl kwa kyŏljŏng* (Political Line of the Party and Party Activities and Resolutions) (Chŏngnoji Press, 1946), pp. 20-21.

socialist forces that would gain the active support of the peasantry through a radical land reform. This shift represented the moment when the policies of the Northern Branch of the KCP and the Soviet Union joined forces with peasant radicalism. This peasant radicalism had originated in the peasant rebellions of the late Chosŏn period and, more recently, developed through the revolutionary peasant union movement of the 1930s.

When Japan dismantled the feudal Chosŏn state, it preserved its socioeconomic foundation, the landlord system. Japan's exploitative agricultural policies in Korea used the landlord system to turn Korea's farming villages into food suppliers to Japan. On the one hand, Japanese imperialism supported the increase of Japanese landlords by implementing a policy of agricultural colonization,[21] but on the other hand, it also promoted the export of rice to Japan by using the landlord system to maintain the Korean landlords' control over the peasantry.

Japan's agricultural policies accelerated both the accumulation of land by large landholders and the decline and differentiation of the peasant class. Small and medium Korean landowners and peasants declined to the status of small landowners and tenants or became landless peasants who emigrated to places like Manchuria and Japan. Conducted under the auspices of the Government-General, land improvements and irrigation projects increased the accumulation of and investment in land by large landlords and capitalists, but they also contributed to the acceleration of the peasants' decline in socioeconomic status because of the added pressure of union fees and irrigation taxes. The majority of farmers, whether they were tenants or self-cultivators, ended up cultivating less than one *chŏngbo* of land.

Self-cultivators amounted to 21.7% of farm households in 1915, and their percentage declined to 19.9% in 1925 and then to 17.9% by 1935.[22] In the same years, the percentage of semi-tenants fell from 40.1% to 33.2% and then 24.1%, respectively. Conversely, the number of tenants increased from 35.9% to 43.2% to 51.9% in the same period. In 1935, 2.5% of farm households were *hwajŏnmin* (fire-field people or slash-and-burn farmers), and 3.6%

---

21. Kim Yong-sop (Kim Yongsŏp), "Ilje ŭi ch'ogi nong'ŏp singminch'aek kwa chijuje" (The early agricultural policies of the Japanese and the landlord system), *Han'guk kŭnhyŏndae nong'ŏpsa yŏn'gu* (Seoul: Ilchogak, 1992); Choe Won-kyu (Ch'oe Wŏnkyu), "Ilje ŭi ch'ogi Han'guk singminch'aek kwa Ilbon'in nong'ŏp imin" (Japan's early colonial policy toward Korea and Japanese agricultural migrants), *Tongbang hakji*, nos. 77-78-79 (combined issue, 1993).

22. The 1935 statistics on independent farmers includes landlords. Therefore, in reality, the proportion of independent farmers was actually smaller than this figure indicates.

were farm laborers. In total, the number of farmers who were tenants or of lower status had increased to 58% of all farm households. The population of farm families had been mainly owners and small owner-cultivators in the early colonial period. The composition of the peasant class, which had been dominated by self-cultivators and semi-tenants, came to consist of mainly tenant farmers by the mid-1930s. In short, during the occupation period, all levels of the peasant class suffered a decline in economic status.

Statistics indicate that the development of the landlord system in northern Korea lagged behind that of other regions. However, these statistics were just relative figures; the decline of the peasant class was also accelerating in the north.

In South and North Hamgyŏng provinces, the proportion of owner-cultivators and semi-tenants was relatively high; in particular, North Hamgyŏng was the only region in Korea where the percentage of owner-cultivators exceeded 50 percent. The landlord system had not yet expanded greatly in this region. Despite the slow growth of the landlord system and the wide distribution of the owner-cultivator class in this region, Hamgyŏng province was the region where the revolutionary peasant movement was the most active. One of the socioeconomic factors behind the radicalization of the peasant movement was the rapid decline of the peasant class that occurred in this region in the late 1920s and early 1930s.[23] In the case of South Hamgyŏng province, taking the year 1917 as the base level of 100, the number of owner-cultivators declined to 90 in 1927, while the number of semi-tenants and tenants increased to 106. Just five years later in 1932, the index for owner-cultivators declined again to 71, while the indices for semi-tenants and tenants increased to 105 and 188, respectively. There was no significant change in the proportion of semi-tenants from 1927-32, but the number of tenants nearly doubled compared to the 1917 figure while the number of self-cultivators declined drastically. The rapid decline of the peasantry seems to have been one of the main reasons that the peasants were attracted to a revolutionary movement.[24]

23. Yi Chunsik, "Ilje ch'imnyakgi nongming undong ŭi inyŏm kwa chojik—Ham'gyŏng-namdo pyŏngjidae ŭi kyŏng'u" (Ideology and organization of the peasant movement during the Japanese invasion period—the case of P'yŏngjidae, South Hamgyŏng province) (Ph.D. diss., Department of Sociology, Yonsei University, 1991), pp. 65-76.

24. Department of Agriculture and Forestry, Chosŏn Government-General, *Chosen ni okeru kosaku ni kansuru sanko jiko tekiyo* (Summary of the conditions of tenant farmers in Chosŏn) (1934), pp. 60-61.

In contrast to Hamgyŏng province, the landlord system had undergone significant growth in North and South P'yŏng'an provinces. The revolutionary peasant movement was weak as the socialist movement was not active there. Even in this region, the number of tenant conflicts rapidly increased after 1932. In 1937, the year of the most severe tenant conflicts, there were 1,527 disputes in South P'yŏng'an, 1,575 in North P'yŏng'an, and 1,378 in Hwanghae province—more than 1,000 cases in each of the three northwestern provinces.[25] In North and South P'yŏng'an provinces, the leader of the peasant movement was the Korean Peasant Society (Chosŏn nongminsa), which had close ties to the Ch'ŏndogyo religion.[26] While Christianity had spread mainly in the towns and cities of the province, Ch'ŏndogyo, the successsor to Tonghak, had a strong presence in the countryside. After the defeat of the Tonghak Peasant Movement (aka, the Kabo Peasants' War) of 1894-95, Tonghak believers moved in large numbers to P'yŏng'an province, and the region became the center of Ch'ŏndogyo in Korea. Although Ch'ŏndogyo did not strongly resist Japan, its conception of state and society was extremely idealistic and radical. After liberation, politically ambitious Ch'ŏndogyo leaders in North Korea formed the North Korean Ch'ŏndogyo Young Friends' Party (Puk Chosŏn Ch'ŏndogyo Ch'ŏng'udang), and they were a radical group that advocated the nationalization of all the means of production, including land. Thus, the revolutionary peasant union movement in Hamgyŏng province and the Ch'ŏndogyo peasant movement in P'yŏng'an province were the two historical foundations that enabled the rapid organization of peasant unions and the development of the peasant movement in all areas of the North after liberation.

Immediately after liberation, people's committees were established all over the country, and they granted peasants cultivation rights to land appropriated from the Government-General, Japanese landowners, and pro-Japanese collaborators. The peasants also engaged in a struggle with ordinary landlords to implement the "3-7" tenancy fee system. Because of such efforts, peasants were able to establish a central organ to represent their interests with the

---

25. Department of Agricultue and Forestry, Chosŏn Government-General, *Chosen nochi geppo* (Korean Agricultural Yearbook) (1938), pp. 8-9.

26. According to a report on the character of peasant movement organizations in 1933, South and North P'yŏng'an contained 985 of the 1096 Korean peasant organizations were considered "Nationalist/Communist". Chi Sugŏl, *Iljeha nongmin chohap undong yŏn'gu—1930 nyŏndae hyŏkmyŏngjŏk nongmin chohap undong* (The peasant union movement under Japanese rule—the revolutionary peasant union movement of the 1930s) (Seoul: Yŏksa pip'yŏngsa, 1993), p. 59.

founding of the North Korean National League of Peasant Unions (NLPU, Puk Chosŏn nongmin tongmaeng). Formed mainly by former activists in the revolutionary peasant union movement of the 1930s, this league enabled the continued mobilization of peasant radicalism.

The demands of the peasants were even more radical and explicit than the policies announced by Kim Il Sung, the chairperson of the NKPPC. On February 18, 1946, the peasant council in Sŏngch'ŏn County, South P'yŏng'an province, drafted a "Letter to Secretary General Kim Il Sung of the North Korea Bureau of the Korean Communist Party," and the letter fundamentally rejected the legitimacy of the landlord class's right to own land. The landlords' right to ownership was just "a monopoly or an allotment passed down from feudal times through violent means" which the Japanese imperialists had recognized through the Cadastral Survey Ordinance. Their next resolution proposed that "land should be confiscated land from landlords and nationalized, and then rights to cultivation should be granted appropriately according to the abilities of the peasants."[27] It is important to keep in mind that this proposal targeted all landlords for land confiscation. The leaders of the peasant movement who had been organizing peasants in this area demanded confiscation of all land belonging to landlords.

The Kangdong County Peasant Conference, which opened on the same day, was not as explicit in its demands, but it still adopted a position criticizing all landlords. Following a demonstration in which more than 12,000 peasants participated under the slogan "Land to the Peasants," the peasants adopted the "Resolution on Peasant Demands in Kangdong County." They criticized the landlord class, saying that "a government of all the people, a progressive democratic state is now being built after Liberation, but the only elements obstructing national unification are feudal large landlords and their spokespeople." The resolution also demanded "free distribution of land only to those who till the fields in the villages." The peasants completely rejected the alternative of making the peasants pay for their allotments of land, insisting on the free distribution of land. These efforts constituted the beginning of the peasants' petition drive for land reform.[28]

Because of political considerations such as the need to cooperate with the U.S. and the South on the agreed policy of a unified Korea, the Soviet Occupation Army and the northern branch of the KCP had difficulty settling on

---

27. *Chŏngno*, February 25, 1946.
28. *Chŏngno*, February 25, 1946.

the scope and method of land reform. However, since rural peasants were free of such political concerns, they could forcefully assert their simple and fundamental demand for free distribution of all land belonging to landlords.

The opinions of the peasants were not the only concern of Kim Il Sung and the Soviet Occupation Army. They also had to consider the objectives of Soviet headquarters. In February 1946, Meretzov and Shtykov of the Maritime Military District reported the following four-article plan for land reform to Molotov and Bulgarin of Soviet headquarters:

A. Nationalization of land exceeding five *chŏngbo* owned by all Korean landlords and private individuals.

B. Complete prohibition of the tenancy system in which half the harvest was given to the landlord and nationalization of all tenant land.

C. Confiscation of all land belonging to Japanese landlords and all the traitors to the Korean people.[29]

D. In order to eliminate landlord influence in the villages, the draft law will stipulate that landlords will receive the redistributed land in another county.[30]

This plan for a thorough land reform was based on the results of the village cadastral survey mentioned above. As the results showed, North Korea, unlike other countries, did not have large landlords with vast private estates; rather, landowners with more than five *chŏngbo* employed tenants according to "feudal" practices. The analysis of the survey emphasized the necessity to confiscate land from landlords with more than five *chŏngbo* of land in order for the land reform to have a significant effect. It was estimated that the confiscation of land would affect about seven percent of all households and amount to 53% (1,100,000 *chŏngbo*) of the total amount of cultivated land in the country and that 559,000 peasant households with little or no land would receive an average of two *chŏngbo* each.

This land reform plan was different from the land reforms in Eastern Europe that were part of the effort to construct "People's Democracies." Land reform in Eastern Europe tended to involve the confiscation without compensation of land belonging to fascist groups but payment for the land of

29. This included land belonging to those who had fled to south Korea. The Soviet Military Government's own report did not have statistics on the number of refugees to the south, but according to American statistics the number of such people was 8,000,000.

30. Meretskov and Shtykov, "Proposal for Land Reform in North Korea," February 1946. TsAMORF, Fond 379, Opis 166654, Delo 1.

ordinary large landowners (generally those with more than 50 *chŏngbo* of land). Eastern European countries also adopted a policy of distributing land ownership rights to the peasants, rather than nationalizing land ownership. The objective was to create a popular democratic agricultural system by minimizing the opposition of the landlord class and by satisfying the demands for land of the peasant class. The Soviet Foreign Ministry, which was considering the establishment of an Eastern European-style "people's democracy" in North Korea, presented an alternative to the land reform proposal of the Soviet Maritime Military District. S.A. Lozovskii, the Vice-Minister of the Foreign Ministry, agreed with the policy of confiscation without compensation but advocated restricting the scope of land seizure. In addition, he proposed a system in which peasants would pay the equivalent of one year's average production in long-term annual installments, as a condition for receiving an allotment of land. Table 1 is a comparison of the land reform proposals of the Soviet Maritime Military District and of the Foreign Ministry.

When Lozovskii presented his land reform plan, the Central Committee of the CPSU proposed the adoption of the following proposal:

1. Ratify the draft law on land reform in North Korea [Lozovskii's plan; author's note].
2. Authorize Meretzkov and Shtykov to have this law added to the deliberations of the Korean Peasant Congress through organizations of Korean political activists.
3. Assign Meretzkov and Shtykov to send a summary of all revisions to the draft law put forth by the NKPPC and Peasant Congress and to add their own conclusions to the ratification of the Party's Central Committee.[31]

With the emergence of the opposition between the Foreign Ministry's land privatization plan and the Maritime Military District command's land nationalization plan, the final decision fell into the hands of the NLPU and the NKPPC.

The first group to be consulted was the representatives of the peasantry. The approach that was increasingly adopted throughout the country was to accommodate the demands of the peasants in order to build support for land

---

31. S.A. Lozovskii, "Problems for Consideration Regarding the Draft Plan for Land Reform," March 12, 1946, AVPRF, Fond Ministra Y.A. Malika, Opis 8, Papka 6, Por. 81.

TABLE 1

COMPARISON OF LAND REFORM PLANS,
MARITIME MILITARY DISTRICT COMMAND AND THE
PEOPLE'S COMMISSARIAT FOR FOREIGN AFFAIRS

	Maritime Military District	Foreign Ministry
Type of Land Reform	Appropriation and Free Distribution (Nationalization)	Compensation and Distribution by Purchase (Privatization)
Scope of Confiscation	1. Confiscation of all land from landlords owning more than five *chŏngbo* 2. Confiscation of all land cultivated by tenant farmers	1. Confiscation of all land from landlords owning more than ten *chŏngbo* 2. For landlords with up to ten *chŏngbo*, only property exceeding five *chŏngbo* will be confiscated 3. For all landlords with tenants, only property exceeding two *chŏngbo* will be confiscated
Distribution Method	Nationalization of land, cultivation rights given freely to peasants	Property rights given to landless peasants, land-poor peasants, agricultural workers
Compensation	None	Average of one year's production paid in long-term yearly installments (landless peasants, agricultural workers 1/25th per year for 25 years; land-poor peasants 1/15th per year for 15 years)

SOURCE: Meretskov and Shtykov, "Proposal for Land Reform in North Korea," February 1946, TsAMORF, Fond 379, Opis 166654, Delo 1; S.A. Lozovskii, "Problems for Consideration Regarding the Draft Plan for Land Reform," March 12, 1946, AVPRF, Fond Ministra Y.A. Malika, Opis 8, Papka 6, Por 81.

reform and settle on a concrete plan. The Congress of the North Korean NLPU opened on February 23, 1946. From the 23rd to the 26th, provincial and county representatives met in subcommittees for discussion, and after the results were collected on the 27th, the main session of the Congress convened for three days from February 28 to March 2.[32]

In the subcommittee meetings, the peasant representatives unanimously called for the nationalization of land belonging to landlords. Only a representative from South Hamgyŏng province voiced a different opinion, adding a provision that when land is taken from landlords, they should be left with enough land to cultivate themselves.[33]

One hundred fifty delegates from every province in Korea attended the main session of the Congress, and they all belonged to the North Korean NLPU, representing all the peasants of the North.[34] They consisted of ninety-three poor peasants, sixteen medium-scale farmers, thirty-six intellectuals, two petty capitalists, one field hand, and two rich peasants.[35] Reflecting the composition of the peasant class at the time, a large majority of the delegates were poor peasants, but medium-scale and rich peasants also participated.

The Congress discussed the land issue and the long-term development of agriculture, and on March 3, 1946, it passed the "Resolution of the Congress of the North Korean Peasant League." This resolution included six "Demands," five of which were related to the NLPU's position on land reform. They stated their support for 1) the confiscation of land from Japanese and "traitors to the people" who collaborated with the Japanese and 2) the confiscation of land that was cultivated entirely by tenant farmers or hired laborers and of land belonging to temples and other religious organizations. They also requested that the NKPPC 3) turn over all the land to farm workers, landless peasants, and peasants with small landholdings as their "permanent possession," 4) cancel the peasants' debts to landlords, and 5) nationalize all irrigation facilities and forest land.[36]

The land reform plan adopted by the representatives of the North Korean NLPU called for the confiscation of all land cultivated by tenant farmers and

---

32. *Chŏngno*, February 27, 1946; March 2, 1946.

33. TsAMORF, Fond 142, Opis 551975, Delo 5, pp. 17-19.

34. Most of the people in the executive committee of the first North Korean Peasant League had been involved with either the socialist movement or the revolutionary peasant union movement in Myŏngch'ŏn, Yŏnghŭng, and elsewhere in the Hamgyŏng region.

35. Political Headquarters, Maritime Military District, Bureau Seven. "North Korean Land Reform," 1946, RTsZhNDNI, Fond 17, Opis 128, Delo 1119, 14-15.

36. *Olt'a*, March 10, 1946.

then the free distribution of that land to the peasants. In this respect, it coincided with the land reform plan of the North Korean Communist Party and the Maritime Military District. The important difference was that the North Korean NLPU representatives decided not to nationalize the land and instead adopted a land privatization plan that granted ownership rights to peasants. The decision reflected the desire of ordinary peasants to become the owners of their own land, rather than for the nationalization of land. After adopting this resolution, the North Korean NLPU formed a committee of thirteen members to draft a land reform law and submit it to the NKPPC.[37] After the draft law was received by the NKPPC, the final version of the land reform bill was submitted to the main session of the NKPPC under the names of Chairman Kim Il Sung and Vice-Chairman Kang Yang'uk.

Significant differences existed between the land reform proposal of Romanenko's Maritime Military District command (Meretskov and Shtykov's first draft) and the NLPU Congress' revised land reform plan presented to the NKPPC (the second draft).[38] The most fundamental difference in the second draft was the change in the recipient of land ownership rights. According to the first draft, appropriated land would become "the property of the Korean state," but in the final draft, the phrasing was changed to "the property of the peasants" (articles two and three). It was a change from a nationalization of land to private ownership.

There were two important changes concerning the scope of land seizure. In the first draft, "lands owned by schools, research institutes, hospitals, churches, Buddhist temples and monasteries, and other religious organizations" (article four) were all not targeted for appropriation. However, in the final draft, the lands of churches, monasteries, and other religious organizations were removed from the category of land that would not be appropriated. These religious organizations were included in the range of confiscation of "land of more than five *chŏngbo*" (second draft, article three, paragraph four).[39] Religious organizations, especially large landowners like the Catholic Church and the Buddhist orders, were originally not included within the scope of land confiscation in Romanenko's draft but were first added to that category by the NLPU Congress on March 4.

37. "Puk Chosŏn nongmin yŏnmaeng taehoe kyŏljŏngsŏ" (Resolution of the North Korean Peasant League Congress), paragraph six.

38. The first draft and second draft plan are both included in Meretskov and Shtykov, *op. cit.*, pp. 4–10.

39. Ibid.

Another change concerned the treatment of self-cultivated land. The first draft stipulated that "land will not be confiscated, if it belongs to peasants who cultivate it by themselves and does not exceed five *chŏngbo*" (article six, paragraph two). Only individual ownership of land exceeding five *chŏngbo* was not permitted. The second draft, however, deleted this section. By allowing the continued ownership of land exceeding five *chŏngbo* if it was self-cultivated, the drafters of the land reform law were giving rich peasants special consideration.

In the first draft, the administration of the transfer of land ownership rights was to be handled by the "county (*kun*) people's committees," but it was later changed to the "provincial people's committee." And instead of using the term "nationalization" for the confiscation of orchards, forests, and irrigation facilities, the second draft said that they were to be "transferred to the people's committees."[40]

Debate on the land reform bill in the NKPPC began on March 5, 1946.[41] First, the NKPPC chairman read the draft law aloud, and then eleven members voiced their opinions in the discussion that followed. The far majority of the speakers supported the land reform plan. But Minister of Industry Yi Munhwan and Minister of Finance Yi Pongsu, independents who were not affiliated with any political party, were critical of the method of land reform.[42] Hong Kihwang, vice-chairman of the people's committee of South P'yŏng'an province and a member of the Korean Democratic Party, also voiced opposition to the plan.[43] People such as Yi Munhwan, Yi Pongsu, and Hong Kihwang presented an alternative plan that called for compensation to landlords. Yi Pongsu felt that a distinction must be made between medium and large landowners and that their

40. Ibid.

41. B. Sapozhnikov, "On Issues Relating to the Draft Law for Land Reform," 12 March 1946. AVPRF, Fond Ministra Y.A. Malika, Opis 8, Papka 6, Por. 81, pp. 4–6.

42. Yi Pongsu and Yi Munhwan were evaluated by the Soviet military government as "pro-Soviet". The Soviet Military government had this assessment of them: "Yi Munhwan: born 1897 to a landlord family. Graduated technical school. No party affiliation. Electrician. Excellent electrical engineering expert. Highly competent. [Faithful to] the Soviet Union." "Yi Pongsu: Born 1892 to peasant household. No party affiliation. Participated in anti-Japanese movement and jailed several times. Pro-Soviet." T.F. Shtykov, "Disposition and Background of Leaders of North Korean Political Parties and Social Organizations," 17 June 1946, RTsKhIDNI, Fond 17, Opis 128, Ed. 61, pp. 56–57.

43. Hong Kihwang was 63 years old in 1946. He had participated in the nationalist movement before liberation, and after liberation managed the Samhŭng Textile Factory. "Records of the Congress of North Korea Provincial, City, and County People's Committees, 17 February 1946," *Puk Han kwangye saryojip* (Kyŏnggi-do, Kwach'ŏn-si: National History Compilation Committee), vol. 8, p. 135.

numbers must be clearly determined. He proposed that the land of large land-owners be confiscated while that of medium landowners be purchased. Their opposition reflected a concern that the current draft law, which involved the confiscation and free distribution of land, was too radical and would make land reform appear to be part of a socialist revolution. The majority's response to their concern was to clarify that the objective of land reform was not to encroach upon the capitalist order but to eradicate the "feudal system." After the debate ended, the NKPPC unanimously passed the land reform law, and it was promulgated the next day, March 6.[44]

Despite the fact that the Soviet Foreign Ministry supported a moderate, Eastern Europe-style land reform, the Maritime Military District Command and the leaders of the Northern Bureau of the KCP successfully passed a land reform law that involved the confiscation without compensation of all land cultivated by tenant farmers and the free distribution of that land. Its passage was made possible by the firm support of the peasant organizations that were dominated by poor peasants.

Land Reform: The Fall of the Landlord Class and the Revolutionization of the Peasant Class

The peasant class, whose power was growing through its alliance with the socialist forces, took over the landlord class' role as the leaders of rural society in North Korea. Urban workers, social organizations such as the Democratic Youth League (Minjujuŭi ch'ŏngnyŏn tongmaeng), and political parties such as the Communist Party were all mobilized for the land reform. But the organization that, with the support of these groups, was in charge of executing land reform in every village was the Village Committee. Before the land reform, every village held "peasant assemblies" (nongmin ch'onghoe) at which Village Committees were formed of the most dedicated individuals among the poor farmers, tenant farmers, and agricultural laborers.[45] In all of North Korea, 11,930 Village Committees were formed, with a total of 197,485 peasants participating.[46]

44. B. Sapozhnikov, *op. cit.*, pp. 4-6.

45. *Puk Chosŏn nongmin sinmun*, March 20, 1946.

46. Soviet Civil Administration in North Korea, *Three-Year Summary Report of the Soviet Civil Administration in North Korea, August 1945-November 1948*," Volume One: *Politics*, (Pyongyang, 1948). AVPRF 0480, Opis 4, Papka 14, Delo 47, p. 118.

"Peasant Self-Defense Corps" were also organized in rural villages, consisting of youths and adults aged eighteen to thirty-five.[47] According to the "Regulations of the Peasant Self-Defense Corps," units were composed of eight to ten members each. There were three to five units stationed in each village, three or four platoons in each township, and three to five battalions in each county, and a battalion command was established in each province.[48] While the Village Committees in each *ri* (natural village) were responsible for implementing the land reform, the Peasant Self-Defense Corps were responsible for any use of force against the landlords. The state, which did not penetrate yet to the *ri* level, used the land reform as a pretext to expand its power to the natural village level.

As peasants who had been oppressed by the landlord class actively participated in the land reform, they began to release their pent-up revolutionary fervor. Primary documents provide many examples of how difficult it was for authorities to control the peasants' revolutionary outbursts even in P'yŏng'an province where there was no tradition of a revolutionary peasant union movement. The following was taken from a Public Security Bureau report on peasant activities in Simch'ŏn township, Sŏnch'ŏn county, North P'yŏng'an province:

> In this region, there are many landlords with more than five *chŏngbo* of land. Religions such as Christianity and Ch'ŏndogyo are very strong (the religious leadership is from the landlord class), and the number of believers totals 1,247 people. Therefore, since class conflict between the landlords and the tenants has always been very strong, the peasants who have been liberated through the implementation of the historic land reform are extremely agitated and have begun to oppress the landlord class. As their understanding of the organs of the people's government is weak and their hostility so strong, they are sweeping away the landlords, thinking that they cannot trust the organs of government (the peasants have formed their own judicial organs). Just last year, on May 1 (May Day), it was reported that it was not easy to extinguish the strong blaze of uprisings organized by peasants against all of the past exploiting classes. While the class consciousness of the masses in this region is very strong, they went beyond leftist extremism and were acting blindly.[49]

47. *Puk Chosŏn nongmin sinmun*, March 20, 1946.
48. *Puk Chosŏn nongmin sinmun*, April 13, 1946.
49. "1947 nyŏn saŏp kwangye sŏryu (Poanch'ŏ)—Sŏnch'ŏn kun Simch'ŏn myŏn punjuso saŏp kŏm'yŏl" (Documents relating to activities in 1947 (Ministry of Public Safety)—inspection of

Sŏnch'ŏn County was a region where the landlord system developed as wet-field cultivation became widespread. Christianity was so strong that Sŏnch'ŏn was called the "Jerusalem of Korea," and among the Christians, there were many large landlords. Within Sŏnch'ŏn County, many large landlords, such as the prominent O family, resided in Simch'ŏn township. After the land reform began, peasants there spontaneously created their own organs of justice and attacked the landlords. Although the peasant movement during the colonial period had not been very active in Sŏnch'ŏn County, the peasants did not trust the organs of government—not even the people's committees—and engaged in hostile actions toward the landlords when land reform was enacted after liberation.

The people's committees functioned as a kind of united front organization in which both socialists and figures from other political parties and social organizations participated. Having been oppressed for a long time, the peasants preferred the radical method of attacking the landlord class themselves, rather than depending on a government organ of such ambiguous politics. In this turbulent situation, the long-simmering conflict between landlords and tenants exploded instantaneously.

Faced with a revolutionary peasantry, the landlord class had to find a way to protect its interests. However, it was impossible to deny the urgency of land reform, and it was difficult to attempt an effective response in the face of the armed strength of the Soviet military and the Village Self-Defense Corps. At the time, there was no political or social organization in North Korea that could represent the landlords' interests. Because of such factors, the resistance of the landlord class was disorganized and sporadic.

As the land reform progressed, outbreaks of resistance became even more frequent. In all regions, there were sporadic cases of attacks on Soviet Military Government organs and Communist Party buildings, of terrorism against officials carrying out the land reform, of student demonstrations, and of the spread of propaganda, pamphlets, and rumors. Even within the people's committees, there were instances of non-cooperation from national-capitalist elements such as the Korean Democratic Party.[50] In his report of March 24,

---

Simch'ŏn Township, Sŏnch'ŏn County local office," *Puk Han kwangye saryojip*, volume 9, pp. 356-58.

50. The following article gives some examples of landlord resistance: Chŏn Hyŏnsu, "Haebang chikhu Pukhansa yŏn'gu ŭi myŏt kaji munje e taehayŏ" (Several issues in the study of post-liberation North Korea," *Yŏksa wa hyŏnsil*, no. 10 (1993), pp. 302-03.

1946, Ignati'ev noted that landlords and opposition forces were increasing their anti-land reform activities in several counties.[51]

The Soviet Military Government and the legislative organ of the NKPPC collected reports on activities in the North, and the following is an overview of cases of resistance in each region.

In Pyongyang, on the night of March 7, 1946, just two days after the announcement of the land reform, someone threw a grenade at the building housing the Communist Party Committee. There was an instance of arson at the two-story house next to the Garrison Command in Kangsŏ County, South P'yŏng'an province. When the people's committee of South P'yŏng'an deliberated on the land reform law, KDP members showed little interest, and some even walked out of the Committee hall when the discussion began. In Kangdong County, a group of landlords decided among themselves to arrest the local police chief, who was actively participating in the land reform.[52] There was even a case of murder in which Kim Hyesŏn, the chairperson of a village committee in Sŏngt'ae township, Kangsŏ County, was killed.[53]

In the city of Sinŭiju, North P'yŏng'an province, Chŏng Talhŏn, the chairperson of the provincial people's committee, discussed the land reform law at a student meeting on March 11, but not a single one of the 150 students present supported it. People's committee leaders from landlord families that opposed the law refused to carry out their duties. There were some landlords who thought, "Who elected and formed the people's committees that adopted this land reform law? I will not give up my land, and as long as I have strength, I will fight." Even some rich peasants thought, "In the end, this law will not be of much benefit to the peasants. No matter how hard the peasants work, they will not be able to own anything, and their whole harvest be taken away by the Red Army."

In Hwanghae province, there were rumors that 200 middle school students in Haeju refused to attend classes for several days and that all the harvest from the land distributed to the peasants would be seized. At a student meet-

---

51. Ignati'ev, "March 24 Summary Report on the Progress of the Land Reform and Local Tendencies," March 25, 1946, TsAMORF, Fond USGASK, Opis 102038, Delo 2, p. 183.
52. Ibid., pp. 183–84.
53. "Puk Chosŏn kongsandang Pyŏng'annamdo Kangsŏ kun wiwŏnhoe ch'aekim ilgun ege chun chisi" (Instructions to the Leaders of the Kangsŏ County, South P'yŏng'an Province People's Committee from the North Korean Communist Party, April 9, 1946), *Kim Il Sung chŏnjip* (The complete works of Kim Il Sung) vol. 3 (Korean Workers' Party Press, 1992), pp. 261-62.

ing, someone asked, "Whom do the Communists work for? Do they work for the Soviet Union or for the Korean people?" On March 10, students decided to raid the people's committee and the local branch of the Communist Party, and on the night of March 12, there was an attack on one of the officers' residences.[54] In Haeju county, township committees (*myŏnwiwŏnhoe*) did not cooperate with the land reform in Kŭmsan, Changgok, and Sŏsŏk.[55]

In South P'yŏng'an province, leaflets were scattered in the town of Sariwŏn that criticized the land reform and Kim Il Sung.[56] In Sinmak, eight sons of landlords who moved to the South formed an armed organization and threatened local residents so that they would not participate in the land reform.[57] In An'ak County, one landlord assaulted a member of the Peasant Committee.[58] There were cases of farm supervisors in Kŭmch'ŏn County who tried to continue to use tenant farmers despite the enactment of the land reform.[59] In Chaeryŏng County, there was an incident where leaflets against land reform were scattered, and the main suspects were middle school students. More than half the students in the local middle school were children of landlord or capitalist families.[60]

In Kangwŏn province, the "Anti-Communist, Anti-Soviet, Anti-Land Reform Propaganda Incident" occurred in Kŭmhwa. After the Public Security Bureau of the Kangwŏn Provincial Inspectorate collected evidence on the

54. Shtykov, "Implementation of Land Reform and Local Tendencies," 15 March 1946, AVPRF, Fond Referentura po Koree, Opis 6, Por. 16, Inv 200, Papka 3, pp. 1-3.

55. Haeju People's Inspectorate, "Minutes of the Meeting of Legal Affairs Officers," April 10, 1946, Materials on Minutes of the Meeting of Legal Affairs Officers (Hwanghae Provincial Court, Prosecutor's Office), no page number given.

56. Ignati'ev, "March 25 Summary Report on the Progress of the Land Reform and Local Tendencies," TsAMORF, Fond USGASK, Opis 102038, Delo 2, p. 187.

57. Ignati'ev, "March 24 Summary Report," pp. 183-84.

58. Ibid.

59. Kŭmch'ŏn People's Court Chairman, Kŭmch'ŏn People's Inspectorate, "T'oji kaehyŏk pogo" (Report on Land Reform), April 7, 1946, Materials on Minutes of the Meeting of Legal Affairs Officers (Hwanghae Provincial Court, Prosecutor's Office), no page number given. In Koksan and Changyŏn, landlords and tenants reportedly agreed in secret to maintain the tenant system as it was. "Minutes of the Second Meeting of All Provincial Security Bureaus," *Puk Han kwangye saryojip*, vol. 9, p. 245.

60. Chaeryŏng People's Inspectorate, "Sabŏp kigwan ch'aek'imja hoeŭi pogosŏ" (Report of Minutes of Legal Affairs Officers), April 10, 1946, no page number given.

incident, the investigation was transferred to the Soviet Military Counter-Revolutionaries Supervisory Office.[61]

In terms of geographical location, what the above instances of resistance have in common is that nearly all of them, except for Kŭmhwa in Kangwŏn province, occurred in the northwest plains region of Hwanghae and P'yong'an provinces. In contrast, there were hardly any reported cases of resistance in the mountainous eastern portions of P'yŏng'an province and in South and North Hamgyŏng province. Outbreaks of resistance were relatively more frequent in regions where the landlord system was strong.

Nevertheless, on the whole, land reform was completed without any setbacks in its schedule. The far majority of landlords chose to flee to South Korea rather than to resist. Especially in Hwanghae and Kangwŏn provinces, the two provinces near the 38th Parallel, the extent of migration to the South was striking. The Chaeryŏng People's Prosecutor's Office reported that "the number of people who have fled to the South has reached about fifty-nine, and as they mainly consist of large landlords, large-scale businessmen, and pro-Japanese elements, it is probable that there are still quite a few people who are preparing to flee."[62] In Kangwŏn province, there was a report that among landlords who had lost their land, there were many who were migrating to the South.[63]

Although their numbers were small, there were landlords who accepted the policies of the NKPPC. In commentaries on the land reform, the NKPPC recognized landlord households that had distributed land to peasants before the land reform as "patriotic landlords" and did not confiscate their houses or farming equipment.[64] Of the 29,683 landlord households in North Korea with more than five *chŏngbo* of land whose property was seized, 3,911 households (13.2% of the total) moved to another county and became ordinary peasants. These landlords received a total of 9,622 *chŏngbo* of land for an aver-

---

61. Kangwŏn Province Chief of Inspectorate, "Puk Chosŏn che 2 ch'a sabŏp ch'aek'imja hoeŭi Kangwŏndo saŏp pogosŏ" (Second Meeting of the North Korean Legal Affairs Officers, Kangwŏn Province Activity Report), April 20, 1946, p. 19.

62. Chaeryŏng People's Inspectorate, "Sabŏp kigwan ch'aek'imja hoeŭi pogosŏ."

63. "Puk Chosŏn che 2 ch'a sabŏp ch'aek'imja hoeŭi Kangwŏndo saŏp pogosŏ," p. 24.

64. There was also a report that mentioned "scenes of patriotic landlords tilling the fields just like peasants who had received [allotments of] land." "Chŏng'chi pogo (Hwanghae Provincial Court, Prosecutor's Office)," *Puk Han kwangye saryojip*, volume 9, p. 138.

age of 2.5 *chŏngbo* per household.[65] In some regions, landlords were encouraged to invest in industrial capital.[66]

The division of the country was one of the major reasons that the resistance of the landlord class was weak in the North. Rather than engaging in resistance under the rule of the Soviet Military Government, the landlord class, which opposed the land reform, had the option of seeking a new life by moving to the South. Thus, the division of the country—particularly, the occupation by the Soviet Army—was the most important factor in weakening the resistance of the landlord class.[67]

There were a few other important factors behind the weakness of landlord resistance. Their potential for resistance had already been weakened by the time of the land reform. First, immediately after liberation, there had been attacks on pro-Japanese collaborators in all regions. For example, in Kosŏng and Yangyang counties in Kangwŏn province, where there was no formal legal apparatus, residents subjected "national traitors" to "People's Courts," and people's committees seized the property of pro-Japanese collaborators.[68] Moreover, the landlord class received an economic blow because of the "3-7" system of tenancy fees and the "honor system" of rice collection. The South P'yŏng'an provincial branch of the Communist Party reported that in the process of implementing the "3-7" system, there were "small 'local wars' in a few places because of the opposition of small landlords" and that it solved this problem under the principle of "public security first."[69] During

65. Central Statistics Bureau, State Planning Committee, *1946-1960, Chosŏn Minjujuŭi Inmin Konghwaguk inmin kyŏngje paljŏn t'onggyejip* (Collection of statistics on people's economic development, Democratic People's Republic of Korea 1946-1960) (Pyongyang: Kungnip ch'ulp'ansa, 1961), p. 59.

66. An'ak Chief of People's Court-Chief Inspector, "Chibang sajŏng ch'ŏngch'wi sahang pogo ŭi kŏn" (Report on things heard about local conditions), April 7, 1946, no page number given.

67. Pak Myŏngnim, *op. cit.*, p. 201.

68. In Kosŏng in mid-September 1945, one Korean was sentenced to death as a "national traitor" by an eleven-member "People's Court." In early November, the Kangwŏn Provincial Inspectorate in Ch'ŏrwŏn enforced a stay of execution in the name of the Soviet military. In Yangyang, three "national traitors" (including one Japanese) were sentenced to "re-education" by a People's Court. "Second Meeting of the North Korean Legal Affairs Officers, Kangwŏn Province Activity Report," p. 11. At the beginning of liberation, Koreans who had collaborated with Japanese imperialism, and of course Japanese themselves, were deemed "national traitors" by the People's Courts.

69. Korean Communist Party, South P'yŏng'an Provincial Committee, "Chosŏn Kongsandang Pyŏngnamdo che 1 ch'a taep'yo taehoe pogo yŏnsŏl" (Report on speeches at the first representatives' congress of the South P'yŏng'an Province Korean Communist Party," *Chosŏn kongsandang mungŏn charyojip*, p. 67.

the land reform, there were even cases of investigations and arrests of "hidden" landlords or those who failed to participate in rice collections—in order to contain the opposition of the landlords.[70] Most of all, right-wing nationalists had already become weakened before the land reform because of their clash with the Soviet Occupation Army during the anti-trusteeship movement. In an extremely short period of time, land reform revolutionized the peasantry and brought about the collapse of the landlord class that had dominated agrarian society.

Conclusion

After World War II, programs of land reform were implemented all over the world, and the North Korean land reform was the most radical and thorough. The radicalism of the North Korean land reform was the result of a combination of international, domestic, and local factors: the worsening of the conflict between the U.S. and Soviet Union, the conflict between socialism and capitalism in the Korean peninsula, and the explosion of peasant radicalism in rural villages.

Immediately after liberation in August 1945, the USSR and mainstream North Korean communists did not assume that the division of the country would be permanent, nor did their plans call for a radical land reform to achieve that goal. Their basic approach was to establish a "provisional governing apparatus" in North Korea that would be friendly—or at least not opposed—to the Soviet Union while preparing for the possibility of establishing a unified government as agreed upon by the Allies. Socioeconomic reform was limited to the elimination of pro-Japanese and extreme right-wing forces that would be an obstacle to the establishment of a unified government. On land reform, their platform proposed only the confiscation of land from Japanese imperialists and pro-Japanese collaborators and its distribution to the peasantry. These measures do not necessarily indicate that the ultimate goal of the Soviets and the socialists was not to communize the Korean peninsula. Rather, it means that the Soviets and the socialists, who had to cooperate with the U.S. and bourgeois nationalist forces, recognized the limits of their power and lowered their goals. The premise behind their

---

70. "Puk Chosŏn che 2 ch'a sabŏp ch'aek'imja hoeŭi Kangwŏndo saŏp pogosŏ," p. 19.

thinking was the fluidity (temporary nature) of the division at the 38th parallel.

However, actual events unfolded in a different direction. From the time of the London Conference, relations between the U.S. and Soviet Union became severely strained over Japan and other northeast Asian issues. The growing power of the right wing in the South made the Soviets concerned that the U.S. was making a de facto separate government in the South—with the formation of the KDP in September, the U.S. military government's support of the KDP, and the return of Syngman Rhee and KPG leaders. In addition, the lack of support for reform within North Korea and the Sinŭiju Incident of November 23 contributed to a sense of crisis that it would be impossible to create a stable base of support in North Korea unless large landlords were purged from rural society. At the Moscow Foreign Ministers' Conference in late December 1945, the U.S. and USSR agreed on a policy to establish a unified government in Korea. But at the same time, the Maritime Military District Command in charge of the North Korean military occupation reported to their superiors that they were carrying out a centralization of power and a land reform against large landlords. U.S.-Soviet conflict on the Korean peninsula and left-right conflict among Koreans was already severe even before the trusteeship crisis erupted in early 1946. It was within this context that North Korea moved toward a more fundamental and radical direction in land reform.

When the Cho Mansik group did not actively support the Moscow accords during the "Trusteeship Crisis" of 1946, bourgeois nationalist forces became further weakened within the North Korean power structure. Until that point, the policy of the USSR and the KCP had been to work toward the creation of a pro-Soviet regime through a left-right coalition with the bourgeois nationalist forces. In February 1946, they changed their policy to one of creating a stable power structure dominated by socialists by granting the peasantry's radical demands for land and gaining their support.

This shift in policy meant that communism joined forces with a peasant radicalism whose roots went back to the peasant rebellions of the late Chosŏn period. More recently, peasant radicalism in the Liberation period was a descendant of the revolutionary peasant movements of the 1930s. Through the people's committees set up throughout Korea, peasants had already received cultivation rights to land appropriated from the former colonial state, individual Japanese, and pro-Japanese collaborators. Peasants had also struggled against landlords to establish the "3-7" system of tenancy fees.

With the establishment of the "North Korean Peasant League" after liberation, the peasants created a central organ to represent their interests. The NKPL, led by activists from the revolutionary peasant union movement of the 1930s, continued to mobilize peasant radicalism. The first group to call for a radical land reform that involved the confiscation and free distribution of all land belonging to landlords was not the Communist Party, but county-level peasant councils. Despite the fact that the Soviet Foreign Ministry advocated an Eastern European-style moderate land reform, the support of peasant organizations, which were mainly composed of poor peasants, enabled the Soviet Maritime Military District Command and Northern Branch of the Korean Communist Party to carry out a policy of confiscation without compensation and free distribution of all land cultivated by tenant farmers.

As soon as the land reform law was promulgated, it was carried out very rapidly. Despite its complex policy on redistribution, the reform was completed within one month because the peasants, who understood the complicated local relationships of ownership and cultivation, created *ri*-level Peasant Committees to decide all matters themselves. As can be seen in the case of Sŏnch'ŏn County in North P'yŏng'an province, some of the peasantry became so radicalized through the land reform that even the people's committees could not control them. After the land reform, the NKPPC and Kim Il Sung gained tremendous support among the peasantry.

Through the land reform, the North Korean state came to possess a unity in which the state leadership had the strong support of the ordinary masses. In addition, the state had an internal homogeneity in which most heterogeneous factors were eliminated. The foundation of the unity and homogeneity evident in North Korea society today had already been established in the process of land reform.

However, this foundation was far from secure in 1946. The landlord class had been rendered powerless, but it did not accept the legitimacy of the NKPPC's land reform. The landlord class believed that when a unified government would be established in Korea, land reform would be enacted again but according to a different method. They had the option of going to South Korea where right-wing forces were concentrated and which was under the rule of the U.S. military government. For them, migration to the South was not a permanent escape; South Korea was just a temporary base to prepare for their counterattack. The peasants could not ignore the threat that the landlords had left behind as they left for the South. A full-scale conflict between socialism/peasant radicalism and capitalism/landlord reformism would explode four years after the land reform with the outbreak of the Korean War in 1950.

translated by Charles K. Armstrong

Index of Terms

Choguk kwangbokhoe 祖國光復會 Fatherland Restoration Society
Cho Mansik 曹晩植 (1883-?)
Chosŏn nongminsa 朝鮮農民社 Korean Peasant Society
Hong Kihwang 洪基璜
hwajŏnmin 火田民 "fire-field people" or slash-and-burn farmers
inmin minjujuŭi 人民民主主義 people's democracy
Kang Yang'uk 康良煜
kun 郡 county
nodongnyŏk 勞動力 labor power
"*Minjok taedangyŏl e taehayŏ*" 民族大同團結에 對하야 "On the Grand
    Unity of the Nation"
Minjujuŭi ch'ŏngnyŏn tongmaeng 民主主義青年同盟 Democratic Youth
    League
myŏnwiwŏnhoe 面委員會 township committees
Nongmin chawidae 農民自衛隊 Peasant Self-Defense Corps
Pak Hŏnyŏng 朴憲永 (1900-1956)
Puk Chosŏn imsi inmin wiwŏnhoe 北朝鮮臨時人民委員會 North
    Korean Provisional People's Committee
Puk Chosŏn nongmin tongmaeng 北朝鮮農民同盟 North Korean
    National League of Peasant Unions (NLPU)
Yi Munhwan 李文煥
Yi Pongsu 李鳳洙
yŏngnyang 力量 capacity

PART III

INTELLECTUALS

CHAPTER 7

Paek Nam'un and Marxist Scholarship during the Colonial Period

Pang Kie-chung
方基中

The scientific socialist thought of Marxism was introduced into Korea in the late 1910s, after it had become a colony of Japan. Along with nationalism and other capitalist ideologies, Marxism was one of the most influential ideologies on the political thinking and activities of Koreans during the colonial period, because of its theories of national liberation and social revolution. After liberation, it became the state ideology for the socialist regime in North Korea. Marxism has had a significant impact on the political, social, and cultural thinking of Koreans for the past eighty years, continuing beyond the end of the cold war into the present time. One of the most important tasks facing historians is to examine the historical development and characteristics of Marxist thought in Korea. This research is necessary to gain a systematic understanding of the fundamental trends of modern Korean history from the late nineteenth century—when Korea failed to establish a modern nation-state—to the period of Japanese colonial rule, and finally to liberation and the division of the country. It is also necessary in order to achieve an in-depth understanding of the problems of reunification, which have become more pressing in recent years.[1]

---

1. In the past, research on socialism has mainly focused on political and social movements, but recently, it has been expanding into intellectual thought, which is a positive development. There is not enough space to mention all of this research, but notable studies of socialist and Marxist thought include: Sŏ Chungsŏk, *Han'guk hyŏndae minjok undong yŏn'gu* (Studies on contemporary nationalist movements in Korea) (Seoul: Yŏksa pip'yŏngsa, 1991); Kim Yong-sop (Kim Yongsŏp), *Han'guk kŭnhyŏndae nong'ŏpsa yŏn'gu* (Studies on the agricultural history of modern and contemporary Korea) (Seoul: Ilchogak, 1992); Pang Kie-chung (Pang Kijung), *Han'guk*

As part of this effort, this chapter examines the economic thought and scholarship of Paek Nam'un (1894-1979; *ho* Tong'am), the most prominent Marxist economic historian of the colonial period. He was a professor in the Department of Commerce at Yŏnhŭi Junior College (the precursor to today's Yonsei University) and was the founder of Marxist historiography in Korea. He was also one of the pioneers of modern Korean historiography who, along with the nationalist historian Sin Ch'aeho, developed an autonomous, scientific perspective on Korean history.[2]

With the publication of *Chosŏn sahoe kyŏngjesa* (*The Socioeconomic History of Chosŏn*, 1933) and *Chosŏn ponggŏn sahoe kyŏngjesa* (*The Socioeconomic History of Feudal Chosŏn*, 1937), he not only laid the foundation for Marxist historiography in Korea but also exposed, theoretically and empirically, the historical fallacies and bourgeois, imperialist nature of studies on Korean history by Japanese government researchers. In fact, by focusing on the logic of Korean history's internal development, he was the first scholar to develop a historical methodology and vision that enabled an understanding of both the universal and the uniquely Korean aspects of its history. In other publications, I have undertaken a theoretical examination of his historical materialism and his theories on the developmental stages of Korean history in order to examine his theoretical limitations and the importance of his contributions to historiography.[3]

kŭnhyŏndae sasangsa yŏn'gu (Studies in the intellectual history of modern and contemporary Korea) (Seoul: Yŏksa pip'yŏngsa, 1992); Kim Tongch'un, "Sasang ŭi chŏngae rŭl t'onghae pon Han'guk ŭi 'kŭndae' mosŭp" (The form of modernity in Korea as seen through the development of its thought), *Han'guk ŭi 'kŭndae' wa 'kŭndaesŏng' pip'an* (Seoul: Yŏksa pip'yŏngsa, 1996).

2. Studies on Paek Nam'un's theory of history and historical thought include: Kim Yong-sop, "Ilbon Han'guk e issŏsŏ ŭi Han'guksa sŏsul" (The depiction of Korean history in Japan and Korea), *Yŏksa hakpo*, no. 31 (1966); Kang Man'gil, "Ilche sidae ŭi pansingmin sahaknon" (Anti-colonial historiography during the colonial period), *Hanguksahaksa ŭi yŏn'gu* (Seoul: Han'guksa yŏn'gu-hoe, 1986); Kang Chinch'ŏl, "Sahoe kyŏngje sahak ŭi toip kwa chŏngae" (The introduction and development of socioeconomic historiography), *Kuksagwan nonch'ong*, no. 2 (1989); Chŏng Ch'angnyŏl, "Hanguk esŏ minjung sahak ŭi sŏngnip.chŏn'gae kwajŏng" (The establishment and development of *minjung* historiography in Korea), *Han'guk minjungron ŭi hyŏndan'gae* (Seoul: Tolbegae, 1989).

3. Pang Kie-chung, "Paek Nam'un ŭi yŏksa iron kwa Han'guksa insik" (Paek Nam'un's theory of history and conception of Korean history), *Yŏksa pip'yŏng*, no. 9 (summer 1990); Pang Kie-chung, *Han'guk kŭnhyŏndae sasangsa yŏn'gu*; Pang Kie-chung, "Ilcheha Paek Nam'un ŭi Han'guk chabonjuŭi paldal saron" (The conception of the history of the development of capitalism in Korea by Paek Nam'un during the colonial period), *Tongbang hakji*, nos. 77-78-79 (combined issue, 1993); Pang Kie-chung, "Paek Nam'un ŭi hangmun kwa sasang" (The scholarship and thought of Paek Nam'un), *Yŏnse kyŏngje yŏn'gu*, no. 1 (1994).

Although Paek Nam'un's scholarship focused on history, the significance of his work and thought goes beyond his empirical contributions to Korean historiography. He clearly had the most sophisticated understanding of Marxist theory and historical materialism among socialist intellectuals during the colonial period. He did not follow Marxist theory dogmatically but grounded it in the historical realities of Korea's situation to develop a theory for "understanding Chosŏn" (*Chosŏn insik*). He was an exemplar of the intellectual who stressed the autonomy of intellectual practice while pursuing the ultimate objective of national liberation and the establishment of a socialist state. Although some of his colleagues and some scholars in the younger generation shared his ideas on intellectual practice, they differed from mainstream Marxists who were the leaders of socialist political and cultural movements at the time. The mainstream conception of practice meant a dogmatic acceptance of Stalinism and an extreme leftist classism.

In this context, an examination of Paek Nam'un can reveal some important aspects of the introduction of Marxism in Korea. During the Liberation period, he was active, both politically and intellectually, in moderate leftist organizations, serving as the director of the Chosŏn Academy (*Chosŏn haksulwŏn*), the chairman of the South Korean New People's Party (*Sinmindang*), and the vice-chairman of the Worker-People's Party (*Kŭllo inmindang*). After the division of the country, he played an important role in laying the intellectual foundations of North Korean socialism as an elder statesman of its intellectual world. As his career suggests, differences in epistemology and conceptions of praxis were closely related to differing conceptions of the future of the nation and of the direction of socialist political and cultural movements.

An examination of Paek Nam'un's scholarship and thought during the colonial period can provide a systematic analysis of the general thinking of socialist intellectuals in terms of their political-economic ideology and their conceptions of state and society which were fundamentally different from those of bourgeois nationalist intellectuals. At the same time, his life and work also provide an opportunity to examine differences among socialist intellectuals in their understanding of Marxism and praxis as well as the historical and political significance of such differences. The interrogation of this problematic is the underlying concern of this chapter.

The first section of this chapter examines the development of Paek Nam'un's thought during the colonial period and his theoretical contribution to a Marxist approach to "understanding Chosŏn." The second section examines his views on modern Korean economic history which most clearly reveal his understanding of historical materialism. This section will cover topics such as the breakdown of feudal society, the internal dynamics and failures of the movement toward capitalism, and his conception of "transplanted capitalism" (*isik chabonjuŭi*) under conditions of colonialism.

Of course, restricting my examination to such scholarly topics makes it impossible to draw a complete picture of Marxist thought in Korea during the colonial period and, more specifically, to give a full analysis of the debates on Marxist theories of revolution. Another limitation is the fact that Paek Nam'un did not participate in any political movements during the colonial period and was only active in cultural and scholarly movements. These limitations to my approach can be overcome only through a comprehensive analysis of his political activities after liberation and of his conception of the state based on the principles of "new democracy" (*sin minjujuŭi*).[4] Whatever Paek's shortcomings may be, they do not diminish the historical importance of Paek Nam'un's scholarship and thought in the history of Marxist thought in Korea and, more generally, in the history of political thought in modern Korea.

The Development of Paek Nam'un's Marxist Scholarship

INTRODUCTION TO MARXISM IN THE 1920S

Paek Nam'un was born on February 11, 1894 as the second son of Paek Nakgyu in the village of Pan'am, Asan *myŏn*, Koch'ang county, North Chŏlla province. His family was a provincial yangban family that had belonged to the Noron faction for several generations. Although they were poor, they were a typical Confucian household that stressed education in Neo-Confucianism and adherence to ritual. His father was also a Confucian scholar who was a disciple of Song Pyŏngsŏn, an orthodox descendent of the Noron faction's scholarship.[5] Spending his childhood in extreme poverty, he learned classical Chinese and received a strict education in Neo-Confucian

---

4. Because of limitations of space, this article will not give an analysis of Paek Nam'un's conceptions of state and of "new democracy." For more on this topic, see Pang Kie-chung, *Han'guk kŭnhyŏndae sasangsa yŏn'gu*, Chapter 3.

5. Song Pyŏngsŏn (1836-1905) was an official in the Great Han Empire and committed suicide to protest the Protectorate Treaty of 1905. Paek Nakgyu was deeply moved by his teacher's martyrdom as an act of resistance against the Japanese. *Hŭngsŏngji*, book 3, *haengŭi*.

family rituals at the local school (*sodang*) run by his father. His family environment had a significant influence on the formation of his young mind and provided an important foundation for his future academic research. From his father, who deplored Japanese imperialist aggressions—albeit with a feudal mind-set—Paek Nam'un gained an understanding of Korea's political situation as well as an anti-Japanese consciousness. His exposure to Confucian thought in this period influenced his later interest in the history of Korea's economic thought.[6]

Paek Nam'un's transition from a feudal worldview to a modern one began when he enrolled in the Suwŏn Agricultural and Forestry School (Suwŏn nongnim hakgyo) in 1912. It was a government school under the jurisdiction of the Model Farm for the Promotion of Agriculture (Kwŏn'ŏp mobŏmjang). The Japanese operated the model farm as part of its policy to control Korean agriculture as the basis for its exploitation of the colony,[7] and the school sought to legitimize Japan's control of the Korean rural economy and to maintain the dominance of the landlord system. Its educational ideals were based on the agrarianism (*nongbonjuŭi*) advocated by landlords whose goals were to increase productivity and to ease class tensions. The school's objective was to train Koreans to be leaders in rural areas and low-level functionaries who would carry out the exploitative agricultural policies of the Government-General.[8] Paek learned about modern natural science and the basic principles of capitalist agriculture and economics.

After the beginning of the Japanese occupation, the contradictions in the agricultural economy became even further aggravated. At Suwŏn Agricultural and Forestry School, Paek Nam'un acquired a concrete understanding of Korean agriculture's fundamental problems as he directly observed the actual condition of rural villages. It was at this time that he became deeply concerned about the state of the nation and began to devote himself to scholarship. After his graduation in 1915, he worked for a while as a teacher at the Kanghwa Public Normal School and as a technician at the Kanghwa Forestry Association. After resigning these positions, he went to Japan in October

6. Paek Nam'un, "*Chosŏn sahoe kyŏngjesa* ch'ulp'an e taehan sogam" (Thoughts on the publication of The Socioeconomic History of Chosŏn), *Chungang*, no. 1 (November 1933), p. 105.

7. Kim Tohyŏng, "Kwŏnnong mobŏmjang ŭi singminji nong'ŏp chibae" (Control of colonial agriculture by the Model Farm for the Promotion of Agriculture), *Han'guk kŭnhyŏndaesa yŏn'gu*, no. 3 (1995).

8. Pang Kie-chung, ibid., pp. 37-40; Pang Kie-chung, "Ilcheha Yi Hun'gu ŭi nong'ŏpnon kwa kyŏngje charip sasang" (The views on agriculture and conception of economic self-sufficiency of Yi Hun'gu during the colonial period), *Yŏksa munje yŏn'gu*, no. 1 (1996), pp. 119-20.

1918 to study and enrolled at the Tokyo Higher Commercial School (Tokyo Kodo Shogyo Gakko) in March 1919. The school was elevated to the status of a college in 1920, changing its name to Tokyo Commercial College (Tokyo Shoka Daigakko).

Paek Nam'un studied at Tokyo Commercial College during an extremely turbulent period in world history. With the success of the Russian revolution and the end of the First World War, national liberation movements became widespread in former colonial and semi-colonial regions. In Korea also, the desire for national independence exploded in the March 1st Movement. In Japan, the "Taisho democracy" movement captured the sentiment of the masses. Liberal thought and calls for social reconstruction were popular, and interest in socialist thought grew together with the labor and agrarian movements. The fact that Paek Nam'un entered Tokyo Commercial College at such a time is deeply significant on several levels. Tokyo Commercial College was one of the most important public educational institutions serving the needs of Japanese capitalism after the Meiji Restoration.[9] However, some of the school's faculty were also leaders in the Taisho democracy movement such as Minobe Tatsukichi (1873-1948), Fukuda Tokuzo (1874-1930), and Ueda Teijiro (1879-1940). Through them, the school served as a channel for the introduction of various kinds of Western bourgeois thought and democratic ideologies.[10] Having gathered an influential group of economists led by Fukuda Tokuzo, it became the center of the "social policy" faction and the German Historical School of Economics in Japan.[11]

9. For more about Tokyo Commercial College, see sources such as Sakai Tatsuo, *Hitotsubashi goju nensi* (The fifty year history of Hitotsubashi) (Tokyo: Tokyo Shoka Daigaku Hitotsubashikai, 1925); Tokyo Shoka Daigaku, ed., *Tokyo Shoka Daigaku Ichiran* (Overview of Tokyo Commercial College) 1,2,3 (Tokyo: Tokyo Shoka Daigaku, 1925).

10. Mitani Taichiro, "Taejŏng demokŭrasi ŭi chŏngae wa nolli" (The development and logic of Taisho democracy), *Ilbon hyŏndaesa ŭi kujo*, eds. Ch'a Kibyŏk and Pak Ch'ungsŏk (Seoul: Han'gilsa, 1980), pp. 254-55; Imai Seiichi, "Taishoki no siso to bunka" (Thought and culture in the Taisho period), *Koza Nihonshi* 7 (Tokyo: Tokyo Daigaku Shuppankai, 1971), pp. 158-59.

11. Ouchi Hyoe, *Keizaigaku gojunen jo* (Fifty years of economics, vol. 1) (Tokyo: Tokyo Daigaku Shuppankai, 1959), pp. 34-40. The German Historical School of Economics critiqued both classical economics and Marxian economics; it was characterized by its emphasis on historical and ethical methods. Fukuda Tokuzo (1874-1930) went to Germany in 1898 and studied under the Historical School economist Lujo Brentano at the University of Munich. He quickly gained fame with his Ph.D. dissertation ("Social and economic development in Japan," 1900) in which he emphasized the correspondence in the stage of economic development of Germany and Japan and Japan's universal social development. After his return to Japan, he lectured at Tokyo Higher Commercial School and Tokyo Commercial College. Together with Kawakami Hajime of

When Paek Nam'un was studying in the school's regular course (undergraduate division), his advisor was Takata Yasuma (1883-1972), who taught sociology and the history of economics. An anti-Marxist, Takada was one of the main figures of Japanese bourgeois economics and sociology from the latter half of the 1920s and was active as a theorist of fascism in Japan.[12] Tokyo Commercial College in the early 1920s promoted a bourgeois social science grounded in a social reformism that provided intellectual support for the development of Japanese capitalism. Paek was exposed to a wide variety of bourgeois social science, and it was at this school that he also decided to focus his scholarly efforts on history, specifically economic history.[13]

However, Paek Nam'un did not follow the intellectual trends at Tokyo Commercial College; rather, he formulated his research agenda in the process of adopting a critical distance toward them. From the beginning of his college days, he was attracted to Marxist ideas and began to adopt Marxism as his theoretical perspective. When he was in the preparatory division, he audited the lectures on Hegel in an introductory philosophy class taught by Kihira Tadayoshi (1874-1949), a professor at Gakushuin University who also gave lectures at Tokyo Commercial College. Paek soon became interested in a dialectics. After he entered the regular course in 1921, he was increaseingly absorbed in the study of Marxist philosophy and economics. Paek Nam'un avidly read the debates on value between Fukuda Tokuzo and Kawakami Hajime (1879-1946) of Kyoto Imperial University. Agreeing with the arguments of Kawakami, a Marxist, he decided to devote himself to the study of Marxism. When he took seminars taught by Fukuda and Takata Yasuma,

Kyoto Imperial University, he formed the Shakai seisaku gakkai and played a central role in the development of economics in Japan. With Yoshino Sakuzo of Tokyo Imperial University, he formed the Reimeikai and was one of the leaders of the Taisho democracy movement. On Fukuda's life, see Fukuda Tokuzo sensei kinenkai, ed., *Fukuda Tokuzo sensei no tsuioku* (Tokyo: Fukuda Tokuzo sensei kinenkai, 1960).

12. On Takata Yasuma, see Usui Jisho, "Takata Yasuma hakushi no shogai to shakaigaku" (The life and sociology of Dr. Takata Yasuma), *Takata Yasuma hakushi no shogai to gakusetsu* (Tokyo: Sobunsha, 1982); Yi Chunsik, "Paek Nam'un ŭi sahoe insik kwa Malksŭjuŭi" (Paek Nam'un's Marxism and conception of society), *Sahoehak yŏn'gu*, no. 6 (1990), pp. 319-20.

13. Paek Nam'un stated that he began to have a serious interest in history when he audited a class during his first year as an undergraduate on the history of ancient European civilizations that was taught by Miura Shinshichi, who lectured on economic history and the history of civilization at Tokyo Commercial College. Kyŏngsŏng Sŏdaemun kyŏngch'alsŏ (Seoul Sodaemun police station), "Kamsangnok" (Record of impressions), *Yi Sunt'ak oe iin pulgiso sagŏn sŏryuch'ŏl*, 1938.

who were critical of Marxism, he had theoretical disagreements with their views and became even more drawn to Marxist theory.[14]

Another influence on Paek Nam'un was Yamamoto Sanehiko (1885-1952), the president of Kaizosha, who gave him much help, both financially and emotionally, from the beginning of his studies in Tokyo. Through cultural events and publishing activities such as the founding of the journal *Kaizo* (Reconstruction) in 1919, Yamamoto, a progressive liberal, was an important figure in spreading democratic thought and Marxism in Japan during the Taisho democracy period.[15]

With the maturation of Paek Nam'un's political consciousness, he developed a critical attitude toward the intellectual atmosphere of his school and decided to devote himself to the study of Korean economic history. He came to realize that the Historical School of Economics, which was espoused at his school, was an imperialist social science providing intellectual support to Japan's occupation and rule of Chosŏn. The school advanced a theory of the stagnation of Korean society, by fabricating historical "facts" such as the assertion that Korean history lacked a feudal period. The purpose of their research was to whitewash and rationalize Japan's aggressions and imperialist policies by providing support to the argument that its "modernization" policies enabled Korea to undergo capitalist development and a commercial revolution.

One of the pioneering proponents of "stagnation theory" (J. *teitairon*) was Fukuda Tokuzo, one of Paek Nam'un's teachers. Based on his observations and knowledge gained from a roughly twenty-day trip to Korea in 1902, Fukuda argued in 1904 that Korea was a stagnant society, stuck at the stage of the ancient village economy, without a national economy or a

---

14. Kyŏngsŏng Sŏdaemun kyŏngch'alsŏ (Seoul Sodaemun police station), "P'iŭija Paek Nam'un sinmun chosŏ che il hoe" (Record of the first interrogation of suspect Paek Nam'un), "P'igoin Paek Nam'un sinmun chosŏ che i hoe" (Record of the second interrogation of suspect Paek Nam'un), "Kamsangnok" (Record of impressions), *Yi Sunt'ak oe iin pulgiso sagŏn sŏryuch'ŏl*, 1938.

15. The person who introduced Paek Nam'un to Yamamoto Sanehiko was Yamamoto's younger brother, Yamamoto Shigehiko. At the time that Paek Nam'un left for Japan, Yamamoto Shigehiko worked as the clerk to Ishizuka Eizo, who was director of the Home Affairs Bureau of the Government-General in Korea. Kyŏngsŏng Sŏdaemun kyŏngch'alsŏ (Seoul Sodaemun police station), "P'iŭija Paek Nam'un sinmun chosŏ che il hoe" (Record of the first interrogation of suspect Paek Nam'un), *Yi Sunt'ak oe iin pulgiso sagŏn sŏryuch'ŏl*, 1938. Through this introduction, Paek developed a close relationship with Yamamoto Sanehiko, and as is well known, both of Paek's books were published by Kaizosha. Pang Kie-chung, *Han'guk kŭnhyŏndae sasangsa yŏn'gu*, pp. 44–47; Yamamoto Sanehiko, *Mansen* (Manchuria and Chosŏn) (Tokyo: Kaizosha, 1932), pp. 26–28.

conception of the state. Providing the basic arguments for "stagnation theory," he asserted that the cause of Korea's stagnation was the lack of feudalism, and the lack of the concept of private land ownership, and the "national character of the Korean people" which was deficient in rationalism.[16] Even into the 1920s, before research on Korea's socioeconomic history had been done by Koreans themselves, the influence of Fukuda's views was absolute. His view held sway not only in the classrooms of Tokyo Commercial College but also in the field of economic history in Japan and in government research institutions, enabling them to survive and be propagated.[17] Paek Nam'un strongly disagreed with the imperialistic justifications of Japan's colonization and colonial policy put forth by his teacher and his school. He was especially critical of the Historical School of Economics and bourgeois scholarship, which formed the methodological and epistemological foundation for their views.

Paek Nam'un's interest in Marxism fundamentally resulted from his uncompromising political views, whose goal was to overcome the political and social situation of his country under foreign domination. When he stated that it was necessary for the "Chosŏn nation [to undergo] a historical self-criticism" based on scientific theories he meant that its purpose should be to achieve an understanding of the nature of Japan's occupation of Korea and of the dire situation in Korea's rural areas and to illuminate the future path of the nation.[18] His position reflected the main intellectual currents that burst onto the scene after the March 1st Independence Movement and were popular among young intellectuals.

As is well known, the social contradictions that had emerged during the late Chosŏn and Hanmal periods in Korea became even more pronounced as they were intricated with the problem of national liberation after the beginning of the Japanese occupation. In particular, the contradictions were concentrated in problems in the agricultural economy arising from the landlord system. By pursuing capitalist development through the preservation of the existing landlord system, the Japanese sought to co-opt the Korean landlord and capitalist classes, turning them into partners in colonial rule. Through a

16. Fukuda Tokuzo, "Kangoku no keizai soshiki to keizai tani" (The economic organizations and economic units of Korea), *Keizaigaku kenkyu*, 1925 edition, pp. 119-20, 143-44, 151-61.

17. Hatada Takashi, *Chosenjin to Nihonjin* (The Chosŏn people and the Japanese people) (Tokyo: Keiso shobo, 1983), pp. 68-78.

18. Kyŏngsŏng Sŏdaemun kyŏngch'alsŏ (Seoul Sodaemun police station), "P'igoin Paek Nam'un sinmun chosŏ che i hoe" (Record of the second interrogation of suspect Paek Nam'un), *Yi Sunt'ak oe iin pulgiso sagŏn sŏryuch'ŏl*, 1938.

large-scale transfer of capital, Japan attempted a violent integration of the Korean economy within a system of "transplanted capitalism." It regarded Korea as a supplier of raw materials, a market for commodities, and a source of exploitable labor for Japanese capitalism. These policies brought the petty farmer class, who comprised the great majority of the population, to the brink of bankruptcy.[19]

The problems facing Korea under Japanese rule would not be solved simply by national liberation but also required a structural reform of society to resolve social contradictions and class issues. The structural problems of Korean society were the objective factor that underlay the adoption of socialism and Marxism by populist and progressive groups. They became the new guiding principles of the national liberation movement after the Russian Revolution.[20] Young intellectuals in Korea and students in Japan, who were concerned about the state of their country, were seeking a fundamental solution to national and class issues from a peasant and populist perspective. They found in socialism and Marxism an ideology and a system of thought that offered a solution to overcome such problems. Their interest in Marxism was natural and understandable since various capitalist ideologies and bourgeois economics were providing intellectual justification for Japan's occupation and exploitation of Korea. Paek Nam'un had grown up in a struggling rural area, and during his days at the Suwŏn Agricultural and Forestry School, he directly observed the dire situation in rural areas and the deception of Japan's exploitative agricultural policies. Like many others in his generation, he was also caught up in the intellectual trends of the times.

At the end of his early intellectual development, Paek Nam'un came to the conclusion that Marx's historical materialism was the proper methodology

19. Kim Yong-sop, ibid.; Choi Won-kyu (Ch'oe Wŏn'gyu), "Hanmal ilche ch'ogi t'oji chosa wa t'ojibŏp yŏn'gu" (An examination of cadastral surveys and land laws in the Hanmal and early colonial periods) (Ph.D. diss., Yonsei University, 1994); Chŏng Yŏnt'ae, "1910 nyŏndae ilche ŭi nong'ŏp chŏngch'aek kwa singminji chijuje" (Japan's agricultural policies and the colonial landlord system in the 1910s), *Han'guk saron*, no. 20 (1988); Chŏng T'aehŏn, "1910 nyŏndae singmin nongjŏng kwa kŭm'yung sut'al kigu ŭi hwangnip kwajŏng" (Colonial agricultural management and the establishment of exploitative financial institutions in the 1910s), *3-1 minjok haebang undong yŏn'gu* (Seoul: Ch'ŏngnyŏnsa, 1989).

20. Kim Yong-sop, ibid., pp. 398–410; Im Kyŏngsŏk, "Koryŏ kongsandang yŏn'gu" (A study of the Koryŏ Communist Party) (Ph.D. diss., Sŏngkyunkwan University, 1993), chapters 1 and 4. This trend was a worldwide phenomenon that was common in countries that were in a colonial or semi-colonial situation. In addition to the Russian Revolution, the failure of the March 1st Liberation Movement, which was based on bourgeois nationalist principles, was another impetus for the rapid spread of socialist thought as the new ideology of the national liberation, peasant, and labor movements.

for understanding Japan's imperialist ideology and for a scientific understanding of Korea's history and current situation.[21] He felt that research and theoretical work on Korean society and history—what can be called *Chosŏn insik* (understanding Chosŏn)—was a matter of praxis that needed to be accomplished by Koreans themselves in order to overcome their colonial situation. With such an independent attitude toward scholarship, he devoted himself to the lifelong task of developing a scientific understanding of Chosŏn and systematizing "Chosŏn economic history."[22]

There are two aspects to Paek Nam'un's Marxism in this period that are important to understand. First, although he adopted a Marxist perspective, he was opposed to an extreme classism that viewed Korea's problems only from a class perspective. An uncompromising anti-imperial nationalist, he viewed the Japanese occupation as being no different from slave domination. To him, there could be no social revolution that was not premised on national liberation, which was the task of the entire people. As socialist thought spread rapidly in the early 1920s, his position was that the nationalist and socialist movements, two groups that were opposed to each other, should establish a united front to oppose the Japanese.[23] His scholarly activities after his return from Japan were consistent with such views.

Second, his understanding of Marxism was still at a relatively low level, reflecting the early theoretical level of Marxism and the general situation of the academic world in Japan in the early 1920s. Since there were few translations of Marx's original works at the time, Marxist theory was spread mainly through introductory works or journals. A foundation had not yet been established for an intellectually systematized Marxist school or science. Marxist analyses of society were at the level of a mechanical application of Marxist economic principles to social issues without any historical research based on historical materialism.[24] As will be explained below, although Paek

---

21. Paek Nam'un, "Pujŏng wŏlli e taehan koch'al" (An investigation of negative principles), *Yŏnhŭi*, no. 5 (October 1925), pp. 98-99; Paek Nam'un, "Chosŏn sahoeryŏk ŭi tongjŏk koch'al" (A dynamic investigation of the strength of Chosŏn society), *Chosŏn ilbo*, January 3, 1926.

22. Paek Nam'un, "'Chosen keizai no kenkyu' ŭi tokgam" (Impressions on reading "Research on the Chosŏn economy"), *Chosŏn chi kwang*, no. 89 (January 1930), p. 24; Paek Nam'un, "*Chosen shakai keizaishi* ch'ulp'an e taehan sogam" (Impressions on the publication of *The socioeconomic history of Chosŏn*), *Chung'ang*, no. 1 (November 1933), p. 105.

23. Paek Nam'un, "Chosŏn sahoeryŏk ŭi tongjŏk koch'al."

24. Yamakawa Hitoshi, "Wagakuni ni okeru marukusizumu no hattatsu" (The development of Marxism in our country), *Kaizo* (March 1933), pp. 34-35; Moriya Norio, *Nihon Marukusushugi no keisei to hatten* (The formation and development of Japanese Marxism) (Tokyo: Aoki shoten,

had already created his own framework for Korean economic history during his college years, he had at this point done no more than establish a basic research perspective and work out the fundamentals of his view of history. The empirical study and theoretization of all periods of Korean economic history, based on historical materialism, were tasks for the future.

Appointed as a professor at Yŏnhŭi Junior College (Yŏnhŭi chŏnmun hakgyo) in April 1925, Paek Nam'un began in-depth work on Korean economic history. Among his various scholarly activities, he participated in the Institute for Research and Surveys on Korean Issues (Chosŏn sajŏng chosa yŏn'guhoe) and undertook a systematic review of what he had learned in Japan.[25] It was not until the latter half of the 1920s that he gained a full theoretical understanding of Marxist epistemology and social science which he then concretized into a methodology for studying Korea.

After 1927, when the socialist movement and socialist thought reached a new stage of development in Korea, many socialist intellectuals undertook theoretical examinations of materialist dialectics and historical materialism. There was lively discussion on the strategy and tactics of the "Korean revolution" in connection with debates on class, social contradictions, and united front politics. In the course of these debates, a general consensus emerged supporting the Comintern's theory of colonial revolution, which advocated an anti-imperial and anti-feudal bourgeois democratic revolution.[26] In response to such developments, Paek Nam'un devoted himself to the collection and analysis of historical materials for his research on Korean economic history. At the same time, he deepened his understanding of materialist

---

1967), pp. 21-22, 60-65; Toyama Shigeki, "Yuibutsu shikan shigaku no seiritsu" (The establishment of historical materialist historiography), *Nihon rekishi koza* 8 (1957), pp. 289-319.

25. On Paek Nam'un's scholarly work and activities and his conception of political action after his appointment at Yŏnhŭi, see Pang Kie-chung, *Han'guk kŭnhyŏndae sasangsa yŏn'gu*, pp. 73-82.

26. O Miil, "Ilje sigi sahoejuŭijadŭl ŭi nong'ŏp munje insik" (The conception of agricultural issues by socialists during the colonial period), *Yŏksa pip'yŏng*, no. 7 (winter 1989), pp. 266-78; Yi Kyun'yŏng, *Sin'ganhoe yŏn'gu* (Seoul: Yŏksa pip'yŏngsa, 1993), Chapter 2; Mizuno Naoki, "Kominterŭn ŭi minjok t'ong'il chŏnsŏn kwa Singanhoe undong" (The Comintern's united front and the Sin'ganhoe movement), *Yŏksa pip'yŏng*, no. 1 (spring 1988); Han Sanggu, "1926-1928 nyŏn sahoejuŭi seryŏk ŭi undongnon kwa Sin'ganhoe" (The Sin'ganhoe and theories of movement of socialist groups, 1926-1928), *Han'guksa yŏn'gu*, no. 86 (1994). In Japan, whose developments had a direct influence on Korean intellectuals, the situation was more developed. As the works of Marx, Engels, and Lenin were more and more being translated into Japanese, Marxist science was beginning to establish itself as a distinct school of scholarship. Moriya Norio, ibid., chapter 3; Nagaoka Shinkichi, *Nihon shihonshugi ronso no gunzo* (The group of debates on Japanese capitalism) (Kyoto: Mineruva shobo, 1984), chapters 1 and 2.

dialectics and historical materialism through close readings of the major works of Marxism. He also tackled the theoretical problem of how to apply Marxism to the study of Korean history.[27] From 1930, with the completion of his theoretical journey and the onset of the Great Depression, he advocated scholarship from a Marxist perspective and opened a new era in Korean academia.

PAEK NAM'UN'S MARXIST SCHOLARSHIP IN THE 1930S

(1) Changes in the Intellectual World during the Great Depression

In the early 1930s, Paek Nam'un published a series of articles, beginning with "The origins and duties of the establishment of sociology,"[28] that analyzed the current state of the academic world and its political and intellectual aspects. In these writings, he presented a methodology for doing research on Korea and delineated the tasks that the social sciences would have to undertake in order to overcome Korea's colonial situation. His ideas were wide-ranging in scope, beginning with general theories of knowledge and scholarship and extending to all fields of the social sciences including history, sociology, and economics.[29] In his view, the Korean intellectual world during the Great Depression was going through a "period of critical cleansing"

27. The works that he read in this period include Marx's *Capital, Theories of Surplus Value, The German Ideology, A Contribution to a Critique of Political Economy, Wage Labor and Capital*, writings on China and India; Engels' *Anti-Dühring, The Origin of the Family, Private Property, and the State*; Lenin's *Materialism and Empirico-Criticism, State and Revolution*, notes on philosophy, and *The Agrarian Problem in Russia*. He also did in-depth examinations of works by scholars such as Madiar, Karl Wittfogel, Guo Moruo, and Kawakami Hajime. Kyŏngsŏng Sŏdaemun kyŏngch'alsŏ (Seoul Sodaemun police station), "P'iŭija Paek Nam'un sinmun chosŏ che il hoe" (Record of the first interrogation of suspect Paek Nam'un), *Yi Sunt'ak oe iin pulgiso sagŏn sŏryuch'ŏl*, 1938.

28. Paek Nam'un, "Sahoehak ŭi sŏngnip yurae wa immu" (The origins and duties of the establishment of sociology), *Chosŏn ilbo*, August 20-24, 1930.

29. "'Chosen keizai no kenkyu' ŭi tokgam;" "Kwahak paljŏn ŭi yŏksajŏk p'ilyŏnsŏng" (The historical inevitability of the development of science), *Tongbang p'yŏngnon*, no. 2 (January 1932); "Chosŏn sagwan surip ŭi chech'ang" (A proposal for the establishment of view of Chosŏn history), *Kyŏngje yŏn'gu*, no. 4 (February 1933); *Chosŏn sahoe kyŏngjesa* (The Socioeconomic History of Chosŏn) (Tokyo: Kaizosha, September 1933), preface; "Chosŏn kyŏngjesa ŭi pangbŏpnon" (A methodology for Korean economic history), *Sin Tonga* 3, no. 2 (December 1933); "Iron kyŏngjehak ŭi chaegŏn" (The reestablishment of theoretical economics), *Chung'ang* 2, no. 10 (October 1934); "Chosŏn t'ŭkyu ŭi sahoe chedo" (Social systems peculiar to Korea), *Tonga ilbo*, October 20-28, 1934; "'Sutja Chosŏn yŏn'gu' che o chip e taehan tokhugam" (Impressions after reading 'Quantitative research on Chosŏn' no. 5), *Tonga ilbo*, May 28-29, 1935; "Chŏng Tasan paeknyŏnje ŭi yŏksajŏk ŭiŭi" (The historical significance of the 100th anniversary of Chŏng Yagyong's death), *Sin Chosŏn*, no. 12 (August 1935).

(pip'anjŏk ch'ŏngsangi) in which there was a sharp conflict between two currents—what he termed "confusion" and "cleansing"—which differed politically and intellectually in terms of their worldviews and methodologies of analyzing society and history. The term "confusion" referred to the state of crisis and reactionary turn of the various ideological bourgeois sciences, and "cleansing" signified the founding and development of a Marxist science.

Paek Nam'un's views were deeply shaped by the political-economic and intellectual changes that emerged during the Great Depression. As Japan faced, one after another, the financial panic of 1927, the world-wide Great Depression in 1929, and then an agricultural depression in 1930, the structural contradictions of Japanese capitalism clearly reached unprecedented levels. In this period, countries all over the world were moving toward state monopoly capitalism as the imperialist powers created economic blocs and implemented a system of economic controls to overcome the depression. Japan also tried to solve its systemic crisis through economic controls and the creation of a Far Eastern economic bloc (linking Japan and Manchuria), beginning with its invasion of Manchuria in September 1931.[30] Japan began to build a system of imperial fascism, intensifying its repression of socialism and the mass movements of the peasant and worker classes. Since the effects of the economic contradictions caused by the depression were ultimately shifted and concentrated onto Korea, the exploitation of the Korean people became far more severe. The heightening of contradictions and the intensification of exploitation led to the outbreak of class struggles by the masses against the Japanese and the landlord-capitalist classes as well as to the unprecedented rapid increase of tenant farmer protests.[31]

The changes brought about by the Great Depression were reflected in ideological trends and in the academic world. In both Japan and Chosŏn,

30. Kajinishi Mitsuhaya, et al., *Nihon shihonshugi no botsuraku* (The collapse of Japanese capitalism) III (Tokyo: Tokyo Daigaku Shuppankai, 1963); Eguchi Keiichi, "Sinryaku senso to fuasizumu no keisei" (The war of aggression and the formation of Fascism), *Koza Nihonshi* 7 (Tokyo: Tokyo Daigaku Shuppankai, 1971); Oishi Ka'ichiro, ed., *Nihon teikokushugi 2: sekai daikyokoki* (Japanese imperialism 2: the period of worldwide Great Depression) (Tokyo: Tokyo Daigaku Shuppankai, 1987), chapter 2.

31. Cho Tonggŏl, *Ilcheha Han'guk nongmin undongsa* (The history of Korean peasant movements during the colonial period) (Seoul: Han'gilsa, 1979); Chi Sugŏl, *Ilcheha nongmin chohap undong yŏn'gu* (A study of the peasant cooperative movement during the colonial period) (Seoul: Yŏksa pip'yŏngsa, 1993); Yi Chunsik, *Nongch'on sahoe pyŏndong kwa nongmin undong–Ilche ch'imnyakgi Hamgyŏngdo ŭi kyŏng'u* (Social change in rural society and the peasant movement—the case of Hamgyŏng province during the Japanese invasion period) (Seoul: Min'yŏngsa, 1993).

bourgeois groups rapidly became more conservative, supporting the preservation of the capitalist state system and imperialist expansion. In the academic world, the increasing conservatism involved efforts to strengthen the intellectual justifications of Japan's increased exploitation of Korea and its policy of turning Koreans into "imperial citizens" (*kominka*). For Koreans, this conservatism also was directly related to hopes for the future path of the nation.

Paek Nam'un's critique of contemporary ideological and intellectual trends necessarily focused on two mutually related factors. The first was the growth of Japanese government research that provided the scholarly and ideological basis for Japan's exploitative colonial policies; Japan was actively pursuing a colonialist policy of conducting research on Chosŏn. The second was the growing conservatism of bourgeois nationalist intellectuals under the influence of this government research and the intensification of a methodological opposition on how to study Korea. These were the issues that Paek Nam'un was most concerned about and were also the reason he felt that the early 1930s needed to be a period of "critical cleansing" in scholarship and ideology.

With the intensification of the contradictions of Japanese capitalism and the growth of Marxism, various bourgeois intellectuals in Japan who had been leaders in the Taisho democracy movement began to join the establishment and openly support the development of Japanese capitalism. During the Great Depression, when leftist professors were being oppressed, bourgeois intellectuals actively criticized Marxism and provided intellectual support for Japan's policy of "ideological guidance" (*shiso sendo*).[32] After the Manchurian invasion in 1931, with the rise in statism and nationalism, Japan moved toward the establishment of a fascist system. Responses to Marxism focused on formulating a theory of the state that would emphasize the absoluteness and permanence of the capitalist, imperialist state.[33]

32. Otsuka Torao, "Sayoku kyoju jishoku no rimen," *Gakkai ibun* (Strange stories from the academic world) (Tokyo: Senshinsha, 1931), pp. 91-130; Omori Yoshitaro, "Siso zendo no tetsugaku" (The philosophy of thought guidance), *Kaizo* (September 1932); Omori Yoshitaro, "Yuibutsu shikan no boei no tameni" (For a defense against historical materialism), *Chuo koron* (November 1932). In particular, in response to Marxism's conception of the state, Takata Yasuma, Paek Nam'un's advisor at Tokyo Commercial College, declared the absoluteness and permanence of the state and actively supported imperial statism and fascism. Takata Yasuma, *Marukisizumu no keizaigakuteki hihan* (An economic critique of Marxism) (Tokyo: Seinen kyoiku hukyukai, 1932); Takata Yasuma, *Kokka to shakai* (State and society) (Tokyo: Iwanami shoten, 1934).

33. Yanaihara Tadao, "Minzokushugi no hukko" (The revival of nationalism), *Kaizo* (November 1933); Kawakami Hajime, "Kokka shakaishugi no rironteki kento" (A theoretical

In the 1930s, bourgeois scholarship in Japan began to decline to the level of official government scholarship. It functioned as a spokesperson for the state ideology of fascism in its formative period and provided intellectual legitimization for or, at the very least, tacitly approved of Japanese aggression. In short, it fell to the level of official propaganda. As a result, two of the prototypical methodologies of bourgeois scholarship—"theories of national character" and textual exegesis—underwent further development. With the rise of statism, ultra-nationalism, and spiritualism, the critical autonomy and intellectual nature of scholarship became severely compromised.[34]

As part of its reactionary shift, Japan intensified its cultural policies toward Korea. Above all, such policies meant an increase in colonialist research on Chosŏn and increased support for Japanese government scholarship, the center of such research. A major focus was the rewriting of "Chosŏn history as a part of Japanese history," and the Japanese devoted a great deal of energy and resources to the compilation of *The History of Chosŏn* (*Chosŏnsa*). The colonial government had already founded the Society for the Compilation of a History of Chosŏn (Chosŏnsa p'yŏnch'anhoe) in 1925. It mobilized a large number of Japanese government scholars and Koreans for this project,[35] publishing their results beginning in 1932. The compilation of *The History of Chosŏn* was the material realization of colonial historiography. The Japanese sought to affect Koreans' sense of identity and to prepare the scholarly and spiritual foundation for the "imperial citizen" policy.[36]

As an integral part of its effort to rewrite Korean history, the Japanese also created an institutional structure for Japanese government research on Chosŏn. The central institution was Kyŏngsŏng (Keijo) Imperial University (J. Keijo teikoku daigakko) whose mission was to contribute to the

---

examination of state socialism), *Chuo koron* (June 1932), p. 13; Fujiwara Akira, ed., *Nihon minshu no rekishi* 8 (The history of the Japanese masses) (Tokyo: Sanseito, 1975), pp. 284–91.

34. Ienaga Saburo, "Taisho-Showa no rekishi siso" (The historical thought of the Taisho and Showa periods), *Nihon ni okeru rekishi siso no tenkai*, ed. Nihon shisoshi kenkyukai (Sendai: Tohoku shuppan, 1961), pp. 277–79, 286–88.

35. For an overview of this project, see Chosŏn Ch'ongdokbu Chosŏnsa p'yŏnch'anhoe, ed., *Chosŏnsa p'yŏnch'anhoe saŏp kaeyo* (An overview of the work of the Society for the Compilation of a History of Chosŏn), 1938 (reprint, Seoul: Siinsa, 1986).

36. Kim Yong-sop, "Ilbon-Han'guk e issŏsŏ ŭi Han'guksa sŏsul," p. 134; Pak Kyŏngsik, *Ilbon chegukjuŭi ŭi Chosŏn chibae* (The rule of Chosŏn by Japanese imperialism) (Seoul: Ch'ŏng'a ch'ulp'ansa, 1986), p. 404.

formation of colonial policy.[37] At Kyŏngsŏng Imperial, the Japanese professors in the history department were mainly followers of the "textual exegesis" (J. *bunken kosho*) school of historiography which was advocated by the "National History Faction" (J. *Kokushi gakuha*) at Tokyo Imperial University. Together with the researchers at the Society for the Compilation of a History of Chosŏn, they formed the Ch'ŏnggu Society (J. Aooka; E. Blue Hill) in 1930, and they were the main scholars conducting imperialist research on Korean history. They believed in the theory of the "common ancestry" of Japan and Korea, and in their view of history, Korea and Manchuria were treated as a single territorial unit. Both of these aspects were creations of the "National History Faction."[38]

Professors in the law department at Kyŏngsŏng Imperial established the Institute of Chosŏn Economic Studies (Chosŏn kyŏngje yŏn'guso) in 1928. In terms of their general approach to Korea, these scholars followed the Historical School's economic historiography, using its empirical, statistical research methods and adopting the theory of stagnation of Korean society. The Institute's objective was to refute Marxist scholarship and to contribute to the formation of colonial policy. It conducted a tremendous amount of research on socioeconomic changes in Korea from the Hanmal to the colonial period.[39] This research contributed to Japan's efforts to justify its colonization as a modernizing force, asserting that Korea before the occupation was corrupt and stagnant and only began to experience growth and development under Japanese rule. On another level, it also aimed to refute Marxist theories of the state and to demonstrate the superiority of the capitalist state.

As Japan intensified its thought control and colonialist research on Korea, radical changes occurred in both the Korean nationalist movement and the intellectual world. From the late 1920s, in response to the active participation

37. Kim Yong-sop, ibid., pp. 135-36; Chŏng Sŏn'i, "Kyŏngsŏng cheguk taehak ŭi sŏnggyŏk yŏn'gu" (A study of the character of Keijo Imperial University) (Ph.D. diss., Yonsei University, 1997).

38. Kim Yong-sop, ibid., p. 135.

39. Kyŏngsŏng cheguk taehak pŏpmun hakhoe, "Chosen keizai kenkyujo ni tsuite" (About the Institute of Chosŏn Economic Research) (afterword), *Chosen keizai no kenkyu* (Research on the Chosŏn economy, 1929). Ten books were published from 1928 until 1938, beginning with the first *Kyŏngsŏng cheguk taehak bŏphakhoe nonjip* (Collection of papers by the Institute of Legal Studies at Kyŏngsŏng Imperial University). The second book, *Chosen keizai no kenkyu*, the sixth book, *Chosen shakai keizaishi kenkyu* (Research on the socioeconomic history of Chosŏn, 1933), and the seventh book, *Kokka no kenkyu* (Research on the state, 1934) were publications of the results of their research that clearly show the objectives of the Institute of Chosŏn Economic Studies.

of the worker and peasant masses in political movements, bourgeois nationalists became markedly more moderate in both their politics and ideology. In 1929, moderate nationalists began their third campaign for colonial self-rule, explicitly revealing their class interests and their willingness to compromise with the authorities. Through their efforts to undermine the united front led by leftist and left-leaning groups, the moderates brought about a split within the nationalist movement and contributed to the dissolution of the Sin'ganhoe.[40]

As part of this effort, the moderate nationalists, together with a group of leftist nationalists, organized an "Immediate Benefit Movement" (*Tangmyŏn iik hoekdŭk undong*), which brought them into sharp conflict with the socialists who were organizing a revolutionary worker-peasant movement.[41] The "Immediate Benefit Movement" included the rural literacy and "V Narod" movements as well as the organization of cooperatives and movements for agricultural improvements, saving the poor, and improving the standard of living. By causing a rift between radical nationalists and socialists, the moderates sought to weaken the socialist movement and to create a political situation in which they could assume leadership of the nationalist movement.

While bourgeois reformers were becoming more moderate, radical groups, which had joined forces in the Sin'ganhoe, also underwent significant changes. These changes became apparent with the shift in political strategy by the socialists and the signs of disunity among radical nationalists. Lacking centralized leadership after the dissolution of the Chosŏn Communist Party in 1928, the socialists attempted to change their strategy to one of rebuilding the Communist Party and organizing revolutionary worker-peasant movements, rather than working within a united front. The main factors in their decision were the new conditions caused by the Great Depression and the "December theses," which had been adopted by the Sixth Congress of the Comintern and set strategy for colonial liberation movements. At the same time, they engaged in an all-out struggle with moderate nationalists

---

40. Pak Ch'ansŭng, *Han'guk kŭndae chŏngch'i sasangsa yŏn'gu* (A study of the history of political thought in modern Korea) (Seoul: Yŏksa pip'yŏngsa, 1992), pp. 343-55; Kang Tongjin, *Nihon no Chosen shihai seisakushi kenkyu* (A study of the history of Japan's ruling policies toward Chosŏn) (Tokyo: Tokyo Daigaku shuppankai, 1979), pp. 419-29; Chi Sugŏl, "1930 nyŏndae ch'oban'gi sahoejuŭijadŭl ŭi minjok kaeryangjuŭi undong pip'an" (Socialists' criticism of the moderate nationalist movement in the early 1930s), *80 nyŏndae Han'guk inmun sahoe kwahak ŭi hyŏndangye wa chŏnmang* (Seoul: Yŏksa pip'yŏngsa, 1988), p. 272.

41. Chi Sugŏl, ibid., pp. 274-78; Sŏ Chungsŏk, *Han'guk hyŏndae minjok undongsa yŏn'gu*, pp. 137-43.

who supported self-rule. The moderate nationalists were trying to make the Sin'ganhoe a more moderate organization and intensified their attacks on the socialists.

As clear evidence of their shift to classism, the socialists emphasized the need for class struggle in a fascist society and came to view the radical nationalists within the Sin'ganhoe as being no different from the moderate nationalists. Rejecting the possibility that radical nationalists could play a revolutionary role within the liberation movement, the socialists took a leading role in the dissolution of the Sin'ganhoe.[42] Because the radical nationalists represented petit bourgeois interests, lacked a broad mass base, and felt that class cooperation was the only path for the nationalist movement,[43] they were not able to exert any political influence outside of united-front politics and legally sanctioned arenas. It was the socialists' change in political strategy that led to the rapidly increasing conservatism of the radical nationalists. Around the time of the Sin'ganhoe's dissolution, some of the radical nationalists participated in non-political educational movements together with the moderates. Others engaged in cultural activities as they became even more drawn to a nationalist ideology that was no different from the civicism and statism they had earlier criticized for their fascist character.[44]

In the early 1930s, during the Great Depression, the united front politics of the late 1920s gave way to an all-out confrontation between moderate nationalists and socialists, both within the nationalist movement and in the intellectual world. It was a conflict between the worldviews and conceptions of the nation of two social forces with mutually different class bases. It was also a conflict between differing conceptions of state and society concerning Korea's response to Japanese colonialism and the path of Korea's future develop-

42. U Tongsu, "1920 nyŏndae mal-30 nyŏndae Han'guk sahoejuŭijadŭl ŭi singukga kŏnsŏllon e kwanhan yŏn'gu" (A study of the ideas on building a new state of Korean socialists in the late 1920s and 1930s), *Han'guksa yŏn'gu*, no. 72 (1991); Sŏ Chungsŏk, ibid., chapter 1, section 3; Han'guk yŏksa yŏn'guhoe, *Ilcheha sahoejuŭi undongsa* (The history of the socialist movement under Japanese rule) (Seoul: Han'gilsa, 1991); Yi Kyun'yŏng, ibid., chapter 5. Scholars have slightly different opinions on the nature of the classist tendencies of socialists, but they generally agree that such tendencies had a negative effect on the national liberation movement.

43. Lee Ji-won (Yi Chiwŏn), "Ilcheha An Chaehong ŭi hyŏnsil insik kwa minjok haebang undongnon" (The conception of society and views on the national liberation movement of An Chaehong dur-ing the colonial period), *Yŏksa wa hyŏnsil*, no. 6 (1991).

44. Lee Ji-won, "1930 nyŏndae chŏnban minjokjuŭi munhwa undongnon ŭi sŏnggyŏk" (The nature of the conception of the nationalist culture movement in the early 1930s), *Kuksagwan nonch'ong*, no. 51 (1994); Pang Kie-chung, "1920-30 nyŏndae Chosŏn mulsan changnyŏhoe yŏn'gu" (A study of the Native Products Promotion Society in the 1920s and 1930s), *Kuksagwan nonch'ong*, no. 67 (1996); Chi Sugŏl, ibid., pp. 273-74.

ment. In theoretical terms, the conflict was between the capitalist modernization espoused by bourgeois nationalists and the anti-imperialist, anti-feudal bourgeois democratic revolution advocated by socialists. Both sides engaged in a heated debate on philosophy and religion and were in sharp conflict because of their fundamental differences on the most important economic issue of the time, the livelihood of the Korean peasantry.[45] Because bourgeois nationalists argued for the necessity of "moderate reforms" using the slogan of nationalism, an intense debate arose over the meaning of the concept of the "nation," and the national question became a pressing topic of interest.[46]

Two main factors were behind Paek Nam'un's view of the Great Depression years as a period of "critical cleansing" in the intellectual world. First, as fascist ideology spread to Korea, he felt that it was necessary to refute Japanese government scholarship on Korea, which was justifying and whitewashing Japan's occupation of Korea, as part of the struggle against colonialism. Second, it was also necessary to provide an alternative to the increasingly conservative tendencies and scholarship of nationalist intellectuals, as part of the struggle within the nationalist movement. As he saw it, the only way to accomplish these tasks was to establish a scientific "knowledge of Chosŏn" (*Chosŏn insik*) based on Marxist theory that would solve the problems faced by the nation and clarify its future path. These were the tasks that he set for himself in response to the ideological and academic trends of the time. At the

---

45. *Sin ingan*, special issue on a critique of Marxism (January 1933); *Sin kaedan* (January 1933): special issue on a critique of Ch'ŏndogyo; *Sin kaedan* (February-July 1933, combined special issue on a critique of religion); *Pip'an* 21-22 (March 1933, combined issue on a critique of religion); O Miil, ibid., pp. 283-90; Ha Wŏnho, "1930 nyŏndae sahoejuŭijadŭl ŭi nong'ŏp-nongminnon" (The views of agriculture and peasants of socialists in the 1930s), *Iljemal Chosŏn sahoe wa minjok haebang undong* (Seoul: Ilsongjŏng, 1991), pp. 169-74; Kim Yong-sop, "Ilche kangjŏmgi ŭi nong'ŏp munje wa kŭ t'agae pangch'aek" (Agricultural problems and proposed solutions during the Japanese occupation period), *Han'guk kŭnhyŏndae nong'ŏpsa yŏn'gu*. See chapter 4 in this volume for an abridged translation of this article.

46. In particular, these debates were triggered by Yi Kwangsu, the theorist of moderate nationalism; see Yi Kwangsu, "Minjok undong ŭi sam kich'o saŏp" (The three basic tasks of the nationalist movement), *Tonggwang*, no. 30 (February 1932). Marxists' responses to Yi Kwangsu's arguments include Chŏng Chŏlsŏng, "Int'elligench'ya wa minjok undong—Yi Kwangsu ŭi minjok undong ŭi iron ŭl bunswoeham" (The intelligentsia and the nationalist movement—destroying Yi Kwangsu's theory of the nationalist movement), *Pip'an*, no. 14 (June 1932); Sin Namch'ŏl, "Minjok iron ŭi sam hyŏngt'ae" (The three forms of theory on the nation), *Sinhŭng*, no. 7 (1932). In the course of these debates, it became clear that moderate nationalists held a defeatist conception of the nation, increasingly becoming followers of fascism and that socialists had a classist conception of the nation of socialists, dogmatically accepting Stalin's conception of the nation.

same time, his work was meant to provide intellectual support for the social-ist movement.

In particular, Paek Nam'un emphasized two aspects necessary to achieve his goals. First, he felt that it was essential to establish an autonomous under-standing of Korea.

In other words, scholarship with Chosŏn as its object—the understanding of Chosŏn—can be seen as both a social responsibility and a kind of privileged arena of the Chosŏn people—[in particular], among them, students of science—who have immediate experience of its history and current situation.[47]

His emphasis on scholarly autonomy was natural since his objective was the refutation of colonialist research by the Japanese government that distor-ted Korean history and justified Japan's occupation by "demonstrating" that it brought about modernization and an industrial revolution. He was also trying to highlight the significance of scholarly praxis in overcoming colo-nialism as well as the fact that the Koreans themselves are the agents of their own history.

Second, he felt that it was important to establish and disseminate a Marxist scholarship that could develop a scientific "knowledge of Chosŏn." From the late 1920s, the theoretical understanding of Marxism underwent significant development together with the development of the socialist movement in Korea, and a number of Marxist theorists and intellectuals emerged in the intellectual world. However, a true Marxist understanding of Korea had not yet matured into a school of scholarship that could critique the views of Korea advocated by Japanese government scholarship or bourgeois nationalist intellectuals. Even as the ideological conflict between the left and the right intensified, the forms of bourgeois thought espoused by nationalist intellectuals still remained the leading force in the Korean scholarly world.[48] It was a reflection of the circumstances of the intellectual world at the time that Paek Nam'un advocated the promotion of Marxist science and emphasized that the early 1930s needed to be a period of "critical cleansing."

Paek Nam'un's efforts to promote a Marxist scholarship of Korea in-volved three different projects. The first was the theoretical project of devel-oping a Marxism that could achieve a transformation of the views of Korea advanced by bourgeois scholarship. Second, he sought to give concrete,

47. Paek Nam'un, "'Chosen keizai no kenkyu' ŭi tokgam," p. 24.
48. Pang Kie-chung, Han'guk kŭnhyŏndae sasangsa yŏn'gu, pp. 98-100.

empirical content to the Marxist methodology and view of history that he was advocating, by developing a framework that could encompass all periods of Korean economic history. Lastly, he was active in scholarly organizations whose activities could contribute to overcoming Japanese colonialism and to developing a vision for the nation's future.

(2) Critique of Bourgeois Scholarship and the Theory of the "Understanding of Chosŏn"

Paek Nam'un understood science to be a factor of productivity in a broad sense of the term. He defined science and scholarship as the structured totality of experience adapted to the demands of life in human society. More specifically, he saw them as part of the systematized theoretical knowledge of things and the concepts that express human knowledge. By ordering and re-creating the experience of society and nature for humanity, science serves as a systematic method of developing interactions among humans and between humanity and nature. Since the foundation of science lay in human life as a social existence, he felt that the critique of the experience of life is the fundamental condition for the establishment of science. As science is the reflection of the social relations of production, he felt that a specific science in a certain period is a product of the objective social relations of that period. Similarly, the position of scientists is also historically and socially determined. In his materialist understanding of thought, he rejected bourgeois conceptions of science that viewed it as the product of absolutist thinking. He also completely rejected the notion of a humanity and idealist thought that transcends history.[49]

Building on this conception of science, Paek Nam'un noted that science has three fundamental characteristics: uniformity (*pŏpch'iksŏng*), historicity (*yŏksasŏng*), and "classness" (*kyegŭpsŏng*).[50] By the term "uniformity," he meant the abstraction of laws of causality from inchoate phenomena—a process which was part of the universalization of the logic of the critique of experience. The "laws of causality" were simply the workings of the dialectic, as discussed by the founders of Marxism, a necessary, dependent relationship between phenomena.

---

49. Paek Nam'un, "Kwahak paljŏn ŭi yŏksajŏk p'ilyŏnsŏng," pp. 36-38; Paek Nam'un, "Sahoehak ŭi sŏngnip yurae wa immu" 1-2, *Chosŏn ilbo*, August 20-21, 1930; Paek Nam'un, "Chŏng Tasan ŭi sasang" (The thought of Chŏng Yagyong), *Tonga ilbo*, July 16, 1935.

50. Paek Nam'un, "Kwahak paljŏn ŭi yŏksajŏk p'ilyŏnsŏng," pp. 36-39; Paek Nam'un, *Chosŏn sahoe kyŏngjesa*, pp. 8-9.

The term "historicity" referred to the principles of social science that are applicable to history, in contrast to those of natural science. The principles of social science were the laws of social development governing the transformation of one social formation into another. They explained the historical inevitability of the current society's emergence and of the future society that it will necessarily develop into. The "historicity" of science was another term for the theory of historical materialism as a methodology of social science; i.e., the principles of social formation that theorized the mutual relationship between the universal laws of social development and the characteristics of a specific historical context.

The term "classness" referred to Paek's belief that in a class society, science develops in accordance with class interests and under the domination of a particular class. When science and scientific thought develop to the point where they can finally undermine the prevailing mode of domination, the ruling class will suppress science, as can be seen in past artistic renaissances and in the history of science. He argued that these factors explained the origins of the "partisan nature" of science and scholarship.[51]

Paek Nam'un argued that even though a "newly-rising science"— namely, Marxism—was being oppressed by the dominant class, it had been developing according to its own dynamism and would continue to develop in the future. This "new science" represented the new productive force of the oppressed classes and a progressive political perspective. He explained his views on the inevitability of scientific development as follows:

> Social organizations in all periods undergo a period of development to prepare for [the emergence of] a future society. At the same time, the oppressed class embarks on a reform of these organizations, on the one hand, and demands spiritual liberation, on the other. In this way, an exact science emerges for the first time. It clarifies the positive and negative aspects of existing science by revealing the contradictions of society, and it carries out the task of a newly rising science by demonstrating the trends of history.[52]

To Paek Nam'un, historical materialism (aka, the theory of social formations) was the "only scientific methodology" for doing research on Korea that could overcome the effects of colonialism and reveal the future path of the nation. Only based on such knowledge and methods would Chosŏn be

---

51. Paek Nam'un, "Iron kyŏngjehak ŭi chaegon," p. 8.
52. Paek Nam'un, ibid.

able to delineate the outlines of a new state and society rather than serve as an "old tool of a fallen capitalist republic."[53] In other words, his conception of Marxist science turned Marxist theories of state and society into a methodology of social science. The heart of the methodology was the elucidation of the dialectic development of social relations; i.e., the historical laws determining the inherent inevitability of the transformation of social formations based on class struggle. Transformation in the present stage necessarily involved the negation of capitalist society, as expressed in the phrase "the exploiters will be exploited."[54]

Paek's conviction in the inevitability of social transformation was expressed in phrases emphasized repeatedly in his writings, such as "active measures that know no despair" and "the irreversibility of historical laws."[55] He sought to establish an autonomous, scientific scholarship on Korea because he believed that it would be possible to envision a new state that could simultaneously achieve both national and class liberation only when all the social contradictions of the Japanese occupation were revealed and when the intellectual and scholarly basis of colonial exploitation was analyzed and critiqued.[56]

It was only natural that Paek Nam'un's "critical cleansing" began with a critique of the bourgeois scholarship and epistemology of Japanese government scholarship that was rooted in the ideology of the ruling class. He identified four general aspects of bourgeois science and scholarship in the imperialist stage which were common to all its various schools of thought. First, bourgeois science posited a duality between an absolute world of abstraction and pure, individual human nature, on the one hand, and actual social life which is the basis for science's existence, on the other. Second, it lacked methodological unity since the internal unity among its disciplines was fragmented. Third, it denied both the "partisan nature" (socially determined) of science and the universality of class development in human history.

---

53. Paek Nam'un, *Chosŏn sahoe kyŏngjesa*, pp. 181, 447.

54. Paek Nam'un, "Sahoehak ŭi sŏngnip yurae wa immu" 3, *Chosŏn ilbo*, August 22, 1930. This phrase refers to the "negation of negation" that Marx discussed. Karl Marx, *Capital*, vol. 1, chapter 32, translated by Kim Suhaeng (Seoul: Pibong ch'ulpansa, 1989), pp. 959-69.

55. Paek Nam'un, *Chosŏn sahoe kyŏngjesa*, p. 9; Paek Nam'un, "Chosŏn t'ŭkyu ŭi sahoe chedo."

56. Paek Nam'un, "Sahoehak ŭi sŏngnip yurae wa immu (wan)," *Chosŏn ilbo*, August 24, 1930; Paek Nam'un, *Chosŏn sahoe kyŏngjesa*, p. 445.

Fourth, it was ultimately a class ideology that rationalized the permanence of capitalist relations of production and the imperialist system.[57]

Paek thought that there were, in turn, three epistemological bases for these aspects of bourgeois science: an abstract view of history that emphasizes individual characteristics such as race and historical accident, a methodology based on metaphysical idealism or agnostic positivism, and a liberal conception of society based on Social Darwinism, natural law, and a belief in free competition among individuals.[58] He emphasized that social reformism, *Nationalökonomie* (K. *kungmin kyŏngjehak*, national economics), and the economic history developed by the German Historical School in its imperialist stage were all essentially the same, being offshoots of classical bourgeois science. He now clearly adopted a critical stance toward the various strands of the scholarly lineage that he had been exposed to in college.[59]

Based on this problematic, Paek Nam'un undertook a critique of the methodologies employed by bourgeois schools of thought in researching Korea.[60] The primary object of his critique was the positivist methodology of Japanese government scholarship that was being promoted in the name of academism and "pure scholarship" and of those Korean scholars who accepted its premises. Noting that "there are many people who confuse scientific theory and positivism," he emphasized that empirical evidence is no more than an illustration that enables generalizations of concrete aspects of history and is, therefore, no guarantee of scientificity by itself.[61] In particular, his critique of Japanese government scholarship attempted to expose the political and ideological factors underlying the apparently "objectivist" empiricism. Although positivism, as a general theory of historical knowledge, was a "powerless

57. Paek Nam'un, "Sahoehak ŭi sŏngnip yurae wa immu" 2-5, *Chosŏn ilbo*, August 21-24, 1930; Paek Nam'un, "Iron kyŏngjehak ŭi chaegon," pp. 8-10.

58. Paek Nam'un, ibid.; Paek Nam'un, "Itani kyoju no 'Chosen ni okeru sangyo kakumei' wo yomu" (Reading "the industrial revolution in Chosŏn" by Professor Itani) in Itani Zen'ichi, *Chosen keizaishi* (The economic history of Chosŏn) (Tokyo: Daitokaku, 1928), p. 271. Paek was trying to emphasize the fact that the liberal view of history of Social Darwinism, which idealized the principle of "survival of the fittest," was not only an intellectual justification of Japanese aggression but also the basis of the "understanding of Chosŏn" of both Japanese government studies and national capitalists.

59. Paek Nam'un, "Sahoehak ŭi sŏngnip yurae wa immu" 2-5, *Chosŏn ilbo*, August 21-24, 1930; Paek Nam'un, "Iron kyŏngjehak ŭi chaegŏn," pp. 8-10; Paek Nam'un, "Chosŏn kyŏngjesa ŭi pangbŏpnon," pp. 123-24.

60. Paek Nam'un especially focused on their view of history and methodologies, and since previous studies have sufficiently covered their conception of history (see the articles mentioned in footnotes 2,3), I will focus on his critique of methodology here.

61. Paek Nam'un, *Chosŏn sahoe kyŏngjesa*, p. 428.

methodology" rooted in the absence of theory,[62] the ideological essence behind this powerlessness lay in its justification of Japan's colonial occupation through the dissemination of a view of Korea as stagnant and lacking in autonomy.

Furthermore, Paek emphasized that the predatory positivism of Japanese government scholarship was not restricted only to its historical research but was also prevalent in its studies of Korea's current socioeconomic situation. He felt that two methodologies, quantitative and scientific, were in conflict with each other in research on contemporary Korea.

> At the present time, when people are talking about Chosŏn's "rapid progress," it is possible to observe that two conflicting methodologies of studying Chosŏn are emerging. One is a quantitative method that seeks to verify this "rapid progress" through "statistical research" on contemporary Chosŏn, and the other is a scientific method that seeks to examine the underlying factors by critiquing the research on "statistical Chosŏn." Of these two contrasting methods of researching the unique aspects of Chosŏn's current situation, the second method is of course the correct one.[63]

The positivism of Japanese government scholarship was a methodological weapon for the dissemination of the ideology of colonial modernization. It attempted to justify Japan's colonial domination as the bestower of modernization by proving the "rapid progress" of Korea's society and economy under Japanese occupation through statistical, quantitative analyses. As mentioned earlier, the leading figures in this research were the Japanese professors in the Institute of Chosŏn Economic Studies at Kyŏngsŏng Imperial University.

The critical, scientific method that was opposed to the statistical, quantitative methods of positivism was, of course, the methodology of Marxism. Paek Nam'un emphasized that it was the only suitable method for uncovering the predatory, imperial nature of colonial domination hidden behind statistics of immediate phenomena. He saw the fundamental confrontation in the Korean academic world in the early 1930s as one between the positivism of Japanese government scholarship and the Marxist theory of social formations. He advocated the latter as the only method of "understanding

---

62. Paek Nam'un, "Chosŏn kyŏngjesa ŭi pangbŏpnon," p. 123.

63. Paek Nam'un, "'Sutja Chosŏn yŏn'gu' che o jip e taehan tokhugam (sang)" (Impressions after reading "Quantitative research on Chosŏn" no. 5, part 1), *Tonga ilbo*, May 28, 1935.

Chosŏn" that could refute the arguments of the former. It could also provide a scientific vision of the inherent possibilities of overcoming Korea's colonial situation.

Japanese government scholarship was not the only target of Paek Nam'un's "critical cleansing;" he also took aim at the bourgeois academism and methodologies of Korean nationalist scholars. These scholars sought to turn "Chosŏn cultural history into its own microcosm (Mikrokosmos),"[64] and their efforts were particularly evident in their conceptions of Tan'gun Chosŏn. Beginning in the Hanmal period, intellectuals had disseminated stories of Tan'gun Chosŏn among the masses. These stories served as an ideological foundation of the nationalist movement and formed the basis of bourgeois nationalist conceptions of state and nation. For example, this view of Tan'gun had a strong influence on both the "national heritage preservation movement" (minjok munhwa suho undong) and the "Chosŏn Studies Movement" (Chosŏnhak undong) which were organized by nationalists in the first half of the 1930s. Paek's critique was not restricted to historical interpretations of Tan'gun or to the search for the origins of the Korean race, but it also intended a sweeping critique of bourgeois conceptions of the state, the nation, and history.[65]

Paek Nam'un's focus was to refute views of Tan'gun that emphasized national development and national uniqueness based on "transcendent, absolute" ideals and to reveal the bourgeois class interests inherent in metaphysical and ethical conceptions of the nation. His method was to demonstrate that the basis of the nation lay in class relations through the emergence of the family and clan systems and the formation of a class state.[66] He regarded the nationalists' belief in racial uniqueness as a reactionary view of history and the nation that was in essence no different from the views of Japanese government scholarship. To him, both ignored the laws of historical development.[67] If the oppressed themselves began to emphasize their uniqueness at a time when Japanese policy was increasingly pursuing a "reactionary turn against historical law," "that [emphasis] would not be the so-called path to revival, but they would instead be unconsciously falling into the evil path of

---

64. Paek Nam'un, Chosŏn sahoe kyŏngjesa, p. 7.
65. Chosŏn sahoe kyŏngjesa was an effort to clarify these very issues.
66. Paek Nam'un, "Chosn kyŏngjesa ŭi pangbŏpnon," p. 124; Paek Nam'un, Chosŏn sahoe kyŏngjesa, pp. 71–72.
67. Paek Nam'un, Chosŏn sahoe kyŏngjesa, p. 7.

slavery."[68] In other words, it would be impossible to discover the potential for national liberation and the construction of a "new Chosŏn" through the nationalist intellectuals' methodology of researching Korea or through the conceptions of scholarship and the nation that emphasized Korea's unique cultural history.

This section has analyzed Paek Nam'un's critique of bourgeois scholarship that led to his call for the development of a Marxist science and an understanding of Korea in the early 1930s. Most of all, his critique attempted to undermine the "Culture Policy" (*Bunka seisaku*) of the Government-General, which was devoting increased resources to its colonialist "research on Chosŏn" and to refute Japanese government scholarship which was based on a positivist methodology. He expressly called for a transformation in the methodology of research on Korea so that it could uncover the potential for a simultaneous national and class liberation. He saw the tension within Korea between the moderate nationalists and the socialists as a conflict of worldviews and conceptions of state and society over the future social composition of the "new Chosŏn." He regarded the conflicting views on Korea as the scholarly reflection of this political confrontation between the right and the left. He was uncompromising in his belief that the promotion of a scientific study of Korea based on Marxism was the only path to national revival. In this sense, he played a vanguard role in providing intellectual support to the socialist movement for national liberation. His scholarly work opened, for the first time, the path for the adaptation of Marxist thought to the study of Korean society and history.

(3) Internal Divisions among Marxist Intellectuals

Published by Kaizosha in Tokyo in September 1933, Paek Nam'un's *The Socioeconomic History of Chosŏn* appeared at a time when Japan's ideological suppression and ideological conflict within the nationalist movement were becoming more severe. Kim Kwangjin, a professor at Posŏng Junior College, commented, "since this book has scientifically determined the developmental laws of Chosŏn society from a Marxist perspective, it has achieved a complete cleansing of existing histories of Chosŏn."[69] As Kim's remarks suggest, the publication of his book was a landmark moment in the history of modern scholarship in Korea. Its significance lies in its success,

---

68. ibid., pp. 444-45.

69. Kim Kwangjin, "Paek Nam'un kyosu ŭi sinjŏ *Chosŏn sahoe kyŏngjesa*" (Prof. Paek Nam'un's new work *The Socioeconomic History of Chosŏn*), *Tonga ilbo*, September 21, 1933.

after many years of effort, at developing a Korean Marxist historiography and in its declaration of the pursuit of a Marxist "understanding of Chosŏn."

The years 1933-34 were also a turning point in modern Korean scholarship in another sense. The academic world reached a new stage of development in 1933 as the number of scholars increased significantly during the Great Depression era. Interest in conducting research on Korea peaked as many intellectuals recognized the importance of "understanding Chosŏn." The Society for Chosŏn Economics (Chosŏn kyŏngjehoe) was established on June 9, 1933, and its founders were twenty-seven professors at junior colleges and economic journalists from newspapers and journals. Their purpose was to research and conduct surveys on economics and the Korean economy in particular. In addition to its chief officer Paek Nam'un, the key figures in the society included Kim Kwangjin, Kim Up'yŏng, Yi Yŏsŏng, Sŏ Ch'un, and Yi Kŭngjong.[70] Growing to forty-six members in 1934, the Society for Chosŏn Economics became a relatively large scholarly organization considering the conditions of its time and was known as the "headquarters of the scholarly corps" (*haksul pudae ŭi ch'ammo pon'yŏng*).[71]

In late 1933, nationalist intellectuals such as An Chaehong and Chŏng Inbo organized a "Chosŏn Studies Movement."[72] Its objective was to promote "understanding of Chosŏn" by conducting research on its "unique cultural trends," in order to overcome the "backward features of Chosŏn" and to understand "Chosŏn within [the context of] the world."[73] The Chosŏn Studies Movement attracted a good deal of interest in 1934-1935 through a series of events conducted to commemorate Silhak scholar Chŏng Yagyong (1762-1836; *ho* Tasan).[74] As a cultural movement that arose when radical

---

70. *Tonga ilbo*, June 10, 1933; *Tonga ilbo*, January 1, 1935. For more on these figures, see the Biographical Notes toward the back of the book.

71. *Tonga ilbo*, January 1, 1935.

72. The term *Chosŏnhak* (Chosŏn studies) was first used by Ch'oe Namsŏn in the 1920s in imitation of the term "Chinahak" (China studies), but in this period, it was actively promoted by An Chaehong. Han Yŏng'u, "An Chaehong ŭi sinminjokjuŭi wa sahak" (An Chaehong's new nationalism and historiography), *Han'guk tongnip undongsa yŏn'gu* 1 (1987), pp. 262-65.

73. An Chaehong, "Chosŏnhak ŭi munje" (The problem of Chosŏn studies), *Sin Chosŏn*, no. 7 (December 1934), pp. 2-4.

74. These projects included the 1934 "Lectures on the 99th Anniversary of Chŏng Tasan's [Death]," the "100th Anniversary of Chŏng Tasan's [Death]" in 1935, and the publication of the collected works of Chŏng Yagyong, *Yŏyudang chŏnsŏ*. See Kim Yong-sop, "Uri nara kŭndae yŏksahak ŭi paldal" (The development of our country's modern historiography), *Han'guk ŭi yŏksa insik*, vol. 2 (Seoul: Ch'angjak kwa pip'yŏngsa, 1976), pp. 475-76; Sin Chosŏnsa, "Chŏng Tasan sŏnsaeng sŏgŏ e chehayŏ" (On the 100th year since the passing of Chŏng Tasan), *Sin Chosŏn*, no. 10 (August 1935). The most prominent Silhak scholar from the late Chosŏn period,

nationalists were in turmoil during the ideological conflicts of the early 1930s, the movement was also political in nature. In this context, the Chosŏn Studies Movement had a dual nature. On the one hand, it was a cultural response by nationalist intellectuals to the colonialist knowledge of Korea produced by Japanese government scholarship, and, on the other hand, it was also a response to the rise of Marxist science.[75]

The founding of the Chindan Society (Chindan Hakhoe) in May 1934 was another response to Japanese scholarship on Korea. Its founders were scholars in the humanities who were graduates of Japanese universities or of Kyŏngsŏng Imperial University. Its "purpose [was] to do research on Chosŏn culture defined broadly," and it published their work in their own journal, the *Chindan hakbo*.[76] As is well known, its main figures were disciples of the National History School of historiography, which constituted the mainstream in Japanese government scholarship. They were cultural nationalists who faithfully followed the bourgeois conception of history and the positivist methodology of documentary exegesis that they had learned from their teachers.[77] The Chindan Hakhoe did not undertake any active efforts to overcome Korea's colonial situation but instead pursued "pure scholarship" focusing on research on Korean culture. It was a prototypical bourgeois academic organization that worked within the system.[78] As the society developed ties with moderate nationalist groups associated with the *Tonga ilbo* and moved toward a reactionary cultural traditionalism, its work provided the scholarly foundation for the bourgeois nationalists' cultural movement of the 1930s. In other words, behind the pure scholarship and rational positivism of the Chindan Hakhoe lay the ideology of moderate nationalism

---

Chŏng Yagyong (*ho* Tasan, Yŏyudang; 1762-1836) broke with the feudal framework of Confucian thought and prepared a stepping-stone for modern thought; he was a Confucianist who can be called the Rousseau of Korea. Paek Nam'un's view of Chŏng Yagyong will be treated in the next section.

75. Lee Ji-won (Yi Chiwŏn), "1930 nyŏndae chŏnban minjokjuŭi munhwa undongnon ŭi songgyŏk."

76. "Huibo" (News items), *Chindan hakpo*, no. 1 (November 1934), p. 224.

77. Kim Yong-sop, "Ilbon Han'guk e issŏsŏ ŭi Han'guksa sŏsul," p. 139; Cho Tonggŏl, "Minjok kukga kŏnsŏl undonggi ŭi yŏksa insik" (Historical understanding in the period of the state-building movement), *Han'guk ŭi yŏksaga wa yŏksa insik* (ha) (Seoul: Ch'angjak kwa pip'yŏngsa, 1994).

78. Kim Yong-sop, ibid., pp. 139-40; Pang Kie-chung, "Haebang hu kukga kŏnsŏl munje wa yŏksahak" (Historiography and the issue of state-building after liberation), *Han'guksa insik kwa yŏksa iron* (Seoul: Chisik san'ŏpsa, 1997), pp. 84-85.

which was influenced by modernism and nationalism while being rooted in a feudal traditional consciousness.[79]

The years after 1933 were a formative period for modern Korean scholarship. During this time intellectual trends emerged that differed in their theoretical positions on and methodologies for "understanding Chosŏn." With the development of the academic world, interest in conducting research on Chosŏn grew tremendously. Closely connected with the political developments of nationalist forces, the Chosŏn Studies Movement and the Chindan Hakhoe served as gatherings of bourgeois scholars. Though they differed from each other in terms of scholarly views and political positions, what they held in common was the fact that they were all responding to the rise of Marxist scholarship. This was a reflection of the political and intellectual conflict within the nationalist movement during the Great Depression as well as its extension into scholarship. As the Korean intellectual world grew, conflict gradually increased over methods of "understanding Chosŏn" and scholarly praxis. One of the most important of these debates was the in-depth critique by Marxist intellectuals of nationalist intellectuals and the "understanding of Chosŏn" of the Chosŏn Studies Movement.

The common thread among Marxist critiques was the view that the methodology of the Chosŏn Studies Movement was ideological and lacked scientificity and that its scholarly position and view of the nation were ultranationalistic.[80] Marxists even viewed the conceptions of national spirit put forth by the Chosŏn Studies Movement as "Chosŏn variants" of fascist ideology.[81] However, what is striking in this critique is that two different views of Korea became apparent within Marxism.

---

79. Pang Kie-chung, ibid., pp. 85-86.

80. The most important critiques were: Sin Namch'ŏl, "Ch'oegŏn Chosŏn yŏn'gu ŭi ŏpjŏk kwa kŭ chaech'ulbal" (The recent accomplishments in research on Chosŏn and its new beginning), *Tonga ilbo*, January 1-7, 1934; Reporter "T," "Chosŏnhak ŭn ŏddŏk'e kyujŏng halgga—Paek Nam'un ssi wa ŭi ilmun ildap" (How should "Chosŏn studies" be defined?—a question and answer session with Mr. Paek Nam'un), *Tonga ilbo*, September 11, 1934; Ch'ŏnt'ae san'in, "Chinjŏnghan Chŏng Tasan yŏn'gu ŭi kil—aullŏ Tasannon e nat'anan sokhakjŏk kyŏnhae rŭl pip'anham" (The path of serious research on Chŏng Yagyong—along with a critique of nativist views in conceptions of Chŏng Yagyong), *Chosŏn chung'ang ilbo*, July 25-August 6, 1935; Han Ŭngsu, "Maejogun tusang e ilbong" ([Striking] a blow on the heads of those who sell their ancestors), *Pip'an*, no. 25 (December 1935); Yi Ch'ŏngwŏn, "Tan'gun sinhwa e taehan kwahakjŏk pip'an" (A scientific critique of the myth of Tan'gun), *Chosŏn chung'ang ilbo*, March 5-7, 1936.

81. Chŏn Yŏngsik, "Chosŏnjŏk ideollogi munje—t'ŭkhi p'assijŏm kwa ŭi kwallŏn esŏ (1)-(11)" (The problem of Chosŏn ideology—in particular, in its relation to fascism), *Chosŏn chung'ang ilbo*, March 29-April 10, 1936.

First, the tendency towards a radical classism denounced not only the methodology and ideological standpoint of the Chosŏn Studies Movement but also all nationalist notions as being ultra-nationalistic. It denied that nationalist "understandings of Chosŏn" had any value. In general, this classism was accompanied by a view of Chosŏn as stagnant and determined by external forces, ignoring the autonomous nature of Korean history and Chosŏn's development in accordance with the universal laws of history. For example:

At present, the modern thought that is implanted in our minds is not what Chosŏn thinkers of previous generations laid the foundation for. It came from the West. It is an imported commodity. . . . When examining Chosŏn intellectual history, it would be a tremendous mistake to view the Chosŏn thought of previous generations as being of the same kind as the national thought produced by England's classical economics, the thought of the French people as it appears in the history of French sociology, or the philosophical thought of the German people. The reason is that, as can be seen in Chosŏn's history, it has not been possible to have a systematic intellectual life from ancient times onward. . . . Since there were no distinct systems of thought, the thinkers in Chosŏn's history were scholars who were intoxicated with foreign thought such as that of China or India. . . . In this sense, a Chosŏn ideology has not been able to have a systematic history of its own.[82]

Marxist intellectuals with a class-centered mind-set completely dismissed the possibility of the autonomous development of Korean intellectual history and Korean history itself from ancient times to the modern period. Their "understanding of Chosŏn" was a typical example of a scientific theory of stagnation embellished by historical materialism. In other words, their class-centered view of the nation was manifested through an "understanding of Chosŏn" that regarded the nation as a meaningless category.

Although it is impossible to generalize from such an extreme example, such views were deeply held by many Marxists, with differences only in degree. From 1935, a critique emerged of Paek Nam'un's epistemological views and his theory of the developmental stages of Korean history. His critics used the notion of the Asiatic mode of production as a powerful theoretical weapon against him. In the process, the classist "understanding of

---

82. Han Ŭngsu, "Maejogun tusang e ilbong," pp. 50-51.

Chosŏn" became even further entrenched. As Marxists' view of Korea
became increasingly class-centered and as their critique of the Chosŏn Studies
Movement became joined with their critique of Paek Nam'un, the so-called
Marxist theory of Korean uniqueness emerged.[83]

Second, other Marxists intellectuals acknowledged the importance of
"Chosŏn Studies" to the nation. These Marxists advocated the development
of a critical "Chosŏn Studies" based on objective science even though they
were clearly opposed to the ideological scholarship and methodology of the
Chosŏn Studies Movement. The key figure in this group was Paek Nam'un,
and it included other scholars, mainly in the humanities, such as Sin Namch'ŏl (1907-?), Kim T'aejun (1905-1949), and Hong Kimun (1903-1992).
Paek Nam'un felt that even the non-autonomous, nihilistic "understanding
of Chosŏn" of "mainstream" Marxists was reactionary. Assuming the necessity of objective knowledge for a "true love" of Chosŏn, he stressed the importance of an autonomous "understanding of Chosŏn" in order to find "our
true selves."[84] The importance that he placed on the national and political
significance of the "understanding of Chosŏn" was clearly demonstrated in
his utterly indifferent attitude toward the Chindan Hakhoe.[85] To him, the
Chindan Hakhoe's research, which was based on pure scholarship and

---

83. Yi Ch'ŏngwŏn, Pak Sajŏm, Han Hŭngsu, Kim Kwangjin, and other theorists involved in
the socialist movement were the leading figures of this trend. For more on this topic, see Pang
Kie-chung, Han'guk kŭnhyŏndae sasangsa yŏn'gu, pp. 160-70.

84. Paek Nam'un harshly criticized the Chosŏn Studies Movement, saying that it exoticized
the unique conceptions of Chosŏn such as the Chosŏn mind (Chosŏn sim), Chosŏn consciousness
(Chosŏn ŭisik), and Tan'gun. A good indication of his thinking is the fact that he participated in the
activities for the 100th anniversary of Chŏng Yagyong's passing, despite his critique of the movement. He felt that it would be possible to understand the historical laws and inevitability of the
internal development of thought in Korean history through an examination of Silhak and Chŏng
Yagyong, and his position on the "understanding of Chosŏn" was qualitatively different from that
of first group of Marxists. Paek Nam'un, Chosŏn sahoe kyŏngjesa, preface, p. 2; Paek Nam'un,
"Chŏng Tasan paeknyŏnje ŭi yŏksajŏk ŭiŭi," p. 23; Paek Nam'un, "Chŏng Tasan ŭi sasang" (The
thought of Chŏng Yagyong), Tonga ilbo, July 16, 1935.

85. As mentioned above, the focus of Paek Nam'un's critique in his series of works published
in 1934-35 was above all the bourgeois scholarship and positivist methodology that asserted the
purity of scholarship. This was a critique of Japanese government studies, and it also constituted a
critique of the Chindan Hakhoe. In contrast, many Marxists of the time showed little of the hostile
attitude toward the Chindan Hakhoe that they had toward the Chosŏn Studies Movement. In a
book review, Yi Ch'ŏngwŏn criticized the view of pure scholarship and ideological scholarship of
the Chindan Hakhoe; see Yi Ch'ŏngwŏn, "Chindan hakbo che sam kwŏn ŭl ilkko" (After
reading Chindan hakbo, no. 3), Tonga ilbo, November 9, 1935. With this exception, Marxists'
rather favorable attitude toward the Chindan Hakhoe provides an important clue to understanding their intellectual position at the time.

positivism, was typical bourgeois scholarship that lacked even the positive merits of the Chosŏn Studies Movement, differing little from Japanese government scholarship.

Many factors were behind the split among Marxist intellectuals that became apparent in the critique of the Chosŏn Studies Movement. The most important internal factor was the differing conceptions of the nation and Korea's colonial situation. At the time, Korean Marxist intellectuals' understanding of the nation and colonialism was based on the theory of the nation as formalized by Stalin. Many Korean Marxists dogmatically accepted Stalin's "theses" without sufficiently taking into consideration the unique features of the Korean nation. Stalin's conception of the nation generalized the particular experience of the West, arguing that "the nation is a product of class in the formation of capitalism."[86] It is not surprising that Korean Marxists showed classist tendencies in their view of the colonial problem. When the classist tendencies became even stronger because of the emergence of the theory of the international proletariat and the Comintern's "December theses" of 1928, Marxists began to react strongly even to the term "nationalism."[87] They regarded nationalist ideology as merely an alternative form of ultra-nationalism which in turn was closely related to fascist ideology. The severe criticism of the Chosŏn Studies Movement and the particularistic "understanding of Chosŏn" of the majority of Marxists were based on, and were an extension of, a classist conception of the nation and colonialism that was generally held within the socialist movement.

Paek Nam'un also adopted Stalin's theory of the nation and emphasized that nationalism is the class ideology of modern capitalism. As mentioned above, it was based on this position that he criticized the capitalist nature of bourgeois nationalist conceptions of history, the nation, and the state. However, his view of the colonial problem was clearly different from the general views of most Marxists at the time in that he went beyond a dogmatic

---

86. There were two theses in Stalin's discussion of the theory of the nation. First, "the nation is a stable community of people that is formed historically and is based on the psychological character that emerges from a common language, region, economic life, and a common culture." J.V. Stalin, "Malksüjuüi wa minjok munje" (Marxism and the National Problem), *Sŭt'allin chŏnjip* 1 (The complete works of Stalin, vol. 1), trans. by Sŏ Chunggŏn (Seoul: Chŏnjin, 1988), p. 45. Second, "the nation is not just a historical category but a historical category that belongs to a particular era, the era of the development of capitalism." See ibid., p. 50. Of course, it was the latter that defined bourgeois nationalist movements as a struggle for capitalism.

87. Sohongsaeng, "Chapji ch'ongp'yŏng" (Comprehensive critique of magazines), *Sin kaedan*, October 1932; Hwang Yŏng, "Minjok kaeryangjuŭi chido wŏlli ŭi pip'an" (A critique of the principles of leadership of nationalist reformism), *Sin kaedan* (March 1933).

acceptance of Stalin's theory. As he extensively read the theories of thinkers such as Marx, Engels, and Lenin regarding the nation and the state, he developed his own perspective on Korea's colonial situation through concrete research on the historical formation of the Chosŏn nation. His objective was to discover the unique historical aspects of its formation, which differed from that of the West, within the context of the developmental laws of Korean history. He emphasized the applicability of Engels' concept of the proto-nation which predated the establishment of capitalism. Like other Marxists, Paek emphasized the emergence of a class state in ancient times and the class-based nature of the formation of the nation. However, in contrast with the west, he felt that the ancient class state in Korea emerged simultaneously with the formation of the Chosŏn nation and nation-state.[88] He saw the Chosŏn nation as an "early emerging nation" and gave that fact special historical significance.[89]

The main focus of Paek Nam'un's theory of the ancient nation-state was to critique the bourgeois conception of the nation by illuminating the nature of the state in slave society. This conception was based on the notion of Tan'gun and Japanese government studies that fundamentally denied the ability of Korean society to develop in accordance with the universal laws of history. His work was also intended to be an indirect critique of class-centered approaches that mechanically followed Stalin's theory of the nation. He argued that the "Chosŏn nation" was a proto-nation that had been formed during the emergence of a slave state and that the nation had a long history as a homogeneous people. Besides its scholarly importance, his research also expressed his view that a national consciousness, based on knowledge of these unique aspects of Korean history, had an extremely important political role in the goal of national liberation.[90] These were the factors that led Paek Nam'un, in contrast to the majority of Marxists, to emphasize national consciousness and an autonomous "understanding of Chosŏn" based on scientific theory.

---

88. Paek Nam'un, *Chosŏn sahoe kyŏngjesa*, pp. 130, 177-78, 184-85, 311.

89. Paek Nam'un, ibid., p. 447. By adding points of emphasis to the phrase "early emerging nation" in the text, he emphasized the unique features of the formation of the Chosŏn nation that was distinct from that in the West.

90. It was not until after liberation that Paek Nam'un directly discussed the importance of an autonomous conception of nation and understanding of the national problem. Paek Nam'un, *Chosŏn minjok ŭi chillo* (The path of the Chosŏn nation) (Seoul: Singŏnsa, 1946). However, his basic ideas had already been formulated during the occupation period through his work on an "understanding of Chosŏn" (*Chosŏn insik*).

These aspects of his research clarify how his understanding of Marxist theory and thought developed.

Theories of the Development of Capitalism in Korea and the Nature of Colonial Society

THEORIES OF THE INTERNAL BREAKDOWN OF FEUDAL SOCIETY AND OF THE SPROUTS OF CAPITALISM

In the preface of *The Socioeconomic History of Chosŏn*, Paek Nam'un presented his plan to develop a framework for Korean economic history that would focus on economic social formations (*kyŏngjejŏk sahoe kusŏng*). The two main topics of research were to be "the breakdown of the Asian feudal state and the sprout form of capitalism" (*chabonjuŭi maeng'a hyŏngt'ae*) and "the development of foreign capitalism and international relations." The task that he set for himself was to examine these two subjects through a series of analyses of primitive communist society, slave society, and Asian feudal society.[91] As his research plan suggests, he understood the fundamental direction of modern Korean economic history as a movement in which Japanese aggression forcibly incorporated the Korean economy into Japan's system of "transplanted capitalism," although capitalism had begun to develop internally during the late Chosŏn and Hanmal periods. The basic framework of his understanding of early modern Korean economic history, which was directly related to his views on Korea's colonial situation, had already been formed by the mid-1920s after his return from Japan.

In January 1926, shortly after his return from Japan, Paek Nam'un published a short article, "A dynamic investigation of the strength of Chosŏn society" (Chosŏn sahoeryŏk ŭi tongjŏk koch'al). In this article, he fully laid out his conception of early modern economic history, covering the differentiation of classes in Korea before the Japanese occupation and the transition to capitalism.[92] His main point was that Korean feudal society, with 1894 as the turning point, gradually collapsed because of the acceleration of political and socioeconomic differentiation, the development of liberal thought, and the abolishment of class distinctions. A newly rising class (the middle class) emerged from below as a "third class" that had no connections to political power, unlike the privileged classes. The article contained no analysis of the

---

91. Paek Nam'un, *Chosŏn sahoe kyŏngjesa*, preface, p. 3.
92. Paek Nam'un, "Chosŏn sahoeryŏk ŭi tongjŏk koch'al."

changes in the relations of production that the newly rising class went through in the process of its formation. However, he saw it as a new political force whose members, emerging from below, sought to transform themselves into capitalists and to form a bourgeois political party. Together with the "first" and "second" classes who pursued bourgeois development from above, they represented the common interest of the "united Chosŏn bourgeois" under the patronage of feudal power groups.[93] He emphasized that bourgeois thought—referring to individualism and the principle of free competition rooted in Social Darwinism—also developed during the Hanmal period, paralleling changes in the relations of production.[94]

Paek Nam'un's research on the transition to capitalism focused on the open ports period, with 1894 as the main turning point. His earlier work had uncovered the process of the breakdown of the feudal state and society, but the scope of his research now expanded to cover the late Chosŏn period. His focus on the internal dynamics of Korean society was most apparent in his views on Silhak and Chŏng Yagyong. Viewing thought and ideology as reflections of the social relations of production, Paek Nam'un felt that the thought of Chŏng Yagyong and other Silhak thinkers was a reflection of social conditions in the late Chosŏn period. The emergence of Silhak showed that society was undergoing an intensification of feudal contradictions and a breakdown of feudal institutions.[95] More specifically, he argued that the breakdown of feudal society occurred through the intensification of feudal

93. Paek Nam'un, ibid. The term "first class" referred to the central class of aristocratic officials, and "second class" meant the provincial landed yangban. While he recognized the various paths in the formation of the Korean bourgeoisie and the differences in their political-economic bases, he saw the category of "bourgeoisie" in the Hanmal and occupation periods as a combination of the first and second classes, which pursued capitalist development from above from the Hanmal period onwards, and the "third class," which pursued it from below and viewed them as a single bourgeois camp.

94. Paek Nam'un, "Itani kyoju no 'Chosen ni okeru sangyo kakumei' wo yomu," p. 271; Paek Nam'un, "Sahoehak ŭi sŏngnip yurae wa immu" 4, *Chosŏn ilbo*, August 23, 1930. What is notable in his work is that Paek emphasized the particular conditions of Korea's situation and located the newly rising class of capitalist society in the countryside. In his view, bourgeois development was not limited to the urban commercial and manufacturing classes; he saw it in relation to the growth of a so-called "rural bourgeoisie." This argument is an important hint that shows his interest in discovering the internal potential for the transition to capitalism. The emergence of rich peasants in rural areas was predicated on the breakdown of feudal productive relations and land ownership relations and on the general development of a commodity currency economy. It was also the consequence of the growth of the differentiation of the peasant class that accompanied these developments.

95. Paek Nam'un, "Chŏng Tasan ŭi sasang."

exploitation which was based on the growth of a commodity-monetary economy in the late Chosŏn period. Silhak thought of the late eighteenth and early nineteenth centuries was thus a new intellectual trend that emerged in order to escape from the metaphysical tendencies of Neo-Confucianism and ritual studies and from intellectual subordination to China.

The focus of Silhak scholarship was the study of social reform during the breakdown of feudal society. To Paek, the intellectual core of Silhak lay in its theories of economic policy whose goal was to resolve the feudal contradictions of society.[96] He viewed Chŏng Yagyong as the intellectual who systematized Silhak thought. Chŏng analyzed the contradictions of feudal society and expounded on a variety of policies with the objective of achieving social reform. These aspects of the thought of Silhak and Chŏng Yagyong reveal the reasons for Paek Nam'un's interest in them. In terms of his political concerns, his interest reflected a strong sense of the necessity for land and agricultural reform in Korea to solve problems that were becoming extremely severe under Japanese rule.

In his work "Theory of Farmland," Chŏng Yagyong discussed a radical program of land reform that he called the "village-land system" (*yŏjŏnbŏp*). Paek felt that it occupied an important place in the history of Korea's modern economic thought. It was a proto-form of socialist economic theory that expressed, in part, the notion of the "right to the whole product of labor" (*nodong chŏnsugwŏn*).[97] He considered Chŏng Yagyong's thought to be a transitional phase between feudal thought and early modern liberal thought, since it reflected the breakdown of feudalism during the late Chosŏn period. Furthermore, in Chŏng's ideas on social reform, he saw proof of the inevitability of the historical laws of the development of thought and was able to delineate transformations in the social formation of the period.[98]

Another key to understanding Paek Nam'un's theory of the breakdown of feudalism was his theory of the commodity. It was the starting point of Marxist economics on the laws of the functioning of capitalism, and he placed tremendous importance on the theory of the commodity in research on Korean economic history. He once noted, "all the secrets of modern civil

96. Paek Nam'un, *Chosŏn sahoe kyŏngjesa*, preface, p. 2; Paek Nam'un, "Chŏng Tasan ŭi sasang;" Paek Nam'un, "Chŏng Tasan paeknyŏnje ŭi yŏksajŏk ŭiŭi," pp. 22-23.
97. Paek Nam'un, "Chŏng Tasan ŭi sasang."
98. Paek Nam'un, ibid.; Paek Nam'un, "Chŏng Tasan paeknyŏnje ŭi yŏksajŏk ŭiŭi," pp. 22-23; Paek Nam'un, "Hyang'yak ŭi puhwal e taehaya" (On the revival of the community compact), *Ch'ŏngnyŏn* 12, no. 1 (January 1932), p. 6.

society [can be] revealed through an analysis of the commodity."[99] He was not simply expounding the Marxist principle that the secret of capitalist production and increasing capital through the exploitation of surplus value was inherent in commodity production. Rather, he felt that the secret to refuting the "stagnation theory" of Korean history—propounded by both Japanese government scholars and many Marxists—could also be discovered from an analysis of commodity production.

Since commodity production is realized through commodity circulation (i.e., markets), Paek Nam'un's focus was on the development of markets and a commodity-monetary economy. He regarded the "stagnation theory" of Korean markets as crude scholarship that could not provide a theoretical understanding of the Korean market system. Korea's traditional markets were an important key to understanding not only the development of the commodity-monetary economy but also the historical emergence of commercial capital and high-interest capital as well as the class composition of the feudal urban economy.[100] These were the reasons that Paek was interested in feudal society during the Koryo period. His research focused on the development of commodity production within feudal society, the circulation of currency, and the role in the feudal circulation system played by exchange markets as a link between commodity production and monetary circulation.[101]

Based on his initial research, he then extended his examination of these issues—such as the emergence of the circulation and exchange economy and the formation of commercial capital—up to the period of the breakdown of feudalism. His goal was to refute decisively the "stagnation theory" of Korean history, which denied that such developments had occurred. A good example was his critique of the economist Kim Kwangjin, who also argued that Korean society had been stagnant during the feudal and late Chosŏn periods. Kim's argument was that a monetary economy had developed in Korea in

99. Paek Nam'un, *Chosŏn sahoe kyŏngjesa*, p. 11.

100. Paek Nam'un, "'Chosen keizai no kenkyu' ŭi tokgam," p. 30; Paek Nam'un, "Changggun ŭi naeyŏk—Chosŏn ŭi sijang chedo—" (The history of merchants—Chosŏn's market system), *Tonggwang*, no. 30 (February 1932), p. 24.

101. Paek Nam'un, *Chosŏn ponggŏn sahoe kyŏngjesa* (Tokyo: Kaizosha, 1937), section 12, "The various relations of markets of exchange:" chapter 86, "Market Organizations;" chapter 87, "The Currency System;" chapter 89, "Commerce and Commercial Capital;" chapter 90, "High-Interest Capital."

the seventeenth century, but commercial capital did not emerge until the late nineteenth century.[102]

Before defining the process of commodification as a temporary exchange of products, it seems necessary to examine the historical significance of the existence of markets. Furthermore, the view that a monetary economy in Chosŏn began from King Sukjong's reign [1674-1720] seems to overlook the sporadic nature of [the emergence] of Chosŏn's monetary system, and [I] cannot agree with the opinion that high-interest capital appeared only within the capital region. Commercial capital and high-interest capital were twins that emerged in the development of the social relations of production; therefore, the appearance of a monetary economy in Korea cannot be separated from the emergence of commercial capital. Accordingly, [I] cannot agree at all with the opinion that the old society, in which commercial capital had not even emerged, suddenly collapsed because of the invasion of "Western ships," because it would be the same as arguing that [when] European capitalism invaded China, [it] encountered the Asiatic mode of production.[103]

Of course, since, at this point, he had only made general comments on the breakdown of feudalism in the late Chosŏn period, Paek Nam'un still had not undertaken a fundamental examination of an issue that he himself had problematized—the differentiation of the peasant class. Its differentiation was the historical precondition for the emergence of the "rural bourgeoisie." To cover this topic, he would have had to examine changes in agricultural productivity which were the fundamental driving force behind the breakdown of feudalism.[104] Despite this limitation, his focus on the internal dynamics of the transition to capitalism produced an original interpretation of Korean history that no other scholar at the time had managed to develop. This interpretation clearly reveals Paek Nam'un's unique views on Korean history which emphasized the unitary laws of societal development and the inherent inevitability of historical transformation.

102. Kim Kwangjin, "Richo makki ni okeru Chosen no kahei mondai" (Chosŏn's currency in the late Yi Dynasty), *Pojŏn hakhoe nonjip* 1 (1934).
103. Paek Nam'un, "Pojŏn hakhoe nonjip e taehan tokhugam (4)" (Impressions after reading *Pojŏn hakhoe nonjip*), *Tonga ilbo*, May 4, 1934.
104. Although Paek Nam'un must have realized the theoretical significance of the issue of agricultural productivity, he never discussed, during the occupation period, the breakdown of feudalism and the emergence of the rural bourgeoisie in relation to this issue. It was not until after liberation that he first examined agricultural productivity during the late Chosŏn period.

In Paek Nam'un's view, the breakdown of feudalism occurred during the late Chosŏn period. As this process became accelerated after 1894, the internal development of capitalism underwent some progress. Japanese government studies ignored the internal development of capitalism and the development of bourgeois thought in Korea and argued that capitalism first developed in Korea as the result of Japanese policy after the occupation began. Rejecting their findings, Paek emphasized instead that Chosŏn had had the potential to develop capitalism on its own beginning in the late Chosŏn period, but this potential was suppressed and distorted in the process of colonization because of the violence of the Japanese police state and Japanese transplanted capital that supported it.[105] This suppression and distortion were a consequence of Korea's forcible incorporation into a colonial system of foreign transplanted capitalism.

In terms of its scholarly significance, Paek Nam'un's theories of the breakdown of feudalism and the sprouts of capitalism made three important contributions to the establishment of a scientific scholarship on Korea. First, he demonstrated that while the collapse of feudal society had already begun before the Japanese occupation, Korea had also developed the potential for the internal development of capitalism. His objective was to undermine the theory of Korean stagnation promoted by Japanese government scholarship, that was producing even more sophisticated studies of the late Chosŏn and Hanmal periods since the work of Fukuda Tokuzo. Second, his work revealed how this internal development was disrupted and distorted because of the violence of the Japanese occupation. He was attempting to expose the fabrications of Japan and Japanese government scholarship that, based on the theory of stagnation, tried to justify colonial exploitation as a "benefit" that brought about "Chosŏn's progress." Finally, by discovering the historical origins of transplanted capitalism, he tried to provide a key to understanding the nature of society and the form of contradictions in contemporary Chosŏn as well as to envisioning possibilities for political action.[106]

---

105. Paek Nam'un, "Itani kyoju no 'Chosen ni okeru sangyo kakumei' wo yomu," p. 271.

106. Such intentions were clearly expressed in the following passage from Paek Nam'un: "A theory of the present stage of the Chosŏn economy requires, on the one hand, an analysis of existing social institutions and, on the other hand, demands naturally a theory of policy. However, in order to satisfy these demands, it is necessary, at least, to examine carefully the nature of current policies and to analyze comprehensively the historical development of the Chosŏn economy up to the present stage." Paek Nam'un, "Chosen keizai no gendankairon" (On the present stage of the Chosŏn economy), *Kaizo* 16, no. 5 (April 1934); reprinted in *Shiso iho* 17 (December 1938), p. 303.

PAEK NAM'UN'S THEORY OF TRANSPLANTED CAPITALISM AND HIS
CRITIQUE OF THE PLANNED ECONOMY

(1) The Formation and Structure of the System of Transplanted Capitalism

Paek Nam'un noted, as is obvious, that opinions on the current stage of
the Chosŏn economy differed according to the methodological position
taken in investigating such issues. In addition, differences in political views
naturally arose over the future direction of the nation.[107] Paek argued that the
"sprouts" (*maeng'a*) of domestic capitalist development emerged in the late
Chosŏn and Hanmal periods, but "the path for the autonomous development
of capitalism in Chosŏn" became blocked because of the Japanese occupation.
Korea was forced to follow the path of a distorted form of capitalism, that is,
transplanted capitalism (*isik chabonjuŭi*). Emphasizing the historical significance of the loss of political sovereignty to Korea's economic development,
he saw the Japanese occupation as a turning point toward a capitalist social
formation. After the "first age of Chosŏn," which began in 1894, came the
"second age" beginning in 1910, which cast a dark shadow over the prospects of the entire bourgeoisie in Korea. Korean society under Japanese rule
was a "society made heterogeneous by a new power."[108]

Paek conceived of transplanted capitalism in Korea as developing in
three stages from the beginning of the occupation to the early 1930s. First,
there was the stage of the permit system during the administration of Governor-General Terauchi Masatake; second, the liberal stage under Governor-
General Saito Makoto in the 1920s; and third, the monopoly stage during
Governor-General Ugaki Kazushige's rule.[109]

During the first stage, the Company Law (K. Hoesaryŏng, J. Kaisharei,
1911) was the main factor determining the nature of transplanted capitalism.
It implemented a permit system (K. *t'ŭkhŏ chedo*; J. *tokkyo seido*) that did
not allow freedom of enterprise. Paek Nam'un regarded it as a law "that pronounced its power to determine life or death over Chosŏn commercial and
industrial companies." To him, the Company Law represented a policy of
systematic restrictions on enterprise whose objective was both to enable Japanese manufacturing capital to control Korea and to support the activities of

107. Paek Nam'un, "Chosen keizai no gendankairon," pp. 304–05.

108. Paek Nam'un, "Chosŏn sahoeryŏk ŭi tongjŏk koch'al" (A dynamic investigation of the
strength of Chosŏn society), *Chosŏn ilbo*, January 3, 1926; Paek Nam'un, "Itani kyoju no
'Chosen ni okeru sangyo kakumei' wo yomu," p. 263.

109. Paek Nam'un, "Chosen keizai no gendankairon," p. 305.

Japanese businessmen who had political connections. As a result, Chosŏn native capitalists suffered heavy losses during the early period of transplanted capitalism.[110] The permit system meant politics by military police and the pursuit of mercantilist policies under state tutelage.

Another key element of transplanted capitalism was the cadastral survey of the 1910s. Paek Nam'un noted, "the land survey is just the division of the sphere of production by imperialism. That is, [it is] no more than the reorganization of the feudal private ownership system into a capitalist one."[111] In other words, what the cadastral survey accomplished was a conversion of feudal property rights, which already recognized private property, into coercive capitalist property rights. To put it yet another way, it was a reorganization of the feudal landlord system into a capitalist landlord system.

The second stage was the period of liberal rule known as the "Cultural Policy" (J. *Bunka seiji*). Paek Nam'un felt that its historical significance lay in the "institutionalization of transplanted capitalism."[112] In this period, the Program to Increase Rice Production and the irrigation cooperative movement brought about revolutionary changes in the rural economy, and there was a tremendous increase in the entry of transplanted capital into Korea. Although government scholars justified such developments as an "industrial revolution" and as "cultural politics," Paek criticized them for intensifying economic class contradictions and covering up social conflict.[113] The revolutionary changes in rural areas resulted in a severe redistribution of land ownership as shown by the land accumulation of large landlords, the impoverishment of small landlords, the uprooting of small farmers from the land, and the increase in the number of tenant farmers. The changes also brought about a food shortage for the peasant class because of the increase in rice exports.

Under the "Cultural Policy," the Company Law was repealed; however, Paek felt that the repeal was only superficially consistent with the principles of free enterprise. At a time when transplanted capitalism was already institutionalized, the repeal merely "strengthened the institutionalized handicaps" that gave privileges to transplanted capitalists and systematized them into institutions of exploitation.[114] He argued that through the institutionalization

---

110. ibid., pp. 305-06.

111. Paek Nam'un, *Chosŏn sahoe kyŏngjesa*, p. 214.

112. Paek Nam'un, "Chosen keizai no gendankairon," p. 307.

113. ibid., pp. 307-08.

114. Paek Nam'un, "Hujin ch'ujong Chosŏn san'ŏp kyŏnghyang" (Following after dust, trends in Chosŏn industry), *Tonga ilbo*, April 2, 1930; Paek Nam'un, "Chosen keizai no gendankairon," p. 308.

of transplanted capitalism, Korea was turned into a commodity market, a supplier of raw materials, and an investment market, all of which were completely integrated into Japanese capitalism. On the other hand, the number of labor strikes and tenant farmer protests increased rapidly, ushering in a new era for the labor and peasant movements.[115]

According to Paek Nam'un, the fundamental development in Korea's social formation in the 1920s was the complete institutionalization of transplanted capitalism. Capitalist transformation was occurring throughout the Korean economy, "regardless of the type of industry."[116] However, the driving force in the development of transplanted capitalism was the influx of Japanese capital. In his analysis of contemporary society, the point he most emphasized was the fact that the only capitalist development that occurred in Korea was that of transplanted capital.

Of course, Korean native capital had the potential to serve as the basis for the internal development of capitalism beginning in the Hanmal period, and Paek did acknowledge that Korea underwent some capitalist growth during the development of transplanted capitalism.[117] Though the growth was slight, a certain amount of native capital was clearly converted into industrial or financial capital.[118] However, he did not regard this growth as the primary force in transplanted capitalism in Korea because the great majority of industrial and finance capital came from Japan. His argument was that the growth of Korean native capital, which amounted to only 9.6% of the total capital in the country, was simply a temporary phenomenon and that small- to medium- scale native capital was actually undergoing a decline.[119] The leap in the development of Korean industry was the result of transplanted capital's growing control over Korean industrial facilities and of the decline of small- to medium-scale native capital.

Agriculture also underwent similar changes in this period. In Paek's view, the "growth in the area of cultivation, an increase in the number of large

---

115. Paek Nam'un, "Chosen keizai no gendankairon," pp. 303, 307.

116. Paek Nam'un, "Hujin ch'ujong Chosŏn san'ŏp kyŏnghyang" (Following after dust, trends in Chosŏn industry), *Tonga ilbo*, April 2, 1930.

117. For Paek Nam'un, "native capital" was a concept that encompassed all three of the above-mentioned classes that existed before the Japanese occupation. He felt that the largest portion of native capital during the occupation period was formed by landlord capital which was based on land capital. Paek Nam'un, "Chosen keizai no gendankairon," p. 316.

118. Paek Nam'un, "Hujin ch'ujong Chosŏn san'ŏp kyŏnghyang."

119. Paek Nam'un, "Chosŏn sahoeryŏk ŭi tongjŏk koch'al;" Paek Nam'un, "Hujin ch'ujong Chosŏn san'ŏp kyŏnghyang."

landlords, the decline of small-to-medium landlords and self-cultivators, and a large increase in the number of tenant farmers" were all indications of the class differentiation occurring in the rural economy.[120] The underlying factor was the accumulation of land by Japanese landlords and capitalists which caused the decline of even small- to medium-scale landlords. He saw foreign landlords as the central force in agricultural capitalism. They produced around 80% of Korea's rice exports (totaling seven to eight million *sŏk*) and brought about the commodification of rice and the introduction of capitalist methods of agricultural management.[121]

For Paek Nam'un, the fundamental aspect of Korean capitalism under Japanese imperialism was its transplanted nature. Based on this view, he felt that Korea's economic institutions merely functioned for the benefit of the development of an imperialist economy. The economy under Japanese rule was the "particular developmental form of the Korean capitalist economy which was completely and fundamentally united" with Japanese monopoly capitalism.[122]

(2) Critique of the Fascist Control Economy of the 1930s

The third stage in the development of transplanted capitalism occurred during the Great Depression era. In this period, Japan completely revised and intensified its exploitative policies, and Paek Nam'un characterized these steps as a change toward a fascist control economy (K. *t'ongje kyŏngje*) under the monopoly stage of transplanted capitalism.[123] Based on the theory of the general crisis of capitalism, he categorized these changes into three new worldwide trends that reflected the systemic crisis of capitalism during the Great Depression: economic blocs, control economies, and fascism. Regional economic blocs became the units of systemic conflict, and their formation was a worldwide economic trend that arose from the effort to repartition colonies among the imperialist powers that had entered the "final phase of capitalism." Control economies were domestic "planned economies of capitalism" that attempted to overcome the general crisis, and fascism was a

---

120. Paek Nam'un, "Chosen keizai no gendankairon," p. 316.
121. Paek Nam'un, ibid., pp. 314-16. He noted that over 600,000 *chŏngbo* of land, which amounted to one-seventh of the total cultivated area in Korea at the time (4.39 million *chŏngbo*), was owned by Japanese landlords.
122. Paek Nam'un, ibid., p. 304.
123. Paek Nam'un, ibid., p. 308; Paek Nam'un, "Pokgo kyŏngje ŭi immu" (The duties of the atavistic economy), *Tonga ilbo*, September 29, 1935.

"concentrated form of power politics" that developed in response to these domestic and international conflicts.[124]

Among the three trends, the theoretical core linking them together lay in the control economy. Paek Nam'un felt that it was the fundamental factor that could reveal the internal dynamics of monopoly capitalism. Concluding that the control economy represented a shift to the state monopoly stage of capitalism, he regarded the system of economic controls as a planned economy and called it a "dangerous escape route" for the imperialist states facing systemic crises.

> Since "economic controls" represent a capitalist "planned economy," it must be understood that [they are] the unified theoretical basis for these three grand projects. . . . The capitalist planned economy is actually a dangerous escape route on which the current imperialist powers have staked everything. Socially, it is an attempt to overcome the general crisis of capitalism, and psychologically, it represents a mind-set that aims for the stabilization of capitalist institutions.[125]

Monopoly capital determined the concrete nature of this stage of capitalism both domestically and internationally, and its operation resulted in the rise of economic blocs and a fascist political system. The only differences among the imperialist countries were in the manner and degree that the three trends were being pursued. It was only natural that these differences existed because the social characteristics of each country were different and because there were also differences in the conditions of economic depression faced by each country and the political situations caused by it.[126]

Beginning in the Great Depression years, the trend in the world was toward the formation of international economic blocs based on domestic economic controls and the rise of fascism. Paek Nam'un predicted that the conflict of contradictions among the blocs would inevitably intensify because of the uneven development of monopoly capital. Moreover, the growth of these contradictions would be even more accelerated because of factors such as capitalist development in colonial and semi-colonial regions, the rise of national

---

124. Paek Nam'un, "Nyuddil ŭi chŏnmang (1)" (The prospects of the New Deal), *Tonga ilbo*, June 13, 1935.

125. Paek Nam'un, ibid.

126. Paek Nam'un, ibid; Paek Nam'un, "Segye kyŏngje rŭl chibae hanŭn ppullŏk undong ŭi kŭmhu (3)" (The future of the bloc movement that is dominating the world economy), *Tonga ilbo*, January 3, 1934; Paek Nam'un, "Chŏnjaeng kwa kyŏngje (6)" (War and the economy), *Tonga ilbo*, January 9, 1936.

liberation movements in those regions, and the development of the socialist economy in the Soviet Union. Based on this view of current events, he gave the following overview of future developments in the world capitalist system.

Together with the world depression, internal contradictions are growing within the world economic blocs themselves. There is also [a struggle] among the imperial states to capture world markets and raw materials, to acquire colonies and semi-colonies, and to increase gold holdings. Thus, on the one hand, there is competition in armaments and naval construction; on the other hand, tariff wars, foreign exchange dumping, and dumping of commodities are becoming more severe. . . . However, since these measures will undoubtedly be unable to overcome the world economic depression, it is likely that the formation of economic blocs will necessarily develop into a "political recession" and then, ultimately, into a second imperialist war. However, it is only the laws of history that can predict such developments.[127]

Paek predicted that the direction of world events would lead to the outbreak of another world war. Although the League of Nations, which he called a "club of imperialists," had been formed after World War I, only military might could resolve the international conflicts resulting from monopoly capitalism's efforts to redivide the world into economic blocs.[128] His declaration that economic blocs and control economies were just a "preparatory step toward a wartime economy" was based on this view of international trends.[129]

The rise of Japanese fascism and the tightening of its occupation policies toward Korea were part of these international trends. Paek Nam'un saw Japan's fascist policy of economic controls in the 1930s as the intensification of its efforts to create an economic bloc and as an effort to build supply bases to prepare for the transition to a wartime economy. Its objective was to establish the material foundation for its continental aggressions and the creation of a Far Eastern (Japan-Manchuria) bloc, which began with its invasion of Manchuria in 1931. The main elements of the policy of economic controls were

127. Paek Nam'un, "Segye kyŏngje rŭl chibae hanŭn ppullŏk undong ŭi kŭmhu (5)," *Tonga ilbo,* January 5, 1934.

128. Paek Nam'un, "Chŏnjaeng kwa kyŏngje (6)." This was what he meant when he defined economic blocs as "a world historical process in the current stage of the world economy that is of extreme importance in bringing about the end of modern society." Paek Nam'un, "Chŏnjaeng kwa kyŏngje (1)," *Tonga ilbo,* January 1, 1936.

129. Paek Nam'un, "Chŏnjaeng kwa kyŏngje (6)."

the Rural Revitalization Campaign (K. *Nongch'on chinhŭng undong*) of 1932-1940, the revival of feudal institutions (K. *pokgo chŏngch'aek*), the national autarky campaign (K. *kukch'aekjŏk chagŭm chajok*), and the Industrialization policy for the northern regions of Korea. The Rural Revitalization Campaign and its component measures—the Plan to Establish Self-Cultivating Farmers (K. *chajaknong ch'angjŏng kyehoek*), the 1934 Chosŏn Agricultural Land Ordinance (K. Chosŏn nongjiryŏng; aka, Tenant Farmer Law), and the feudal revival policies—were reflections of the fundamental direction of Japan's occupation policies. The autarky campaign and the industrialization policy reflected the nature of Japan's economic exploitation of Korea as well as the nature of the crisis faced by Japanese capitalism in its efforts to create an economic bloc.[130]

Governor-General Ugaki Kazushige implemented measures such as the Rural Revitalization Campaign and the Tenant Farmer Law under the ideology of the "revival of self-sufficiency." As is well known, the publicly stated objective of these measures was to establish a system of small-scale, self-cultivating farmers who would serve as the middle stratum of rural society, by placing some restrictions on the landlord system and providing protection for tenant farmers.[131] However, Paek Nam'un regarded these policies as a deceitful response to the intensification of class conflict in rural areas and the sharp increase in tenant farmers' disputes that occurred as transplanted capitalism became institutionalized.[132]

The rise in peasant protests, such as tenant farmers' disputes, was caused by factors such as the extreme inequities of land ownership brought about by the development of large-scale landlordism and the *nongjang* system, the acceleration of the decline of the peasantry, and the accompanying bankruptcy

---

130. Paek Nam'un, "Chosen keizai no gendankairon," p. 308.

131. Miyata Setsuko, "Chosen ni okeru noson sinko undo" (The rural revitalization movement in Chosŏn), *Kikan gendaishi* 2 (1973); Tomita Akiko, "Junsenjika Chosen no noson sinko undo" (The Rural Revitalization Campaign in Chosŏn in the quasi-wartime period), *Rekishi hyoron*, no. 377 (1981); Chi Sugŏl, "1932-1935 nyŏngan ŭi Chosŏn nongch'on chinhŭng undong" (The rural revitalization movement in Chosŏn between 1932-1935), *Han'guksa yŏn'gu*, no. 46 (1984); Pak Sŏp, "Singminji Chosŏn e issŏsŏ 1930 nyŏndae ŭi nong'ŏp chŏngch'aek e kwanhan yŏn'gu" (An examination of the agricultural policies of the 1930s toward colonial Chosŏn), *Han'guk kŭndae nongch'on sahoe wa nongmin undong* (Seoul: Yŏl'ŭmsa, 1988); Chŏng Yŏnt'ae, "1930 nyŏndae 'Chosŏn nongjiryŏng' kwa Ilje ŭi nongch'on t'ongje" (The "Chosŏn Agricultural Land Ordinance" and Japanese regulation of rural areas in the 1930s), *Yŏksa wa hyŏnsil*, no. 4 (1990); Chi Sugŏl, "1930 nyŏndae chŏnban'gi Chosŏn'in taejijuch'ŭng ŭi chŏngch'ijŏk tonghyang" (The poli-tical tendencies of large-scale Chosŏn landlords in the early 1930s), *Yŏksa hakbo*, no. 122 (June 1989); Kim Yong-sop, "Ilche kangjŏmgi ŭi nong'ŏp munje wa kŭ t'agae pangch'aek."

132. Paek Nam'un, "Chosen keizai no gendankairon," pp. 312, 317.

of peasant life. A telling phenomenon was the existence of "famines in years of bountiful harvests." Small-scale farmers who were uprooted from their land bore the brunt of the burden of the depression. They were faced with a "situation in which it was difficult [to obtain] substitute foods such as foreign rice and Manchurian millet as they were deprived of their own harvests."[133] In rural areas in Korea during the Great Depression, the impoverishment of small farmers and the resulting rural exodus became accelerated. Many became "wage laborers, repeating a grim pattern of change of occupation, wandering, starvation, and return to one's hometown." As a result, tenant farmers' disputes became more organized, and their frequency increased sharply during this period.[134] Paek argued that the peasant movement joined forces with the labor and socialist movements and was transforming from an economic protest into a political movement because inequalities in land ownership were rooted in the nature of transplanted capitalism—i.e., the domination of Korean agriculture by Japanese capital.[135] These structural factors thus explain how the labor and peasant movements transformed into a movement for national liberation.

The exacerbation of class contradictions in rural areas and the intensification of peasant resistance posed a threat to the occupation of Korea by Japanese capitalism which was in a state of crisis. More immediately, these factors made it difficult for Japan to accelerate its efforts to create a Far Eastern economic bloc in preparation for the transition to a wartime economy. Though the public objective of economic controls was a return to self-sufficiency, the policy actually consisted of measures to establish control over the countryside and to enable ideological suppression in response to developments in this period, as clearly shown in Governor-General Ugaki Kazushige's views on agricultural management.[136] This was the point of Paek Nam'un's critique of Japan's control economy policies in the early 1930s.

Paek viewed the Self-Cultivating Farmer Plan, on which Ugaki put much emphasis, as a prototypical measure that reflected the hidden agenda of

---

133. Paek Nam'un, ibid., pp. 314-17; Paek Nam'un, "Chosŏn nodongja idong munje 1" (The problem of the migration of Chosŏn workers 1), *Tonga ilbo*, January 1, 1935.

134. Paek Nam'un, "Chosŏn nodongja idong munje 1"; Paek Nam'un, "Chosen keizai no gendankairon," pp. 312, 317.

135. Paek Nam'un, "Chosen keizai no gendankairon," p. 317.

136. Ugaki Kazushige, *Ugaki Kazushige nikki II* (The diary of Ugaki Kazushige) (Tokyo: Misuzu shobo, 1968-1971), pp. 932, 949-50. For a discussion of Ugaki's views on agricultural policies, see Chŏng Yŏnt'ae, "1930 nyŏndae 'Chosŏn nongjiryŏng' kwa Ilje ŭi nongch'on t'ongje," pp. 247-48; Kim Yong-sop, *Han'guk kŭnhyŏndae nong'ŏpsa yŏn'gu*, pp. 419-20.

Japanese policies. The goal of the Self-Cultivating Farmer Plan was not to provide a fundamental solution to agricultural problems. Rather, it was a politically motivated policy that sought to establish conservative forces in the countryside. Its objective was to quell tenant farmers' disputes and to alleviate peasant discontent in situations where the separation between land ownership and cultivation was severe. The Self-Cultivating Farmers Plan was a deceitful policy that protected the profits of the landlord class, and Paek argued that the plan would inevitably fail in Korea just as history had shown that such plans had failed in all capitalist countries.[137]

Although the protection of tenant farmers was the ostensible purpose of the Tenant Farmer Law and the feudal revival policies, Paek Nam'un noted that they also revealed the true purpose of the control economy. First, the Tenant Farmer Law was meant to be an "antidote" to neutralize the increasing conflict between tenant farmers and landlords. The law was by nature deceptive since it did not contain any guidelines on tenant farming fees. He thus argued that the Tenant Farmer Law was the "most rational legal way to secure 100% of the profit for the landlords" in addition to keeping tenant farmers in feudal legal status.[138] He derided the opposition of Japanese landlords to the Tenant Farmer Law, saying that they were "either ignorant of the spirit of the law or were unbelievably greedy." On the other hand, he criticized the efforts by nationalists to support the law, seeing it as an opportunistic act that outwardly supported the interests of tenant farmers but actually represented the interests of landlords.[139]

Second, Paek felt that the policies to restore feudal institutions, such as the community contract (K. *hyangyak*) or grain storehouses, were significant in two respects. They were both part of the measures that Japan adopted to overcome the heightening rural crisis and part of its political effort to co-opt local elites and the rural middle class into serving as a pro-Japanese force.[140] His argument was that the feudal revival policies were a world historical phenomenon that developed during the rise of Fascism under monopoly capital. In reality, they were measures to enable thought control and to provide

---

137. Paek Nam'un, "Chajaknong ch'angjŏng kyehoek" (The Plan to Establish Self-Cultivating Farmers, *Tongbang p'yŏngnon* 3 (July-August 1932), pp. 24-26; Paek Nam'un, "Chosen keizai no gendankairon," p. 311.

138. Paek Nam'un, "Chosen keizai no gendankairon," pp. 317-18.

139. ibid., p. 318.

140. Paek Nam'un, ibid., p. 321; Paek Nam'un, "Hyangyak ŭi puhwal e taehaya," p. 6.

support for the planned economy in order to maintain the development of transplanted capitalism in the colony.[141]

Implemented in the name of the "restoration of self-sufficiency," the measures for the peasantry seemed to place some constraints on the landlord class. However, Paek Nam'un felt that they ultimately remained within the limits that protected the interests of the landlord class. In a situation where the majority of peasants were already alienated from the means of production, the "path to restoration of self-sufficiency" was merely the "death knell for the economic collapse of the Chosŏn peasantry."[142] In his view, a genuine movement for self-sufficiency would have had to be an organized self-defense movement for tenant farmers who were suffering from oppression by the Japanese. Its purpose would have been the fundamental solution of the inequities in land ownership; that is, the liberation of the peasantry through the abolition of the landlord system. However, he believed that this solution would be possible only with the achievement of the political goal of national liberation.[143] His proposals for solving agricultural problems reflected the general position of socialists at the time who advocated both national liberation and a land revolution, and they were fundamentally different from the proposals of the majority of nationalists.

The exploitative policies of Japanese fascism went beyond the establishment of economic controls. In order to overcome the capitalist crisis, the Japanese also implemented measures for economic exploitation that subordinated Chosŏn even more completely to Japanese monopoly capital as a supplier of raw materials and as a source of exploitable labor power. Paek Nam'un thought that these developments resulted from the structural weaknesses inherent to Japanese capitalism as a late imperial power. The key factor was the structural instability of the textile industry, the only industry in which Japan was competitive within the world capitalist system. Exports of raw silk and cotton products determined the growth or decline of Japanese monopoly capitalism, and Japan was completely dependent on imports for raw cotton and textile machinery. He thought that the international position of the Japanese cotton industry was becoming extremely unstable because of the severity of conflict among economic blocs during the Great Depression and because of Japan's growing inferiority in competing for markets and its

141. Paek Nam'un, "Pokgo kyŏngje ŭi immu."
142. Paek Nam'un, "Chosen keizai no gendankairon," p. 309.
143. Paek Nam'un, ibid., p. 312.

inequality compared to the British cotton industry, its principal rival.[144] Since Japan had no alternative other than to develop new monopolies of raw materials and markets, it had to intensify its exploitation of Chosŏn and to embark on an expansion of the Far Eastern economic bloc through military action.[145]

Through the "state autarky program," Japan pursued policies to transform the structure of production in the Korean economy. It promoted industrialization in northern Chosŏn, cotton cultivation in the south, and wool and hemp cultivation in the north. The promotion of cotton, wool, and hemp cultivation sought to increase production of these materials by establishing controls over production and even marketing. Paek Nam'un viewed these policies as an effort to simplify the structure of agricultural production in Korea, just as the Program to Increase Rice Production had attempted, and to subordinate Korean agriculture to the needs of the Japanese cotton-spinning industry.[146] Industrialization in the north was the consequence of the monopolistic development of transplanted capital that also entailed a monopoly of natural resources and an increased exploitation of labor power by Japanese monopoly capital. He argued that through monopoly capitalism's exploitative industrialization policy, a "transformation of the Chosŏn economy" was occurring that brought about a modern organization of labor within production.[147]

There were four main points to Paek Nam'un's critique of transplanted capitalism in Korea and of the "economic controls" policy in the 1930s. First, under Japanese rule, Korean society underwent a qualitative transformation to a capitalist social formation, and the decisive event in the transformation was the loss of political sovereignty in 1910. His second point was that the potential for the internal development of capitalism in Korea was blocked through violent means, and subsequent capitalist development involved the development of transplanted capitalism, the driving force of which was foreign capital from Japan. His third point was that the institutionalization of

144. "Ilmun ildapgi Yŏnhŭi chŏnmun kyosu Paek Nam'un ssi," *Sin tonga* 2, no. 12 (December 1932), p. 21; Paek Nam'un, "Chosen keizai no gendankairon," pp. 321–22.

145. Paek Nam'un, "Chosen keizai no gendankairon," p. 322. This was the basis for his view that the Far Eastern bloc was the economic bloc with the most serious political and military tensions. Paek Nam'un, "Segye kyŏngje rŭl chibae hanŭn ppullŏk undong ŭi kŭmhu (4–5)," *Tonga ilbo*, January 4–5, 1934.

146. Paek Nam'un, "Chosen keizai no gendankairon," pp. 321–23.

147. Paek Nam'un, ibid., p. 325; Paek Nam'un, "Chosŏn nodongja idong munje 2" (The problem of the migration of Chosŏn workers 2), *Tonga ilbo*, January 2, 1935.

transplanted capitalism in Korea was completed in the 1920s; and then during the Great Depression of the 1930s, when Japan entered the monopoly stage under a control economy because of the crisis of the world capitalist system, it also implemented a policy of fascist economic controls in Korea. Lastly, since class contradictions in transplanted capitalism were rooted in the colonial conflict between Korea and Japan, the nature of the labor and peasant movements was fundamentally political; that is, they were in essence a national liberation movement.

CONCEPTION OF SOCIETY AND THE DIRECTION OF THE NATIONALIST MOVEMENT

In order to understand Paek Nam'un's views on national liberation, it is necessary to reexamine their relation to his work on economic history and contemporary Korea in the context of his conceptions of society and of social contradictions. In general, the main focus of his analysis of contemporary society was the transplanted nature of colonialism that was expressed through class conflict as the system of transplanted capitalism developed and became entrenched. This "transplanted nature" was the aspect of society that determined the nature of the contradictions of the social formation under the present stage of capitalism. Paek Nam'un elaborated his argument as follows.

> Can the current economic institutions of Chosŏn be simply defined as a capitalist society? Not at all. . . . In all the institutions of the Chosŏn economy, there is a mixture of feudal remnants and a capitalist system. However, what matters is not the relative importance of each in the constitution of the economy; rather, they are the expression of class relations in the colony of an imperialist economy. Therefore, [the mixture of feudal and capitalist elements] can be seen as a specific developmental form of a Chosŏn capitalist economy that is completely a unitary whole. Politically, it appears as a conflict between nations, but socioeconomically, it appears as capitalist conflict. In the case of the latter, the class conflicts within the Chosŏn nation are also an important social phenomenon that cannot be ignored. But as long as transplanted capitalism has a dominant presence in the institutions of the Chosŏn economy, national conflicts and capitalist conflicts will almost completely overlap

with each other. The double nature of conflict is the defining characteristic of the Chosŏn economy today.[148]

Paek Nam'un's argument had two general points. First, Korea under
Japanese rule was not a straightforward capitalist society. Rather, it was a society of transplanted capitalism whose dominant feature was the transplanted
nature of colonial capitalism which was completely incorporated into the economy of Japanese monopoly capitalism. The term "dominant" referred to
the mutual determination of the feudal and "transplanted" aspects of society.
As a mixture of two economic systems, the Chosŏn economy possessed the
qualities of both feudalism and transplanted capitalism, but despite the quantitative superiority of the former, he argued that the latter determined the
qualitative nature of the social formation.

Second, under Japanese rule, the fundamental contradictions of Korean
society, which were rooted in the nature of transplanted capitalism, were expressed through the merging of political (colonial) and class (capitalist) conflict. In other words, what was of primary importance in the structure of
contradictions was the merging of national and class contradictions due to the
main features of transplanted capitalism.[149] It was a combination of the total-
izing nature of colonial and economic domination by Japan with the political
and class conflicts that transplanted capitalism caused between Japan and Chosŏn. More specifically, within agriculture, there was a conflict between Japanese landlords and Korean peasants; within commerce and industry, there was
a conflict between Japanese transplanted capital and Korean laborers.

Paek Nam'un categorized class conflict within the nation as a secondary
contradiction, clearly revealing his understanding of society and social contradictions. Class contradictions within the nation were the product of the overlapping of feudal contradictions arising from the landlord system with the
capitalist conflict caused by the movement of native capital into commerce
and industry. Paek tended to de-emphasize the conflict between Korean native capital and landlords, on the one side, and laborers and tenant farmers, on
the other. Rather, as mentioned above, he put more emphasis on the conflict
between colonizer and colonized—that is, between transplanted capitalism
and small- to medium-scale Korean capitalists and landlords. He also

---

148. Paek Nam'un, "Chosen keizai no gendankairon," p. 304.

149. To borrow Mao Tse-tung's usage, it can be said that it was a union of fundamental and
important contradictions. Mao Tse-tung, "On Contradiction" in *Chungguk hyŏkmyŏng kwa Mo
T'aekdong sasang 1*, Bruno Shaw, ed. (Seoul: Sŏkt'ap, 1986), pp. 153-68.

emphasized the decline in status of Korean capitalists and landlords caused by the influx of transplanted capital.

Although Paek's focus on transplanted capitalism appears to have reflected his emphasis on the primacy of the colonial conflict, this focus was also rooted in his rejection of the possibility that Korean native capital could have served as the driving force in the development of national capitalism. In Paek's view, capitalist growth by native capital, though possible for short periods of time, became fundamentally impossible under conditions of colonialism as early as the mid-1920s. In contrast, other intellectuals called for the development of commerce and industry through companies owned by Koreans and for the self-sufficiency of the national economy. Similar to the Native Products Promotion Movement (Mulsan changnyŏ undong) which lasted into the 1930s,[150] they argued for the potential development of "self-sufficient capitalism" or "national capitalism" under conditions of transplanted capitalism. Paek criticized such views as opportunism that would lead only to the emergence of "privileged workers" rather than native capitalists. To him, their policies were fundamentally no different from the Japanese policy of the "revival of self-sufficiency."[151] Paek's argument was that without national liberation, native capital would either become completely subordinated to the colonial state and transplanted capital or end up falling into bankruptcy.

While Paek Nam'un emphasized that class conflict rooted in Korea's colonial situation was the primary contradiction of society, he sought to understand class conflict within the context of the political significance of the feudal remnants contained within transplanted capitalism. In the preface to *The Socioeconomic History of Feudal Chosŏn*, he discussed the mutual relationship between feudal remnants and the transplanted nature of capitalism as follows:

> During this turning point of world history, the form of Eastern society is a mosaic mixture of the persistence of feudal remnants, which appears as Asiatic stagnation, and the dominance of the highest form of capitalism. The dual nature of this society will necessarily undergo rapid transformation.[152]

In short, feudal remnants were structurally integrated with monopoly capitalism, the "highest form of capitalism." The concrete form of these

---

150. Pang Kie-chung, "1920-30 nyŏndae Chosŏn mulsan changnyŏhoe yŏn'gu."
151. Paek Nam'un, "Chosen keizai no gendankairon," p. 325.
152. Paek Nam'un, *Chosŏn ponggŏn sahoe kyŏngjesa*, preface, p. 1.

remnants was the relations of production of the landlord system which was now integrated with a modern land ownership system. Colonial and class conflicts, stemming from the transplanted nature of capitalism during the Japanese occupation, were rooted in the semi-feudal nature of the landlord system. Because the structural features of Japanese capitalism made its development partially dependent on Korean agriculture, it was only natural that the Japanese colonial state sought to control it through the landlord system.[153] Paek used the Japanese expression "mosaic mixture" (J. *yosegizaiku teki konketsu keitai*) to describe the contradictions of a landlord system integrated with monopoly capitalism.

Paek Nam'un's views on the nature of contradictions and society under Japanese rule can be summarized as follows. The fundamental contradiction of Korean society was the conflict between colonizer and colonized, and this conflict was rooted in the transplanted nature of capitalism which led to the merging of national and class contradictions. As feudal contradictions were structurally integrated with the colonial situation, he argued that the ultimate goal of political and social movements should be a national liberation that would be simultaneously "anti-capital" and "anti-feudal." In his view, national liberation was the primary political task facing Korean society because it would be impossible to achieve a fundamental solution to the socioeconomic contradictions of colonial society without political independence.[154] After national liberation, society would be able to move in a non-capitalist direction with the goal of establishing a socialist state. National liberation and the establishment of a socialist state were not separate tasks but constituted a "Chosŏn revolution" in which the two were elements of a single, continuous task. When Paek Nam'un used the phrase "rapid transformation of the dual nature [of society]" in the above-mentioned quote, he was referring to this kind of revolution.

With these political tasks in mind, Paek Nam'un argued that the driving force for national liberation, which would set the future path of the nation, lay in the heightened class consciousness and organized movement of the proletarian worker and peasant masses. They were composed of groups

153. Kim Yong-sop, *Han'guk kŭnhyŏndae nong'ŏpsa yŏn'gu*, pp. 45-47, 390-91.
154. The land problem was the fundamental task of anti-feudal reforms, and Paek emphasized that "unless [it is accomplished] through a political solution, it is absolutely impossible to have a fundamental solution." This statement is another example of his thinking on these issues. Paek Nam'un, "Chosen keizai no gendankairon," p. 312.

such as poor farmers, laborers, and the "industrial reserve army."[155] On the other hand, he regarded moderate nationalists as a completely reactionary force. Their goal was not a fundamental solution to economic problems, and they advocated a course of capitalist development that subordinated the Korean economy to transplanted capitalism. However, Paek did not feel that the proletarian movement was the only force for national liberation. The nationalist bourgeoisie could also play a role in the struggle against imperialism, because conflict existed between Japanese capital and small- to medium-scale Korean capitalists and landlords and because native capital would be unable to develop under conditions of colonialism. Although his thinking later became much more factional than it had been in the 1920s, he consistently maintained his support for a united front in the nationalist movement. One clear example was his attempt in 1936 to build a united front of scholars by proposing the establishment of the Central Academy (K. Chungang ak'ademi). It was to include scholars from both the natural and the social sciences as well as the humanities.[156]

Despite these political ambitions, Paek Nam'un was not able to translate his theories or ideas on the "Chosŏn revolution" into political action. Fundamentally, the problem arose from his own political limitations as he restricted his activities to scholarly praxis. In addition, he was unable to develop a political strategy suited to his conception of society and vision of a new state. Paek seems to have disagreed with Lenin's and the Comintern's theories of colonial revolution. Commonly held by Korean socialists at the time, these theories argued that colonies should pursue a bourgeois democratic revolution that was anti-imperial and anti-feudal.[157] However, Paek was not able to establish a new Marxist perspective on democracy and the state that could articulate, in contrast to the mainstream Marxist view, a conception of anti-imperial struggle that was both anti-capitalist and anti-feudal. During the colonial period, he was unable to continue his efforts to resolve the theoretical limitations in his thinking because of his imprisonment by the Japanese in the Economic Club (Yŏnhŭi Junior College) Incident of 1938 (Yŏnhŭi

155. Paek Nam'un, "Chosŏn sahoeryŏk ŭi tongjŏk koch'al;" Paek Nam'un, "Chosen keizai no gendankairon," pp. 312, 325.

156. Paek Nam'un, "Haksul kigan pudae ŭi yangsŏng—Chung'ang ak'ademi ch'angsŏl" (The cultivation of a corps of scholarly cadres–the establishment of the Central Academy), *Tonga ilbo*, January 1, 1936. His proposal for the establishment of the Central Academy had the intention of establishing a united-front institute for researching policy that would prepare for state-building in a liberated "new Chosŏn."

157. Pang Kie-chung, *Han'guk kŭnhyŏndae sasangsa yŏn'gu*, pp. 221-23, 344-59.

kyŏngje yŏn'guhoe sagŏn).[158] It was after liberation that he resolved these problems, when he found a clue to overcoming his theoretical limitations through Mao Tse-tung's theory of "new democracy."[159]

Conclusion

Paek Nam'un was the pioneer of Marxist scholarship in Korea during the Japanese occupation, and the focus of this chapter has been on the formation of his thought, his conception of scholarship, and his theory of "understanding Chosŏn." It has also examined his understanding of the history of Korea's capitalist development and his views on contemporary Korean society and prospects for national liberation. When he studied in Japan during the early 1920s, he was influenced by socialism and Marxism. He adopted their worldview and scholarship, seeing them as an ideology that could provide a solution to Korea's colonial and socioeconomic contradictions. He began serious scholarly work in the early 1930s during the beginning of the Great Depression. His ambition was to systematize Chosŏn economic history and to promote scientific "understanding and research on Chosŏn" (*Chosŏn insik-Chosŏn yŏn'gu*) that could contribute to overcoming Korea's colonial situation.

Paek's scholarly activities had two main goals. The first was the establishment of the autonomy of scholarship; he asserted that research on Chosŏn must be done by Koreans themselves. The second was the development of a scientific "understanding of Chosŏn" that would make it possible to overcome Japanese colonial ideology and to envision the future of the nation. This scientific knowledge would reveal the contradictions of Korean society and explain the development of Korean history in accordance with universal historical laws. To accomplish these goals, he undertook an in-depth critique of the methodological limitations and the ideological nature of Japanese government scholarship. Through various kinds of institutional support, this scholarship produced a distorted knowledge of Chosŏn that was meant to justify Japan's colonial aggressions and to undermine Koreans' national

---

158. Hong Sung-Chan (Hong Sŏngch'an), "Iljeha Yŏnjŏn sangkwa ŭi kyŏngje hakp'ung kwa 'Kyŏngje yŏn'guhoe sa'gŏn'" (The intellectual atmosphere of the department of commerce at Yŏnhŭi Junior College during the colonial period and the Economic Club Incident), *Yŏnse kyŏngje yŏn'gu* 1, no. 1 (1994).

159. Pang Kie-chung, ibid., pp. 313-42.

consciousness. However, Paek rejected the views of nationalist intellectuals because of their culturalist and essentialist conceptions of the state, society, and Korea. He wanted to demonstrate that a change to Marxist epistemology was the only path to national revival.

Paek's main scholarly concern was the systematization of Korean economic history, which no scholar had yet accomplished. This chapter has focused on a related subject—Paek's theories of the internal breakdown of feudalism and of the sprouts of capitalism and his efforts to expose the predatory nature of transplanted capitalism in Chosŏn. Using positivist, statistical methods, Japanese government scholarship attempted to justify Japan's occupation of Chosŏn and the system of transplanted capitalism by claiming that they brought about Korea's "industrial revolution." As is well known, the basis of the ideology of "colonial modernization" was the stagnation theory of Korean history, which was closely tied to theories of the inferiority of Korean national character.

In this period, the majority of Korean scholars—both nationalists and Marxists—also accepted stagnation theory, as if it were an unavoidable fate, and analyzed Korea's colonial situation and its future based on its premises. Paek Nam'un's theories of the breakdown of feudalism and the sprouts of capitalism aimed to be a total refutation of the stagnation theory. Since his work only sketched the outlines of his argument, it is not surprising that he was unable to discover the specific features of the breakdown of feudalism in Korea nor the internal factors that suppressed the potential for capitalist development in Korea and led to its fall to colonial status. Nonetheless, the scholarly significance of his work on modern economic history is comparable to his contributions to pre-modern economic history.

On the basis of his historical work, Paek Nam'un defined the social formation of Korea under colonial rule as a society of transplanted capitalism completely integrated with the institutions of Japanese capitalism. He then made the following points about the nature of social contradictions in Korea. First, capitalist conflict (class contradictions) became merged with colonial conflict (contradictions between colonizer and colonized) because of the predominant influence of transplanted capitalism in colonial society. Second, the primary contradiction was located in class conflict between nations, while class conflict within a nation was a secondary contradiction.

Third, since feudal contradictions and colonial class conflict were interconnected structurally, the relation between capitalist and feudal contradictions was also inseparable. Fourth, because the growth of native capital was essentially impossible in a system of transplanted capitalism, contradictions were intensifying between transplanted capitalism and small- to medium-scale Korean capitalists and landlords. Finally, one of Paek's most important observations was that because of the nature of contradictions under colonial transplanted capitalism, the labor and peasant movements were fundamentally political in nature. That is, their struggle was part of the national liberation movement.

Paek Nam'un was unable to develop a theoretical framework that could articulate a political strategy for a future suited to the historical and social features of Korea's modernization. His political-economic goal for the nation was the achievement of a "Chosŏn revolution" that would simultaneously liberate the country from the Japanese and overcome the class contradictions rooted in the agricultural economy. It was a path of socialist development whose primary goal was to achieve an anti-imperial national liberation that would be both anti-feudal and anti-capitalist. United with socialist forces, the proletarian movement and the worker and peasant masses would be the fundamental driving force for national liberation.

Paek thought that it was necessary to create a united front against imperialism through an alliance with certain groups of bourgeois nationalists, who were supported by native capitalists. Nevertheless, he completely rejected moderate nationalists' program of capitalist modernization. Their objective was not a fundamental solution of colonial and socioeconomic contradictions; they compromised with the Japanese and asserted the possibility of the development of native capitalism. Paek's political positions and views on a scientific "understanding of Chosŏn" clearly revealed the ideological and political points of contention between the socialists and the nationalists. It is possible to see Paek Nam'un's scholarship as a demanding form of intellectual praxis whose objective was to support the political activities and the labor and peasant movements of socialist forces.

Although Paek Nam'un is just one example of a Marxist intellectual, he is central to a proper understanding of the intellectual history of the colonial period. An analysis of his work can reveal the socioeconomic background and intellectual factors behind the historical introduction of socialism and Marxist thought in Korea. It can also explain how they provided an ideology of national liberation and social revolution. In short, his scholarship was an ideological reflection of Korea's colonial and socioeconomic situation.

During the occupation period, the socialist movement, as well as the peasant and labor movements, broke with the traditions of the peasant-oriented social reform movements of the late Chosŏn and Hanmal periods and adopted socialism as the ideology of the national liberation movement. Within the context of Korean intellectual history, Paek can be seen as the successor to the Silhak tradition of peasant-oriented reform thought that emerged in the late Chosŏn period. His scholarship and thought clearly indicated the intellectual context in which Marxism, the most recently introduced foreign ideology, became a major stream of social reform thought. The other major stream of thought was the "civilization and enlightenment" (*munmyŏng kaehwa*) ideology advocated by landlords who had led top-down reforms to establish a modern nation-state in the Hanmal period. During the occupation period, it developed into a bourgeois nationalist ideology that was baptized in a "deformed" modernism under the system of transplanted capitalism. Paek's thinking also reflected the historical features of socialist and Marxist thought during its period of formation in Korea as it attempted to overcome the class limitations of bourgeois nationalist ideology.

Despite the significance and critical nature of Paek Nam'un's work, not all Marxist intellectuals and socialist activists were in agreement with his political views or his conceptions of Korean society and history. As reflected in the differentiation of Marxist views on Korea in the 1930s, disagreements arose from differences in epistemological perspectives on Marxist thought and from differences in conceptions of the colonial situation. On the other hand, disagreements were also related to their fundamental positions on Korean history and its intellectual traditions. The majority of socialists viewed Korean history as stagnant, rejected all traditional thought, held a classist view of the nation, and reduced class contradictions within the nation to an expression of colonial contradictions (thus rejecting the idea of a united front with bourgeois nationalists). In contrast, Paek emphasized the conformity of Korean history to universal laws of development, the internal foundations for the introduction of modern ideologies, and the historical features of the formation of the Korean nation as well as the merging of colonial and class contradictions. These differences in opinion were not restricted to scholarship but were related to political differences over their visions for the future of the nation. These differences became evident in the state building movements after liberation that eventually led to the division of the country that persists today.

translated by Michael D. Shin

Index of Terms

Aooka (Ch'ŏnggu) gakkai 靑丘學會 Aooka (Blue Hill) Society
Bunka seiji (J.) 文化政治 Cultural Policy
Bunka seisaku (J.) 文化政策 Cultural Policy
bunken kosho (J.) 文獻考證 textual exegesis
chabonjuŭi maeng'a hyŏngt'ae 資本主義 盲兒形態 sprout form of
  capitalism
Chajaknong ch'angjŏng kyehoek 自作農創定計劃 Plan to Establish Self-
  Cultivating Farmers
Chindan hakbo 震檀學報
Chindan hakhoe 震檀學會 Chindan Society
chŏngch'eron 停滯論 stagnation theory
Chŏng Yagyong 丁若鏞 (1762-1836; *ho* Tasan, 茶山)
Chosenshi (J.) 朝鮮史 *The History of Chosŏn*
Chosŏn haksulwŏn 朝鮮學術院 Chosŏn Academy
Chosŏnhak undong 朝鮮學運動 Chosŏn Studies Movement
Chosŏn insik 朝鮮認識 understanding Chosŏn; knowledge of Chosŏn
Chosŏn kyŏngjehoe 朝鮮經濟會 Society for Chosŏn Economics
Chosŏn kyŏngje yŏn'guso 朝鮮經濟研究所 Institute of Chosŏn Economic
  Studies
Chosŏn nongjiryŏng 朝鮮農地令 Chosŏn Agricultural Land Ordinance
  (Tenant Farmer Law)
Chosŏn ponggŏn sahoe kyŏngjesa 朝鮮封建社會經濟史 *The
  Socioeconomic History of Feudal Chosŏn*
Chosŏn sahoe kyŏngjesa 朝鮮社會經濟史 *The Socioeconomic History of
  Chosŏn*
Chosŏn sajŏng chosa yŏn'guhoe 朝鮮事情調查研究會 Institute for
  Research and Surveys on Korean Issues
Chosŏnsa p'yŏnch'anhoe 朝鮮史編纂會 Society for the Compilation of a
  History of Chosŏn
Fukuda Tokuzo 福田德三 (1874-1930)
Gakushuin Daigaku 學習院大學校 Gakushuin University
haksul ponbu ŭi ch'ammo ponyŏng 學術部隊의 參謀本營 headquarters of
  the scholarly army
Hoesaryŏng 會社令 Company Law
Hong Kimun 홍기문 (1903-1992)
isik chabonjuŭi 移植資本主義 transplanted capitalism

Kaizo 改造 Reconstruction

Kawakami Hajime 河上肇 (1879-1946)

Kihira Tadayoshi 紀平正美 (1874-1949)

Kim Kwangjin 金洸鎭 (1902-1986)

Kim T'aejun 金台俊 (1905-1949)

Kim Up'yŏng 金佑枰 (1897-1967)

Kokushi gakuha (J.) 國史學派 National History Faction

kominka 皇民化 imperial citizens

kukch'aekjŏk chagŭp chajŏng 國策的 自給自足 national autarky campaign

kungmin kyŏngjehak 國民經濟學 *Nationalökonomie*; national economics

Kŭllo inmindang 勤勞人民黨 Worker-People's Party

Kwŏn'ŏp mobŏmjang 勸業模範場 Model Farm for the Promotion of
Agriculture

kyegŭpsŏng 階級性 classness

kyŏngje sahoe kusŏng 經濟的 社會構成 economic social formations

Kyŏngsŏng (Keijo) cheguk taehakgyo 京城帝國大學校 Kyŏngsŏng
(Keijo) Imperial University

Minobe Tatsukichi 美濃部達吉 (1873-1948)

Mulsan changnyŏ undong 物産奬勵運動 Native Products Promotion
Movement

nodong chŏnsugwŏn 勞動全收權 right to the whole product of labor

nongbonjuŭi 農本主義 agrarianism

Nongch'on chinhŭng undong 農村振興運動 Rural Revitalization
Campaign

Noron 老論 Noron faction

Paek Nam'un 白南雲 (1894-1979)

pip'anjŏk ch'ŏngsangi 批判的 淸算期 period of critical cleansing

pŏpch'iksŏng 法則性 uniformity

pokgo chŏngch'aek 復古政策 policies to revive feudal institutions

Sin'ganhoe 新幹會

Sinmindang 新民黨 New People's Party

sin minjujuŭi 新民主主義 new democracy

Sin Namch'ŏl 申南澈 (1907-?)

Sŏ Ch'un 徐椿 (1894-1944)

Suwŏn nongnim hakgyo 水原農林學校 Suwŏn Agricultural and Forestry
School

Takata Yasuma 高田保馬 (1883-1972)

Tangmyŏn iik hoekdŭk undong 當面利益獲得運動 Immediate Benefit
Movement

Tan'gun Chosŏn 檀君朝鮮

Tokyo kodo shogyo gakko 東京高等商業學校 Tokyo Higher
Commercial School

Tokyo shoka daigakko 東京商科大學校 Tokyo Commercial College

t'ongje kyŏngje 計劃經濟 control economy

t'ŭkhŏ chedo 特許制度 permit system

Ueda Teijiro 上田貞次郎 (1879-1940)

Yamamoto Sanehiko 山本實彦 (1885-1952)

Yi Kŭngjong 李肯鐘 (b. 1898)

Yi Yŏsŏng 李如星 (b. 1900)

yŏjŏnbŏp 閭田法 village-land system

yŏksasŏng 歷史性 historicity

Yŏnhŭi chŏnmun hakgyo 延禧專門學校 Yŏnhŭi Junior College

Yŏnhŭi kyŏngje yŏn'guhoe sagŏn 延禧經濟研究會事件 Economic Club
Incident

yosegijaiku teki (J.) 寄木細工的 混血形態 mosaic mixture

CHAPTER 8

An Chaehŏng's Thought and the Politics of the United Front

Lee Ji-won
李智媛

The problems that emerged in the course of Korea's modern history brought about complex ideological responses. No matter what form they took, these ideologies all sought to provide concrete solutions to contemporary problems because it was crucial in this period to undertake reform of feudalism and engage in resistance against imperialism. Moreover, they were also concerned with achieving national liberation during the occupation period and with establishing the fundamental framework for state building after liberation. Thus, it is important to examine Korea's intellectual and political history from the occupation period to the post-liberation era in order to gain a comprehensive understanding of modern Korean history and of the underlying factors behind the formation of divided states after 1945.

The objective of this chapter is to examine the thought of An Chaehŏng (*ho* Minse, 1891-1965), a bourgeois nationalist who led movements promoting class cooperation both during the occupation period and after liberation. He began his education in the Hanmal period during the time of self-strengthening movements (*chagang undong*) and entered the middle school of the Hwangsŏng Christian Youth Society, the precursor to the YMCA, in 1907. His father, An Yunsŏp, had a considerable influence on him as a youth. An Yunsŏp was a reader of the *Hwangsŏng sinmun* and the *Tongnip sinmun* and was very interested in new Western ideas. In fact, An Chaehŏng enrolled in that middle school because his father had told him, "since all the high-minded figures are gathered in the Independence Club after its movement began, you should go there and learn its celebrated thought and scholarship." During his three years in middle school, he received instruction from leaders of the Independence Club such as Yun Ch'iho, Yi Sangjae, and Namgung Ŏk. Through his early education and exposure to politics, he learned about the theories of self-strengthening that were popular at the time.[1] After completing middle school, he entered the Department of Political Economy at Waseda University in Japan, graduating in 1914.

In the 1920s, bourgeois nationalists split into two factions: "moderate" or "right wing" nationalists, on the one hand, and "radical" or "left wing" nationalists, on the other.[2] The former group represented the interests of large landlords and subordinate national capitalists and generally sought a political compromise with the Japanese through efforts such as the self-rule movement and the *sillyŏk yangsŏng* (cultivation of abilities) movement. The latter represented peasants, workers, and small-to-medium landlords and capitalists who advocated class cooperation and engaged in political struggle, unwilling to compromise with the Japanese. An Chehong rose to prominence as one of the leaders of the radical nationalists. He was a central figure in journalism through his position at the *Chosŏn ilbo*, and he was one of the leaders in the formation of the Sin'ganhoe in an effort to create a united front with socialist forces.

When moderate nationalists grew in strength and pushed for self-rule in the 1920s, nationalists who opposed self-rule called for uncompromising resistance against the Japanese. These leftist nationalists and socialists wanted to go beyond moderate social reform efforts that essentially operated within the scope of Japanese policies. Their goal was to establish an anti-Japanese front in order to expand the mass base of the national liberation movement. Both socialist and nationalist forces made concrete efforts to create such a front in 1926, resulting in the formation of the Sin'ganhoe in February 1927. The main office of the Sin'ganhoe was located in Seoul, and it established 120-150 branches throughout the country with a membership that varied between twenty to forty thousand. Although it could not operate freely because of Japanese interference, the leaders of the central office organized activities for the masses such as lecture tours in the provinces and support for labor strikes,

1. An Chaehong later recalled that he himself was proud to be a student at that middle school. See An Chaehong, "Haksaeng sidae ŭi hoego" (Recollections of my student days), *Sin Tonga* (April 1935); An Chaehong, "Pit'ong!—Choguk ŭi pokmol" (Bitter sadness! the fall of our fatherland), *Sin ch'ŏnji* (August 1946).

2. The precise differences between the two in terms of class and social base will become clearer as more case studies are done, but it is already evident that this distinction provides a useful way of understanding the various ideological trends of modern Korean history—as well as the various conceptions of the state.

tenant disputes, and student protests through local branches. The Sin'ganhoe, which was dissolved in May 1931, was the largest anti-Japanese social organization during the occupation period, and it was the progenitor of united front movements of the left and the right in modern Korean history.

When the Japanese reduced the scope of legally permitted activities in the 1930s and made it impossible to engage in political organizing, An Chaehong shifted his focus to a culture movement that called for the preservation of national culture and heritage. He also became a central leader of the Chosŏn Studies Movement (Chosŏnhak undong). These movements, along with the work of socialist intellectuals, led to the growth of scholarly and intellectual movements in the 1930s. They also laid the foundation for the nationalist historiography that further developed the pioneering work of Pak Ŭnsik and Sin Ch'aeho as well as for the "neo-nationalist' historiography that emerged after liberation.

Immediately after liberation, An Chaehong worked with Yŏ Unhyŏng to organize the Committee for the Preparation of Korean Independence (Chosŏn kŏnguk chunbi wiwŏnhoe, CPKI), serving as its vice-chair. But he soon left the organization in protest of the growing dominance of the left. Shortly afterwards, he published a book, *Neo-Nationalism and Neo-Democracy (Sin minjokjuŭi sin minjujuŭi*, 1945) in which he advocated building a state through class cooperation—but based on nationalism. Even after liberation, he maintained a moderately rightist position from which he tried to build ties to other groups, including socialists. Because of his political and ideological views, he was able to serve as a member of the Emergency National Council (Pisang Kungmin Hoeŭi), as a representative from the right on the Left-Right Coordinating Committee (Chwau Hapjak Wiwŏnhoe), and as the Chief Civil Administra-tor (*Minjŏng changgwan*) for the American military government. When separate governments were established in the North and the South, moderate forces advocating class cooperation could no longer survive as an independent political force. From 1948, An operated on the fringes of the Syngman Rhee administration, working on educational activities. In the second National Assembly election in May 1950, he was elected as an independent from P'yŏngt'aek *ku* in Seoul. After the outbreak of the Korean War in June, he was kidnapped and brought to the North. He served as the chair of the Council for the Promotion of Peaceful Reunification during the 1950s and died in Pyongyang in 1965.[3]

3. On the life of An Chaehong, see Ch'ŏn Kwan'u, "Minse An Chaehong yŏnbo" (A chronology of the life of An Chaehong), *Minse An Chaehong sŏnjip 4* (Seoul: Chisik sanŏpsa,

Research on An Chaehong is of more than just biographical interest. An examination of his thought and career would also be useful in achieving a systematic understanding of the ideology and politics of national liberation and state building in modern Korean history. However, few serious studies have been done on moderates such as An up to now, mainly because of the political situation in Korea in which neither the North nor the South have favorable views of moderates. Research on An began cautiously in the late 1970s, but these studies tended to have a narrow focus, treating only a particular area of his career.[4] In order to understand his thought as a response to the development of modern Korean history, it is necessary to undertake a close examination of his views on state building and on social and political movements from the occupation period.

As a preliminary step to undertaking this project, this study attempts to analyze An Chaehong's conceptions of society and of the national liberation movement during the Japanese occupation period. This study is part of the broader effort to understand the full spectrum of bourgeois nationalist thought whose objective was the establishment of a modern capitalist state. More specifically, it is an effort to discover the intellectual foundations of the views on political economy and political movements of the radical nationalist groups that participated in the united front led by the Sin'ganhoe in the latter half of the 1920s. Furthermore, it is hoped that this study will be helpful in illuminating the conceptions of national liberation and of the state held by

1980); Lee Ji-won (Yi Chiwŏn), "An Chaehongnon" (A study of An Chaehong), *Singminji sidae chisikin kwa minjok haebang undong* (Hanguk yŏksa yŏn'guhoe haksul tae t'oronhoe palp'yomun, 1991).

4. For studies on An Chaehong's thought and activities, see: Kim Yong-sop (Kim Yongsŏp), "Urinara kŭndae yŏksahak ŭi paltal" (The Development of Modern History in Korea), *Munhak kwa chisŏng* (summer 1971); Yi Chŏngsik, "Kusŏng Minse An Chaehong ŭi chasŏjŏn" (The oral autobiography of An Chaehong), *Sin Tonga* (November 1976); Song Kŏnho, "An Chaehong," *Han'guk hyŏndae inmulsaron* (Seoul: Han'gilsa, 1984); Chŏng Yunjae, "An Chaehong ŭi sin minjujuŭi yŏn'gu" (An examination of the neo-democracy of An Chaehong), *Han'guk hyŏndae sahoe wa sasang* (Seoul; Chisik sanŏpsa, 1984); Yu Pyŏng'yong, "An Chaehong ŭi chŏngch'i sasang e kwanhan chae kŏmt'o" (A reexamination of the political thought of An Chaehong), *Han'guk minjok undongsa yŏn'gu*, no. 1 (1986); Kang Yŏngch'ŏl, "Minse An Chaehong," *Han'guk hyŏndae inmulnon 1* (Seoul: Ŭryu munhwasa, 1987); Han Yŏng'u, "An Chaehong ŭi sin minjokjuŭi wa sahak" (The neo nationalism and historiography of An Chaehong), *Han'guk tongnip undongsa yŏn'gu*, no. 1 (1987). Lee Ji-won, "An Chaehong," *Han'guk ŭi yŏksaga wa yŏksahak, ha* (Seoul: Ch'angjak kwa pip'yŏngsa, 1994).

bourgeois nationalists, as well as the internal differences among them,[5] during the occupation and the liberation periods.

In order to examine these aspects more concretely, this study is divided into three sections. The first section examines a topic that has not been covered in existing research on An Chaehong, focusing on his views on the economy and his theory of a national economy (*minjok kyŏngje*). These aspects provide the key to understanding his conception of bourgeois modernization. The second section analyzes An's views of Korea's colonial situation and of world affairs which constitute the subjective and objective factors underlying his nationalism. Finally, the third section discusses his views on the national liberation movement which developed out of his conception of society and his nationalism.

5. Previous studies have not paid much attention to the internal differences and splits in the bourgeois nationalist movements. One factor is that scholars have tended to see the bourgeois nationalist movement as the sole movement of the time, assuming that the task of the nationalist movement during the occupation period was (bourgeois) modernization. See Cho Kijun, "Chosŏn mulsan changnyŏ undong ŭi chŏn'gae kwajŏng kwa kŭ yŏksajŏk sŏnggyŏk" (The development and historical character of the Native Products Promotion Movement), *Yŏksa hakbo*, no. 41 (1969); Yi Hyŏnhŭi, "1920 nyŏndae kungnae minjokjuŭi yŏn'gu" (An examination of domestic nationalism in the 1920s), *Paeksan hakbo*, no. 20 (1975); Pak, Yong'ok, "Minjokjuŭi undong ŭi sae tan'gye" (The new stage of nationalist movements), *Han'guksa* 22 (Kuksa p'yŏnch'an wiwŏnhoe, 1984). On the other hand, there has also been a tendency to view the bourgeois nationalist movement simply as the preliminary stage of the socialist movement or to focus on its moderate elements and the weakness of the class base of bourgeois nationalism, again leading some scholars to ignore the internal differences. See Kajimura Hideki, "Minzoku sihon to reizoku sihon 2" (National capital and dependent capital 2), *Chosen ni okeru sihonshugi no keisei to tenkai* (1977); Kang Tongjin, *Ilche ŭi Han'guk ch'imnyak chŏngch'aeksa* (The history of Japan's policies to take over Korea) (Seoul: Han'gilsa, 1980); So Chungsŏk, "Hanmal Ilche ch'imnyakha ŭi chabonjuŭi kŭndaehwaron ŭi sŏnggyŏk" (The characteristics of theories of capitalist modernization theory during the Hanmal and occupation periods), *Han'guk kŭnhyŏndae minjok munje yŏn'gu* (Seoul: Chisik sanŏpsa, 1989); as studies by North Korean scholars. Recently, there have been some efforts that have focused on and attempted to explain the differing class bases or ideological development of groups within the bourgeois nationalists. See Sin Ilch'ŏl, "Han'guk tongnip undong ŭi sasangsajŏk sŏnggyŏk" (The characteristics of the Korean independence movement in the context of the history of thought), *Asea yŏn'gu* 21-11 (1978); Naraki Chijin, "Shokuminchiki minzoku undo no kindaikan" (The conception of modernity of the nationalist movement during the colonial period), *Chosenshi kenkyukai ronbunshu* 26 (1989); Pak Ch'ansŭng, *Han'guk kŭndae chŏngch'isa yŏn'gu* (Studies on the history of modern Korean political thought) (Seoul, Yŏksa pip'yŏngsa, 1992); Yun Haedong, "Ilcheha mulsan changryŏ undong ŭi paekyŏng kwa kŭ inyŏm" (The background and ideology of the Native Products Promotion Movement during the occupation period, *Han'guk saron* 27 (1992); Kim Yong-sop, "Ilche kangjŏmgi nong'ŏp munje wa kŭ t'agae pang'an" (Problems in the agricultural economy and their solutions during the Japa-nese occupation period), *Han'guk kŭnhyŏndae nong'ŏpsa yŏn'gu* (Seoul, Ilchogak 1992).

An Chaehong's Views on the Colonial Economy

PEASANT-ORIENTED VIEW OF AGRICULTURAL ISSUES

In An Chaehong's view, agriculture, in which approximately 80 percent of the masses were engaged, determined the quality of life of the people. After Chosŏn became a colony of Japan, the Chosŏn economy was fundamentally under the dominance of capitalist economic institutions.[6] He felt that the situation of agriculture under Japanese rule threatened the survival of the Chosŏn people because the agricultural system now transferred the brunt of the economic contradictions of Japanese capitalism to the colony. He saw the situation as the result of a national conflict between an empire and its colony.

Japan prepared the legal and institutional foundations for its exploitation of Korea through the cadastral survey of the 1910s. In the 1920s, it implemented exploitative agricultural policies that accelerated both land accumulation by capitalist organizations and the decline of the Chosŏn peasantry. An Chaehong observed the decline and impoverishment of the peasantry and thought that the fundamental cause lay in the Program to Increase Rice Production (Sanmi chŭngsik kyehoek, PIRP) through which Japanese imperialism tried to use the colony to solve the problems of over-population and a diminishing food supply.[7] With the objective of enabling Japan to exploit even greater quantities of rice, the PIRP was a state-led effort to bring about a drastic increase in rice production through the forced implementation of land improvements, irrigation projects, and new seed varieties.[8]

An Chaehong felt that the Chosŏn peasantry was falling into poverty and starvation because the outflow of rice caused by the PIRP was so great that the very existence of the peasantry was endangered.[9] The devastation of the Chosŏn people were thus not a natural disaster but a human one, and he described their situation as the "rock below the water [*amch'o*] contained in

---

6. An Chaehong, "Nongmindo ŭi kojo" (Elevating the way of the peasantry), *Chosŏn ilbo*, December 5, 1926.

7. An Chaehong, "Ilbon imin changnyŏ munje" (The problems with encouraging Japanese immigration), *Chosŏn ilbo*, May 13, 1927.

8. Hori Kazuo, "Nihon teikokushugi ni okeru nogyo seisaku" (The agricultural policies of Japanese imperialism), *Nihonshi kenkyu* 171 (1976); Kawai Kazuo, *Chosen ni okeru sanmai zoshoku keikaku* (The plan to increase rice production in Chosŏn) (Tokyo: Miraisha, 1986).

9. An Chaehong, "Kigŭn taech'aegŭn yŏha" (What is the solution to famine?), *Chosŏn ilbo*, September 22, 1924.

Japan's colonial policy."[10] It was hardly unusual for an imperial country to cause the devastation of the colonial agriculture in order to solve its population and food supply problems—as England had done in Ireland and Turkey had done in Greece.[11] But he emphasized that these policies could become the cause of tremendous social catastrophe from both a national and a class perspective.[12]

The fundamental causes of the impoverishment of Chosŏn agriculture were rooted in the land accumulation by Japanese state capital (i.e., the Ministry of Finance) and finance capital (e.g., the Oriental Development Company, the Industrial Bank of Chosŏn). As a result of the PIRP, Japanese and Japanese capital "moved into [Chosŏn] through the support of the state and the machinations of quasi-governmental companies, . . . drove out landless tenants from fertile farmland in all regions, and bought up the land owned by small landlords and owner-cultivators."[13] "Like agricultural overseers [*marŭm*], [they] assigned tenancy rights to Chosŏn peasants and did nothing but collect tenancy fees;" consequently, things reached the point where the land of Chosŏn could no longer feed its people.[14] In a situation where close to half of the agricultural population had already become landless and impoverished tenants, agricultural immigration from Japan and land accumulation simply led to the further decline of the Chosŏn peasantry and an aggravation of tenancy problems. In order to protect the livelihood of Chosŏn tenant farmers, it became necessary to oppose agricultural immigration from Japan and the practices of Japanese agricultural enterprises,[15] and agricultural tenancy became the most pressing social issue of the time.[16]

More specifically, the tenancy problem resulted from the practices of both Chosŏn landlords who depended on the support of the Japanese ruling authorities and quasi-governmental companies that were backed by the state. Therefore, tenancy was simultaneously an economic and class issue concerning the livelihood of farmers and a political issue involving resistance against Japanese imperialism. An Chaehong made his views on the tenancy issue

10. "Ilbon imin changnyŏ munje."

11. "Kigŭn taech'aegŭn yŏha."

12. "Ilbon imin changnyŏ munje."

13. Ibid.

14. An Chaehong, "Mosundoenŭn imin changnyŏ kyehoek" (The contradictions of the plan to encourage Japanese immigration), *Chosŏn ilbo*, August 16, 1929.

15. See footnote 9.

16. An Chaehong, "Chindo sagŏn e taehayŏ" (On the Chindo Incident), *Chosŏn ilbo*, December 7, 1924.

clear in his comments on a tenancy dispute in 1924-25 organized by residents of Chindo county against the Oriental Development Company (Tongyang ch'ŏksik chusik hoesa, ODC) and the Hŭng'ŏp Company (Chosŏn Hŭng'ŏp chusik hoesa).

In Chindo, the Hŭng'ŏp Company had begun to buy up land and operate *nongjang* from 1908, and during the occupation period, individual landlords and *nongjang* run by Japanese companies, such as the Hŭng'ŏp Company, owned over 40 percent of the tenant land in the region.[17] The Japanese landlords not only collected tenancy fees that amounted to 80 percent of the harvest but also imposed the "five-person" system to control their tenants by organizing them into groups of five.[18] In 1924-25, the peasants of Chindo organized a large-scale dispute under the leadership of their tenants' association (*sojakinhoe*). Adopting a more confrontational attitude toward the combined forces of the landlords' association and the colonial authorities, they demanded a reduction of tenancy fees and ultimately sought to bring about a "farmland revolution."[19]

In his commentary on the Chindo tenancy dispute, An Chaehong pointed out the harmful effects of the irrational relationship between landlords and tenants—out of concern for safeguarding the livelihood of the tenant farmers. He deemed the resistance of the tenants to be a legitimate way to solve these problems.[20] In order to improve the dire situation of the tenant farmers, he advocated the abolition of land accumulation by finance capital and speculative capital which served as the "special forces [*t'ŭksu pudae*] of capitalism."[21] In particular, the ODC was a presence that "was intent on sucking the sweat and blood of the white-clothed peasantry [*paekŭi nongmin*] under the banner of the state"[22] and was "incompatible with the

17. Yi Chongbŏm, "1920-30 nyŏndae Chindo chibang ŭi nongch'on sajŏng kwa nongmin chohap undong" (The situation of rural villages and the agricultural cooperative movement in the Chindo region in the 1920s and 1930s), *Yŏksa hakbo*, no. 109 (1989), pp. 65-66.

18. Asada Kyoji, *Nihon teikokushugi to kyushokuminchi jinushisei* (Japanese imperialism and the landlord system in the former colonies) (Tokyo: Ochanomizu shobo, 1968), pp. 161-63.

19. Yamato Kazuaki, "Chosen nomin undo no tenkanten" (The turning point of the Chosŏn peasant movement), *Rekishi hyoron*, no. 413 (1984).

20. "Chindo sagŏn e taehayŏ."

21. An Chaehong, "Nongch'on ŭn ŏdero—hyŏpdong chojap i kajang p'iryo" (Where is rural society headed?—cooperatives are the most necessary), *Tonggwang*, no. 20 (April 1931), p. 582.

22. An Chaehong, "Tasi Tongch'ŏge taehaya" (Another examination of the Oriental Development Company), *Chosŏn ilbo*, November 12, 1924; An Chaehong, "Tongch'ŏk ŭn muŏsinya" (What is the Oriental Development Company?), *Chosŏn ilbo*, February 9, 1925. White clothes were a symbol of the Chosŏn people.

happiness of the Chosŏn masses."[23] He advocated dismantling the Oriental Development Company and distributing its land to tenant farmers and small owner-cultivators for free or for a fee to facilitate the transformation of tenant farmers into owner-cultivators.[24] With the objective of ameliorating the poverty of the peasantry, his proposals called for a fundamental reform of agriculture that would benefit the peasantry, opposing the agricultural policies of the Japanese that served the interests of the landlords and capitalists.

Thinking of Chosŏn's national interest, An Chaehong opposed land accumulation and the establishment of large-scale agricultural enterprises by the institutions of Japanese capitalism. But on agricultural issues internal to Chosŏn, he supported the maintenance of a landlord system based on small-to-medium landlords. In other words, he favored a landlord system that maintained a fair and equitable relationship between landlords and tenants based on the resolution of problems such as the protection of tenants' rights, landlords' assumption of land taxes, an equitable distribution of land and the harvest, and the prevention of immigration by Japanese farmers.[25] In order to protect the interests of small and medium landlords, he advocated using a fair rate for tenancy fees to enable an equitable distribution of the harvest between landlords and tenants.[26] In An's view, while Japan's agricultural policies enabled large landlords to develop by giving them access to Japanese capital and political resources, they also brought about the decline of small and medium landlords as well as of tenant farmers.[27] His position represented a compromise that aimed both to provide tenant farmers with the stability they needed to engage in agriculture and to enable the economic improvement of small and medium landlords by reforming the irrational customs of the landlord-tenant relationship.[28]

23. "Tasi Tongch'ŏge taehaya."
24. "Tongch'ŏk ŭn muŏsinya."
25. "Tasi Tongch'ŏge taehaya"; "Chindo sagŏn e taehayŏ"; An Chaehong, "Tanggukja ege yŏham" (To the authorities), *Chosŏn ilbo*, December 8, 1924; An Chaehong, "Silje undong ŭi tangmyŏn munje" (The immediate tasks of practical movements), *Chosŏn ilbo*, March 27, 1928; An Chaehong, "Hyŏnha Chosŏn nongmin ŭi sam tae kin'gŭpch'aek" (Solutions to the three most urgent problems faced by Chosŏn peasants today), *Nongmin* 1, no. 2 (June 1930); "Nongch'on ŭn ŏdero" (Where is rural society headed?).
26. An Chaehong, "Hyŏnha Chosŏn nongmin ŭi sam tae kin'gŭpch'aek," p. 13.
27. See footnotes 9, 16, and 22.
28. Similarly, among the editorials of *Chosŏn ilbo*, there were many proposals for reform of the cultivation system that reflected the needs of the peasantry and advocated rectifying the irrational elements of the landlord-tenant system. See "Nong'ŏp chŏngch'aek kwa sojak chedo" (Agricultural policies and the tenancy system), *Chosŏn ilbo*, January 13-15, 1925; "Chosŏn nongmin undong ŭi chŏngch'ijŏk kyŏnghyang" (The political tendencies of the Chosŏn peasant

As supplementary measures to give relief to the peasantry, An Chaehong advocated increasing agricultural production and establishing cooperative unions (*hyŏpdong chohap*).[29] To increase production, he emphasized the implementation of improvements in agricultural technology, the encouragement of secondary occupations, and crop diversification.[30] In this period, cooperatives were generally viewed as commercial unions in which peasants would collectively handle sales, purchases, and credit, and potentially, they would enable bankrupt farmers to become owner-cultivators again and impoverished agricultural communities to regain prosperity.[31] At the time, the cooperative movement was a topic of debate among nationalist intellectuals since, if utilized well, cooperatives could serve as a way for small capitalists and producers to withstand competition from large capitalists and producers.

An touted cooperatives as "communities of consumers and producers that could protect and promote [the interests] of consumers from the exploitation of various commercial middlemen."[32] Focusing on the establishment of consumer cooperatives, he envisioned a cooperative movement that could grow to the point where it could solve the financial problems of the countryside. He felt that they could provide an alternative to the credit unions that served as the instruments of Japan's financial penetration of rural society.[33] In

---

movement), *Chosŏn ilbo*, March 24-26, 1925; "Nongch'on ŭi wigi e daehan kuch'ichaek ŭi ilmyŏn ŭl simham" (Considering one aspect of the plan to relieve the crisis in rural society), *Chosŏn ilbo*, August 31, 1925. These proposals contained almost the same ideas as the ones that An Chaehong advocated in his other writings: protection of tenancy rights, assumption of the land tax by landlords, equitable distribution of the harvest, and the prevention of agricultural immigration from Japan. These editorials are good examples of the *Chosŏn ilbo*'s position as the spokesperson for the interests of small and medium landlords and capitalists.

29. "Hyŏnha Chosŏn nongmin ŭi sam tae kin'gŭpch'aek"; "Nongch'on ŭn ŏdero—hyŏpdong chohap i kajang p'iryo"; "Silje undong ŭi tangmyŏn munje."

30. Ibid.

31. Kim Tonghyŏk, "Nongch'on tangmyŏn munje rosso ŭi nongmin chohap" (Farmers' cooperatives as an imminent task of rural society), *Chosŏn chi gwang*, no. 77 (March-April 1928); K S, "Chosŏn ŭi nongch'on kwa sanŏp chohap" (Rural society and Industrial cooperatives in Chosŏn), *Sinmin*, no. 50 (June 1929); Yi P'ungjae, "Chosŏn nong'ŏp kyŏngje e kwanhan hyŏnjae sanghwang kwa changrae taech'aek" (The current situation and plans for the future of the Chosŏn agricultural economy), *Sinhŭng sidae*, no. 1 (April 1931); Ham Sanghun, "Hyŏpdong chohap undong e taehaya" (On the cooperative union movement), *Pyŏlgŏn'gon* 5, no. 7 (August 1930); Ham Sanghun, "Hyŏpdong chohap ŭi chojik kwa silche pangbŏp" (The organization and actual methods of cooperatives), *Hyesŏng*, no. 1 (January 1932); Yun Chonghwa, "Nongch'on ŭi p'ip'ye wa kŭ taech'aek ŭl nonham" (A discussion on the impoverishment of rural society and its solutions), *Tonga ilbo*, December 7-19, 1932.

32. "Silje undong ŭi tangmyŏn munje."

33. "Hyŏnha Chosŏn nongmin ŭi sam tae kin'gŭpch'aek," p. 14.

other words, since rural credit unions provided hardly any assistance to the general peasantry, he sought to establish independent cooperatives that would mainly function as consumer cooperatives. Even though these cooperatives were not as developed as producer cooperatives, An thought that it was necessary to support and organize the peasant class in order to enable small and medium farmers to survive and compete against capitalists and large landlords.[34]

In sum, An Chaehong's understanding of problems in the agricultural economy and his proposed solutions were not very elaborate or detailed. The basic premise behind his ideas was that the general condition of the Chosŏn peasantry was in decline because of the agricultural policies of the Japanese which were fundamentally designed to serve the needs of Japanese capitalism. The major problems facing the agricultural economy were the expansion of the landlord system as one of the foundations of Japanese capitalism and the decline of Chosŏn tenant farmers, owner-cultivators, and small and medium landlords. His proposed solutions focused on a reform of Japan's agricultural policies, the improvement of relations between landlords and tenant farmers, an increase in agricultural production, and a cooperative movement.

PROMOTION OF NATIONAL CAPITAL AND THE NATIONAL ECONOMY

In the transition from a feudal to a modern society, the feudal economic structure is inevitably destroyed, and capitalist relations develop. Just as this transition was gaining momentum in Chosŏn, the intrusions of the foreign powers blocked its autonomous development.[35] In An Chaehong's view, the

34. Yi Sunt'ak, "Chosŏn kwa nong'ŏp" (Chosŏn and agriculture), *Tonga ilbo*, October 23–November 11, 1921; Min Pyŏngdŏk, "Nongch'on ŭi chorak kwa tangmyŏn kwaje" (The decline of rural society and its immediate problems), *Chosŏn chi kwang*, no. 75 (January 1928); Yi Sunt'ak, "Nongch'on chohap kwa yŏndae ch'aegim" (Rural cooperatives and collective responsibility), *Tonggwang*, no. 20 (April 1931).

There were two different positions on cooperative unions in this period. The most common position felt that cooperatives or industrial unions (*san'ŏp chohap*) meant the establishment of consumer cooperatives. Advocates of the second position attempted to transform efforts into a producer cooperative movement. The second can be said to focus on capitalist cooperatives, and the second on socialist cooperatives. See Kim Yong-sop, "Ilche kangjŏmgi nong'ŏp munje wa kŭ t'agae pang'an" (Problems in the agricultural economy and their solutions during the Japanese occupation period).

35. An Chaehong, "Haebang chŏnsŏn ŭl pugam hamyŏnsŏ" (Taking a bird's eye view of the liberation front), *Chosŏn ilbo*, March 1, 1925; "Chŏltaehan sinsaeng ŭi chint'ong" (The absolute pain of a new birth), *Chosŏn ilbo*, May 18, 1935 (reprinted in *Minse An Chaehong sŏnjip* 1 (The selected works of An Chaehong, Vol. 1), pp. 501-04).

economic institutions of Japan were undermining Korea's commerce and manufacturing and obstructing their transition to capitalism.[36]

What was necessary to overcome Chosŏn's dire situation was an increase in productivity which would, as a historical inevitability, bring about the leap to a capitalist economy.[37] An Chaehong believed that the historical tasks facing Chosŏn had to be resolved through the autonomous development of a national (capitalist) economy that could compete with the foreign capital of the imperialist powers. He emphasized that to survive among the large-scale industries of Japanese capitalism, it was necessary to develop independent Chosŏn capital and to promote industry through the small-scale manufacturing and cottage industries of the small and medium capitalists of Chosŏn.[38]

It is clear that the Chosŏn people have the ability to engage in small-scale manufacturing. Textiles, ceramics, and chemicals are industries that have the potential to be developed by the hands of the Chosŏn people. Among the chemical industries, [the production of] daily necessities and food products do not, relatively speaking, require large-scale capital and can be sufficiently developed through small-scale companies. For these industries, the best approach that is most suited for these times is to forgo quick success and to achieve results step by step.[39]

In other words, An advocated the development of national capital in the manufacturing industries—textiles, ceramics, and chemicals—in which Chosŏn had a competitive advantage within the overall industrial structure.[40] In a

36. An Chaehong, "Paengnyŏn taegye wa mokchŏn munje" (The grand 100-year plan and immediate problems), *Chosŏn ilbo*, August 25, 1926.

37. An Chaehong, "Paeg'yŏl, kŭrŏna ŏmsukhan pandong ŭi ch'oejung ŭi sin ilnyŏn" (Climax: but a new year in the midst of stern reaction), *Chosŏn ilbo*, January 1, 1926. From early on, An Chaehong had shown interest in promoting capitalist development, and after coming back from Japan in 1914, he participated in the Chosŏn sanjik changnyŏ kye, which was formed with the purpose of promoting the development of Chosŏn national capital through economic self-reliance. See also footnote 85.

38. In the 1920s, most of the industrial enterprises in Chosŏn were very small-scale manufacturing companies that still depended on handicraft technology. Chŏn Sŏkdam and Ch'oe Yun'gyu, "19 segi huban'gi-Ilche t'ongch'i malgi ŭi Chosŏn sahoe kyŏngjesa" (The socioeconomic history of Chosŏn from the late nineteenth century to the end of Japanese rule) (Seoul: Isŏng kwa hyŏnsilsa, 1989), pp. 153-55.

39. "Paengnyŏn taegye wa mokchŏn munje."

40. In the 1920s, the condition of Chosŏn factories and industries was very low compared to those of the Japanese, but among them, dyeing and weaving, paper, and chemicals were industries in which Chosŏn industrial producers had a comparative advantage. Yun Haedong, ibid., section 1, part 1.

situation in which "it is impossible for the native, national bourgeois class to experience significant growth under foreign capitalism,"[41] he envisioned the growth of the existing productive classes in Chosŏn through the promotion of native products such as hemp cloth, ramie cloth, silk, paper products, wool, and bamboo goods.[42]

An Chaehong's ideas on the national economy constituted one of the guiding theories of the Native Products Promotion Movement of the 1920s. He became a director of the Native Products Promotion Society in April 1924,[43] and one of his objectives was to provide an alternative to the model of economic development through the growth of large-scale manufacturing.[44] By contrast, the *Tonga ilbo* strongly advocated the pursuit of modern civilization through the development of capitalist industry—as a means of increasing production. While An agreed on the need to raise productivity, he felt that the material development of capitalism would also have to involve the maintenance of the economic livelihood of Chosŏn and the preservation of the autonomy of the national economy. Otherwise, in his view, the pursuit of a purely material capitalist modernization would result in the subordination of the Chosŏn economy to Japan. If the "national bourgeoisie," whose growth was limited in a colony, wanted to maintain an autonomous existence and to avoid subordination to the Japanese, it would be necessary to cooperate and build alliances with other classes.[45] In particular, it would be necessary to create a base for mass support among the peasants and laborers who were not yet subordinated under the Japanese economy, and the Native Products Promotion Movement had the potential to become an economic movement in which such a mass base could facilitate inter-class cooperation.

Until the early 1930s, An Chaehong mainly focused on realizing his ideas on developing small and medium capitalists and preserving the national

---

41. An Chaehong, "Kiroe sŏn Sin'ganhoe" (The Sin'ganhhoe at the crossroads), *Chosŏn ilbo*, May 16, 1931.

42. "Paengnyŏn taegye wa mokchŏn munje."

43. "Chosŏn mulsan changnyŏhoe che 2 ch'a chŏnggi ch'onghoe hoerok" (The minutes of the second regular general meeting of the Native Products Promotion Society), *Sanŏpgye*, no. 4 (June 1924), p. 68.

44. For more on the two competing theories within the Native Products Promotion Movement, see the article by Yun Haedong mentioned above.

45. Based on this perspective, An Chaehong felt that an ideal situation was the united front between the Kuomintang and the communists in China through which merchants and industrialists, who were fundamentally anti-Japanese national capitalists, joined forces with like-minded landlords. An Chaehong, "T'ongil nan kwa t'ongil ŭi ŏryŏum" (The challenges of unification and the difficulty of unification), *Chosŏn ilbo*, June 30, 1929.

economy through the Native Products Promotion Movement. In the first half of the 1920s, the Native Products Promotion Society had been very active, but by the end of the decade, it was virtually defunct. In 1931, it built a new headquarters behind Pagoda Park (Tapgol Kongwŏn) and started publishing a journal, *Changsan*, to stimulate a revival of the movement.[46] While he pushed for its continuation, he emphasized that the movement, which had focused on the abstract ideas of the educated classes, should become more of a mass movement devoted to increasing production and to promoting the use of native Chosŏn products.[47]

Though An saw small-scale factories and industries as the basis of national capital and encouraged their development, they increasingly fell into decline after the Manchurian incident in 1931. Japan established an economic bloc linking Japan to Chosŏn, Manchuria, and Taiwan, and the penetration of Japanese capital and commodities into these areas occurred at an even greater scale.[48] In the process, the conditions for the autonomous development of Chosŏn manufacturing grew worse. Even under these conditions, An continued to stress the autonomy of a Chosŏn economy that could compete with the industrial economy of Japanese imperialism.[49] "Even though the impetus for industrialization was coming from outside," he felt that "there were aspects to Chosŏn industry that required progress from an autonomous position and that could not be undermined by Japanese capitalism since it was a part of existing real life."[50] Demonstrating the strength of his conviction in the importance of the national economy, he noted that even if national capital becomes weak, "it is no reason to reject it as the basis of the nation."[51]

An Chaehong's views on the national economy were deeply rooted in his conception of modernity which emphasized the potential for autonomous development within the nation during the process of capitalist modernization. He was aware of the difficulties of capitalist modernization under imperial

46. Yi Chongrin, "Sinnyŏnsa" (Comments on the new year), *Changsan* 2-1 (January 1931), p. 2.

47. An Chaehong, "Mulsan changnyŏ undong ŭi il chinjŏn" (Progress in the Native Products Promotion Movement), *Changsan* 2-1 (February 1931), p. 3.

48. Chŏn Uyong, "1930 nyŏndae 'Chosŏn kongŏphwa' wa chungso kongŏp" (Industrialization and small- to medium-scale industry in Chosŏn in the 1930s), *Han'guk saron*, no. 23 (1990).

49. An Chaehong, "Kwahak kisul kannŭng" (Science, technology, craftiness), *Chosŏn ilbo*, June 13, 1935 (reprinted in *Minse An Chaehong sŏnjip* 1, p. 522).

50. Ibid.

51. An Chaehong, "Chosŏn'in ŭi ch'ŏji esŏ" (From the standpoint of the Chosŏn people), *Chosŏn ilbo*, December 2, 1932.

rule, and his model for development was not simply a blind imitation of the paths taken by the West or Japan.[52] To achieve capitalist modernization, Chosŏn should pursue an autonomous development suited for its own situation.[53] Modernization in Chosŏn should not be an external, material development of capitalism but should be directed inwardly so that all members of the nation can develop modern ways of thinking and enjoy a modern life. To An, the universality of capitalist modernization lay in the abolition of the feudal ways of the yangban gentlemen (*yangban to, saennim to*), which represented the harmful customs and life of the past, and in the production of modern individuals through the promotion of the ways of the commoner and of labor (*sangnom to, ilggun ŭi to, nodong to*).[54] His conception of a national economy was a complex one that encompassed not only a modern economic structure and the promotion of industry but also the development of a modern consciousness and the enlightenment of the nation.[55] According to An's views, even if imperialist domination blocked modern development externally, it would be impossible to stop the process of modern development within the nation, and thus, it was necessary to find a suitable method to stimulate this development.

An Chaehong's Views on World Affairs and Korea's Situation

VIEWS ON IMPERIALISM AND WORLD AFFAIRS

An Chaehong's interest in world affairs stemmed from his belief that the problems faced by Chosŏn were the result of competition among the world powers and thus no longer just concerned the Chosŏn people but were faced

52. An Chaehong, "Yaindo wa nodongdo" (The way of barbarian and the way of labor), *Chosŏn ilbo*, March 5, 1928.

53. In the above-mentioned article, Naraki Chijin referred to this thinking as "modern skepticism." His comment was correct in drawing a distinction from moderate nationalists who adopted a subordinate, compromising position toward Japan and advocated capitalist modernization. However, it was inaccurate to assert that An Chaehong rejected capitalist modernization itself. An was an anti-imperial nationalist who aimed at an autonomous capitalist development through the promotion of small-scale industry.

54. "Yaindo wa nodongdo" and "Nongmindo ŭi kojo."

55. An Chaehong, "Kŭmnyŏn ŭi minjung kyoyang undong" (This year's mass enlightenment movement), *Chosŏn ilbo*, October 9, 1927. On the problems in agriculture as well, he emphasized the education and the enlightenment of the peasantry. It seems that these views stemmed from the nationalism which focused on self-strengthening that was deeply embedded in his thought and epistemology. This point will be discussed in detail in section 3 of this chapter.

by all the oppressed peoples of East Asia.[56] In his view, the world system in the modern age was structured into two groups: the aggressive world powers and the oppressed nations that resisted them.[57]

An was interested in the following four aspects of the changes in world affairs after World War I, "the great historical event of the modern period." The first aspect was that imperialist, capitalist powers established a new world order and entered a period of relative stability. Second, a socialist order appeared with the rise of the Soviet Union as a new world power. The third was the possibility of the recurrence of an imperialist war. The last aspect was the rise of nationalist, anti-colonial movements in colonial and semi-colonial regions; in particular, the world historical signifiance of liberation movements in northeast Asia.

After World War I, imperialist countries restructured the international order by adjusting the relations of power among them through the Versailles Treaty, the Washington Conference, and the Locarno Conference. An Chaehong saw the realignment of the imperialist, capitalist powers and the stabilization of the world order as a movement toward reactionism.[58] Internally, reactionism meant blocking the union of the propertyless class and suppressing the Communist Party that was providing leadership; externally, it meant the reconstruction and expansion of a new military order through a military build-up and the oppression of weak and small countries.[59] The imperialist, capitalist states, such as England, Germany, France, and the United States, were embarking again on an "eastward expansion" into Africa and Asia in order to restore the energy, resources, and other foundations of the state that had been lost during the world war. An saw this development as a return to "reactionary statism" (*pandongjŏk kukgajuŭi*).[60]

On the other hand, after the Russian Revolution, a socialist order emerged as a threat to the capitalist and imperialist system. An felt that imperialism would inevitably begin to suppress socialist class movements as it became stronger; in addition, the expansion of the power of the Soviet Un-

---

56. An Chaehong, "Pandong sŏnsang ŭi segye wa mit kŭ ch'use" (The world from the perspective of reaction and its tendencies), *Kaebyŏk*, no. 55 (January 1925), p. 28.

57. An Chaehong, "Tongbang che minjok ŭi kaksŏng" (The awakening of the nations in the east), *Chosŏn ilbo*, June 28, 1925.

58. "Pandong sŏnsang ŭi segye wa mit kŭ ch'use"; "Tongbang che minjok ŭi kaksŏng"; "Paeg'yŏl, kŭrŏna ŏmsukhan pandong ŭi ch'oejung ŭi sin ilnyŏn."

59. "Pandong sŏnsang ŭi segye wa mit kŭ ch'use."

60. Ibid.

ion would prevent capitalist, imperialist forces from seizing hegemony in world affairs uncontested, as they had done before World War I.[61]

In An's view, the ranks of the central world powers were rearranged during the changes in the world system after the mid 1920s—i.e., the relative stability of the capitalist imperialist system and the growth of the socialist order. He regarded England, the U.S., and the Soviet Union as the "three great centers of the world," revealing his fundamental views on international affairs. England was the reigning imperialist power; America was a newly rising imperialist state that was fighting to occupy the top spot in the world; and the Soviet Union was a proletarian state that loomed as a nightmare to the great capitalist powers.[62] He began to be aware of the contradictions in the world system that emerged through the conflict between the capitalist and socialist systems, and he viewed those countries as the strongest powers of the two opposing camps.

An Chaehong's conception of the world system contained both a class-oriented perspective and a state-oriented one.[63] He felt that capitalism and socialism were similar in that both sought to achieve hegemony in the conflict of differing systems since they both emerged through the formation of nation-states. The capitalist camp would strength its rule over its colonies as one aspect of the reactionism of capitalist imperialism, and the socialist camp would attempt to expand its influence to oppressed nations and classes under the banner of world revolution.[64] Demonstrating the double nature of his worldview, An saw the world situation both as a conflict between systems and ideologies and as a conflict among states. However, the state-oriented perspective[65] sometimes led to problems when it resulted in misconceptions of the actual state of world affairs.[66]

61. "Pandong sŏnsang ŭi segye wa mit kŭ ch'use" and "Tongbang che minjok ŭi kaksŏng."

62. "Pandong sŏnsang ŭi segye wa mit kŭ ch'use."

63. An Chaehong, "Pandong chonsŏn ŭl pugam hamyŏnsŏ" (Looking over the reactionary front), *Chosŏn ilbo*, March 1, 1925.

64. "Pandong sŏnsang ŭi segye wa mit kŭ ch'use."

65. His view of both capitalism and socialism from a statist perspective is deeply connected with his views on nationalism and the colonial situation, which will be discussed in the next section. From a nationalist perspective focusing on self-strengthening, the state is equated with the nation, and all history transcends class and society, unfolding through the unit of the "nation." An himself referred to this perspective as an "encompassing sense of the nation" (*minjok pŏmnon*). An Chaehong, "Hŏguhan tongmu-minjogae nŭn chon'gwi" (A long-standing comrade—love for the nation is noble), *Chosŏn ilbo*, November 10, 1931.

66. A typical example was his views on fascism. While he saw fascism as a form of bourgeois dictatorship, he thought that the international situation brought about by its emergence could be characterized as simply a revival of statism and populism. In short, in his view, fascist dictatorships

An Chaehong predicted that the reorganization of the world system after the 1920s had the potential to bring about the outbreak of another world war. The impetus for a world war would primarily come from the military build-up that accompanied the reactionary turn by the capitalist, imperialist states.[67] In the 1920s, the capitalist powers enjoyed world economic prosperity and embarked on a new military buildup, clearly laying the groundwork for future strife among the capitalist states. Because of the worldwide "third crisis of capitalism" that began in the late 1920s, the fascist movement gained momentum in the 1930s, and as the threat of war loomed over Europe and Asia, the economic crisis pushed events to the brink of another world war. An saw the military expansion of Germany and Italy in Europe[68] and the naval buildup of Japan and the United States in Asia[69] as part of the military buildup of reactionary capitalism. At the time, the rivalry among the powers in Asia centered on the struggles between England and the U.S., between Japan and the U.S., and between Japan and Soviet Russia.[70] He felt that the conflicts among the four countries focused particularly on China because of the movement into Asia by England and America, "soon to be the greatest power in the world;" Japan's continental ambitions; and the eastern expansion of the Soviet Union which opposed the other three powers.[71]

An thought that the struggle for hegemony among the capitalist powers would occur in the Pacific Rim and that the battle lines would fall between capitalism and socialism. For one thing, as the U.S. developed into the leading capitalist imperial power after World War I, its interests were increasing in the Pacific. Japan attempted to create a niche for itself within the competition between England and the U.S., but it was difficult to accomplish as

emerged as a form of statism. Accordingly, he viewed the political systems of all countries in the 1930s as fascist dictatorships—including Stalin in the Soviet Union, Mussolini in Italy, Hitler in Germany, and Roosevelt in the U.S.. An Chaehong, "Tokchae kwan'gyŏn 1" (My view of dictatorship 1), *Chosŏn ilbo*, February 6, 1936.

67. An Chaehong, "Pobo chŏnjin ŭi sin ilnyŏn" (A new year of gradual progress), *Chosŏn ilbo*, January 1, 1928.

68. An Chaehong, "Kukje chŏngguk ŭi chŏnmang" (Prospects of the international situation), *Sin Chosŏn* 5, no. 1 (January 1936).

69. An Chaehong, "Ch'oegun kukche wiguk ŭi sam chungsim" (The three centers of recent international crises), *Sin Chosŏn*, no. 6 (October 1934).

70. "Pandong sŏnsang ŭi segye wa mit kŭ ch'use."

71. His views on the fundamental dynamics of world affairs were consistent throughout the 1920s and 1930s. Especialy after the Manchurian Incident, he felt that tensions between the U.S. and Japan and between Japan and the Soviet Union were growing sharper, intensifying the international crisis. "Ch'oegun kukche wiguk ŭi sam chungsim" (The three centers of recent international crises), p. 3.

long as the Soviets threatened to expand southward.[72] In 1925, Japan concluded a new treaty with the Soviet Union in an attempt to settle the issue of national borders, but in fact, it was worried that the Soviets, who had lost their hegemony in Manchuria and Mongolia after the Russo-Japanese War, might expand southward again under the pretext of spreading world revolution and block Japan's advance into the Asian continent. After the 1920s, relations between Japan and the Soviet Union became "tense and difficult over the issue of China, as they had in the past after the Sino-Japanese War."[73]

For these reasons, China was the primary focus of international crises involving Asia, and An Chaehong showed great interest in China's political situation.[74] As he explained, the issue "was not whether or not he had a favorable view of events in China but that [China] was deeply connected to the direction of trends in the Far East."[75] More specifically, he felt that "the majority of the masses needed a double liberation from the unresolved problems of the present time—as subjugated nations and as oppressed classes. Almost all of them lived as the citizens of the eastern countries, and the revolutionary movement of the Chinese people was a historical inevitability in both of these senses."[76]

An also took great interest in the rise of nationalism and nationalist movements of oppressed peoples that were under a state of domination as a result of changes in international affairs after World War I.[77] As a result of the war, the colonies of Russia and Austria were liberated, and nationalist movements arose throughout the East in places such as Turkey, Egypt, Morocco, India, China, and Mongolia. An felt that these developments were events of great importance that had the potential to cause tremendous upheaval in the

---

72. An Chaehong, "Chŏngno tongch'im chonghoeinggwan" (Examining all aspects of the eastern aggressions of Communist Soviet Union), *Chosŏn ilbo*, November 22-26, 1924.

73. An Chaehong, "Chungguk hyŏngse wa Ilbon ŭi chiwi" (The condition of China and Japan's position), *Chosŏn ilbo*, December 9, 1926.

74. See writings such as: "Tongbang che minjok ŭi kaksŏng"; "Pandong sŏnsang ŭi segye wa mit kŭ ch'use"; "Chungguk hyŏngse wa Ilbon ŭi chiwi"; An Chaehong, "Chungguk hyŏngmyŏng ŭi chŏngch'ijŏk kach'i" (The political significance of the Chinese Revolution), *Hyŏndae p'yŏngnon* (January 1927); An Chaehong, "Chungguk choch'aji munje wa pan chegukjuŭi undong" (The problem of the leased territories in China and the anti-imperialism movement), *Hyŏndae p'yŏngnon* (March 1927); An Chaehong, "Winan Chungguk ŭi pyŏksang taegwan" (General prospective of China in Crisis), *Sin Chosŏn*, no. 7 (December 1934).

75. "Chungguk hyŏngse wa Ilbon ŭi chiwi."

76. "Chungguk hyŏngmyŏng ŭi chŏngch'ijŏk kach'i," p.36.

77. An Chaehong, "Salgi e ssain munhwa chŏngch'i" (The bloodthirstiness of culture politics), *Chosŏn ilbo*, May 22, 1924; "Paeg'yŏl, kŭrŏna ŏmsukhan pandong ŭi ch'oejung ŭi sin ilnyŏn."

world.[78] The rise of nationalist movements by oppressed nations as a world-wide phenomenon and the conflicts among the world powers over China gave legitimacy to the anti-Japanese nationalist movement in Chosŏn and acted as a stimulus. Already in the late 1920s, An predicted that the situation on the Far Eastern continent would change greatly by the early 1940s and that the role of Korea in the Far East would be a matter of keen interest—as much as that of China and Japan.[79] Although he did not elaborate concretely on the changes that would raise such interest, he clearly had insight into the dynamics of international affairs and prospects for the national liberation movement.

To sum up, An Chaehong saw the fundamental dynamic of the world system as a conflict between the capitalist and socialist camps as the reactionary policies of the capitalist imperial powers aimed to create stability after World War I. However, his views also simultaneously contained a state-oriented perspective that viewed both capitalism and socialism as similar in their efforts to expand their hegemony at the state level. In his dualistic worldview, An also looked favorably on the rise of class and nationalist movements of oppressed peoples that resisted hegemonic aggressions. An's view of international affairs was an important component of his thought—along with his conception of nationalism and of the colonial situation—that produced an optimistic view of Chosŏn's prospects for liberation, enabling him to maintain an unyielding position of resistance toward Japan.

VIEWS ON KOREA'S COLONIAL SITUATION AND CONCEPTION OF NATIONAL SELF-STRENGTHENING

Since the international problems in the modern era appear as national matters rather than as class issues,[80] An Chaehong felt that "half of the problems in world affairs occur in the form of national issues."[81] His views were the result of a national awakening that was, in turn, based on the premise that saw contradictions in world system as a conflict among nations.[82]

However, An's interest in national issues was not limited to the nation's potential for external resistance against other nations. It also stemmed from a

78. Ibid.

79. An Chaehong, "Chosŏn kumhu ŭi chŏngch'ijŏk ch'use" (The political direction of Chosŏn's future), *Chosŏn ilbo*, December 19, 1926.

80. "Tongbang che minjok ŭi kaksŏng."

81. An Chaehong, "Minjok chŏnmang" (Prospects of the nation), *Chosŏn ilbo*, October 2, 1931.

82. "Paeg'yŏl, kŭrŏna ŏmsukhan pandong ŭi ch'oejung ŭi sin ilnyŏn."

nationalist concern for self-strengthening (*chagang*) through the adoption of anti-feudal, capitalist civilization. Influenced by Social Darwinism, the self-strengthening movements of the Hanmal period advocated cultivating the abilities of the people and pursued the creation of a modern capitalist civilization.[83] Through the influence of his father, An was deeply involved in self-strengthening movements in his youth, going back to his days in the Hwangsŏng Christian Youth Society.[84] In the 1910s, even after he came back from Japan, his work continued to focus on self-strengthening efforts such as education.[85] In terms of his intellectual genealogy, theories of self-strengthening had a substantial influence on the formation of his views on the nation, the state, and the masses.

An Chaehong felt that in order to build a modern state, the primary internal task facing the people was the formation of a nation. He used the concepts *minjok* (nation), *kungmin* (people or citizenry), and *kukga* (the state) interchangeably, and his conception of the nation corresponded with the

83. For more on the self-strengthening movement and the introduction of social Darwinism in the Hanmal period, see: Yi Kwangnin, "Kuhanmal sahoe chinhwaron ŭi suyong kwa kŭ yŏnghyang" (The introduction and influence of Social Darwinism in the Hanmal period), *Serim Han'gukhak nonch'ong*, 1 (1977); Yi Songhŭi, "Taehan cheguk malgi aeguk kyemong hakhoe yŏn'gu" (An examination of the Patriotic-Enlightenment Study society in Great Han Empire period) (Ph.D. diss., Ewha Women's University, 1986); Kim Tohyŏng, "Taehan cheguk malgi kukgwŏn hoebok undong kwa kŭ sasang" (The movement to restore sovereignty and its ideology at the end of the Great Han Empire period) (Ph.D. diss., Yonsei University, 1988); Chu Chin-Oh (Chu Chin'o), "Tongnip hyŏphoe ŭi sahoe sasang kwa sahoe chinhwaron" (The social ideology of the Independence Club and Social Darwinism), *Son Pogi paksa chŏngnyŏn ki'nyŏm Han'guk sahak nonch'ong* (1988); Pak Ch'ansŭng, "Hanmal chagang undong ŭi kyeyŏl kwa kŭ sŏngkyok" (The factions within the self-strengthening movement in the Hanmal period and their views), *Han'guksa yŏn'gu*, no. 68 (1990).

84. At the school, he became an avid reader of the *Taehan maeil sinbo* and the *Hwangsŏng sinmun*, and he read books such as *Miguk tongnip chŏnsa* (The history of the American war for Independence), *Tansa kŏngukji*, *It'aeri kŏnguk yŏng'ungjŏn* (Biography of the heroes in the founding of Italy), Wŏllam mangguksa (The history of the fall of Vietnam), and Liang Qichao's (1873-1929) *Yinbing shi wenji* (*Yin ping shih wen chi*) and *Ziyou shu*. An Chaehong, "Haksaeng sidae ŭi hoego" and "Pit'ong!—Choguk ŭi pokmol."

85. After finishing his studies in Japan in 1914, he frequented the Sinmun'gwan which was run by Ch'oe Namsŏn and met with other young intellectuals who had studied abroad or received a Western education in Chosŏn. He started to engaged in activities to prepare the stepping-stone for the restoration of national sovereignty through the establishment of modern capitalist civilization. Consequently, in 1915, he became the principal of Chung'ang Academy, which had been taken over by Kim Sŏngsu and participated in the Chosŏn sanjik changnyŏ kye (Association for the promotion of the textile industry in Chosŏn) whose purpose was to develop native Chosŏn capitalists. Lee Ji-won, "An Chaehong non" (An examination of An Chaehong), *Singminji sidae ŭi chisig'in kwa minjok haebang undongnon* (Han'guk yŏksa yŏn'guhoe che 3 hoe haksul taet'oronhoe palp'yomun), 1991, p. 8).

vision of a sovereign state (i.e., a self-strengthened state) that has undertaken efforts to enrich the country and strengthen the military (*puguk kangbyŏng*). It was consistent with the principles of self-strengthening theories that were popular in the Hanmal period. An stressed that "in the transitional period from a state of backwardness to modern society, intentional destruction and construction is inevitable, and through this process, it is also necessary, to undergo, one time, a national intensification and purification."[86] He called this process the "maturation of nationalism" (*minjokjuŭi seryŏn kwajŏng*).[87] However, the Chosŏn masses had not been able to complete this process of maturation to overcome their state of feudal backwardness. Because they were in a state of economic decline and spiritual unrest,[88] he felt that it would still be beneficial to continue the internal task of "nationalist maturation" even though Chosŏn had become a colony of Japan.

An's thinking developed out of his critique of—and his reflection upon the failures of—modernization movements from above and national liberation movements that did not go through the process of nationalist maturation. In his opinion, from the enlightenment movements after the port opening in 1876 to the March First Movement, all movements were doomed to fail since the internal abilities of the people remained undeveloped.[89] Thus, the fundamental task of the nation was to continue to cultivate the abilities of the people, no matter what the obstacles, and to lay the foundation for national self-strengthening.

To achieve these goals, An Chaehong emphasized the growth of capitalist production and the development of a modern consciousness. As mentioned above, his emphasis on the preservation of the national economy under colonialism was closely related to his focus on overcoming Chosŏn's colonial situation through self-strengthening. Furthermore, it was necessary to establish a patriotic mindset rooted in the national spirit (*kukhon*) in order to build a nation-state that would be an "organic entity constituted by the national spirit."[90] An emphasized that the immediate task of the nation was to

---

86. An Chaehong, "Kurŏmyŏn i irŭl ŏjjiharya" (Now, what should we do about this?), *Chosŏn ilbo*, June 4, 1924; "Haebang chŏnsŏn ŭl pugam hamyŏnsŏ."

87. An Chaehong, "Kungminjuŭi wa minjokjuŭi" (Patriotism and nationalism), *Chosŏn ilbo*, February 18, 1932.

88. An Chaehong, "Sinnyŏm hŭisaeng nodong - minjung kuje ŭi chŏngsinjŏk p'yoch'am" (Conviction, sacrifice, labor—the spiritual model for saving the people), *Sidae ilbo*, May 17, 1924.

89. "Haebang chŏnsŏn ŭl pugam hamyŏnsŏ."

90. The conception of the state as an "organic entity constituted by the national spirit" came from the notion of "state spirit" in Liang Qichao's *Xinmin shuo* (*Hsin min shuo*), and beginning

disseminate education to the masses in order to stimulate both a national and a modern consciousness.[91]

As a natural outgrowth of his focus on national self-strengthening, he viewed the masses of Chosŏn as a target of education and cultivation who still needed to undergo "nationalist maturation." If a broad section of the masses gained a modern and a nationalist consciousness through the spread of education, it would make it possible to lay the foundation for the "recon-struction of the irrational social life" and for the "construction of a new future society." However, An did not consider the masses to be a purely pas-sive object of education or agents of history who lacked subjectivity. To An, the masses were the central force in the "nationalist maturation" of moderni-zation and the central group within the nation. Consequently, he emphasized the need for a movement to elevate the consciousness of the masses as the foundation for mass organizing.[92]

His optimism on the potential of the masses was one of the main factors that prevented his outlook on Korea's situation from falling into a defeatist attitude through the adoption of the principles of Social Darwinism. He ac-cepted the Darwinian notion of "fitness," but he rejected the way it could be used to justify the conquest of peoples whose level of fitness was weak. He defended the resistance of oppressed peoples as the same as other forms of nationalism that sought to preserve the survival of a country in the age of capitalism and imperialism.[93] An stressed the uniqueness and equality of all

with Sin Ch'aeho (1880-1936), it became a central aspect of the conceptions of the nation and the state of nationalist ideologies that focused on self-strengthening in Korea. Sin Ilch'ŏl, "Sin Ch'ae-ho ŭi kŭndae kukgagwan" (Sin Ch'aeho's conception of the modern state), *Sin Ch'aeho ŭi sasang kwa minjok tongnip undong*, Tanje Sin Ch'aeho sŏnsaeng ki'nyŏm saŏphoe, ed. (Seoul: Hyŏng-sŏl ch'ulp'ansa, 1986).

91. He encapsulated his ideas in slogans such as *kyoyuk ŭi minjunghwa* (教育의 民衆化) and *minjung ŭi saenghwalhwa* (民衆의 生活化). An Chaehong, "Sidae kwanggu ŭi sin ilnyŏn" (A new year for rectifying the age), *Chosŏn ilbo*, January 1, 1925.

92. An Chaehong, "Kwihyang haksaeng munja pogŭpban" (Teams of students returning to their hometowns to spread literacy), *Chosŏn ilbo*, July 14, 1929; An Chaehong, "Saenghwal kae-sin undong ŭl kojoham" (Improving the movement reform [daliy] life), *Chosŏn ilbo*, May 2, 1929. An Chaehong conceived of the mass education movement as a preparatory step to organizing the masses, giving it the most emphasis among the various daily life movements. In this aspect, his ideas can be clearly distinguished from those of An Ch'angho (1878-1938) and Yi Kwangsu (1892-1951) whose educational movements focused on self-cultivating activities mainly for the elite. For more on An's and Yi's education movements, see: Sŏ Chungsŏk, "Hanmal ilche ch'imnyakha ŭi chabonjuŭi kŭndaehwaron ŭi sŏnggyŏk" (The nature of views on capitalism modernization in the Hanmal period and under Japanese aggression), *Han'guk kŭnhyŏndae ŭi minjok munje yŏn'gu* (Seoul: Chisik sanŏpsa, 1989).

93. See footnote 76.

nations, and he also focused on the nation's potential for resistance. In this aspect, his views contrasted with those of moderate nationalists whose goal was the achievement of "civilization and enlightenment" and who tended to collaborate with the Japanese even as they called for the "development of the abilities" of the people and "national self-strengthening."[94] In fact, because he viewed the resistance of oppressed peoples as one of the main components of their nationalism,[95] he understood the world in terms of a conflict among nations and consistently emphasized, to the point of stubbornness, the preservation of ethnic uniqueness—i.e., the national economy, national history, and the national language.[96] An's conception of the nation was close to an abstract notion of it as a "totality in which [the members] are conscious of a spiritual existence that is unified historically and culturally."[97] These aspects constituted the common elements—and the limitations—in the thinking on the nation of radical nationalists in the early modern period.

To An Chaehong, national self-strengthening meant reform of feudal customs and resistance against foreign aggressions, and from a state-oriented perspective, what it fundamentally aimed at was the establishment of a modern capitalist state. In such cases, the hegemony of the bourgeoisie naturally

94. An Chaehong's conception of national self-strengthening contained the notions of "independence" and "resistance" along with an emphasis on the development of abilities and a social development that aimed at capitalist modernization. By contrast, Yi Kwangsu and other like-minded nationalists also advocated the establishment of a capitalist, modern civilization, but they only called for "civilization and enlightenment" and a social reform that did not question the fact of Japanese rule in order to achieve this modernization.

95. The conception of self-strengthening that emphasized the nationalist resistance of oppressed peoples based on the equality of all nations was systematized by Sin Ch'aeho in the Hanmal period. The patriotic emphasis on nationalist resistance was maintained as the central feature of An's views on Chosŏn's colonial situation. This aspect of An's thought became even more firmly established as he observed the advanced capitalist states again embarking on programs of imperialist domination after World War I. He felt that the imperialist patriotism of the advanced capitalist states and the nationalism of the oppressed countries of East Asia were "the same in nature, different in form." But the latter was the target of "execration," and the former was a goal to be achieved by oppressed peoples. An's theories provided a defense of the national resistance and liberation movements of oppressed peoples. An Chaehong, "Kungminjuŭi wa minjokjuŭi."

96. An Chaehong, "Chosŏn'in kwa kugŏ munje" (The Chosŏn people and the issue of the national language), Chosŏn ilbo, May 28-29, 1925; "Chosŏnsa munje" (Problems in Chosŏn history), Chosŏn ilbo, August 8, 1926; An Chaehong, "Charip chŏngsin ŭi che il bo" (The first step of the spirit of self-reliance), Chosŏn ilbo, November 4, 1926; "Chosŏn'in ŭi ch'ŏji esŏ" (From the standpoint of the Chosŏn people); "Minse p'iltam—minjung simhwa kwajŏng" (A conversation in writing with An Chaehong-), Chosŏn ilbo, May 2-19, 1935 (reprinted in Minse An Chaehong sŏnjip 1, pp. 470-513).

97. An Chaehong, "Sahoe wa chayŏnsŏng" (Society and naturalness), Chosŏn ilbo, October 16, 1935 (reprinted in Minse An Chaehong sŏnjip 1, p. 537).

became an issue. However, An saw class conflict within colonial Chosŏn society as a secondary concern. In large capitalist states, class divisions arose among its citizens between the oppressors and the oppressed as a result of social development, but in the case of Chosŏn, the masses had not yet undergone a widespread, autonomous process of modern class differentiation because of colonial rule and thus were suffering a total decline that transcended class.[98] He believed that neither the capitalist class nor the laborers class could develop into an independent class under colonialism. Since the capitalist class could not develop sufficiently under the domination of foreign capitalism, it would have to join forces with the Japanese ruling authorities in order to achieve a bourgeois class dictatorship.[99] Because the propertyless classes (i.e., laborers and peasants) lacked political power and were fragmented, they also were not developed enough to act as an organized force.[100]

In a situation where class development was in its early stages, An Chaehong regarded the middle class—namely, the small-to-medium landlords and capitalists—as the class in Chosŏn whose level of development was the most "normal." They constituted a national petit-bourgeois class that had already partially modernized in terms of their economic activities and mindset and was able to engage in resistance against the Japanese.[101] In his view, the petit-bourgeois class was a "middle" or "central" class that was in the politically worst position under imperial rule. Nevertheless, they "refused to enter into a rightist alliance with the Japanese and had acted as an independent force from feudal times that would not join an international front out of a purely proletarian class consciousness."[102] An acknowledged that the petit-bourgeois class lacked the basic conditions to act autonomously either as political actors or as

98. "Tongbang che minjok ŭi kaksŏng"; see also footnote 88.

99. An Chaehong, "Kiro e sŏn Sin'ganhoe" (The Sin'ganhoe at a crossroads), *Chosŏn ilbo,* May 16, 1931.

100. An Chaehong, "Haesoron naeng'an'gwan" (A dispassionate look at calls for the dissolution [of the Sin'ganhoe]), *Chosŏn ilbo,* December 26, 1930; An Chaehong, "Haesoron kwa oryu" (Calls for the dissolution [of the Sin'ganhoe] and their fallacies), *Chosŏn ilbo,* April 17, 1931.

101. An Chaehong, "Haesop'a ŭige yŏham" (To the faction calling for the dissolution [of the Sin'ganhoe]), *Pip'an,* no. 4 (combined issue, July-August 1931); "Kiro e sŏn Sin'ganhoe."

102. Ibid. In An Chaehong's conception of the economy, the petit-bourgeois class was composed of the Chosŏn independent farmers, small landlords, and small-to-medium merchants and industrialists that he saw as the central force in the development of the national economy. Examining his views on national self-strengthening and the economy together, it is possible to conclude that among the two main courses of modernization that emerged in the nineteenth century, his conceptions of modernization and a modern state followed the "peasant course," which also represented the interests of independent cultivators and small landlords, while aiming for capitalist modernization.

a class, but he saw it as a force that would resist the Japanese and as the most suitable group to undertake the task of national self-strengthening.[103] He did not deny that under the Japanese occupation, workers and peasants could grow in strength and develop into the central force of the national liberation movement.[104] However, he emphasized that the political maturation of the bourgeoisie must occur first. The Chosŏn people lacked the political capabilities for a movement since they had not yet gone through the "process of democratization" which normally would occur as a result of class conflict within the nation.[105] In short, the fundamental objective of An's program of national self-strengthening—which was to be led by the petit-bourgeois class—was also to promote bourgeois nationalism and to pursue capitalist modernization.

Theory of National Liberation and An's Political Activities

THE SIN'GANHOE AND THE "LEFTIST NATIONALIST FRONT"

Developing out of his views of society and the nation, An Chaehong's vision for the nationalist movement was the creation of a "leftist nationalist front."[106] In his unique conception of movements, the contradictions of imperial rule were seen primarily in terms of the relations between nations, and social groups were distinguished according to whether they were nationalist or anti-nationalist, anti- or pro-Japanese in their political orientation. To An, there were only two political positions that the Chosŏn people could adopt under imperial domination—i.e., collaboration or resistance. The term "right wing" referred to groups that collaborated with the Japanese, and "left wing" denoted those that resisted.[107] An asserted that a "liberation front" of both

103. "Haesoron kwa oryu."
104. An Chaehong also was not against the pursuit of the interests of the masses, including laborers and peasants, in order to protect their livelihoods. See "Haesoron kwa oryu."
105. An Chaehong, "Kich'i put'o sŏnmyŏnghi haja" (Let's first make our position clear), *Tongbang p'yŏngnon*, no. 1 (April 1932).
106. An Chaehong, "Sin'ganhoe ŭi ch'angnip chunbi" (Preparations to establish the Sin'ganhoe), *Chosŏn ilbo*, January 10, 1927.
107. An Chaehong, "Chosŏn'in ŭi chŏngch'ijŏk punya" (The political arena of the Chosŏn people), *Chosŏn ilbo*, Janaury 21, 1925; "Chosŏn kumhu ŭi chŏngch'ijŏk ch'use" (The political direction of Chosŏn's future). In distinguishing between nationalism and socialism, he viewed socialism as leftist and nationalism as rightist. If the two were distinguished according to the criteria of thought, ideology, and position toward the Japanese ruling authorities, then socialism would constitute the far left; nationalism, a "central party' (中央黨); and collaborators, the far right. After

nationalists and socialists was necessary for the oppressed masses and that it was also necessary to form a strong united front through struggle.[108]

The immediate impetus for An's organization of a leftist national front was the rise of the self-rule movement (*chach'i undong*). Around the time of the March First Movement, Government-General officials and bourgeois nationalists began to discuss the possibility of granting Chosŏn autonomy.[109] An noticed that an increasing number of Chosŏn people were thinking seriously about self-rule and drifting into the collaborationist camp. From late 1923, Song Chin'u and Yi Kwangsu of the *Tonga ilbo* and Ch'oe Rin of the Ch'ŏndogyo religion became the leading figures of the movement and built ties with leaders living abroad such as An Ch'angho. When the Government-General decided to conduct a study on the implementation of self-rule in late 1925, it became a matter of urgent concern among domestic activists.[110] An defined the self-rule movement as a compromise with the government authorities. Such movements could "exist only through the consent and inducement of the ruling authorities [which were attained] by building connections and good relations with them," and they were a "conciliatory measure by the ruling authorities to appease the Chosŏn people."[111] He predicted that a self-rule movement would emerge through the combination of a change in Japan's colonial policies—which took into account a long-term rule over Chosŏn, its plans to move into mainland China, and the spread of communist movements—with "utilitarian gradualists" among the Chosŏn people.[112]

liberation, he called the political thought based on the ideas of neo-nationalism and neo-democracy as "ideology of a central party"—stemming from his conception of the national liberation movement during the occupation period.

108. "Chosŏn'in ŭi chŏngch'ijŏk punya."

109. For more on the self-rule movement, see: Kang Tongjin, *Ilche ŭi Han'guk ch'imnyak chŏngch'aeksa* (The history of Japan's policies to take over Korea), Chapter 4; Han Paeho, "3.1 undong chikhu ŭi Chosŏn singminji chŏngch'aek" (Chosŏn colonial policies immediately following the March First Movement), *Ilche ŭi Han'guk singmin t'ongch'i*, Ch'a Kibyŏk, ed. (Seoul: Chŏng'ŭmsa, 1985); Pak Ch'ansŭng, "Ilcheha ŭi chach'i undong kwa kŭ sŏnggyŏk" (The self-rule movement under Japanese rule and its characteristics), *Yŏksa wa hyŏnsil*, no. 2 (1989).

110. In three installments beginning on November 26, 1925, the president of the *Kyŏngsŏng ilbo*, Fukushima Michimasa, published an article, "Chosen tochi no konpon gi" (The fundamental significance of [Japanese] rule of Chosŏn), which reflected the thinking of the Government-General. It appeared after the Government-General had consulted with figures at the *Tonga ilbo*. See Kang Tongjin, ibid.; Pak Ch'ansŭng, ibid., pp. 180-83.

111. See footnote 109.

112. Ibid.

In An's view, the fate of efforts to collaborate with the Japanese would be determined by how much the objective and subjective factors of the various political and economic conditions in Chosŏn could be shifted to the left (i.e., against compromise). If resistance movements could gain hegemony over the national liberation movement, An believed that people would naturally abandon collaboration movements. He even asserted that the self-rule movement was doomed to fail in view of both objective and subjective conditions. While Japan seemed to be open to permitting autonomy in Chosŏn, it was actually a deception designed to facilitate the expansion of the institutions for its rule and the strengthening of its economic control over Chosŏn.[113] As Japan toughened its rule, the masses of Chosŏn would grow even more impoverished and come increasingly into conflict with the Japanese. An predicted that under such conditions, collaboration movements would not be able to gain mass support and would not last for long.[114] Expecting that the international situation in East Asia would become favorable for the national liberation movement in the future, he was optimistic about the prospects of success for resistance movements.[115] Based on this optimism, An argued for the organization of a mass movement for political resistance by forming a "leftist nationalist front" that could undermine the strength of collaboration efforts. In the 1920s, his vision for a leftist nationalist front was realized through the establishment of the Sin'ganhoe.

An Chaehong saw the Sin'ganhoe as the precursor to a "united national party"[116] that would engage in political struggle and serve as the sole organization for political movements in order to prevent groups from collaborating with the Japanese.[117] An began to plan the establishment of a united political party under the leadership leftist nationalists from the time he became involved in efforts to organize the Yŏnjŏnghoe in January 1924. In early 1924, Ch'oe Rin and Yi Sŭnghun of the Ch'ŏndogyo religion; Kim Sŏngsu, Song Chin'u, and Choe Wŏnsun from the *Tonga ilbo*; Sin Sŏg'u and An Chaehong from the *Chosŏn ilbo*; Sŏ Sang'il from Taegu, and Cho Mansik from

113. An Chaehong, "Aeran munje wa Chosŏn munje" (The problems of Ireland and Chosŏn), *Chosŏn ilbo*, November 4, 1926.

114. Ibid.

115. See part 3, section 1 of this chapter.

116. An Chaehong, "Minjok tan'ildang ŭi munje" (The issue of a united national party), *Chosŏn ilbo*, August 7, 1927; An Chaehong, "Sin'ganhoe ŭi Kyŏngsŏng chihoe" (The Kyŏngsŏng [Seoul] branch of the Sin'ganhoe), *Chosŏn ilbo*, December 10, 1927.

117. An Chaehong, "Sin'ganhoe ŭi kŭpsokhan paljŏn" (The rapid growth of the Sin'ganhoe), *Chosŏn ilbo*, December 23, 1927.

Pyongyang gathered to discuss the problems related to organizing a political association.[118] Despite their common intentions, they were already split into two groups according to their differing visions for a political movement—one wanted to create a political association for a leftist nationalist movement, and the other wanted to pursue a self-rule movement that had already been discussed in secret. After the meeting, An resolved to block efforts to organize a self-rule movement, and from the second half of 1926, he consulted with Hong Myŏnghŭi and Sin Sŏg'u on "forming a true national party in the near future."[119] With the support of Kwŏn Tongjin, Pak Raehong, Pak Tong'wan, Han Yong'un, Choe Ikwan, and Sin Ch'aeho, he began preparations to organize the Sin'ganhoe.[120]

In its early days, An thought that the Sin'ganhoe could not become more than an intellectual organization and would remain in a transitional stage halfway between an ideological and a political organization in character. His plan was to turn the Sin'ganhoe into a political party that would become the central political organization coordinating and guiding the national liberation movement and that would engage in political struggle and resistance against the Japanese.[121] To develop it into a united national party, it was necessary to transform it from an ideological organization into a political one, and An felt that such a transformation would be possible only by going into

118. Saito Makoto, "Dokuritsu undo shusoku go ni okeru minzoku undo no gaiyo" (A summary of the nationalist movement after the suppression of the independence movement), *Saito Makoto bunsho* 10 (Seoul: Koryŏ sŏrim, 1990), pp. 225-37.

119. Around October 1926, An Chaehong, Kim Chun'yŏn, and others informed the Minhŭnghoe about the plans for a self-rule movement led by Ch'oe Namsŏn and Yi Kwangsu, successfully foiling those plans. North Kyŏngsang Province Department of Police, ed., *Kodŭng kyŏngch'al yosa*, p. 47.

120. Kan Tokusan (Kang Tŏksang), ed., *Gendaishi shiryo* (Documents on contemporary history) 29 (Tokyo: Misuzu shobo, 1970), p. 95.

121. Ever since the March First Movement, there had been a conflict within the independence movement over the kind of central organization needed to coordinate and lead the movement. Some proposed establishing a government, and others supported founding a political party. Ultimately, proponents of a government prevailed, and the Korean Provisional Government (Taehan Minguk Imsi Chŏngbu) was formed in Shanghai. However, there were still many who believed that a party organization would be an effective way of carrying out the independence movement. In China in 1926, there was a movement in China to create a pan-national political party that would seek to unity all the various groups in the movement. No Kyŏngch'ae, "Han'guk tongnipdang ŭi kyŏlsŏng kwa kŭ pyŏnch'ŏn" (The formation of the Korean Independence Party and its changes), *Yŏksa wa hyŏnsil*, no. 1 (1989); No Kyŏngch'ae, "Kug'oe minjok undong ŭi nosŏn kwa i'nyŏm ŭi pyŏnch'ŏn kwajŏng" (Changes in the ideology and course of nationalist movements abroad), *3.1 Minjok haebang undong* (Seoul: Ch'ŏngnyŏnsa, 1989).

the masses and raising their level of consciousness.[122] According to An, the path to creating a political party was to "gather vanguard elements such as petit-bourgeois intelligentsia and, after unifying them, gradually organize a wide spectrum of classes such as laborers, peasants, and capitalists."[123]

Based on these plans, the immediate goals for the Sin'ganhoe were to organize the masses and to raise their level of consciousness. More specifically, the pressing issues that it had to address were: 1) the elevation of the peasantry; 2) the protection of cultivation rights and the prevention of foreign immigration; 3) dissemination of education for the Chosŏn people; 4) attainment of freedom of the press, publication, association, and organization; 5) guidance and support of a cooperative union movement; and 6) changes in attire and elimination of topknots.[124]

What was striking was the emphasis placed on the first task, the elevation of the peasantry. Since peasants composed eighty percent of the population, they constituted the "base of the organizing potential of Chosŏn."[125] However, what he meant by mass organization was not the organization of a proletariat by raising their class consciousness but the cultivation of the masses through self-realization and the development of an anti-feudal, modern consciousness. In his writings on this subject,[126] he noted that it was necessary for the masses to have exposure to anti-feudal modernization in order for political movements to develop in Chosŏn and that the basis of a united national party would have to be masses who possess greater sophistication through organizing and a heightened level of consciousness. In this sense, An felt that the Sin'ganhoe would have to be involved in the sphere of daily life and engage in educational movements and the cultivation of the masses.[127]

122. "Sin'ganhoe ŭi kŭpsokhan paljŏn."

123. "Sin'ganhoe ŭi Kyŏngsŏng chihoe."

124. An Chaehong, "Silche undong ŭi tangmyŏn munje—Sin'ganhoe nŭn muŏsŭl halka" (The immediate tasks of the movement—What should the Sin'ganhoe do?), *Chosŏn ilbo*, March 27, 1928.

125. Ibid.

126. An Chaehong, "Kumnyŏn ŭi minjung kyoyang undong" (This year's movement to cultivate the masses), *Chosŏn ilbo*, October 9, 1927.

127. See footnote 124. During the occupation period, he continually advocated movements for the cultivation of the masses, and his ideas were some of the main reasons that beginning in 1929, the *Chosŏn ilbo* organized life improvement movements (*saenghwal kaesŏn undong*) and literacy movements (*munja pogŭp undong*) by sending students into the countryside. "Nongmindo ŭi kojo"; An Chaehong, "Haksaeng ŭi tankyŏl" (Student unity), *Chosŏn ilbo*, March 4, 1927; "Kŭmnyŏn ŭi minjung kyoyang undong"; An Chaehong, "Saenghwal kaesin ŭl kojoham" (Upgrading life circumstance), *Chosŏn ilbo*, July 14, 1929; "Kwihyang namyŏ haksaeng chegun ege" (To students returning to their hometowns) *Chosŏn ilbo*, July 18, 1929;

In An's conception of the Sin'ganhoe's political ideology, organization, and activities, what kind of relationship did he envision with the socialists whom he saw as allies in a leftist national front? In March 1926, he met with Kang Tal'yŏng and other leaders of the second Korean Communist Party, and they reached an agreement on forming a united front of nationalists and socialists that would build an organization similar to the Kuomintang in China.[128] However, it seems that they did not have any concrete discussions on the method of unifying the two camps. An simply presumed that in a time of crisis when collaborators were becoming dominant, an alliance between nationalists and socialists would naturally occur since they were the two main groups in the national liberation movement.[129] In the early days of the Sin'ganhoe, it used slogans such as "unconditional unity," "a single front," and "a united party" without any detailed explanations of how to accomplish these goals.[130] When socialists called for the dissolution of the Sin'ganhoe and conflicts emerged over the direction of the movement, An began to search for more concrete ways of maintaining a united front with the socialists.

In the process, An Chaehong revised his views on a united front and instead sought to promote unity by making both sides see that it would be in their political interest to enter into an alliance. In a situation where ideological conflict between capital and labor was growing sharper, it would be impossible to achieve inter-class unity; thus, An felt that a class alliance could be achieved based on shared political interest.[131] But he emphasized that the petite bourgeoisie would be the leaders of the class alliance. Since the labor class had not yet developed to the point where it could take control of social movements and lead the masses, it was still necessary for the "petite bourgeoisie or leftist intelligentsia" to assume a leadership role.[132] The Sin'ganhoe was the first pan-national alliance that had the support of the people, and its growth was more rapid than that of the Chosŏn Worker-Peasant League (Nonong ch'ong tongmaeng). Emphasizing the role of the petit-bourgeois

An Chaehong, "Yakjin kŭrŏna mullŏsŏsŏ" (A leap, but a step back), Chosŏn ilbo, August 9, 1929; An Chaehong, "Nong-min hakgyo wa kajŏng hakkyo" (Peasants' schools and home schools), Chosŏn ilbo, September 3, 1930.

128. "Che 2 ch'a Chosŏn kongsangdang sagŏn chŏmgŏ pogo ch'ŏl" (File of reports concerning the second Chosŏn Communism Party incident), Han'guk kongsanjuŭi undongsa saryo 2, p. 121.

129. "Haebang chŏnsŏn ŭl pugam hamyŏnsŏ."

130. See footnotes 116, 117; An Chaehong, "Kajŭnghal p'ajaeng" (Despicable factional strife), Chosŏn ilbo, February 28, 1928.

131. "Kiro e sŏn Sin'ganhoe."

132. An Chaehong, "Chosŏn chisikgun ŭi wigi" (The crisis of Chosŏn intellectuals), Chosŏn ilbo, September 2, 1931.

class, An felt that the reason for its rapid growth was that "petite bourgeoisie in leadership positions could envision the path to future change, rather than just having an acute desire for rash adventurism."[133]

An Chaehong firmly criticized those who called for the dissolution of the Sin'ganhoe in the name of the interests of the labor and peasant classes.[134] To explain the situation caused by the economic depression that began in the late 1920s, socialists put forth a "theory of the third crisis of modern capitalism" and used it as the basis for their critique of the Sin'ganhoe. An acknowledged that the general arguments of the theory were sound.[135] However, a certain amount of time and deliberate effort would be necessary to turn their ideas into reality. In his view, to call for the dissolution of the Sin'ganhoe in support of class interests was no different from the musings of Henri Saint Simon (1760-1825) who believed that the rise of capitalism could lead immediately to the creation of an ideal society.[136] Although the socialists viewed the petite bourgeoisie as not engaged in struggle, An criticized views that did not take into account the role of the petite bourgeoisie as an "infantile fallacy."[137] An felt that the petite bourgeoisie not only assumed central roles in the formation of the Sin'ganhoe but also were a group that would choose not to compromise with Japan even as it tightened its rule. At the time, a consolidation of rightist forces was imminent as a result of efforts such as Japan's policy to create independent farmers (Chajaknong Ch'angjŏng Kyehoek), the reform of the Privy Council (Chungch'uwŏn), and the implementation of a new system of provincial administration. An felt that under these circumstances, the creation of a union of (leftist) forces that would not compromise with the Japanese was still an important and urgent task.[138]

An's conception of a leftist nationalist front, however, could not serve as the guiding principles for the Sin'ganhoe because of the conflict between maintaining an uncompromising resistance against the Japanese and pursuing a movement of struggle that conducted only legally sanctioned activities. The fundamental purpose of organizing the masses was to engage in struggle

133. An Chaehong, "Haeso pihaeso" (For or against dissolution [of the Sin'ganhoe]), *Chosŏn ilbo*, April 14, 1931.
134. An Chaehong, "Haesoron kwa oryu," *Chosŏn ilbo*, April 17, 1931.
135. "Haeso pihaeso."
136. An Chaehong, "Chae kaksŏng kwa chae insik" (Reawakening and rethinking), *Chosŏn ilbo*, January 1, 1932; "Haeso pihaeso."
137. "Kiro e sŏn Sin'ganhoe."
138. An Chaehong, "Chiphoe kyŏlsa munje chaeŭi" (A reexamination of the problems of assembly and association), *Chosŏn ilbo*, September 5, 1931.

against the Japanese, but as Japan tightened its rule and as the scope of the national liberation movement became more and more limited, it became extremely difficult to remain within legal boundaries and, at the same time, refuse to compromise with the Japanese. Despite their level of political commitment, the necessity to pursue legal activities ultimately pushed them into a more moderate direction. In the early 1930s, when calls for the dissolution of the Sin'ganhoe emerged, An began to argue for a "rectification" that would sweep away all systemic and class contradictions in one stroke and for the necessity of moderate reforms (*kaeryang*) to elevate the basic skills of the masses through legally permitted activities.[139] During the debate over the dissolution of the Sin'ganhoe, this conception of movements was behind his continual emphasis on the effectiveness of legal struggle and his defense of the Sin'ganhoe as an organization for "multiple paths of simultaneous" struggles.

This drift toward moderation was partially the consequence of An Chaehong's conception of class in which he assigned hegemony in the liberation movement to the petit-bourgeois class which was in the most central and intermediary position in Chosŏn in terms of class potential. His argument was that the petit-bourgeois class in Chosŏn would not be able to exert any political power outside of a united front or legally permitted activities because it lacked a mass base and had not yet developed to the point that it constituted an independent class.[140] As a result, in his conception of the national liberation movement, it was impossible to abandon the objectives of pursuing both a mass enlightenment movement and a united front with socialist forces.[141]

THE CULTURE MOVEMENT AND THE CHOSŎN STUDIES MOVEMENT

Along with the nationalist leftist front, An Chaehong also pursued the so-called "Culture Movement" to put his ideas on nationalism into practice. Early on in his career, he had stressed the importance of national spirit and national culture, based on his conception of national self-strengthening.

139. An Chaehong, "Sudo pyŏngjin ŭi sin ilnyŏn" (A new year of simultaneous progress on multiple paths), *Chosŏn ilbo*, January 1, 1930; An Chaehong, "Ch'ongch'ul ch'onggyŏl ch'ongch'al" (Complete exposure, final settlement, total insight), *Chosŏn ilbo*, January 1, 1931; An Chaehong, "Ch'ongch'ul esŏ ch'onggŏmch'al ro" (From complete exposure to complete investigation), *Chosŏn ilbo*, January 4, 1931.

140. An Chaehong, "Haesoron kwa oryu."

141. For these reasons, he did not abandon efforts at cooperation with socialist forces even after the dissolution of the Sin'ganhoe. See "Chae kaksŏng kwa chae insik" (Reawakening and rethinking).

However, his interest in culture did not develop into involvement in a concrete movement until the 1930s. After the dissolution of the Sin'ganhoe, An withdrew, for the moment, from social and political movements. He tried to organize another movement led by leftist nationalists but without success. His own career was going through difficulties as he was virtually forced to resign from the presidency of the *Chosŏn ilbo*.[142] Because of changes in movements and the intellectual world in Chosŏn at the time, this period was a turning point in his ideological standpoint and involvement in movements.

In intellectual and political circles in the early 1930s, leftist nationalist forces were in a state of turmoil as socialists were shifting to a more class-based strategy and moderate nationalists were becoming increasingly reactionary. Judging that the current situation was unfavorable to the progress of political movements, he promoted the Culture Movement as the "best secondary option" (*ch'oesŏnhan ch'asŏnch'aek*).[143] The Culture Movement would aim for the "cultural refinement, intensification, and purification of the Chosŏn people" in a way that completely eliminated any trace of politics. An's vision for the Culture Movement was quite moderate; it was a part of his "theory of the simultaneous pursuit of rectification (*hyŏkjŏng*) and moderate reforms" that he advocated in the first half of the 1930s.[144] In other words, he acknowledged the moderate nature of the Culture Movement but emphasized the realities faced by movements.

Nationalism was facing a crisis because of the thinking of socialists was becoming increasingly class-centered, leading them to renounce nationalism. Based on his conception of "pan-nationalism" in the mid 1930s, An Chaehong criticized the class-centered approach of socialists and hoped for a union of all classes under overarching banner of the nation.[145] He asserted that "interest in and the study of Chosŏn or ethnic things do not always [stem from] reactionary conservatism, sentimental atavism, or petit-bourgeois exclusivism," emphasizing the importance of understanding the nature of the

142. In March 1932, An was arrested along with Yi Sŭngbok, the business manager of *Chosŏn ilbo*, under the charge of misappropriation of funds raised for Chosŏn expatriates in Manchuria. In April, while still in jail, An resigned as the president of the *Chosŏn ilbo*. In November, he was sentenced to eight months in jail and was released for time already served. After his release, he took time off to recuperate. Ch'ŏn Kwan'u, "Minse An Chaehong yŏnbo" (A chronology of the life of An Chaehong), *Ch'angjak kwa pip'yŏng* (winter 1978).

143. An Chaehong, "Chosŏn kwa munhwa undong" (Chosŏn and the culture movement), *Sin Chosŏn*, no. 8 (January 1935), p. 3.

144. An Chaehong, "Segye ro put'ŏ Chosŏn e" (From the world to Chosŏn), *Chosŏn ilbo*, June 6, 1935 (reprinted in *Minse An Chaehong sŏnjip* 1, p. 510).

145. See footnote 66.

nationalist movement as well as international and class unity.[146] He felt that class and nationalist movements must co-exist and be unified with each other, writing that the terms "internationalism and nationalism refer to their co-existence, overlapping, and mutual compatibility in their realization."[147] However, An's views emphasized national unity and took into account class issues—but under the fundamental assumption that the nation was of primary importance. In the end, at a time when it became impossible to engage in political organizing within legal bounds, the essence of the Culture Movement was to promote the rebirth of the Chosŏn people as a nation suited to the changed reality.[148]

In the 1930s, An Chaehong began to devote even more attention to nationalism, seeing it as the last stronghold of resistance against the Japanese and as the basis of critique against those who argued for the primacy of class. Further extending his ideas on national self-strengthening, he felt that it was necessary for oppressed countries struggling against the great powers to strengthen their nationalism at a time when mass populism was rampant in fascist countries and "Japan-ism" (*Ilbonjuŭi*) was on the rise in the 1930s. His reasoning was based on the belief that each nation ultimately had to co-exist within world history according to its own particular national interests. However, nationalism of the future should establish a new "Chosŏn self,"[149] and it would be "based not on cultural remnants of past ages that are feudal and exclusivist but on a conception of the self that is open to the world."[150] He developed a theory of a more open nationalism that saw the traits of backward societies as an instance of diversity within a global universality and recognized the overlapping and co-existence of various political systems and cultures despite cultural uniqueness.[151] From the second half of the 1930s, he

146. An Chaehong, "Chosŏn kwa Chosŏn'in" (Chosŏn and the Chosŏn people), *Sin Tonga* (January 1935), p. 14.

147. Ibid.

148. "Chosŏn kwa Chosŏn'in."

149. An Chaehong, "Chosŏnhak ŭi munje" (The issue of Chosŏn Studies), *Sin Chosŏn* (December 1934), p. 3.

150. Ibid.

151. An Chaehong, "Kukche yŏndaesŏng esŏ pon munhwa t'ŭksu kwajŏngnon" (The theory of unique development of culture from the perspective of international solidarity), *Chosŏn ilbo*, January 1, 1936.

called this nationalism "a kind of *minsejuŭi* in which the nation and the world would be constituted through their interaction with each other."[152]

For the Culture Movement, the two activities that An Chaehong stressed were the promotion of "Chosŏn Studies"[153] and the organization of a cultural foundation. Believing that the first step in national awakening was an accurate understanding of its own situation, he advocated a more objective understanding of Korea in the context of its relations with other nations and states.[154] The Chosŏn Studies Movement and the cultural foundation were concrete attempts to put these ideas into action.

An defined "Chosŏn Studies" as "the attempt by a single collective of a certain homogeneous cultural system to investigate and illuminate the cultural trends of its particular history and society as an academic discipline."[155] There were two approaches to engaging in Chosŏn Studies, and he felt that both should be the objective of rigorous scientific research on Chosŏn. The first was statistical research on social dynamics, and the second involved the study of the unique aspects of traditional culture.[156] Although he often noted the "evils of the national character" to point out the objective deficiencies of

152. Ibid. These ideas on nationalism formed the central theory of his book *Sin minjokjuŭi sin minjuŭi* (Neo nationalism, neo democracy) (Seoul: Min'usa, 1945) which was written after liberation.

153. After 1925, moderate nationalists also argued for the necessity of "research on Chosŏn" (*Chosŏn yŏn'gu*) and undertook a systematic examination of it at a scholarly level. Within historical circles, the first person to argue the necessity of Chosŏn Studies was Ch'oe Namsŏn, and he showed a defeatist conception of nationalism and a focus on national reconstruction and spiritual reconstruction in his general discussions on Chosŏn Studies in his 1931 work *Chosŏn yŏksa* (History of Chosŏn). See Kim Yong-sop, "Urinara kŭndae yŏksahak ŭi sŏngnip" (The establishment of modern Korean historiography), *Han'guk ŭi yŏksa insik*, ha (Seoul: Changjak kwa pip'yŏngsa, 1976); Han Yŏng'u, "Minjok sahak ŭi sŏngnip kwa chŏn'gae" (The establishment of nationalist history and its development), *20 segi ch'o ŭi yŏksa insik* (Papers from the 11th conference on Korean history hosted of the National Historical Compilation Committee, 1988). However, the Chosŏn Studies envisioned by An Chaehong was different from that of Ch'oe Namsŏn in its emphasis on the universality within uniqueness. An's work represented a more developed stage compared to the nationalist historiography of Pak Ŭnsik and Sin Ch'aeho, and it formed the foundation of the neo-nationalist conception of history after liberation. See Yi Chiwŏn, "Sin minjok-juŭi sagwan, muŏsŭl kyesŭnghan kŏsin'ga" (The neo-nationalist conception of history—what did it emerge from?), *Yŏksa pip'yŏng*, no. 14 (Autumn 1991).

154. "Chosŏn kwa Chosŏn'in," p. 14; An Chaehong, "Segye munhwa e Chosŏn saeg ŭl jjanŏch'a" (Let's weave the colors of Chosŏn into world culture), *Tonga ilbo*, September 12, 1934.

155. "Chosŏnhak ŭi munje," p. 2.

156. Ibid.

the Chosŏn people, he did not regard them as fundamental flaws.[157] Since Chosŏn Studies would adapt a world-oriented sense of self to Chosŏn's situation in a way that would respect the unique development of cultures, it should begin with research that would enable new interpretations of Chosŏn's past history.[158] It was at this time that An began his own research on Chosŏn history. From 1934, he compiled and edited the *Yŏyudang chŏnsŏ* (Complete works of Chŏng Yagyong) with Chŏng Inbo and published it through the Sin Chosŏn Company, which was run by Kwŏn T'aehŭi. Until 1936, he conducted research on Chong Yagyong and Sin Ch'aeho and wrote a series of articles on ancient Korean history.[159]

An Chaehong himself felt that the Culture Movement should be run as a business enterprise rather than as a political organization. He envisioned the establishment of a "Chosŏn Cultural Foundation" to conduct the Culture Movement. The Chosŏn Cultural Foundation would operate with a fixed endowment, and its main purpose would be to promote and popularize research on Chosŏn culture. Its main activities were to focus on the study of the various developments in contemporary Chosŏn society and culture and the publication of critical studies of culture in general, writings and critical studies on Chosŏn culture, and the works of past scholars.[160] Since its activities not only sought to facilitate cultural projects but also to promote scholarly work, they would emphasize the scientific nature and professional level of research on Chosŏn, and the choice of activities seems to have been related to

---

157. An Chaehong, "Uri minjoksŏng ŭi pyŏngp'ye (3)" (The evils of our nation character), *Chosŏn ilbo*, 1935 (reprinted in *Minse An Chaehong sŏnjip 1*, p. 497). By contrast, Ch'oe Namsŏn wrote on the inferior and deformed national character of Chosŏn in his *History of Chosŏn*, indicating his defeatist conception of nationalism.

158. In the context of the development of modern historiography, the Chosŏn Studies Movement was important in two senses. It was both a reaction to the colonialist research on Chosŏn by Japanese government scholars and a response to the development of Marxist scholarship. See Han Yŏng'u, "Minjok sahak ŭi sŏngnip kwa chŏn'gae" (The establishment of nationalist history and its development), p. 12.

159. An Chaehong, "Tan'gunnon kwa Ŭnkija malssalnon" (The theories of Tan'gun and of the rejection [of the existence] of Kija of Yin), *Sin Chosŏn*, no. 11 (June 1935); An Chaehong, "Asadal sahoe ŭi palchŏn" (The development of Asadal society), *Chogwang* (February 1936); An Chaehong, "Chŏng Tasan sŏnsaeng ŭi hak kwa saeng'ae" (The life and scholarly work of Chŏng Yagyong), *Sin Chosŏn*, no. 6 (October 1934); An Chaehong, "Chŏng Tasan sŏnsaeng kwa kŭ saeng'ae ŭi hoego" (Recollections on Chŏng Yagyong and his life), *Sin Tonga* (October 1934); An Chaehong, "Chosŏn sahak ŭi sŏn'guja—Sin Tanjae haksŏl sagyŏn" (My personal views on the theories of Sin Ch'aeho, pioneer of Chosŏn historiography), *Chogwang 2*, no. 4 (April 1936).

160. An Chaehong, "Munhwa hyŏphoe soŭi" (A brief discussion on a cultural foundation), *Chosŏn ilbo*, June 20, 1935 (reprinted in *Minse An Chaehong sŏnjip 1*, pp. 533-34).

the sudden rise in the number of scholarly organizations, a trend in the intellectual world at the time.[161] An felt that the cultural foundation should have a status comparable to that of the Ohara Institute for Social Research (Ohara Shakai Mondai Kenkyujo) in Japan.[162] "Despite differences in their missions," the Ohara Institute, whose scholarship was based on Marxism, played a "very significant role culturally," and he felt that it could serve as a model of a "cultural organization where prominent intellectuals in the private sector could work freely and whose standards equalled that of institutions of higher learning."[163] However, his plans for a Chosŏn Cultural Foundation never came to fruition. Not only was he not able to raise the necessary funds, but around that time, he was also arrested twice by the Japanese police in the Military Academy Student Incident and the Hŭng'ŏp Club Incident.[164]

An Chaehong's turn to the Culture Movement reflected a deepening of his theoretical interest in nationalism, and it served as an alternative to a more directly politically-oriented movement. But at a time when Japanese fascism was gaining strength, it was impossible for a culture movement based

---

161. The years after 1933 can be seen as a period of rapid growth in the history of modern Korean scholarship. The Chosŏn Kyŏngje Hakhoe was founded in June 1933, followed by the Chindan Hakhoe in May 1934, and these years also constituted the period of the Chosŏn Studies Movement. On the trends in the intellectual world in this period, see Pang Kie-chung, *Han'guk kŭnhyŏndae sasangsa yŏn'gu* (Studies in the intellectual history of modern and contemporary Korea) (Seoul: Yŏksa pip'yŏngsa, 1992), chapters 1 and 2. A variety of scholarly trends emerged that differed in epistemology and research methodlogy, but An Chaehong welcomed the general rise of interest in research on Chosŏn in all areas of society. "Chosŏnhak ŭi munje," p. 4.

162. "Munhwa hyŏphoe soŭi," *Minse An Chaehong sŏnjip 1*, pp. 523-24. The Ohara Institute for Social Research was founded in Osaka in 1920 by Ohara Magosaburo, president of Kurashiki Cotton Spinning Company, with his contribution of one million yen. The researchers of this institute were mainly graduates of the Economics Department at Tokyo Imperial University, and they conducted a wide range of scholarly work ranging from studies on Marxist theory to research on social problems. The most active researchers included scholars such as Kushida Tomizo, Kuruma Samezo, Morito Tatsuo, Hosokawa Karoku, and Ryu Shintaro. Members of the institute were regarded to be equal in status to university professors, and it was one of the main intellectual centers in Japan during the 1920s and 1930s. Otsuka Torao, *Gakkai ibun* (Tokyo: Senshinsha, 1931), pp. 204-06; Ouchi Hyoe, *Keizaigaku gojunen*, vol. 1 (Tokyo: Tokyo Daigaku Shuppankai, 1954), pp. 170-72.

163. "Munhwa hyŏphoe soŭi," *Minse An Chaehong sŏnjip 1*, pp. 523-24.

164. In 1936, An Chaehong was arrested for referring a young man, Chŏng P'ilsŏng, to Kim Tubong of the National Revolutionary Party (*Minjok hyŏngmyŏngdang*) in Nanking, China, receiving a two-year jail sentence. In 1938, he was jailed in Sŏdaemun police station during the Hŭng'ŏp Kurakbu Incident. Until 1939, he was constantly in conflict with the Japanese authorities. After his release, he returned to his hometown in the countryside and devoted himself to research on Chosŏn's ancient history. Ch'ŏn Kwan'u, "Minse An Chaehong yŏnbo" (A chronology of the life of An Chaehong).

on *minsejuŭi* to mobilize significant resistance. Unable to gain any room to maneuver within legal limits and without an arena within which to realize its ideology, his version of a culture movement ended up emphasizing "spiritual matters" and had much potential to develop into subjective escapism. Fascism concealed class contradictions and produced nationalist and pro-state propaganda as a way of mobilizing the masses. Just as fascism drew in various elements of the petite bourgeoisie and rendered the labor class powerless, An's nationalism also contained the danger of diverting the colonial masses' potential for resistance into support for the existing system, by failing to recognize the nature of Japanese fascism. For these reasons, An's critics in the 1930s called his Culture Movement a "form of Korean fascism" and labelled him a "social Fascist."[165] Even leaving aside the issue of the accuracy of this critique, it seems clear that An's conception of the Culture Movement as the "best secondary option," despite his subjective intentions, had aspects that made it difficult to maintain resistance against the Japanese because the shift to a moderate line led to a weakening of its political stance.[166] During the Japanese occupation period, the movements of petite bourgeoisie within the

---

165. At the time, all sorts of socialists made critiques of the Chosŏn Studies Movement and other scholarly efforts led by nationalist intellectuals. For specific critiques of An Chaehong, see Kim Namch'ŏn, "Chosŏn ŭn kwayŏn nuga ch'ŏndae hanŭn'ga" (Who actually views Chosŏn with contempt?), *Chosŏn chungang ilbo*, October 18-27, 1935; Sŏ Kyŏngbaek, "P'asijŭm ŭi ch'anyang kwa Chosŏn hyŏngjŏk P'asijŭm" (Admiration for Fascism and Chosŏn Fascism), *Chosŏn chungang ilbo*, February 19, 1936; Chŏn Yŏngsik, "Chosŏnjŏk ideollogi munje" (The ideological issues of Chosŏn), *Chosŏn chungang ilbo*, March 29-April 10, 1936; Han Ŭngsu,"'Maejosang' tusang e ilbong" ([Striking] a blow on the heads of those who sell their ancestors), *Pip'an*, no. 25 (November 1935). Their arguments were based on the theory of social fascism (as a critique of social democracy) which was adopted at the Sixth Congress of the Comintern in 1928. The theory of social fascism, which became the basis for adopting the strategy of "class against class," expanded the notion of "bourgeois" to include the supporters of social democracy who advocated class cooperation. Based on this theory, socialists adopted a strategy of "class against class" to separate the worker class from other classes and viewed the establishment of soviets as the only program for revolution. The theory of social fascism demonstrated a tendency to leftist extremism, and the critiques of An Chaehong by socialist commentators were also based on this theory, strongly suggesting the existence of such tendencies among Korean socialists. See Kim Yŏngsun and Yi Yong'u, *Kukga iron* (Theory of the state) (Seoul: Han'gilsa, 1991), pp. 143-57.

166. Of course, another factor that has to be considered is the repression of the Japanese which did not tolerate even such moderate movements. Because of the nature of the Government-General's policies, it is possible to view these movements as resisting the Japanese, in a relative sense, and other subjective and objective factors would have to be taken into consideration in order to do so. However, in this chapter, I will not attempt a comprehensive evaluation of social movements, and I will restrict myself to just mentioning their moderate nature in terms of their politics.

national liberation movement ultimately ended in failure, and the trajectory of the Culture Movement traced the path of their decline.

Conclusion

Of all the various aspects of An Chaehong's thought and career, this chapter has focused on an examination of his political-economic thinking and his conception of the national liberation movement. The objective was to clarify, through An Chaehong, one of the major streams of bourgeois nationalist thought in Korea. Though it pursued capitalist modernization, this stream rejected a worldview centered on the interests of capitalists and promoted a unique form of nationalism, seeking to resist imperialism. An's views on contemporary society and social movements can be summarized as follows.

An felt that the current state of the Korean economy was one in which the feudal economic system was being strengthened while capitalist growth was being blocked under the Japanese occupation. The key agricultural issue was the decline of Chosŏn small and medium landlords, independent cultivators, and tenant farmers—which was the result of the strengthening of the landlord system to serve as one of the foundations of Japanese capitalism. As a solution to this problem, he proposed a reform of the agricultural policies of the Japanese, betterment of relations between landlords and tenants, increased production, and the establishment of cooperative associations. What he focused on most in the economy was the fact that the institutions of Japanese capitalism were undermining national capital of Korea, obstructing its development. He saw the petty bourgeoisie—small- to medium-scale capital—as the central force in national capital since their development was blocked and since they were not subordinated under the economic structure of Japanese colonialism.

One of An Chaehong's main interests was international affairs, and he viewed them from the perspective of an oppressed colonial nation. He felt that after World War I, the fundamental dynamic of the world system was the conflict between capitalism and socialism which emerged during the process of the reorganization and stabilization of the imperialist powers. However, his view of the world was also deeply state-centered in perspective. Based on this dualistic understanding of the world, An emphasized that class movements resisting imperialism and the resistance movements of oppressed nations were universal phenomena of world history.

An's views on the economy and world affairs were ultimately concerned with political issues and Chosŏn's colonial situation. The central element of his political thought was his conception of the nation as the totality of historical outcomes. His view of Korea's colonial situation was state-oriented and focused on self-strengthening, but it also had the characteristics of the nationalism of an oppressed people who were seeking to promote resistance and equality. Accordingly, the agents of resistance and reform could not be conceived separately from the totality of the nation, and the goal of this self-strengthening was the development of a modern bourgeois nation. However, the petite bourgeoisie were to be the central force of the modern nation because of the nature of bourgeois development under Japanese rule. In his view, the petite bourgeoisie constituted a centrally positioned group whose mindset and economic activites were partially modernized and who still possessed the capability to resist.

Though An saw the "national petite bourgeoisie" as the central force of resistance, they were unable to achieve sufficient growth as a class under Japanese rule. Because of their weak class base, the petite bourgeoisie had to join with other classes, such as the peasant and labor classes, in order to exert political influence. Therefore, he emphasized the importance of class cooperation and a united front with socialist forces. He called for the formation a "nationalist leftist front," and his vision for such a movement was realized through the Sin'ganhoe. Intermediate groups, such as the petite bourgeoisie, can function as a catalyst in the formation of a united front, but when the front splits, they tend to be the first to collapse. In the end, the "national petite bourgeoisie" could not stop the dissolution of the Sin'ganhoe, whose original purpose was to serve as a transitional organization to the unitary national party that An envisioned. After the failure of political resistance movements, he turned to the Culture Movement as an alternative. In the 1930s, he faced a storm of criticism, being viewed as a "social fascist," and the movements that he organized went further down the path of decline.

During the occupation period, An Chaehong developed an internally consistent system of thought that aimed at nationalism for self-strengthening and capitalist modernization under the leadership of the petite bourgeoisie. The reasons why he could not maintain a position of uncompromising resistance against the Japanese were rooted in the foundations of his intellectual views. In this sense, An's conception of organized movements can be regarded as a typical reflection of the political and ideological positions taken by bourgeois nationalist groups within Chosŏn that resisted the Japanese. These views developed into one of the programs for state building in the Liberation period. They also served as the intellectual foundations for the politics of moderate rightist groups and for the "ideology of neo nationalism" that emerged after 1945. This is the historical context in which the ideology of "neo-democracy and neo-nationalism" and the politics of the moderate right after liberation must be understood.

translated by Paul S. Nam with Jeong-Il Lee

Index of Terms

amch'o 暗礁 rock below the water

chach'i undong 自治運動 self-rule movement

chagang undong 自强運動 self-strengthening movements

chajaknong ch'angjŏng kyehoek 自作農創定計劃 policy to create
independent farmers

Changsan 奬産

ch'oesŏnhan ch'asŏnch'aek 最善한·次善策 best secondary option

Chŏng Yagyong 丁若鏞 (1762-1836; *ho* Tasan, 茶山)

Chosŏnhak undong 朝鮮學運動 Chosŏn Studies Movement

Chosŏn hŭng'ŏp chusikhoesa 朝鮮興業株式會社 Hŭng'ŏp Company

Chosŏn kŏnguk chunbi wiwŏnhoe 朝鮮建國準備委員會 Committee for
the Preparation of Korean Independence

Chosŏn nonong ch'ong tongmaeng 朝鮮勞農總同盟 Chosŏn Worker-
Peasant League

Chosŏn sanjik changnyŏ kye 朝鮮産織奬勵契 Association for the
Promotion of the Textile Industry in Chosŏn

Chosŏn yŏn'gu 朝鮮研究 research on Chosŏn

Chungch'uwŏn 中樞院 Privy Council

Chwau hapjak wiwŏnhoe 左右合作委員會 Left-Right Coordinating
Committee

hyŏkjŏng 革正 rectification

hyŏpdong chohap 協同組合 cooperative unions

Ilbonjuŭi 日本主義 Japan-ism

It'aeri kŏnguk yŏng'ungjŏn 伊太利建國英雄傳 Biography of the heroes
in the founding of Italy

kaeryang 改良 moderate reforms

Kodŭng kyŏngch'al yosa 高等警察要史

kukga 國家 state

kukhon 國魂 national spirit

kungmin 國民 people or citizenry

kyoyuk ŭi minjunghwa 敎育의 民衆化

marŭm 마름 agricultural overseers

Miguk tongnip chŏnsa 米國獨立戰史 The history of the American war
for independence

Minhŭnghoe 民興會

minjok 民族 nation

minjok kyŏngje 民族經濟 national economy

minjokjuŭijŏk seryŏn kwajŏng 民族主義的 洗練過程 maturation of nationalism

minjok pŏmnon 民族汎論 encompassing sense of the nation

Minjŏng changgwan 民政長官 Chief Civil Administrator

minsejuŭi 民世主義

munja pogŭp undong 문자보급운동 literacy movements

Nonong ch'ong tongmaeng 勞農總同盟 Korean Labor-Peasant League

Ohara Shakai Mondai Kenkyujo 大原社會問題硏究所 Ohara Institute for Social Research

paekŭi nongmin 白衣農民 white-clothed peasantry

pandongjŏk kukgajuŭi 反動的國家主義 reactionary statism

Pisang Kungmin Hoeŭi 非常國民會議 Emergency National Council

puguk kangbyŏng 富國强兵 wealthy country, strong army

saenghwal kaesŏn undong 生活개선운동 life improvement movements

sangnom to, ilggun ŭi to, nodong to 상놈道, 일꾼의道, 勞動道 the ways of the commoner and of labor

Sanmi chŭngsik kyehoek 産米增殖計劃 Program to Increase Rice Production

san'ŏp chohap 産業組合 industrial unions

sillyŏk yangsŏng 實力養成

Sin'ganhoe 新幹會

Sin minjokjuŭi sin minjujuŭi 新民族主義 新民主主義 *Neo-Nationalism and Neo-Democracy*

sojak'inhoe 소작인회 tenants' association

Tansa kŏngukji 瑞士建國誌

Taehan Minguk Imsi Chŏngbu 大韓民國臨時政府 Korean Provisional Government

Tongyang ch'ŏksik chusikhoesa 東洋拓殖株式會社 Oriental Development Company

t'ŭksu pudae 특수부대 special forces

Wŏllam mangguksa 越南亡國史 The history of the fall of Vietnam

Xinmin shuo (Hsin min shuo) 新民書

yangban to, seannim to 兩班道, 샌님道 the ways of yangban gentlemen

Yinbing shi wenji (Yin ping shih wen chi) 飮氷室文集

Ziyou shu 自由書

Yi Sunt'ak and Social Democratic Thought in Korea

Hong Sung-Chan
洪性讚

After Korea's liberation in 1945, three political groups, broadly speaking, contended with each other to gain control over the newly independent state. First, right-wing nationalists wanted to maintain a capitalist state by continuing the economic system of the colonial period. The second group consisted of left-wing socialists who completely rejected the colonial economic system and aimed to establish a socialist state. Lastly, moderates attempted to create a left-right coalition, carry out far-reaching reforms of the economic system, and establish a unified state built upon social democratic ideas. Despite their efforts at left-right collaboration, both the left and the right severely attacked the moderates. To leftists, moderates appeared to waver between internationalism and social chauvinism. In their view, although moderates expressed support for internationalism, their actions tended more toward social chauvinism and opportunism. Leftists criticized such behavior because it undermined the political front of the proletarian liberation movement and the development of a class consciousness by seeking the continued existence of capitalism.[1] Moderates were also criticized for constantly urging cooperation and opposing division in class struggles; they were viewed as reformists who clung to legal means and representative politics.

As the division of the country became a reality and socialist and capitalist systems were established in the North and South respectively, moderates were no longer able to operate as a distinct political force. They became

---

1. Yi Sŏkt'ae, ed., "Chungganp'a" (The moderate faction), *Sahoe kwahak taesajŏn* (Seoul: Mun'uin sŏgwan, 1948), p. 628.

354 | *Hong Sung-Chan*

absorbed into one of the two other groups, leaving them fragmented and marginalized. Because of their political fate, scholarly interest in the moderates declined after the Korean War as the division of the country became hardened. However, scholars have come to realize the necessity of understanding the historical background of Korea's division as the prospect of unification has recently become a serious subject of debate. Recently, there has been a revival in research on the political-economic thought of the moderates, resulting in a growing number of studies on this topic.[2]

The objective of this chapter is to contribute to this growing body of research by examining the political-economic thought of Yi Sunt'ak (1897-1950, *ho* Hyojŏng), an active figure in moderate political groups in the post-liberation period. During the first half of the twentieth century, he led a varied life as both a scholar and a politician. In the early 1920s, he studied Marxism under the Japanese economist Kawakami Hajime (1879-1946) and played a pioneering role in its introduction into Korea. In 1938, he was arrested as one of the leaders in the Economic Club (Kyŏngje yŏn'guhoe) Incident, also known as the "Campus Communization Incident" (Haknae chŏkhwa sagŏn), at Yŏnhŭi Junior College (aka Chosun Christian College), the precursor to today's Yonsei University.[3]

Although Yi Sunt'ak joined the right-wing Korean Democratic Party (KDP) after liberation, he quickly left it and participated in the formation of the People's League (Minjung tongmaeng), a political organization of moderate political groups, in fall 1946. Until January 1948, he was active in

2. Kim Kisŭng, "Pae Sŏngryong ŭi chŏngch'i kyŏngje sasang yŏn'gu" (A study of the political economic thought of Pae Sŏngryong) (Ph.D. diss., Korea University, 1990); Cho Sŏnghun, "Chwau hapjak undong kwa minjok chaju yŏnmaeng" (The right-left coalition movement and the National Autonomy Alliance), *Han'guk tongnip undongsa ŭi yŏn'gu* (Seoul: Paeksan Pak Sŏngsu kyosu hwagap ki'nyŏm nonch'ong kanhaeng wiwŏnhoe, 1992); To Chinsun, "1945-48 nyŏn uik ŭi tonghyang kwa minjok t'ong'il chŏngbu surip undong" (Trends of the right wing and the movement to establish a unified national government, 1945-48) (Ph.D. diss., Seoul National University, 1992); Pang Kie-chung (Pang Kijung), "Haebang chŏnggukgi chungganp'a nosŏn ŭi kyŏngje sasang–Kang Chin'guk ŭi san'ŏp chaegŏnnon kwa nong'ŏp kaehyŏknon ŭl chungsim ŭro" (The economic thought of the moderate faction during the Liberation period—with a focus on the industrial revival and agricultural reform proposals of Kang Chin'guk), *Kyŏngje iron kwa Han'guk kyŏngje*, Ch'oe Hojin paksa kangdan 50chu'nyŏn ki'nyŏm nonmunjip kanhaenghoe, ed. (Seoul: Pakyŏngsa, 1993).
3. Hong Sung-Chan (Hong Sŏngch'an), "Iljeha Yŏnjŏn sangkwa ŭi kyŏngje hakp'ung kwa Kyŏngje yŏnguhoe sa'gŏn" (The intellectual atmosphere of the department of commerce at Yŏnhŭi Junior College during the colonial period and the Economic Club Incident), *Yŏnse kyŏngje yŏn'gu* 1, no. 1 (1994). "Economic Club" is the organization's own romanization of its name.

right-left coalition efforts such as the Democratic Independence Front (Minjujuŭi tongnip chŏnsŏn) and the Democratic Independence Party (Minju tongnipdang). Rejecting both the right-wing KDP and the left-wing Korean Communist Party (KCP), he supported the moderate stance of building a right-left coalition in order to establish a unified democratic state based on the principle of national autonomy. However, when the Syngman Rhee (Yi Sŭngman) administration took power in the South in August 1948, Yi became the first head of the Planning Office (Kihoekch'ŏ), and, in 1949, he became the chairperson of the Union of Korean Financial Cooperatives (Chosŏn kŭmyung chohap yŏnhaphoe). In short, he was co-opted by the right wing regime of South Korea. When the Korean War broke out in June 1950, he was kidnapped by the North, and little is known of what happened to him afterwards.

As befits a figure who was involved in a wide range of intellectual and political activities, scholarly opinion on Yi Sunt'ak is diverse.[4] Looking at his whole life and career, it is possible to discern some common threads. Politically, his career followed a path common among moderates. Intellectually, he can be characterized as a social democrat or reformist who, although he was different from a typical Western social democrat, was committed to the ideals of class cooperation, national unity, constitutionalism, and reformism, beginning in the colonial period. Yi is an important figure in modern Korean history through whom it is possible to examine the intellectual background of moderate politics as well as the history of the introduction, development, and ultimate failure of social democracy in Korea. Although scholarship has devoted much attention to tracing the major trends of modern Korean intellectual history, there has been relatively little research on the

---

4. Kim Myŏngsŏn, "Yi Sunt'ak kyosu" (Professor Yi Sunt'ak), *Wŏlgan Sebŭransŭ* 11 (1979); Im Yŏngt'ae, *Singminji sidae Han'guk sahoe wa undong* (Korean society and movements during the colonial period) (Seoul: Sagyejŏl, 1985); Yun Kijung, "Kyŏngje kyŏng'yŏnghak ŭi hangmunjŏk chŏnt'ong" (The intellectual traditions of economics and management studies), *Kyegan Yonse chilli chayu* (autumn 1989); Yun Kijung, "Yi Sunt'ak," *Kyegan Yŏnse chilli chayu* (spring 1993); Hwang Myŏngsu, "Yi Sunt'ak," *Han'guksa taebaekgwa sajŏn*, vol. 18 (Seoul: Han'guk Chŏngsin Munhwa Yŏn'guwŏn, 1992); Hong Sung-Chan, "Ilcheha Yi Sunt'ak ŭi nong'ŏpnon kwa haebang chikhu ipbŏp ŭiwŏn ŭi t'oji kaehyŏk pŏp'an" (Yi Sunt'ak's views on agriculture during the Japanese occupation period and the proposal of the land reform law of the South Korean Interim Legislative Assembly in the post-liberation period), *Kyŏngje iron kwa Han'guk kyŏngje* (1993); Hong Sung-Chan, ibid., 1994; Hong Sung-Chan, "Han'guk kŭnhyŏndae Yi Sunt'ak ŭi chŏngch'i kyŏngje sasang" (The political economic thought of Yi Sunt'ak during Korea's modern and contemporary history), *Yŏksa munje yŏn'gu*, no. 1 (1996).

moderate faction or social democracy. This chapter hopes to help remedy that situation.

Yi Sunt'ak's Intellectual Development

NATIONALISM AND EDUCATION IN TOKYO

Yi Sunt'ak was born on November 30, 1897 in Haenam county, South Chŏlla province as the fifth son of Yi Hŭimyŏn. The Yŏn'an Yi family was one of the three most prominent families in this region, along with the Haenam Yun and Yŏhŭng Min families. But by the time of his birth, the family had declined to the status of independent farmers, and when his father died in 1904, they ended up becoming tenant farmers.[5] Later, he recollected that his childhood experiences had made him aware of the extreme differences between rich and poor and implanted within him a hatred of social inequality.

The Yi family remained strongly Confucian up to the Hanmal period, and Yi Sunt'ak received a classical education at a local Confucian school (*sŏdang*). Working to support his mother, he had his first contact with modern education when he enrolled in Mokp'o Public Normal School. In 1910, when he was thirteen, he experienced the shock of Japan's occupation of Korea, and he developed anti-Japanese feelings. Despite such feelings, he believed Japanese propaganda that the annexation embodied the brotherhood between the Korean and Japanese nations and would contribute to the establishment of peace in the East, and he had high expectations for the future of Koreans.

Graduating from normal school in March 1913, he entered Mokp'o Public Commercial School but dropped out after a semester because he could not pay the tuition. Returning home, he worked as a clerk (*sŏgi*) in Samsan

5. *Yŏnhŭi chŏnmun hakgyo haknae chŏkhwa sagŏn sŏryu* (Documents on the Campus Communization Incident at Yŏnhŭi Junior College) 1938-1940. This is a record of documents made by the police, the prosecutor, and the court at the time of the Economic Club incident. Below, if there are no footnotes appended, all information about his life is taken from this document. I also will use books such as Kida Tadae, *Chosŏn insa hŭng sinnok* (Seoul: Chosŏn sinmunsa, 1935) and Yi Sunt'ak, *Ch'oegun segye iljugi* (A recent trip around the world) (Seoul: Hansŏng tosŏ chusik hoesa, 1934). Yi Sunt'ak's book was recently republished, and all quotations are taken from the reprint edition, *Ch'oegun segye iljugi* (Seoul: Hakminsa, 1997). For a chronology of his life and list of his publications, see *Yŏnse kyŏngje yŏn'gu* 4, no. 2 (1997), an issue commemorating the 100th anniversary of his birth.

myŏn and as a low-level assistant (*kowŏn*) in the Haenam county office. At the time, the Japanese were suppressing the tenacious anti-Japanese resistance movements that arose in the early occupation period. He felt guilty because he had attended a public school built by the Japanese and worked in the lowest level offices of the Japanese administrative structure. Although he performed his job while hiding his anti-Japanese feelings, he became aware of the discriminatory nature of Japanese policies in politics, the economy, society, and education, becoming dissatisfied with Japanese rule.

Yi Sunt'ak left Korea in July 1914 to study in Japan but again had problems paying the school's tuition.[6] He received financial assistance from another Korean student, Kim Yŏnsu (1896-1979), who was in the fifth year at Azabu Middle School in Tokyo. As is well-known, Kim was the son of the large landlord Kim Kyŏngjung of the Honam region and the younger brother of Kim Sŏngsu.[7] Through Kim's financial support, Yi began the third year at Seijo Middle School in Tokyo in April 1917. He spent four and a half years in Tokyo, associating with other nationalist Korean students, until he left to enroll in the preparatory division of Kobe Higher Commercial School in April 1919.[8] He was in Tokyo when the Declaration of Independence of the Korean Youth Independence Corps was announced on February 8, 1919 and when the March First Movement broke out in Korea, and his nationalist sentiments grew even stronger.

The influence of his two older brothers, Yi Sangho and Yi Sŏng'yŏng, was also important in the development of his nationalism. From the 1910s, they were both active in Poch'ŏngyo, a new national religion that was an

---

6. Hyojŏng, "Tong'yu kuŏk" (Old memories of travel to Japan), *Sintonga* 5, no. 1 (1935). According to the *Yŏnhŭi chŏnmun hakgyo haknae chŏkhwa sagŏn sŏryu*, he left for Japan in August 1916, but I have decided to use the information from the *Sintonga* article. Hyojŏng is the *ho* (pen name or civic name) of Yi Sunt'ak.

7. The brothers Kim Yŏnsu and Kim Sŏngsu (1891-1955) were the most prominent Korean capitalists during the colonial period; they managed and at least partly owned companies and organizations such as Kyŏngsŏng Spinning and Weaving Company, Samyang Company, the *Tonga ilbo*, and Posŏng Junior College, the precursor of today's Koryŏ (Korea) University. See Kim Sanghyŏng, *Sudang Kim Yŏnsu* (Seoul: Sudang Kim Yŏnsu ki'nyŏm saŏphoe, 1971); Kim Yong-sop (Kim Yongsŏp), *Han'guk kŭnhyŏndae nong'ŏpsa yŏn'gu* (Seoul: Ilchogak, 1992); Carter J. Eckert, *Offspring of Empire: The Koch'ang Kims and the Colonial Origins of Korean Capitalism, 1876-1945* (Seattle and London: University of Washington Press, 1991).

8. In autumn 1918, Yi Sunt'ak passed the equivalency examination for middle school graduation and dropped out of Seijo Middle School during the second term of the fourth year. He was going to enter Third Higher School in Kyoto, but on Kim Yŏnsu's advice, he enrolled in Kobe Higher Commercial School instead.

offshoot of Chŭngsangyo.[9] Poch'ŏngyo began a reorganization in the late 1910s, and by the early 1920s, it became a large-scale religious organization with several hundred-thousand followers. Around the time of the March First Movement, it underwent vigorous expansion at the same time that it was being suppressed by the Japanese authorities.[10] In 1921, it proclaimed the foundation of a new dynasty, called "Siguk," and spread the belief that the founder of the religion would someday ascend to heaven. The belief in a messiah gave hope to the common people who were in despair over the future of the nation after the failure of the March First Movement.

The growth of the religion suggested new possibilities for the development of the nationalist movement to intellectuals who were engaged in debates over its future direction.[11] As two of the central, most capable leaders of the religion,[12] Yi's two brothers were entrusted with important positions within the organization and converted other nationalist intellectuals to the religion such as Yi Chong'ik, Ko Yonghwan, and Chu Ik. They functioned as

---

9. Yi Sangho (1888-1966, *ho* Ch'ŏng'ŭm) had a classical education until he was sixteen, and for three years beginning in 1908, he studied at Misan Middle School in Haenam. After the occupation of Korea began, he spent three years abroad in places such as Shanghai and Beijing and was active in Poch'ŏngyo after his return to Korea in 1915. Yi Sŏng'yŏng (1895-1968, *ho* Namju) received a classical education until he was ten, graduated from Yonghung Elementary School in Mokp'o, and taught at Haenam Normal School when he was eighteen. He entered Poch'ŏngyo in 1914, and leaving the same year for Japan, he studied in the historical geography department at Tokyo Higher Teachers' School. After he graduated in 1919, he devoted himself to Poch'ŏngyo, and after 1945, he changed his name to Yi Chŏngnip.

10. Both of Yi Sunt'ak's brothers suffered hardships because of the Japanese in this period. When the Japanese undertook a large-scale suppression of Poch'ŏngyo in 1921 (which the religion refers to as "the third ordeal"), Yi Sangho was arrested by Japanese police and was imprisoned for forty days. Yi Chŏngnip, *Chŭngsangyosa* (The History of Chŭngsangyo) (Seoul: Chŭngsangyo ponbu, 1977).

11. Yi Chŏngnip, ibid.; Han'guk minjok chonggyo hyŏpŭihoe, "Poch'ŏngyo," *Han'guk minjok chonggyo ch'ongnam* (Seoul: Han'guk minjok chonggyo hyŏpŭihoe, 1992).

12. Surprised by the enormous expansion of Poch'ŏngyo, the Japanese decided that it was no longer possible to suppress it and forced the organization to go public in August 1921. The legalization of the organization was accomplished quickly under the leadership of Yi Sangho, and it established a mission in Seoul, the Kyŏngsŏng chinjŏngwŏn, in February 1922, with Yi Sangho as its director. In January 1923, it decided to establish missions in each province and county of the country called "chinjŏngwŏn" and "chŏnggyobu" respectively. In May of that year, it established a company, Pogwangsa, with Yi Sŏng'yŏng as its president, and published a journal, *Pogwang*, the official organ of the religion. In September of the same year, according to the code of laws established by Yi Sŏng'yŏng, Poch'ŏngyo decided to establish the Ch'ongjŏngwŏn and Ch'ongnyŏngwŏn as its central administrative organ, and Yi Sangho was appointed as the chairman of the Ch'ongryŏngwŏn whose duty was to supervise the provincial *chinjŏngwŏn*.

a bridge between Poch'ŏngyo and the nationalist movement.[13] Of his two brothers, Yi Sunt'ak was especially close with Yi Sŏng'yŏng, who also went to study in Japan in 1914, and they seem to have had a strong influence on each other.[14] When the Native Products Promotion Society was formed in January 1923 mainly through the efforts of the *Tonga ilbo*, Yi Sunt'ak was one of the founding members and served on its board of directors, and his close relationship with his brother is one of the reasons that the Poch'ŏngyo organization gave its complete support to the Native Products Promotion Movement (Mulsan changnyŏ undong).[15]

As a result of these influences, Yi Sunt'ak's nationalism was similar to that of right-wing bourgeois nationalists associated with the *Tonga ilbo*. In general, they were opposed to armed resistance against the Japanese and thought that it was more important to focus on educational and commercial activities in order to overcome the country's backwardness. In August 1920, he published an article in the *Tonga ilbo* that proposed a plan for Korea's

13. Yi Chŏngnip, ibid. Chu Ik participated in the March First Movement and the Korean Provisional Government in Shanghai. Yi Chong'ik was the head of the Kyŏngsŏng (Seoul) chinjŏngwŏn in January 1923. Yi Kyun'yŏng, *Singanhoe yŏn'gu* (A study of the Singanhoe) (Seoul: Yŏksa pip'yŏngsa, 1993), p. 86; Yi Chŏngnip, ibid., pp. 105-6. When the two brothers were expelled from the religion because of conflicts with Ch'a Kyŏngsŏk, the founder, they formed the Poch'ŏngyo hyŏksinhoe (committee chair, Yi Sangho) together with Yi Chong'ik, Ko Yonghwan, and Chu Ik, and began a movement to reform Poch'ŏngyo. In response, the founder and his supporters asked the Japanese authorities to suppress this organization and formed a pro-Japanese organization called the Siguk taedongdan, becoming a de facto governmental group. In the end, both brothers left for Manchuria in October 1923. Returning to Korea in 1925, Yi Sangho established a new religion called Tonghwagyo and served as its leader, and in 1926, he compiled the scripture of Chŭngsangyo, *Taesun chŏn'gyŏng*. Believing in the imminent defeat of the Japanese, Yi Sŏng'yŏng sought to organize a group called the Tonga hŭngsansa in 1942 with the objective of unifying the various religious organizations after liberation. However, he was arrested for violating the Peace Preservation Law and remained in jail until liberation. Yi Chŏngnip, ibid.

14. For Yi Sŏng'yŏng's views on politics, society, and the economy, see Yi Chŏngnip, *Taesun ch'ŏlhak—Han'gukin pon'ui ŭi segyegwan* (Taesun philosophy—a view of the world for Koreans) (Seoul: Chŭngsangyo ponbu, (1947) 1984).

15. Some important members of Poch'ŏngyo served as directors of the Native Products Promotion Society (NPPS) such as Im Kyŏngho, head of the chinjŏngwŏn in South Ch'ungch'ŏng province; Ko Yonghwan, an employee of the Kyŏngsŏng (Seoul) chinjŏngwŏn; and Chu Ik, a manager at the Kyŏngsŏng chinjŏngwŏn. When the NPPS established consumer cooperatives, Ko Yonghwan was one of the five members of the preparatory committee. Both the Kyŏngsŏng chinjŏngwŏn and Pogwangsa bought advertisements in the initial issue of *Sanŏpgye*, the official organ of the NPPS, that printed messages of congratulations, and Ko Yonghwan and Im Kyŏngho were managers of *Sanŏpgye*. When Poch'ŏngyo's takeover of the newspaper *Sidae ilbo* caused controversy, Yi Sunt'ak and Chu Ik acted as third-party mediators. See *Chosŏn ilbo*, July 13, 1924.

economic development.[16] As far as is known, it is his first published piece of writing. He believed that a country that is unified politically, culturally, and racially must possess the natural, human, and social conditions in order for its economy to develop. His argument was that Korea's economic development had been slow because it lacked the necessary social conditions. Unlike Korea, the West based its economy on laissez-faire thought, emphasized consumption, and advocated the unrestrained play of desire. By contrast, following Confucian principles of altruism and of restraining desire, Korea forbade luxury and produced only the minimum of products necessary; it ignored the benefits of commerce and a monetary currency and systematized these ideas in its economy and social philosophy. Based on these views, he presented three proposals for the development of the Korean economy.

His first proposal called for the dissemination of knowledge of economics. He felt that the level of economic knowledge was an important factor in determining success in the age of capitalism. It was necessary to establish commercial schools and institutions to teach laissez-faire thought in all regions of the country and ultimately to develop Korea's international competitiveness by developing the people's conceptions of labor. His second proposal focused on changing the mind-set of Korean capitalists. He believed that the monied class in Korea was not active in building factories, companies, or large agricultural estates because it lacked knowledge of the principles of capitalism. He proposed that the wealthy should either employ people who had such knowledge or educate their children or other promising young people and encourage them to establish their own businesses.

Yi Sunt'ak's third proposal was concerned with the restoration of Korea's commercial rights. In his view, the main reasons for Japan's almost complete dominance of Korean commerce were Korea's loss of sovereignty and its failure to establish an autonomous national economy. Although restoration of national sovereignty was absolutely necessary to regain full control over commercial rights, he felt that it would be difficult to accomplish at the time. Instead, he emphasized a plan that would enable Koreans to outcompete foreign merchants. He stressed the need to disseminate "new education" and new knowledge to develop the abilities of the people and the need to establish consumer and producer cooperatives in all cities in order to provide goods to people at low prices. His plan avoided direct confrontation

16. Yi Sunt'ak, "Pando ŭi kyŏngjesang chiui rŭl nonhayŏ kŭmhu kyŏngje paljŏnch'aek e kŭpham (chŏn 5 hoe)" (On Korea's economic position and proposals for its future economic development), *Tonga ilbo*, August 4-11, 1920.

with the Japanese, seeking to restore Korea's sovereignty by indirect means. By targeting educational efforts at national capitalists and leaders in each field of society, the abilities of the people would develop, and through a movement to establish commercial cooperatives, foreign merchants would be driven out of Korea. Ultimately, Yi believed such development would result in the restoration of both commercial rights and national sovereignty.

Yi Sunt'ak expressed similar views in an article on the effects of the post-war recession of 1920 on the Korean people.[17] Although recessions were worldwide phenomena that followed the laws of economics, he felt that their severity would differ according to the effectiveness of the state's response to the crisis and the people's ability to endure their effects. Korea's situation was especially dire not only because the people lacked the ability to endure recessions but also because the state's response was not adequate. Why then was Korea unable to respond adequately to the recession? He believed that the main reasons were Korea's occupation by Japan and its inability to develop its own "unique national economic organizations." Korea was in a "state of disarray and unable to unify its national economic organizations because only a few had been developed in connection with Japan [i.e., subordinated to the Japanese economy]." Accordingly, the most pressing issues were the "establishment of national economic institutions suited to Chosŏn society" and the restoration of the "power of a stable state sovereignty."[18] What he meant was the restoration of national sovereignty. Since the restoration of commercial rights would have been a difficult task by itself, the prospects for the restoration of sovereignty were even less realistic. Therefore, he proposed that Korea should accumulate capital and stimulate commerce and industry by organizing a movement centering on national capitalists and nationalist leaders to develop the abilities of the people. The most urgent task facing Koreans was the acquisition of the skills necessary for a capitalist economy.

While in Tokyo, Yi Sunt'ak associated with Koreans who were right-wing bourgeois nationalists and shared their intellectual views. As a solution to the problems of Korean society, he emphasized the development of the national economy and the restoration of state sovereignty. However, since it would be difficult to accomplish these goals through direct confrontation

17. Yi Sunt'ak, "Mokha ŭi konghwang kwa pando kyŏngje sahoe ŭi ch'amsang (chŏn 5 hoe)" (The current economic recession and the sad state of Korea's economy and society), *Tonga ilbo*, May 26-30, 1921.
18. Yi Sunt'ak, "Chosŏn'in musanhwa ŭi t'ŭkjing" (The characteristics of the proletarianization of the Chosŏn people), *Sinmin* 2, no. 8 (1926).

with the Japanese, he put his hopes on educational efforts, cultural projects, and the promotion of native industry that aimed to change the mind-set of the national bourgeoisie.

MARXISM AND EDUCATION IN KYOTO

In September 1919, Yi Sunt'ak left Kobe Higher Commercial School and enrolled in the special program of the economics department at Kyoto Imperial University on the advice of Kim Yŏnsu, who was a student in the department.[19] One of his professors at Kyoto was Kawakami Hajime, the most famous economist in Japan at the time, who published *Binbo mono-gatari* (Tale of Poverty) in 1917. He was known as an authority on Marxism in Japan and was one of the foremost scholars at Kyoto Imperial University as well as in the Japanese intellectual world. Yi came to view Kawakami as the only true economist in East Asia, past or present, and as the dominant figure in the Japanese intellectual world. He was such a devoted student of Kawakami's that he earned the nickname of "the Kawakami Hajime of Cho-sŏn." He extensively read Kawakami's writings such as *Shakai mondai kan-ken* (Opinions on Social Issues, 1918), *Kinsei keisai siso siron* (Historical Treatise on Modern Economic Thought, 1920), and *Yuibutsu sikan kenkyu* (Studies in Historical Materialism, 1921). *Tale of Poverty*, in particular, had a considerable emotional impact on him, and theoretically, *Studies of Histor-ical Materialism* was a strong influence.[20]

Although Yi Sunt'ak had been dissatisfied with the state of society from his childhood, he did not show much interest in social problems both because of his poverty and because of his devotion to his studies. While he was studying in Tokyo and Kobe, various anti-state ideologies such as socialism, communism, and anarchism were introduced into Japan after the First World

19. In April 1921, he entered the regular course (English economics department) and graduated in March 1922. The most important courses that he completed were: Principles of Economics (I+II), Economic History, Colonial Policy, Statistics, Readings in Economics (first foreign language), Agricultural Economy, Industrial Economy, Commercial Economy, Theories of Foreign Trade, Social Problems and Social Policy (I+II), Public Finance, History of Economics, Finance, Theories of Transportation, Insurance, Commercial Law, and Accounting. See Kyoto Teidai sekidan (Register of Kyoto Imperial University).

20. Yi Sunt'ak, "Sahoe munje e taehan Hasang Cho paksa ŭi taedo wa kyŏnji" (The attitude and position of Dr. Kawakami Hajime on social issues), *Sinsaenghwal* 1, no. 6 (June 1922); Hanyang hakin, "Chwagyŏng kyosu ugyŏng kyosu—Yŏnhŭi chŏnmun kyosu ch'ŭngp'yŏng (sok)" (Left-leaning professors and right-leaning professors—a survey of professors at Yŏnhŭi Junior College), *Samch'ŏlli*, no. 12 (1931); *Yŏnhŭi chŏnmun hakgyo haknae chŏkhwa sagŏn sŏryu*, 1938-1940.

War. He witnessed the unprecedented turmoil of the Japanese intellectual world and the development of Marxism as both a legal and an underground movement. Up to that time, he had not reached any "conclusions" about his own views, but as he attended Kawakami's lectures and read about Marxism, his conception of justice and his theoretical standpoint gradually developed through his interaction with Marxism, which emphasized "struggle between the two classes of the rich and the poor" and believed in the "victory of the impoverished class."[21]

Yi Sunt'ak studied Marxist economic thought at Kyoto before Kawakami embarked on a "new journey" to continue his study of Marxism in 1923-24. Kawakami first encountered Marx's historical materialism through the works of E.R.A. Seligman. Accordingly, Kawakami separated historical materialism from dialectic philosophy and understood Marxism not as a world-view or philosophy but simply as an economic theory.[22] Until the mid-1910s, Kawakami's thought showed the combined influences of liberalism, historicism, and *Nationalökonomie*. Even after he started publishing his journal *Shakai mondai kenkyu* (Studies on Social Issues) in 1917, he was not yet a committed Marxist. He was still in the process of transforming from a bourgeois economist into a Marxist economist until around 1927-28 when he became a truly "indomitable Marxist" and a "warrior seeking after truth." During his approximately twenty years at Kyoto Imperial University, he repeatedly wavered as he searched for the "haven" of Marxism. After 1927-28, his lectures focused entirely on an exposition of Marxism, but until then, he also lectured on bourgeois economics, otherwise known as "vulgar economics."

21. As a result of these influences, while he was a student at Kyoto Imperial University, he formed the Kyoto Korean Labor Mutual Aid Association (Kyŏngdo Chosŏn'in nodong kongjehoe) in May 1920 and became its chairman. His efforts were devoted to improving the welfare of Korean laborers in the area. Therefore, the Japanese police kept a close surveillance of Yi Sunt'ak, who "held anti-Japanese ideas." See Hong Sung-Chan, *ibid.*, 1994.

22. From 1923, Japanese Marxists such as Kushida Tomizo and Fukumoto Kazuo began to criticize severely the limitations of Kawakami's understanding of Marxism. Thus, Kawakami left on a "new journey" to study dialectics. Unless there is a footnote appended, information about Kawakami is taken from the following sources: Kawakami Hajime, *Keizaigaku taiko* 1 (General principles of economics) (Tokyo: Aoki shoten, 1928); Kawakami Hajime, *Jijoden* 1 (Autobiography) (Tokyo: Iwanami shoten, 1952); Furuta Mitsuru, *Kawakami Hajime* (Tokyo: Tokyo University Press, 1959); Ouchi Hyoe, *Kawakami Hajime* (Tokyo: Chikuma shobo, 1966); Yamanouchi Yasushi, "Taisho demokurasi to Marukusu shugi" (Taisho democracy and Marxism), *Kindai Nihon keizai shisoshi* I, Cho Yukio and Sumiya Kazuhiko, ed. (Tokyo: Yuhikaku, 1969); Inoue Kiyoshi, ed., *Fukutsu no Marukusu shugisha Kawakami Hajime* (The indomitable Marxist, Kawakami Hajime) (Tokyo: Gendai hyoronsha, 1980).

After graduating from Kyoto Imperial University in March 1922, Yi Sunt'ak returned to Korea and published several articles on Marxist theory before he became a professor at Yŏnhŭi Junior College the following year.[23] Clearly demonstrating a commitment to Marxism, these articles were mainly abridged translations or adaptations of Kawakami's writings. Yi's main sources were Kawakami's *Historical Treatise on Modern Economic Thought* and *Studies in Historical Materialism*. Yi Sunt'ak felt that reading these two books was absolutely necessary to understand Marxist thought, scientific socialism, and historical materialism.[24] Consequently, these articles by Yi are useful in examining both Kawakami's influence on Yi's view of economics and Yi's understanding of Marxism.

In the early 1920s, Kawakami considered the three main principles of Marxist thought to be historical materialism, as a theory of the past; economics, as a theory of the present; and policy studies, as a theory of the future (referred to as social democracy or the theory of socialist movements). What united these three principles was the theory of class struggle. It is striking that he referred to Marxist policy as "social democracy." To Kawakami, the term "social democracy" (*shaminshugi*) represented Marx's ideal society, a society in which no distinction would exist between capitalist and laborer. In such a society, capitalists would be unable to exploit workers, and everyone would subscribe to the notion that one had to work in order to eat. Kawakami referred to this Marxist conception of policy as the "theory of exterminating capitalists" or the "theory of requiring everyone in the country to do labor." However, this did not mean the literal extermination of capitalists. Rather, the class with a monopoly on land and capital would be eliminated by a thorough implementation of free competition and antimonopoly principles, and a society would be created in which all people would be able to develop their natural abilities in free competition. To accomplish these goals, it was necessary to eliminate the capitalists' monopoly

23. Yi Sunt'ak, "Malk'ŭssŭ ŭi yumul sagwan" (Marx's historical materialism), *Tonga ilbo*, April 18-May 8, 1922; Yi Sunt'ak, "Makssŭ sasang ŭi kaeyo" (A summary of Marxist thought), *Tonga ilbo*, May 11-June 23, 1922 (This article is an abridged translation of Kawakami's book, *Kinsei keisai sisosiron* (History of Modern Economic Thought (Tokyo: Iwanami shoten, 1920). Below, this article will be referred to as "1922a," and references to quotations from this article will only give the number of the serialization); Yi Sunt'ak, "Makssŭ ijŏn ŭi kyŏngje sasang" (Economic thought before Marx), *Tonga ilbo*, July 12-August 7, 1922; Yi Sunt'ak, "Chabonjuŭi saengsan chojik ŭi haebu" (An analysis of the organizations of capitalist production), *Tonga ilbo*, January 19-February 9, 1923.

24. Yi Sunt'ak, ibid., 1922a, installment #1.

of capital and to have a "capital communalism" (*shihon kyoyushugi*) in which "the principles of communism would be applied to the type of property known as capital."[25]

Kawakami felt that "capital communalism" could be achieved only through the efforts of workers engaging in class struggle. Unlike neo-historicist economists like Fukuda Tokuzo, who advocated class cooperation between capitalists and workers, he refused to advocate class cooperation. He felt that socialism must be realized through the workers' oppression of opposing forces. The method for achieving these goals should not be a moral or religious movement through which the ruling class reconstructs society on their own. Rather, the propertyless class should gather their strength in political movements; after "a minority takes state power in its hands," they should implement socialism forcibly through the exercise of their authority.[26] Nevertheless, he did not think that a political movement should engage in violent revolution. The reason was that, as Marx had pointed out, a social revolution was a change in the entire superstructure that can occur "rapidly or slowly" according to changes in the economic base.

Kawakami's opposition to violent revolution was also apparent in his views on the history of socialist movements. In its early stages, according to him, such movements had focused on reform of people's character through moralistic sermons. Later, they developed into political movements with the objective of gaining control of the state. Political movements initially aimed at building a new society through a rebellion that would overthrow the old one. However, in cases where prospects for success were clearly low, they adopted rational, constitutional methods instead. They spread their ideology and thought in newspapers and magazines, demanded the right to vote, and formed political parties. They tried to seize political power by capturing a majority in elections for representative assemblies.[27]

For Kawakami, the fundamental objective of social reconstruction was the achievement of socialism. A society would be built in which monopolies of land and capital would be strictly prohibited, and people would be able to live and develop their natural abilities in a state of free competition. His goals would be achieved not through class cooperation but through class struggle; the propertyless would seize hegemony and accomplish their goals through the exercise of state power. Instead of violent revolution, he searched

25. Yi Sunt'ak, ibid., 1922a, installment #37.
26. Yi Sunt'ak, ibid., 1922a, installments #7, 12, 37.
27. Yi Sunt'ak, ibid., 1922a, installments #7, 8.

for a method of achieving these goals through gradual, constitutional means; in other words, Kawakami supported the social-democratic line of the Second International.

As examined above, during his school days in Japan, Yi Sunt'ak was influenced by two opposing worldviews. The first was nationalism. In the nationalist worldview, it was necessary to build a distinct national economy through the restoration of sovereignty which, in turn, would be accomplished through the recovery of commercial rights. It called for a reformist movement through legal means, such as the promotion of education and the establishment of business cooperatives, led by the nationalist bourgeoisie. The second was Marxism or, more accurately, social democracy. Maintaining their commitment to class struggle, the propertyless would form a political party through gradual, constitutional methods. This worldview called for the realization of "capital communalism" by the use of state authority after the propertyless class seized political power in elections. In other words, nationalism deeply affected his emotions and instincts while his intellect was influenced by the science and theory of social reconstruction of Marxism.

Yi Sunt'ak wavered between these two contradictory worldviews. However, at the time, he was becoming more deeply drawn to nationalism. Vacillating between a class-based internationalism and a patriotic nationalism, his intellect followed a Marxist worldview, but his activities consistently fell within the bounds of nationalism. Saying that Kawakami's ideas of social reconstruction were "not at all a dangerous [form of] thought," Yi Sunt'ak accepted almost all of Kawakami's ideas. Yi completely agreed with his argument that social reconstruction would require considerable preparation and time and that his ideas would have to be implemented gradually in proper sequence.[28] However, in contrast to Kawakami, Yi Sunt'ak believed in the necessity of class cooperation and, in particular, of cooperation between laborers and capitalists.

An article from 1921 on social reconstruction clearly shows that Yi already held these ideas when he was a student at Kyoto Imperial University.[29] He stated that the most important consequence of the First World War was that it put the world on a path of social reconstruction and showed that social reconstruction could be accomplished through reform rather than through the

28. Yi Sunt'ak, "Sahoe munje e taehan Hasang Cho paksa ŭi t'aedo wa kyŏnji."

29. Yi Sunt'ak, "Kuju chŏnjaeng i sahoe sasang sang e kŭphan yŏnghyang ŭl nonham" (A discussion of the influence of the European war on social thought), *Sinmin kongnon* 2, no. 7 (1921).

sort of violent change that occurred in the French and Russian revolutions. He discussed three phenomena as proof of his argument. First, in all countries before the war, the proletariat had advocated socialist ideas of internationalism and anti-statism and opposed the war. But once war broke out, they renounced socialism and participated in the war to defend their homelands. After the war, with their newly acquired self-confidence and moral authority, they began to demand reforms in return for their sacrifice. Since no government could afford to ignore these demands, social reconstruction increasingly could be accomplished through reformist methods with the cooperation of the entire society instead of a revolution led by a single class.

Second, as the war grew longer, it became more imperative for governments to have the support of the labor class, and governments changed their treatment of laborers and began to regard them as partners in civic life. In politics, governments let representatives of laborers' organizations participate in the cabinet or gave them other important political positions. In the economy, they gave laborers a voice and a certain degree of participation in the management of enterprises along with material improvements through equitable distribution of wealth and resources. Although these measures were not all successful and became insufficient to deal with problems in the post-war period, he felt certain that these changes had a substantial effect in strengthening former labor movements and in developing social thought and social movements "materially as well as spiritually."

Third, since the standard of living of workers became equal to or even rose higher than that of the educated class during the war, existing forms of class thinking and conceptions of material well-being broke down. Workers sought a wage increase through continual labor agitation in response to rising prices during wartime, and the economic status of the intellectual class became similar to or fell below that of the workers.

In sum, in several articles from the early 1920s, Yi Sunt'ak discussed trends in social thought and social movements after World War I and put forth the following view on the future path of social reconstruction:

> Still possessing traditional, conservative ideas, we should not try to reconstruct society through violent means only, if capitalists can stop being obsessed with their own profits, if they try to provide material support to workers without discrimination through equitable distribution, if they give workers a voice and the right to participate in the management of companies by treating them as equal partners, and if

they can also give workers spiritual satisfaction by not abusing the power that capitalists have enjoyed up to now. However, I do not deny that there may be unavoidable circumstances where it is necessary to use violent means. The main point is that since our attitude toward social reconstruction up to now has been ambiguous, we should not be swept up by our desires for revolution, and we should devote ourselves to achieving only a certain degree of reform.[30]

Although Yi Sunt'ak did not reject revolution, he remained committed to social democratic ideas of class cooperation or, more accurately, to social reformism and social chauvinism. Then, why did he, unlike Kawakami, emphasize class cooperation, although he agreed with almost all of Kawakami's ideas on social reconstruction? Why did he advocate a more reformist program than Kawakami's social democracy? What are the underlying reasons that he moved toward reformism and support for class cooperation in the early 1920s, at a time when, within Marxism, the Third International criticized the reformism of the Second, leading to a split within its ranks?

Yi Sunt'ak and Social Democracy

VIEWS ON CLASS COOPERATION AND UNITED-FRONT POLITICS

As new types of thought were introduced into Korea in the early 1920s, there emerged, broadly speaking, two political groups and two political ideologies that came into conflict with each other. These two groups were the national capitalists and the socialists. They were the successors of, respectively, the landlord course and peasant course of reform from the late Chosŏn and Hanmal periods. Interest in socialism grew tremendously as an alternative ideology and political movement after the failure of the March First Movement.[31]

It was in the midst of these changes that Yi Sunt'ak returned to Korea in March 1922. Yi quickly became known in academic and journalistic circles because of his status as a graduate of Kyoto Imperial University, the aura of being a student of Kawakami's, and his long-standing relation with Kim Yŏnsu. After working at Kyŏngsŏng Spinning and Weaving Company

---

30. Yi Sunt'ak, ibid.
31. Kim Yong-sop, ibid.; Pang Kie-chung, *Han'guk kŭnhyŏndae sasangsa yŏn'gu* (Studies in the intellectual history of modern and contemporary Korea) (Seoul: Yŏksa pip'yŏngsa, 1992).

(Kyŏngsŏng pangjik chusik hoesa), which was owned and run by Kim Yŏnsu, and the Chosŏn Commercial Bank (Chosŏn sang'ŏp ŭnhaeng), he became a professor in the department of commerce at Yŏnhŭi Junior College in April 1923. In November of that same year, Yi became the acting chair of the department as the successor of Paek Sanggyu, who had moved to Posŏng Junior College. This position could be considered the equivalent of being the dean of the business school. The following year, in November 1924, he was formally appointed department chair and became an influential administrator, also becoming a member of the school affairs committee.

After his return to Korea, Yi Sunt'ak mainly devoted himself to two types of activities. The first was education and scholarly work, and the second was social and intellectual organizations whose ultimate objective was national independence. First, he was active in introducing Marx's historical materialism and economics into Korea through newspapers, journals, and lectures at Yŏnhŭi.[32] It was in this period that he published the articles most strongly suggesting that he was a Marxist. He also devoted himself to building up the faculty and establishing the intellectual direction at Yŏnhŭi's department of commerce. He built a department committed to scholarship that was anti-Japanese, anti-imperialist, and against government-sponsored research with the hiring of Paek Nam'un (graduate of Tokyo Commercial College, the precursor of Hitotsubashi University) and Cho Pyŏng'ok (Columbia University) in 1925 and of No Tonggyu (Kyoto Imperial University), one of his former Yŏnhŭi students, in 1928.[33]

Second, throughout the 1920s, he participated exclusively in organizations of bourgeois nationalists or in united-front organizations. These included the Min'uhoe, Native Products Promotion Society, Research Institute on Chosŏn Affairs (Chosŏn sajong yon'guhoe), the Korean branch of the Institute of Pacific Affairs, and the Sin'ganhoe. The one exception was his appointment in February 1927 as an editorial advisor of the journal *Labor Movement*, which was published by socialists belonging to the Seoul Youth Corps (Sŏul ch'ŏngnyŏnhoe).[34]

---

32. At Yŏnhŭi, he taught courses such as Principles of Economics, Customs and Warehousing, Commercial History, Japanese Commercial Letter Writing, Statistics, Insurance, and Commercial Policy.

33. Hong Sung-Chan, ibid., 1994.

34. *Chosŏn ilbo*, February 14, 1927. It is unclear whether or not he actually participated in the editing of this journal.

Why did an economist like Yi Sunt'ak not participate in socialist or communist political movements and organizations even though he felt that no economic theory rivaled Marx's?[35] Some years later, he gave three reasons for his decision.[36] First, his personality was not suited for illegal, extremist political movements as he lacked the courage to be an activist. Second, as a Christian school, Yŏnhŭi Junior College did not tolerate open efforts at political propaganda nor anti-Christian scholarship such as socialism and Marxism. Third, he did not agree with the position of the Third International, i.e., the Comintern's advocacy of world revolution. Among the three, the main reason was most likely the third one, and it is a telling indication of Yi Sunt'ak's views during this period.

Yi Sunt'ak was one of the founding members of the Native Products Promotion Society, which was organized by the *Tonga ilbo* in January 1923, and served on its board of directors. When socialists criticized the movement, he came to its defense with his extensive knowledge of Marxism. His opponent in this debate was the socialist Yi Sŏngt'ae (1901-?). In a March 1923 article, Yi Sŏngt'ae argued that the movement was fundamentally anti-revolutionary since it was a movement led by the middle class and a small number of capitalists. He felt that socialists and the proletariat should oppose this movement because, even if it did succeed, Korean capitalists and the middle class would monopolize its benefits.[37] However, Yi Sunt'ak did not regard the Society as merely a middle class movement. He saw it as a national political movement organized by all classes "gathering under a single umbrella" including Korea's capitalists and proletariat, the intellectual class, nationalists and internationalists, communists and anarchists, and men and women. He also felt that not all middle class movements were inherently

35. Yi Sunt'ak, "T'ŭksu sajŏng e kamhan kyŏngjehak ŭi Chosŏnjŏk yŏn'guron" (Economic Research on Chosŏn based on its Special Situation), *Chosŏn ilbo*, July 8, 1935.

36. *Chŏnhyangnok* (Record on Conversion), June 23, 1939 in *Yŏnhŭi chŏnmun hakgyo haknae chŏkhwa sagŏn sŏryu* (1938-1940).

37. Yi Sŏngt'ae, "Chungsan kyegŭp ŭi igijŏk undong—sahoejuŭija ka pon mulsan changryŏ undong" (The selfish movement of the middle class—a socialist's view of the Native Products Promotion Movement [NPPM]), *Tonga ilbo*, March 20, 1923. For more on the debates surrounding the movement, see: Cho Kijun, "Chosŏn mulsan changryŏ undong ŭi chŏn'gae kwajŏng kwa kŭ yŏksajŏk sŏngkyŏk" (The development of the NPPM and its historical significance), *Yŏksa hakpo*, no. 41 (1992); Yun Haedong, "Iljeha mulsan changnyŏ undong ŭi paegyŏng kwa kŭ inyŏm" (The background and ideology of the NPPM during the colonial period), *Han'guk saron*, no. 27 (1992).

anti-revolutionary in nature.[38] A middle-class movement could also become revolutionary if the people involved realized that they were all being turned into a proletariat and consciously decided to participate in such a movement.

Yi supported the Native Products Promotion Movement for reasons beyond his personal relationships with right-wing nationalists, such as Kim Sŏngsu and Kim Yŏnsu. He had known them since his student days in Tokyo, and they were the leaders of the movement. First, there was his understanding of Marx's theory of revolution. He felt that Marx's historical materialism contained two completely different theories of revolution. There was the political revolution which Marx expounded as a theorist of revolution, and there was also the social revolution that Marx discussed as a Social Darwinist. According to Yi Sunt'ak's interpretation, the former referred to a proletarian revolution whose aim was to seize state power, and the latter referred to a change of the social formation.

Yi thought of political revolutions as "an unusual episode in the process of social evolution" and thus no more than "a single historical incident arising within the realm of politics." It was reckless to "try [to accomplish] social revolution through a simple political revolution" at a time when productivity was not sufficiently developed. Korean society was at a stage in which it "was necessary to plant seeds of revolution within current economic institutions that would be able to produce 'newer, more developed' economic institutions since current institutions could not be eliminated overnight." In his view, Korea was not at a stage where it could achieve socialism since productivity was not sufficiently developed, and social evolution could not be accomplished through the will of one or two individuals but consisted of stages that all societies must pass through in their inevitable evolution. He believed that the Native Products Promotion Movement, whose goal was to encourage domestic production, stimulate industry, and develop productive facilities, was not at all in contradiction with the objectives of socialism.

Second, Yi Sunt'ak supported the NPPM because he believed that, in terms of class position, all Koreans belonged to the proletariat. It was the so-called theory of the "total proletariat" (*ch'ongch'ejŏk musanja*). He felt that all the accumulation of wealth, industrialization, and population increase in Korea after the occupation were accomplished by Japanese capitalism and not through Korea's own economic efforts. Since development under colonialism

---

38. Yi Sunt'ak, "'Sahoejuŭija ka pon mulsan changnyŏ undong'—Yi Sŏngt'ae ssi ŭi nonmun ŭl p'yŏngham" ("A socialist's view of the NPPM"—a critique of Yi Sŏngt'ae's article), *Tonga ilbo*, March 30, 1923. From this point on, this article will be referred to as "Yi Sunt'ak, 1923a."

had no benefits to Koreans themselves, if the occupation continued, all of them would eventually fall to the status of industrial or agricultural laborers. In addition, an increase in Japanese immigration would likely lead to increased foreign migration by Koreans.[39] Such views were apparent in an article in which he examined the status of land and capital ownership in Seoul in late 1926 according to nationality:

> Kyŏngsŏng [Seoul] is already no longer the center of Korea. It is not the center of Koreans. That is, Kyŏngsŏng. . . is not the Kyŏngsŏng of Koreans but the Kyŏngsŏng of the Japanese. It is true in economic aspects and will be even more so in other areas of society. Therefore, it is natural that Kyŏngsŏng is not "Kyŏngsŏng" but Keijo [author's note: the Japanese pronunciation of the characters for Kyŏngsŏng]. . . . In Kyŏngsŏng, although there are approximately three times as many Koreans as Japanese, [Koreans] will no longer be masters of the house called Kyŏngsŏng, if [they] cannot become owners of the house or can only be an employee of that house.[40]

He understood the structure of class conflict under Japanese imperialism to be a confrontation between Japanese and Koreans, thus demonstrating his view that Koreans were a "total proletariat."

Based on such views, Yi was skeptical about the internationalism of Marxism. Because of the nature of the Japanese occupation, "Korean workers [were] in a doubly disadvantageous position." No matter how developed the class consciousness of the workers was and no matter how common their interests were as an exploited group, Korean and Japanese laborers were "not in a situation [where they] can shake hands." He noted that even Marx urged Polish communists, who were under the rule of another nation, to support a political group whose primary goal was not class revolution but national liberation. Thus, he felt that Korean socialists should also participate in the Native Products Promotion Movement even though it was a nationalist political movement.

> Since Korea today has been placed under imperialism, that is, since Korea is, in a sense, in a situation that aids the inevitable unifying movements of the laborers, it is not "possible to make clear the battle

---

39. Yi Sunt'ak, "Chosŏn'in musanhwa ŭi t'ŭkjing."

40. Yi Sunt'ak, "Kyŏngsŏng inya? Keijo nya?" (Kyŏngsŏng or Keijo?), *Tonga ilbo*, January 5, 1927.

lines of the class struggle," and it seems that there is also no "need to make the battle lines of the class struggle clear."[41]

This quotation is a revealing example of his thinking. Since Korea was polarized into Japanese, who were capitalists, landlords, the wealthy, and the ruling class, and Koreans, who were made up of laborers, tenant farmers, the poor, and the dominated class, he felt that it was necessary to have a national political movement or a national revolution before a social revolution.

> I thought that the communist movement in Korea was a struggle of Koreans, who were the dominated class and impoverished class, against the Japanese, who became the ruling and wealthy class because of Korea's special situation. Therefore, I felt that the communist movement in Korea must begin with a national political revolution. . . . There are two reasons why I held such opinions on a revolution in view of Korea's special situation. First, at the time, in rural areas in Korea, Korean landlords were rapidly losing status, and their lands were almost all taken over by Japanese. In such a situation, I felt that in Korea, landlords would soon [all] be Japanese, and tenant farmers and agricultural laborers would be Korean. Second, as Japanese monopolized almost all small- and large-scale commercial and industrial enterprises in the cities, capital was concentrated in [the hands of] the Japanese. On the other hand, since Koreans were being displaced from the center of cities and falling into the status of the proletariat, I felt that in the near future, Japanese would become capitalists and Koreans would become workers in Korea. In other words, I expected that the two races of Japanese and Koreans would eventually form the classes of rich and poor in Korea. With my nationalist sentiments reinforcing such views, I became a so-called national communist and held the opinion that communist revolution in Korea must first pass through the stage of national political revolution before entering the stage of social revolution.[42]

This section has examined the formation of Yi Sunt'ak's intellectual and political views during the 1920s. I have sought to examine why he did not agree with the Comintern's position on world revolution, why he did not participate in the political and organizational movements of socialists or communists while joining national capitalist and united-front movements,

---

41. Yi Sunt'ak, ibid., 1923a.
42. *Chŏnhyangnok* (Record on Conversion).

and why he was committed to united-front movements, unlike Kawakami who criticized them. Since he had to take into account Korea's special situation, i.e., the national contradictions that occurred under foreign occupation, he faced a different situation than Kawakami, who had left on a new journey, "determining to stake [his] life on [achieving] a jump" in his thought and practice around 1923-24. In 1927-28, Kawakami suddenly re-signed from his post at Kyoto Imperial University and directly participated in the communist movement.[43]

In Yi's opinion, political revolution in Korea would not take the form of a direct seizure of state power by the proletariat who sought the realization of socialism. Rather, it had to be a national political movement or a national political revolution that sought the liberation and independence of the nation. By substituting his conception of national political revolution for Marx's proletarian revolution, Yi Sunt'ak was able to reconcile the two worldviews of internationalism and classism, on the one hand, and of nationalism and patriotism, on the other. No longer troubled by the conflict between his mind and his actions, he supported the united-front policies and principles of class cooperation. Furthermore, he was able to develop a theory of two-stage revolution which posited that a revolution in Korea would have to pass through the stage of national political revolution first and then enter the second stage of social revolution.[44]

Yi Sunt'ak supported cooperation not only between capitalists and laborers but also between farmers and laborers. On April 15, 1924, when the Chosŏn Worker-Peasant League (Chosŏn nonong ch'ong tongmaeng) passed a resolution on the union of the labor and tenant farmers' movements at their inaugural meeting, he supported it enthusiastically. Although laborers and farmers were classes with different interests, he felt that they needed to form a united class front because they were both being exploited by the leisure classes of capitalists and landlords. There were two reasons behind his position.[45]

43. Kawakami Hajime, ibid., 1952.

44. Kawakami also made a distinction between social and political revolutions. Although these views were the result of theoretical efforts to reconcile Marx's thesis on the movement between social formations (*Preface to A Critique of Political Economy*) with the fact that socialist revolution has occurred in economically backward Russia, it seems that they were also a reflection of his hopes that the movement to socialism could be achieved peacefully through the development of productivity. Yamanouchi Yasushi, "Taisho demokurasi to Marukusu shugi." Yi Sunt'ak probably also held similar hopes.

45. Yi Sunt'ak, "Nodong undong kwa sojak undong ŭi hyŏpdong" (The unity of the labor movement and the tenant farmers' movement), *Kaebyŏk*, no. 47 (May 1924).

First, as mentioned above, he viewed class conflict during the colonial period as a confrontation between Japanese landlords and capitalists, on the one hand, and Korean laborers and tenant farmers, on the other. Second, he thought that even if the agricultural population, which comprised eighty-five percent of the total population, particularly the tenant farmers, could not be considered agricultural laborers, neither could they be regarded as agricultural managers. Tenant farmers were "falling day by day to the status of a kind of hired laborer"; they were just "a type of hired laborer" and "agricultural laborers who had freedom in law only" in terms of social status and income derived from cultivation. Because tenant farmers were no different from hired laborers, unity would be possible between Korean laborers and tenant farmers. Because they were both being exploited by Japanese landlords and capitalists, an alliance between the labor and tenant farmers' movements would also be possible. He felt that such a union and alliance would be one of the keys to achieving national political revolution.

Out of his support of left-right collaboration and united-front politics, Yi Sunt'ak participated in the Sin'ganhoe in January 1927 as one of its founding directors and as an official. However, with the announcement of the "December theses" in 1928, the activities of socialists and communists began to focus more on class struggle, and both left-wing nationalists, who supported a united-front, and right-wing nationalists became their main targets of attack. In the end, the Sin'ganhoe was formally dissolved in May 1931, and the political base for left-right collaboration was significantly reduced.

When the students in the department of commerce at Yŏnhŭi Junior College all withdrew from the school in protest in June 1929, Yi Sunt'ak was criticized as a person of low character by progressives who said that he "who had once adhered to Marxist thought for his food, clothing, and social status had changed and converted."[46] Coming at a time when united-front politics were breaking down, such criticism must have caused him tremendous disappointment. When he visited Shanghai in 1933, he noted that, among all the foreigners there, only Koreans were not able to establish a secure livelihood—because they lacked an enterprising spirit, because the older generation of Koreans was not able to provide sound leadership, and because they were still not able to overcome the evil nature of factional strife.[47] Similarly,

46. Hong Sung-Chan, ibid., 1994; Hanyang hak'in, ibid.
47. Yi Sunt'ak, *Ch'oegŭn segye iljugi*, p. 41.

when he visited India in the same year, he expressed a sincere wish that the Indian people would overcome class struggle, religious friction, and England's divisive policies.[48] As he lamented the fact that Koreans were not able to establish comprehensive principles of national leadership and did not recognize the evils of factionalism, he wished that they could quickly overcome the struggle between the classes.

When Japanese thought control in Korea became more severe in the 1930s, Yi Sunt'ak ended his involvement in academic and social organizations and devoted himself fully to school administration and scholarly work. At the same time, in the early 1930s, both the right-wing and left-wing nationalists focused their efforts on cultural reform in order to discover the core of national identity or anti-Japanese elements in Korean society by finding the unique aspects of the nation's culture, language, and history.[49] Yi actively participated in such activities. In January 1931, he joined the compilation committee of the Chosŏnŏ sajŏn p'yŏnch'anhoe (Society for the compilation of a Korean language dictionary), and in April 1935, he became a founding member of the Chosŏn ŭmsŏng hakhoe (Society of Korean Phonetics), which did research on the Korean language.[50] In addition, he participated in the formation of the Chosŏn kyŏngje hakhoe (Korean Economics Society) whose purpose was to refute the findings of Japanese governmental research on the Korean economy along with other economists of varying ideologies such as Yu Okgyŏm, Paek Nam'un, No Tonggyu, Kim Toyŏn, Kim Kwangjin, Kim Up'yŏng, Yi Yŏsŏng, So Ch'un, and Yi Kŭngjong.[51] His life and career followed a path typical of supporters of united-front politics. He moved more toward reformism than he had in the 1920s, but he was still consistent in his support for national unity and a united-front.

THEORY OF ANTI-MONOPOLISTIC DEMOCRACY

Another important element in Yi Sunt'ak's political economic thought during the colonial period was his views on democracy. Visiting England in 1933, he was amazed that people were freely able to express support for

48. Ibid., p. 67.
49. Yi Chiwŏn, "1930 nyŏndae minjokjuŭi kyeyŏl ŭi kojŏk pojon undong" (The nationalists' movement to preserve cultural artifacts in the 1930s), *Tongbang hakji* 77-78-79 (combined issue, 1992).
50. *Chosŏn ilbo*, January 8, 1931, April 26, 1935.
51. Pang Kie-chung, *Han'guk kŭnhyŏndae sasangsa yŏn'gu*, pp. 112-13; Hong Sung-Chan, ibid., 1994. For more on Paek Nam'un, see the chapter on him in this volume. For more on the other figures, see the Biographical Notes toward the end of this book.

various political ideologies and discuss sensitive issues such as freedom of religion, Indian independence, communism, socialism, anarchism, pacifism, and anti-imperialism. "Ah—freedom of thought, freedom of ideology, freedom of expression," he wrote, "[I] had to come to England to see such freedoms." He had earlier seen in Japan, Italy, and Germany that fascist states were severely suppressing various anti-fascist groups such as labor unions, social-democratic parties, and the communist party; therefore, he was especially interested in the fact that the conflict of ideologies was not a problem in England, where even communism could be disseminated freely. These experiences confirmed to him that freedom of expression and a democratic tolerance of ideologies were the best way to overcome the crisis caused by conflicting ideologies.[52] In this sense, Yi can be viewed as a kind of intellectual pluralist. His intellectual pluralism was evident in the fact that he gave equal treatment to Marxist and anti-Marxist works in his lectures and that he hired scholars of various academic standpoints who had studied in Japan and the U.S. to be professors at Yŏnhŭi Junior College when he was chair of his department.[53]

Yi Sunt'ak had an intense hatred of fascism as the enemy of democracy and freedom of thought. He viewed fascism as a general political phenomenon of capitalist states; it was a form of violent dictatorship that occurred during general crises of capitalism. He felt that in terms of politics, the essence of fascism was statism (*kukga chisangjuŭi*), and in terms of the economy, it was state capitalism. Accordingly, he thought that a fascist revolution would result in absolute obedience to the state, recognition of the importance of capital, affirmation of the private management of production and distribution, support for private property, rejection of internationalism, opposition to communist class struggle, and armed struggle against other nations.[54] For these reasons, he compared Hitler to the despotic Shih Huang Ti, the first emperor of the state of Chin, and he warned about the possible outbreak of a second world war.[55]

As mentioned above, Yi Sunt'ak's ideas on social reconstruction were influenced by Kawakami. In Yi's conception, the proletariat would disseminate their ideology freely through newspapers and magazines and demand

---

52. Yi Sunt'ak, ibid., pp. 202-05.

53. Hong Sung-Chan, ibid., 1994.

54. Yi Sunt'ak, "Kŭm'il ŭi p'asijŭm undong" (Today's fascist movements), *Tongbang p'yŏngnon*, no. 3 (1932).

55. Yi Sunt'ak, ibid., pp. 182, 189.

the right to vote. After they become the majority party in elections for the representative assembly, they would seize state power to reconstruct society through constitutional, rational methods. To Yi, political democracy was an essential precondition of social reconstruction; however, political democracy in itself would be sufficient. Political freedom without economic democracy would amount to no more than purely legal, formal democracy, and genuine democracy could be achieved only through economic democratization, that is, when "economic conditions are partially rectified" and all people are given "as much" freedom and equality "as possible" in the pursuit of their livelihoods.[56] He thought that the rectification of economic conditions was the key to actual democracy.

Yi Sunt'ak's idea of democracy was not a bourgeois democracy but one in which all members of society would enjoy economic equality. Its premise was the rectification of the current state of economic conditions; that is, a reform of economic institutions. He also referred to such reform as "material reconstruction" (*muljŏk kaejo*). In a short essay published in October 1930, he wrote that the greatest social problem of the time was poverty and argued that since social parasites such as the leisure and wealthy classes were responsible for causing such poverty, it was more urgent to undergo a material reconstruction in which "wealth would be collectively produced and equitably distributed" rather than a spiritual reconstruction or reform in which the "haves" would give to the "have-nots."[57] When the Korean economy was in danger of collapsing in early 1925 because of a bad harvest, he discussed last-resort measures for saving the economy and suggested that "all private capital in Korean society should be combined and [used] to resist foreign capital."[58] What he was advocating was a type of cooperative movement. He thought that it would be difficult to achieve such a combination of capital at the present time and that even if it were possible, it could not be accomplished in all areas of the country at the same time. Furthermore, if it were done on a small scale and in a partial manner, the capital accumulated would not amount to much. "Only after a fundamental reform of existing social insti-

---

56. Yi Sunt'ak, "Chosŏn ŭi kyŏngje minjuhwa (chŏn 2 hoe)" (The economic democratization of Korea), *Tonga ilbo*, December 1+5, 1946. Below, this article will be referred to as "1946a."

57. Yi Sunt'ak, "Kisaengch'ung ugam" (Random thoughts on parasites), *Ch'ŏngnyŏn* 10, no. 8 (1930).

58. Yi Sunt'ak, "Kŏja tanhap—oerae chabon taehang. Kyŏngsŏng Yonjŏn kyosu Yi Sunt'ak ssi tam" (Combination of large-scale capital—resistance against foreign capital. A conversation with Mr. Yi Sunt'ak, professor at Yŏnhŭi Junior College in Seoul), *Tonga ilbo*, January 1, 1925.

tutions" would a combination of capital be substantial and large amounts of capital be utilized efficiently. He had in mind two objectives for this "fundamental reform." The first was the restoration of Korea's sovereignty from Japan, that is, from foreign capitalism, and the second was to achieve a noncapitalist reform, one that "did not stand in the position of capitalism."[59]

In early 1931, when the Great Depression was at its height, Yi Sunt'ak developed a theory of socialist producer cooperatives. First, to improve conditions in rural areas, he suggested immediate measures such as the exemption or reduction of various taxes paid by self-cultivators, provision of low-interest loans, the maximum reduction of tenant farming fees, the encouragement of secondary occupations, prohibition of alcohol and tobacco, the use of colored clothing, and the prevention of early marriage. For fundamental reform, he proposed the organization of an agricultural cooperative movement at the rural village level. In a cooperative system, all members of the community would be collectively responsible for tasks such as finance, acquisition of tenant farming land, purchase of agricultural equipment and fertilizer, sale of farm products, cultivation, and payment of tenant farming fees.[60] What he meant by "producer cooperative" was a kind of socialist producer cooperative. The cooperative movement would encourage the "combination all private capital in our society" in order to resist foreign capital, emphasizing the restoration of Korea's sovereignty and non-capitalist reform.

Yi's other writings from this period contain similar examples of such views. For instance, an article from 1932 stated that the fundamental cause of the Great Depression lay in the deficiencies of capitalist economic institutions, and he felt that even if the problems caused by the depression could be somewhat alleviated without a reform of capitalism, a fundamental solution would be impossible.[61]

For Yi Sunt'ak, democracy was not simply a matter of politics. Rather, democracy meant a reform of capitalism and the realization of a non-capitalist economic democracy in which poverty would be solved by eliminating the rich and elite classes and in which wealth would be collectively produced and equitably distributed. Years later, he recollected that the ultimate goal of his vision of social reconstruction was the "elimination of private ownership

59. Yi Sunt'ak, ibid.

60. Yi Sunt'ak, "Nongch'on chohap kwa yŏndae ch'aek'im" (Agricultural village cooperatives and collective responsibility), *Tonggwang*, no. 20 (April 1931).

61. Yi Sunt'ak, "Mulga tŭnggui wa kyŏnggi chŏnhwan" (Rise in prices and changes in economic trends), *Ch'ŏngnyŏn* 12, no. 8 (1932).

of important productive institutions such as factories, land, and railroads by nationalizing them, and a decrease in the gap between the rich and the poor through the equitable distribution of commodities according to each person's abilities."[62] He was seeking the establishment of a socialist system in which major productive facilities would be nationalized and the products of labor would be distributed according to a person's abilities. As a concrete method of achieving such a society, he planned to "build a communist society" legally through the power of a "communist political party." The party would be created by "educating" the Korean masses "in communism" through legal means and leading them to self-awakening by instilling class consciousness in them.[63] Of course, what he meant by "legal methods" was educational efforts through means such as newspapers, magazines, pamphlets, and public meetings at a level tolerable to the authorities.

Yi Sunt'ak's views on political economy during the 1920s and early 30s can be regarded as a form of social democratic thought. However, his conception of social democracy differed from that of Western thinkers. In their conception, the proletariat would seize state power through elections (political revolution) and then achieve socialism by gradual reforms through their control of the state. By contrast, because Korea was under imperial rule, Yi felt that the propertyless and propertied, socialists and nationalists should join forces. They should first bring about a national political revolution to restore national sovereignty, and then society could be reconstructed gradually by the state. Because of the nature of the Japanese occupation, social democracy in Korea changed and became more moderate in nature.

The Culmination of Yi Sunt'ak's Thought: Moderate Politics

Left-Right Collaboration

In August 1945, when the Japanese were defeated and the U.S. military government was established in the South, Yi Sunt'ak was reinstated as a

---

62. "P'igoin Yi Sunt'ak sinmun chosŏ" (April 22, 1940) (Record of the interrogation of the defendant Yi Sunt'ak) in *Yŏnhŭi chŏnmun hakgyo haknae chŏkhwa sagŏn sŏryu* (1938-1940). Since these words were spoken in front of a judge, it may be difficult to accept their truthfulness, but I feel that they roughly reflect his thoughts at the time.

63. Ibid. Since these materials are court documents and police records, it is probably more accurate to consider their use of the term "communism" to mean "social democracy."

professor at Yŏnhŭi Junior College.[64] While working on the reconstruction of Yŏnhŭi, which lay in ruins at the end of the colonial period, he became the first dean of the College of Commerce in 1946 after the school was elevated to the status of a university, laying the foundation for the development of higher education in Korea after liberation.

Yi also was active in politics. In September 1945, he participated in the formation of the Korean National Party (Han'guk kungmindang) and soon afterwards joined the Korean Democratic Party (KDP, Han'guk minjudang), becoming the chair of its finance committee.[65] His decision to join the KDP was likely due to his relationships with people such as Kim Yŏnsu, but he did not remain a member for long. When the KDP rejected the "Seven Principles" of left-right collaboration established by the Left-Right Coordinating Committee in October 1946, he left the party in protest.

Yi then became involved in the People's Alliance (Minjung tongmaeng), one of the main political organizations of the moderate faction at the time, and he became a member of its standing committee, head of its general affairs section, and head of its financial affairs section. In December 1946, he

64. In April 1938, Yi Sunt'ak, along with colleagues such as Paek Nam'un and No Tonggyu, was arrested for violating the Peace Preservation Law in the Yŏnhŭi Professor Campus Communization Incident, also known as the Economic Club Incident. In July 1940, he was released on bail, and in December of that year, still out on bail, he received a sentence of two years of jail time and three years of probation. Forced to resign from his post because of the incident, he earned a living by working as a full-time instructor and as the head of the general affairs section (*sŏmu kwajang*). During the late 1930s and early 1940s, Yŏnhŭi Junior College suffered from a suppression of thought that was unprecedented in the history of Korean academia. The Japanese arrested, one after another, the vice-principal of the school, chairmen of the humanities, commerce and business, and science departments, and regular professors or forced them to leave the school, by implicating them in the Economic Club Incident as well as other incidents such as the Hŭng'ŏp Club Incident, the Tonguhoe Incident, and the Chosŏnŏ Hakhoe (Chosŏn Language Association) Incident. In 1942, the Japanese seized the school's property as enemy property (it had been established by an American missionary), and finally in 1942, even its name was changed to Kyŏngsŏng Kong'ŏp Kyŏng'yŏng Chŏnmun Hakkyo (Kyŏngsŏng junior college of industrial management). Hong Sung-Chan, ibid., 1994.

65. Yi also was the South Chŏlla representative and a member of the finance committee of the Emergency National Council (Pisang Kungmin Hoeŭi), and he was on the economic committee of the Democratic Council. Song Namhŏn, *Han'guk hyŏndae chŏngch'isa I* (Contemporary Korean Political History 1) (Seoul: Songmungak, 1980), Chapter 3. In November 1945, Yi was appointed as an economic advisor to the military government along with other scholars such as Paek Nam'un, Hong Sŏngha, and Yun Haengjung. They warned the military government that liberalization of the grain market would worsen grain supply problems and proposed that the government restore the regulated distribution system, but when their proposal was rejected, they all resigned from their positions. Han Kyuhun, "Chosŏn unhaeng 40 nyŏn" (40 years of the Bank of Korea), *Kŭm'yung kyŏngje*, no. 4 (1979).

was nominated by the People's Alliance and then selected by the military government to be one of the representatives of the South Korean Interim Legislative Assembly (SKILA). In February 1947, he became a member of the standing committee of the Democratic Independence Front, which was formed through a union of moderate political groups. In addition, he became a member of the central affairs committee of the Korean Republican Party (May 1947), a member of the inaugural political platform committee as well as a member of the central executive administrative committee of the Democratic Independence Party (Minju tongnipdang), which was the central group of the National Autonomous League (Minjok chaju tongmaeng, November 1947). His political activities were characterized by his consistent support for left-right collaboration until he left the Democratic Independence Party on January 25, 1948.[66]

Why did Yi Sunt'ak, who had refrained from political activities during the colonial period, take a prominent role in politics after liberation? He essentially began his involvement in politics by joining the KDP; what, then, are the reasons that, from late 1946, he was continually active in moderate, united-front political groups while rejecting both the KDP and the KCP, the two main political groups of the time?

The reasons for his political choices were rooted in his views on the contemporary situation in Korea.[67] First, he felt that the defeat of the Japanese created a revolutionary situation in which the capitalist and landlord classes were suddenly swept away, that is, in which the greatest obstacle to the achievement of economic democracy was eliminated. With the defeat of the Japanese, class conflict no longer existed between the Japanese (capitalists) and Koreans (proletariat), and although the U.S. military government seized Japanese property and capital, they would be transferred to Korea and become the common property of all the people. "Even looking at the current

---

66. The Democratic Independence Party was formed through the combination of five moderate political parties, and their major political principles were complete independence, democracy, and national unification. In November 1947, it passed a resolution calling for the establishment of an autonomous, democratic, unified government; independence without trusteeship; and the withdrawal of both U.S. and Soviet troops. Even after he left the party, he signed two petitions that supported similar principles: one signed by 108 notable figures opposed the establishment of a separate government and supported participation in North-South negotiations, another signed by 330 figures criticized the U.S.'s policies toward Korea and Japan and advocated the simultaneous withdrawal of U.S. and Soviet troops. He continued to wish for the establishment of a unified government.

67. Unless there is a footnote added, all material in this section is taken from Yi Sunt'ak, ibid., 1946a.

situation," the prospects for economic democratization were optimistic if a unified government could be established through left-right collaboration and if economic policies could be implemented democratically.

Second, Yi Sunt'ak did not think that national capitalists would pose a serious obstacle to economic democratization in the post-liberation period. For him, the term "national capitalist" encompassed two different groups. The first was Korean capitalists in finance, commerce, and manufacturing, and the second was the landlord class. He felt that the former would not be a hindrance to economic democratization because they had little power. He was not even concerned about large-scale capitalists who had made fortunes quickly through the acquisition of former Japanese property. While they could be a problem if the status quo remained unchanged, there was nothing to worry about because companies had no inducement to build new facilities or expand existing ones due to the lack of fertilizer, raw materials, and opportunities for speculation. People would also find it difficult to get permits for new large-scale enterprises, and most of all, their assets could be "frozen" and the capitalists could be properly "handled and managed" at a suitable time by the state. However, his views differed on the landlord class, who formed the main body of national capitalists and were the principal owners of national capital after liberation. He felt that land reform was absolutely essential. However, it was also necessary to be careful about the concrete method of land reform since the landlords did form the "main body" of national capitalists.[68] Even though he was optimistic about the prospects for economic democratization, he emphasized that "the land problem [needs] to be suitably resolved" and that "future economic policies [need] to be established and implemented in accordance with a democratic course [of development]."

Third, he thought that it was impossible to side with either of the two countries occupying Korea, the U.S. or the Soviet Union, or with either of the two systems, capitalism and socialism, that they represented. He did not believe that Korea should ignore the presence of the two foreign armies in Korea and just follow one model of state building—either the Western and U.S. model of capitalism or Soviet-style socialism. Rather, it was necessary to establish a unified democratic state through a compromise between the

68. As will be mentioned below, he had a leading role in the drafting of SKILA's land reform law, and the draft proposal called for land reform to be conducted by compensating landlords for their land—a position that he had advocated even during the colonial period. Such proposals were based on his views that landlords after liberation were the "main body" and "foundation" of national capital.

two, that is, through a combination of U.S.-style and Soviet-style democracies. He felt that "it is necessary to consider both viewpoints"—capitalism and socialism, the U.S. and Soviet Union—as models for Korea's development.

Yi's support for left-right cooperation was rooted in his distinctive views on the U.S. and the Soviet Union. When he visited the U.S. in 1933, he was impressed with the world-leading level of American civilization and culture in terms of both quantity and quality. He wrote, "if anyone doubts it, [you] should go to America. [You] will discover something beyond your imagination." He had the highest praise for the U.S. educational system, noting its methods of self-teaching, focus on development, pragmatism, and voluntary nature in contrast with the cramming, standardization, focus on desk work, and compulsory nature of Japanese education. He confessed that the misunderstandings that he had had of the American educational system disappeared when he observed it for himself. His views on America were strongly positive.[69]

His impressions of the Soviet Union were similar. In his writings in the 1920s, he had already introduced the religions and labor system of the Soviet Union to a Korean audience. Later, through his position at the Commercial Research Institute (Sang'ŏp yŏn'guso) at Yŏnhŭi, he steadily bought and studied books on the Soviet Union over the years and developed a strong impresssion of it as a country that had repeatedly undergone periods of "strengthening and growth" and became the most powerful socialist country in the world.[70] When the U.S. and Soviet Union normalized diplomatic relations in November 1933, he noted that the future world order in politics, the economy, and foreign relations would follow a different path than before, and he warned of the dangers of being slow in paying attention to these developments.[71]

This section has been an examination of Yi Sunt'ak's views on Korea's situation immediately after liberation. Beginning from the colonial period, he had thought that the decisive moment for the realization of his political ideas would be the seizure and exercise of state power in a constitutional

---

69. Yi Sunt'ak, *Ch'oegŭn segye iljugi*, pp. 264–67.

70. Yi Sunt'ak, "Ssobet kukga ŭi chonggyo" (The religions of the Soviet state), *Yŏnhŭi*, no. 5 (1926); Yi Sunt'ak, "Sobiet'ŭ kukga ŭi nodong chedo" (The labor system of the Soviet state), *Hyŏndae p'yŏngnon* 1, no. 4 (1927); Yi Sunt'ak, *Ch'oegŭn segye iljugi*, p. 272; Hong Sung-Chan, ibid., 1994.

71. Yi Sunt'ak, *Ch'oegŭn segye iljugi*, p. 273.

political system. Therefore, he placed tremendous importance on the role of the state in social reconstruction and economic democratization. He felt that it was first necessary for the left and right in North and South Korea to compromise and work together to establish a unified government and then for that government to implement a series of economic democratization policies, such as land reform. Looking at "all the objective conditions in Korea today," he expected that political and economic democratization would be quickly realized with the establishment of a unified government since there was "almost complete agreement" on the ideology for the establishment and implementation of democratic economic policies, on both the left and the right and in both the North and the South.[72] It was both possible and necessary that political and economic democracy in post-liberation Korea be achieved through consensus rather than social revolution.

Yi reiterated these views in an article he published in early December 1946, after the general strike of September and the October uprisings of that year. He "believed that even if Korea will definitely not follow the path of social revolution through revolutionary means, [it] will achieve a genuine democracy through consensus with the strength of the people."[73]

When the U.S. changed its policy toward Korea in the latter half of 1946, it attempted to strengthen the political position of moderate political groups and supporters of left-right collaboration, by excluding both the domestic far right and far left. The U.S. military government then centered the SKILA around the moderates and attempted to solve the issues of political and economic democratization facing Korea, and Yi enthusiastically participated in these efforts. Having consistently supported legal, constitutional political action since the colonial period, he thought that this was a golden opportunity to establish a government in Korea that would be based on the principles of left-right collaboration.

THEORY OF A PLANNED ECONOMY

What kind of economic system did Yi Sunt'ak envision for a unified democratic state in Korea? In December 1946, he was one of the representatives selected by the American military government to participate in the SKILA (joining the Industry, Labor, and Agriculture Committee and the Public Finance Committee), and from early 1947, he dedicated himself to

---

72. Yi Sunt'ak, 1946a.
73. Ibid.

preparing a land reform law. His dedication was not surprising since he believed that a solution to the land problem was a precondition to economic democratization.

When the Japanese formed the Chosŏn san'ŏp chosahoe (Society for the Investigation of Korean Industry) in August 1921, he published an article in response entitled "Chosŏn kwa nong'ŏp" (Chosŏn and agriculture), in which he discussed his policy proposals and ideas on agricultural reform.[74] In his view, the most important task facing Korean society was to find a solution to the land problem: a small number of large-scale Japanese landlords were "creating an intolerable large-farm system in Korea" and engaging in agricultural management. He firmly believed that agricultural policies fundamentally had to address the reform of the landlord system and the establishment of an agricultural system based on small- to medium-scale cultivators. The reason was that such an agricultural system had the most advantages economically, socially, and politically.[75] He felt certain that the way to establish such an agricultural system rapidly was for the government to pass a land redistribution law and to purchase from landlords as much as possible that was "considered to be of excessive acreage." Then, land reform would be conducted by distributing this land, along with reclaimed land and government-owned land, to small cultivators among farmers with sufficient labor power.

Nevertheless, he felt that such measures by themselves would not be sufficient. An agricultural system based on small- to medium-scale cultivators would be likely to fail if bad harvests or other unforeseen events forced farmers without financial resources to sell the land they had received. Land reform needed to be accompanied by two policies for the protection of small- to medium-scale farmers. The first policy was the introduction of a household property/agricultural land system in which the minimum amount of land necessary for the subsistence of a single household would be fixed. In such a system, the sale, alienation, or mortgage of that land would be forbidden,

---

74. Yi Sunt'ak, "Chosŏn kwa nong'ŏp—changnong kigwan sŏlch'i ŭi kŭpmu rŭl nonham (chŏn 15 hoe)" (Chosŏn and agriculture—a discussion of the urgent need to build facilities for promoting agriculture), *Tonga ilbo*, October 12-November 2, 1921. For more on the relation between this article and the land reform law made by SKILA after liberation, see Hong Sung-Chan, 1993. Unless there is a footnote, the next section is taken from this article.

75. An emphasis on small- to medium-scale cultivators is a characteristic of the agricultural policies of social democrats. During the colonial period, Paek Nam'un, in contrast to Yi Sunt'ak, advocated large-scale agriculture. See Pang Kie-chung, "Iljeha Paek Nam'un ŭi Han'guk chabonjuŭi paldalsaron" (Paek Nam'un's views during the colonial period on the history of Korean capitalism), *Tongbang hakji*, nos. 77-78-79 (combined issue, 1992).

and the government would have the first option of buying land when it was being sold. The objective was to establish strict state regulation over the country's land. The second was the establishment of special financial institutions for agriculture that would furnish low-interest loans to farm families.

Having given thought to these plans for many years, Yi Sunt'ak participated in the preparation of SKILA's land reform law beginning in February 1947. Until it was sent to the legislature in December 1947, it was Yi who led the debates on it and established the framework of the draft law. On January 12, 1948, during a regular session of the SKILA, Pak Kŏn'ung, who was the chair of the Industry, Labor, and Agriculture Committee as well as the chair of the U.S.-Korea Land Reform Liaison Committee,[76] praised Yi Sunt'ak for his leadership in all aspects of the drafting of the law and said that all questions about sections of the law that were unclear should be directed to Yi. Pak was emphasizing Yi Sunt'ak's central intellectual role in the drafting of the law.

The main aspects of the law were nearly the same as his proposals on agriculture from the early 1920s: purchase of land for redistribution, establishment of small- to medium-scale agriculture through the distribution of purchased lands, and the establishment of a household property/agricultural land system and special financial institutions for agriculture in order to protect small- to medium-scale farmers.[77] According to this law, the government would purchase land—in installments over many years—that was not cultivated by the owner or exceeded three *chŏngbo* in area at an average price of 300 percent of the land's yield. That land would then be distributed to tenant farmers, subsistence farmers, and agricultural laborers.

The land reform law gave the government first priority in being able to purchase land if it had been owned, cultivated, and inherited as household property by a farm family and was up for sale because of the lack of an heir, rural migration, or a change of occupation. The objective was to establish a household property/agricultural land system. The land reform law completely forbade the free sale and purchase, mortgaging, donation, and other transactions involving farmland. It also forbade tenancy and the leasing of all

76. Pang Kie-chung, "Haebang chŏnggukgi chungganp'a nosŏn ŭi kyŏngje sasang—Kang Chin'guk ŭi san'ŏp chaegŏnnon kwa nong'ŏp kaehyŏknon ŭl chungsim ŭro"; Hong Sung-Chan, ibid., 1993.

77. For more on the draft of SKILA's land reform law, see Han'guk nongch'on kyŏngje yŏn'guwŏn, *Nongji kaehyŏksa yŏn'gu* (A study of the history of agricultural land reform) (Seoul: Han'guk nongch'on kyŏngje yŏn'guwŏn, 1989), pp. 1188-95.

farmland as well as the granting of collateral rights, surface rights, and preferential rights to farmland.

In addition, the law called for the establishment of special financial institutions for the protection of small- to medium-scale farmers that would handle agricultural finance by establishing public corporations that would serve as rural depositories—ideas that were taken almost exactly from his proposals from the colonial period.

When Pak Kŏn'ung presented the land reform law to the legislative assembly, he emphasized the inevitability and necessity of land reform for capitalist development, noting that people have the erroneous idea that it is only the slogan of extremists.[78] Pak also emphasized that the members of the committee were all in agreement that land reform was not the slogan of the communist party or the proletariat class but was actually what the capitalist class needed to liberate the peasantry and develop agriculture. The objective of this law was to enable Korea to eliminate large-scale landlords and to build a system of small- to medium-scale agriculture centered on self-cultivating farmers as capitalist development became the model for the economic system. However, this system was not a completely capitalist one. It was a combination of the KDP and a right-wing plan of monetary compensation for seized land and sale of land for distribution using the North Korean system of state regulation of farmland that had been instituted after its land reform.

In his proposals for commercial and industrial development, Yi Sunt'ak similarly envisioned a society that was based on small- to medium-scale industry. In December 1947, Pak Kŏn'ung announced that the U.S. Military Government, the U.S. State Department, U.S. economic advisors, and other high officials had reached a consensus that all former enemy property would be turned over to the Korean government. In accordance with world trends, large industries would be nationalized, and small- to medium-scale industries would be transferred or leased to individuals who would run them as private enterprises.[79] Pak worked closely with Yi Sunt'ak in the Industry, Labor, and Agriculture Committee of the SKILA, the U.S.-Korea Land Reform Liaison Committee, and the Korean Industrial Reconstruction Association, which was formed in September 1947.[80] Pak must have picked Yi's brains for information and perspectives on a wide range of economic proposals. In

78. Hong Sung-Chan, ibid., 1993.

79. *Nam Chosŏn kwado ipbŏp ŭiwŏn sokgirok 4* (Records of the South Korean Interim Legislative Assembly 4) (Seoul: Yŏgang ch'ulp'ansa), record no. 190, December 22, 1947.

80. Pang Kie-chung, "Haebang chŏnggukgi chungganp'a nosŏn ŭi kyŏngje sasang—Kang Chin'guk ŭi san'ŏp chaegŏnnon kwa nong'ŏp kaehyŏknon ŭl chungsim ŭro."

addition, Yi had been proposing the nationalization and state management of major industrial facilities ever since the Japanese occupation period, and after liberation, he argued that it was necessary to utilize former enemy property for national production by distributing it equitably among the citizens.[81] In this sense, Pak and Yi were of one mind on economic issues, and moderate political groups, such as the National Autonomous League, agreed on the nationalization of large industry and the private management of small and medium enterprises.[82]

To regulate the economy, Yi Sunt'ak envisioned a planned economy that would be managed according to a comprehensive plan established by the state, rather than a liberal, laissez-faire economy. It was necessary to have state planning since current problems could not be solved through liberal economic policies. In order to provide a fundamental solution to problems in agriculture, population, and food supply, he emphasized several factors: the necessity of an adequate distribution of the agricultural population, a solution to the agricultural labor shortage by preventing concentration of the population in cities, and proper distribution of capital among industries and between urban and rural areas—all under a comprehensive state plan. He also placed importance on financing, reorganization of cultivated land, and agricultural improvements.[83]

The economic system that Yi Sunt'ak proposed for post-liberation Korea was capitalist but not a fully liberal one. In agriculture, he wanted to establish a strict system of state regulation of farmland in which the state would eliminate large-scale landlords by conducting a land reform with compensation. The state would also forbid the sale, purchase, mortgaging, donation, tenancy, and leasing of farmland by introducing a household property/agricultural land system, and it would have first priority in purchasing household farmland. For commerce and industry, he planned a system in which large-scale industries would be nationalized and small- to medium-scale industries would be run through private enterprise. He wanted to establish a social democratic society, a type of planned economic system, in which small- to medium-scale farmers and industry would serve as the foundation of society. The state would run the economy by creating comprehensive plans; the

---

81. Yi Sunt'ak, 1946a.
82. Pang Kie-chung, ibid.
83. Yi Sunt'ak, "Minjok chŏk kyŏnji esŏ pon kyŏngje chŏngch'aek (ingu siknyang munje)" (A national perspective on economic policies (population and food supply problems)), *Minjŏng* 1, no. 1 (September 1948).

resulting society would be neither a dictatorship of capitalists nor a dictatorship of the proletariat, nor would it be either a society of monopoly capitalism or a proletariat society.[84]

On August 7, 1948, Yi Sunt'ak was unexpectedly chosen to be the first head of the Planning Office in the Syngman Rhee (Yi Sŭngman) administration. In this position, he was in charge of all affairs related to the organization of the budget and the making of comprehensive plans on the public finance, the economy, banking, manufacturing, natural resources, and commodities of South Korea. Around April 1949, he drafted the Five Year Plan for industrial revival and the Five Year Plan for mobilization of material resources. He also made a "comprehensive plan for cooperatives" in which cooperatives would be established as lower-level organizations in all industries such as agriculture, commerce, and mining to provide institutional support for the five-year plans. Material resources necessary for industrial revival would be mobilized and regulated through these cooperatives.[85] Yi also participated in all legislative aspects of the government's land reform law, serving as the vice-chairman of its drafting committee which was launched in September 1948.[86]

Despite such efforts, all of his plans ended in failure. Within the first economic team of the First Republic, there were two opposing groups: right-wing supporters of a liberal economy who had studied in the U.S. and politically moderate supporters of a planned economy who were reformist and

---

84. Pang Kie-chung, ibid. The fundamental doctrine of the National Autonomous Alliance was the building of a Korean democratic society that was neither a society of monopoly capitalism nor a proletarian society. Yi Sunt'ak was a member of the founding political platform and policy committee and the central executive administrative affairs committee of the Democratic Independence Party, the central group of the National Autonomous League.

85. Chŏng Chin'a, "Che il konghwaguk ch'ogi (1948-1950) ŭi kyŏngje chŏngch'aek yŏn'gu" (A study of the early economic policies of the First Republic (1948-1950)), *Han'guksa yŏn'gu*, no. 106 (1999). Among these proposals, the plan for mobilization of material resources and the cooperative plan were passed in cabinet meetings (*kungmu hoeŭi*) on April 17 and April 26, 1949, respectively, but the latter came to naught when deliberation by the National Assembly was delayed.

86. He also played a leading role in the drafting of the "Request for Reparations from Japan." In autumn 1948, he established the guidelines for war reparations, and in February 1949, established the Investigating Committee for Reparations from Japan. Using materials collected from each government office, he drafted the "Request for Reparations from Japan" (Tae-Il paesang yogu chosŏ, 2 volumes). Yu Chin'o, "Han'il hoedam" (Korea-Japan negotiations), *Chung'ang ilbo*, August 30 and September 1, 1983.

had studied in Japan.[87] Yi's plans failed because the latter group gradually lost influence in the administration. In February 1949, the draft of the government's land reform law was passed in a cabinet meeting. When it was brought to the National Assembly, Yi supported it, saying that it "is the law that is the most suited to Korea's current situation." He was genuinely shocked when a significant portion of the public regarded it as a pro-landlord law.[88] Even though the law did not retain his proposal for state regulation of farmland and did not institutionalize his long-cherished idea of a system of household property farmland, he was satisfied with the final version of the law. As an example of his belief in the necessity of compromise, it could be said that compromise was the philosophical basis of Yi's conception of social democracy and social reform.

Yi resigned as the head of the Planning Office on July 22, 1949, and on the same day was appointed as chair of the Chosŏn Financial Union (soon to change its name to the Korean Financial Union). He remained in that post until February 15, 1950.[89] This move was logical, considering his consistent support for the establishment of special financial institutions for the protection of small- to medium-scale farmers. He became a member of the food supply section of the U.S.-Korea Economic Stability Committee, which was officially launched on January 26, 1950, and he also participated in the drafting of the Fifteen Principles for Economic Stability which were announced

87. Examples of the former include Kim Toyŏn (minister of finance), Im Yŏngsin (Louise Yim, minister of commerce and industry), and Ch'oe Sunju (president of the Bank of Korea). Examples of the latter include Cho Pong'am (minister of agriculture and forestry) and Yi Sunt'ak (head of the Planning Office). Chŏng Chin'a, ibid. Yi Sunt'ak became head of the Planning Office through the recommendation of Yi Pŏmsŏk, the first prime minister of South Korea (the Planning Office was a vice-ministerial level organ that was under the prime minister's office), and one of the reasons for his appointment was to check the power of the groups of officials who had studied in the U.S. Interview with Yi Hansu, the oldest son of Yi Sunt'ak.

88. *Saehan minbo* 3-4, February 21, 1949, p. 25. On March 24, 1950, after he had resigned as the chair of the Korean Financial Union, Yi Sunt'ak participated in the Central Land Reform Committee (Chungang nongji wiwŏnhoe) as a civilian representative and engaged in debates on measures concerning land reform. Han'guk nongch'on kyŏngje yŏn'guwŏn, ibid., p. 620.

89. Nong'ŏp hyŏpdong chohap chunganghoe, *Han'guk nong'ŏp kŭm'yungsa* (The history of agricultural finance in Korea) (Seoul: Nong'ŏp hyŏpdong chohap chunganghoe, 1963). He was also asked to serve as a member of the Committee for the Management of Foreign Aid Goods (Oeguk wŏnjo mulsan unyŏng wiwŏnhoe, August 1949), as a member of the Central Committee for Labor Mediation (Chungang nodong chojŏng wiwŏnhoe November 1949), as an official for the higher civil service examinations (kodŭng kosi wiwŏn, in economics, December 1949), and as a member of the Committee for Codification of Laws (Pŏpjŏn p'yŏnch'an wiwŏn). An Yongsik, ed., *Taehan minguk kwallyo yŏn'gu I* (A study of civil-service bureaucrats of the Republic of Korea) (Seoul: Yŏnse taehakgyo sahoe kwahak yŏn'guso, 1995), p. 619.

by the government on March 4, 1950.[90] A few months later, in May of that same year, he ran but lost as an independent candidate in the second general election, in which the moderate politicians participated in large numbers. Around July 1950, immediately after the outbreak of the Korean War, he was kidnapped to the North.

Yi had followed the prototypical path of a moderate after liberation: in the immediate post-liberation period, moderates began their political activities, seeking to establish a unified, democratic state through left-right collaboration, but when capitalist and socialist states were established in South and North Korea, they were no longer able to maintain their existence an independent political group and were absorbed by one or the other of the two systems, leading to the failure of their efforts.

Conclusion

Yi Sunt'ak's intellectual development was influenced by two contrasting worldviews. First, he absorbed nationalism and patriotism through his association with nationalist, pro-capitalist Korean students in Tokyo. Second, he learned Marxism and class-based thought through his contact with Kawakami Hajime in Kyoto. Marxism was perhaps the major influence on his theoretical standpoint and conception of morality. In his youth, he wavered agonizingly between these two opposed worldviews. His intellect was drawn toward class-based thought, but his instincts and behavior tended toward nationalism. As he struggled with this conflict, he attempted to develop his own thinking by reconciling these two worldviews.

The key elements in Yi Sunt'ak's political economic thought during the colonial period were his theories of class cooperation and united-front politics, both of which differed from the positions of internationalism and class-oriented ideologies. The allure of nationalism prevailed over the appeal of classism. There were two underlying reasons why he was drawn to nationalism and advocated class cooperation and united-front politics. The first was his understanding of Marx's theory of revolution. Distinguishing between Marx's conceptions of social and political revolution, he thought that Korea's stage of development at the time called for a political revolution rather than a social one. Although he thought that social revolution, reform of capitalism,

---

90. *Tonga ilbo,* January 30, 1950.

and social reconstruction were absolutely necessary, he felt that Korea was not yet at a stage of readiness for these changes. Second, there was his view of Koreans as a "total proletariat." He viewed the class structure in Korea during the colonial period as a confrontation between Japanese (landlords, capitalists, the rich) and Koreans (tenant farmers, workers, the poor). He concluded that under domination by the Japanese empire, Korea would not be able to determine a clear line of class struggle, nor was it necessary to do so.

Yi thought that revolution in Korea could not be a social revolution that would bring about a shift to socialism, nor could it be a simple political revolution in which the proletariat class would directly seize state power. Because of the nature of the Japanese occupation, revolution in Korea would have to be a national political movement or revolution that would restore Korea's sovereignty from the Japanese through the cooperation and union of all the capitalists, proletariat, intellectuals, nationalists, socialists, communists, anarchists, and men and women of Korea. In this sense, Yi Sunt'ak's theory of revolution substituted Marx's idea of a political revolution with a national political revolution; it called for a two-stage revolution in which Korea would first undergo a national political revolution and then reach the stage of social revolution. This reasoning was based on his rejection of the Comintern's line of internationalism and class struggle and on his support of national unity, class cooperation, and united-front politics. The development of Yi Sunt'ak's thought, in effect, demonstrates how social democratic thought was introduced into Korea and changed during the occupation period.

Another major element of Yi's thought during the occupation period was his theory of democracy. He thought that genuine democracy meant the simultaneous realization of political and economic democracy. It would be a society in which the main criminals of poverty—the rich and privileged classes—would be eliminated and wealth would be collectively produced and equitably distributed. It would be a society in which the gap between rich and poor would be reduced by nationalizing major productive facilities and by distributing goods according to a person's abilities. It called for a fundamental reform of capitalism. Nevertheless, he did not think that revolutionary methods were the only means to achieve such a society, emphasizing instead constitutional, legislative, and reformist methods. A political party would be created through legal means, and its ideology would be disseminated through newspapers and magazines. After the party attained a majority in the legislature through elections, it would seize state power and use it to reconstruct society. In this sense, the political economic thought of Yi

Sunt'ak corresponded to the social democratic line of the Second International, or, more accurately, to social reformism.

When Japan was defeated in August 1945, Yi viewed liberation as a golden opportunity to realize his political and social ideals. The ruling class of Japanese landlords, capitalists, and wealthy would withdraw from Korea with the defeat of the Japanese. Former enemy property would then be transferred to the Korean government and would become the common possession of the entire nation, and Korean capitalists would not pose an obstacle to the realization of economic democratization since their power was weak. He thought that the left and the right should join forces and, as quickly as possible, establish a unified, democratic government that would be a combination of American-style capitalism and Soviet-style socialism. If this government adequately pursued economic policies such as land reform through democratic principles, he felt that the prospects for economic democracy would be optimistic. Such optimism was the reason that he rejected both the KDP and the KCP, the two major political groups on the right and the left, and that he was active in moderate political groups, such as the People's Alliance and the Democratic Independence Party, whose goal was the establishment of a unified, democratic state through left-right collaboration.

In the post-liberation period, his plan for the economic system of a unified, democratic Korean state was neither a society of monopoly capitalism nor a proletarian society. He envisioned an agricultural system of small- to medium-scale cultivators that would be established through abolishing the landlord system by land reform and introducing a household property/farmland system and in which the state would strictly manage all farmland. It was a compromise between the right-wing's plan for land reform with compensation to landlords and North Korea's state management methods. Furthermore, he wanted to establish a planned economy in which the state would manage the economy through comprehensive planning, rather than a liberal, free-market capitalist system. It was a kind of social democratic economic system.

In August 1948, he was chosen to be the first head of the Planning Office in the Syngman Rhee administration. However, he was not up to the task of realizing his agenda within a government dominated by the right wing. He followed the typical path of the political moderates who, as Korea was becoming a divided nation, were unable to maintain an independent existence and whose efforts ended in failure as they were absorbed into both leftist and rightist political groups. As the head of the Planning Office, he became the vice-chair of the Drafting Committee for the Land Reform Law and participated in the drafting of the land reform law of the South Korean government. He combined the drafts of the Ministry of Agriculture and Forestry and the Planning Office and even took into account the opinions of the KDP group within the government, leaving out the household property farmland system and state management of farmland that he had originally envisioned. When the land reform bill was submitted to the National Assembly, he supported it, believing that it was the law most suited to Korea's current situation. It seems true that the principle of compromise formed the philosophical basis of Yi's social democracy and social reform.

translated by Michael D. Shin

Index of Terms

chabonga pangmyŏllon 資本家撲滅論 theory of exterminating capitalists

chinjŏngwŏn 眞正院

ch'ongch'ejŏk musanja 總體的 無產者 total proletariat

chŏnggyobu 正教部

Ch'ongjŏngwŏn 總正院

Ch'ongnyŏngwŏn 總領院

Chŏnhyangnok 轉向錄 Record on Conversion

Chosŏn kŭmyung chohap yŏnhaphoe 朝鮮金融組合聯合會 Union of Korean Financial Cooperatives

Chosŏnŏ hakhoe 朝鮮語學會 Chosŏn Language Association

Chosŏn nonong ch'ong tongmaeng 朝鮮勞農總同盟 Chosŏn Worker-Peasant League

Chosŏn sajong yŏn'guhoe 朝鮮事情硏究會 Research Institute on Chosŏn Affairs

Chosŏn sang'ŏp ŭnhaeng 朝鮮商業銀行 Chosŏn Commercial Bank

Chosŏn san'ŏp chosahoe 朝鮮産業調査會 Society for the Investigation of Korean Industry

Chungang nodong chojŏng wiwŏnhoe 중앙노동조정위원회 Central Committee for Labor Mediation

Chungang nongji wiwŏnhoe 中央農地委員會 Central Land Reform Committee

Chŭngsangyo 甑山敎

Haknae chŏkhwa sagŏn 學內赤化事件 Campus Communization Incident

Han'guk kungmindang 韓國國民黨 Korean National Party

Han'guk minjudang 韓國民主黨 Korean Democratic Party

ho 號 pen name or civic name

Hŭng'ŏp kurakbu 興業俱樂部 Hŭng'ŏp Club

Kawakami Hajime 河上肇 (1879–1946)

Kihoekch'ŏ 企劃處 Planning Office

Kim Sŏngsu 金性洙 (1891–1955)

Kim Yŏnsu 金秊洙 (1896–1979)

Kobe kodŭng sang'ŏp hakgyo 神戸高等商業學校 Kobe Higher Commercial School

kodŭng kosi 高等考試 higher civil service examinations

kŏguk nodongnon 擧國勞動論 theory of requiring everyone in the country to do labor

Kongnip mokp'o kani sang'ŏp hakgyo 公立木浦簡易商業學校 Mokp'o
    Public Commercial School
kowŏn 雇員 low-level assistant
kukga chisangjuŭi 國家至上主義 statism
kungmin kyŏngjehak 國民經濟學 *Nationalökonomie*
kungmu hoeŭi 國務會議 cabinet meetings
Kyŏngdo Chosŏn'in nodong kongjehoe 京都朝鮮人勞動共濟會 Kyoto
    Korean Labor Mutual Aid Association
Kyŏngje yŏn'guhoe 經濟研究會 Economic Club
Kyŏngsŏng 京城 Seoul
Kyŏngsŏng chinjŏngwŏn 京城眞正院
Kyŏngsŏng pangjik chusikhoesa 京城紡織株式會社 Kyŏngsŏng Spinning
    and Weaving Company
Minjok chaju yŏnmaeng 民族自主聯盟 National Autonomous League
Minjujuŭi tongnip chŏnsŏn 民主主義獨立前線 Democratic Independence
    Front
Minjung tongmaeng 民衆同盟 People's League
Minju tongnipdang 民主獨立黨 Democratic Independence Party
Min'uhoe 民友會
muljŏk kaejo 物的改造 material reconstruction
Mulsan changnyŏhoe 物産獎勵會 Native Products Promotion Society
Mulsan changnyŏ undong 物産獎勵運動 Native Products Promotion
    Movement
Nam-Chosŏn kwado ipbŏpŭiwŏn 南朝鮮過渡立法議院 South Korean
    Interim Legislative Assembly
Oeguk wŏnjomulsan unyŏng wiwŏnhoe 外國援助物産運營委員會
    Committee for the Management of Foreign Aid Goods
Pisang kungmin hoeŭi 非常國民會議 Emergency National Council
Poch'ŏngyo 普天敎
Poch'ŏngyo hyŏksinhoe 普天敎革新會
Pŏpjŏn p'yŏnch'an wiwŏn 법전편찬위원 Committee for Codification of
    Laws
Sang'ŏp yŏn'guso 商業研究所 Commercial Research Institute
Seijo chunghakgyo 成城中學校 Seijo Middle School
shaminshugi 社民主義 social democracy
shihon kyoyushugi 資本公有主義 capital communalism
Siguk 時國
Siguk taedongdan 時局大同團

Sin'ganhoe 新幹會

sŏdang 書堂 local Confucian school

sŏgi 書記 clerk

sŏmu kwajang 庶務課長 chief of general affairs section

sŏngwa 選科 special program

Sŏul ch'ŏngnyŏnhoe 서울靑年會 Seoul Youth Corps

tae-Il paesang yogu chosŏ 對日賠償要求調書 Request for Reparations from Japan

Tonga hŭngsansa 東亞興産社

Tonguhoe 同友會

Yi Sŏngt'ae 李星泰 (1901-?)

Yi Sunt'ak 李順鐸 (1897-1950)

Yŏng kyŏngjegwa 英經濟科 English economics department (regular course)

Yŏnhŭi chŏnmun hakgyo 延禧專門學校 Yŏnhŭi Junior College

Afterword

Bruce Cumings

History has an immediacy in Korea that is remarkable: a textbook revision here, a reversal of historical verdicts there, or just a minor departure from orthodoxy, can send shock waves through the whole body politic. Did the Japanese have a colony in Korea called Mimana, shortly after the birth of Christ? So says a new "rightwing" or "nationalist" Japanese schoolbook; this and a handful of other offensive passages were enough to have the Korean Ambassador to Japan recalled in the year 2000, almost two millennia removed from Mimana (which may or may not have existed—anywhere—just as people called "Japanese" and a country called "Korea" had a similarly questionable existence in this remote site of antiquity). History has a palpable actuality in Korea—it is alive, it matters, it echoes and reverberates, and therefore every Korean citizen is a custodian of the past.

Was the peninsula now known as Korea unified in the seventh century, or the tenth? To answer the question one way is to identify with one Korean state calling itself *Han'guk*, and to answer it the other way is to identify with another Korean state calling itself *Chosŏn*. "Who started the Korean War?" That was the question put to an American by a North Korean guide on the way in from the airport, and when the American chuckled and said, "You like to get right to the point, don't you?" the guide barked back that this question was no laughing matter. Indeed, it isn't: answer it the wrong way and you can still go to jail in either half of Korea. A few days later this American visited a beautiful mountaintop near P'yŏngyang, where hundreds of busts of fallen anti-Japanese fighters overlook the capital city. What will happen to these monuments after unification—since most of the deceased were communists? Now a coherent national narrative divides into two incommensurate, separate rivers, flowing in opposite directions; a pool of unanimity on one account (*contra* Japan) now divides into streams of difference about everything else. Rare is the person honored in both Korean narratives.

But some are, like An Chunggun. On South Mountain in Seoul, his statue stands, honoring his sole if singular historical act, the assassination of Ito Hirobumi—heroic Meiji elder to Japanese historians, prime author of Korea's colonization to Korean historians. Going backward to 1945, this same mountaintop was the site of the most magnificent Shinto shrine in all of Korea (even if there is no hint of it now). Going forward to 1979, seventy years to the day after Ito died of his gunshot wounds at Harbin station, Kim Chaegyu put a bullet into the head of President Park Chung Hee. A mere coincidence that this happened on October 29? Hadn't Park been an officer in the Japanese Imperial Army? But, the interlocutor asks, what does that make of Kim Chaegyu, then director of the reviled KCIA, who was also an officer in the Japanese Imperial Army? And what do we make of Park and Kim both graduating in the second class of the military school set up by the American Military Government, which ruled south of the 38th parallel from 1945 to 1948?

Now another narrative intrudes: the master narrative of the post-World War II years, that is, the American narrative. One Korea gets colored white and deposited in the Free World, not without some warts and peccadilloes to be sure, but nonetheless a staunch ally and friend to the victor in the Cold War (which won because it is free, liberal, democratic, and market-oriented). The other Korea gets colored red and deposited first on the losing side—the Communist bloc—and then on the dustbin of history. (It lost because it is unfree, illiberal, totalitarian, and statist. But it still exists? It should erase itself.) North Korea might not be the worst place in the world (although over the past decade you wouldn't find many objections in the American media), but its sins are not mere warts and peccadilloes, and its time has come and gone: therefore it should do the right thing and get rid of itself—just be gone, dissolved in the stream of an unfortunate history.

When great powers trifle with the lifeblood of an ancient and dignified people who take history seriously, sooner or later they get their recompense. Japan has gotten it every day since Emperor Hirohito capitulated on August 15, 1945. Imagine: a country admired from afar as Asia's star example of modernity, but loathed by its near neighbors for sins committed more than half a century ago. The United States also got a kind of recompense in the

1980s, as its massive embassy in Seoul, perched right next to the seat of government, came to resemble an embattled legation in war-torn Beirut, and a new generation shouted itself hoarse about American crimes. No doubt it wasn't easy to take, this slap on the face from such a staunch Free World ally. But this decade marked a new departure, a new step in Korea's independence. That step is at the root of the remarkable historical departures included in this volume. Before 1980, you couldn't find this new historiography anywhere, but soon you found it everywhere—and the reason was that neither the master American narrative, nor the particular South Korean version (replete with interpretations that only a South Korean would believe), could explain modern Korean history.

If this departure had its punctuation on October 29, 1979, with an act that instantly demolished the fiction that all Koreans marched in lockstep toward the Valhalla of modern industrial development, led by a man named Park Chung Hee whom regime scribes likened to Bismarck, Ataturk, and Japan's industrial sovereigns (for example, Ito), it accelerated dramatically in the aftermath of America's most craven moment in recent history, as a liberal Democratic administration in Washington aided and abetted another *coup d'état* by the Korean military, accomplished over the dead bodies of thousands of protesters in Kwangju. Suddenly every question about Korea's modern history was up for grabs, and a new generation of historians got busy. Two decades later, we have a maturing historiography on just about every important question of modern Korean history.

The chapters in this volume on An Chaehong and Yi Sunt'ak are particularly poignant ones for an American to read. Both of them were men of moderate and even scholarly temperament, open to experience, worldly, and generally pro-American. Like so many other people of their generation, the history of the post-World War I period had turned them into radicals, if only briefly in An's case, and only intellectually in Yi's case. The war to end all wars came to a close with two clarion calls for self-determination, imbedded in Woodrow Wilson's Fourteen Points (free, liberal, democratic, but not meant for the colonized in Japan's sphere) and Lenin's theories of national liberation (illiberal, undemocratic or democratic in a very different meaning, and written for all the colonized of the world). An Chaehong's own ideas about the post-World War I situation, as discussed by Lee Ji-won (see pp. 320-24), are clear elaborations of Lenin's theories. Yi Sunt'ak's radicalism was perhaps more characteristic of the Korean left, in abjuring materialism in favor of the idea that all real change originates in the realm of human thought—first of all people need to change their "mind-set" (p. 356), and after that everything will be alright. If that seems naïve, the idea that correct thought takes precedence over everything else became the ruling doctrine in Kim Il Sung's North Korea (perhaps illustrating the lingering intellectual influence of Korean Neo-Confucianism).

Another point that comes out of these chapters, of course, is that all the well-educated young people of the 1920s knew each other. Kim Yŏnsu helped with Yi Sunt'ak's tuition at a middle school in Tokyo, long before Kim became one of the leading Korean industrialists of the Japanese period. An Chaehong took the political economy curriculum at Waseda University, like any number of other young Koreans who later became prominent political activists. In the mid-1920s, An associated with Kim Sŏngsu, Song Chin'u, Cho Mansik and Hong Myŏnghŭi during his preparations for the founding of the Sin'ganhoe (pp. 332-33): all of these people became critically important figures two decades later in the politics of Liberation. Paek Nam'un, however, seems to have summed all this up in one lifetime: not only was his perspective "representative of the main intellectual currents among young students" in the 1920s (p. 249), but he knew everyone and everyone knew him. I was struck to learn that at one point, he taught in the same department as Cho Pyŏng'ok (p. 369). After Cho became head of the National Police under the Americans, no two people seemed farther apart politically than these two.

In the 1920s, as Paek's distinguished career shows, to be young and involved and concerned with the fate of one's country, was to be a radical— most likely a socialist of one sort or another. We see this in one prominent Korean biography after another, but poignantly in people like An Chaehong and a more important figure from the period, Kim Kyusik. Kim was an eloquent pamphleteer for revolution in the 1920s, but a man returned to his proper self in the late 1940s: moderate, scholarly in temperament, worldly, by then deeply experienced, willing to work with Americans for the good of their country. Another figure out of Yŏnsei University's past, Chŏng Inbo, sought to convince Americans of the likely outcome of their tendency to rely on the same Koreans that the Japanese did—a civil war.[1] These people were the natural leaders of the middle class, and therefore natural friends to the United States. The problem was that no middle class had been allowed to

---

1. See Bruce Cumings, *Korea's Place in the Sun: A Modern History* (New York and London: W.W. Norton, 1997), p. 203.

develop, either by the landed aristocrats of the Chosŏn period, or by the Japanese. Thus their personal narratives run toward admirable but unrewarded efforts to bridge ideological differences under the American Occupation, followed by their utter disappearance, one after another, in the oblivion of a thoroughly divided nation: "abducted" to North Korea in 1950 and forgotten. (Can you be so sure? None went willingly? None joined the North?)

Kim Yong-sop's (Kim Yongsŏp) lifelong *oeuvre*, however, does not fit this particular narrative. Instead, there is a steady accretion of historical interpretation from a distant but determining starting point—the 1930s—that develops according to its own internal logic, quite apart from the national division, or what North or South Koreans might think, or what Americans or Japanese might think. Initially Professor Kim's departure was to subject Japanese justifications of their rule in Korea to the test of a thorough empirical inquiry, on the question of overriding importance for modern East Asian history: how is it that Japan got off the mark first? How could two neighboring civilizations of such antique origin, of such long, distinguished and continuous histories, have diverged so dramatically in a mere few decades, such that one swallowed the other? Japanese historians found the answer in a remarkably mimetic trope: *stagnation*. That is, they picked up the primary conceit of the West, going back to the division of the Roman Empire into eastern (stagnant and Oriental) and western (progressive and Occidental) parts, which culminated in a general theory known as the Asiatic mode of production and adhered to by one enlightenment figure after another (Montesquieu, Adam Smith, Mill, Hegel, Marx). Then these Asians turned the theory not against themselves, but against Koreans: Eureka, we have found it—the secret of their misery, not to mention the secret of our success. While the Japanese were busy industrializing, Koreans had been vegetating in the teeth of time.

Kim Yong-sop examined this shibboleth through detailed inquiries into the main source of wealth in Korea for centuries, the land, its product, and the relations of production, including the vexed discourse about the "sprouts of capitalism" that Michael Shin analyzed in the Introduction. Professor Kim's concern was with the internal mechanisms of change and development in Korea, and the result of his inquiries and those of his students is a rather complete picture of Korean agrarian history (in books and articles already catalogued by several of our contributors). What is remarkable to me, though, is the thread of continuity that Kim Yong-sop picks up and sustains, to create a narrative that bears few traces of Korea's national division.

This is serious history that can be appreciated by serious people in South and North, and by intellectuals everywhere. It is work that properly lays much of Korea's modern problematic at the feet of its elites, especially landed aristocrats who were not so much "feudal," "stagnant" or backward-looking, as *controlling* (as evidenced in Hong Sung-Chan's chapter). They created and sustained an agrarian system that squelched incentives for creative labor and enterprise, and militated against talent rising from below. They put their interests above those of their fellow Koreans and the Korean nation, seeking to monopolize production and distribution, that is, marketing, without spreading and broadening the wealth. Then they collaborated with imperial occupiers to perpetuate their hold on wealth and influence, by any means necessary. Peasants by the millions were prevented from using the market for their own ends, and thus the vast majority of Koreans remained subsistence-oriented quite "late" in world time, up until 1945 at least, and long after Japanese farmers had become entrepreneurial ("being a tenant farmer was synonymous with being destitute and hungry," pp. 147-48). There was but the smallest hint of a real middle class, and even the modern thing that Japan unquestionably brought to Korea, commercial and industrial capitalism, was tainted by the auspices of its introduction. Thus, Korean historians saw the central system of modernity, the thing that made the wheels go round, as an alien implant, a foreign graft, just another aspect of Korea's "deformed modernism" (p. 301).[2]

Korea's agrarian history thus assured that landlordism and tenancy would be the critical social and political question of the Liberation period, culminating in the quick land revolution in the North that Kim Seong-bo so ably analyzes (with much new information), and a messy sequence of half-hearted and failed reform efforts in the South. First, the U.S. Military Government distributed the land owned by the Oriental Development Company to peasants who could pay the cost, then a land reform plan cleared the legislature in 1949, but was not implemented. During the northern occupation in the summer of 1950, a revolutionary redistribution ensued under harsh wartime conditions, followed finally by a reformist redistribution pushed through at the behest of Americans in the spring of 1951. Still and all, it *was* a

---

2. Of course, recent work by scholars like Carter Eckert and An Pyŏngjik has shown that Koreans also had an important role in developing capitalism during the colonial period, but here I am talking about the perceptions of earlier historians.

redistribution, and in short order the way was open to some measure of development and prosperity for Korean farmers.

Kim Yong-sop's work is one of the rare places where the complicated sequence of modern agrarian history can be appreciated in its fullness, from the late Chosŏn period through the differing agrarian outcomes in North and South. Professor Kim's deft thread of continuity goes further than that, however. His footnotes are packed with references from the 1930s and 1940s to authors that are very familiar to me: Yi Hungu, In Chŏngsik, Pak Mungyu, Pak Insu, and, above all, Paek Nam'un. These were the people I read as a graduate student in the early 1970s, courtesy of kindly booksellers in Seoul who would retreat to a back room and come out with a dusty volume written by one of these people, often wrapped in cheap brown paper to hide the author and title.

At the time, I thought their work was excellent, convincing, full of analysis and comparisons that rang true. It amazed me to see the degree to which Korean history then, in the hands of people who wrote and published before the great dividing line that came in 1950, was widely understood to be an essential part of world history, and especially part and parcel of the tremendous blows meted out by the Great Depression to every nation, but especially the weaker nations of the world. Japan was correctly seen as both an imperial nation and a weak nation, a subordinate part of a world order dominated by England and the United States.[3] They all thought that the colonial period was synonymous with a capitalist period, foisted on Korea by the Japanese. But at the time, I did not know really who these authors were, or that many of them ended up in North Korea (clearly a voluntary decision in the cases of Paek Nam'un and Pak Mungyu).

It was easy for me, in my relative freedom as a foreigner, to cite them and use their work. It is an act of continuous courage for Professor Kim to rely so much on their work, given their subsequent political history, but in many ways his concern for continuity of interpretation is also a tribute to his mentors figurative and otherwise (including Paek Nam'un and those mentioned above), and to other stellar members of the Yŏnsei University history faculty. The best thing to be said about Kim Yong-sop's courageous and committed scholarship, however, is what he himself says at the end of his chapter: the root cause of the national division is to be found in the history of lord and peasant, and the remedies that both Koreas took (or did not take)

---

3. See for example Paek Nam'un's arguments, pp. 287-89 in Pang Kie-chung's chapter.

to deal with the fundamental problems that arose from those longstanding relationships.

My one regret about this volume is the evidence it provides as to the continuing distance between Korean and American work on modern Korean history. The two historiographies still move along separate paths. The footnotes carry next to no citations of American work, even though many volumes are of direct relevance to the issues at hand. James B. Palais, for example, has devoted much of his fine career to detailed inquiries into Korean land relations in the Chosŏn period, making frequent reference to the work of Korean and Japanese historians who work on the same subjects. He is as much a student of Kim Yong-sop as Kim was of Paek Nam'un, and does Professor Kim the honor of disagreeing with him, if only after the most rigorous kind of empirical work. Edwin Gragert's fine work on agrarian relations in the 1920s and 1930s is also of great relevance to this volume. There are many other examples that might be mentioned. Here I do not think Americans can be faulted: we have read and digested the work of Korean historians, but Koreans have not done us the same favor.

So there is yet another step that Korean historiography needs to take, which is to break with the essentialist notion that only Koreans can understand Korean history.[4] This, too, is part of the repertoire of every Korean citizen-historian; any man in the street, let alone the established historians, considers himself to be the arbiter of all historical interpretation, great and small. This is perfectly understandable, given the damage done to Korea and its history by foreign powers. But it isn't conducive to good history, and to the extent that it persists, Koreans are not custodians of the past so much as the prisoners of their own conceits.

The appearance of this volume in translation, however, is testimony to the blurring of nationalities and identities that is ongoing in the United States, and to the emergence of a new generation of historians, many of them Korean-Americans. Their generation is the harbinger of a full, many-sided modern history of Korea that is slowly emerging, among scholars who have few language barriers and excellent training in the best American universities. Soon this volume should have its opposite, in other words, a book of articles written by young historians in English, translated for a Korean audience.

---

4. The reader might want to have another look at Paek Nam'un's critique of such notions as "Chosŏn mind" and "Chosŏn consciousness" (p. 273 n. 84 in Pang Kie-chung's chapter).

Contributors

CHOI WON-KYU (CH'OE WŎNGYU) is currently a professor in the Department of History at Pusan University. The focus of his research is early modern socioeconomic history. His major publications include "Ilcheha ŭi nong'ŏp kyŏng'yŏng e kwanhan yŏn'gu" (An examination of agricultural management under Japanese rule, *Han'guksa yŏn'gu*, nos. 50-51, 1985) and "Taehan chegukgi yangjŏn kwa kwan'gye palgŭp saŏp" (The cadastral survey and issuance of land deeds during the Great Han Empire period in *Taehan cheguk ŭi t'oji chosa saŏp*, Seoul: Minŭmsa, 1995), from which his chapter in this volume was adapted.

CHU CHIN-OH (CHU CHIN'O) is a professor in the History Department at Sangmyung University in Seoul. His main area of interest is the political and intellectual history of the early modern period. His major articles include: "1898 nyŏn Tongnip hyŏphoe undong ŭi chudo seryŏk kwa chiji kiban" (The leaders and foundation of support of the Independence Club movement in 1898, *Yŏksa wa hyŏnsil*, no. 15, 1995) and "Haesan chikhu Tongnip hyŏphoe hwaldong e taehan kak kyech'ŭng ŭi pan'ŭng" (The reactions of each class to the activities of the Independence Club after its dissolution, *Silhak sasang yŏn'gu*, no. 9, 1997).

BRUCE CUMINGS is Norman and Edna Freehling Professor of International History and East Asian Political Economy at the University of Chicago. He is the author or co-author of eight books, including the two-volume study, *The Origins of the Korean War* (Princeton University Press, 1981, 1990), *War and Television* (Visal Routledge, 1992), *Korea's Place in the Sun: A Modern History* (Norton, 1997), *Parallax Visions: Making Sense of American—East Asian Relations at Century's End* (Duke University Press, 1999), and *North Korea: Another Country* (The New Press, 2004).

HONG SUNG-CHAN (HONG SŎNGCH'AN) is Professor of Economic History in the Department of Economics at Yonsei University. His research focuses on early modern and contemporary economic history. He is the author of *Han'guk kŭndae nongch'on sahoe ŭi pyŏndong kwa chiju-ch'ŭng* (The landlord class and the transformation of the rural society in modern Korea, Chisik san'ŏpsa, 1992), a co-author of *Han'guk kŭndae kŭm'yungsa yŏn'gu* (The history of finance in early modern Korea, Segyŏngsa, 1996), and the editor of *Nongji kaehyŏk yŏ'ngu* (Studies on south Korean land reform, Yonsei University Press, 2001).

KIM SEONG-BO (KIM SŎNGBO) is a professor in the Department of History at Yonsei University. The focus of his research is the contemporary socioeconomic history of North and South Korea. From 1997 to 2002, he served as the research director of the Yŏksa munje yŏn'guso (The Institute for Korean Historical Studies). He is the author of *Nam-Pukhan kyŏngje kujo ŭi kiwŏn kwa chŏn'gae* (The origins and development of the economic structures of north and south Korea, Yŏksa pip'yŏngsa, 2000).

KIM YONG-SOP (KIM YONGSŎP) began his teaching career in 1958 at Seoul National University and then moved to the Department of History at Yonsei University in 1975, where he remained until his retirement in 1997. His main field of research is late Chosŏn period and early modern socioeconomic history. He is the author of several books, including: *Chosŏn hugi nonghaksa yŏn'gu* (The history of the science of agriculture in the late Chosŏn period, Ilchogak, 1988), *Chŭngbop'an Han'guk kŭndae nong'ŏpsa yŏn'gu* (The agricultural history of early modern Korea, revised edition, Ilchogak, 1990), *Chŭngbop'an Chosŏn hugi nong'ŏpsa yŏn'gu I* (The agricultural history of the late Chosŏn period I, revised edition, Chisik sanŏpsa, 1995); and *Han'guk chungse nong'ŏpsa yŏn'gu* (The agricultural history of Korea in the middle ages, Chisik san'ŏpsa, 2000).

LEE JI-WON (YI CHIWŎN) is a professor in the Department of Liberal Arts at Taelim College in Anyang, Kyŏnggi province. She does research on the early modern period, focusing on intellectual and cultural history and the history of the nationalist movement. She is the co-author of *Han'guk munhwasa* (A cultural history of Korea, Hyean, 1998), and her major articles include: "1930 nyŏndae minjokjuŭi kyeyŏl ŭi kojŏk pojon undong" (The national heritage preservation movement of nationalists in the 1930s, *Tongbang hakji*, nos. 77-78-79, combined issue 1993) and "1930 nyŏndae chonban minjokjuŭi munhwa undongnon" (The conception of the nationalist culture movement in the first half of the 1930s, *Kuksagwan nonch'ong*, no. 51, 1994).

PANG KIE-CHUNG (PANG KIJUNG) is a professor in the Department of History, Yonsei University. His field of interest in the intellectual history of the early modern and contemporary period. He was also the president of the Han'guk yŏksa yŏn'guhoe (The Organization of Korean Historians) from 2000-2001. He is the author of *Han'guk kŭnhyŏndae sasangsa yŏn'gu* (Studies in the intellectual history of modern and contemporary Korea, Yŏksa pip'yŏngsa, 1992) and *Pae Minsu ŭi nongch'on undong kwa Kidokgyo sasang* (The rural movements and Christian ideology of Pae Minsu, Yonsei University Press, 1999).

MICHAEL D. SHIN is an assistant professor in the Department of Asian Studies, Cornell University.

Translators

CHARLES K. ARMSTRONG is Associate Professor of History and Director of the Center for Korean Research at Columbia University. His published works include *The North Korean Revolution, 1945-1950* (Cornell University Press, 2002) and, as editor, *Korean Society: Civil Society, Democracy and the State* (Routledge, 2002).

KELLY YOOJEONG JEONG is an assistant professor of English at John Jay College of Criminal Justice, CUNY. Her research areas are modern and contemporary Korean literature, Korean cinema, and popular culture. She is currently working on a book about gender, modernity, and the question of the nation in Korean literature and film.

HOWARD KAHM is a graduate student in the Department of Asian Languages and Cultures at UCLA. He is interested in working on the economic history of colonial Korea.

JEONG-IL LEE is a graduate student in the Department of Asian Languages and Cultures at UCLA. His dissertation will focus on culture, ethnicity, historiography, and intellectual discourse in the late Chosŏn and early modern periods.

PAUL S. NAM is a graduate student at UCLA specializing in the socio-economic history of colonial Korea.

MIN SUH SON is currently a Ph.D. candidate in Korean history in the Department of Asian Languages and Cultures at UCLA. She is writing her dissertation on the cultural impact of the introduction of electric lights, streetcars and telegraph to Seoul in the late nineteenth to early twentieth century.

Biographical Notes

KIM KWANGJIN (1902-1986) was born Kwangju, South Chŏlla province. He graduated from the Department of Political Economy at Waseda University and became a professor at Posŏng Chŏnmun Hakgyo, the precursor to today's Korea University. After liberation, he went to the North and became a professor at Kim Il Sung University.

KIM TOYŎN (1894-1967) was born in Kimp'o, Kyŏnggi province. While he was attending Keio University, he was jailed for two years for his involvement in the Declaration of Independence by Chosŏn students in Tokyo on February 8, 1919. After graduating from Columbia University in 1927, he received his doctorate in economics from American University in 1931. After returning to Chosŏn, he became a lecturer at Yŏnhŭi chŏnmun hakgyo in 1932. In 1942, he was jailed in the Chosŏnŏ Hakhoe Incident. After liberation, he became one of the leading figures in the Korean Democratic Party and became increasingly involved in politics. In 1948, he became the vice-minister of finance in the Syngman Rhee administration and later served as the vice-speaker of the National Assembly.

KIM UP'YŎNG (1897-1967) was born in Yŏsu in South Chŏlla province. He attended Ohio State University and received his MA degree from Columbia University. He is the author of *Kŭmyung chohapnon: Chosŏn sŏmin kŭmyung kigwan ŭi haebu* (1933).

NO TONGGYU (1904-?) was born in Yonggang, South P'yŏng'an province. He entered the Department of Commerce at Yŏnhŭi chŏnmun hakgyo in 1921. After graduating in 1924, he entered the Department of Economics of Kyoto Imperial University, receiving his degree in 1927. He became a lecturer in the Department of Commerce at Yŏnhŭi in 1928 and became a professor the following year. In 1938, he was jailed in the Economic Club (Kyŏngje yŏn'guhoe) Incident. He is believed to have died in the early 1940s after his release from jail.

SŎ CH'UN (1894-1944) was born in Chŏngju in North P'yŏng'an province. From a poor family, he caught the attention of Yi Sŭnghun and was able to enroll in Osan Academy. He was influenced by Yi Kwangsu, who was a teacher at Osan at the time. At the end of the 1910s, he went to study in Japan. After attending the Tokyo Higher Normal School and studying in the Department of Philosophy at Toyo University, he en-tered Kyoto Imperial University in 1923 and graduated from its Faculty of Economics in 1926. After returning to Chosŏn, he worked as a journalist writing commentary on economic issues for the *Tonga ilbo*, the *Chosŏn ilbo*, and the *Maeil sinbo*.

YI KŬNGJŎNG (b. 1898) was born in Yŏngi County, South Ch'ungch'ŏng province. He graduated from the Kyŏngsŏng Junior College of Law (Kyŏngsŏng Pŏphak Chŏnmun Hakgyo) in 1917 and continued to study law at Meiji University. He received an MA degree from Columbia University in economics. After returning to Chosŏn, he worked at the Bank of Chosŏn and was on the board of directors of Hwashin Department Store. He was also the president of the *Chosŏn sanggong sinmun*.

YI YŎSŎNG (b. 1900) was born in Taegu and graduated from Chungang High School in 1918. He participated in independence move-ments in Manchuria and returned to Taegu with the outbreak of the March 1st Movement. He tried to continue such activities in Taegu but was ar-rested and served three years in jail. After his release, he went to Japan and enrolled in the department of political economy at Rikkyo University where he participated in various student societies. Around 1930, he returned to Korea where he worked at the *Chosŏn ilbo* and the *Tonga ilbo*. He also formed the company Segwangsa, wrote the series *Sutja Chosŏn yŏn'gu* (Statistical research on Korea, five volumes) with Kim Seyong, and wrote a his-tory of the movement of small and weak nations. As the suppression by the Japanese became more severe, he began to withdraw from society and became a genre painter as well as doing research on ancient arts and the history of clothing in Korea.

Index

CORNELL EAST ASIA SERIES

Order online: www.einaudi.cornell.edu/eastasia/CEASbooks, or contact Cornell East Asia Series Distribution Center, 95 Brown Road, Box 1004, Ithaca, NY 14850, USA; toll-free: 1-877-865-2432, fax 607-255-7534, ceas@cornell.edu

IBT/10-05/1.2M pb/.3M hc